And the Light Became so Bright

And the Light Became so Bright

The Influence of C.H. Douglas on the Writings of Ezra Pound

LORNE A. REZNOWSKI, STL, PHD

WITH CONTRIBUTIONS AND EDITING BY THEODORE REZNOWSKI, STB, AND M. OLIVER HEYDORN, PHD

AROUCA PRESS

Waterloo, ON N2J 0A5
www.aroucapress.com

ISBN: 978-1-998492-45-9 (pbk)
ISBN: 978-1-998492-46-6 (hc)

Dedicated to those who strive for Economic Justice and Economic Democracy, through the distribution to all — men, women, and children — of the wealth created by the Cultural Heritage through the Increment of Association.

and the light became so bright and so blindin'
in this layer of paradise
that the mind of man was bewildered.
—Ezra Pound, Canto XXXVIII

CONTENTS

The writer thanks the late Mr. Ezra Pound for his encouragement in the undertaking of this study. He also thanks the late Mrs. Dorothy Pound for her kind assistance in directing the writer to source material and in sending material. Thanks is also given to Mary de Rachewiltz for her kind encouragement to complete this work. Gratitude is expressed to all others who have assisted in making this work possible.

INTRODUCTORY LETTERS

April 6, 1965
Mr. Lorne A. Reznowski

Ottawa 14, Ontario
CANADA
Mr. Ezra Pound
c/o Princess de Rachewiltz
Brunnenburg, Tirolo
Merano, Italy

Dear Mr. Pound,

I have been a student of the philosophy of Douglas Social Credit since my early boyhood. At present I am engaged in graduate work in English literature at the University of Ottawa (Canada).

In reading a biography on you, I was struck by the great influence Major Douglas had upon you. You mention Social Credit in so many letters to your literary friends and there are allusions to Social Credit in your Cantos.

It seems to me that many doctoral theses in English literature have been written on the influence of Fabian Socialism on Shaw, Wells, etc. However, there seems to be a conspiracy of silence with regard to the influence of Social Credit on modern literature.

I know that you brought Social Credit to the attention of T. S. Eliot, Wyndham Lewis, Marianne Moore, Archibald Macleish [*sic*] etc.

I know that Eliot refers to Social Credit in his introduction to *The Rock*.[1]

I would like to write my doctoral thesis on "The Influence of C. H. Douglas on the Cantos of Ezra Pound". Do you think that Douglas was a strong enough influence in your career to justify a thesis such as this?

---

[1] Editor's note: Eliot, *The Rock*, 12. T. S. Eliot refers to C. H. Douglas and his theory of Social Credit in Part I of the play, *The Rock*, in the voice of the character Ethelbert.

If you feel this is too narrow, I could perhaps write on the "influence of C. H. Douglas on the writings of Ezra Pound", or the "Influence of C. H. Douglas on Modern Literature".

I would appreciate your advice on this matter.

The head of my department approves of a thesis on this general subject, and I feel that if it were published in book form it might help to counteract the all-pervasive Fabian Socialist strangle-hold on much of modern literature and criticism.

I am also a candidate for the doctorate in Theology from the Catholic University of America in Washington, D. C. I am a lecturer in English literature at the University of Ottawa. I wrote my Master's thesis in English on "The Death of Hope in H. G. Wells" dealing with his last "Discussion Novels", and the general debate between Shaw and Wells vs. Belloc and Chesterton.

Yours truly,

Lorne A. Reznowski

P. S. I also know Social Credit influenced John Drinkwater, John Buchan etc.

P. P. S. I am a personal friend of Martin Hattersley who is the son of C. Marshall Hattersley, one of the original writers on Social Credit along with C. H. Douglas and Maurice Colbourne. C. Marshall Hattersley was a friend of T. S. Eliot's. Martin Hattersley tells me that Compton MacKenzie also came under the influence of Social Credit.

P. P. P. S. The two most prosperous provinces (without any direct interest-bearing debt) in Canada are the Social Credit provinces of Alberta and British Columbia. They are forced to work within the framework of the debt-money system, but they are an example to the world.[2]

[2] Reznowski, "Letter to Ezra Pound."

20 april 1965
Rapallo

Dear Mr Reznowski

Try your 2nd suggestion.
i.e. "The influence of C.H.D on the writings ~~f~~ of E.P.

best wishes.

Ezra Pound

FOREWORD
Lorne Reznowski and the History of this Study

Theodore Reznowski

> The first part of Dante's *Divine Comedy* is many things: a moving human drama, a supreme expression of the Middle Ages, a glorification of the ways of God, and a magnificent protest against the ways in which men have thwarted the divine plan. One of the few literary works that has enjoyed a fame both immediate and enduring, The Inferno remains powerful after seven centuries. It confronts the most universal values—good and evil, free will and predestination—while remaining intensely personal and ferociously political, for it was born out of the anguish of a man who saw human life blighted by the injustice and corruption of his times.[3]

MUCH OF THE ABOVE QUOTE CONCERNING Dante's *The Inferno* could similarly be applied to *The Cantos of Ezra Pound.* Before my father, Lorne Reznowski, died, I had several conversations with him about his Pound thesis. He explained that if Pound had written a textbook on economics, it would *not* have been read or printed past the generation alive at the time. Pound understood from Dante that one must write an artistic monument. Only then, would the story, *the anguish of a man who saw human life blighted by the injustice and corruption of his times* be read in ages to come. As an artistic masterpiece, the story could not be forgotten or hidden away.

Lorne Anthony Reznowski, *Sonny,* was born January 5, 1929, in Winnipeg, Manitoba, Canada. His father, Lorne William Reznowski, was the son of a mixed Ukrainian and Polish father Anton Rzesnoski (Rzezniowski) from Kosiv, in the Chortkiv district of Austro-Hungary, and his Ukrainian mother, Maria Michaleska, from the village of Bilo-boznitsia, Chortkiv, Austro-Hungary. His mother was the daughter of a mixed Polish and Ukrainian father, Tryfon Brokowski, and a

[3] Penguin Random House, "The Inferno by Dante Alighieri," publisher's description for *The Inferno.*

mixed Czech and German mother, Catherine Weselak. Tryfon was from Mietnice, Czarist Russia, and Catherine was from the village that bordered Mietnice, Komoriwka, in Austrian Galicia.

Lorne, for his first two years, lived with his parents in Beausejour, Manitoba. Around the age of two, he moved to Winnipeg and was then raised for most of his youth at 390 Boyd Ave., in the North End. His father set up his practice at times on Selkirk Ave. and for a while south on Main St., just past the old CPR railroad station. The so-called *North End* was home to many East European immigrants, and the poorest district of the city, as it is today.

Lorne spoke often of how his section of Boyd Ave. was largely Jewish, and he grew up learning many Yiddish words, a foundation he expanded on later in life. Lorne would recall enjoyable games of cricket or *shinny* hockey, playing with any old stick and ball in the back alleys of his neighbourhood. His best friend, Eddy Diamond, lived next door on the lower floor, while the Jewish *Shochet* (kosher ritual slaughterer) and his wife, lived above Eddy.

Eddy attended kindergarten at the Peretz School. Lorne, not attending kindergarten and missing his friend, would wait all day for Mrs. Diamond to walk him over to the school to meet Eddy on school days. Lorne would remember *graduating*, or at least wearing a graduation hat, during Eddy's own kindergarten graduation. Mrs. Diamond would be remembered by Lorne as a saintly mother-like figure whom he adored. The tragic death of Eddy, his long-time childhood companion, was something Lorne would often recall with sadness years later.

Lorne remembered first hearing of Social Credit while sitting on his father's lap, when his father would read the Winnipeg newspapers and laugh at the cartoons poking fun of William Aberhart, otherwise known as *Bible Bill.* As the leader of the Social Credit movement, Aberhart and his party, running under the name of *Social Credit,* faced its first election. The party was promising a National Dividend, which in the disillusionment of the Depression, seemed to be another empty promise. At this time, Lorne's own father, along with many other Ukrainians and other East European immigrants, were supporters, if not members, of the Communist Party, and other related Socialist movements. Winnipeg was known for its strong labour movement and the violent Winnipeg Strike of 1919. When the Jewish kids of the neighbourhood had asked Lorne whom he was voting for in the election, Lorne would remember, with a smile, telling them "Tim Buck" at the tender age of six. The other children answered "Sonny, you're a communist!" The 1935 election in the federal Riding of

Winnipeg North was famous in Canadian politics, as it appeared that Tim Buck[4] would be elected to Canada's federal parliament.

During the Great Depression, Lorne's parents began to plan their new home and office on Selkirk Avenue. Lorne's father's brother, Edward Reznowski, was a Communist Party member. Edward was convinced by others to go to Spain to fight for the Communists on the Republican side against Francisco Franco and the Nationalists, joining the Mackenzie-Papineau Brigade. He returned, as with others, scarred by the experience of the death and destruction he witnessed. Likewise, Lorne's maternal grandfather, Tryfon Brokowski, was a communist supporter if not a member. He died while working at the Canadian Pacific Railyards in the North End.

Despite the sympathies in Lorne's extended family for Communism, especially during the Great Depression of the 1930s, his father, mother and extended family were faithful Roman or Ukrainian Greek-Catholics, and like so many, were only desperate for an answer to the poverty around them. Lorne remembers his father coming home early one morning during the Depression, from a late-night house call, and his mother asking him why he did not insist on payment for the visit. In response, his father answered, "They had nothing, and I left them money for milk for their baby." Lorne would recount how during the Depression, his maternal grandmother, would open her door to the itinerant, hungry, incomeless men, who came by asking for food, rather than be influenced by others who were scared to feed them. Despite the struggles of the period, the Reznowski family was well off compared to most of their neighbours.

In 1941, Lorne recalled his father and mother coming home from an evening outing. They had been to a Social Credit meeting in Winnipeg, in which the French Métis[5] engineer, Paul Prince spoke.[6] Lorne remembers asking if this was the same political party they had always laughed at, but his father answered that he was impressed

[4] Lorne often commented that in Whittaker Chambers's book *Witness*, 308, Chambers mentions seeing Buck, the secretary of the Communist Party of Canada, during a visit to Dr. Philip Rosenbliett. This Doctor was a handler for the Soviet underground in America.

[5] The Métis people of western Canada and the U. S. are of mixed ancestry, i.e., Native American and European. They formed their own distinct culture on the western prairies. Twice they rebelled against the Canadian government for their local rights, in 1869–1870 and 1885. Lorne would comment that he had the honour to be a candidate in the federal Riding of Provencher, for the Social Credit party in the 1968 election, where its former MP, Louis Riel, had led both western rebellions.

[6] A collection of Paul Prince's 1944 radio broadcasts: Prince, *Think and Conquer!*

by the speaker and the ideas. From this time, his father and mother became active in the Social Credit movement.

Lorne would recount how, by age twelve, he would give impassioned speeches on Social Credit, which were memorized William Aberhart speeches. He recalled giving the speeches at Social Credit gatherings in Dauphin, and Winnipeg, Manitoba.

In 1944, his favourite uncle, Captain Ted Brokowski, ran for the Social Credit party in the federal riding of Selkirk, Manitoba. Ted was a physician in the Sherbrooke Fusiliers Regiment, a Canadian armoured unit. Ted had studied at Cardiff, Wales, where he met and married Ellen Levinsohn. She was an only child who hailed from the Jewish community of The Hague, Netherlands. Both her parents had died in the Holocaust. Ted was wounded by shrapnel in the battle to take Caen, France, during the Normandy invasion and breakout. Family encouraged Ted to run for the April 1945 federal election in the riding of Selkirk. This would bring him home for at least the campaign, once Ted had been officially nominated as the Social Credit candidate at the Winnipeg Beach Hotel. The morning following the unsuccessful election, they took down the large Social Credit banner on Doctor Lorne's home and office building on Selkirk Ave in Winnipeg, which proclaimed *Social Credit or Slavery*. Ted, always one with a good sense of humour commented, "Well, I guess there is no question; *slavery* wins again."

Most of Lorne's early education was at St. Nicholas Ukrainian Greek-Catholic school, with some post high school education at St. Paul's College in Winnipeg. Lorne often attended church with his mother at the Polish parish when not at the Ukrainian church with his father or friends. At home, Czech was mostly spoken. Lorne loved the varied and rich cultural heritage of his family, and within the culturally rich, if economically poor, multi-ethnic North End of Winnipeg. He loved languages and developed a class on the History of the English language when he taught later at the University of Manitoba. He acquired a love for French Canadian culture studying in Montreal at the English-speaking Loyola College, run by the Jesuits. While there, he often encouraged his fellow students to question their economics professor on accepted *orthodox* economic policies, something that would get him into trouble with the professor as an instigator.[7] When he gave a speech in class, in French, support-

[7] It is possible that this professor was intimately familiar with Social Credit, as the task was largely given to the Jesuit community of Quebec in 1939 to investigate Social Credit theory to see whether it was tainted by socialism, something that

ing Duplessis and the Union Nationale concerns, Lorne was one of the few at the English-speaking college that supported the Quebec Nationalist demands for provincial rights. Following his studies in Montreal, Lorne would return to study for a brief period at the University of Manitoba.

Lorne moved west, to British Columbia, where he worked loading grain on ships as a longshoreman and then worked as a stevedore on the Princess Joan ferry. While he was in British Columbia, the Social Credit party won the provincial election. He often explained that he had been shocked by this, not really believing it was possible for Social Credit to win in British Columbia. He remembered hearing kids at play chanting what must have been a provincial party campaign slogan: "You said it, Social Credit" leading up to the election, but like most others, never thought they would form the government.

Lorne went on to study and obtain a degree in theology at the Catholic University of America, as a seminarian for the Ukrainian Greek-Catholic Eparchy of Saskatoon. He lived at the Ukrainian College of St. Josaphat. While there, Lorne met his wife-to-be Joan Heslop, an American from upstate New York. They would move to Ottawa, where Lorne would continue his studies. Lorne later would be ordained as a Deacon, serving in the Ukrainian Greek-Catholic Archeparchy of Winnipeg.

Lorne was studying and working as an assistant professor at the University of Ottawa, during the 1960s, when Social Credit elected the largest contingent of MPs to the federal parliament. The party became divided during this time between the Quebec French faction and the English faction. Lorne assisted the federal leader Robert Thompson during this period from the English-speaking wing of the party. At the same time Lorne was a great admirer of Réal Caouette, the leader of the French-speaking Quebec based wing of the party. Lorne had the opportunity to meet Caouette as a messenger from Thompson. He was sent to speak to Caouette in Ottawa. Lorne felt that the Quebec MPs saw him as not trustworthy if not an outright spy for Thompson.

In 1966, Lorne moved his young family back to his home city of Winnipeg. He himself would run unsuccessfully as a candidate

---

was banned in Catholic Quebec. Their judgement was *negative* to the accusation. The report from the nine theologians regarding Social Credit is an interesting read, not only for Catholics but also for others. Various English translations are online, though the original was published in French, in the November 15, 1939, issue of the Montreal weekly *La Semaine Religieuse* (The Religious Weekly).

for Social Credit in the federal Riding of Provencher, Manitoba in 1968. Lorne would recall driving with one of the Mennonite farmers, a speaker attached to the roof of a car, and the cows along the road bellowing back, to which his local aide exclaimed, "*They must be Liberals!*"

Lorne was elected the leader of the Canadian federal Social Credit party in 1978. He ran unsuccessfully in a by-election for the federal Riding of St. Boniface, Manitoba. He would serve as party leader for eight months until he resigned from his position, partly due to growing opposition from the Quebec federal MPs. They had been his biggest supporters, but now desired a Quebec leader during a time of increased cooperation between the provincial separatist *Parti Québécois* and the Quebec wing of the federal Social Credit party. Lorne was also mentally exhausted by the constant travel and became dispirited by being away from his wife and children.

Lorne remained out of party politics from 1980 until his death from cancer on Nov. 9, 2011. From his experiences in politics, Lorne would often state that Douglas was right about the need for Social Credit to be a movement, a pressure group, rather than a political party. He was familiar with the Pilgrims of St. Michael movement (The "Bérets Blancs" of Louis Even) and would mention at times that a lot of money and effort was wasted in party politics, where many who did not understand Social Credit became involved only to advance their own political fortunes rather than the cause. He would state that the party was gone, so the critics who used to laugh at the Bérets Blancs have little to show, while the Pilgrims' movement had spread beyond Canada, educating individuals concerning the proposals of Social Credit theory. He would cite, as an example, an encounter he had had while he was leader of the federal party with a concerned gentleman who had asked him what he would do to *create jobs*. The correct answer, that Social Credit wanted to give *monetary credit dividends* to all citizens, not *create* unnecessary work and a waste of resources, would have been beyond the man's understanding without some study. Lorne stated that he was dispirited as leader by the need to win elections when the real need was to educate the public about Social Credit philosophy and policies.

To know Lorne, you must know what he enjoyed teaching, reading, and speaking about in conversation. He loved history and was always borrowing from the library, to read again, the various volumes of the *Jesuit Relations*, i.e., their early reports from their missions in New France. He loved teaching both American and English literature. He enjoyed speaking about Chaucer, Shakespeare, Jonathan Swift, Samuel Johnson and Boswell, Charles Dickens, Gerard Manley Hopkins, Mark Twain, Arthur Miller, Graham Greene, and Flannery O'Connor. He often reread and spoke about the Radical William Cobbett, or the political and religious journey of Whittaker Chambers.

He always spoke of the Distributists, Chesterton-Belloc together. He was a long-time reader of the Chesterton Review, from St. Thomas More College, Saskatoon, Saskatchewan. He tended to glorify those who farmed and their rural communities. This was from his own Catholic theological background and the Tory, Distributist influence from those he read. He believed that the death of rural livelihood in Canada and worldwide was undermining of both faith and family.

He never spoke of being a *Tory*, but often spoke negatively of the *Whig interpretation of history*. He was a supporter of the monarchy in Canada, though if he read some Jacobite book recently, he would make some negative references to the *German upstart House of Hanover*. As for Ukrainian history and politics, Lorne always spoke fondly of the Polish-Lithuanian Commonwealth period, and the Habsburg period in western Ukraine. He had sympathy for the monarchists among the Ukrainians, such as the Old Ruthenian and Hetmanate viewpoints. He would remember fondly the visit to his elementary school, the Ukrainian St. Nicholas School in Winnipeg,[8] when the Hetmanych, Danylo Pavlovych Skoropadskyi (Данило Павлович Скоропадський) visited on December 13, 1937. He also would speak fondly about the possibilities that might have been, from the close relationship between the Ukrainian Greek-Catholic Metropolitan Andrey Sheptytsky of Lviv, with the young Habsburg Archduke Wilhelm Franz of Austria,[9] in achieving Ukrainian independence under the Habsburgs. Both hopes would be considered archaic, if not laughable, by most Ukrainians today, but men are permitted to hope and dream.

Lorne began his work on Ezra Pound and Douglas in 1965, during a time of transition back to Winnipeg from Ottawa, Canada. He was offered a position at the University of Manitoba's St. Paul's College. Despite living in Winnipeg, even years later, he always pined for a

[8] Б/а, За Україну, 205.

[9] Wilhelm Habsburg died on August 18, 1948. He was arrested in the American zone of Vienna by the Soviets. They accused him of aiding the Organization of Ukrainian Nationalists (OUN) and Western intelligence. Snyder, *The Red Prince*.

return to Ottawa. In a letter written in 1967, he approached the University of Ottawa about the possibility of returning to teach. In their response, the university encouraged him to apply for an open position, while also advising that he do all he could to expedite the completion of his thesis on Ezra Pound, something difficult to do now from afar in Manitoba, with his four children and setting up new roots. In a draft of a letter, Lorne mentions that he was twice encouraged by the faculty at the University of Ottawa to complete his thesis in *haste*, as two English professors who served as key members of his thesis committee were soon to leave on sabbatical.

As the date of his expected thesis defence approached, a letter dated September 18, 1967, advised Lorne that the defence would be postponed due to "discovery of faulty documentation, punctuation and grammar". The letter was signed by Richard N. Pollard, chairman of the PhD Committee, and chairman of the Thesis Defence Board, with copies to professors Batzer (Pollard's partner and future wife), Marcotte, McGuinty, and O'Neill. This was followed by a letter from Pollard dated October 19, 1967, stating: "it now appears that parts of your thesis are plagiarised", with copies sent to the same individuals mentioned above, plus Pierre-Yves Boucher.

Lorne never denied there were problems with the thesis. In a draft letter he wrote dated July 18, 1968, he accepts much of the criticism levelled at the work in chapters one and two and summarizes: "I do plead guilty to stupidity but there was no intent on my part to plagiarize or to deceive Dr. McGuinty." My father explained that Pollard himself had proposed that McGuinty had never gone over the first two chapters of the Pound thesis but had only reviewed the last chapters on *The Cantos.* As would be expected, the first two should have been the easiest for Lorne. As he himself states, it was only a matter of clearly stating facts related to what Douglas and Pound had each stated in their writings on Social Credit. It was the interpretation of *The Cantos* that Lorne spent all his time on and which gave him, as it would give anyone, the most difficulty. Until my father died, he still felt that the episode poisoned his relationship with Dr. McGuinty, about whom Lorne always spoke with great admiration and respect.

The notion that Lorne was deliberately deceiving McGuinty is a bizarre fabrication, as McGuinty himself had a copy of the thesis, as did other faculty responsible for approving the scheduling of the final defence. McGuinty and anyone else on the thesis committee would have had the opportunity to examine the thesis for any errors. The main problem discovered in chapters I and II was that while properly quoting Pound or Douglas, Lorne had indirect quotes, which properly were direct quotes. He did not recall years later, but I suspect that he had written the work while planning to revise the quotes later on, which did not happen. The errors were obvious, which made the charges over the top. Lorne does not mention that he likewise was under pressure to apply to return to the University of Ottawa to teach, something that created a lot of stress between his parents, who wanted him to remain in Winnipeg, and his wife and himself. His wife Joan wanted to return to Ottawa, where she would be closer to her family in upstate New York. There are several letters from Ottawa and one from his own parents showing the pressure he was under to decide. In the chaos of resettling in Winnipeg as well as the personal mental depression he was in, he failed to reformat these direct quotes, or to adequately review the final typed version that his mother had completed.

My father realized there were other problems with the acceptance of his thesis, besides the one just mentioned. Pound was a controversial writer. At the time, Douglas and Social Credit were likewise controversial topics in Canada. In the 1960s, the federal Social Credit party was revitalized. This was causing trouble for the Liberals in their traditional stronghold of Quebec, just across the river from Ottawa. The Cuban Missile crisis had brought the question of whether nuclear warheads should be placed in Canada. Social Credit members from Quebec opposed the introduction of American supplied nuclear weapons into Canada, a response more in keeping with Canada's Left, but they were coming from their own unique Douglasite-French-Catholic-Nationalist position.

Lorne wrote how his professor of Irish literature, Dr. Michael O'Neill, had warned Lorne that his thesis would be controversial. Despite the political loyalties of several other English Department faculty being with other Canadian political parties, Lorne considered them not only fellow faculty, but friends. Lorne always felt a sense of loyalty to the professors at the University of Ottawa and respect for them as men of Faith. Dr. McGuinty, for example, was always a strong Liberal party supporter, but Lorne revered him and his large family of twelve children. McGuinty was elected as a member of Provincial Parliament for the Liberal party in Ontario, leading to his own family's dominance of the Ontario Liberal party and Ontario politics for years. Lorne did write, however, that he felt that the hiring of Pollard and Batzer had occurred because Marcotte and

McGuinty were opposed to the influence of Dr. Emmett O'Grady, former head of the English Department. They had both travelled to the US to personally meet Pollard and Batzer and encouraged and recommended their hiring.

From Lorne's own writings, and conversations I had with him, it was the new committee chair, Dr. Richard N. Pollard and his partner, Dr. Hazel Batzer, both hired together by agreement with the University of Ottawa, who opposed the thesis. Sensing Pollard's disdain for him and his research, Lorne had asked to transfer to another university, but was told, coming from Pollard, that the English Department would do all they could to stop his admittance to another college, be it on the Pound thesis or any other topic. The only choice they would support was to find a new subject for his doctorate, and to remain at St. Paul's at the University of Ottawa. In a conversation my father related that he had met Pollard once during the time of this controversy, and he was treated with respect by him. Pollard mentioned though how his own French *Doctorat d'État* State Doctoral thesis had been saluted by the French Academy with high honours. In a letter to my father from Dr. Campbell, who was, at the time, in France, Campbell mentioned that he was afraid that, with himself gone on sabbatical, Lorne would be given trouble by others in the English Department. But Lorne never mentioned that any other English Department staff had treated him unfairly during his time at the university up until the problems he encountered with the thesis. In a letter written by Professor Campbell to Lorne, he writes: "I don't see how the thesis can be rejected, if that is what happened. You have been around long enough to know that this is irregular even at Ottawa.... If they signed the project, they not you, should be held responsible and made to defend the project. What happened to Dalton? Did he give the direction over to another? Had he not okayed the final printing one way or another? Was Dr. O'Neill not supposed to be one of the readers? You would not be supposed to know that, but he should come to your aid."

Who was Pollard? Our family would hear from several individuals following Pollard and his wife's departure from the University of Ottawa that Richard Pollard, it had been found, did not possess a doctorate as he claimed when hired. Only one member of the English Department approached my father directly soon after, and another later spoke to my brother, expressing the same. They related that Pollard had deceived the university into believing he had obtained his Doctorate at the University of Paris. Is this true?

In 1974, less than a year before they left the University of Ottawa, Pollard and Batzer published a book.[10] On the book jacket it does not mention that Pollard obtained his PhD at the Sorbonne in Paris, but states: "*Richard Pollard* received his PhD from the University of Strasbourg." This contradicts his academic claim that is found at the University of Ottawa archives, which clearly states he held his doctorate from the University of Paris. This likewise contradicts what Pollard stated when he supposedly obtained his doctorate, while teaching at Adams State College, a community college in Alamosa, Colorado. In an article in the college newspaper,[11] the following is written:

> If Dr. Richard N. Pollard, assistant professor of English, had only hung his hat somewhere in France during the year 1951 he would have been the holder of the much esteemed and difficult to get French doctoral degree in literature ten years sooner.
>
> ...The reason for this much belated honor is that even though Dr. Pollard had satisfactorily completed all requirements for the degree in 1950 he failed to satisfy a French ruling which demands all candidates for the doctoral degree to have at least two years residence in France.
>
> A particular requirement of European universities concerning doctoral dissertations is that all published, existing sources of information dealing with the subject, must be investigated, and included in the dissertation. The delay has been due to the difficulty in establishing the existence of a volume dealing with the topic discussed in Dr. Pollard's dissertation.
>
> Its non-existence has finally been accepted through affidavits to this effect from various culture attaches and libraries throughout the world. Thus, the final delay has been obliterated.
>
> The Orestes-Electra Dilemma has been historically traced by Dr. Pollard from its beginning in Homer's Illiad [sic] to modern times. In this dissertation, Dr. Pollard examined instances throughout European literature (the psychological dilemma of avenging the murder of one's father by killing one's mother).
>
> During 1957–58 Dr. Pollard returned to France for further study at the University of Paris and to gain that very troublesome second year of French residency....

---

10 Pollard and Pollard, *From Human Sentience.*

11 "Dr. Richard Pollard Receives," *The South Coloradan.*

> During the 1949–50 he attended the University of Straubourg [*sic*], France, where he became enthused with the European approach to study. His thesis which was written in French, was on the Orestes-Electra dilemma.... Dr. Pollard said in reference to the French system, "I like the scholarship requirements of thesis that must be unique and original and a contribution to the field of study."...
>
> ...Dr. Pollard hopes that his thesis will be published within the year. The thesis will serve as an introductory volume for a thirty volume work dealing with comparative studies in the Orestes-Electra story.

Pollard's thesis was never published. This is bizarre considering what is stated in the above article in praise of his work and its future publication along with thirty additional volumes. Likewise, it is bizarre that he would collaborate to have his wife's thesis published,[12] while not making any effort to publish his own already completed work. One can search for Pollard's work at the University of Paris Library website and find nothing. One can search for any reference to his allegedly important work and find no citations by others, neither quoting nor referencing the thesis. Correspondence was undertaken by me with both the University of Paris and their library, asking if there was any evidence of a doctorate being received by Pollard at the Sorbonne, or even the existence of his thesis; both replies came back in the negative. As to the book jacket claim that he possessed a "Ph.D from the University of Strasbourg" and to my request to Strasbourg for evidence that Pollard obtained a doctorate from that institution, or if a thesis existed, the reply was also negative to both questions. He had been a student there, as he would be later in Paris, but that is all. Pollard's master's thesis had been on a similar topic.[13]

The University of Ottawa betrayed my father and the other students and staff, *via* the English Department's gross negligence in hiring Pollard, thereby aiding Pollard's deceit. In my ongoing correspondence with the English Department at the University of Ottawa, they were not interested in investigating the issue further, even after I provided the above evidence. The last letter received was dated January 26, 2012, and written by Antoni Lewkowicz, the Dean of the Faculty of Arts. In it he writes: "Richard Pollard is deceased and unable to respond to these allegations, the evidence to

[12] Pollard, "From Heroics to Sentimentalism."
[13] Pollard, "The Electra Theme."

date is insufficient to confirm that he did not hold the degree that he claimed, and even if I were to obtain additional evidence, the sort of statement you are requesting likely would not be permissible under privacy laws."

Knowing that there does not seem to exist a thesis by Pollard, no evidence that he obtained his Docteur des Lettres at the University of Paris, one can read Pollard's book *From Human Sentience . . .* , as a manual justifying his actions. It is, in totality, a rejection of the practice of students drafting a thesis to obtain their degree. From the preface,[14] where they break all writing conventions by writing eighteen lines with no periods, they make it clear that this is something that will not conform to academic standards. They write later: "To achieve the present work, we have pooled a century of sentience, nine decades of intense study, and half a century of teaching experience. Some may object to the absence of footnotes, bibliography, and other scholarly paraphernalia . . . but the essential material of this study comes from experience that can not be attributed to any particular authority."[15] One could cite several quotes from their work showing that they are rejecting the traditional concept of an academic thesis. For them, anything that is not something totally *new,* such as a critique of another's artistic creation rather than writing one's own play, is considered as a "substitution" for real artwork. "Substitution assumes that interpretation is superior to the art that it acts upon; it arrogates unto itself the function of art improvement, to bring art up to standards it sets."[16] Finally, they write on their novel concept of plagiarism, which would apply to any literary based thesis: "Substitution, or any of the qualities that make up substitution, steals from art, exercises a sort of reverse plagiarism by inserting into art conditions and meanings contrary to those it lifts from art."[17] The consequences of the Pollard incident in relation to the Pound thesis had lasting effects on Lorne and his family. Today, Pollard's behaviour could certainly be considered a form of academic bullying. He engaged in posturing to present himself as something that he was not.

I spoke to my father about the response from Ezra Pound to my father's letter. He smiled and replied that he felt compelled to follow what Pound suggested, but he realized it was a monumental task. He decided to drop anything that obviously was Social Credit related

---

14 Pollard and Pollard, *From Human Sentience*, v.

15 Pollard and Pollard, *From Human Sentience*, vii.

16 Pollard and Pollard, *From Human Sentience*, 256.

17 Pollard and Pollard, *From Human Sentience*, 257.

from Pound's prose writing, as the Douglasite influence on Pound in those instances would have been self-evident to any reader. My father stated that even *The Cantos* on its own, as it related to Douglas's influence, was too large; there was so much to comment on. Lorne suggested that he should have kept it to just a part of *The Cantos,* but felt compelled as a young student to be faithful to Pound's letter. The letter was a blessing, but a curse too, if one was trying to complete it in two years. Despite this, my father was fascinated by the project, i.e., seeing throughout Pound's monumental written output the influence of Douglas on Pound.

Despite all Lorne endured, he still enjoyed teaching at St. Paul's College at the University of Manitoba, as well as spending time with his family and friends. Lorne had a humility that is evidenced in some of his comical self-referential statements, such as "I never had an original thought in my life." He would jest that "most professors are educated far beyond their own intelligence." Lorne stated that he enjoyed speaking more to the janitors at the university, rather than to fellow professors. Especially he singled out Stefan Korytko, who had suffered much from both Soviet and Nazi occupation of Ukraine and who could hold his own against any professor when it came to a discussion on Eastern European history or Canadian politics.

I am certain my father would agree, based on Pound's dismissal of universities as mere *Beaneries*, that above the door of most North American Liberal Arts Colleges should be placed the warning of Dante's Inferno:

Abandon All Hope Ye Who Enter Here[18]

My father, as mentioned, never received any further letters from Ezra Pound. He received several from Dorothy Pound, in which she would kindly answer his questions and support him with copies of material she thought would be of interest to his work.

My father at some time wrote to Ezra Pound's daughter, Princess Mary de Rachewiltz. We can find letters dated from 1972 to 1989. She was always kind and supportive. When our family was in Europe my father was invited to visit. In June 1975, he travelled with my brother and me, age 11, by train from Garmisch-Partenkirchen, Germany. The few days we spent were, for a young boy, quite magical. I remember staying in a small family-run hotel in Dorf Tyrol. I recall attending

[18] Alighieri, *The Inferno*, Canto III, 9.

Mass at the local church, it being full and having to stand outside. It was the feast of Corpus Christi, and, at this time, there was a local festival with food and games. Eventually, one day, we walked down to the castle below, Brunnenburg Castle which to me, as a child, seemed like the sort of castle one would see only in storybooks with its parapets. Eventually we met Pound's daughter, Mary, climbing upstairs within a tower to an office. There we all sat down while my father spoke. Mary was kind enough to take us to the parapets from which there was an incredible view.

My father always hoped to finish his work; he was still writing and received an encouraging reply from Mary de Rachewiltz in 1989. Unfortunately, it was never to be. He found it too much, having to take early retirement, trying to write his own biography, family history, and enjoying time with his grandchildren. Shortly before he died, Lorne mentioned that Mary was surprised that Lorne had received a letter dated April 20, 1965, from her father, Ezra Pound. Pound at that time was not known to respond often to letters, especially from individuals he did not personally know.

As to the present work, in 2011, when Lorne was already sick with cancer, I made some tentative steps looking at this and other works Lorne had written. It was only possible following his death to begin more seriously. Every time I thought it was nearly finished, I would see problems. His first chapter was taken exclusively from Douglas's *Economic Democracy*. Now I can remember entering a used bookstore on Academy Ave. in Winnipeg, in the late 1990s or early 2000s. In a locked cabinet, there were many books by C. H. Douglas. When I asked the store clerk she explained that they were selling for hundreds of dollars, especially to buyers in Japan. Currently, with the internet and many of Douglas's works well past their copyright restrictions, it is much easier to find passages of C. H. Douglas that had an influence on Ezra Pound beyond what Lorne was able to reference in the 1960s.

I am no expert in economics and Douglas's theories. I therefore approached Dr. M. Oliver Heydorn, whom I knew from his writings on Social Credit, to help with my father's work, especially concerning Douglas. I had already begun to add references to Douglas's works directly into the appropriate sections of Pound's works, and Dr. Heydorn continued to find and to add what seemed the best sections to take from Douglas's works.

The Pound sections are mostly my father's work. Even so, some additions were needed, mostly to incorporate current research on sections of *The Cantos* referenced. The following chapters on *The Cantos* are all the allusions Lorne had referenced, minus one or two he had not explained and were therefore deleted. Additional passages were added from the work of other Pound researchers regarding allusions Lorne had already referenced. As will be noted in the work, Lorne covered Canto I to Canto CIX, which is what was in print circa 1967. This did not include the Italian Cantos, nor the blacked-out sections of Canto LII, nor Canto CX and what followed. Some of Pound's allusions, and Lorne's references to them, had to be changed, as there has been so much study done on Pound since the late 1960s. We tried to be faithful to Lorne's writing and comments, but also to bring new research into his work in accordance with what he would have written himself. Even so, there will be much we leave unanswered. Pound's written output is so vast, and there are major differences in opinion concerning many allusions that are found in Pound, either to what they reference or, more often, to their meaning.

I likewise approached my sister Gabriella Reznowski for help, to read and correct some of my own writing, to provide advice, and to do some research when questions arose. She was always supportive of this project.

As for any errors in this work, I take responsibility for them. As for anything of value, the credit goes especially to my father who saw in many places what others had not seen: the influence of Douglas on Pound. Likewise, credit goes to Dr. Heydorn for providing an accurate presentation and interpretation of Douglas's writings and thought.

GENERAL INTRODUCTION

The purpose of this work is to show that no other influence so powerfully affected the content of Ezra Pound's writings as that of C. H. Douglas.[19] Ezra Pound first met Douglas in 1918 at the very time that Douglas's first articles on what he named *Social Credit* were beginning to appear. Pound was introduced to Douglas by the Guild Socialist Alfred Richard Orage, who was to become Douglas's first prominent convert to the philosophy and policy of Social Credit.

[19] C. H. Douglas was a "Consulting Engineer and Economist; . . . Chief Engineer and Manager in India, British Westinghouse Co., Ltd.; Assistant Chief El. Engineer, B. A. and Pacific Ry.; Assistant Superintendent Royal Aircraft Factory; witness, Canadian Banking Enquiry, 1923; MacMillan Committee, 1930, etc.; Chief Reconstruction Adviser, Government of Alberta, 1935; late Major R. F. C. and R. A. F." "Douglas, Clifford Hugh" *Who's Who 1938*, 937–38. The *Ottawa Citizen* newspaper and the Southam family who published it had been instrumental in having him invited to appear before the Canadian Banking Enquiry. Irving, *The Social Credit Movement*, 74.

As a result of his meeting with C. H. Douglas and his introduction to the philosophy of Social Credit, Pound became profoundly interested in monetary-economic history. He became convinced that it was essential for the artist to understand the nature and history of money. He also became convinced that usury, as Pound understood it in its modern usage, was the direct cause of decadence which he saw all around him in the realm of arts and letters.

The theme of his great masterpiece, *The Cantos*, is that of the age-old struggle between the creator of goods and the man who gets a corner on the market, a monopoly. The most vicious cornering of the market—as we will see—according to Pound, is that to be found in the cornering of the money-market, i.e., the monopoly of money, the monopoly of credit.

Pound, in *The Cantos*, traces this epic struggle between the usurer and the rest of humanity, through ancient Chinese history, Medieval, and Renaissance Italian history, the early history of the United States, particularly as seen in the Jefferson-Adams correspondence, and finally up to the Bretton Woods agreement, drafted by Harry Dexter White. This is seen in the Chinese *Cantos*, the Italian *Cantos*, and the American *Cantos*. The contemporary scene is also dealt with in the *Rock Drill Cantos* and in the *Throne Cantos*.

This work will attempt to show the nature and extent of the impact of C. H. Douglas on the poetry and prose of Ezra Pound. It will seek to show that the philosophy of C. H. Douglas was a most powerful influence on *The Cantos* and on much of the other poetry and prose of Ezra Pound. The writer hopes to contribute to a deeper understanding and more profound appreciation of *The Cantos* in particular, and of the writings of Ezra Pound in general. Pound's close collaborator in printing his works, James Laughlin, states "Pound's economic theories were a mishmash of eccentricities."[20] In contrast to Laughlin and others, this work will attempt to show that Douglasism is the uniting factor in Pound's study of economics, history, art, leisure, causes of war, control of the press, control of education, fashion, etc.

This will be achieved *via* the presentation of Douglas Social Credit philosophy and policy and an examination of the impact that these had upon Pound's writings. The Social Credit influence will be identified by first examining some of Pound's prose works dealing with Douglasism. Afterward, *The Cantos* will be carefully examined for direct influence of the philosophy and policy advocated by Douglas.

---

[20] Laughlin, *Pound as Wuz*, 166.

In examining *The Cantos*, it will be necessary to quote from them at length. This is due primarily to the fact that there has not yet been a book or thesis done on the influence of Douglas on Pound. Richard G. Landini's dissertation "A Guide to the Economic Thought in Ezra Pound's Cantos" merely scratches the surface of the Douglasite influence, though with great insight that provided much guidance in this present work. In addition to this, Landini makes some significant errors due to his not being fully conversant with Douglas Social Credit.

CHAPTER I

The Douglas Social Credit Vision for Finance and the Economy

M. Oliver Heydorn, Ph.D.

In order to properly understand the influence of Douglas Social Credit on Pound, one must first understand what Douglas Social Credit entails—hence the necessity of this brief introduction.[1]

IN SPITE OF THE INITIAL INTIMIDATION FACTOR that Douglas Social Credit might possess as a body of thought—one that is (1) relatively new in economic history (having emerged only in the last one hundred years or so), (2) relatively unknown, and (3) radically different from other alternatives in both its approach and its prescriptions—Douglas's financial and economic ideas are really not that difficult to comprehend. Indeed, when the Social Credit vision of the world is presented in terms of certain everyday realities—realities with which most modern people are intimately familiar—the intellectual passage from the unknown to the known is easily traversable. I am thinking, of course, of the world of computers as the basis for an extended analogy. From that world we can draw a variety of comparisons that should effectively illuminate the Douglas analysis and proposals in a manner that will make the seemingly complex and abstruse luminously intelligible.

THE NATURE OF THE ECONOMY

Let us start with the simple and straightforward observation that the economy has two distinct dimensions to it. To begin with, there is the real, or *physical* economy, involving the actual production, distribution, and consumption of goods and services that answer to human needs or desires. This more tangible aspect is composed of raw materials, labour, real capital (machines, equipment, and tools), know-how, and so forth. In the second place, there is the more intangible dimension to the economy that sits 'above' the physical economy as a virtual reality, and this is the financial economy. The financial

[1] Douglas Social Credit has nothing to do with the much more recent CCP 'social credit' system introduced in China. If anything, they are opposites.

economy consists of money (which exists mainly in the form of the enumerated abstraction known as bank credit), of costs and prices, of inflation and deflation, of securities (bonds and shares), of taxation, of derivatives, and of many other things of a similar nature.

Thankfully, for our purposes, these two dimensions of our economic life can be likened to the two basic dimensions that define the world of computers: hardware and software. The hardware refers to the more tangible, material component of the computer, the parts having mass and occupying space, while the software is the more intangible, formal element, consisting in the coding of a particular programme. Thus, the real or physical economy is akin to the different elements that make up the hardware of a computer, i.e., the motherboard, the CPU, the keyboard, the mouse, the screen, and so forth. The financial economy, on the other hand, is analogous to the software that may be loaded onto the computer and which allows the user to direct the computer's hardware to perform certain tasks in keeping with the programming contained in the software. Just as a computer's software gives form, direction, and a certain sort of limitation or determination as to how its hardware is to be deployed, the financial system is a means by which we conceive of the physical potential of the economy's hardware and then set it into motion to produce and distribute certain desired results to the end users, i.e., the consumers, in keeping with the specific financial rules or 'programming' that have been put in place.

The foregoing suffices as a general description of the nuts and bolts of the economic system and its two basic dimensions. But these dimensions, the real and the financial, the economy's hardware and software, can be related to one another in a number of different ways. These varying configurations are not all of equal worth or of equal utility. In order to evaluate how these two dimensions *ought* to be related, that is, which arrangement is the best arrangement that will yield optimal results, we need to introduce the normative notion of purpose. What is the purpose of the economy? Once we know what the true purpose of an economy is we will also know what constitutes a good economy and what is necessary for its achievement. For as Aristotle observed, something is a good exemplar of its kind when it fulfils its purpose well. Thus, just as a good knife is one which cuts well, i.e., one which fulfils its due function well (the purpose of a knife being to cut), so too a good economy is one which fulfils its due function or purpose well.

Douglas says that the true or fundamental purpose of the economy may be defined as follows: it exists for the sake of delivering the goods and services that people need to survive and flourish with the least amount of resource consumption and of human labour. As he explains in *Warning Democracy*:

> . . . the policy of the world economic system amounts to a philosophy of life. There are really only three alternative policies in respect to a world economic organisation:
>
> The first is that it is the end in itself for which man exists.
>
> The second is that while not an end in itself, it is the most powerful means of constraining the individual to do things he does not want to do; e.g., it is a system of government. This implies a fixed ideal of what the world ought to be.
>
> And the third is that the economic activity is simply a functional activity of men and women in the world; that the end of man, while unknown, is something towards which most rapid progress is made by the free expansion of individuality, and that, therefore, economic organisation is most efficient when it most easily and rapidly supplies economic wants without encroaching on other functional activities.
>
> You cannot spend too much time in making these issues clear to your minds, because until they are clear you are not in a position to offer an opinion on any economic proposal whatever.[2]

Thus, a good economy is one which fulfills this due function well in view of its real or physical possibilities. If what is physically possible and desirable is easily made manifest and people receive the goods and services they require in order to survive and flourish with the least amount of labour and resource consumption, then the economy may be deemed a success. But this success, this fulfillment, is dependent, in turn, on the *proper* relationship obtaining between the real, physical economy on the one hand, and the financial economy on the other.

For there are two differing roads, two paths, as it were, that can be followed here. There is what we might call "the path of truth", where the financial software is designed in such a way that the figures it projects reflect, as an adequate, accurate instrument should, whatever is happening in terms of the actual or potential rate of production relative to the real demand for that production. But there is also, as an alternative, "the path of the lie", where the financial software is poorly designed and, as a result, it does not accurately represent the physical facts in its operation, but paints a picture of the real economy that is artificially limited and hence distorted or misleading. *The difference in question is thus the difference between an honest financial system and a dishonest financial system.*

---

2 Douglas, *Warning Democracy*, 37–38.

HONEST VS. DISHONEST FINANCIAL SYSTEMS

When the financial system is properly designed as an honest system, one that gives a truthful reading of the physical economic facts, something new comes into being: the functional order of the economy can be and is fulfilled. For when the financial software is truthful in its functioning, the financial dimension of the economy becomes subordinate, i.e., subservient to the real economy (as it should be, since the real economy is objectively and necessarily more important than its symbolic representation). This puts the agents for whom the real economy exists, i.e., the individual citizens in their role as consumers, in the driver's seat, and it allows the whole mechanism of the economy to perform to its fullest physical potential in response to the directing power of those agents. There is no artificial limitation or distortion accruing to the use of an inadequate financial software that conditions what the agents can and cannot do. The path of truth thus turns out, quite appropriately, to be the path of goodness, the path of fulfillment.

On the level of production, this would mean that whenever there is, on the one hand, a legitimate desire for some good or service, and, on the other hand, the physical capacity (the raw materials, labour, machinery, know-how, etc.) to satisfy that desire, then the financial system should automatically supply or make available sufficient producer credit so that that production can be catalyzed. In other words, there should be no artificial limits on production. The financial software should function in such a way that financial credit, the capacity to deliver credit, as when and where required, will be issued in a sufficient volume so as to mirror in full the real credit of a society, i.e., the capacity to deliver goods and services as when and where required. *If one hundred trillion in goods and services is desired in the world in the course of a year and the physical economy can handle that demand, then sufficient credit to catalyze the production of that one hundred trillion should be automatically forthcoming, ceteris paribus.* This is the very purpose of the financial software, i.e., to serve as a neutral tool that simply presents an accurate picture of the physical economic potential in conjunction with the desire to make use of that potential.

On the level of consumption, an honest financial software would operate in such a way that whatever is produced at whatever remunerative price (i.e., costs plus a reasonable profit margin) is mirrored by a sufficient flow of consumer income to liquidate all the relevant costs of production in full and to thereby distribute the entire inventory of goods and services to consumers. Only when this condition is fulfilled is the financial system accurately representing the value of goods and services with their due counterpart in the form of income. *If one hundred trillion in consumer goods and services at remunerative prices has been produced in the world in the course of a year, then the financial system should automatically supply one hundred trillion in income with which those goods and services could be purchased.* The result of this truthful financial representation would be the establishment of an inherent balance between the flow of costs/prices on the one hand, and the flow of consumer buying power in the form of incomes on the other, i.e., a self-liquidating equilibrium.

When, by contrast, the financial system is not properly designed and functions instead as a dishonest system, the picture it paints of the real economy hampers the ability of economic agents to fulfill the true purpose of economic association. This is because the inaccurate picture of the economy that is then presented is a limited and distorted one. In this case, the physical economic system becomes subservient to the financial system. A metaphysical inversion takes place where the more real (the physical economy) is at the mercy of the less real (the financial economy) and indeed the former ends up being, to some significant extent, sacrificed for the latter. This puts those who have a vested interest in the financial system and its operation in the driver's seat in lieu of the common individuals who make up an economic association. The path of the lie turns out to be the path of both dysfunction (inadequate fulfillment), and exploitation/oppression.

On the level of production, 'following the path of the lie' means that the financial software would often fail to make the needed producer credit available and, as a result, some proportion of the real credit would remain unactualized and some people would go without needed goods and services—even though the physical resources to meet those needs are all present. The financial software would systemically underestimate, if you will, the physical or objective capacity of the real economy to provide needed goods and services, and thus their production is not fully catalyzed. Perhaps, to refer to the previous example we used, only sixty trillion of the one hundred trillion of desired goods and services that could and should be produced is actually produced.

Why does this lack of producer credit occur? One of the key limiting factors here has to do with the lack of effective demand that would support the kind of organic economic growth, or retooling, which would actualize the real credit of society in full. This brings us to examine the second major issue concerning the malfunctioning of an improperly designed, i.e., a structurally dishonest, financial software: the artificial limitations it imposes on the power to consume.

As far as consumption is concerned, a dishonest system fails to automatically supply a sufficient flow of income to match the flow of goods and services with remunerative prices attached. Instead, only a certain proportion of those goods and services is represented by corresponding income. That is, the value of goods and services is systematically or structurally underestimated by the financial software in terms of the consumer buying power which it simultaneously or automatically renders available and with which those goods and services are to be purchased. The resultant deficiency is known in Douglas Social Credit literature as the price-income gap.[3] It is not that the system cannot supply more consumer buying power in order to clear the market, but that it doesn't do so simply in virtue of the production itself and can only do so by getting someone to contract additional debt. Additional production financed via more debt-money has to be undertaken to release the additional money required to fill the gap, or else consumers have to obtain more money by some other means (we will return to a fuller discussion of the conventional methods of managing the gap shortly).

THE NATURE OF THE CURRENT FINANCIAL SYSTEM

Unfortunately—but not surprisingly—the reigning financial system in the world has, according to its faulty design, embodied the path of the lie: the financial software does not properly mirror the physical economic reality, but rather limits and distorts it. The physical economic reality is thus subordinated to the financial software. The results are less than fully functional, as we have seen: the software fails to enable or to facilitate the fulfillment of the economy's purpose in an optimal way (i.e., to the extent that such a realization is physically or objectively possible). Instead, by limiting and distorting the physical economic facts in the picture it paints of those facts, it actively interferes with the fulfillment of the economy's purpose and sets it on a different path, a path that falls short, that misses the mark. Economic life is more inefficacious, inefficient, unfair, and harmful to persons, the social order, the political order, and the environment than it otherwise would be. One of Douglas's core claims is precisely this: the economic system simply cannot properly fulfill its true purpose of delivering the goods and services that people need to survive and flourish (with the least amount of labour and resource consumption)

[3] Please note that the gap is not caused, in the main, by usury, but by cost accountancy conventions as applied to real capital (machines and equipment, etc.).

so long as the current financial system utilises the faulty software with which we are attempting to run our economies.

The state of affairs just described would be bad enough even if it were the whole story, but there is a flipside to the dysfunction which demonstrates that the situation is, unfortunately, even worse. The poor design of the financial software, "poor" from the point of view of the economy's true purpose, is actually a "good" design if one were running the economy for a different purpose at the expense of its true purpose. The alternative purpose in question is the centralization of wealth, power, and privilege in the hands of those who own the private financial system and those on whom they bestow their largesse. In other words, the current financial software governs the real economy in such a way that it disproportionately enfranchises a small group of plutocrats at the top of the social hierarchy at the expense of all those who occupy any rung beneath them.[4] The result is a pyramidical societal structure built fundamentally on one qualifier: the possession of money or the size of one's bank account as determined by the current rules. All who produce and consume under the financial pyramid serve the pyramid and especially those at the top of the pyramid. Depending on their degree of alacrity and competence in serving the pyramid, they are rewarded proportionately and are permitted to move up the rungs. This describes, in the most general sense, the usurious dimension of existing economic arrangements that Ezra Pound, in particular, railed against so vehemently. Naturally, a usurious financial and economic regime bears its own characteristically negative social, cultural, and, above all, political implications.

Thus, the general consequences of running the economy according to the rules of a dishonest financial software is that while it yields suboptimal results with respect to the true purpose of economic association, it yields more or less optimal results from the point of view of those who have positioned themselves to usurp, as much as possible and for their own private purposes, the unearned increment of economic association (which is an aspect of the commons).[5]

---

[4] It may be that the 'error' of the price-income gap largely emerged as a kind of 'bug' that was not intended by anyone, but then, when the bug was pointed out to those responsible for running the system by C. H. Douglas and others, there was no desire to change it because they realized that they were profiting handsomely—albeit illegitimately—from it.

[5] The commons refers to the cultural and natural resources that are accessible to all members of a society. The commons land in the medieval village, for example, delivered various benefits to the peasants on a generous and customary basis.

CONVENTIONAL METHODS OF BRIDGING THE PRICE-INCOME GAP

The great opportunity for the usurers arises from this fact: the main method that the existing financial system employs in order to fill the price-income gap is to induce someone to borrow more money into existence from the banking system in order to directly supplement the flow of consumer buying power (*via* the issuance of consumer loans and lines of credit, including mortgages, car loans, student loans, credit cards, installment buying plans, etc.) or else to induce governments and/or businesses to borrow additional money into being for the purpose of expanding public or capital production. This latter approach would distribute additional wages, salaries, and dividends, i.e., additional consuming buying power, without, in the same period of time, increasing the rate of flow of consumer goods and services. In order to properly appreciate this reliance on increasing debt as a method of compensating for the gap, one must already understand that under the existing debt-money system every bank loan creates money *ex nihilo* in the form of bank credit and every repayment of a bank loan destroys bank credit. The vast majority of the money supply exists in the form of bank credit (rather than notes and coins) and most of that bank credit is issued in the form of a repayable debt.[6]

An alternative to further indebtedness is to seek the establishment of a 'favourable balance of trade.' By exporting in monetary terms more than what one imports, it becomes possible to narrow the gap in both directions, i.e., by (1) getting rid of some of the surplus production that is not otherwise sellable, and by (2) distributing additional wages, salaries, and dividends *via* the activities of the exporting companies. This is, however, a zero sum game, with both winners and losers and it thus induces its own problems, including trade wars and military conflicts.

Let it therefore be stressed once again that the Douglas Social Credit claim that there is a 'deficiency of purchasing power' does not mean that there is not or never can be enough purchasing power to buy all the goods on offer, but only that the necessary purchasing is not *automatically* distributed in full. Instead, the extra purchasing power must come from investment in additional cycles of production, and/or from the extension of consumer loans, and/or from favourable trade balances. Douglas broke down these matters as follows:

---

[6] Cf. Bank of England, Money Creation in the Modern Economy, *Quarterly Bulletin* 2014 Q1, https://www.bankofengland.co.uk/-/media/boe/files/quarterly-bulletin/2014/money-creation-in-the-modern-economy.pdf.

> We are often told that it is obviously absurd to say that the financial system does not distribute sufficient purchasing power to buy the goods that are for sale. *We* never said it! What we do say is that, under the present monetary system, in order to have sufficient purchasing power to distribute goods for consumption, it is necessary to make a disproportionate amount of capital goods and goods for export.
>
> Sweden is held up as a wonderful example of how well the monetary system can work. Sweden is producing about three times as much as she is actually consuming, but owing to vagaries of exchange she is able to export the remaining two-thirds. She has to take three times as much trouble as is really necessary in order to make the monetary system work.
>
> That is, broadly speaking, the situation. In this country, and in every modern country, in order to make the present monetary system work at all, you have got to make a whole lot of things that are not immediately bought in order to distribute what is already available.[7]

DELETERIOUS CONSEQUENCES OF CONVENTIONAL METHODS OF BRIDGING THE GAP

We have already mentioned that the conventional methods of filling the gap, while enabling the economy to hobble along, provoke all sorts of economic, social, environmental, political, cultural, and international problems. It is now time to specify in some greater detail what these are and to discuss exactly how these difficulties arise. Since the gap is not always filled adequately, there can be recessions. There can also be demand-pull inflation if too much compensatory money is issued, and the gap is overshot. This is what occurs in a boom and the economy "overheats." The tremendous increase in public and private debts which accompany the filling of the recurring price-income gap also leads to periodic financial crises as the aggregate debt can become too large and the economy becomes incapable of carrying it. Banks then cease to lend as confidence declines, a credit crunch ensues, and bankruptcies and an economic slowdown/contraction follows. This does allow, however, for some of the debt to be written off and for the economy to return to a path of growth once the pain subsides.

The steady increase in debt also drives another kind of inflation, known as cost-push. The more debt there is, the more income is diverted to servicing repayments and interest charges, and the more

---

[7] Douglas, *The Approach to Reality*, 26–27.

income is diverted, the more difficult it becomes to maintain the standard of living on the basis of existing incomes. This leads to demands for wage and salary increases to compensate. But since wages and salaries must eventually be recovered in costs and hence prices, this causes prices to increase. Cost-push inflation is one of the ways we try to relativize the size of the ever-increasing societal debt load that is a by-product of conventional methods of filling the price-income gap.

These methods of dealing with the gap are also inefficient in a physical sense because it means we have to work harder and longer than would otherwise be necessary on things that no one really wants or would not want under a saner system (which implies a tremendous amount of waste and sabotage) in order to obtain the additional buying power necessary to distribute the surplus of those goods and services that are desired and needed.

For the same reason, the existing system is unjust insofar as it does not automatically enfranchise the consuming public with the sufficient buying power which should be theirs by right. Whatever has been paid for in physical terms (and everything that has been produced and is waiting for purchase must have been paid for already in physical terms, otherwise it would not exist), should, if the financial system accurately reflected reality, be capable of being purchased in full in financial terms while leaving no residue of debt. To deny the public the consuming power to match their producing power is to fail to give citizens their due; it is a gross injustice.

Beyond that, filling the gap with debt-money combined with the need for constant economic growth plays a huge role in the heavy and often increasing taxation under which we labour, installs servility in the form of wage and debt-slavery, centralizes economic wealth, privilege, and power into fewer and fewer hands (i.e., the hands of those who own the financial system or otherwise profit from its operations), induces forced migration, cultural dislocation, unnecessary stresses and strains, social conflict, environmental degradation, and can provoke international economic conflict (since not all countries can simultaneously enjoy favourable trade balances) which can then lead to war, etc. We pay a very heavy price in dysfunction at all levels of our human existence for the running of the financial system as a private monopoly that alone possesses the means of alleviating the price-income gap. Poverty in the midst of plenty, as bad as that is, is merely one of the more salient features of the dysfunctional financial and economic regime under which we are forced to toil.

DOUGLAS'S MONETARY REFORM PROPOSALS

If the financial software is, at present, the great limiting and distorting factor, that which is obstructing the fulfillment of the economy's true purpose and simultaneously delivering wealth, privilege, and power into the hands of the few, then the proper rectification of the economy must involve a rewriting of the financial software. Douglas's specific proposals for monetary reform might be thought of, therefore, as a set of guidelines for re-engineering the economic system by rewriting and redesigning its financial software. We need a new and better financial programming if we wish to obtain more satisfactory results for the people. Douglas Social Credit provides the fundamental principles and a set of suggested mechanism for orchestrating this change.

The first and most general rule that should be followed by a new and improved financial system would be that it should function as an honest system; i.e., it should embody accuracy by mirroring in the world of intangible numbers the facts of the real economy as these change from period to period. The financial system is not to limit or to distort our conception of either our economic potential, or of the real flow of wealth that is available at any moment in time, but must rather serve as a transparent and faithful representation of the objective facts concerning both.

To this end, Douglas proposed the establishment of a National Credit Authority whose main task would be to introduce, monitor, and regulate a National Monetary Policy. This policy would be the new objective to which the whole of the financial system would be directed.

On the level of production, whenever there is, on the one hand, a legitimate need for some good or service, and, on the other, the raw material, real capital, labour, know-how, etc., to meet that need, then the National Credit Authority should ensure that sufficient producer credit will be created and issued to the relevant productive agencies in order to guarantee that the desired production will, in fact, be catalyzed. If, in a given nation, ten trillion dollars' worth of physical assets is available to be monetized, then that forms the backing against which ten trillion dollars could be issued for production purposes. This would require the introduction of a National Balance Sheet. On the side of the assets, all productive resources that might find their way into production could be given a value in terms of their replacement costs. On the side of the liabilities, the existing money supply might be registered as that which makes a demand on the country's assets. The net worth, determined by subtracting the value of the liabilities from the assets, would provide some indication as to how much additional money might be created with productive assets as their ultimate backing.

On the level of consumption, whenever there are goods and services coming into the market, with remunerative prices attached, there should be a sufficient flow of income available to consumers to transfer those goods and services from the retailers to the consumers and thereby liquidate once and for all the retailers' costs of production. If, in a given nation, ten trillion dollars' worth has been produced, ten trillion dollars in income should be automatically distributed to consumers. In order to achieve this end, the National Credit Authority would need to establish a National Profit and Loss Account. This would measure the value of available goods and services on the one hand, and the value of consumer buying power (incomes) on the other. In case of a societal profit, i.e., where the value of goods and services on offer exceeds the available income that could be used to purchase them (which would be the normal state of affairs), the National Credit Authority would monetize the difference *via* the creation of debt-free credit (or credit that does not need to be repaid by recipients directly to the issuer) that would be distributed to consumers *via* a National Dividend, or on their behalf, *via* a National Discount.

The National Dividend is perhaps the best known of Douglas's proposals. It would consist of a certain amount of money that would be distributed on a periodic basis, such as monthly, to each individual citizen, who is considered as a shareholder in society. The dividend would differ from the more well-known universal basic income in at least two ways: (1) the dividend would be financed through monetary reform involving the creation of new, 'debt-free' credit (as opposed to conventional methods of financing involving redistributive taxation and/or an increase in public indebtedness), and (2) the dividend would not represent a guaranteed amount but would increase or decrease depending on the size of the price-income gap. The greater the gap (which, in turn, would depend on how profitable the society was, in terms of its level of productivity), the greater the dividend. The smaller the gap, the smaller the dividend. There is thus a built-in negative feedback mechanism where the dividend and the physical necessity of work is concerned. While the dividend is meant not just to help fill the recurring price-income gap, but to do so in a way which allows people whose work is no longer needed by the productive system to retain access to goods and services (by providing them with an income that is delinked from work), it nevertheless ensures that if too many people seek to live off the dividend alone, the dividend itself will decrease in size, thus indicating the need for more labour in the productive system (by making it more difficult to live off the dividend alone).

The National Discount, the second method for filling the gap, is built on the observation that the true cost of producing anything is the consumption incurred in the course of its production. The true cost of making a violin, for example, is the wood, labour, wear and tear on tools, etc., that is 'consumed' in the process of making the violin. Now, if the financial system accurately reflected physical reality, the violin should only cost in financial terms what it cost in real terms; i.e., it should cost no more than the figures that might be attached to the wood, labour, depreciation of tools, etc. Unfortunately, in one way or another, the present financial system often adds purely financial costs to cover the repayment of financial capital, investments, or loans, and this elevates the financial cost of production above its real cost as measured in financial terms. By only charging the consumer with the real cost while reimbursing the retailer with the full financial cost, we can simultaneously lower the cost to the consumer (thereby increasing his purchasing power) while, at the same time, ensuring that all of the retailers' costs are fully covered and indeed liquidated. This is achieved by applying the price factor or the consumption/production ratio to retail prices. By measuring the value of what is consumed in comparison with what is produced we can determine how much prices are incorrectly financially inflated on average in the economy as a whole. The resulting percentage discount will show how much prices needed to be lowered to bring them into alignment with the real costs of production.

The message of C. H. Douglas to our civilisation can therefore be summarized as follows:

> *Money is not a commodity, not something to be bought and sold at interest, and it is not something that should be treated as an idol, as the determining factor of all human activity. Instead, money is a neutral informational tool that should accurately represent the physical economic reality. Accordingly, there should always be enough of it in the form of producer loan credit to catalyze the production of whatever goods and services are both physically produce-able and desirable. Similarly, there should always be enough of it in the form of income to consume in full whatever is produced and offered to consumers on the market. Once these desiderata have been fulfilled, the economic system will deliver far more satisfactory results to all members of an economic association on a basis that is more efficient, effective, and fair. Money must cease to be master and become a servant.*

SOME WORDS OF CLARIFICATION AND CAUTION

For those who are newcomers to Douglas Social Credit, it is vital to recognise that the aspects we have been discussing, and which form the theme of this book, i.e., the financial and economic aspects, constitute only one part (albeit the major part in terms of volume) of the Douglas corpus and of Social Credit doctrine in general. There is also a strong philosophical dimension (including, most especially, an elaborate social philosophy) to Douglas Social Credit, as well as a relatively well-developed political theory, and a historical theory. Indeed, in order to properly understand Major Douglas's financial analysis and proposals one must understand that, in the words of Douglas himself, "Social Credit is the policy of a philosophy". It is, in other words, the outworking of a certain conception of human association based on the underlying philosophy of Social Credit. Things such as the dividend and the discount are not ends in themselves, but are rather a means to greater ends, namely, the emancipation of the individual (considered collectively) from the illegitimate domination of the group and thus the optimization of human satisfaction in association. Monetary reform must serve the greater purpose of enfranchising and empowering people with both increasing purchasing power and increasing leisure over and against the state and the private business sector.

With respect to the present manuscript: *And the Light Became So Bright: The Influence of C. H. Douglas on the Writings of Ezra Pound* by Lorne Reznowski, a few further clarifications regarding the intricacies of Douglas Social Credit are in order.

In some contexts, Reznowski gives the impression, or might be interpreted as claiming that, under Douglas Social Credit, there would be no possibility of debt-money (money created by a bank with a corresponding debt). Let it be clear, however, that Douglas Social Credit does not abolish debt-money entirely. Producer credit, created by the banking system, would still be issued as loans to productive agencies. What Douglas Social Credit does do is to enable these producer loans to be redeemed in full by supplementing the regular flow of consumer incomes obtained *via* wages and salaries with 'debt-free' credit issued in the form of the National Dividend and the National Discount. In other words, Douglas Social Credit does indeed eliminate debt, but not by eliminating the use of debt-money as such, but by ensuring that all debts associated with production can be paid as they come due with a sufficiency of consumer buying power and without necessitating, therefore, the contraction of additional debt-money. In this way, Douglas's proposals do away with the irredeemable quality of aggregate debt which characterizes the existing system and which worsens exponentially over time.

By eliminating much of the long-term compensatory debt, whether of government, businesses, or consumers (i.e., debt-money that is currently relied on to fill the recurring price-income gap), Douglas Social Credit would also automatically eliminate the compound interest that is currently charged on that mountain of debt. Much of the usury embodied in the system, involving as it does the transfer of purchasing power from the greater part of society to the plutocratic elite who own the banking system, would thereby fall away.

Second, and in close connection with the preceding point, sometimes both Reznowski and Pound give the impression that usury is THE problem *par excellence* with which Douglas was concerned, when, in fact, the gap between prices and incomes which Douglas identified is not caused in the main, or in any special way, by the practice of charging interest on loans, but rather by the many cost accountancy charges (financial, depreciation, and maintenance charges, etc.) associated with real capital that are not "provided for" by the system. For this reason, eliminating the charging of interest on loans is not sufficient to resolve the problem of the gap.

Finally, Reznowski might sometimes be read as suggesting that there would not be, or might not be, any room for private banks in a reformed financial system. However, Douglas Social Credit does not support the nationalization of the private banking system either. Privately owned banks would continue to evaluate the credit-worthiness of applicants and issue credit to producers on a for-profit basis while using the same set of criteria that they presently employ when determining whether loans should be granted: the financial viability of the business in question. What is essential, however, is that the private banks fully co-operate with the National Monetary Policy that would be the *leitmotiv* of a Douglas Social Credit Commonwealth. This would involve holding National Dividend deposits, honouring compensated price reimbursements, borrowing electronic reserves from the National Credit Office to match their loans (should a full reserve system be introduced), not expanding their balance sheets to lend for consumptive purposes, and so forth. To this end, Douglas once suggested that private bankers should be licensed by the state and that the license should be cancelled if they did not fulfill the requirements of the National Monetary Policy.

CHAPTER II

An Examination of Pound's Prose Works in the Light of His Reaction to the Philosophy and Policy of C.H. Douglas

IN THIS CHAPTER, THE AUTHOR HAS USED material from Pound's collection of essays entitled *Impact: Essays on Ignorance and the Decline of American Civilization.* These writings represent Pound's mature views as they were circa 1940. In the interest of maintaining moderate length, it was impossible to include material from every work of Pound showing an influence by Douglas, such as *ABC of Economics.* However, the essays chosen are sufficient to show the extent of Douglas's influence on the prose writings of Ezra Pound. The following examples have been carefully examined and will be presented in a different order than Pound presented them in *Impact.* Finally, some excerpts from Pound's radio broadcasts delivered from Rome during the Second World War will be analyzed.

The influence of Douglas as reflected in Pound's prose writings alone is a vast subject, and more than adequate as a thesis topic in itself. If one consults Donald Gallup's bibliography of Pound's writings,[1] one is amazed at the volume of books, articles, reviews, letters, etc., which Pound produced on the subject of monetary reform in general and Douglas Social Credit in particular. In this connection, it is important to recognize that Pound's later interest in the Gesell scrip plan of the monetary reformer Silvio Gesell[2] must be considered as supplementary to his interest in Douglas Social Credit and not as a substitute for Social Credit.

A VISITING CARD

In his essay "A Visiting Card" written in 1942, Pound maintains that the financial establishment aims at the obfuscation of history. He refers to this financial power structure as *the power of putrefaction*. The

---

[1] Gallup, *Ezra Pound: A Bibliography.*

[2] Silvio Gesell was a one-time finance minister of Bavaria and the originator of the Gesell scrip monetary reform proposals.

financial establishment seeks to destroy all religion, by destroying its symbols, by causing theoretical argument. As a result, "[t]heological disputes take the place of contemplation. Disputation destroys faith, and interest in theology eventually goes out of fashion: not even theologians themselves take any interest in it."[3]

Pound sees this power of putrefaction as destroying all *intrinsic beauty*. It is spread like any disease "carried by rats, wholly unconscious of their role." He sees the financial power structure as iconoclastic in nature and warns us to "[s]uspect anyone who destroys an image, or wants to suppress a page of history."[4]

Pound accuses the usurocracy of destroying the mystery of fecundity, and the mysteries within the Church itself: "Latin is sacred, grain is sacred. Who destroyed the mystery of fecundity, bringing in the cult of sterility? Who set the Church against the Empire? Who destroyed the unity of the Catholic Church with this mud-wallow that serves the Protestants in the place of contemplation? Who decided to destroy the mysteries within the Church so as to be able to destroy the Church itself by schism? Who has wiped the consciousness of the greatest mystery out of the mind of Europe, to arrive at an atheism proclaimed by Bolshevism?"[5] In these bitter words, Pound the artist and medievalist condemns the institution of usury as an influence corrosive of art and religion.

Like Douglas, Pound maintains that usury can be eradicated by going back to a state credit system.[6] He constantly uses history, both ancient and modern, to prove his point. He points out that right "[f]rom the day when the T'ang Emperors began to issue their state notes," circa 656 AD, gold as money was no longer needed. These T'ang notes "kept their original form" from 656 to 841–7 AD.[7]

Pound maintains the importance of terminology that is understood by all, especially in economics. He states that "[o]ne should distinguish between the fraud" of interest on money that was "created out of nothing," and the fraud of raising the value of money by monopoly manipulation, thereby causing debtors to pay double on the property or articles they purchased with the loan. He also points to another "ancient fraud," that of making a nation buy items for double their

---

[3] Pound, *Impact*, 55.
[4] Pound, *Impact*, 55.
[5] Pound, *Impact*, 55.
[6] Editor's note: as far as Douglas's proposals are concerned, a "state credit system" should be understood as involving a National Monetary Policy imposed on private banks in favour of the genuine common good, not a state monopoly on money.
[7] Pound, *Impact*, 54.

value.[8] Pound hammers on the need in economics for terminology that is precise and not misleading: "With a clear and exact definition of money, a clear understanding of the nature of money, years of economic bewilderment and stupidity will be avoided. Add definitions of credit and circulation, and you will practically arrive at an economic erudition that can be recorded in a few pages and really understood in a few months of study."[9]

This insistence on definitions in economic discussions especially was likewise of great concern to Douglas:

> A speaker on a technical subject, if speaking to a technical audience, has a common ground of agreed knowledge. Or, alternatively, in speaking to a general audience, is generally conceded the advantage of expert knowledge. But, curiously enough, neither of these situations is generally found to be the case in regard to a discussion of the money system. There is practically no agreed body of expert opinion; and the average business man, engaged in "making" or perhaps losing money is, perhaps naturally, apt to regard himself as being equipped to discuss the matter at length with anyone. The result of this, however, too frequently, is the creation of mental confusion and verbal argument, arising from the clash of two capable logicians arguing from different premises; and, therefore, naturally unable to come to any agreement or understanding. In order to avoid, so far as is possible, this position to-night I propose to ask you to memorise, or, better still, to write down, certain definitions.
>
> These definitions are not necessarily orthodox, and you are, of course, at liberty to question them at your leisure. But they are the definitions and conceptions from which I am arguing in speaking to you. The first definition to which I would draw your attention is that of Wealth, and is, "The rate at which a nation or any other corporate body or individual can *deliver* goods and services esteemed conducive to well-being." I would ask you particularly to notice that the word "*deliver*" is used in this definition, and not the word "produce," and also to notice the inclusion of the word "rate." The second definition is that, "The objective of an industrial system is to deliver goods and services to the whole of the individuals included in the Nation, or other corporate body, to which the system is attached, with the minimum amount of trouble to those individuals."[10]

---

8 Pound, *Impact*, 60–61.
9 Pound, *Impact*, 61.
10 Douglas, *Warning Democracy*, 90–92.

Pound works out his own *Kulturmorphologie* on the basis of Douglas's philosophy. He maintains that there is a strict relationship between usury and art. Usury corrodes art just as it corrodes humanity. He maintains that "an expert, looking at a painting (by Memmi, Goya, or any other), should be able to determine the degree of tolerance of usury in the society in which it was painted."[11]

Pound maintains that without understanding economics, one cannot understand history. He points out that "[t]he emphasis given to economics by Shakespeare, Bacon, Hume, and Berkeley does not seem to have been enough to have kept it prominent in the Anglo-Saxon public conscience. After the arch-heretic Calvin, it seems, discussion of usury has gone out of fashion. A pity! As long as the Mother Church concerned herself with this matter one continued to build cathedrals. Religious art flourished."[12] One cannot begin to understand the influence of Douglas on Pound, unless one realizes the extent to which Pound, the artist, and medievalist, was convinced of the corrosive effect of usury on art.

Repeatedly, in his prose writings, Pound emphasizes the basic Douglasite postulate that: "The credit of the nation belongs to the nation, and there is not the slightest reason why the nation should have to pay rent for its own credit.... When the state understands its duties and powers it does not leave its sovereignty in the hands of private interests that are irresponsible or arrogate to themselves unwarranted responsibilities."[13]

Pound sees money as "a title and a measure."[14] For Pound, the beauty of ancient coins was due to royals understanding their sovereign power and responsibility, while the loss of beauty in coinage is due to "the corruption of the governments concerned."[15] He then gives examples of such corruption, such as the Rothschilds and their financing of armies against Venice, Romagna, and the Roman Republic. Pound then, to show his great love for Rome as the centre of culture and civilization, inserts suddenly here a cryptogram, formed by two words "R O M A—A M O R" (i.e., "ROME—LOVE").[16]

```
R O M A
O     M
M     O
A M O R
```

[11] Pound, *Impact*, 61–62.
[12] Pound, *Impact*, 61.
[13] Pound, *Impact*, 65.
[14] Pound, *Impact*, 65.
[15] Pound, *Impact*, 65.
[16] Pound, *Impact*, 65–66.

Pound goes on to say that any good economic system or economic procedure must be just in order to be sound. Money is only a notice to the public concerning how much is due to the one with a coin or note. In producing these coins or paper notes that are a "means and a measure of exchange," the state is performing work and it is right and just that the employees and officials of the state are rewarded, rather than that taxes are collected from other people's products produced from work performed.[17] In other words, Pound maintains that "[t]he ethical and intellectual work that goes into determining the measure of the just price deserves its due reward,"[18] i.e., that the state employee or official performs a function that benefits all. Pound states: "It is unjust that money should enjoy privileges denied to goods. Monetary theory is worthy of study because it leads us to the contemplation of justice."[19]

Pound points out that going into debt is a path to a career in politics. He goes back to ancient Chinese history to show just how old this particular vice is. He quotes the Mandarin Wu Yung who states that when he was made Governor, the bankers insisted that he take a loan from them. Wu Yung showed them that he could never repay them from his salary. "That was a mere detail that didn't worry them in the least."[20] This anecdote illustrates Pound's belief in the Douglasite concept of the control of politicians by the financial power, undermining any government, be it democratic or otherwise. Pound's unique contribution to Social Credit, as we will see throughout this work, is that Pound constantly points out the historical basis for Douglas's position, in ancient and modern world history.

Pound emphasizes that the state with a sound monetary policy, can provide materially for all people and for all work that is useful and needed by the state. The only limit imposed is a nation's raw materials and the people's physical and intellectual power. There is no need to seek the permission of the usurer before beginning a needed state project.[21] A footnote in Pound's essay entitled "Italy's Policy of Social Economics" provides a clue, in relation to this point, as to why Pound was interested in Mussolini: "The family allowances provisions approach steadily nearer and nearer to C. H. Douglas's Social Credit principles. They do not constitute obviously, a national dividend per capita as Douglas proposes, but they are definitely consumer credit.

---

[17] Pound, *Impact*, 68–69.
[18] Pound, *Impact*, 69.
[19] Pound, *Impact*, 69.
[20] Pound, *Impact*, 68.
[21] Pound, *Impact*, 68.

On Feb. 11, 1941, the allowances were extended far beyond the working class and made to include college graduates, sons, and daughters of professional men, who weren't yet earning their own livings."[22]

Pound had hoped that Italy and Mussolini would move to the policy of monetary reform outlined by Douglas. Douglas himself never shared these hopes in Mussolini. In Douglas's writings and speeches, there are several examples where he expressed clearly his disdain for Mussolini and Fascism, such as the following: "Our own financiers (if there can be said to be any ownership in financiers) gave Italy terms equivalent to cancelling five-sixths of the debt. You will not fail to notice that these extremely favourable terms to Italy coincide with the apotheosis of one of the most fantastic tyrannies (not excepting that of Russia) which history has ever known."[23]

AN IMPACT

In his essay "An Impact," which appeared in 1935, Pound begins the essay by giving the definitions for two Douglasite concepts: "*Increment of association*: Advantage men get from working together instead of each on his own, e.g., crew that can work a ship whereas the men separately couldn't sail ships each on his own. *Cultural heritage*: Increment of association with all past inventiveness, e.g., thus, crops from improved seed; American wheat after Carleton's researches; a few men hoisting a locomotive with machinery."[24]

Pound is using *cultural heritage* in the very narrow technical sense in which Douglas uses it in his writings. Of course, both Pound and Douglas recognize that culture goes far beyond human inventiveness and human co-operation. Pound goes on to say: "An epic is a poem including history. No one can understand history without understanding economics. Gibbon's History of Rome is a meaningless jumble till a man has read Douglas. My generation (that born in the 1880's) was dragged up in black ignorance of economics, an ignorance in part the product of malice, in part of sheer sloth and incompetence."[25]

Pound sees all "in high office in England" as accomplices to thieves' but they are ignorant, he says, as to why he declares them so. He realized that he would be accused of immoderate language, yet he cannot think of any other conclusion knowing the facts, i.e., the monetary facts of money creation in England.[26]

---

22 Pound, *Impact*, 266.
23 Douglas, *Warning Democracy*, 69.
24 Pound, *Impact*, 142.
25 Pound, *Impact*, 142.
26 Pound, *Impact*, 142.

Pound goes on in his second point to speak of the cheapness of goods: food, clothes, etc, when measured by the cost of physical effort and the difficulty of obtaining the material to produce them when compared to the experience of earlier generations. It is Douglas's *just price,* Pound declares, that accurately perceives the economic truth: "The parts of his system, all those details which deal with price adjustment are, fundamentally, a recognition and registration of realities, of the real cost (in effort) of forks, spoons, automobiles, grain fit to eat, eggs promptly delivered, and not carried liquid from China."[27]

Pound in his third point returns to his insistence on the need for clear-cut definitions of terms in economics. He feels that nowhere is the breakdown of language and definition more evident than in *the dismal science* of economics. He accused the *orthodox economist* of fuzziness of thought and expression in their definitions of fundamental terms which they use over and over again: "A thousand volumes a year ooze from dead minds all rendered dull, tangled, useless by the failure to make a few rudimentary dissociations, to distinguish, that is, between capital and property, between gold as deposit, and gold as measure, between demand wishing for, and demand meaning power to get."[28] He emphasizes that "[p]roperty is not capital. The increment of association is not usury." He says that "[h]istorians have been too lazy to seek the facts, and too bull-witted to understand them."[29]

Throughout his prose works, as throughout *The Cantos*, Pound hammers home the basic Douglasite principle that "[t]he state has credit. Distribution is effected by little pieces of paper."[30] But these facts are not in school books and therefore it is for Pound's generation to see to it that no child is ignorant of the monetary-economic facts concerning the *little pieces of paper*: "If you don't watch these, you will be slaves. If you don't know how they are made; who makes them; who controls them; you will be diddled out of your livings . . . The sword can 'protect the furrow,' . . . etc. . . . against foreign invasion, but not against the usurer's cunning. Against usury it has availed never at all."[31]

Pound points out that the medieval Church condemned usury and sodomy together to the same hell, because they are "both against

---

27 Pound, *Impact*, 143.
28 Pound, *Impact*, 143.
29 Pound, *Impact*, 143.
30 Pound, *Impact*, 143.
31 Pound, *Impact*, 143–44.

natural increase". He states that "Dante knew this and said so."[32] Pound sees it in Shakespeare's *The Merchant of Venice* where Shylock the usurer wants in return no shinbone or elbow, but desires that Antonio never have children. He refers us back to the Lombard Chronicles, and its law against causing one to be a eunuch."[33]

Pound, the artist, returns to the fact that the necessities of life are now cheap. It is only with the effort to provide high quality products that man may trouble himself and here is enough work for all:

> No man has outdistanced Homer. But for everything that is not great art, participant in that form of undyingness, for all that is used and used up, all that is worn, worn out, dwelt in, we must know the new cheapness, we must know that its cost in effort, in toil, in sweat, in difficulty, has dwindled, and dwindles.[34]

As an example of the perversion and suppression of the facts of monetary history, Pound gives the example of President Martin Van Buren's memoirs. The memoirs provide the records of the American bank war, "the death struggle between the bank and the people," and though written circa 1860, it would not be until 1920 that they would be printed. For Pound, this is an example of how the knowledge of the honest issue of coin was known but allowed to be forgotten. It is Pound's and his generation's duty to hammer these truths in human consciousness, so they will never be forgotten. He feels that certain facts, i.e., the monetary-economic facts, must become so well known that it enters "into the folk-lore, into men's proverbs."[35]

Pound records his disillusionment with the American New Deal, which had initially raised the hopes of many monetary reformers. He feels that, as of January 1935, the New Deal "has shown no comprehension of fundamentals, no perception of the basic relations of currency system, money system, credit system to the needs and purchasing power of the whole people."[36]

---

[32] As Dante was faithful to scholastic philosophy, especially to that of Thomas Aquinas, so is Dante's pupil, Ezra Pound. Concerning usury and its relation to sodomy, and ultimately to *Geryon*—Fraud, see: Ravenscroft, *Usury in the Inferno.* Sodomy and usury are linked and both condemned by the Greek philosopher Aristotle (*Politics* 1.10, 1258b) and in Christian philosophy (See, for example, the works of St. Thomas Aquinas). Dante is in this Western philosophical and Christian tradition.

[33] Pound, *Impact*, 144.

[34] Pound, *Impact*, 144.

[35] Pound, *Impact*, 144.

[36] Pound, *Impact*, 145.

Pound emphasizes next that "*[t]he earth belongs to the living*," a quote from Thomas Jefferson, with which Pound opens his essay "An Impact".[37] So while slavery has disappeared, why is it now replaced by slavery to printed paper and metal disks? He insists that the good of the state is "'over and above'" that of the individual but not as though it means statal good is "'counter to'" the good of the individual.[38]

Pound answers the charges of those who attack *fiat* money by answering: "'Fiat' is bad only if it means 'let there be grain or wood, where grain is not, or where there is nothing.' Intended in that sense, fiat money would be an evil. Like every other economic term it has been used as a scarecrow and used with two or more meanings. You can issue valid money against any commodity (or against services) up to the amount people want. The commodity must be there; services must be available."[39]

Pound distinguishes between two kinds of banks in history: banks built to benefit and build the community and banks created to despoil. The best example of a beneficent bank is the Monte dei Paschi of Siena founded by Cosimo de Medici. Pound says that for three hundred years the wisdom of the Medici family was employed for the benefit of Siena, to restore the city after its destruction by Florence. Cosimo, first Duke of Tuscany, guaranteed the capital of the Bank with the living property of Siena, and some awkward collateral:

> That is to say, Siena had grazing lands down towards Grosseto, and the grazing rights worth 10,000 ducats a year. On this basis taking it for his main security, Cosimo underwrote a capital of 200,000 ducats to pay 5 percent to the shareholders, and to be lent at 5 1/2 percent; overhead kept down to a minimum; salaries at a minimum and all excess profit over that to go to hospitals and works for the benefit of the people of Siena. That was in the first years of the 17th century, and that bank is open today. It outlasted Napoleon. You can open an account there tomorrow.[40]

What one can learn from this, Pound says, is the foundation of good banking: "Credit rests *in ultimate* on the abundance of nature, on the growing grass that can nourish the living sheep."[41] He points out that the moral of this piece of Renaissance monetary history is

37 Pound, *Impact*, 142.
38 Pound, *Impact*, 146.
39 Pound, *Impact*, 146.
40 Pound, *Impact*, 147.
41 Pound, *Impact*, 147.

in the intention of the Medicis. This bank did not seek immediate profit, "but to restart the life and productivity of Siena."[42]

The second kind of bank which Pound distinguishes in history is that bank which is created to "strangle the last ounce of profit out of their debtors."[43] He calls this kind of bank a hell bank. Pound says that the chief and most glorified of these hell banks in history is the Banca S. Georgio of Genoa. Pound describes this institution as "the pitiless company of Genoese creditors, the model bank among bankers":[44]

> 'About the year 1200 there existed in Genoa, divers societies....
>
> 'In 1252 they united....
>
> 'In 1451, 9th April. The commune of Genoa vested in perpetuity its dogana (that is the collection of all import tax), in the Banca S. Georgio." That means that the bank got all the proceeds.
>
> '1539. The Doge, governors and procurators confirmed and anew conceded and assigned to the protectors of S. Georgio all the proceeds of the salt tax ... approving the addition of the taxes on oil and grain, meat, wine, etc.... with the right to sell the same if they chose.
>
> '1749 the bank got the right to tax church property also, but at a fourth less than the secular.
>
> 'The revolution of 1797 disorganized its collection of taxes, the provisional government leaving the bank (of St. Georgio) provisionally its internal administration, and the collection of customs, took from its directors *their absolute civil and criminal jurisdiction* as incompatible with the unity of the republic and the sovereignty of the people.'[45]

Pound quotes this from the "Memorie sulla Banca di S. Georgio, Genoa, 1832. Compiled by their keeper of archives, Antonio Lobero." He points out that "Lobero seems rather indignant at this infringement of bankers' omnipotence," and gives this as an example of "what bankers will placidly do if you let 'em."[46] "The great company of St. George could be both plaintiff and judge in a civil or criminal suit against its interests."[47]

Pound emphasizes that "[t]he arts did not flourish in Genoa, she took almost no part in the intellectual activity of the renaissance. Cities

---

42 Pound, *Impact*, 147.
43 Pound, *Impact*, 147.
44 Pound, *Impact*, 148.
45 Pound, *Impact*, 148.
46 Pound, *Impact*, 148.
47 Pound, *Impact*, 149.

a tenth her size have left more durable treasure.[48] Thus, Pound again gives this as an illustration of one of his important applications of Douglas's theory to the world of arts and letters, i.e., that usury has a corrosive effect on the arts and that no great art can be produced in a society which is under the control of usury.

Pound reiterates that "[y]ou can issue sound money to express the will of the people" for desired services.[49] But he also emphasizes that sound money does not have to be state money. Pound gives the following examples of private and local money: "Scovil metal dollar, 1842; Lockport, Mills, 1851; my grandfather's money against 'lumber or merchandise'; Larkin & Co. 'merchandise bonds' issued before the recent American bank holiday."[50] In a footnote, Pound states that he is not calling for "a 'return' to private money in place of government money."[51] Nevertheless, we must learn from the history of private money. Neither banks nor governments are a necessary preliminary to the existence of money: "States fail or fall into the hands of ignorant men or of scoundrels. The banks have tried to throttle communities over which they have bloody and armed power of militia or police armed with machine-guns, fire-hoses and gas-bombs; sane men and free merchants have issued their own paper or metal implements of exchange and accountancy, and will do so whenever the light of reason penetrates or the spirit of manhood co-exists with a minimum of necessary knowledge."[52]

Pound is of the opinion that neither rhetoric nor a poem denouncing a military tyrant is too strong for "the devils of finance, in whose hands lie the tyrants and for whose fist military prowess is merely a knuckleduster."[53]

Pound accuses the financiers of creating a desert—the modern economic wasteland. As an example of this wasteland, he turns his attention to sabotage, i.e., the wholesale destruction of "surplus" goods. He cites the case of the Austrian Charity League which had asked Brazil for its surplus coffee but had found that it would "cost three shillings and nine pence a pound even if Brazil GIVES 'em the coffee instead of destroying it."[54] Pound gives this as an example of the complete failure of the debt-money system to distribute the plenitude

[48] Pound, *Impact*, 149.
[49] Pound, *Impact*, 149.
[50] Pound, *Impact*, 149.
[51] Pound, *Impact*, 149.
[52] Pound, *Impact*, 149–50.
[53] Pound, *Impact*, 150.
[54] Pound, *Impact*, 150.

of nature's abundance. It is from Douglas that Pound obtained this notion of sabotage: the insane destruction of goods demanded by the debt-money system and the production of goods not made to last, but only to waste human productive effort and the earth's resources on the altar of an economic system that demands increased output to hobble along. Pound comments: "This situation is the glory and boast of Messrs. Norman and Rothschild. It is the certificate of efficiency. Deterding, Herbert Lawrence, Duff Cooper, Sarvazy, Sieff, De Wendel, Robert Protot, the brothers Schneider of Creusot, and ten thousand fatted bankers proclaim the virtues of 'orthodox' economics, assisted by 500 curs, and titled straw men waiting for something to break."[55]

Repeatedly in his prose Pound hammers home the basic Douglasite postulate that the "state has credit," that the state need not borrow its own credit from private sources: "'Just as I have credit at the Albergo Rapallo, I could eat there for three months without the proprietors presenting a bill or feeling any uneasiness. I do not have to go to the Bank of Chiavari and borrow money and pay the bank usury on that money, in order to lunch and dine'."[56] He charges that for a hundred years states have sabotaged their credit, by using it at "less than its value," or by paying private companies an offering (i.e., interest) for its use. He compares the imbecility of the government to "hypnotized rabbits" and that finally there is "no greater treason to the people" than the nation refusing to give its own people debt-free credit.[57]

Pound maintains that the theory of debt-free money has been known before. He points out that debt-free money was known to Andrew Jackson and Martin Van Buren. However, it was the tragedy of the American Civil War which destroyed the tradition of debt-free money in the United States. Following the Civil War, America experienced: "[A] dead loss of cultural heritage of which she was uterly and unspeakably unconscious. The war of the 1830's is not to be found in the school books. Jackson is regarded as a tobacco-chewing half-wit, or a tuppeny militarist, the murderer of a few Indians, and the victor of New Orleans; Van Buren either vilified or forgotten. Only abnormal Englishmen have ever heard of such presidents."[58]

Pound sees much the same need for a reform in economics that he and his modernist followers had worked out in literature, such as simplifying and articulating terminology, "less intolerance" with

---

[55] Pound, *Impact*, 150.
[56] Pound, *Impact*, 151.
[57] Pound, *Impact*, 151.
[58] Pound, *Impact*, 151.

similar movements and emphasis on the important ideas. Pound states that prosperity is from "exchange of goods" so any banking system that sabotages exchange "is evil." Pound mourns the fact that often he comes across foolish comments in economics that he explained long ago in his book *ABC of Economics.* He charges that "Inadequate monetization has made 'inaccessible islands' of fields lying adjacent one with the other; it has created barriers between garden and factory."[59]

Pound maintains that C. H. Douglas and Silvio Gesell "have ended the Marxist era." C. H. Douglas in understanding "that the cultural heritage, the increment of association with all past inventiveness, is the great and chief fountain of value," displaced the Marxist theory of value.[60] Gesell exposed the great weakness in Marxism as a reform movement in showing "that 'Marx never questioned money. He just took it for granted'."[61] In other words, Pound sees Marxism as failing to get down to the root of the problem, which is a monetary problem.

In this connection Pound maintains that we must make a clear distinction between property and capital and not use it as received from "false economics":

> Properly understood capital is liquid. The great division is between whatever is a lien on the other men's services, and what is either completely neutral and passive, or constitutes a potential responsibility, whereof the weight leans on the owner. Land can lie fallow, houses decay at various speeds, industrial plants depreciate both from decay and standing still while invention goes past them. The increment of association is not usury. To see clearly one must divide capital from everything that is not capital. The moment money is spent, whatever thing is purchased is no longer capital, it is property; it has but three possibilities: You may keep it, use it, or lose it. Many vast and heavy books have ended in muddle from failure to see that property and capital are *radically* different. Property does not imply the enslavement of others.[62]

Pound bluntly states that we grow food to feed, we weave cloth to clothe. Therefore, the aim of a monetary system is to move goods from where they exist to people in need. This, of course, is the essence of Douglasism. Pound claims that money has been considered as if it "were goods" and even honoured "above all other goods." He sees this

---

[59] Pound, *Impact,* 152.
[60] Pound, *Impact,* 152–53.
[61] Pound, *Impact,* 153.
[62] Pound, *Impact,* 153.

as unjust and states that if "free men" understood this, they would not allow it. Again, he attacks those who use "fiat money" to frighten people. He refers us to his Cantos and the emphasis he puts on the connection between money and real goods that exist to be purchased. Pound quickly once again runs through criticisms of modern sabotage, repeating some earlier ones he stated, but adding here: "If the American Government owned crops sufficiently to order their destruction, it owned them quite enough to order their delivery."[63]

Pound, referring back to his statement on fiat money, emphasizes that purchasing power must be made adequate to buy goods for sale. He scoffs at the *orthodox economists* who scream inflation and quotes A. R. Orage: "Would you call it inflation to print tickets for every seat in a theatre, regardless of the fact that the house had hitherto been always two-thirds empty simply because no tickets had been printed for the greater number of seats?"[64] He continues, stating that "inflation" happens when money is created beyond what is available in desired goods or services. Like Andrew Jackson before him, Pound asserts that "[t]he safest place for a reserve purchasing power is in the pockets of the people."[65] He scoffs at the adamant position of the *orthodox economists*: "Agglomerates of protoplasm, listed as professors in the phone book, still bleat that money is just false teeth, metal and spectacle frames. Professors! they started as boys who said 'yes' to their teachers 30 years ago, and therefore got taken on as assistants."[66]

Pound maintains that Douglas was not someone who just makes up a theory to explain reality, but sees reality as it is and draws out conclusions: "He observed that *that* company was creating prices faster than it gave out power to buy. Having the concrete case before him, he considered its consequences. And if that happens in every other factory, every other industry? It needs no fancy algebra to prove that the purchasing power of the whole people can never catch up with the price of goods that they bring into being. There is one way for any serious man to refute this, he can show us the books of two, three or one prospering company where such is not the case."[67]

Pound ends this essay, stating that England will be the last nation to employ a recommendation created in London (i.e., Social Credit) and the reason is for "local pathologists" to study. He remarks that

---

63 Pound, *Impact*, 154.
64 Pound, *Impact*, 155.
65 Pound, *Impact*, 155.
66 Pound, *Impact*, 155.
67 Pound, *Impact*, 155–56.

"if a man were a royalist he would believe (I mean the theory he would think he believed would imply), that the king is boss of the coinage. If he were a 'democrat' he would believe that the power to issue money is delegated *by* the people *to* its representatives. Neither of their beliefs can sanction the mere leaving it in the hands of irresponsible men."[68]

IN THE WOUNDS: MEMORIAM A.R. ORAGE

In his essay entitled "In the Wounds: Memoriam A. R. Orage," which appeared in 1935, Pound pays tribute to the late Alfred Richard Orage who may be regarded as C. H. Douglas's closest collaborator in the origin of Social Credit. Here Pound gives Douglas's policy and philosophy as his own view. Pound begins the essay by describing the origins of Social Credit:

> Sometime in 1918 or thereabouts an ex-engineer, ex-head of Westinghouse's Indian branch, then managing an airplane factory noticed that his factory was creating prices faster than it emitted the power to buy.
>
> Say that in a month the factory produced £20,000 "worth" of airplanes, but distributed only £17,000 as purchasing power, in wages, dividends, etc. Douglas saw that if his factory was doing so, all other successful factories must be doing so in greater or lesser degree. If factories don't, they go "bust."
>
> The Major's first observation is on a par with the observation of the falling apple or of the kettle lid lifted by steam: a point of departure.
>
> No one, so far as I know, has attempted to disprove this part of Douglasism either to Douglas, to Orage or to the present writer by the simple presentation of the accounts of a firm.
>
> Douglas's perception was that under the present accounting system the actual money available can never buy all the available goods.[69]

Pound maintains as with Douglas, that the gap between prices and purchasing power constantly widens and that the on again off again "idiocy" of issuing of money by the banking system, can never bridge the gap. Only that which Pound calls the "irrigation system" of Douglas is the answer.

Pound deals with the main complaint against Douglasism:

---

68 Pound, *Impact*, 156.
69 Pound, *Impact*, 157–58.

> [W]here will the state get the money to pay dividends? Why isn't it merely "persistent, never-ending inflation"?
>
> For Douglasism (itself part of a thought-heritage) proposes to distribute purchasing power to the public via national dividends. And this strikes some people as absurd, or at least impossible.
>
> These same people, often receive dividends from their "investments in industrial or national bonds." They often read in newspapers that "government subsidies have been granted" or that "doles," etc., etc. are being provided or that "relief" is being provided. But the spectacle of nations pouring our purchasing power by the million through specific grants, emergency measures and as "charity" causes no mental cohesion, or no mental activity based on convergence and interaction of thoughts."[70]

Pound does admit that except for "deliberate cheats and fools," it is understandable that one should ask how is it possible to pay all citizens in a nation a continuous monetary dividend "without going bankrupt"? He points out that in order to understand where the state could draw its power to pay continual dividends, one must understand the Douglasite concept of the "increment of association": "When small merchants could not fill each his own ship, they banded together, and shared in marine adventure, both peril and profit. When savages hunted, they now and again hunted in bands. A group of men acting together can, in some circumstances achieve more than the sum of the possible attainments of the same hundred men acting each on his own. The difference between these sums is the 'increment of association.' That increment is essential to the comprehension of the Douglas plan, for which Orage gave his life."[71]

Pound then goes on to illustrate the Douglasite concept of the *cultural heritage* by the following example: "Five thousand Basutos cannot sling a Baldwin locomotive forty feet into the air, and put it down gently on the other side of the factory. When men associate not only with other live men, but with the aggregate of all acquired skills and inventions, the increment of association with all these skills and inventions adds another dimension to the 'increment of association,' an increment so enormous that popular imagination is still incapable of understanding it, and many people are still scared, as of a bogey man. The new increment is the 'cultural heritage' of Douglas's economics."[72]

[70] Pound, *Impact*, 158–59.
[71] Pound, *Impact*, 159.
[72] Pound, *Impact*, 159–60.

Pound states that "the Douglas solution of poverty, slums, industrial tyranny" is found in the simple statement: "the cost of production is consumption." With this, Pound explains, Douglas is saying that a nation's only loss is what is yearly consumed, destroyed, or exported. Douglas's aim is "economic justice," and Pound states that however unimaginable this may sound, so once was "[r]adio and flying."[73]

Pound's great admiration for Orage is based in part on Orage's selfless dedication to the cause of Douglasism. Orage, like Douglas, emphasized economic justice. To illustrate the righteousness of Orage, Pound mentions how Orage was enraged to learn that biologists were trying to find a cure for pellagra, an illness caused by a poor diet, that was "cheaper than food" itself.[74] Pound describes Orage with the Latin word *rectitudo*, one with moral rectitude, uprightness:

> Orage's *rectitudo* demanded justice, justice in the division of the "eredità culturale," the cultural heritage; of the increment of association.
>
> It demanded that the price charged the plain man and consumer should have a just ratio to the real cost of his food and clothing, and that adequate monetary-tickets should exist....
>
> Those of us who saw the Major's point in the first weeks of his first declarations find it rather difficult to unsee it, or to put ourselves in the role of non-perceivers.
>
> For three or four years after that, Orage repeated, now soft, now loud, now irate, now ironic: "consumption is the cost of production. You cannot cure unemployment. Unemployment is not a disease. We could get all the food and goods needed if the banks would get out of our way, if the banks wouldn't sabotage our exchange and consumption.[75]

Pound emphasizes that Douglas's philosophy is but a part of an older thought-tradition. He mentions that in Thomas Jefferson's era, the public were conscious and remarked on how an increase in supply of money was needed when there was an increase of desired commodities in the market. Pound interprets this as meaning that for a higher standard of living and desired exchange of goods, there must be adequate *tickets* (money, i.e., as tickets in Orage's earlier statement of tickets for theatre seats) and therefore bank accounting

---

[73] Pound, *Impact*, 160.

[74] Pound, *Impact*, 160. Brewer's yeast was the *cure* for pellagra, but it did not treat the true cause of pellagra; *poverty—malnutrition*: Bryan and Mull, "Pellagra Pre-Goldberger."

[75] Pound, *Impact*, 161.

must meet the increase of goods for sale.[76] As Pound approaches the end of this essay, he wants to return again to seeing Orage as a just man who understood the need "to equate the nation's purchasing power to available goods."[77] That is, as Douglas taught, a debt-free influx of money to every citizen in the form of the Social Credit dividend, a share in the wealth of one's nation, its *increment of association*, would bridge this gap. Likewise, by means of the just price, the actual cost of any good on sale would be the price charged.[78]

Finally, it is proper to end with the last words Pound heard from his friend Orage. These faint words were heard from Britain over the radio in Italy, spoken by Orage mere hours before his death, what Pound called "a fine sentence to die on": "in the gap between Price-values and Income is enough gunpowder to blow up every democratic Parliament."[79]

THE JEFFERSON-ADAMS LETTERS AS A SHRINE AND A MONUMENT

Ezra Pound's essay "The Jefferson-Adams Letters as a Shrine and a Monument" appeared in 1937 and is helpful as background reading for the *Adams Cantos*. Pound emphasizes that the heart of Jefferson's story can be found in a letter the latter had written to Crawford in 1816:

> . . . and if the national bills issued be bottomed (as is indispensable) on pledges of specific taxes for their redemption within certain and moderate epochs, and be of *proper denominations for circulation*, no interest on them would be necessary or just, because they would answer to every one of the purposes of the metallic money withdrawn and replaced by them.[80]

Before this, in the same paragraph, Pound writes that literature must not be divorced from reality. He maintains that neither Jefferson nor Adams "would have thought of literature as something having nothing to do with life, the nation, the organization of government." He insists that no first-rate author would ever think of his own works this way: "If he was a lyrist, he was crushed under a system; or he was speaking of every man's life in its depth; if he was Trollope or Flaubert he was thinking of history without the defects of generic

[76] Pound, *Impact*, 161.
[77] Pound, *Impact*, 164.
[78] Pound, *Impact*, 164–65.
[79] Pound, *Impact*, 158.
[80] Pound, *Impact*, 174.

books by historians which miss the pith and point of the story."[81] It must be borne in mind that for Pound, *the pith and point* of history's story is very often the monetary-financial *pith and point*. This the historians have neglected with monotonous regularity. Behind this, once again, lies Pound's search for and finding of the Douglasite *thought-heritage* throughout history.

Pound insists that Europe entered World War I because it had not absorbed the insights by Jefferson, and "because the canon law had been buried, because all general knowledge had been split up into useless or incompetent fragments. Because literature no longer bothered about the language 'of law and of the state' because the state and the plutocracy cared less than a damn about letters."[82]

In the light of the strong American tradition in favour of a debt-free money system, as evidenced in the Jefferson-Adams correspondence, Pound is impatient with some of the theories of Freud. He points out that for each man who may have some anxiety illness "due to sex, there are nine and ninety with an anxiety state due to lack of purchasing power, or anticipation of same. It is typical of a bewildered society that it should erect a pathology into a system."[83]

Pound comments that Flaubert, Trollope and Henry James understood money. These men in their works were not oblivious of the monetary aspect. However, he is amazed that Karl Marx and La Tour du Pin are blind to this. Before Voltaire's "totalitarian writings" Pound does not find this kind of ignorance. With respect to the Church Fathers and Duns Scotus, Pound says they see and understand the money problem. He further states that in Latin there is much written "on Intrinsic and Extrinsic value of money."[84]

Pound charges that in popular American history the monetary aspect is not given importance. He points out that Van Buren's memoirs, which stressed the monetary factor and were historically important writings, remained unpublished for sixty years. Pound emphasizes that he cannnot understand how any nation can exist without a "national culture." An integral part of any nation's "national culture", for Pound, is its monetary tradition and monetary history. He quotes from Jefferson's correspondence to give us yet another

[81] Pound, *Impact*, 174.
[82] Pound, *Impact*, 175.
[83] Pound, *Impact*, 177. Cf. Douglas in *The Monopoly of Credit*, 50: "It is poverty and economic insecurity which submits human nature to the greatest strain, a statement which is easily provable by comparing suicide statistics with bankruptcy statistics and business depression."
[84] Pound, *Impact*, 178.

luminous detail which will only take on added significance as we widen our background in American monetary history: "'Congress will then be paying six percent on twenty millions, and receiving seven percent on ten millions, being its third of the institution; so that on the ten millions cash which they receive from the States and individuals, they will, in fact, have to pay but 5% interest. This is the bait.' (Monticello, Nov. 6, 1813)."[85]

Ezra Pound, in devoting his time and energy to working for the spread of Douglas's philosophy, was convinced that he was simply returning to an old American tradition, which had been lost sight of in the carnage of the American Civil War. He quotes two further passages from the Jefferson-Adams correspondence:

> The same political parties which now agitate the United States, have existed through all time'; precisely. And this is precisely the complaint in the first volume of my defence. (John Adams quoting, Priestly to Jefferson, July 9, 1813).
>
> By comparing the first and last of these articles (this follows a table of figures) we see that if the United States were in possession of the circulating medium, as they ought to be, they cd. redeem what they cd. borrow from that, dollar for dollar, and in ten annual installments; whereas usurpation of that fund by bank paper, obliging them to borrow elsewhere at 7 1/2%, two dollars are required to reimburse one. (T. J. from Poplar Forest, Sept. 11, 1813).[86]

Pound has profound respect for medieval canon law. He points out that "[t]he just price" came from the Church's canon law. An important part of Douglas's theory has to do with his own understanding and application of the concept of the Just Price.[87] Pound emphasizes that the good structure of the Roman Empire came from the curtailing of usury rates. The Romans concerned themselves with freeing the understanding "of usury from that of marine insurance."

---

85 Pound, *Impact*, 179.

86 Pound, *Impact*, 180.

87 Cf. Douglas in *Programme for the Third World War*, 30: "Perhaps the cleavage in outlook between the East and West is most practically exemplified in the idea of 'price' as simply the haggling of the market, or as Sir Marcus Samuel put it, 'the price of an article is what it will fetch,' on the one hand, and the struggles of the Mediaeval Church (the foundation of Europeanism) with the concept of the Just Price. Whether St. Thomas Aquinas achieved any stable mechanism for this doctrine, I do not know—probably not. But the philosophy of it is basic. There is no part of the Social Credit thesis which has roused such rancour as the demonstration that the Just, or what we now prefer to call the Compensated Price, is at the root of economic democracy."

As an example of the Roman attempt Pound cites "the scandal of Cato the censor" in Roman history.[88]

AMERICA AND THE SECOND WORLD WAR

Pound's essay "America and the Second World War" appeared in 1944. The main events dealt with in this essay are: "1. The suppression of the paper-money issue in Pennsylvania AD 1750. 2. The American Revolution (1776) and its subsequent betrayals. 3. The fall of the United States under the control of the international usurocracy during the Civil War, somewhere about 1863."[89]

In this essay, Pound maintains that if you can understand what led to any war, you will understand what leads to others if not all wars. Pound charges that the real reason for wars is not given enough attention. The texts of schools do not explain how banks function: "The mystery of economics has been more jealously guarded than were ever the mysteries of Eleusis."[90] Pound states that the Second World War "is part of the secular war between usurers and peasants, between the usurocracy and whomever does an honest day's work with his own brain or hands."[91]

Pound constantly emphasizes the fact that the usurocracy has perverted, twisted, and suppressed the facts of history. He points out that the pivotal cause of the American Revolution of 1776 was the abolishment in 1750 of money issued in some colonies, such as Pennsylvania. Instead, history as taught in the United States speaks of "more picturesque matters," e.g. "the Boston Tea Party." This would be a prime example, for Pound, of the way in which history deals with the effects rather than causes. Pound insists that history must deal with causes, and that in most cases the causes will be found to be monetary causes.[92]

Pound states that the proper basis of credit was already known at the start of the 17th century, as practiced by "the Monte dei Paschi of Siena." We have already noted the importance of the Monte dei Paschi in Pound's thinking. The proper basis of credit "was, and is, the abundance of the productive capacity of nature, taken together with the responsibility of the whole people."[93]

---

88 Pound, *Impact*, 181.
89 Pound, *Impact*, 184.
90 Pound, *Impact*, 185.
91 Pound, *Impact*, 185.
92 Pound, *Impact*, 185.
93 Pound, *Impact*, 186.

In opposition to the Monte dei Paschi and its sound basis of credit is the private Bank of England with its concept of credit based on usury. Pound quotes the prospectus of Paterson, one of the bank's founders:

> "[T]he bank hath benefit of the interest on all moneys which it creates out of nothing." Paterson, in other words, proposed to lend not money but notes, gambling on the very likely probability that only a small fraction of the "depositors" would ever want to withdraw their money at the same time.
>
> The trick came off, and in a grand way. But the Quakers of Pennsylvania were beginning to enter into competition with the Bank of England *pro bono publico Pennsylvanico*. That is to say, they lent their paper money to farmers for purposes of land reclamation up to an amount equal to half the value of the farm in question, requiring payment in ten annual instalments.
>
> The bank in the mother country, through the instrumentality of the British Government, had this beneficial competition, which had brought prosperity to the colonies, suppressed in 1750.
>
> After various other vexations, the colonies declared their independence.[94]

In this essay, Pound also gives his famous thirty-line introductory study of American history. This is a 'book' consisting of four chapters worth quoting in full:

> Chapter I: "All the perplexities, confusion, and distress in America arise, not from defects in their constitution or confederation, not from want of honour or virtue, so much as from downright ignorance of the nature of coin, credit, and circulation." (John Adams)
>
> Chapter II: " . . . and if the national bills issued be bottomed (as is indispensable) on pledges of specific taxes for their redemption within certain and moderate epochs, and be of proper denomination, for circulation, no interest on them would be necessary or just, because they would answer to every one of the purposes of the metallic money withdrawn and replaced by them." (Thomas Jefferson, letter to Crawford, 1816).
>
> Chapter III: " . . . and gave to the people of this Republic the greatest blessing they ever had—their own paper to pay their own debts." (Abraham Lincoln)

[94] Pound, *Impact*, 187.

> Chapter IV: The Congress shall have Power
> To coin Money, regulate the Value thereof, and of foreign Coin, and fix the Standard of Weights and Measures.
>
> Constitution of the United States, Article 1 Legislative Department, Section 8, Clause 5.
>
> Done in Convention by the Unanimous Consent of the States present the seventeenth Day of September in the Year of our Lord one thousand seven hundred and eighty seven and of the independence of the United States of America the Twelfth. In witness whereof We have hereunto subscribed our Names. (George Washington — President and deputy from Virginia).[95]

Pound states that only chapter IV can with ease be known by Americans in this "denatured democracy."[96] He points out that for a long time, Congress has not recognized the competency granted to it by the American Constitution, i.e., the power to coin money. He also notes, in a sarcastic voice, that "some crank from Nebraska or Dakota raises an uncouth voice to demand a little of the liberty proclaimed by the Fathers of the Republic, but the roar of the rotary presses soon drowns such rustic vociferations."[97]

In this essay Pound also deals with the role of Abraham Lincoln in American monetary history. He points out that Lincoln was assassinated after he made the statement: "and gave to the people of this Republic. . . . " Booth, Pound notes, never did explain how he fled Washington and knew about the one unguarded route. Pound feels that the orchestration of Lincoln's assassination, timed with the attempt on Seward, the Secretary of State, and other details cannot be explained by Booth's theatrics. For Pound, it was Lincoln's opposition to the usurocracy that would seem to be the cause of his death.[98] Of interest is that the Lincoln biographer, Emil Ludwig, also cites Lincoln's letter in fuller detail, concerning the creation of the

---

[95] Pound, *Impact*, 188–89.
[96] Pound, *Impact*, 189.
[97] Pound, *Impact*, 190. Charles Gustav Binderup, a Democrat from Nebraska, is probably referenced here. He served in the U. S. Congress from 1935 to 1939. Several of Binderup's letters can be found at the *Gorham Munson Papers on the American Social Credit Movement*. The "Dakota" most likely is the Republican Gerald Prentice Nye, Senator for North Dakota. He chaired the "Special Committee on Investigation of the Munitions Industry," which inquired also into banking involvement: States Congress, "Nye, Gerald Prentice."
[98] Pound, *Impact*, 190.

greenbacks, which is quoted here by Pound.[99] Ludwig also states that Booth obtained "money from unknown sources," but that Booth claimed it had come from his "successful speculations in petroleum."[100]

The British government's seeming support for the Confederacy always made them suspect. London banking houses were also known to have financed the South, making them suspect. From testimony following the assassination of Lincoln, we learn of the substantial amounts of money at the Montreal Branch of the Ontario Bank, besides at other banks, available to agents of the Confederacy in Canada.[101] The funds at the Ontario Bank branch in Montreal, it was testified, "were exclusively raised by drafts of the secretary of the treasury of the Confederate States upon London, deposited in their bank to the credit of Thompson."[102] The referenced Jacob Thompson was an agent for the Confederate Secret Service in Canada.

Pound maintains that the usurers, routed by Jackson and Van Buren in 1830–40, used the issue of Black slavery to distract from the banking question.[103] Prior to the Civil War, the debates in Congress showed knowledge of the usury problem. However, following Lincoln's death, the debate became obscured. The great financial debt of the South to the City of New York before the war was no longer newsworthy:[104] "Usurocracy had discovered that the slave-owning system was less profitable than that of 'free' labour. Anyone who possessed a slave had to keep him alive and in fit condition to work. This cost more than 'free' labour, in respect of which, under the capitalist system, the employer had no responsibility whatsoever. The defeat of the slave owners was already determined, predetermined."[105]

Pound also deals with Bolshevism in this essay. He states that Stalin's criticism of capitalism in his *Foundations of Leninism* is worthy of study. Pound admits that Stalin thoroughly understands what Pound considers the crimes of the different Roosevelts, Churchills, Blums, and others. However, Bolshevism is criticized by Pound for

---

99 Ludwig, *Lincoln*, 448–49. Thomas F. Schwartz, the past Illinois State Historian and curator of the Henry Horner Lincoln Collection, used to have a column entitled "Lincoln Never Said That." He believes this Lincoln letter to be a forgery according to the criteria he uses to verify Lincoln documents. Others posit the claim of forgery has not been substantiated: Carr, "The Mysterious Col. Edmund."

100 Ludwig, *Lincoln*, 476.

101 Harris, *Assassination of Lincoln*, 368–69.

102 Harris, *Assassination of Lincoln*, 369.

103 Pound, *Impact*, 190

104 Pound, *Impact*, 191.

105 Pound, *Impact*, 191.

using economic warfare, "flooding foreign markets with goods and foodstuffs at cut prices."[106] The purchase of Suez Canal shares by the U. S. S. R is likewise economic war. Pound charges that Bolshevism collaborates with liberalism, for they both agree to export labour, people, in exchange for food. Pound gives the example of Stalin's willingness to work humans to death, building a canal. Only "economic detail" differentiates Liberalism and Bolshevism. He compares them both to just different tentacles of a "monster."[107] Thus, Pound is attacking Bolshevism and Liberalism because of their disregard for the dignity of the individual. The freedom and dignity of the individual is a basic feature of Douglasism.

Pound next summarizes his theory as to the cause of wars thus: "(1) Wars are made to create debts. (2) War is the highest form of sabotage. (3) A nation that will not get itself into debt drives the usurers to fury."[108] It must be borne in mind that Pound's reference to sabotage must be understood in the Douglasite sense of the word, the creation of artificial scarcity by the destruction of goods.[109]

In a postscript, that is followed by a list of suggested reading, Pound summarizes what has been missing with regard to the knowledge of the economic facts of life as they impinge on the individual and upon nations:

> What has been lacking, especially among practical people, among industrialists, large as well as small, among businessmen, and not only small business men, is a comprehensive survey of the usurocratic mechanism, an awareness of the relationships between commercial transactions, of the relationships between the management of a factory or business and the international monetary system, not on a short-term basis, at three-monthly or three-yearly intervals, but over periods of centuries or half-centuries: and always with the same object: lucre. And always with the same mechanism

[106] Pound, *Impact*, 193.
[107] Pound, *Impact*, 193.
[108] Pound, *Impact*, 193.
[109] War is used as a pretext to "create" tickets, i.e., money, and what better articles to make than ones that will be destroyed and need to be replaced by more weapons of war. In this insane debt system, one can only buy food, clothing, and shelter by constantly producing goods, often undesired production or of poor quality, in order to bridge the gap between prices and money available, between production and consumption. Pound condemns this waste of human effort. Instead of replacing *sabotage*—this production of useless products—with the debt-free dividends of Douglas, the financial system continues its destructive policies leading to debt, poverty, trade wars and ultimately, military conflict.

> too, namely the creation of debts for the extortion of interest, of monopolies so that they can keep prices continually fluctuating, including the prices of the various monetary units, of the various national currencies.[110]

Pound maintains that, after the death of Lincoln, power in the United States went from the government "into the hands of an evil combine." Democracy was lost.[111] For Pound, since that time the United States is no longer self-determining and the British Empire likewise. He goes on to explain how these two democracies really work, with the power hidden from public view:

> It is so much waste of time to talk of this or that 'democracy.' The real government was, and is, to be found behind the scenes. The system works as follows. Two or more parties appear before the public. As a matter of form, and to reassure the simpletons, some honest men are allowed to do a little clean work as long as they don't touch the big rackets. The biggest rackets are those of finance and monopolization, including the monopolization of money itself, both within the nation and in combination with the various foreign currencies.[112]

Pound points out that even before the First World War Anatole France in *L'Ile des Pingouins* explained how "'commercial' wars" function:

> "Certainly," replied the interpreter, "there are industrial wars. Nations without commerce and industry have no reason to go to war, but commercial nations are forced to adopt a policy of conquest. Our wars must, of necessity, increase in number as our industrial activity increases. When one of our industries fails to find an outlet for its products, we must have a war to open up new markets. This year, in fact, we have had a coal war, a copper war, and a cotton war. In Third Zealand we have massacred two thirds of the natives to force the remainder to buy umbrellas and braces."[113]

NATIONAL CULTURE, A MANIFESTO

In his essay entitled "National Culture, a Manifesto" which appeared in 1938, Pound maintains that America had a national

---

[110] Pound, *Impact*, 193–94.
[111] Pound, *Impact*, 195.
[112] Pound, *Impact*, 196.
[113] Pound, *Impact*, 196.

culture from 1770 until 1861, if not possibly longer. A few remnants remained, but as the usurocracy gained power in America it no longer was a national culture.[114] Pound cannot foresee American culture rejuvenating, while books by Marx and Lenin are sold cheaply by the thousands and Adams's and Jefferson's writings still remain unknown. He points out that for three years he has been trying to purchase John Adams's letters, without success.[115] He states: "Men who impede the examination of the monetary and financial causes of historic events are a seething corruption."[116]

Pound repeats his call for clear definitions of "economic terms", as the first step to creating order out of the chaos of the financial system: "An administration that can not or dare not define money, credit, debt, property, capital, is unlikely to provide a durable solution of national chaos or evolve a durable system of national order."[117]

Near the end of this essay, Pound draws attention to the U. S. Constitution, i.e., "the right of congress to determine the value of money," which he states "has not been tried." America had a basis for such a national program in the time of Jackson and Van Buren. Pound states that materialism cannot be its basis, as "it is merely subhuman." Even "Charlie Marx couldn't carry materialism into his theory of values, and as a working system Russia knows it is a washout."[118]

DESTRUCTION BY TAXATION

Pound's short essay entitled "Destruction by Taxation" is made up of three short pieces written in 1938, 1939 and 1959, respectively. Pound prefaced the essay by a letter sent to him by C. H. Douglas: London, January 7, 1936: "Dear E. P., Pending engaging a whole-time secretary to correspond with you, I suggest that you concentrate on the subject of taxation as a form of modern highway robbery combined with iniquitous interference with the freedom of the individual. Yours ever, C. H. Douglas."[119]

In this essay Pound maintains that the British tax system is "black infamy." He states that the British taxpayer is taxed two pounds for every sovereign the government spends. Pound makes a sharp distinction between a tithe and a tax:

---

[114] Pound, *Impact*, 3.
[115] Pound, *Impact*, 4.
[116] Pound, *Impact*, 4–5.
[117] Pound, *Impact*, 5.
[118] Pound, *Impact*, 9.
[119] Pound, *Impact*, 12–13.

> A tithe is a payment made in something the payer has. A tax is normally paid in money.
>
> A tithe is strictly proportional to production. Justice from time immemorial has limited tithe to a tenth or a ninth. More was considered evil and less inadequate for the good conduct of the state.
>
> Extortion is forced payment of an exaggerated sum. One of the prime means of extortion is that of insisting on payment in something which the payer has not, and which he can only obtain at a price unjustly high.
>
> In present circumstances your taxes are to be paid in money. And the taxpayer is too illiterate in matters of money to ask what money is; who issues it; under what circumstances is it obtainable? (1938)[120]

This passage is a pure reflection of what Pound had learned from Douglas. The following are examples of Douglas writing on the same theme of a tithe versus a tax:

> [T]here is no relation between facts and money. It is essential to begin by a consideration of real, i.e., physical, economics as distinct from money economics. For instance, the old and original tithe was a genuine and justifiable tax. It consisted of one-tenth of the agricultural production of the taxed land, and this agricultural production so collected was handed over to the Church for the physical maintenance of the clergy and their dependents, it being assumed that the clergy were too busy with other matters to raise their own crops. It may be recalled that the word "clergy" is derived from "clerk" and that it is to clerks that we owe (and pay) our taxes.
>
> Now it is obvious that the physical meaning of this to those who paid the tithe was that they did a small amount of extra work or, alternatively, had a little less to eat themselves. There was nothing in such an arrangement which could, or did, result in a loss to the community on the one hand, or, on the other, make it impossible for the agriculturists to live.
>
> But now consider the fact of a money tax upon agricultural land, which is the form the tithe has now taken. It is imposed quite irrespective of the value of anything which is produced upon the land, and its effect is simply that of an overhead charge upon anything which is produced. If a farmer owns the land he farms and has to pay tithe upon it, the tithe

120 Pound, *Impact*, 12–13.

> appears as a cost of production and increases the price that he must charge in order to live off his farm. If he cannot raise the price, which is generally the case, he makes a money loss, and ultimately ceases to farm, because he does not grow money, he grows produce, and money is demanded from him.
>
> This is exactly what has happened in England, where three million acres of farming land has gone out of cultivation since the War. But the evil does not stop there. Since the farmer does not make a reasonable living, he does not keep his land in good order and he has no money to spend upon the products of other industries.[121]

In a sub-heading of this essay entitled "The Dismantled Manor House," Pound states that no completely sincere monetary policy has come from the British Parliament since the establishment of the Bank of England. What England must bear from taxes is without justification. The farm worker does not dine better because the manor house paintings were sold due to "a black and iniquitous inheritance tax": "The obscuring of the sense of the *nature* of money has destroyed all these fine things uselessly. The dismantled Manor House, that could be and ought to show a model of how to live, is made a skeleton for no purpose."[122]

Pound maintains that a good system of taxation should be only for a part of the produce, not in a set monetary charge. The collection of taxes itself should be inexpensive, instead of creating further expense and "encourage production, not sabotage it." It should not cause criminal activity by penalizing needed production. Pound gives the example of bootlegging, which only exists because of taxes or prohibition of liquor.[123]

AN INTRODUCTION TO THE ECONOMIC NATURE OF THE UNITED STATES

In "An Introduction to the Economic Nature of the United States" which appeared in 1944, Pound reviews some basic American monetary history. Pound calls it an essay "of the struggle between the people and the usurers, or financiers, in the colonies, and then in the United States of North America."[124] He begins the history thus:

---

[121] Douglas, *Dictatorship by Taxation*, 2–3. Brewer, *The Sinews of Power*, supports Douglas's contention that taxation, especially to support foreign wars, led to a loss of liberty.

[122] Pound, *Impact*, 13.

[123] Pound, *Impact*, 16.

[124] Pound, *Impact*, 16.

> The settlers, or colonizers in Pennsylvania and in other colonies, irritated by the disappearance of metal money, understood that any other document could be used for book-keeping and as a certificate of what the bearer was entitled to receive in the market. The agriculturists who arrived in the new country, while they cleared the forests and prepared their camps, lacked the power to buy what was necessary to build houses, to buy ploughs, and to make a living. So the governments of several colonies began to lend paper-money for these purposes. Pennsylvania chose the best method adapted to the conditions—repayment in ten or twelve years, and lending amounts up to one half the value of the farm. Those who lent the money, living near to those who had received the loan, could judge the character of the borrowers. This arcadian simplicity displeased the London monopolists and the suppression of this competition, together with other irritants, provoked the 1776 "Revolution."[125]

Pound points out that John Adams confronted the problem of inflation. Pound says that Adams stated "that a diminishing buying power of the paper money functioned as an unevenly distributed tax, a tax that hit those with a fixed salary, or living on an income ... in any event, an inflation of this kind would not have created a public debt *with interest.*"[126]

Pound states that "[i]t was understood that the base of the real credit of the thirteen colonies was their capacity to work, taken together with the truly great possiblity of future production limited then, not by nature, fields, vegetation, but only by the number of inhabitants."[127] Pound goes on to state: "History, as seen by the monetary economist, is a continuous struggle between producers and those who try to make a living by inserting a false system of book-keeping between the producers and their just recompense."[128] Pound states that the Bank of England realized that it did not need to loan money but to loan its own paper. In Philadelphia, financiers copied this money practice as their monopoly, learned from overseas. "Financiers and congressmen" purchased the promises-to-pay of states, at 20% of face value though the nation had to pay at a full 100%. This was the 'scandal of the assumption,' post the revolutionary war.[129]

---

125 Pound, *Impact*, 16.
126 Pound, *Impact*, 17.
127 Pound, *Impact*, 17–18.
128 Pound, *Impact*, 18.
129 Pound, *Impact*, 18.

Pound maintains that "the true history of the economy of the United States" is to be found in the letters written between Adams and Jefferson, the other personal letters written between the Fathers of the Republic, and the writings of Van Buren. The main points of all these writings are in agreement on: "debts, altering the value of monetary units, and the attempts, and triumphs of usury, due to monopolies, or to a 'Corner' [on the market]."[130] Pound considers the economic history of the United States post the Civil War to the present as a game of the Exchanges in New York and in Chicago, a game of speculation. The interests of the common American to have a fair and "fixed price" is not desired by those who make money by speculating on the market.[131]

Pound points out that fraudulent book-keeping, monopoly, etc., can be found throughout history. He says this is why the usurers are opposed to study of the classics: "Aristotle, in his *Politics* I.4/5, relates how Thales, wishing to show a philosopher could easily 'make money' if he had nothing better to do, foreseeing a bumper crop of olives, hired by paying a small deposit, all the olive presses on the islands of Miletus and Chios. When the harvest arrived, everybody went to see Thales. Aristotle remarks that this is a common business practice. And the exchange frauds are, nearly all of them, variants on this theme—artificial scarcity of grain and of merchandise, artificial scarcity of money, that is, scarcity of the key to all the other exchanges."[132]

Pound insists that usury ruined the American Republic. Though usury has traditionally "been defined as too high interest on money,"[133] Pound defines usury as "a charge for the use of purchasing power, levied without regard to production, sometimes without regard even to the possibilities of production."[134]

This is an important distinction in the controversy over Pound and his understanding of Douglas. Pound uses the word "usury" to indicate all that is wrong with bank created finance, from the usually accepted definition of usury as an unjust interest charged, to the fact that the money created is often not for the consumption of needed goods, and finally incorporating the reality of the A+B theorem: the sabotage of the economy via the premature withdrawal of credit from circulation. The latter factor results in an economy that always

130 Pound, *Impact*, 19.
131 Pound, *Impact*, 20.
132 Pound, *Impact*, 22–23.
133 Pound, *Impact*, 26.
134 Pound, *Impact*, 210.

demands further money creation in order to consume goods already produced. This is important in understanding Pound's condemnation of the Catholic Church, in the 20th century, for failing to condemn usury, except in an increasingly narrowly limited accepted definition. Pound is clear that usury, as he understands the traditional teaching from the Greek philosophers down through the fathers of the Church, is forever and always an evil. Pound says that "finance" replaced the word "usury" in "polite conversation" in America. He says that Jefferson references this when he states: "'No one has natural right to be money-lender save him who has it to lend."[135]

Pound observes that near the conclusion of World War I: "C. H. Douglas insisted on the opportunity of potential abundance and demanded national dividends, that is a distribution of family or individual allowances so as to permit the public to buy what the public had produced."[136] Pound notes that this was termed "insane" by the press controlled by the financiers. He refers to the statistics of the Loeb Report in 1935 that confirmed Douglas's position. Before World War II, in the midst of the depression, a family of four in the U. S. would have received a $4,000 to $5,000 a year dividend, with no charge, with no tax (in accordance with the Douglas proposal), just to be able to consume the abundance produced by the nation.[137]

The great lesson taught by American history and world history, says Pound, is that "*it is idiotic to leave the pocket-book of the nation in the hands of private irresponsible individuals, perhaps foreign; it is idiotic to leave the nation's sources of information in the hands of private irresponsible individuals, sometimes foreign.*"[138] Pound goes on to attack *free enterprise* as it existed, because it led to the mass of humanity working to greatly profit financiers: "The aim of finance is to gain by the labour of others. In the last four decades, the aim of finance, in order that the gains of a small group be greater, has been the retention of all the profits of mechanical inventions and the lowering to a minimum of the workers' rewards. And this was done in the open market through free enterprise."[139]

---

[135] Pound, *Impact*, 26.
[136] Pound, *Impact*, 31.
[137] Pound, *Impact*, 31.
[138] Pound, *Impact*, 31.
[139] Pound, *Impact*, 32. Editor's note: "[T]he profits of mechanical inventions" is what Douglas called the *Cultural Heritage* that should benefit all citizens financially, not a privileged class that has stolen the privilege. It underlies the great Douglasite proposals of a debt-free dividend to all citizens and the compensated price discount to producers.

In this essay, Pound provides a series of quotations to show the actions taken by finance. Pound quotes Van Buren:

> The expedient resorted to . . . was nothing less than a largely increased line of discounts. . . . In October 1830 they stood at $40,527,523. Between January 1831 and May 1832 they were increased to $70,428,007: the highest figure ever reached.
>
> Mr. Webster said: "Thirty millions of the capital of the bank are now on loan and discount in the States on the Mississippi. These will all have to be called in within three years and nine months if the charter is not extended."
>
> ". . . the annual operations of the bank . . . amounted to three hundred and forty one millions of dollars. . . . The public money subject to the individual control of the President . . . was limited to fifteen or twenty thousand dollars." (Note: The president controlled thousands not millions.)
>
> ". . . demoralization of the public mind by means of a pecuniary panic." ". . . this Committee, whose doings were confidential and from whose councils the Government directors were invariably excluded."
>
> ". . . funds of the institution, including the money of the Government, as means for operating upon public opinion . . . application of the money over the public press, over influential individuals and over members of Congress."
>
> ". . . to derange the credits of the Country and to spread the pecuniary embarrassments over the length and breadth of the land by which the desired panic was produced."
>
> ". . . total reduction in thirteen months . . . $17,100,851 upon a discount line of sixty four millions. . . . [140]

These quotations are taken from Martin Van Buren's autobiography,[141] which provides us with the best chronicle of the Bank War. This was the great struggle fought by Andrew Jackson and Martin Van Buren against the rechartering of the private Bank of the United States. Jackson and Van Buren wanted the United States Treasury to issue its own credit without borrowing from the Bank of the United States. The above quotations record the efforts of the money power to interfere with the plans of Jackson and Van Buren.

As an example of the *rottenness* which is corroding the soul of America in monetary affairs, Pound refers to the "'Annual Reports of the Secretary of the Treasury,' June 1932 to June 1939":

---

140 Pound, *Impact*, 32–33.

141 Van Buren, *The Autobiography*, 621, 623, 633, 641–42, 654.

> [T]he Treasury of the United States bought ten billion dollars of gold at thirty-five dollars per ounce instead of $21.65 as in former times. The Treasury does not issue any reports regarding the source of this gold and, even if the Secretary of the Treasury himself wanted to find out where the gold came from, all he could find in his files would be names of the last sellers. This means that the government, or the American people, paid ten billion dollars for gold that, before the change in price, could have been bought for six billion. This amounts to a gift of four billion dollars to merchants of gold among whom are, as has always been the case, many foreign merchants.[142]

In this same essay Pound provides us with a basic outline of American economic history:

> 1620–1750: Beginning and development of colonial prosperity based finally upon a system of loans by some of the Colonial Governments to those who tilled the land. This prosperity stimulated gluttony, and the London monopolists tried to impose their monetary monopoly;
>
> 1750–1776–1778: Preparation for the Revolution, formation of the American system;
>
> 1789: Washington president. Struggle between Hamilton, conservative agent of finance and Jefferson's democratization. "Scandal of the assumption";
>
> 1801–1825: Jefferson and his disciples in the White House. The Louisiana Purchase. Second war against England;
>
> 1829–1841: Jackson and Van Buren in the White House. Fight between the banks and the people. The people won;
>
> 1841–1861: Gold discovered in California, in 1849. Debts contracted by the South to New York bankers and elsewhere. Negro slavery, symptoms of the Civil War. From 1861 war of secession, triumph of finance;
>
> 1869–1877: Grant president. Scandals. Gold against people; 1890: The silver question. Trusts;
>
> 1914: Industrial development. Technocracy. The menace of abundance;
>
> 1935: Chart of Potential Product Capacity;

[142] Pound, *Impact*, 34.

> 1939: "*War is his only way out*", phrase pronounced by a Congressman to signify that Roosevelt had made such a mess of things that war was his only way of escape. In other words, the only way to hide his past and maintain his political power.[143]

Pound also gives another chronological table regarding other events in monetary-financial history. Both these tables will be useful later in examining *The Cantos*:

> 1684: England suppressed the mint of Massachusetts which had coined silver.
>
> 1814: Calhoun opposed the process in which the government was forced to get its own credit on loan.
>
> 1819: Crawford issued Treasury bills bearing no interest.
>
> 1825: The Industrial crisis in England led to dumping on the American market, glutting it with merchandise at bankrupt prices.
>
> 1832: Jackson: "The real value of land is due to labour."
>
> 1834–5: Jackson eliminates the national debt. The United States was left with no debt whatever.
>
> Upon examining the receipts and expenditures of the government between 1816 and 1833, even Dewey admits that the great decrease of expenditures was due to the reduction and finally to the elimination of the payments of interest on public debt.
>
> Briefly:

1816: receipts	$47,677,000
1816: expenditure	$31,196,000
1833: receipts	$33,948,000
1833: expenditure	$23,017,000

> Interest on the public debt:

1816:	$ 7,823.000
1833:	$303,000

> and later ZERO.
>
> 1836: The National Treasury having an active balance, distributed this money to the different states. Without going back to the legendary Mohammedan Calif, those who, because of ignorance, shouted that C. H. Douglas's proposal of a

143 Pound, *Impact*, 35–36.

> National Dividend was a scandal and a novelty, may consider the following facts: Massachusetts distributed its share of the money to the various cities and towns; Boston used it for current expenses; Salem built a municipal Building; Groton repaired a bridge, and Maine made a per capita distribution.
>
> 1863–4: Chase favoured the maximum distribution of the National Loan among the people instead of trafficking with the banks.
>
> 1878: The Greenback party was in favour of the National Bills and against the bankers' monopoly. This party received a million votes.
>
> 1884: The end of the Greenback party.[144]

Pound points out, while making a criticism of D. R. Dewey, that credit does not automatically make one rich, but it does provide the ability to purchase. He goes on to explain how anything can become money and be accepted in commerce so long as "whoever issues them have the means to honour them."[145]

A VISITING CARD

We return again to Pound's earlier discussed essay "A Visiting Card." Pound pays tribute to Brooks Adams, great-grandson of John Adams and author of *The Law of Civilization and Decay*. Brooks Adams's history of Western civilization boils down to "a consecutive struggle against four great rackets, namely the exploitation of the fear of the unknown (black magic, etc.), the exploitation of violence, the exploitation or monopolization of cultivable land, and the exploitation of money."[146] Pound states that Adams unfortunately fell for the error made likewise "by Mill and Marx, of money as an accumulation of energy." Pound maintains that this is to deny "both God and nature," and to falsify the "word" which betrays all else.[147] Pound insists that products are made with basic physical resources, in contrast to "spoken poetry and unwritten music" that are made without physical matter. Pound believes that money lenders misled Brooks Adams, "who was fighting for the peasant and humanity against the monopolists," via their "satanic transubstantiation, their Black Mass of money."[148]

---

144 Pound, *Impact*, 37–39.
145 Pound, *Impact*, 39.
146 Pound, *Impact*, 45.
147 Pound, *Impact*, 45.
148 Pound, *Impact*, 45.

Pound insists that "[m]oney does not contain energy. The half-lira piece cannot *create* the platform ticket, the cigarettes, or piece of chocolate that issues from the slot-machine."[149]

Pound may have been first drawn to the writings of Brooks Adams through conversations with C. H. Douglas, or from Douglas's writings. One reference to Brooks Adams in Douglas's writings and speeches reads as follows:

> In a remarkable book first published in 1896, *The Law of Civilisation and Decay,* by Brooks Adams, which is not so well known as it ought to be — the antiquity and the invariable result of political centralisation are demonstrated in a manner which must convince any reasonable reader as to the facts. The thesis is presented in rather a mechanistic dressing, quite possibly because of the intellectual atmosphere prevailing at the time of its publication. We are not so hypnotised by mechanistic conceptions of the Universe as were the Victorians, and we can perceive that mechanisms are merely extensions of purpose, human, divine, or diabolical and that by themselves, they explain nothing.[150]

Pound insists that this sleight of hand, that tries to convince us that money holds "energy" for any enterprise leads to confusion. It is a "black myth" that only a study of history can clear. Pound brings our attention to the Monte dei Paschi, the bank of Siena. Here in history we discover the real foundation of credit, "'the abundance of nature and the responsibility of the whole people.'"[151] For Pound, the present war, World War II, started in 1694 with the creation of the Bank of England.[152] Pound again quotes Paterson, one of the Bank's founders, and his statement to prospective shareholders: "'the bank hath benefit of the interest of all moneys which it creates out of nothing.'"[153] This scam, says Pound, was to charge an interest of 60 percent.[154] Pound focuses on Lord Overstone (Samuel Lloyd). Lloyd explained, how, in the past, currency amounts available were synchronised "to meet the real wants of commerce, and to discount all commercial bills arising out of legitimate transactions." However,

149 Pound, *Impact*, 46.
150 Douglas, *Major Douglas Analyzes*, 5.
151 Pound, *Impact*, 46.
152 Pound, *Impact*, 46.
153 Pound, *Impact*, 47.
154 Comment will be made later in this work concerning Pound's claim of 60% interest by the banking system.

Brooks Adams states that following Waterloo, "'nature herself was favouring the usurers'"[155] with no opposition for over 100 years to the banking "monopoly of money":

> Perhaps no financier has ever lived abler than Samuel Lloyd. Certainly he understood as few men, even of later generations, have understood, the mighty engine of the single standard. He comprehended that, with expanding trade, an inelastic currency must rise in value; he saw that, with sufficient resources at command, his class might be able to establish such a rise, almost at pleasure; certainly that they could manipulate it when it came, by taking advantage of foreign exchange. He perceived moreover that, once established, a contraction of the currency might be forced to an extreme, and that when money rose beyond price, as in 1825, debtors would have to surrender their property on such terms as creditors might dictate.[156]

Pound is sorry if what he quotes from Adams is cryptic to the educated, "but one cannot understand history in twenty minutes. Our culture lies shattered in fragments, and with the monetology of the usurocracy our economic culture has become a closed book to the aesthetes. The peasant feeds us and the gombeen-man[157] strangles us—if he cannot suck our blood by degrees.... We are still in the same darkness which John Adams, Father of the Nation, described as 'downright ignorance of the nature of coin, credit, and circulation.'"[158]

Pound insists that the *cultural tradition* concerning money never should have been removed from the major currents of *literary culture.* He points out that this monetary-cultural tradition may be found "from Demosthenes to Dante; from Salmasius to M. Butcharts' *Money* (an anthology of opinions of three centuries); from the indignation of Antoninus Pius, that people should attempt to exploit other people's misfortunes (e.g., shipwrecks), to... *il duol che sopra Senna induce, falseggiando la moneta.* (Par.XIX, 118–119)."[159]

---

155 Pound, *Impact*, 47.

156 Pound, *Impact*, 47, quoted from Adams, *The Law of Civilization.*

157 A usurer in Ireland. *Merriam-Webster*, s.v. "gombeen-man."

158 Pound, *Impact*, 47–48.

159 Pound, *Impact*, 48–49. This last part in Italian, is from Dante's *Paradiso*: "The pain brought upon the Seine, due to the falsifying of coinage." It refers to Philip the IV of France and his debasing of coinage. Brown, "Philip IV, king of France," *Encyclopaedia Britannica*. The Seine river divides Paris. Without knowing economic history, Pound believes that one cannot understand Dante or other great works of literature.

Pound goes on to say that it is absurd when it is claimed that the state cannot do something due to lack of money. It is the same as saying that the state, "'can't build roads because its got no kilometres.'" It is nature, the actual existence of goods, or the possibility of producing them, that really determines the capacity of the state. Yet it resides above all in the will and physical force of the people.[160] Pound quotes from Mazzini's *Duties of Man*: "'The establishment of public storehouses or depots from which, the approximate value of the commodities deposited having been ascertained, the Associations would issue a document or *bond*, similar to a banknote, capable of circulating and being discounted, so that the Association would be able to continue its work without being thwarted by the need of quick sales, etc.'"[161] Pound points out that Mazzini speaks also of "'a fund for the distribution of credit,' thus anticipating the theories of the Scotsman C. H. Douglas."[162] And then Pound quotes Mazzini again: "'The distribution of this credit,' . . . 'should not be undertaken by the Government, nor by a National Central Bank; but, with a vigilant eye on the National Power, by *local banks administered by elective Local Council.*'"[163]

Pound goes on to insist, in this essay, on the power of the state to lend. He points to historical facts, such as that the fleet that won the Battle of Salamis was built by money loaned by the State of Athens. This state prerogative was misused by the dissolute Roman Empire, when money was lent to unfit borrowers who failed to repay. The Colony of Pennsylvania was able to lend its paper money to farmers, repaid yearly in instalments of ten percent, and the resulting bounty was acclaimed throughout the Western world. Pound mentions the similarly acclaimed method of the Jesuits in Paraguay.[164]

MURDER BY CAPITAL

In his essay "Murder by Capital" which appeared in 1933, Pound deals with the relationship between the arts and the current credit system. He mentions that the greatest writers of his era only were in print due to the initiative of small groups started for that purpose and

---

[160] Pound, *Impact*, 49.
[161] Pound, *Impact*, 49–50.
[162] Pound, *Impact*, 50.
[163] Pound, *Impact*, 50.
[164] Pound, *Impact*, 52. This has to do with the famous Jesuit-governed mission lands in Paraguay. The Jesuits brought unprecedented prosperity to the Paraguayan Indians by means of a debt-free money system. This system continued until the suppression of the Jesuits in the 18th century: Huonder, "Reductions of Paraguay," *The Catholic Encyclopedia*.

contra the large publishing houses.[165] He lists "Joyce, Eliot, Wyndham Lewis" and himself when he intended to break from the "immediate past."[166] Pound asks:

> What drives, or what can drive a man interested almost exclusively in the arts, into social theory or into a study of the "gross material aspects" videlicet economic aspects of the present? What causes the ferocity and bad manners of the revolutionaries?....
>
> Why should a peace-loving writer of Quaker descent be quite ready to shoot certain persons whom he never laid eyes on?....
>
> What specific wrong has the present order done to writers and artists *as such*, not as an economic class or category, but specifically *as artists*? And why should some of them be "driven" to all sorts of excessive opinion, or "into the arms of" groups who are highly unlikely to be of use to them?[167]

Pound does not believe that those who govern and wrong art can continue forever.[168] He insists that he has "blood lust because of what I have seen done to, and attempted against, the arts in my time." He traces all of this back to the modern system of credit. "Artists are the race's antennae. The effects of social evil show first in the arts."[169] For Pound, at the root of the majority of "social evils" is the economic system.[170] Social evils can be cured, or mostly cured, *economically*:

> "The lack of printed and exchangeable slips of paper corresponding to extant goods is at the root of bad taste, it is at the root not of bad musical composition, but at the root of the non-performance of the best music, ancient, modern and contemporary; it as the root of the difficulty in printing good books *when* written.... But with a decent fiscal system the few hundred people who want work of first intensity could at any rate have it, whether it were supposed to leaven the mass or not."[171]

Pound insists that the passion for economics that he professes is due to the "crimes" he has seen committed against the arts. Pound

---

[165] Pound, *Impact*, 83–84.
[166] Pound, *Impact*, 84.
[167] Pound, *Impact*, 84–85.
[168] Pound, *Impact*, 85.
[169] Pound, *Impact*, 86.
[170] Pound, *Impact*, 85–86.
[171] Pound, *Impact*, 86–87.

is not concerned about "minority culture." He insists that, at least from his recollection, he was not a snob writing for a few. "Perhaps that is an exaggeration. Perhaps I was a worse young man than I think I was. Serious art is unpopular at its birth. But it ultimately forms the mass culture."[172]

In his sub-heading "To Recapitulate," he charges that capitalism has "affected art or letters" by: "(1) the non-employment of the best artists and writers; (2) the erection of an enormous and horrible bureaucracy of letters, supposed to act as curators, etc., which bureaucracy has almost uninterruptedly sabotaged intellectual life, obscuring the memory of the best work of the past and doing its villainous utmost to impede the work of contemporary creators."[173]

In Douglas's writings and speeches, one can see statements which must have appealed very much to Pound, the artist. Ezra Pound, the exile, felt very deeply the isolation which the artist suffers at the hands of a world in which materialism predominates:

> It is one of the most curious phenomena of the existing economic system that a large portion of the world's energy, both intellectual and physical, is directed to the artificial stimulation of the desire for luxuries by advertisement and otherwise, in order that the remainder may be absorbed in what is frequently toilsome, disagreeable and brutalizing work; to the end that a device for the distribution of purchasing power may be maintained in existence. The irony of the situation is the greater since the perfecting of the organization to carry on this vicious circle carries with it as we have just seen a complete negation of all real progress.
>
> The common factor of the whole situation lies in the simple facts that at any given period the material requirements of the individual are quite definitely limited—that any attempt to expand them artificially is an interference with the plain trend of evolution, which is to subordinate material to mental and psychological necessity; and that the impulse behind unbridled industrialism is not progressive but reactionary because its objective is an obsolete financial control which forms one of the most effective instruments of the will-to-power, whereas the correct objectives of industry are two-fold: the removal of material limitations and the satisfaction of the creative impulse.[174]

---

172 Pound, *Impact*, 88–89.
173 Pound, *Impact*, 90.
174 Douglas, *Economic Democracy*, 63–64.

Pound had long felt that the position of the artist in the modern world was well-nigh impossible due to an environment completely out of sympathy with his aims and objectives. Pound could not have helped being impressed with the following statement of Douglas:

> In order to arrive at a sound conclusion in these matters it is necessary to start where all things start—in Nature—and to decide what are the motives which actuate men in this connection with the economic and industrial systems; and it is true, as well as proverbial, that self preservation is the first law of nature. Man does not live by bread alone, but he does not live very long without a reasonable amount of food, clothes and shelter. Secondly, and subsequently, he requires, and this increasingly, an outlet for the creative spirit. It may be noted in passing that it is just at this point that the "intellectual" is apt to fail in interpreting the great mass of humanity engaged in a deadly grapple with the weekly household bills, a battle which must in most cases be won decisively before the surplus energy becomes available for the satisfaction of the need of self-expression.[175]

Pound therefore would state that C. H. Douglas is the "first economist to include creative art and writing in an economic scheme, and the first to give the painter or sculptor or poet a definite reason for being interested in economics; namely, that a better economic system would release more energy for invention and design."[176]

INTEGRITY OF THE WORD

In his essay entitled "Integrity of the Word" which appeared in 1939, Pound defines money as a "MEASURE OF PRICE.... MEANS OF EXCHANGE.... GUARANTEE OF FUTURE EXCHANGE."[177] Credit, Pound says, is something we have when we do not have to give money at once for goods or services. It is a "belief that we can and will" pay.[178] Again, Pound refers to money as tickets, as Douglas does, whose use and purpose must be known: "Statally speaking, that is from the point of view of a man or a party that wants to govern justly, a piece of money is a ticket, the country's money is a mass of tickets for getting the country's food and goods justly distributed.... The aim of a sane and decent economic system is to fix

---

[175] Douglas, *These Present Discontents*, 7.
[176] Pound, *Impact*, 90.
[177] Pound, *Impact*, 91–92.
[178] Pound, *Impact*, 92.

things so that decent people can eat, have clothes and houses up to the limit of available goods."[179]

Pound is of the opinion that the authority of the state, backing paper money, is the prime way to create "a just and honest currency." He notes how in China, at least a thousand years before, it was understood, as is evident by "the Tang state (not bank) note."[180] Pound insists that "[s]overeignty inheres in the power to issue money and to determine the value thereof. American interests hide the most vital clause in our constitution. The American government hasn't, they say, the right to fix prices. But it has the right to determine the 'value' of money and this right is vested in Congress. This is a mere difference in legal formalities and verbal arrangements. The U. S. government has the right to say 'a dollar is one wheat-bushel thick, it is one serge-foot long, it is ten gallons of petrol wide."[181]

Pound insists that the practice of making new money in order to *distribute wealth* is not new:

> If you don't believe the Emperor Tching Tang issued the first national dividend in B. C. 1766 you can call it something else. It may have been an emergency dole, but the story will at least clear up one muddle. The emperor opened a copper mine and issued round coins with square holes and gave them to the poor "and this money enabled them to buy grain from the rich," but it had no effect on the general shortage of grain.
>
> That story is 3,000 years old, but it helps one to understand what money is and what it can do. For the purpose of good government it is a ticket for the orderly distribution of what is available. It may even be an incentive to grow or fabricate more grain or goods. But it is not in itself abundance.[182]

Pound charges that the word *inflation* is used only to scare people from expanding the money supply. True inflation is only when more money than "goods or services" available or desired, are created: "Money can be expended as long as each measured claim can be honoured by the producers and distributors of the nation in goods and services required by the public, when and where they want them."[183]

---

[179] Pound, *Impact*, 92–93.
[180] Pound, *Impact*, 94.
[181] Pound, *Impact*, 94.
[182] Pound, *Impact*, 94–95.
[183] Pound, *Impact*, 95. Cf. Douglas, *Money and the Price System*, 12: "Inflation is not an increase of *purchasing power*, it is an increase in the number or amount of money tokens, whether paper or otherwise, accompanied by an increase in price, so that both the money-to-spend side is, in figures, raised and the price side is also, in figures, raised.

Again, Pound returns to the need of defining terms used in discussing economics. Pound asks: what is the purpose of an economic system? He answers that its purpose is that all should eat healthy food, be adequately housed according to the climate, and be sufficiently clothed.[184] Pound goes on to state that the Left believes that *private ownership* is that which has caused the destruction of the economic system's true end. However, Pound says that it is the *demoliberal usurocracy* that destroyed the right of ownership granted to all, and therefore the economic system. Its "doctrine of capital" gave "unprincipled thieves and anti-social groups" the ability "to gnaw into the rights of ownership." From the time of Moses usury has been condemned. Unfortunately, this corruption or perversion of economics is the most powerful force today. By contrast, it is the granting of a right to a share in the fruit of our "common cooperative labour"[185] that most differs from usury and its effects.[186]

THE ENEMY IS IGNORANCE

In his essay "The Enemy is Ignorance" which appeared in 1944, under a sub-heading entitled "The Way of Utopia," Pound describes the working of the Gesell scrip plan (which has been referred to as being complementary to Pound's interest in Social Credit, and not as a substitute for Social Credit). The people of this "Utopia" claim that their prosperity is due to collecting only one tax, a tax on currency. Every paper bill of one hundred units must have a stamp added each month, worth a unit. As the government issues new currency to pay for its expenses, no other tax is needed. Currency is not "hoarded" as it would lose all value after one hundred months. Therefore, in this Utopia, money circulates.[187]

The victory of the Social Credit movement in the Canadian province of Alberta as a result of the 1935 election was followed by the government trying to implement Social Credit policies. In Alf Hooke's book on the Social Credit governance in the province of Alberta, in chapter 12,[188] he lists the legislation that was passed by the elected representatives, only to be disallowed. Reasons for the different pieces of legislation being denied included:

---

[184] Pound, *Impact*, 95–96.

[185] Editor's note: This is a Poundian reference to Douglas's doctrines of the unearned increment of association and the cultural heritage.

[186] Pound, *Impact*, 96.

[187] Pound, *Impact*, 99.

[188] Hooke, *30 + 5, I know*, 135–42.

1) Disallowed by Federal Government.
2) Assent withheld by Lieutenant Governor.
3) Declared unconstitutional by Supreme Court of Canada.
4) Appeal by the Province from Supreme Court decision to Privy Council dismissed (or refused to hear Alberta's argument by their counsel).
5) Declared ultra vires of the Province by the Courts.
6) Disallowed by Mackenzie King government.

As to the common misperception by those critical of Social Credit, that "it didn't work in Alberta," it is not true. The implementation of the policies were never allowed at the provincial level. One policy that was tried was the printing of *Prosperity Certificates* according to the Gesell scrip plan. These acted as money, worth one dollar, and were given out as a dividend to residents of Alberta. This is one reason Douglasite Social Credit policy is often mis-identified with Gesell scrip. Douglas himself criticized Gesell scrip:

> Gesell's theory was that the trouble with the world was that people saved money so that what you had to do was to make them spend it faster. Disappearing money is the heaviest form of continuous taxation ever devised.
>
> The theory behind this idea of Gesell's was that what is required is to stimulate trade—that you have to get people frantically buying goods—a perfectly sound idea so long as the objective of life is merely trading. When a 10s. note becomes worth only 9s. 11d. to-morrow, a man will go and buy something and so stimulate trade. In fact you have exactly the same state of affairs as existed at the time of the stupendous German inflation of the mark. When a waiter received payment in millions of marks he hardly waited to throw down his napkin before dashing out to buy something, because the value was disappearing so rapidly that what he bought one minute would require a billion marks ten minutes hence.[189]

James Laughlin relates how he with Ezra Pound and Olga Rudge visited Herr Unterguggenberger, the onetime mayor of Wörgl who had helped implement the Gesell scrip, bringing three years of prosperity.[190] Pound was still considering the practicality of the scrip, as late as 1970, writing to Laughlin: "'Stamp scrip is impractical as, even when the bills were printed on really good paper, they wore out and went back to treasury to be pulped at end of six months. Also the bother of looking

[189] Douglas, *The Approach to Reality*, 9.
[190] Laughlin, *Pound as Wuz*, 159–60.

at each separate note to see if it was properly stamped. This does not exclude the use of local money in an emergency. . . .'"[191]

For Pound, it is not that Gesell scrip is the best solution, but that it is an historical case of the local community taking back financial sovereignty as a benefit to the community. It showed, proved, that the community, the nation, has credit. It was based on *the abundance of nature and the responsibility of the whole people* within the town of Wörgl. It was proof in our day of the historical truths concerning money creation by the state that Pound would read in Del Mar. It was evidence that Douglasism was a thought heritage that extended into the present. As seen in the Alberta case, it eased the burden of poverty during the depression and made it possible for the province to continue improving roads, while providing a source of purchasing power to the province.[192] The same occurred in Wörgl, Austria, according to the historical record. In Wörgl and Alberta, it helped to bridge the gap between prices and consumer purchasing power within the local economy. We will revisit this when we come to an examination of Pound's *The Cantos*.

Pound goes on to attack the usurocracy and its causing of "wars in succession" in order to place nations and individuals in debt: "For every debt incurred when a bushel of grain is worth a certain sum of money, repayment is demanded when it requires five bushels or more to raise the same sum. This is accompanied by much talk of devaluation, inflation, revaluation, deflation, and a return to gold. Mr. Churchill forced the Indian peasant to pay two bushels of grain in taxes and interest which a short time before he had been able to pay with only one."[193]

---

[191] Laughlin, *Pound as Wuz*, 160.

[192] Editor's note: My father mentioned at times his chance meeting with a gentleman who had grown-up on a poor struggling farm during the depression in Alberta. The man mentioned his remembrance of walking with his father to collect the monthly one dollar prosperity certificate and its importance for the family in surviving those difficult years. See: Hooke, *30 + 5, I know*, 115–16, concerning *Prosperity Certificates*.

[193] Pound, *Impact*, 101. Although it was not a strict Social Credit policy from Douglas, but rather a just tax (as Pound states), the Social Credit party in Alberta had passed legislation to end the practice of charging farmers a tax in money, supplementing a tax in kind, something that would not fluctuate with the market: "In the new legislation the theory was established that a bushel of wheat, whether bringing on the market two dollars or only thirty-five cents, is still just one bushel of wheat and represents to the farmer the same amount of effort in each case." Hooke mentions that this guaranteed "to the farmer that he could never lose his land for non-payment of taxes, and that he could always be assured of the return to him of at least the cost of production." Hooke, *30 + 5, I know*, 151.

Pound sees war as the greatest method of sabotage. Sabotage here has the Douglasite meaning of anything that contributes to wasted human effort or unnecessary costs created by the financial system itself, and hinders the economy's true purpose: to deliver needed goods and services. He charges that usurers cause wars in order to create monopolies beneficial to themselves. Usurers cause wars to put others in debt, in order that they can gain interest payments and profit from the change in currency rates that wars cause.[194] As an illustration of this he quotes the *Hazard Circular* of 1862: "The great debt that (our friends the) capitalists (of Europe) will see to it is made out of the war must be used to control the volume of money.... It will not do to allow the greenback, as it is called, to circulate... for we cannot control them" (i.e., their issue, etc.)."[195] The *Hazard* (or *Hazzard) Circular* was claimed to have been written by an agent of London bankers and distributed among the professional money lenders of America and U. S. Senators and Congressmen. The greenback referred to here is the Congressional money issued debt-free under President Lincoln during the Civil War. For Pound, it testifies to the money power's desire to bring a new slavery into America, debt-slavery, *via* the Bank of England model.

Pound charges that the whole of current popular literature and journalism are in the hands of "international usurocracy," which wants to keep the public ignorant of the usurocratic system. He also charges that "Liberalism and Bolshevism" are both agreed in their rejection of humanity as individuals. Stalin discards truckloads of men as mere instruments to die building a canal. Liberals talk of exporting "'labour'" not the export of men.[196] Pound ends this section of the essay, with five lines printed thus:

A NATION
THAT WILL NOT
GET ITSELF INTO DEBT
DRIVES THE USURERS
TO FURY[197]

Pound defines the usurocracy as "the rule of the big usurers combined in conspiracy."[198] He states that the those who traffic in money cause wars, not those who traffic in guns, be it the present war (World

[194] Pound, *Impact*, 104.
[195] Pound, *Impact*, 104.
[196] Pound, *Impact*, 106.
[197] Pound, *Impact*, 107.
[198] Pound, *Impact*, 107.

War II) or past wars, all for "their own pleasure, to create debts so that they can enjoy the interest on them, to create debts when money is cheap in order to demand repayment when money is dear."[199] Pound is convinced that usury is a "vice, or a crime, condemned by all religions and by every ancient moralist."[200] He quotes the following dialogue from Cato's *De Re Rustica*: "'And what do you think of usury?' 'What do *you* think of murder?!'"[201]

He quotes Shakespeare: "Or is your gold . . . ewes and rams?" It is not money, Pound declares, that is at the root of this evil, but "[t]he root is greed, the lust for monopoly." He quotes St. Ambrose who howled at the usurers, "'Captans annonam, maledictus in plebe sit!' . . . 'Hoggers of harvest, cursed among the people!'"[202] Pound declares that we have made of money a god. This has happened by assigning to money powers it could never have, i.e., "a process of denaturalization."[203] The claim that gold can reproduce itself is one of these false attributes: "[N]ot even if you put two bits of it together, one shaped like a cock, the other like a hen. It is absurd to speak of it as bearing fruit or yielding interest. Gold does not germinate like grain."[204]

Pound admits that industry should pay interest on borrowed capital as it is a means to increase output. However, we no longer understand the difference "between production and corrosion": "Give money its correct potential; make it last as long as things last in the material world; give it, above all, its due advantage (i.e., that of being exchangeable for any goods at any moment, provided the goods in question exist); but do not give money, beyond this advantage, powers that correspond neither to justice nor to the nature of the goods it is issued against or used to purchase. This is the way that leads to social justice and economic sanity."[205]

Pound sums up his thought on this matter by returning again to the importance of defining words, distinction in meaning, in order to think clearly. He recommends the study of Aristotle's and Confucius's writings, for proper learning of clear thought and word definition.[206] He ends with referring to the damaging effect of economic knowledge, as a *crude* science, with poor distinction between words:

---

199 Pound, *Impact*, 107.
200 Pound, *Impact*, 112.
201 Pound, *Impact*, 113.
202 Pound, *Impact*, 113.
203 Pound, *Impact*, 114.
204 Pound, *Impact*, 115.
205 Pound, *Impact*, 116.
206 Pound, *Impact*, 116–17.

> Everywhere there is the hidden work of interest, gnawing away, corroding. This is not the interest paid to the private individual on his bank account, but interest on money that does not exist, on a mirage of money; interest equivalent to sixty percent and over, as opposed to money that represents honest work or goods useful to mankind.
>
> To repeat: the distinction between production and corrosion has been lost; and so has the distinction between the sharing-out of the fruits of work done in collaboration (a true and just dividend, called *partaggio* in the Middle Ages) and the corrosive interest that represents no increase in useful and material production of any sort.[207]

WHAT IS MONEY FOR?

In his essay "What Is Money For?" which appeared in 1939, and is under the heading "Social Credit" within *Impact,* Pound states that "labour and nature" are the only sources of value: "Wheat from ploughing, chestnuts from being picked up. But a lot of work has been done by men (mostly inventors, well-diggers, constructors of

---

[207] Pound, *Impact,* 117. Editor's note: Pound had an interesting way of looking at "bank charges." Douglas does not often use the word usury, but may have had interest exclusively in mind when he spoke about "bank charges." Douglas discounted such bank charges as the main reason for the gap between buying power in a nation and the nation's ability to purchase, *via* its citizens, all needed and desired goods and services, though it was acknowledged by him as one of the minor reasons for the gap. Among the various reasons for the gap, Douglas cites the A+B theorem as the main cause, which is explained elsewhere in this book. Pound speaks of "60%" interest in places, which certainly would be "hyperusura": "For 25 years I have been up against the USURERS' class, wherever USURY, not moderate usury on metal coin, but 60% usury on real money called 6% usury on chequebook and bank money, has dominated, LEISURE has been cut down, the leisure class wiped out" (Pound, *Impact,* 274). Pound is referring, for example, to money creation where $1000 dollars held in the bank can be used as the basis for loans up to ten times that amount. Loaning $1000 at 6% interest may sound reasonable to some as a charge. But every loan is newly created money by the stroke of the pen or the computer keys of a bank teller. If they use the $1000 deposit to loan $10,000 dollars, it is now 6% × 10 = 60% interest charged to the community on the original sum of $1000 that was used to back the creation of new money. An individual can loan you $1000, but this is already existing money that is taken out of his account. An individual cannot loan you from his $1000 in his bank account a sum of $10,000. In bank loans, no one touches the bank's reserve. All the bank loans are new money, created in the act of loaning, and destroyed when paid back by the ones who took out the loans. In the end, when $10,000 is paid back and destroyed, written off the books, there exists the original $1000 at the bank, plus the bank's 60% interest, i.e., $600 interest collected by the bank on its loans. In Canada, 60% interest is legal, but any more is criminal: "Consultation on Fighting Predatory Lending," *Department of Finance Canada.*

factory plant, etc.) now dead, and who therefore can not eat and wear clothes. In respect of this legacy of mechanical efficiency and scientific advance we have at our disposal a large volume of social credit, which can be distributed to the people as a bonus over and above their wage packet. Douglas proposed to bring up the total purchasing power of the whole people by a *per capita* issue of tickets proportional to available goods."[208]

LETTERS TO AMERICA

In a letter to T. C. Wilson from Rapallo, dated November 28, 1936, Pound writes: "You do not yet understand the difference between a tax and a share. Douglas offers every man, every bloody-minded tovarisch, kumrad whatnot, his share in the fruits of the nation. What more does communism offer?"[209]

ON MILITARY VIRTUE

In this essay, dated by Pound "1936?", he stresses that wars are caused by "economic pressure": "A financial system wherein it is more profitable to sell guns than to sell farm machinery, textiles or food stuff is fundamentally vicious."[210] In the essay Pound is critical of pacifists who attack the wrong causes of war or go about it the wrong way: "The place to regenerate an Empire is at home. Pacifists who refuse to consider Confucius' formula for world peace are not worthy of respect. *To promote the peace of the world by the good internal government of one's country.*"[211]

OF MISPRISION OF TREASON

Pound prefaces his book *Impact: Essays on Ignorance and the Decline of American Civilization* with a highly significant short essay from Sir Edward Coke's writings entitled "Of Misprision of Treason." This short essay is significant in that it indicates Pound's great

---

[208] Pound, *Impact*, 266.

[209] Pound, *Impact*, 272. Cf. Douglas in C. H. Douglas, *Money and the Price System*, 15:

> "We believe that the most pressing needs of the moment could be met by means of what we call a National Dividend. This would be provided by the creation of new money—by exactly the same methods as are now used by the banking system to create new money—and its distribution as purchasing power to the whole population. Let me emphasise the fact that this is *not* collection-by-taxation, because in my opinion the reduction of taxation, the very rapid and drastic reduction of taxation, is vitally important."

[210] Pound, *Impact*, 252.

[211] Pound, *Impact*, 253.

interest in the late 16th century and early 17th century commentator on the common law, Sir Edward Coke. It also is highly significant in explaining why Pound has dedicated his life and artistry to the Douglasite cause. Pound is convinced that he would be guilty of concealing high treason if he did not do all in his power to expose the high treason of counterfeiting the "King's coin" which is carried on daily with impunity by the banking system. This counterfeiting of the king's coin is done by the creation and issuing of bank credit (or bank I. O. U.'s) and the carrying on of the vast majority of the nation's commerce by means of this counterfeit legal tender. Pound quotes Coke to the effect that by common law, concealment of high treason was treason. Coke cites the statute of 1 & 2 Ph and Mar. to prove his point and then continues: "It is misprision of High Treason, for forging of money, which neither is the Money of this Realm of England nor currant within the same . . . . *See John Coniers Case Dier 296.* That the receiving of one that hath counterfeited the King's Coin, and comforting of him knowing him to have counterfeited the King's Coin, is but misprision."[212]

Thus, Pound's great and more recent interest in the work of Sir Edward Coke is due to his earlier and continuing interest in the work of C. H. Douglas.

POUND'S ROME RADIO BROADCASTS

Ezra Pound's Rome radio broadcasts during the Second World War are arguably likewise part of his prose work. As with Pound's written works, so do his radio broadcasts show a profound Douglasite influence. From the April 9, 1942, broadcast entitled *Indecision*: "SOVEREIGNTY inheres in the right to issue money, and the American sovereignty belongs by LAW to the people, and their representatives in CONGRESS have the right to issue money and to determine the value thereof. And one hundred and twenty MILLION suckers, have lamentably failed to insist on the observation of this quite 'DECIDED law,' . . . The point at which embezzlement of the nation's funds on the part of high officers becomes treason can probably be decided only by jurists, and not by hand picked set of JUDGES hired to support illegality."[213] This quotation clearly shows the basic Douglasite insistence upon the right of the supreme public authority, i.e., the King, Parliament, or Congress, to issue money.

---

[212] Pound, *Impact*, vii–viii.
[213] Pound, "*Ezra Pound Speaking*," 84.

The Douglasite contention that publicity is controlled by finance and that history is falsified by the forces of usury is revealed in this excerpt from the April 13, 1942, Rome radio broadcast entitled *Question of Motive*:

> Figure out this affair of the ruin of language, the falsification of all reports in the well-paid magazines, the falsification of newsprint, and ALSO the attack on historic knowledge.... Note when American history went out of fashion. When the kids in the lower grades heard of Lenin and Marx and Trotsky and not so much of Lincoln and Washington. Watch the gradual creep up of obscurantism, the neglect, ab initio, from the start, of John Adams, Van Buren and Johnson.[214]

In his broadcast entitled *The Keys of Heaven* dated June 8, 1942, Pound emphasizes the Douglasite theme of enslavement through debt:

> Well, my heart, does it bleed for my country? I would rather have my head work for my country.
>
> If you can't or won't think of the cause of your misery and of this conducement to the slavery of your children for ten generations, God help you.
>
> You are in for billions of DEBT and you have NOT got your own paper money to pay for it. You, most of you, haven't the groggiest idea what Lincoln was sayin.' You don't know what he meant by it. Sheer ignorance of coin, credit and circulation, said John Adams 80 years before Lincoln.[215]

In his broadcast of July 26, 1942, entitled *Axis Propaganda* Pound quotes Jefferson, Lincoln, and William Jennings Bryan, all of whom shared with Douglas an antagonism to the banking system:

> [Q]uotes Thomas Jefferson:
>
> I believe that banking institutions are more dangerous to our liberties than standing armies....
>
> I have two great enemies, the Southern army in front of me and the financial institutions in the rear. Of the two the one in the rear is the greatest foe.
>
> That was Abraham Lincoln. Quote, that is again quote:
>
> The money power preys upon the nation in times of peace and conspires against it in times of adversity. It is more despotic than monarchy, more insolent than autocracy, more

[214] Pound, "*Ezra Pound Speaking*," 93.
[215] Pound, "*Ezra Pound Speaking*," 164–65.

> selfish than bureaucracy; it denounces as public enemies all who question its methods, or throw light upon its crimes.'
> That was William J. Bryan.[216]

In his broadcast of March 25, 1943, entitled *To Recapitulate*, Pound continues the Douglasite themes of the true basis of credit and of enslavement by debt:

> The true basis of credit consists in the abundance of nature and the responsibility of the whole people.... Wars in old time were made to get slaves. The modern implement of imposing slavery is DEBT. Usury is an instrument for increasing debt, and for keeping the debtor in debt perpetually or at least for the longest possible period. It is foetid hypocrisy to prattle of liberty unless that liberty includes the freedom to KEEP OUT OF [DEBT].[217]

In the broadcast of March 26, 1943, entitled *Financial Defeat: U. S.*, Pound states:

> The sovereign power over the issue of money CAN of course be used for maintaining justice. Kitson's study related to flagrant injustice. He found that men who had become indebted in cheap or depreciated currencies had been forced on more than one occasion to pay those debts in money worth twice or much more than the money wherein the debts had been contracted. In Kitson's opinion this was not by accident. He thought it was the fruit of design. He cited a good deal of conclusive evidence in support of his view.
>
> Now supposing that Kitson's view was correct, would it not be interesting to pursue the subject further? Would it not be of interest to know whether the SAME banking firms had indulged in this little practice or wheeze, several times over? Let us say after the wars of Napoleon, after the great and terrible Civil War in America of the 1860's and after the "diktat" of Versailles?[218]

In the broadcast of March 30, 1943, entitled *Usurocracy*, Pound continues the Douglasite critique:

> Brooks Adams observed that after Waterloo, the battle of Waterloo, no power had withstood the power of the usurers.
>
> We will try to maintain a distinction in our own minds between the production system, the system of exchange of

216 Pound, "*Ezra Pound Speaking,*" 218.
217 Pound, "*Ezra Pound Speaking,*" 259, 261.
218 Pound, "*Ezra Pound Speaking,*" 264.

> actual goods, and the wangles or corruptions of accountancy or the money wangles that corrode both the system of production and the processes of exchange.
>
> The page of the usury system which we are trying to analyze dates more or less Patterson's perception that the "Bank" (of England) would have benefit of the interest on all the money that it creates out of nothing....
>
> The quite exquisite spirit of illegality and treason, these manifestations of a usurer, SHOULD need no comment....
>
> The American citizen can, of course, appeal to his Constitution, which states that: "Congress shall have power to coin money, regulate the value thereof and of foreign coin." Such appeal is perhaps quixotic.[219]

In the broadcast of July 6, 1943, entitled *Credit: Legality*, Pound hammers home yet another Douglasite theme: "What is economic justice? Is it based on property? Do the communists answer that in the negative? Is economic justice material justice? In modern society I think the answer must be: economic justice means an equitable distribution of purchasing power. It means a living wage for all labor in all places where the means of subsistence exist."[220]

In the broadcast of July 17, 1943, entitled *Audacia/Audacity*, Pound discusses economic aggression:

> How do you prevent economic aggression INSIDE a nation? If you can't prevent it inside a nation, how do you expect to prevent it on the world base? How do you expect to prevent it internationally if you can not prevent it internally inside the territory already squashed and defiled by the plutocracy, by the usury system, by the rump end of the mercantilist system, which has been diseased and worm eaten by the cancer of usury (at 60 PER cent) and by the wheeze of varying the purchasing power of the government money, at the airy whim of the kikes and financiers? And if you won't, or if a given gang of profiteers, sometimes called politicians, WILL not even try to prevent it INSIDE their own countries, how the Sam Hill do you expect the rest of the world to expect 'em to do anything about preventing it OUTSIDE the borders of their own oppressed and unhappy countries?....
>
> Parts of the world prefer LOCAL control, of their own money power and credit.[221]

---

219 Pound, "*Ezra Pound Speaking,*" 265, 267.

220 Pound, "*Ezra Pound Speaking,*" 366.

221 Pound, "*Ezra Pound Speaking,*" 368–69.

This is sufficient to show the impact of Douglas's philosophy and policy on the prose works of Ezra Pound. In chapter III, approximately the first third of *The Cantos* will be examined to determine the nature and the extent of the influence of Douglas on that portion of Pound's work.

SUMMARY

Ezra Pound's prose output on the subject of Social Credit and monetary reform has been tremendous. Donald Gallup's *Ezra Pound: A Bibliography* lists a large number of books, essays, articles, letters to the editor, letters, book reviews, editorials, radio broadcasts, etc. dealing with monetary economics in general and Douglasism in particular. This Douglasist-oriented prose output started circa 1918 after Pound had met Douglas and continued to his death.

The most representative volume of Pound's monetary-economic prose is that entitled *Impact: Essays on Ignorance and the Decline of American Civilization.* Many of these essays had earlier appeared as *Money Pamphlets by £* published by Peter Russell. This volume of essays represents Pound's mature view as it existed circa 1940.

Pound prefaces this volume of prose by an excerpt from Sir Edward Coke's writings entitled "Of Misprision of Treason." This essay is a significant one in that Pound quotes Sir Edward Coke to the effect that concealment of treason is misprision of treason, and that counterfeiting the king's coin is treason. Pound then quotes Coke to the effect that anyone having knowledge of counterfeiting of the king's coin and concealing that fact is guilty of misprision of treason.

Following Douglas, Pound believes that the creation of credit by the banking system is in fact counterfeiting of the king's coin since this bank credit circulates as if it were legal tender. Pound then reasons that since he has knowledge of this counterfeiting of the king's coin, he also has the obligation to make known this act of treason. If he failed to do to so, Pound reasons, he would be guilty of misprision of treason. An understanding of this reasoning is absolutely essential to a grasp of the motivation behind Pound's herculean efforts in the cause of Douglasism.

In the essays contained in *Impact,* Pound emphasizes the basic Douglasite concepts of the cultural heritage and the increment of association. He defines the cultural heritage as the increment of association (i.e., the advantage men derive from working together rather than singly) plus all past inventiveness. It is this cultural heritage which is the basis of Douglas's concept of real credit, and which provides the basis for the national dividend and compensated price discount.

Pound, following Douglas, maintains that the usurocracy, the rule of the big usurers gathered in conspiracy, has appropriated to itself the increment of association and the cultural heritage. Pound argues that the cultural heritage is the inheritance of the whole human race and cannot in justice belong to and benefit one particular group, i.e., the usurocracy.

Pound argues that the modern banking system inflicts an interest rate of sixty percent on its victims. He calculates this on the six percent bank interest rate on credit, which is created out of nothing, by creating credit ten times greater than the cash reserves of the bank. Pound argues that a sixty percent interest rate is usury. He maintains that usury is a destructive, corrosive force which frustrates consumption and the equitable distribution of nature's abundance. He holds that usury is responsible for the decadence of art and letters in the modern world. Pound further maintains that usury is a destructive, corrosive force which frustrates consumption and the equitable distribution of nature's abundance. He insists that usury has *bitched* sixteen civilizations and that usury is responsible for the decadence of art and letters in the modern world.

Pound, following Douglas, maintains that the state has credit and that the state should lend not borrow. He holds that, in a monarchy, the king should issue the money debt-free, and that, in a democracy, Parliament should issue the money debt-free. Pound insists that the power to issue money is the basis of sovereignty and asks when the king will be *boss* of the coinage again.

Pound, following Douglas, traces most of the modern world's socio-economic woes to the founding of the Bank of England in 1694. He defines the Bank of England as a gang of usurers formed to gain interest at sixty percent. The founding of the Bank of England marked the beginning of the age of usury in the western world. Pound maintains that there have been two kinds of banks in history, i.e., the *hell banks*, e.g., the Banco Sancto Georgio, and the *benevolent banks*, e.g., the Monte dei Paschi of Siena founded by Cosimo de Medici.

Pound maintains that there is normally an artificial shortage of purchasing power in the body economic, as the modern economic system creates prices faster than it creates the power to buy. This chronic artificial shortage of purchasing power is primarily due to most money coming into existence *via* the banking system as a debt and must be paid back to the banking system with interest.[222] Pound advocates closing the gap between prices and purchasing power by means of national dividends paid to consumers, and compensated price discounts paid to sellers. These are to be paid for by the creation of debt-free credit by the supreme public authority.

Pound regards the struggle for foreign markets to be the primary cause of that commercial warfare which has always preceded military warfare in modern times. He insists that usury is the main cause of war, and that world peace can only be attained by individual nations adopting Douglasism.

Pound, following Confucius, maintains that the best way to work for world peace is to work for the good internal administration of one's own country. For Pound, the good internal administration of one's own country would involve the adoption of Douglasist policy and philosophy. He regards all peace movements that fail to recognize this principle as doomed to failure.

[222] Editor's note: Douglas held that the gap was caused primarily by the premature cancellation of credit representing real capital such that real capital has to be paid for at least twice: once for its construction or purchase and the second time to cover its depreciation, maintenance, etc. The creation of money as debt has something to do with this cancellation (as money is destroyed when debt is repaid), but this phenomenon is entirely independent of the question of usury or interest-charges.

CHAPTER III
Cantos I-LI

THE CANTOS IS AN EPIC. EZRA POUND HAS emphasized this fact many times. Pound is convinced that since an epic is a tale of the tribe, it must contain history. History without economics is, for Pound, meaningless. Pound puts the case thusly: "An epic poem is a poem which contains history. Anyone who does not understand economics can have no comprehension of history. Dante was concerned with coin and measure. Homer noticed the problem of food, of pig-rearing, and of the provisions of Odysseus and his companions."[1]

Richard Landini's work on Pound's economic thought is an excellent study that illuminates Pound and the creation of *The Cantos.* Much of what follows on *The Cantos* includes many of Landini's insights.

Like the *Divine Comedy, The Cantos* is a tale of humanity, but with *purposeful focus* on a specific people in a specific locale. In the *Divine Comedy* Dante focuses on the Florentine Republic. In *The Cantos* Pound's main focus is on the American Republic and, as is done in the *Divine Comedy,* Pound wants to manifest the errors of his age and offer solutions.[2] However, it is obvious in the light of Pound's statement above that monetary-economic history will play a significant role in Pound's tale of the tribe. This study will focus on that monetary-economic history of the tribe, as revealed by Pound, to show the Douglasite influence on Pound.

Pound uses the word *periplum* in several places in *The Cantos.* Landini remarks that "Odysseus' journey is something of a *periplus,* a circumnavigating of the Mediterranean islands. I understand Pound's *periplum* as his journey, 1908–1959, among the islands of personal and intellectual experience."[3] In *The Cantos,* in his *periplum,* Pound seeks "to find the permanent and enduring in the history of civilization; to probe history in search of answers to the problems of his own time; to determine the 'right thinkers' in history whose actions

---

[1] Pound, "The Central Problem," 15.
[2] Landini, "A Guide," 46.
[3] Landini, "A Guide," 90.

are benevolently directed."[4] Certainly, C. H. Douglas has an extremely high place in Pound's list of *right thinkers*.

In Pound's conversations with Douglas, and in Douglas's own writings, Pound would have found the inspiration to examine history and verify the contentions of Douglas and his philosophy. As Douglas writes:

> If the preceding survey of some of the more salient facts of the general economic and social situation as it exists at present has been to any extent successful in indicating a general principle, it will be evident that the real antagonism which is at the root of the universal upheaval with which we are faced is one which appears under different forms in every aspect of human life. *It is the age-long struggle between freedom and authority, between external compulsion and internal initiative, in which all the command of resource, information, religious dogma, educational system, political opportunity, and even apparently economic necessity, is at the disposal of the will-to-power, and only history offers grounds for the expectation of any measure of success on the side of freedom.* [emphasis added]. This antagonism does, however, appear at the present time to have reached a stage in which a definite victory for one side or the other is inevitable.[5]

It is important that we understand the method that Pound uses in *The Cantos*. He has described his method as one of *purposeful focus* or *luminous detail.*[6] As Landini states, Pound is concerned with history, historiographers, and the method most valuable for bringing the historically significant to light.[7] As early as 1911, Pound saw the need for more intelligent historical investigation:

> When I bring into play what my late masters and pastors would term, in classic sweetness, my "unmitigated gall," and by virtue of it venture to speak of a "New Method in Scholarship," I do not imagine that I am speaking of a method by me discovered. I mean, merely, a method not of common practice, a method which has been intermittently used by all good scholars since the beginning of scholarship, the method of "luminous detail," a method most vigorously hostile to the prevailing mode of today—that is, the method of multitudinous detail, and to the method of yesterday, the method of sentiment and generalization. The latter is too inexact and

[4] Landini, "A Guide," 90.
[5] Douglas, *The Pyramid of Power*, 57.
[6] Landini, "A Guide," 12.
[7] Landini, "A Guide," 12.

> the former too cumbersome to be of much use to the normal man wishing to live mentally active.[8]

Landini states that Pound's "idea is this: if the historian is to record accurately the period with which he is dealing, he must bring together into a unified whole all of the available facts. He must also be a sensitive interpreter of these facts."[9] Landini goes on to quote from Pound: "... the past should be a light for the future.... The purpose of history is instruction, that is to make people think and to guide their thought toward what will elucidate to-day and to-morrow. We should distinguish between historic study having purposeful focus on life as we know it, and a sort of extension of books of reference, 'mines' as they are called, for those who want to collect matter which can be so focused. 'Purposeful focus' does not mean distortion."[10]

Landini goes on to discuss how Pound points out "that the method of 'multitudinous detail' is, compared with the method of 'luminous detail' and 'purposeful focus,' relatively ineffectual."[11] Landini then goes on to quote Pound's example of *multitudinous detail*: "So-and-so was, in such-and-such a year, elected Doge. So-and-so killed the tyrant. So-and-so was banished for embezzling State funds. So-and-so embezzled but was not banished. These statements may contain germs of drama, certain suggestions of human passion or habit, but they are reticent, they tell us nothing we did not know, nothing which enlightens us. They are of any time and any country. By reading them with the blanks filled in, with the names written, we get no more intimate acquaintance with the temper of any period."[12]

Landini provides Pound's example of *luminous detailing*. Pound does not state the source, but it was paraphrased from *The Civilization of The Renaissance In Italy*, by Jacob Burckhardt:[13] "In this year the Venetians refused to make war upon the Milanese because they held that any war between buyer and seller must prove to be profitable to neither."[14] Pound, Landini states, accepts that "such historical writing through the method of interpretive detail is invaluable. It permits of the reader's fuller comprehension of the people of the period under discussion, their intellectual environment, and the ethical forces in

---

[8] Pound, "I Gather the Limbs," 130.
[9] Landini, "A Guide," 10–11.
[10] Pound, "John Buchan's Cromwell," 149.
[11] Landini, "A Guide," 12.
[12] Pound, "I Gather the Limbs," 130.
[13] Burckhardt, *The Civilization Of The Renaissance*, 58. Concerning the use by Pound of Burckhardt: Casillo, "The Italian Renaissance."
[14] Pound, "I Gather the Limbs," 130.

action at the time."[15] Landini explains that Pound is convinced that through the method of luminous detail as exemplified in the above quotation,[16] we can learn, as Pound writes: "[T]he old order changes, one conception of war and of the State begins to decline. The Middle Ages imperceptibly gave ground to the Renaissance. A ruler owning a state and wishing to enlarge his possessions could, under one régime, in a manner opposed to sound economy, make war; but commercial sense is sapping this régime."[17] Thus, we are better able to understand the problem of the transition from the Middle Ages to the Renaissance within an economic framework. The methods of luminous detailing and purposeful focus Landini hopes to demonstrate are the methods Pound has used in *The Cantos*, at least in the cantos Landini includes.

Landini explains how Cantos IV–XXX were written and published between 1920 and 1930. During these years Pound was "digging down into history" to corroborate a thesis developed in Douglas's Social Credit theory. The thesis Landini states thus: "[W]here in history one finds individual responsibility, beneficent government in control of its own currency, and non-centralization of credit and financial power in the hands of a small group of bankers and financiers, there one finds also economic justice (equitable purchasing power among the whole people) a proper relationship between the ruler and the ruled, and above all flourishing art."[18]

Landini states that Pound's "[T]he *Cantos* reflects these historical investigations, even if his prose writings (1920–1930) do not."[19] Pound's creative process in writing *The Cantos* followed a particular pattern. As Landini explains: [H]e would study some history, some economics, include personal observation of the contemporary scene and some reflection of previous studies, and then crystallize it as part of the 'luminous detail' of his famous epic poem."[20] On the day the war ended in Europe, Pound would explain himself with respect to his delving into history in a letter to the American Counter Intelligence Corps, which he wrote while he was held at their headquarters in Genoa: "Incidentally Mr Amprim has used the word 'theories' in ref/ to my position. I am not interested in theories but in specific historic facts; and in known results of known processes."[21]

---

15 Landini, "A Guide," 12.
16 Landini, "A Guide," 13.
17 Pound, "I Gather the Limbs," 130.
18 Landini, "A Guide," 87.
19 Landini, "A Guide," 88.
20 Landini, "A Guide," 4.
21 Pound, *Ezra and Dorothy*, 71.

As we begin *The Cantos* below, a great resource the reader may wish to follow is The Cantos Project: ezrapoundcantos.org. We often refer to another excellent resource, *A Companion to the Cantos of Ezra Pound, Volume I & II*, by Carroll F. Terrell. Even when we do not refer to them explicitly, they are still the go-to resources for further information, especially concerning the sources Pound used for each canto. A link to online PDFs to *A Companion* and other Pound resources is found at "The Student's Shelf" of The Ezra Pound Society: ezrapoundsociety.org.

Cantos V and VIII–XI, the "Malatesta Cantos," are the result of Pound's study of the Italian city states during the first half of the Fifteenth Century. In these cantos Pound gives us a picture of the turmoil that results as each of the warring factions attempts to create a centralized power, by means of credit and financial control, in their own city state and in the others.[22] The various city states mentioned are ruled in a tyrannical manner, without moral guidance. Sigismundo Malatesta, the Lord of Rimini, stands out as one willing to challenge the orthodox views of the day.[23] What Sigismundo endures is caused by his challenge to economic abuses:

> With the church against him,
> With the Medici bank for itself,
> With wattle Sforza against him
> Sforza Francesco, wattle-nose,
> Who married him (Sigismundo) his (Francesco's)
> Daughter in September,
> Who stole Pèsaro in October (as Broglio says "*bestialmente*"),
> Who stood with the Venetians in November,
> With the Milanese in December,
> Sold Milan in November, stole Milan in December
> Or something of that sort,
> Commanded the Milanese in the spring,
> the Venetians at midsummer,
> The Milanese in the autumn,
> And was Naples' ally in October,
> He, Sigismundo, *templum ædificavit*
> In Romagna, teeming with cattle thieves,
> with the game lost in mid-channel,
> And never quite lost till' 50,
> and never quite lost till the end, in Romagna,
> So that Galeaz sold Pèsaro "to get pay for his cattle."
> (Canto VIII)

[22] Landini, "A Guide," 88.
[23] Landini, "A Guide," 88–89.

In Canto XII Pound comes back to the contemporary period. The first part of the canto shows usury at work in the contemporary scene. The second part is a ribald story dealing with sodomy. By juxtaposing the theme of usury with that of sodomy, Pound implies that these sins are similar, i.e., that sodomy "is as much a crime against God and nature and her bounty as is the crime of usury."[24] Pound, as we have seen from his prose writings, emphasizes that usury and sodomy are both sins *Contra Naturam*. He also is convinced that the Catholic Church got on the wrong track when it softened its stand on usury.[25] Canto XII opens with an account of Baldy Bacon[26] who engaged in usury in Cuba:

Baldy Bacon
          bought all the little copper pennies in Cuba:
Un centavo, dos centavos,
          told his peons to "bring 'em in."
"Bring 'em to the main shack," said Baldy,
And the peons brought 'em;
"to the main shack brought 'em,"
As Henry would have said.
          Nicholas Castano in Habana,
He also had a few centavos, but the others
Had to pay a percentage.
          Percentage when they wanted centavos,
Public centavos.
          Baldy's interest
Was in money business.
          "No interest in any other kind uv bisnis,"
Said Baldy.

(Canto XII)

Thus, Baldy Bacon got a corner on the money market and charged people interest for a public medium of exchange, i.e., the *public centavos*.[27] This is precisely what the banker does. We leave Baldy Bacon and attend a banker's meeting with Jim X:[28]

Jim X...
     in a banker's meeting,
     bored with their hard luck stories,

[24] Landini, "A Guide," 113.
[25] Landini, "A Guide," 137–38.
[26] Also known as, Francis Bacon: Stock, *The Life of Ezra Pound*, 90.
[27] Landini, "A Guide," 18.
[28] Also known as, John Quinn: Terrell, *A Companion*, Vol I, 60.

Bored with their bloomin' primness
        and the little white rims
They wore around inside the edge of their vests
To make 'em look as if they had on two waistcoats,
Told 'em the Tale of the Honest Sailor.
Bored with their proprieties,
        as they sat, the ranked presbyterians,
Directors, dealers through holding companies,
Deacons in churches, owning slum properties,
Alias usurers in excelsis,
        the quintessential essence of usurers,
The purveyors of employment, whining over their 20 p.c.
        and the hard times,
And the bust-up of Brazilian securities
        (S. A. securities),
And the general uncertainty of all investment
Save investment in new bank buildings,
        productive of bank buildings,
And not likely to ease distribution,
Bored with the way their mouths twitched
        over their cigar-ends,

(Canto XII)

The reference to the "ranked presbyterians" is indicative of the Douglasite belief that Calvinism and the so-called Protestant Reformation were responsible for the acceptance of usury in Christian society.[29] Douglas often refers to this in his writings and Pound likewise. Pound is of the opinion that the Catholic Church softened

---

[29] As an example of Douglas's views on Calvinism and its conception with financial capitalism, consider the following: "It is frequently objected that the sins of the financial system are blamed upon the Jews exclusively, whereas it is a matter of common observation that many of the world's largest bankers are, at any rate, so far as can been seen, non-Jewish, not merely in name, but in fact. This is true but it raises the curious problems as to the nature of the relationship between Judaism and Puritan-Calvinistic-Whiggism. Werner Sombart, who, with Bagehot, is perhaps the most competent writer on capitalism, expressed the opinion that the whole of the Puritan and Quaker conceptions so valuable to the system could be traced to Jewish influence. It was the Calvinist Whigs associated with Cromwell who brought the Jews back to England, in the main supported and profited by the industrial revolution with its horrors of child labour and general degradation. The textbook of Cromwell's army and its authority for vandalism and cruelty, was the Old Testament. The Communist-Quaker-Whig Junta of the Cromwellian Stanley Baldwin, with the Calvinistic Archbishop of Canterbury, played a typical part in the constitutional crisis which resented criticism of industrial policy and asserted unmistakably the supremacy of finance." Douglas, *Whose Service*, 14.

its strict canonical stand on usury in the post-reformation period to accommodate itself to Calvinism, which had come to dominate the commercial world. In other words, Pound sees a kind of perverted ecumenical dialogue in the post-reformation period, in which the Church ends up giving at least its tacit consent to a practice against which she had thundered all through the medieval period.

The reference to the "investment in new bank buildings, productive of bank buildings, / And not likely to ease distribution," also has its origins in Douglasite thought. Douglas stresses that the vast profits of the banks are channelled into new grandiose bank buildings. Douglas ironically compares the magnificent new bank buildings with the shoddy materials going into British housing: "[P]unitive taxes frequently paid directly to insurance companies as premiums on insurance against Death Duties. *These have transferred the eligible land in this country from the hands of private administrators, who had a sentimental as well as material incentive to proper administration, into the hands of soulless corporations, whose works are evident by ribbons of jerrybuilt houses punctuated by magnificent corner edifices raised in the honour of the Religion of Mammon, displacing the churches in which, on occasions, unpleasant things were said about the money-changers.*"[30]

Douglas also stressed that the siphoning off of bank profits into the building of new banks, on the best sites in town, does nothing to correct the problem of the distribution of purchasing power and the social unrest it causes: "Three hundred thousand so-called Fascisti are preparing to start a civil war with about a similar number of striking coal-miners, who cannot produce coal at a profit while charging the consumer twice what he paid ten years ago, and all that we can show, I think, on the other side of the ledger, is that we have 8,600 branch banks on most of the corner sites of the country, and the most elaborate and successful insurance offices in the world."[31]

Now Pound stresses the unnatural quality of usury by telling the tale of the honest sailor:

> Said Jim X...:
> There once was a pore honest sailor, a heavy drinker,
> A hell of a cuss, a rowster, a boozer, and
> The drink finally sent him to hospital,
> And they operated, and there was a poor whore in
> The woman's ward had a kid, while
> They were fixing the sailor, and they brought him the kid

[30] Douglas, *Tyranny*, 4.
[31] Douglas, *Warning Democracy*, 60.

When he came to, and said:
    "Here! this is what we took out of you."
An' he looked at it, an' he got better,
And when he left the hospital, quit the drink,
And when he was well enough
        signed on with another ship
And saved up his pay money,
        and kept on savin' his pay money,
And bought a share in the ship,
        and finally had half shares,
Then a ship
        and in time a whole line of steamers;
And educated the kid,
        and when the kid was in college,
The ole sailor was again taken bad
        and the doctors said he was dying,
And the boy came to the bedside,
        and the old sailor said:
"Boy, I'm sorry I can't hang on a bit longer,
"You're young yet,
        I leave you re-sponsa-bilities.
"Wish I could ha' waited till you were older,
"More fit to take over the bisness . . . "
        "But, father,
"Don't, don't talk about me, I'm all right,
"It's you, father,"
        'That's it, boy, you said it.
"You called me your father, and I ain't.
"I ain't your dad, no,
"I am not your fader but your moder," quod he,
"Your fader was a rich merchant in Stambouli."
(Canto XII)

This tale of sodomy which like usury, is a sin *contra naturam*, is taken from Dante.[32] In Canto XI of the *Inferno*, Dante places the usurer and the sodomite together in Hell: "Violence against the Deity may be done / In the heart denying and blaspheming blind; / In Nature, too, spurning his benison. / The smallest ring hath therefore sealed and signed / For its own both Sodom's and Cahors'[33] offense, / And all who speak with scorn of God in mind."[34]

---

[32] Landini, "A Guide," 113.
[33] "Cahors is a city in France, notorious in Dante's age for its usurers." Alighieri, *The Inferno*, 91.
[34] Alighieri, *The Inferno*, 122–23.

Dante is simply reflecting the teaching of medieval theology and canon law towards usury. A perusal of the *Summa Theologica* of St. Antoninus, the *Summa Pastoralis* of St. Raymond of Peñafort, *The Catechism* of John Hamilton, Archbishop of Saint Andrew's, etc., will give some idea of the uncompromising attitude of medieval theology in this matter. Along with the condemnation of usury there was a highly developed doctrine on the concept of the just price in medieval theology. For example, St. Antoninus of Florence, in his *Summa Theologica*, deals at length with the concept of the just price. It is significant that the concept of the just price is a cornerstone of Douglas's theory. Douglas calculated the just price based on the consumption/production ratio. In other words, the true cost of production equals the value of the consumption which made that production possible.

The *Summa Pastoralis* of St. Raymond of Peñafort is considered one source for Chaucer's *Parson's Tale*. Here is a portion of what St. Raymond directs the archdeacon to inquire regarding usury: "First, inquiry is to be made whether there are notorious usurers, or persons reputed to be usurers, and what sort of usury they practise, whether any one, that is to say, lends money or anything else . . . on condition that he receive anything above the principal, or holds any pledge and takes profits from it in excess of the principal, or receives pledges and uses them in the meantime for his own gain."[35]

The Catechism of John Hamilton, Catholic Archbishop of St. Andrew's, Scotland, stipulates that under the seventh commandment are denounced: "Saxtlie, all usuraris and ockiraris synnis aganis this command that wil nacht len thair geir frelie, bot makis conditione of ockir, aganis the command of Christe."[36]

It is important that we bear in mind that Dante's *Divine Comedy* gives Pound's *The Cantos* its overall structure. It is true that the *Odyssey* of Homer is also a major influence on *The Cantos*. However, the general pattern of *The Cantos* in its overall structure is that of the Inferno, Purgatorio, Paradiso pattern of the *Divina Commedia*. Pound had been quoted as saying, "It is difficult to write a paradiso . . . when all the superficial indications are that you ought to write an apocalypse."[37]

---

35 Quoted in Tawney, *Religion and the Rise*, 244.

36 Hamilton, *The Catechism of John Hamilton*, 97–98. A translation of the quote: "In the sixth place, all usurers and those seeking a greater return for a loan sin against the commandment if they will not lend their money freely but demand interest, against the commandment of Christ."

37 Kearns, *Guide to Ezra Pound's*, 213.

Cantos XIV and XV are the famous Hell cantos. It is significant that the locale of Pound's Hell is the London of 1919:

Io venni in luogo d'ogni luce muto;[38]
  The stench of wet coal, politicians
. . . . e and . . . . . n, their wrists bound to
        their ankles,
Standing bare bum,
Faces smeared on their rumps,
        wide eye on flat buttock,
Bush hanging for beard,
        Addressing crowds through their arse-holes,
Addressing the multitudes in the ooze,
    newts, water-slugs, water-maggots,
And with them . . . . . . r,
        a scrupulously clean table-napkin
Tucked under his penis,
        And . . . . m
Who disliked colloquial language,
Stiff-starched, but soiled, collars
        circumscribing his legs,
The pimply and hairy skin
        pushing over the collar's edge,
Profiteers drinking blood sweetened with sh-t,
And behind them . . . . . . f and the financiers
        lashing them with steel wires.
And the betrayers of language
        . . . . . . n and the press gang
And those who had lied for hire;
the perverts, the perverters of language,
        the perverts, who have set money-lust
Before the pleasures of the senses;
howling, as of a hen-yard in a printing-house,
        the clatter of presses,
the blowing of dry dust and stray paper,
fœtor, sweat, the stench of stale oranges,
dung, last cess-pool of the universe,
mysterium, acid of sulphur,
the pusillanimous, raging;
plunging jewels in mud,
        and howling to find them unstained;
sadic mothers driving their daughters to bed with decrepitude,
sows eating their litters,

---

38 "I came to a place stripped bare of every light." Alighieri, *The Inferno*, Canto V, 28.

and here the placard ΕΙΚΩΝ ΓΗΣ
          and here: THE PERSONNEL CHANGES.
melting like dirty wax,
          decayed candles, the bums sinking lower,
faces submerged under hams,
And in the ooze under them,
reversed, foot-palm to foot-palm,
          hand-palm to hand-palm, the agents provocateurs
The murderers of Pearse and MacDonagh, ...
          Captain H. the chief torturer;
The petrified terd that was Verres,
          bigots, Calvin and St. Clement of Alexandria!
black-beetles, burrowing into the sh-t,
The soil a decrepitude, the ooze full of morsels,
lost contours, erosions.
          Above the hell-rot
the great arse-hole,
          broken with piles,
hanging stalactites,
          greasy as sky over Westminster,
the invisible, many English,
          the place lacking in interest,
last squalor, utter decrepitude,
the vice-crusaders, fahrting through silk,
          waving the Christian symbols,
. . . . frigging a tin penny whistle,
Flies carrying news, harpies dripping sh-t through the air,

The slough of unamiable liars,
          bog of stupidities,
malevolent stupidities, and stupidities,
the soil living pus, full of vermin,
dead maggots begetting live maggots,
          slum owners,
usurers squeezing crab-lice, pandars to authority,
pets-de-loup, sitting on piles of stone books,
obscuring the texts with philology,
          hiding them under their persons,
the air without refuge of silence,
          the drift of lice, teething,
and above it the mouthing of orators,
          the arse-belching of preachers.
          And Invidia,
the corruptio, fœtor, fungus,
liquid animals, melted ossifications,

slow rot, fœtid combustion,
            chewed cigar-butts, without dignity, without tragedy,
..... m Episcopus, waving a condom full of black-beetles,
monopolists, obstructors of knowledge,
            obstructors of distribution.

(Canto XIV)

The whole of Canto XIV is quoted to convey the unified impact of Pound's vision of hell. T. S. Eliot had charged that Pound's vision of hell lacks dignity. Pound replied in defence of his vision of hell: "[T]hat *section* of Hell precisely has *not* any dignity. Neither had Dante's fahrting devils. Hell is not amusing. Not a joke. And when you get further along you find individuals, not abstracts. Even the XIV–XV has individuals in it, but *not* worth recording as such .... My 'point' being that not even the first but only last letters of their names had resisted corruption."[39]

The strong Douglasite influence can be seen throughout Canto XIV. Throughout his works, Douglas emphasized the control of politics and politicians by Finance. He had delivered a series of lectures on this very topic:

> Now, the result of all this, interlocking with the control of finance over patronage in politics as elsewhere, has been to produce a peculiar situation, which, so far as my knowledge goes, is not precisely paralleled elsewhere. Considered as an institution, the Government of the United States has never relinquished its sovereignty over finance. Finance has, as usual, and by the simple method of supplying the campaign funds of all the political parties impartially, managed to make its own views prevail, but while being a Government "de facto," it has not succeeded in becoming, as in Great Britain, a Government "de jure." You do not hear in the United States timid and apologetic assurances that on no account would the Government think of criticising, much less of interfering, with the banks or the great credit institutions, although for the reasons which we have just noticed, such interference does not usually materialise, and criticism remains largely ineffective.[40]

The Douglasite influence can also be seen in the reference to "the betrayers of language / ...... n and the press gang / And those who had lied for hire; / the perverts, the perverters of language." Even

[39] Pound *The Letters of Ezra Pound*, 385–86.
[40] Douglas, *Warning Democracy*, 157–58.

as early as *Economic Democracy* Douglas had stressed the financial control of the press and of publicity, and he never ceased to focus attention on this problem. Pound's reference to "the perverts, who have set money-lust / Before the pleasures of the senses;" is an echo of Pound's strong conviction that Christianity under the influence primarily of Calvinism, had focused its attention on condemning sins of impurity rather than sins of usury. Ezra Pound, the Medieval and Provençal scholar, could never accept the idea of *money-lust* being supplanted by the pleasures of the senses. His reference to "sadic mothers driving their daughters to bed with decrepitude," was to be echoed later in the famous "Usury Canto," Canto XLV, "It (usury) hath brought palsey to bed." In other words, usury also frustrates the abundance of nature by wedding youth with age, May with January.

John Calvin and Clement of Alexandria, an early Christian philosopher and theologian, are condemned by Pound for their puritanical writings and teaching. Calvin is well known for this, but as Pound writes: "[F]anaticisms and excess that produce Savonarola, asceticisms that produce fakirs, St. Clement of Alexandria, with his prohibition of bathing by women."[41] Clement is not curently honoured as a Saint in the Western Catholic and Eastern Orthodox Churches, but is honoured as such, for example, by the Coptic Christians of Egypt. Pound knows from Dante that sexual sins, such as adultery and fornication, may be the most common mortal sins, and they may put you in the first circle of hell. They induce evil consequences on marriage and family life. But Pound's anger towards current Christianity in much of his writing is sparked by the fact that it allows a sin to fester that will take you into the innermost part of Dante's hell, the seventh circle—the sin of usury. In allowing this sin to flood the earth we have released this seventh circle of hell on the world. Usury destroys beauty, art, and joy. It leads to many of the same consequences as sexual sins, but on a massive scale. Homes are lost to debt, lives are lost to suicide, marriages are strained or broken, life in the womb is destroyed. Trade wars lead to actual war, debt, both personal and national, become burdens for every generation. Yet we still are unwilling to call this Demon by its name: *Usury*. Calvinism encouraged usury, and Clement never spoke against it in his writings.

Both the "betrayers of language" and those who are guilty of "obscuring the texts with philology, hiding them under their persons," have contributed to the obstruction of knowledge through imprecision of language and definition. The "monopolists, obstructors of

[41] Anderson, *Pound's Cavalcanti*, 208.

knowledge, obstructors of distribution" are in this hell for interfering with the distribution of nature's abundance and for preventing the dissemination of knowledge which could lead to this distribution. It is obvious that included in this *knowledge* are the monetary-economic facts of history, *knowledge* of the actual working of the money system, and *knowledge* of the Douglas solution to the problem.

Canto XV, the second of the two Hell Cantos, continues with Pound's portrayal of a Hell without dignity:

> the cowardly inciters to violence
> .....n and ....h eaten by weevils,
> ....ll like a swollen fœtus,
>   the beast with a hundred legs, USURIA
> and the swill full of respecters,
>   bowing to the lords of the place,
> explaining its advantages,
>   and the laudatores temporis acti
> claiming that the sh-t used to be blacker and richer
> and the fabians crying for the petrification of putrefaction,
> for a new dung-flow cut in lozenges,
> the conservatives chatting,
>   distinguished by gaiters of slum-flesh,"
>
> (Canto XV)

The image of *USURIA*, the beast with a hundred legs, dominates the two Hell Cantos. The respecters of usury, the laudatores temporis actis, the fabians crying for the petrifaction of putrefaction, and the chatting conservatives distinguished by gaiters of slum-flesh, all pay homage to usury.

Here again the Douglasite influence is evident particularly in the linking of the Fabian Socialist movement with the usurocracy. Douglas, throughout his works, and notably in his *Credit Power and Democracy*, drives home the point that the Fabian Socialists do not concern themselves with the problem of centralized financial control.[42] We have seen in Chapter II of this work, that Pound castigated Marx for seeing nothing wrong with the money system. Douglas emphasizes that economists of the Marxist school write as if money were unimportant and take money to be only a reflection of the economic facts of production. In other words, Douglas accuses the Marxists of thinking that when a farmer grows a bushel of potatoes, he also grows the purchasing power with which to buy that bushel of potatoes.[43]

---

[42] Douglas, *Credit Power and Democracy*, 145–46.

[43] Cf. Douglas, *The Monopoly of Credit*, 14: "A student of the preceding pages will have grasped the important fact that money is not made by industry. Neither

Douglas writes the following concerning the conventional right and left of politics:

> UNDER whatever name the parties to political controversies may pass locally, whether that of Conservative, Tory, Liberal, Radical, Socialist, Communist, Republican, or Democrat, it does not require very much acquaintance with the subject to recognise that they represent, wherever found, certain broad attitudes of mind which are conveniently described by the continental terms "Right Wing," "Centre," and "Left Wing."
>
> This is generally recognised. To a lesser degree, it is also recognised that extremes meet, that the extreme Right Wing reactionary, and the extreme Left Wing revolutionary, are fundamentally similar. There is little but a difference in form and mechanism between the ideas of a Mussolini and a Lenin or Trotsky, and they are identical in their contempt for liberty, and passion for the rule of centralised force.
>
> It is elementary to observe that in such cases as the political systems of Russia and Italy, we are spectators of the ultimate incarnation of a system of thought. Since the distribution of this system of thought is not confined to the countries in question, we should expect to find evidences of it elsewhere. I think we do find such evidences, and as they are specially plentiful in the field of taxation, that field will fully repay a little attention.
>
> To observe that the extreme revolutionary has a passion for the imposition of taxes is to state the obvious, and it would be true enough to say that this passion might be explained, firstly as an exhibition of the revenge complex, and so far as intellectual processes enter into it, as being based on the idea that the poverty of the poor is due to the richness of the rich. Similarly, the acquiescence of the Right Wing reactionary in taxation, so long as it penalises the less fortunately situated, might be put down to a more or less conscious recognition of the fact that as taxes have to be paid in money, the mass of the population can, by taxation, be kept in a position of subservience to those from whom alone money can be obtained.[44]

Canto XVIII, completed in 1925, has been called a *Geryon Canto*, i.e., a *Fraud Canto*, by Pound and he cites its importance as containing

---

is it made by agriculture, or by any manufacturing progress. The farmer who grows a ton of potatoes does not grow the money whereby the ton of potatoes may be bought, and if he is fortunate enough to sell them, he merely gets money which someone else had previously."

[44] Douglas, *Warning Democracy*, 173–74.

material that elucidates the "Hell Cantos" XIV and XV.[45] The first part of Canto XVIII is based on an incident recorded by Marco Polo:[46]

> And of Kublai:
> "I have told you of that emperor's city in detail
> And will tell you of the coining in Cambaluc
> that hyght the secret of alchemy:
> They take bast of the mulberry-tree,
> That is a skin between the wood and the bark,
> And of this they make paper, and mark it
> Half a tornesel, a tornesel, or a half-groat of silver,
> Or two groats, or five groats, or ten groats,
> Or, for a great sheet, a gold bezant, 3 bezants,
> ten bezants;
> And they are written on by officials,
> And smeared with the great khan's seal in vermilion;
> And the forgers are punished with death.
> And all this costs the Khan nothing,
> And so he is rich in this world.
> And his postmen go sewed up and sealed up,
> Their coats buttoned behind and then sealed,
> In this way from the voyage's one end to its other.
> And the Indian merchants arriving
> Must give up their jewels, and take this money
> in paper,
> (That trade runs, in bezants, to 400,000 the year.)
> And the nobles must buy their pearls"
> —thus Messire Polo; prison at Genoa—
> "Of the Emperor."
>
> (Canto XVIII)

In 1933 Pound referred to the Khan-Polo incident in these words: "Why should a country or a government rent and pay rent for MONEY? . . . It shouldn't. No intelligent government would pay rent for its own money. No more than I pay rent for the language I am now writing. The cost of money to a government should be the cost of the paper and the engraving and not one damn cent more. Kublai Khan didn't pay rent for the legal tender receipts he gave foreign merchants for pearls. They worked. Those receipts functioned as money."[47]

In other words, Pound sees the Kublai Khan passage in Canto XVIII as offering proof of the fundamental Douglasite precept that

---

[45] Pound, *The Letters of Ezra Pound*, 273.
[46] Polo, *The Travels of Marco Polo*, 202–5.
[47] Pound, "Questions," 4.

the state has credit and need not borrow its own credit. Pound points out that as far back as the 13th century, Kublai Khan was issuing his own paper money without the aid of bankers. Pound also stresses the fact that Kublai Khan's currency system worked.

The second part of Canto XVIII deals with the scheming of Sir Basil Zaharoff (i.e., Zenos Metevsky),[48] financier and seller of armaments:

> European munitions magnate. He started selling arms (ca. 1876) for Nordenfeldt & Co. and later joined Maxim, an early competitor; by 1913 both Zaharoff and Maxim had joined Vickers. Zaharoff also had interests in oil, international banks, and newspapers. He had a spotty career, rising from poverty to immense wealth and spending time in prison in England and Greece. But he was able to rebound from all adversity and by extreme cunning (as well as crookedness) defeat his enemies and come out ahead. Zaharoff, who as a boy in Constantinople was kicked by a Britisher and later was imprisoned and tried in England, hated the British secretly all his life... a repeat in history of Napoleon's experience with the French.[49]

The juxtaposition of the sound currency policy of Kublai Khan with the unsavoury story of Zaharoff would seem to be Pound's way of pointing out the abuses, which take place when a private monopoly of credit is allowed to cut the community off from its own credit. Pound admits that Zaharoff probably didn't know much of what he was doing. However, worldwide control by the money-power inevitably brings about careers like that of Zaharoff.

Since Zaharoff's activities were surrounded with such great secrecy, Pound makes it clear that what he writes of Zaharoff is often from second-hand sources and gossip. However, Pound maintains that Zaharoff is representative of a type that has a regrettable role to play in contemporary history. The second-hand nature of Pound's sources is indicated by Pound juxtaposing certain incidents with brief allusions to spurious accounts of the life of Napoleon, e.g., that of de Bourrienne:[50]

---

[48] "Metevsky is definitely Zaharoff, so far as the facts could be ascertained at the time—none of them essentially contradicted since. Tho of course he stands for a type and a state of mind; and an error in detail wdn't invalidate him." Pound, *The Letters of Ezra Pound*, 320.
[49] Terrell, *A Companion*, Vol. I, 76.
[50] Landini, "A Guide," 150–51.

> There was a boy in Constantinople,
> And some britisher kicked his arse.
> "I hate these french," said Napoleon, aged 12,
> To young Bourrienne, "I will do them all the harm
> that I can."
> In like manner Zenos Metevsky.
> And old Biers was out there, a greenhorn,
> To sell cannon, and Metevsky found the back door;
> And old Biers sold the munitions,
> And Metevsky died and was buried, *i.e.* officially,
> And sat in the Yeiner Kafé watching the funeral.
> About ten years after this-incident,
> He owned a fair chunk of Humbers.
> (Canto XVIII)

According to Landini's reading of Robert Neumann's; *Zaharoff, the Armaments King*, and Richard Lewinsohn's; *Basil Zaharoff, Munitions King*, the Zenos Metevsky of this passage is Zaharoff; Biers is probably Sir Hiram Maxim, described as a rival munition's agent. The Yeiner Kafé incident is part of stories concerning Zaharoff and Humbers is identified with the Vickers company.[51]

Pound points out the discrepancy between Zaharoff's career and his reputation as a philanthropist. Financial power was able to set Zaharoff above ethical or moral rebuke. The great journals of the world spoke kindly of him:

> So La Marquesa de las Zojas y Hurbara
> Used to drive up to Sir Zenos's place
> in the Champs Elysées
> And preside at his dinners, and at *las once*
> She drove away from the front door, with her footmen
> And her coachman in livery, and drove four blocks round
> To the back door, and her husband was the son of a bitch,
> And Metevsky, "the well-known philanthropist,"
> Or "the well-known financier, better known,"
> As the press said, "as a philanthropist,"
> Gave—as the Este to Louis Eleventh,—
> A fine pair of giraffes to the nation,
> And endowed a chair of ballistics,
> And was consulted before the offensives,
> (Canto XVIII)

Again, Pound stresses the Douglasite position of the control of the press by finance. Pound stresses the almost impenetrable veil of secrecy

[51] Landini, "A Guide," 149.

that surrounds Zaharoff's work in arms sales and international finance:

> So I said to the old quaker Hamish,
> I said: "I am interested." And he went putty colour
> And said: "He don't advertise. No, I don't think
> You will learn much." That was when I asked
> About Metevsky Melchizedek.
> . . . .
> "Qu'est-ce qu'on pense. . .?" I said: On don't pense.
> 'They're solid bone. You can amputate from just above
> The medulla, and it won't alter the life in that island."
> But he continued, "Mais, qu'EST-CE qu'ON pense,
> "De la metallurgie, en Angleterre, qu'est-ce qu'on
> "Pense de Metevsky?"
> And I said: "They ain't heard his name yet.
>
> (Canto XVIII)

"[O]ld quaker Hamish" is a reference to David Lloyd George. He was neither a Quaker nor named Hamish. Pound is referencing George's mother's "old quaker" and Banking family, the Lloyds. Quakers were known for their opposition to war. Despite this, several British banking Quaker families, such as the Lloyds, prospered from financing British foreign wars. Lloyd George would *supplant*, *usurp*, and take the place of H. H. Asquith, as Prime Minister of Britain in the power struggle of 1916. Pound implies with the name *Hamish* that this took place by some force or trickery. *Hamish* is an anglicized spelling for the Scottish Gaelic name *Seumas*. In Hebrew, Jacob, *the holder of the heel*.[52]

Pound thus reiterates the Douglasite postulate that wars are caused because of the machinations, both systemic and *ad hoc*, of the Money Power. The system of debt-finance causes nations to struggle for foreign markets and this leads ultimately to military conflict, which is a very profitable outcome for both the bankers and the arms dealers.

> War, one war after another,
> Men start 'em who couldn't put up a good hen-roost.
> Also sabotage . . .
>
> (Canto XVIII)

The reference to sabotage must be understood in the light of the Douglasite concept of sabotage discussed, i.e., the willful destruction of goods in order to bring about the artificial scarcity of goods and

---

[52] Hanks, Hardcastle, and Hodges, *A Dictionary of First Names*. See a similar allusion in Canto 93 concerning Lloyd George and the relationship he had with Zaharoff—*Metevsky*.

services in line with a chronically and artificially scarce supply of purchasing power. Pound, like Douglas, sees war as the highest form of sabotage: "[T]he climax of war only occurred in the moment when a culminating exhibition of organised sabotage was necessary to preserve the system from spontaneous combustion."[53]

In Canto XXII Pound brings C. H. Douglas directly into *The Cantos* and shows him in conversation with John Maynard Keynes who is referred to as Mr. Bukos:

> And C. H. said to the renowned Mr. Bukos:
> "What is the cause of the H.C.L.?" and Mr. Bukos,
> The economist consulted of nations, said:
> "Lack of labour."
> And there were two millions of men out of work.
> And C.H. shut up, he said
> He would save his breath   to cool his own porridge,
> But I didn't, and I went on plaguing Mr. Bukos
> Who said finally: "I am an orthodox
> "Economist."
> Jesu Christo!
> Standu nel paradiso terrestre
> Pensando come si fesse compagna d'Adamo!![54]
> And Mr. H.B. wrote in to the office:
> I would like to accept C.H.'s book
> But it would make my own seem so out of date.
> Heaven will protect
> The lay reader.
>
> (Canto XXII)

The C. H. of the above Canto is obviously C. H. Douglas and the Bukos is Keynes. Douglas asks Keynes, "What is the cause of the H. C. L." (High Cost of Living) and Keynes's answer is the "Lack of labour." Pound was present at the interview and Keynes's response lashed Pound into a fury. He reminded Keynes that there were two million men out of work and kept on demanding a reasonable explanation from Keynes. Keynes finally replied that he was an "orthodox economist" and this closed the interview. Pound never forgot this interview as an example of the blindness of the orthodox economist in the face of economic facts. In a letter to H. G. Wells, Pound wrote: "[I]f you are ass enough to consider Keynes a reliable writer,

---

53 Douglas, *Economic Democracy*, 70.

54 "Jesus Christ! Standing in the garden of paradise, thinking of how to make a mate for Adam!!"

Khrrist and all ———— help you.... Keynes on H. C. L.: '*caused* by LACK of labour.' In my hearing.... An orthodox economist."[55] Landini mentions that Keynes probably was speaking of "skilled labor."[56] Landini's defence makes Keynes's statement more bizarre, as if the few jobs that may have needed *skilled* labor could have increased the cost of living for all. Today, in the modern economy, many argue that the cost of training workers is more than compensated by increased company profits from the new skills training. In any case, it shows the sharp difference between what Keynes and other "orthodox economists" accept and the "reassessment of the basic tenets upon which the economic reality subsists,"[57] that Douglas and Pound desired.

Many today who have never heard of Douglas have heard of Keynes and are unaware of the connection between Douglas and Keynes. As is evident from Pound, Keynes and Douglas had met each other, outside of any official capacity. Douglas criticized Keynes in his own writing. An example can be provided concerning this very same issue, i.e., labour and employment. Douglas writes:

> Mr. J. M. Keynes states that the outstanding faults of the economic society in which we live are its failure to provide for full employment and its arbitrary and inequitable distribution of wealth and income.
>
> That is a very typical instance of what I am referring to as misrepresentation—a tendency to draw a picture which is not a true picture of things as they are. It suggests that the perfect economic system should provide full employment and absolutely equitable distribution of wealth and income. Now that sounds very attractive, doesn't it?
>
> But suppose you say that the object of the economic system is not to provide employment at all, then what importance can you attach to a statement that the job of the economic system is to provide full employment for all? The job of the economic system is not to provide employment at all. It is to provide and distribute goods and services with the minimum amount of inconvenience and loss of time to everybody.[58]

The following from Douglas is another example:

---

[55] Pound *The Letters*, 337. In later editions, see Letter to H. G. Wells, 3 February 1940.

[56] Landini, "A Guide," 61.

[57] Landini, "A Guide," 61.

[58] Douglas, *The Approach to Reality*, 7–8.

> [T]he curious atmosphere of scarcity, with which, in common with everything else, the land question has been surrounded, is, or could be a delusion also. It might be useful to recall that Mr., now fittingly, Lord Keynes predicted that owing to the disappearance of Russian wheat from the European market, wheat would rise to £5 per quarter and would be practically unobtainable, the event being that there was so much surplus wheat in Canada and the Argentine that it was burnt for fuel and the growers were financially ruined by the fall, to the lowest on record, of the price.[59]

For Douglas and for Pound, this is the sabotage that the orthodox economic system provokes, when it is based on ideas that are not reflected in the real economy. If the earth should provide a bountiful harvest, it is an obvious blessing. For the orthodox economist, like Keynes (who claim economics as a science), instead of the predicted rise in prices, the prices drop in such a scenario. Instead of this being accepted as a blessing, it is seen as a curse by the false economy of finance that demands the destruction of a nation's true wealth to maintain the price level. Wheat that could be eaten must be destroyed because the economy must operate according to the economist's rules of imposing scarcity for the sake of inflated prices, not according to the reality of the fruitfulness of nature in conjunction with the existence of real demand.

The connection and conflict between Douglas and Keynes is well explained by Edward Minton in his discussion of the origins of Keynes's claim that a shortage of purchasing power in the hands of consumers needed to be addressed by government borrowing:

> During the 16 years prior to the publication of "The General Theory of Employment Interest and Money" Douglas had written 3 major works, given evidence at Royal Commissions in Canada, New Zealand and England [on 1st May 1930, to a Parliamentary Enquiry of which Keynes was a Member and questioned Douglas] and had by invitation addressed audiences in Japan, Norway, Australia and the United States. Douglas was recognised across the world as the man who was saying that poverty amidst plenty was a result of a shortage of purchasing power. Malthus's quibble with Say was gathering dust in the dismal science's historical dustbin.
>
> Douglas's Statement of Evidence to the MacMillan Committee of Finance and Industry, and his full cross

---

[59] Douglas, *The "Land for the (Chosen),"* 12–13.

> examination before that Committee are available[60]. . . It was chaired by Lord MacMillan and Mr. J. M. Keynes was noted as one of the 12 members.
>
> Douglas had put forward his explanation of the occurrence of a shortage of purchasing power in his written evidence submitted prior to his appearance in person, and all members had been made familiar with it. This is normally referred to as the A + B theorem. It contends that overheads paid in previous stages of a products manufacture are not now available in the hands of consumers to meet their full retail cost. After explaining this by reading what he called "the shortest form in which this statement can be put," Keynes asked him, "By whom are the overhead charges paid?"
>
> Douglas answered, "They are put into the cost of the product. They are not paid to anybody. They have in previous cycles of production appeared in the cost of the factory."
>
> With that Keynes folded his tent, as it were, and asked nothing more. This was the final clang of the penny dropping, it would seem. Keynes had "his" diagnosis of the problem in a deficiency of purchasing power.
>
> Of course a diagnosis is one thing. Recommending a cure is quite another.
>
> Douglas saw money as pretty much a ticket system, whereby products were elected for consumption by consumers. If there were not sufficient "money votes" in the community to enable the available and desired production to be elected for use, then one produced more. But his ideas of equity saw all benefiting either by the issuance of a National Dividend, or through his Just Price mechanism, both of which increased purchasing power relative to prices.
>
> These were NOT financial objectives. They were a practical attempt to give efficiency in terms of human satisfaction, by subduing and submitting finance to this end.
>
> Government had long withdrawn from responsibility for a national policy of issuing credit, and had enshrined through ineptitude private monopoly in this area. This oligarchy, this Golden Internationale, would not accept any democratisation of credit, so Keynes was faced with "political" practicalities.[61]

In the *Social Crediter* newspaper, circa two years before his death, Douglas commented concerning Keynes:

---

[60] Douglas, "Evidence Submitted to the MacMillan."
[61] Minton, "Keynes and Douglas," 2.

> To anyone closely in touch with affairs in the ten years before the outbreak of the second phase of the War, it was obvious that Keynes, and the Keynesian distortion of the Social Credit Thesis, were the Financiers' Answer to the attack on the Banks. Lord Keynes was an able man, and was furnished with the best assistance unlimited money could provide; and the Keynesian Proposal for Deficit Spending, by which the under-distribution of purchasing-power disclosed by the A plus B Theorem, and rather cleverly admitted by Keynes, was paralleled by money issued to finance public works which were not for sale . . . were a brilliantly devised trick to put the population permanently to work for Lord Keynes's employers.[62]

Did Keynes ever write about Douglas himself? In chapter 23 of *The General Theory of Employment, Interest, and Money,* Keynes states the following:

> Since the war there has been a spate of heretical theories of under-consumption, of which those of Major Douglas are the most famous. The strength of Major Douglas's advocacy has, of course, largely depended on orthodoxy having no valid reply to much of his destructive criticism. On the other hand, the detail of his diagnosis, in particular the so-called A + B theorem, includes much mere mystification. If Major Douglas had limited his B-items to the financial provisions made by entrepreneurs to which no current expenditure on replacements and renewals corresponds, he would be nearer the truth. But even in that case it is necessary to allow for the possibility of these provisions being offset by new investment in other directions as well as by increased expenditure on consumption. Major Douglas is entitled to claim, as against some of his orthodox adversaries, that he at least has not been wholly oblivious of the outstanding problem of our economic system. Yet he has scarcely established an equal claim to rank—a private, perhaps, but not a major in the brave army of heretics—with Mandeville, Malthus, Gesell and Hobson, who, following their intuitions, have

[62] Douglas, "Lord Keynes," 1. The Keynesian economist, John Kenneth Galbraith, admitted in his own writing that Keynes was preceded by Douglas. Likewise, he unknowingly granted Pound's thesis, i.e., that the Douglasite monetary philosophy was already present in America's cultural heritage/tradition: "The operative feature of Social Credit was a social dividend, meaning the equivalent of cash payable to citizens at large—a reprise of the pioneering idea of colonial Maryland. The social dividend would surely be spent. It involved none of the passiveness of monetary policy. So Douglas anticipated Keynes—as Keynes himself observed." Galbraith, *Money Whence It Came,* 224.

> preferred to see the truth obscurely and imperfectly rather than to maintain error, reached indeed with clearness and consistency and by easy logic but on hypotheses inappropriate to the facts.[63]

To Keynes's criticism of Douglas, Minton offers the following explanation:

> It is of significance I think, that in the last Chapter in which Keynes deals with technical matters (Chapter 23) he devotes the whole of the last page to Major Douglas. [The last Chapter 24 only deals with social questions.] Is it that in this page he reaches his object; the heading off of Douglas from public acceptance of the nature of the solutions he proposed to the acknowledged problem of a deficiency of purchasing power?
>
> In this page Keynes denies that Douglas's B-payments, which went to liquidating the costs of previous production cycles, create the significant deficiency of consumer purchasing power that Douglas maintains....
>
> The answer (in part) to the first sentence is that "current expenditure on replacements and renewals" are, in the main, made on purchasing inventories of prior cycles of production, or they would not yet exist. In the case of the second sentence, when there is a deficiency of consumer purchasing power already existent, buying more than the existent funds have the power to do so, or financing investment from sales which consequently cannot be made, is only possible in one of two ways; in increasing the national debt in Keynes's model, or issuing a national dividend in the Douglas model.
>
> Douglas's social credit is antimatter to Keynesian social debt.[64]

---

63 Keynes, *The General Theory*, 370–71.

64 Minton, "Keynes and Douglas," 5. Note: What arises from this can only be considered an admission of Douglas's contention: that there is typically a gap between prices and the money available to meet them. This is reflected in the Keynesian call to "prime the economy"—that is, to increase government spending by borrowing, and perhaps also to lower taxes during an economic downturn. When the financial sector's usual methods of filling this gap—such as increased consumer borrowing, among other means—fail, they resort to priming: a large increase in government debt. Douglas offered a saner solution, one that did not create debt but rather issued credit directly to society: the consumer dividend and the compensated price discount, both of which would have an immediate effect.

The protest from other economic schools against the Keynesians—"stop inflationary government money printing!"—is both true and false. Yes, it can

In the final passage of Pound, we read: "And Mr. H. B. wrote in to the office: / I would like to accept C. H.'s book / But it would make my own seem so out of date. / Heaven will protect / The lay reader." We only know who H. B. is from a document Pound submitted to the U. S. military on the 8th of May, 1945, while he was held in detention.[65] This Hobson is John Atkinson Hobson.[66] How can this be, when in the referenced section above of *The Cantos*, Pound gives the initials "H. B."? One can only surmise from Pound's statement that H. B. perhaps stands for *Hobson the Boer*. Hobson, at least for the British public, was most known for his stance against British involvement in the Boer war, writing as a war correspondent for the *Manchester Guardian*.

Hobson and Douglas certainly disagreed and obviously Orage, as a convert to what became known as Social Credit, would take the side of Douglas. Douglas wrote a short booklet as a reply to some criticisms by Hobson: *The Douglas Theory: A Reply to Mr. J. A. Hobson*. This letter that Pound references from Hobson cannot be found, but there is a later letter, not dated, but probably from 1932, that is from *Hobson*.[67]

"A Draft of XXX Cantos," i.e., the first thirty of the cantos, was written between 1920–1930. During these years Pound had been reading very deeply into monetary-economic history to verify for himself the soundness of Douglas's position. The Eleven New Cantos XXXI–XLI are mostly based upon Pound's close reading of the Jefferson-Adams Correspondence. Pound maintains that this correspondence along with the Martin Van Buren *Autobiography* provides the clearest picture of American monetary-financial history. Pound's method here is most definitely that of purposeful focus and luminous detail. All through these cantos, passages are taken from the writings of Jefferson, Adams, and Van Buren's and by means of *superposition* (Pound's preferred term in place of juxtaposition) of

lead to inflation when pursued haphazardly, but in reality, the government borrows money; it does not print it. To claim the government is "printing money" is as inaccurate as claiming that you are printing money when you take out a loan. Such a charge obscures the deeper truth: that the sovereign right to create money has been handed over to private interests.

65 Pound, *Ezra and Dorothy Pound*, 71.

66 Townshend, *J. A. Hobson*, 6.

67 The letter, from what can be read, must be from Samuel George Hobson, who had worked closely with Orage in the early days of *The New Age*. Orage, "Letter from Hobson to Orage." It is possible that Pound confuses J. A. Hobson as the author of a letter from the lesser known S. G. Hobson, as suggested by Kimpel and Eaves, "Some Curious 'Facts'," 630.

passages, the reader is enticed to study America's monetary history more deeply.

Jefferson's concern with the iniquity of the debt-money system is seen in a passage from a letter written in 1813 to Mr. Eppes and incorporated into Canto XXXI by Pound. Jefferson "is attacking the National Bank proposal then before Congress. The proponents of the bill argued that increasing the public debt would be a good thing for business and would lead to increase of commerce and thus to increase of public revenues":[68]

> But observe that the public were at the same time paying
> on it an interest of exactly the same amount
> (four million dollars). Where then is the gain to either
> party which makes it a public blessing?
> to Mr. Eppes, 1813.
>
> (Canto XXXI)

In Canto XXXIII Pound quotes John Adams writing to Thomas Jefferson in 1816 concerning the reaction to the death of George Washington, then Jefferson in 1781 writing to Nathanael Greene concerning the fact that for $75 of paper currency in circulation there was only the equivalent of $1 of gold (specie):[69]

> but to keep in countenance the funding and banking system...
> orations, prayers, sermons . . . not that they loved General
> Washington, but merely to disgrace the old Whigs . . .
>
> $75,000 equal to 1,000 specie. (Feb. 1781) settler will be worth
> to the public 20 times as much every year as in our old
> plan he would have paid in a single payment.
>
> (Canto XXXIII)

It is worthwhile to quote the passage that Pound used to create this allusion to Adam's letter: "The death of Washington diffused a general grief. The old tories, the hyperfederalists, the speculators, set up a general howl. Orations, prayers, sermons, mock funerals, were all employed, not that they loved Washington, but to keep in countenance the funding and banking system; and to cast into the background and the shade, all others who had been concerned in the service of their country in the Revolution."[70]

---

68 Terrell, *A Companion*, Vol. I, 123.
69 Terrell, *A Companion*, Vol. I, 131.
70 Jefferson, *The Writings of Thomas Jefferson*, 68.

Instead of stating "cast into . . . all others who had been concerned in the service of their country," Pound substitutes the words "but merely to disgrace the old Whigs."[71] These words of Adams are not written about Washington's death, but concern the death of Hamilton, which follows this passage on Washington in the very same letter. The *old Whigs* refers to those who were like Hamilton, supporters of a private monopoly in banking, the money-people aristocracy, the financiers, and speculators. Pound therefore has falsified Adams's actual statement concerning Washington, replacing it with what Adams wrote about Hamilton. Pound is obviously stating that he believes that those who loved Washington the most and benefited the most during his presidency were the same people who loved Hamilton, i.e., the money power, the *old Whigs*. In either case, be it in reference to Washington's death or to Hamilton's, it was, from Pound's point of view, the *old Whigs* who truly mourned. Both Adams and Jefferson respected George Washington too much to claim the *old Whigs* were the supporters and the power behind not only Hamilton but also Washington. But Pound will state clearly what he believes to be the case. Washington is not found in Pound's pantheon of righteous Americans who opposed the banking system as a man of the people, but is, like Hamilton, a betrayer of the American Revolution — be it knowingly or unknowingly — to finance. Under Washington's presidency, the First Bank of the United States was created, the project of Hamilton.

Canto XXXIII moves from the Jefferson-Adams correspondence to the contemporary scene:

> Bills discounted at exhorbitant rates, four times or three times
> those offered by the Midland . . . .
> 150 millions
> yearly, merely in usurious discounts . . .
> and he even
> (to change the subject)
> put into the mouths of the directors of the Federal Reserve
> banks the words that they should say . . . "You have got more
> than your share, we want you to reduce, we cannot let
> you have any more."
> (Mr. Brookhart)
> page 34 of the minutes then they adopted another resolution
> page 42 committee of interstate commerce, ask increase
> or railroad rates, said to them: wd. suggest, gentlemen,

[71] Jefferson, *The Writings of Thomas Jefferson*, 69.

> you be careful not to give out anything about any discussion of discount rates disturbs everybody immediate rush never discuss in the newspapers . . . . .
> . . . . . . & Company's banker was in that meeting, and next day he was out after a loan of 60 millions, and got it. Swiftamoursinclair but the country at large did not know it. The meeting decided we were over-inflated.
> (Canto XXXIII)

From Terrell, we learn concerning this reference to *Midland* that it is to the Midland Bank in England: "'These fears of the Politbureau coincided with interests of certain English companies, and of quite a number of high officials of the U. S. S. R. Soviet bills, in London as elsewhere, were discounted at exorbitant rates of interest, three or four times higher than that fixed by the Midland Bank'."[72] 150 million refers to roubles, the amount of interest the Soviets were paying due to Stalin's disastrous policies.[73] The "he even" refers to "W. P. G. Harding, governor of Federal Reserve Board."[74]

These passages that follow refer to the words of the U. S. senator, Smith Wildman Brookhart of Iowa. On the Senate floor in 1931 his message was "that a small businessman is injured, to the advantage of giant corporations, through manipulation of government agencies; private information, denied to the general public, allows a few entrepreneurs to make fortunes."[75] Those on the Federal Reserve Board are given privileges that no others have. Terrell would have done better to call these individuals minimal-risk financiers, not *entrepreneurs*, as money was their business, not goods and services, and they did so with minimum risk since they had inside information. Pound has calculated to provide us with a purposeful focus and luminous detail necessary to appreciate the secret and sinister machinations of the credit monopoly. Here, usury is in complete control and both the common good and the economic freedom of the individual citizen are trampled upon.

In Canto XXXIV Pound quotes John Quincy Adams' account of Madame de Staël's preoccupation concerning the interest on her investments: "I found Lord Cathcart, the newly-arrived British Ambassador, with her . . . . She has lands in the State of New York, upon Lake Ontario, and stocks in the United States funds, and she

---

[72] Terrell, *A Companion*, Vol. I, 132.
[73] Terrell, *A Companion*, Vol. I, 132.
[74] Terrell, *A Companion*, Vol. I, 132.
[75] Terrell, *A Companion*, Vol. I, 132.

wished to enquire how she could continue to receive her interest in England while there is war between the United States and Great Britain."[76] Madame de Staël was the daughter of Necker who was the agent of Finance in its war against the state-issued Assignat at the time of the French Revolution:

> Aug. 14th. to Oranienbaum.
> Where was Ld. Cathcart (that is, at Madame de Stael's)
> And she wanted to know how she cd.
> Receive her interest from United States funds
> While in England, and a war on between them.
> (Canto XXXIV)

Madame de Staël did not care who would win as much as she cared about her monetary interests. She was a true representative of Finance — the banking monopoly — as they do not care who is in power, whether there is peace or war, as long as they receive their interest or profit.

Pound quotes John Quincy Adams to the effect that:

> Banks breaking all over the country,
> Some in a sneaking, some in an impertinent manner . . .
> prostrate every principle of economy.
>
> . . . .
>
> After conversing with Mr. Calhoun, Adams reflected:
> Paper currency . . . reductions of fictitious capital . . . .
> Accumulation of debts as long as credit can be strained . . . .
>
> . . . .
>
> I called upon Nicholas Biddle . . . and recd. two dividends
> of my bank stock . . . . . as I might be called to take part in
> public measures . . . . . I wished to divest myself
> of all personal interest . . . . Nov. 9. '31.
> (Canto XXXIV)

It is only by reading the source that we can fully understand and appreciate Pound's allusions. Pound wishes to draw our attention to the original. He wants us to read America's *paideuma*, the tradition pre-revolutionary and post, the fight for the government to control currency, not allowing the private bank of the United States to take this right on to itself. We cannot understand the force of the statements by Adams, unless we read the source:

> Crawford told me much of the information which he is receiving with respect to the operations of the Bank, and the gigantic frauds practising upon the people by means

[76] Adams, *The Diary of John Quincy*, 97.

> of those institutions. The banks are breaking all over the country; some in a sneaking and some in an impudent manner; some with sophisticating evasions and others with the front of highwaymen. Our greatest real evil is the question between debtor and creditor, into which the banks have plunged us deeper than would have been possible without them. The bank debtors are everywhere so numerous and powerful that they control the newspapers throughout the Union and give the discussion a turn extremely erroneous, and prostrate every principle of political economy.[77]

Adams, in agreement with Pound and Douglas, understood that it was an unequal conflict, as the banking speculators control the press even if they do not outright own it. Next, with respect to the second allusion from above:

> I called upon Mr. Calhoun, and he went with me to Mr. Thomas Law's, in Prince George's County. On the ride we had much conversation upon various topics.... It was a vague but wide-spread discontent, caused by the disordered circumstances of individuals, but resulting in a general impression that there was something radically wrong in the administration of the Government. These observations are undoubtedly well-founded. The disease is apparent, the remedy not discernible. The primary cause is that which has been the scourge of this country from its Colonial infancy—speculations in paper currency, now appearing in the shape of banks; the great multiplication, followed by the sudden and severe reduction, of fictitious capital; then the great falling off in the prices of all our principal articles of exportation, the competition of foreign manufactures carried on by starving workmen, with ours loaded with high wages, the diminution of commerce and the carrying trade, and the accumulation of debt as long as credit could be strained—all this, with ambitious and crafty and disappointed men on the watch for every misfortune and welcoming every disaster.[78]

The third allusion: "I called upon Nicholas Biddle at the United States Bank, and received two dividends of my bank stock, by an order upon the branch bank at Washington. I left with Mr. Biddle my certificate of stock to be sold, and the proceeds to be remitted

---

[77] Adams, John, *The Diary*, 217.
[78] Adams, John, *The Diary*, 241–42.

according to such directions as I may give. I told him that, as I might be called to take part in public measures concerning the bank, and was favorable to it, I wished to divest myself of all personal interest in it. I endorsed my name in blank on the certificate."[79]

John Quincy Adams was anxious to divest himself of all personal interest so that he could take part in *the great bank war* against the re-chartering of the private Bank of the United States.

In Canto XXXV Pound quotes a passage from the monetary-economic history of medieval Mantua:

> Item:
> That there he made a *fontego* (a chamber)
> to lend money on cloth so that they cease not to
> labour for lack of money..Item: that there be made a *scavenzaria*
> and it be furnished with cloth thus pledged
> to be sold *a schavezo* at a price as if wholesale
> plus only the proportion of the tax for the retail so that
> Mantua cloth being cheap as in countries circumjacent and that
> Brescians, Cremonesi, Parmenesi, Resanesi
> who now go to Verona where it is cheaper as also
> our own townsfolk go there, they wd. then come here or
> stay here to the augment of industry and increase in
> the retail tax and all of the other taxes.
> Item: for the increase of this art
> shd. be a man stationed in Venice . . . to sell what we
> can't sell here . . . . Item: a dye works . . . that they can dye
> the pledged cloth . . . and that finding here cloth well coloured
> . . . . inficit umbras . . . .
> the Romagnols wd. come here to Mantua, and the March folk
> who now go to Verona to buy . . . all of which wd.
> be gain to this industry, bring more people to live here
> and be of great use to yr. taxes.
> Mantua 1401, una grida.
>
> (Canto XXXV)

The Douglasite influence in the above passage is quite clear. The reference to the making of a *fontego* "to lend money on cloth so that they cease not to / labour for lack of money" is clearly an example of the Douglasite monetization of real credit. In this case the real credit of Mantua is its cloth, and this real credit is to be monetized by the state lending money on the cloth. The reference to the making of a *scavenzaria* "and it be furnished with cloth thus pledged / to be

[79] Adams, John, *The Diary*, 424.

sold *a schavezo* at a price as if wholesale / plus only the proportion of the tax for the retail" is an example of the Douglasite concept of the *Just Price* as it worked in medieval Italy. In other words, Pound is attempting to show that *there is nothing new about the principles of Douglasism, but that they have prevailed wherever in history economic justice prevailed.*

In Canto XXXVII, Pound returns to American monetary-economic history, particularly to the decade when Andrew Jackson and Martin Van Buren dominated American politics, i.e., 1830–40. This was the time of the great bank war when Jackson and Van Buren fought the powerful forces which sought to re-charter the private Bank of the United States. Pound opens the canto by quoting Martin Van Buren on debt:

> "Thou shalt not," said Martin Van Buren, "jail 'em for debt."
> "that an immigrant shd. set out with good banknotes
> and find 'em at the end of his voyage
> but waste paper . . . . if a man have in primeval forest
> set up his cabin, shall rich patroon take it from him?
> High judges? Are, I suppose, subject to passions
> as have affected other great and good men, also
> subject to esprit de corps.
>
> (Canto XXXVII)

The above passage is an example of the American frontier tradition's natural antipathy to usury and to the usurer. When the American colonists and pioneers carved out their homesteads from the primeval forest, they had nothing else but their hard work plus the abundance of nature. They did not have resources of money or credit. Van Buren objects to the hard-working settler's homestead being confiscated by "the rich patroon." Pound himself was a product of the American frontier tradition, born as he was on the Idaho frontier. His grandfather, Thaddeus Coleman Pound, later a congressman, had fought usury on the Wisconsin frontier by having his company, the Union Lumbering Co. of Chippewa Falls, issue its own paper money. This was done to avoid the usury of the eastern bankers and because the eastern banks simply were not making money available to the Western settlers. Pound's grandfather, by means of this privately issued Chippewa Falls paper currency, built hundreds of miles of railway track in Wisconsin.[80] It is also interesting to note that Thaddeus Pound, during his ten years in Congress,

[80] Cf. Pound, *Impact*, 64–65.

was an avid monetary reformer. Pound never knew this until after he had been converted to Social Credit. He had often commented on the coincidence of his fighting for the same monetary-economic justice his grandfather had fought for in the United States Congress.

Most of Canto XXXVII is directly concerned with the fight against the re-chartering of the private Bank of the United States:

> Authorized its (the bank's) president to use funds at
> discretion (its funds, his discretion) to
> influence press . . .
> veto power, with marked discretion, used no further than
> in objecting to bank under charter existing.
> . . . .
> "To which end, largely increased line of discounts
> 1830, October, 40 million
> May, 1837 seventy millions and then some.
> . . . .
> "30 million" said Mr. Dan Webster "in states on the Mississippi
> "will all have to be called in, in three
> "years and nine months, if the charter be not extended..
> "I hesertate nawt tew say et will dee-precierate
> "everyman's prorperty from the etcetera
> "to the kepertal ov Missouri, affect the price of
> "crawps, leynd en the prordewce ov labour, to the
> embarassement . . . . . ."
> de mortuis wrote Mr. Van Buren
> don't quite apply in a case of this character.
>
> (Canto XXXVII)

The first of the passages refers to the fact that the Bank of the United States used its vast financial power to influence the press during the bank war. Pound makes it even clearer that Andrew Jackson used his veto power, by which he vetoed the Bank Bill in 1832 with great discretion. The last of the separate passages refers to the role played by Daniel Webster in the Bank War. Webster, like Alexander Hamilton, was a great champion of the private banking interests. Pound quotes a barefaced threat by Webster to the effect that if the charter of the private Bank of the United States were not renewed, thirty million dollars in loans in the Mississippi states alone would have to be called in, in the rather short space of three years and nine months. Webster points out that this will depreciate everyone's property, affect the price of crops, etc.

Pound seeks to show the discrepancy between the economic power wielded by this private bank and that power exercised by the President:

4 to 5 million balance in the national treasury
Receipts 31 to 32 million
Revenue 32 to 33 million
The Bank 341 million, and in deposits
6 millions of government money
(and a majority in the Senate)
Public Money in control of the President
from 15 to 20 thousand (id est, a fund for the secret service)
(Canto XXXVII)

In other words, the Bank of the United States had financial power to the extent of 341 million dollars, while the public money in control of the President amounted to fifteen to twenty thousand dollars. Pound ironically points out that this slight amount was a fund for the secret service. It is through its vast financial resources that the Bank can control a majority of the Senate. It is also through this monopoly of the community's credit that the Bank can cause chaos:

"employing means at the bank's disposal
in deranging the country's credits, obtaining by panic
control over public mind" said Van Buren
"from the real committee of Bank's directors
the government's directors have been excluded.
Bank president controlling government's funds
to the betrayal of the nation....
government funds obstructing the government...
and has sequestered the said funds of the government...
(with chapter, date, verse and citation)
acting in illegal secret
pouring oil on the press
giving nominal loans on inexistent security"
in the eighteen hundred and thirties
"on precedent that Mr. Hamilton has
never hesitated to jeopard the general
for advance of particular interests."
"Bank curtailed
17 million on a line of
64 million credits.
(Canto XXXVII)

Here Pound quotes passages from Martin Van Buren[81] to the effect that the bank had employed its power to upset the nation's credit and thus panic the public. Van Buren points out the irony of

[81] Van Buren, *The Autobiography*, 639–41, 648–50, 654.

the bank president controlling government funds to the betrayal of the nation. This refers to the six millions of government money held in bank deposits mentioned earlier. Again, Van Buren returns to the financial control of the press. He also records the arbitrary calling in of the seventeen million dollars of loans out of sixty-four millions. Van Buren's remark that "Mr. Hamilton never hesitated to jeopard the general for advance of particular interests" is significant in light of the fact that Hamilton today is a symbol of integrity. Van Buren, on the other hand, praises Treasury Secretary Taney[82] for resisting the New York branch of the Bank of the United States:

> "Had not Mr. Taney (of the treasury) prevented
> that branch (in New York) from then collecting
> 8 million 700 thousand and armed our city with
> 9 million to defend us (the whole country)
> in this war on its trade and commerce,
>
> (Canto XXXVII)

Pound ends this canto by giving Martin Van Buren the greatest memorial inscription and tribute, a Social Crediter could provide: "HIC JACET FISCI LIBERATOR"—*Here Lies the Liberator of the Treasury*.

Pound quotes the following lines from Dante's Paradiso XIX, 118 as a prologue to Canto XXXVIII: "il duol che sopra Senna / Induce, falseggiando la moneta." The line *falseggiando la moneta—falsifying money* refers to usury and usurers's practices, particularly the lending of promises-to-pay in place of legal tender. In the first part of this canto, Pound returns to the devious ways of Metevsky, the armaments agent and financier. It has already been pointed out that Metevsky is one of Pound's pseudonyms in *The Cantos* for Basil Zaharoff. Most of this canto deals with the machinations of armament interests, e.g., Metevsky, Krupp, and Creusot-Schneider. It is obvious that Pound detests the armaments profiteers and that he seeks peace. However, it is significant that Pound inserts the very heart of Social Credit theory, Douglas's A + B theorem in the middle of his sordid tale of the armament kings. Thus, Pound implies that *there never will be world peace* and an end to the armament makers' bloody harvest *until each nation adopts the Social Credit monetary system*. Pound is convinced that world peace can only be established by means of good government within the individual nations, i.e., governments based on Social Credit.

---

[82] Van Buren, *The Autobiography*, 656.

As an example of the munitions racket, Pound relates one escapade of Metevsky:

> An' that year Metevsky went over to America del Sud
> . . . .
> and he, Metevsky said to the one side
> . . . .
> he said: the other boys got more munitions
> . . . .
> Don't buy until you can get ours.
> And he went over the border
> and he said to the other side:
> The *other* side has more munitions. Don't buy
> until you can get ours.
> (Canto XXXVIII)

Pound superposes over this account, certain obviously second-hand references to Lucrezia Borgia. This, pointed out earlier, is Pound's code for indicating that the Metevsky incident is from second-hand sources and is not known from first-hand experience.[83]

The most direct example of Douglas's influence on Pound is to be had in the middle of Canto XXXVIII. After dealing with a series of completely unsavoury armaments and financial dealings, Pound suddenly stops short and paraphrases a key passage from C. H. Douglas.[84] This is Pound's paraphrasing of Douglas's famous A+B theorem:

> A factory
> has also another aspect, which we call the financial aspect
> it gives people the power to buy (wages, dividends
> which are power to buy) but it is also the cause of prices
> or values, financial, I mean financial values
> It pays workers, and pays for material.
> What it pays in wages and dividends
> stays fluid, as power to buy, and this power is less,
> per forza, damn blast your intellex, is less
> than the total payments made by the factory
> (as wages, dividends AND payments for raw material
> bank charges, etcetera)
> and all, that is the whole, that is the total
> of these is added into the total of prices
> caused by that factory, any damn factory

---

[83] Landini, "A Guide," 150–51.

[84] Douglas, *Credit-Power and Democracy*, 21–22.

and there is and must be therefore a clog
and the power to purchase can never
(under the present system) catch up with
prices at large,
and the light became so bright and so blindin'
in this layer of paradise
that the mind of man was bewildered.[85]
(Canto XXXVIII)

The A+B theorem which is paraphrased above is Douglas's illustration of the chronic shortage of purchasing power under the present monetary system. Douglas maintained that under the present debt-money system, available purchasing power is not adequate to buy all the goods and services produced without further borrowing for further production. Pound is thus intimating, by bringing the A+B theorem in at this point, that the cause of wars is to be found in the chronic shortage of purchasing power.

In Chapter II of this present work, Pound quoted what he had remembered from A. R. Orage's BBC radio address entitled "On Social Credit": "[I]n the gap disclosed between Price-values and Income is enough gun-powder to blow up every democratic parliament."[86] The implication is that there would be no field for the machinations of the war profiters such as Messers. Metevsky, Krupp, Creusot-Schneider, etc., under a Social Credit system. Thus, Pound sees Social Credit as the only *realistic* program for true world peace.

Just prior to the paraphrasing of the A+B theorem in Canto XXXVIII, Pound paraphrases another passage from C. H. Douglas.[87] This is from a section in which Douglas sought to show the fundamental instability of a banking system which issues promises-to-pay as if they were legal tender:

"I have of course never said that the cash is constant
(Douglas) and in fact the population (Britain 1914)
was left with 800 millions of "*deposits*"
after all the cash had been drawn, and
these deposits were satisfied by the
printing of treasury notes.
(Canto XXXVIII)

---

[85] A good, succinct explanation of the A+B theorem can be found here: socred.org/s-c-action/social-credit-views/the-a-b-theorem/the-core-of-the-core-of-douglas-a-b-theorem-and-hence-of-social-credit-s-economic-diagnosis

[86] Orage, *The B. B. C. Speech*, 12.

[87] Douglas, *The New and the Old Economics*, 6–7.

Douglas was describing the bank panic of 1914, during which depositors had demanded gold sovereigns. This would have crippled the country economically, had not the government rescued the banks by printing Treasury currency notes that were to be honoured as legal tender and to be given in place of gold coinage. Douglas makes the point, which Pound reiterates, that even after all the cash had been withdrawn from the banks, the banks still had eight hundred millions in *deposits*. These deposits, of course, simply were and are figures in a book, i.e., entries on the liability side of the banks' ledgers. Douglas had been illustrating that fundamental tenet of banking technique, enunciated by Reginald McKenna, Chairman of the Midland Bank: "[E]very new loan or purchase by a bank creates an equivalent deposit, thus increasing the quantity of money, while every repayment to or sale by a bank destroys a deposit and correspondingly diminishes the quantity of money."[88]

John M. Keynes had been intimately involved in the bank panic of 1914 in England. He had advocated for making it nearly impossible for British citizens to obtain gold: "'Gold should only be available at the head office of the Bank of England,' Keynes wrote to Lloyd George,"[89] while Keynes advocated that any call for gold internationally was to be answered.[90] Douglas had observed and learned from this 1914 crisis that gold was a fetish, that anything can serve, even mere paper, as money, if it was backed by the people and their ability to produce: "The Treasury scrambled to print its new currency before the bank holiday lifted on Friday, August 7. On Thursday, Parliament approved legislation legalizing the new paper money.... It worked. The British public accepted the new paper currency. The Bank of England stabilized. Prices didn't skyrocket."[91]

The phrase right at the end of the paraphrase of the A+B theorem is significant from the standpoint of Douglas's impact upon Pound:

> and the light became so bright and so blindin'
> in this layer of paradise
> that the mind of man was bewildered.
> (Canto XXXVIII)

Here, in Dantesque terms, Pound describes the degree of economic illumination he had received through Douglas. This illumination, by way of analogy to Dante's *lumen gloriae* in the *Paradiso*, was so intense

[88] McKenna, "Midland Bank Limited."
[89] Carter, Zachary, *The Price of Peace*, 16.
[90] Carter, Zachary, *The Price of Peace*, 17–18.
[91] Carter, Zachary, *The Price of Peace*, 17.

that it at first bewildered Pound, as it would any other man.[92] No lines could have been selected from the literary tradition which could have more eloquently portrayed the impact of Douglas on Pound.

In the light of the Cantos being an excursion through the monetary history of the United States and world economic history, through poverty, economic injustice, the purgation of the boom and bust, and the economic wars following the creation of the Bank of England to our own time, it is only in the light of Douglas's A+B theory that Pound offers, in his Cantos, something similar to the "Joy of Divine Light and Presence" that is found at the end of Dante's journey: the key to economic salvation. Pound had planned to continue his Cantos, to include, like Dante, a *Paradiso*, but with Pound's death, one can claim that it was only in this passage that we do have a taste of what may have been in the Divine Light of Pound's *Paradiso*. C. H. Douglas wrote a passage that bears some similarity to Pound's, a passage of hope for economic and social *light* and *splendour*:

> "A comparatively short period will probably serve to decide whether we are to master the mighty economic and social machine that we have created, or whether it is to master us; and during that period a small impetus from a body of men who know what to do and how to do it, may make the difference between yet one more retreat into the Dark Ages, or the emergence into the full light of a day of such splendour as we can at present only envisage dimly."[93]

Immediately after this direct paraphrasing of Douglasite material, Pound returns to the sinister operations of Messers. Krupp, Schneider, Creusot, etc.:

> Said Herr Krupp (1842): guns are a merchandise
> I approach them from the industrial end,
> I approach them from the technical side,
> 1847 orders from Paris and Egypt . . . .
> orders from the Crimea,

---

[92] A. R. Orage, had a four part series in the Jesuit Catholic Journal, *The Commonweal.* The 1926 Vol. III, Issues 14–17. Archive.org has all four issues of *The Commonweal,* available to view. Orage stated: "Douglas himself was actively interested in my instruction. He said many things in our first talk *that blinded me with light*; [emphasis added] and thereafter I lost no opportunity of talking with him, listening to him talk, reading new and old works on finance, with all the zest of an enthusiastic pupil. . . . It was a full year from beginning to study his ideas before I arrived at complete understanding. Then all my time and labor were justified. Orage, "An Editor's Progress," no. 15, 403.

[93] Douglas, *Social Credit*, 217.

. . . .

"The Emperor ('68) is deeply in'erested in yr. catalogue
and in yr. services to humanity"
(signed) Leboeuf
who was a relative to Monsieur Schneider
1900 fifty thousand operai,
53 thousand cannon, about half for his country,
Bohlem und Halbach,
Herr Schneider of Creusot
Twin arse with one belly.
Eugene, Adolf and Alfred "more money from guns than from
tractiles"

. . . .

1885/1900 produced ten thousand cannon
to 1914, 34 thousand
one half of them sent out of the country
always in the chamber of deputies, always a conservative,
Schools, churches, orspitals fer the workin' man
Sand piles fer the children.

. . . .

"faire passer ces affaires
avant ceux de la nation."
(Canto XXXVIII)

In the passages above, Pound summarizes briefly some of the activities of the Krupp (German) and Schneider-Creusot (French) armaments industries. He shows the truly international character of these industries, and the financial inter-alliance involved.[94] The last passage in French above refers to the fact that these international financial and armaments affairs take precedence over humanity, nationality, and the good of any nation.

Canto XL begins with an allusion to Adam Smith's *The Wealth of Nations*[95] concerning the conspiratorial tendencies of guilds:

Esprit de corps in permanent bodies
"Of the same trade," Smith, Adam, "men
"never gather together
"without a conspiracy against the general public."
(Canto XL)

---

[94] See *Defense News*: defensenews.com, to understand the international aspect of the armaments industry.

[95] "People of the same trade seldom meet together, even for merriment and diversion, but the conversation ends in a conspiracy against the public, or in some contrivance to raise prices." Smith, *The Wealth of Nations*, Vol. I, 117.

Pound is implying here that if there is the certainty of conspiracy against the public when ordinary guilds are formed, so much the greater is the certainty and so much greater is the conspiracy when usurers band together.[96] Pound juxtaposes or superposes with the passage above a short passage referring to American and Venetian monetary history:

> Independent use of money (our OWN)
> toward holding OUR bank, own bank
> and in it the deposits, received, where received.
> De banchis cambi tenendi . . . .
> Venice 1361,
> '62 . . . shelved for a couple of centuries . . .
> "whether by privates or public . . .
> currency OF (O, F, of) the nation.
>
> (Canto XL)

In this passage, Pound seeks to show that in the United States of Jefferson's day and in the Venice of 1361, etc., there was an awareness of the fact that public credit belongs to the people and that currency is OF the nation. Further along in this same canto, Pound touches upon the machinations of Mr. Morgan:

> (Case 97) sold to the government the government's arms...
> I mean the government owned 'em already
> at an extortionate profit
> Dollars 160 thousand, one swat, to Mr. Morgan
> for forcing up gold.
> "Taking advantage of emergency" (that is war)
> After Gettysburg, down 5 points in one day—
> Bulls on gold and bears on the Union
> "Business prospered due to war's failures."
> *"If a nation will master its money"*
>
> . . . .
>
> Mr. Morgan: contributions to the Republican Party, largely
> to the republican party.
>
> . . . .
>
> Pujo investigation: Said Mr. Morgan:

---

[96] An example is the charge made today against those who attend the World Economic Forum (WEF) or the Bilderberg meetings that bring together financial oligarchs along with powerful political figures, i.e., that they determine the policy of nations, independently of their elected sovereign representatives. They conspire (synonyms: plot, scheme, intrigue, machinate, collude, connive, contrive [*Merriam-Webster Dictionary*, s.v. "conspire"]) to impose their own plans and goals worldwide.

> "never sold short in my life"
> having learned that a high degree of liquidity....
>
> . . . .
>
> As to the government's arms: they were bought by
> one government office before they had been sold
> (as condemned) by another ditto (i.e. government office)
> passing through a species of profit sieve.
>
> (Canto XL)

Terrell refers us to the 1930 book, *The House of Morgan* by Lewis Corey,[97] as the source for Pound's allusions. In this book we read how the U. S. government, desperate for war supplies, ended up buying arms it already owned. It is detailed in the Congressional Report, Case No. 97:

> Although desperately in need of arms the government was not using any of the Hall carbines, condemned as unfit and dangerous for military use. Simon Stevens offered the carbines for sale in a telegram to General J. C. Frémont, saying "I have 5,000 carbines for sale," which was untrue, no purchase having been made and the carbines being still government property stored in a government arsenal. Frémont needing arms badly and "in business as gentle as a girl and confiding as a woman," accepted Stevens' offer, the price being $22. The day *after* the receipt of Frémont's telegraphic acceptance Arthur Eastman bought the 5,000 carbines at $3.50 apiece from the War Department, payment of $17,486 being made by J. Pierpont Morgan. When the "sale" was made to General Frémont "the arms were still the property of the government,".... After severely castigating the participants in the transaction, the committee allowed $9,678 on Morgan's claim plus brokerage of $1,330. The claim for payment, Morgan insisted, was justified because his House had "made advances in good faith to Mr. Stevens on the security of his agreement with General Frémont." This claim of "good faith" was dismissed by the committee since Morgan "declined to disclose the terms" upon which the advances were made to Stevens.[98]

In Chapter VII of Corey's book, Pound drew his allusions to gold and Gettysburg. The following gives a good summary of this chapter, and how the banking house of Morgan and other financiers,

---

[97] Terrell, *A Companion*, Vol. I, 163.

[98] Corey, *The House of Morgan*, 60–61.

profited from war: "'The love of gain was fed by sacrificing the national credit and encouraging disloyalty,' declared a contemporary observer. 'How would an undertaker be regarded who, acquiring his wealth in burying the dead, rejoiced in the sufferings of those around him? Yet the gold brokers rejoiced over human slaughter and national defeat because their gains were thereby increased.'"[99]

The superposition of the italicized phrase "*If a nation will master its money*" is the clue to this whole passage. If the American nation will assert its sovereignty in monetary matters, as provided for by the constitution, exploiters like Morgan would be rendered impotent.

Superimposed on this tale of the great Morgan are other lines:

> Boutwell decided bonds shd. be sold direct by the treasury.
> . . . .
> Beecher's church organized by realty agents—
> Belmont representing the Rothschilds
> "specie payment's resumption
> "enriched a small group of holders."
> stock subscription (railway construction)
> seldom over 30 percent...
> in '76 default 39% of the total
> that is 39 percent of the
> bonds for railway construction
> said Mr Corey "there being no central institution
> as in London"
> Pujo investigation: Said Mr Morgan:
> "never sold short in my life"
> 1907 "cd. not have been done without Mr Baker
> "we cdnt. have stopped it (the panic).
>
> (Canto XL)

The passage concerning bonds being sold directly by the Treasury refers to bonds replacing U. S. treasury notes as backing for legal tender. Chapter XIII of Corey's book tells the history of U. S. government financing from 1871 to 1879. "Boutwell," George S. was newly elected President Ulysses S. Grant's choice as Secretary of the Treasury and was known for the positive reforms made to the U. S. Treasury. In 1871, competition between banking houses for the right to sell U. S. treasury bonds led to Boutwell's decision to have the treasury alone sell them.[100] National financing was undermined by the House of Morgan. They opposed any government effort to sell bonds on their own and

---

[99] Corey, *The House of Morgan*, 69.
[100] Corey, *The House of Morgan*, 115.

did all it could to oppose other financial houses, such as the banking House of Cooke, from doing so. For the Morgans, financial power could not be shared but only monopolized in their *overlordship.*[101] The result was that the machinations of Morgan hindered the U. S. government's attempt to lower, if not get out of, debt.

This is an example of what Pound considers the gradual, complete emasculation of American economic democracy, and the cutting off of the American people from their own credit. Concerning United States notes, the bankers had:

> won a battle in the Senate for having amendments inserted which made certain exceptions in the legal tender quality of notes. These exceptions were noted on the face of the notes by the infamous trick exception clause, which reads as follows: *This note is a legal tender at its face value for all debts, public and private, except duties on imports and interest on the public debt.* This was the sting of death whereby the bankers were enabled to discredit the greenbacks, and to make a handsome profit on gold. Being crippled in their usefulness as a legal tender the greenbacks were made to depreciate in comparison with specie.[102]

That refers to the banking fraternity's move to undermine the beneficial effect of the three Acts of Congress authorizing the issue of the debt-free National Bank Notes or *greenbacks* as legal tender in 1862 and 1863. The original bill had provided for the recognition of every greenback dollar as full legal tender for all debts. However, due to a number of subservient representatives of the banking fraternity in the Senate, the bankers were able to have the amendment quoted above inserted: *except duties on imports and interest on the public debt.* Terrell explains how the U. S. government could have paid these loans off with its own money, the greenbacks, but the financiers ensured it would not be so: "The banking community after the Civil War made a great killing by defeating the Greenback party, which wanted to pay the national debt in greenbacks rather than to resume the redemption of Civil War Bonds in gold."[103]

Pound's allusion to "Beecher's church," introduces us to a Congregationalist Rev. Henry Ward Beecher, whose preaching gave bankers like Morgan solace by suggesting that their work was God's work: "'Is the great working class oppressed? Yes, undoubtedly it is. God has

[101] Corey, *The House of Morgan*, 117.
[102] Overholser, *A Short Review*, 41–42.
[103] Terrell, *A Companion*, Vol. I, 164.

intended the great to be great and the little to be little .... The trade union, originated under the European system, destroys liberty.... I do not say that a dollar a day is enough to support a workingman. But it is enough to support a man! Not enough to support a man and five children if a man insist on smoking and drinking beer.... But the man who cannot live on bread and water is not fit to live.'"[104]

The allusion by Pound to "Belmont..." and what follows is drawn from Corey,[105] and are meant by Pound to expose the lie made by Pierpont Morgan at the 1912–1913 Pujo investigation concerning the selling of securities. The Pujo Committee was appointed by the United States Senate in 1912 to investigate Wall Street bankers and financiers and their control of the United States, the so-called "money trust." Morgan had stated, he had "never sold short in my life." This refers to the frequent practice of short selling a borrowed security. When you think the price will soon fall, you sell. Once it falls, you buy the same security back. Return it to your broker when it rises again, and the gain is yours. The morality of such transactions is suspect, especially when you are large enough, like the House of Morgan, to cause the rise and fall in price of any security.

As regards the House of Morgan's reaction to the Pujo investigation and those others in the money trust, it is summed up in a description of the younger Morgan: "The hearings would sharpen Jack's hostility toward Jews, reporters, Democrats, reformers—all those troublemakers who stirred up the populace. Scarred by the experience, he would grow disenchanted with democracy and what he referred to as America's 'amateur Government.'"[106] As implied above, the tribalism within the banking community, based on nationality or religion, was not only something we will see as unique to Europe. It existed in America, but with a different flavour. There, the House of Morgan dominated American finance. Jack Morgan, the head of the Morgan bank and an overseer of Harvard University wrote the following in May 1920 to Lawrence Lowell, president of Harvard University: "I think I ought to say that I believe there is a strong feeling among the Overseers that the nominee should by no means be a Jew or a Roman Catholic, although, naturally, the feeling in regard to the latter is less than in regard to the former."[107] Chernow goes on to explain the typical partner of the House of Morgan:

---

[104] Corey, *The House of Morgan*, 123–24.
[105] Corey, *The House of Morgan*, 124–25, 145.
[106] Chernow, *The House of Morgan*, 150.
[107] Chernow, *The House of Morgan*, 214.

> They fit a rough profile—white, male, Republican, Episcopalian, and Anglophile, with an Ivy League education and eastern seaboard antecedents. Harvard was the alma mater of Jack Morgan and his sons and was clearly the preferred school. The bank was perhaps most selective about religion—race wasn't even an issue then, so remote were blacks from the world of banking. Jews were definitely forbidden but had opportunities elsewhere on Wall Street. Private Jewish banks continued to win business, such as retail underwriting, thought vulgar by the blue-blooded Yankee banks....
>
> On the Wall Street of the 1920s, Catholics were borderline cases and often found it harder than Jews to enter high finance. Snubbed by Protestants, they turned to stock market speculation by default, and Jazz Age plungers were disproportionately Irish. Armed with ticker tape and telephones at the Waldorf-Astoria Hotel, Joe Kennedy made a fortune in stock pools but still found Morgan acceptance elusive.[108]

This Morgan Protestant-Episcopalian tribalism is alleged to be, in part, the cause of the then-largest bank failure in US history, the bankruptcy of the Bank of the United States: "Morgan records show that its clientele's [the Bank of the United States] Judaism was very much in the partners' minds. When informing Morgan Grenfell of events in New York, Lamont's son Tommy noted that it was patronized largely by foreigners and Jews. Russell Leffingwell described it as 'an uptown bank with many branches and a large clientele among our Jewish population of small merchants, and persons of small means and small education, from whom all its management was drawn.' Their attitude was short-sighted, for the bank's failure shook confidence across America."[109]

Though article 1 of the U. S. Constitution states: "The Congress shall have Power... To coin Money," we are told by the experts that the U. S. Treasury must be insulated, *via* the Federal Reserve, from direct control over money creation. If the government could just print at will, it would be tempted to print money for every possible need, clearly causing inflation. But cannot the Banks likewise do the same, creating money unrelated to the real economy of goods and services? Could they not loan more, to keep interest payments coming? In December 1982, as Morgan and Citi banks were informed that Brazil could not service its debt coming due, the IMF unveiled a plan. It consisted of:

---

108 Chernow, *The House of Morgan*, 258–59.
109 Chernow, *The House of Morgan*, 326–27.

> a four-part Morgan-Citi plan for saving Brazil. Citibank would reschedule $4 billion in principal; Chase would maintain trade credits; and Bankers Trust would restore short-term "interbank" lines to Brazil. The linchpin was a Morgan-led effort to raise a new $4.4-billion loan for Brazil, the biggest in Morgan history.
>
> The plan set a fateful precedent of "curing" the debt crisis by heaping on more debt. In this charade, bankers would lend more to Brazil with one hand, then take it back with the other. This preserved the fictitious book value of loans on bank balance sheets. Approaching the rescue as a grand new syndication, the bankers piled on high interest rates and rescheduling fees. It was hard to stop the greed so prevalent for so many years.[110]

Is the central bank system, a responsible system? Chernow explains how, in the 1980s, the practice of leveraged buyouts (LBOs) became popular with the banking interest's encouragement. Investors borrow money, using the company to be bought as their collateral.[111] This creates a new infusion of money in the economy, not related to the real economy of goods and services, but the artificial economy of speculation and profiteering. This newly created inflationary money, which had no benefit for society, was legal, though it led obviously to greater costs to consumers and job losses, as for example at Nabisco, to avoid bankruptcy. This forced takeover turned a well-run company into a disaster:

> For a takeover that promised no economic benefit for the company, the RJR Nabisco deal showered bankers with huge rewards—almost $1 billion in fees and expenses. Morgan Stanley came away with a cool $25 million. Like most LBOs, it was executed almost entirely with borrowed money. In return, RJR Nabisco was burdened with over $20 billion in debt. Before it sold a cigarette or a biscuit each year, it was already in the hole for $3 billion in interest payments. It was forced to shoulder debt equal to the combined national debt of Bolivia, Jamaica, Uruguay, Costa Rica, and Honduras. Only ten countries in the world were more indebted. In more innocent days, investment bankers had put companies on a sound footing and jealously guarded their credit rating. Now, even as the Kravis forces

[110] Chernow, *The House of Morgan*, 644.
[111] Chernow, *The House of Morgan*, 693–94.

> toasted their victory, RJR Nabisco bondholders saw their A-rated bonds deteriorate into junk bonds, with $1 billion in value wiped out overnight. And by the summer of 1989, the company had announced plans to fire 1,640 workers as a way to save money to service the oppressive debt burden. That fall, a collapse in the junk bond market suggested that RJR Nabisco had indeed been the era's crowning folly.[112]

In Canto XLI, Pound inserts a passage that takes the reader back to the monetary-economic affairs of Italy in 1442:

> "Where the Pope goes is lack of money
> Because of the mass of clerics
> who bring cheques for the banks to cash,
> And for these the banks must pay money.
> And you must know how they pay, and
> when and on what days there are markets
> and in which seasons are the fairs, and
> when they need money in which where
> and what are the rates of exchange
> (Messire Uzzano in 1442)
> To have shortage neither in time nor in place
> but to have money there ready
> for sailing of ships, wangles of merchants
> and for the due pay for soldiers
> both from commune or overlord,
> and you must work day and night
> to keep up with your letters.
>
> (Canto XLI)

The first part of the section points out the lack of money in 15th century Italy, whenever an excess of cheques was presented at the banks to be cashed. The latter part of the above passage points out the recognition of the necessity, in 15th century Italy, of having an adequate supply of the medium of exchange or legal tender to carry on the economic life of the commune. Implicit here is the Douglasite notion that money is the life-blood of the body economic and must circulate freely throughout that body without being impeded by the blood clot of usury, which can only bring death to the body economic. Further along in Canto XLI, Pound refers to one of his great heroes, Cosimo de Medici, and his organization of the *Monte dei Paschi*. We have seen in Chapter II that the *Monte dei Paschi*

---

[112] Chernow, *The House of Morgan*, 711–12.

is Pound's example of a benevolent bank as opposed to a hell-bank, e.g., the Banca Sancto Georgio of Genoa:

> Cosimo First guaranteed it.
> To pay 5% on its stock, Monte dei Paschi
> and to lend at 5 and ½
> Overplus of all profit, to relief works
> and the administration on moderate pay..
> that stood even after Napoleon.
> Said C.H. "To strangle the bankers . . . ?"
> And Woergl in our time?
>
> (Canto XLI)

The *C. H.* referred to above is, of course, C. H. Douglas, and *Woergl* refers to the town in Austria where Gesell scrip was used successfully until the banks found out and stopped the scrip from circulating.

Towards the end of Canto XLI Pound again gives us a series of luminous details from a letter of Thomas Jefferson to Colonel Monroe:

> Public debt increasing at about one million a year
> You will see by Gallatin's speeches . . . .
> Saddled by bank, led by a bridle
> National property being increased . . .
> must furnish adequate representation . . .
> all imported commodities are raised about 50 percent
> Vol. IX. 337, Lands rose in a vortex of paper,
> not here where the banks do not reach
> Mechanics get 1.50 a day
> But are worse off than with the old wages . . . .
> Independent use of our money . . . toward holding our bank.
> Mr. Jefferson to Colonel Monroe
>
> (Canto XLI)

Terrell provides the 1796 letter quoted above from Thomas Jefferson to the future President James Madison.[113] The passage concerning the public debt increasing at about one million dollars a year refers to the indebtedness of the United States government during the period of the first Bank of the United States from 1791 to 1796. The Gallatin referenced would find himself in the Jefferson camp in opposition to Hamilton. The passage, "Saddled by bank, led by a bridle," refers to the United States being in fact *saddled* by the private Bank of the United States and being led around by the *bridle* of debt. In other words, Pound quotes Jefferson as being

---

[113] Terrell, *A Companion*, Vol. I, 169.

convinced that the economic and hence political sovereignty of the United States were being impugned by the existence and operation of the private Bank of the United States. The repetition of the luminous detail, "Independent use of our money... toward holding our bank," which we have already seen at the beginning of Canto XL, is given as Jefferson's and Pound's solution to these monetary difficulties, i.e., the nation's money must be issued independently of private sources. The bank, as the source of the nation's credit, must be under congressional ownership and control as provided for in principle by the Constitution of the United States: "The Congress shall have Power...To coin Money, regulate the Value thereof, and of foreign Coin, and fix the Standard of Weights and Measures."[114]

The Fifth Decade of Cantos (Cantos XLII–LI) continues the anti-usury theme and in fact contains the two great usury cantos (Cantos XLV and LI). Canto XLII, like most of the others in this section, has its setting in the Italian Renaissance. Canto XLII deals with the history of the *Monte dei Paschi* of Siena. This was the bank referred to above which was founded by Cosimo de Medici. The luminous detail and purposeful focus in this canto are taken directly from the documentary history and chronicles of the bank. Pound, as has been mentioned, gives this bank as an example of a benevolent bank, i.e., a *damn good bank* as distinguished from the *hell banks*, e.g., the Banca Sancto Georgio of Genoa:

> FIXED in the soul, nell' anima, of the Illustrious College
> They had been ten years proposing such a Monte,
> That is a species of bank—damn good bank, in Siena
> A mount, a bank, a fund a bottom an
> institution of credit
> a place to send cheques in and out of
> and yet not yet a banco di giro, and the Bailey
> sought views from the Senate 'With paternal affection
> justice convenience of city what college had with such
> foresight wherefore S.A. (Your Highness) as in register
> Nov. 1624
> following details: as third, a Yearly balance
> as 5th that any citizen shall have right to deposit
> and to fruits therefrom resultant at five percent annual interest
> and that borrowers pay a bit over that
> for services (dei ministri) that is for running expenses
> and book keeping which shall be counted a half scudo

[114] *The Constitution*, art. 1, sec 8, cl. 5.

per hundred per year
(All of this is important)
and 6thly that the Magistrate
give his chief care that the specie
be lent to whomso can best use it USE IT
(id est, piú utilmente)
to the good of their houses, to benefit of their business
as of weaving, the wool trade, the silk trade
And that (7thly) the overabundance every five years shall the
Bailey
distribute to workers of the contrade (the wards) holding in
reserve a prudent proportion as against unforseen losses
though there shd. be NO such losses
and 9th that the borrowers can pay up before the end of their
term whenso it be to their interest. No debt to run more than
five years.
July 1623
Loco Signi
\+ [a cross in the margin]
That profit on deposits should be used to cover all losses
and the distributions on the fifth year be made from remaining
profits, after restoration of losses no (*benché*) matter how
small
with sane small reserve against future idem
(Canto XLII)

In the above passage, Pound is directly paraphrasing the constitution of the Monte dei Paschi as signed on July 18, 1623, by Livio Pasquini, notary and citizen of Siena. This bank is a benevolent bank because its credit is based on *the abundance of nature* and its function is to help equitably distribute that abundance. We have seen in Chapter II of this study that the financial credit of the Monte dei Paschi was based upon the *real credit* of grazing rights toward Grosseto worth 10,000 ducats a year. Based on this real credit, Cosimo de Medici underwrote a capital of 200,000 ducats, to pay five percent to the shareholders, and to be lent at five and a half percent. As the above passage indicates, overhead and salaries were kept at a minimum. All excess profit over this overhead was to go to hospitals and works for the benefit of the people of Siena. The running expenses and bookkeeping were kept at "a half scudo per hundred per year."

Pound emphasizes that the magistrate was to see to it that the specie was lent to whomsoever could best use it for their homes, their businesses, etc. Every five years the overabundance was to be distributed by the bailey (the administrator) to workers of the wards. Thus, from the excess profits of the bank, a dividend was distributed among the workers. This dividend, of course, differs from a dole in that it is not based upon debt or borrowed money but is based upon *real credit, i.e., the grazing lands* toward Grosseto. This is Pound's example of how a benevolent bank operates as distinguished from the operation of *hell banks*, such as the Banca Sancto Georgio of Genoa.

There has been a great deal of confusion in contemporary Catholic moral theology as to the functions of the *Mounts of Piety* in the medieval and Renaissance periods. Some moral theologians have seen these institutions as proofs of the medieval and Renaissance Church's benevolent attitude toward usury. Pound points out that these *Mounts of Pity* or *Monti dei pieta* were simply pawnshops or as Pound calls them *hock shops*:[115]

> That the Mount of Pity (or Hock Shop)
> municipal of Siena has lent only on pledges
> that is on stuff actually hocked . . . wd be we believe useful
> and beneficent that there be place to lend licitly
> MONEY to receive licitly money
> at moderate and legitimate interest
> . . . .
> could accept specie from Universities (id est congregations)
> and individuals and from Luoghi
> i.e. companies and persons both public and private
>   WHOMSOEVER
> not requiring that they have special privilege
> because of their state or conditions but to folk of
> ANY CONDITION
>   that the same Mount cd/lend on good Mallevadoria
> (that is security) at the same rate plus a little over
> to cover current expenses of supervisors and employees
> . . . .
> (in what wd. seem to have been 1622)
> Stating that Siena had no income and Their Highnesses
> had provided credit from customs
> and from miscellaneous taxes
> and that the Grand Duke hadn't lost anything by it
> Plus a list of Sienese assets (coolish)

[115] In agreement with Pound, both Popes Benedict XVI and Francis have referred to *Montes Pietatis*, as examples for today of non-usurious banking, in contrast to some contemporary scholarly opinions. See: Maino, "What Benedict XVI, Francis."

Plus a lien on 'The Abundance'
And knowing that all this is but a little
Pledge the persons and goods of the laity
And leave open door to other towns in the state
who care to give similar pledges
    And that whoso puts in money shall have lots in the Monte
    that yield 5% interest
    and that these shareholders shall receive their due fruit
    And that the Gd Duke make known at Siena
    to the same deputies of the Bailey . . .
    but that it be separate from the Pawn Shop
    and have its own magistrates and employees
    and that YYour HHighnesses send approbation
    commanding their will, we humbly with reverence
    . . . the 29th day of Xember 1622 . . .
            servants of YYour HHighnesses

. . . .

TTheir HHighnesses gratified
the city of this demand to
erect a New Monte
for good public and private and to facilitate . . .
. . . agreed to accommodate
. . . . . . and to lend the fund against the Gd Duke's
public entries to the sum of
200,000 scudi
capital for fruit at 5% annual
which is 10,000 a year
assigned on the office of grazing
on caution of said security offered
leaving ground for other towns that
wish to participate

. . . .

OB PECUNIAE SCARCITATEM
                borrowing, rigging exchanges,
licit consumption impeded
                and it is getting steadily WORSE
others with specie abundant do not use it in business
(to be young is to suffer.
            Be old, and be past that)
do not use it in business and everyone remains here
without work
few come to buy in the market
            fewer still work the fields
Monte non vacabilis publico

shares not to expire with death . . . will TTheir HHighnesses
against public entries
get that straight — capital two hundred thousand
which wd. correspond to 10,000 income
on the entries of the office of grazing
with precautions (cauteles)
to guarantee their same Highnesses against any possible loss
Which idea dates at least to July 1623

(Canto XLII)

This passage is Pound's direct paraphrasing of the petition drawn up by the commune of Siena after its conquest by Florence and presented to Cosimo de Medici, Grand Duke of Tuscany, and the Florentine Bailey. The petition points out that the Mounts of Piety are only hock shops in that they lend only on pledges, i.e., on goods actually hocked. The petition also points out that Cosimo de Medici had set up a Monte, or institution of credit, for Florence and had based this Monte's credit on customs and miscellaneous taxes. The petition stresses that this Monte should be separate from the pawn shop. Cosimo is asked to use his ducal authority and sovereignty to *monetize the real credit* of Siena, i.e., to *provide financial credit* based upon this real credit, i.e., to provide public entries in the public account to the sum of 200,000 scudi.

This concept *of monetizing the real credit of the community* is a basic Douglasite concept. *Real credit*, for Douglas, "is a correct estimate of the rate, or dynamic capacity, at which a community can deliver goods and services as demanded." *Financial credit*, according to Douglas, is "a measure of the rate at which an organization or individual can deliver money. The money may or may not represent goods and services."[116]

At the same time, the petition stresses the grave lack of purchasing power (financial credit) in Siena. This document lists the evils that have befallen Siena *Ob Pecuniae Scarcitatem — from the scarcity of money*, e.g., borrowing, rigging exchanges, and particularly the impeding of licit consumption. The senate and people of Siena inform Cosimo de Medici and the deputies of the Florentine Bailey that the scarcity of money has brought work and commerce to a standstill. Cosimo de Medici, being like C. H. Douglas, a *right thinker*, and like Sigismundo Malatesta, a benevolent prince, did not fail in his sovereign right and duty of giving the people access to their real credit based on the Siena's, as C. H. Douglas coined it, *cultural heritage*, and

[116] Douglas, *The Control and Distribution*, 10.

increment of association. Cosimo de Medici was under no illusion as to any prior rights of usurers to stand between the people of Siena and their credit.

Canto XLIII continues the history of the Monte dei Paschi of Siena. Pound repeats certain passages already seen in Canto XLII:

> OB PECUNIAE SCARSITATEM
> because there was shortage of coin, in November
> because of taxes, exchanges, tax layings and usuries
> legitimate consumption impeded
> ten thousand on the office of pasturage
>
> (Canto XLIII)

Pound stresses this fact a little further along in Canto XLIII:

> Up to the quantity of 200,000
> on the whole people's credit
> for public and private utility
> shares to be called Loca Montis
> which is to say sites on the Mountain
> @ 100 scudi to give 5 scudi a year
> as long as the MOUNT endure
> there first was the fruit of nature
> there was the whole will of the people
> . . . .
> Thus BANK of the grassland was raised into Seignory
> stati fatti Signoria, being present Paris Bolgarini
> credit of the Commune of Siena
> 12 of the Bailey present . . . went into committee
> I cancellarius wrote to his Highness
> A New Mount that shall receive from all sorts of persons
> from Luoghi public and private, privileged and non-privileged
> a base, a fondo, a deep, a sure and a certain
> the City having *'entràte'*
> . . . .
> Dixbre' 22 make responsible
> all persons, and all goods of the laity
> that the Mount have its fund secure
> that whoso puts his coin in it shall hold his luoghi
> bearing 5% fruitage per annum
> Signed Nicolo de Antille
> Horatio Gianfiglioli
> Seb. Cellesi LL AA (Their Highnesses)
> gratify this demand to set up a Monte
> to Public Good and to private

to empower, facilitate, and be licit
were pleased to accommodate, and prestare
the fund on the Grand Duke's public income
to the sum as of capital 200,000
for 5% fruitage that wd. be ten thousand the year
which attain to the Office of Grasslands
Paschi di detta Città
the said sum with cautele
that no one shd/suffer

. . . .

Public debt at the end of the Medici
scudi 14 million
or 80 million lira pre-war.

(Canto XLIII)

The first passage indicates that the buying of shares in the Monte were open to the whole people. Everyone had his right to a *Loca Mantis*, i.e., *a share or place on the mountain*. The line reading "the City having '*entràte*' means that the City of Siena has assets, i.e., *real credit*. In the second-last passage, Pound again emphasizes the lending of "the fund on the Grand Duke's public income / to the sum as of capital 200,000 / for 5% fruitage that wd. be ten thousand the year / which attain to the Office of Grasslands." In other words, the 10,000 ducats of interest a year on the capital of 200,000 ducats was paid from the revenue made on the grazing land. This is stressed because it is an example from the Italian Renaissance of the Douglasite policy dealing with *the monetization of real credit*. The last passage refers to the fact that the Florentine public debt at the end of the Medici reign amounted to fourteen million scudi. There had been a decline in monetary wisdom towards the end of the Medici reign.

Canto XLIV pays tribute to the monetary-economic reforms inaugurated by Pietro Leopoldo and Ferdinando III of the royal house of Habsburg-Lorraine, Grand Dukes of Tuscany. Ferdinando III was the son of Pietro Leopoldo. In this canto, Pound juxtaposes the reforms of Pietro Leopoldo with those of Ferdinando III. Hence, these members of the House of Habsburg-Lorraine join Pound's list of *right thinkers* and *beneficent rulers* along with Sigismundo Malatesta, Nicola d'Este and Cosimo di Medici. The canto opens with a description of some of the Leopoldine reforms:

And thou shalt not, Firenze 1766, and thou shalt not
    sequestrate for debt any farm implement
    nor any yoke ox nor
    any peasant while he works with the same.

Pietro Leopoldo
Heavy grain crop unsold
never had the Mount lacked for specie, cut rate to four and 1/3rd
creditors had always been paid,
that trade inside the Grand Duchy be free of impediments
shut down on grain imports
'83, four percent legal maximum interest
'85, three on church investments, motu proprio
Pietro Leopoldo
Ferdinando EVVIVA!!
declared against exportation
thought grain was to eat
(Canto XLIV)

Pietro Leopoldo made it illegal to confiscate for debt a peasant's means of livelihood or to imprison the peasant himself. The interest rate was cut "to four and 1/3rd" percent. By 1783, the maximum legal interest was four percent and by a *motu proprio* of 1785, was three percent. Due to the heavy grain crop being left unsold, grain imports were stopped. Ferdinando III carried on this beneficent tradition by forbidding the export of grain, on the assumption that *the home market is the best market*. Ferdinando III thought grain was to be eaten, i.e., *consumed as needed at home, and not exported*. This would certainly go against the tenets of our modern *orthodox economics*. Laughlin states: "(Duke Leopold of Siena was one of Pound's heroes because he limited the Monte dei Paschi to 3 percent on loans to the peasants.) Pound had nothing against bank loans that supported any kind of production at a fair rate."[117]

This concept of *the home market being the best market* is of course a basic Douglasite assumption. C. H. Douglas constantly maintained that foreign trade under the present debt system of finance was simply a means whereby a nation exported the cream of its production in order to get enough purchasing power to enable its consumers to buy up the skim milk of its production.[118] Douglas also emphasized that foreign trade did not ease in any way the lack of consumer purchasing

---

[117] Laughlin, *Pound as Wuz*, 162.

[118] Cf. C. H. Douglas, *The New and the Old Economics*, 16. "It is well understood how it has been possible for industry to carry on up to the present time under the faulty financial system we have examined, and the two more important causes are: firstly, the excess of exports over imports, resulting in taking goods out of the country and receiving purchasing power in return for them, thus at one and the same time decreasing the amount of goods in the country and increasing the amount of purchasing power in respect of the remaining goods. . . ."

power for all parties, because foreign trade was largely concerned with the lending and borrowing of credit between nations in order to ensure more foreign trade in favour of the creditors.

Pound describes at length the civic and religious celebrations, which greeted Ferdinando III's *provident law*:

> Flags trumpets horns drums
> and a placard
>   VIVA FERDINANDO
> and were sounded all carillons
> with bombs and with bonfires and was sung TE DEUM
> in thanks to the Highest for this so
> provident law
> . . . .
>   This was a Law called
> Dovizia annonaria
>   to be freed from the Yoke of Licence
> From October 9th until the 3rd of November
> was unforeseen jubilation, four lines of tablet in marble:
>   Frumentorum licentia
>   coercita de annonaria laxata Pauperum aeque
>   divitium bono conservit
>   FERDINANDI 1792
> refused to take with him objects of small bulk which he
> held to be the property of the nation. Ferd III, 1796
> that the sovereign be il più galantuomo del paese
>   (Canto XLIV)

This *so provident law* was the *dovizia annonaria*, an archaic term that can be translated as *abundance of provisions*. This law of Ferdinando il terzo allowed grain to be sold from October 9 until November 3 without a license to sell. The effect of the law was to assist in the domestic distribution and consumption of grain. Earlier in the canto Pound had pointed out that Ferdinando had forbade the export of grain *because he thought grain was to be consumed*. Pound's approval of Ferdinando's policy is based on the Douglasite tenets that *the purpose of production is consumption, that the best market is the domestic market*, that there should be *no export of a false surplus* until all domestic needs are satisfied. When all domestic needs are satisfied then the *true surplus may be bartered for the true surplus of other nations*. The Douglasite distinction between a true-surplus and a false-surplus of goods is a especially important. *A false surplus is one caused by an insufficiency of purchasing power in the hands of the consumer, a true surplus of goods is had when all domestic consumer needs are fully satisfied. Only then is export to foreign countries justified.*[119]

Towards the end of Canto XLIV, Pound brings in the person of Napoleon Bonaparte who also possesses many characteristics of the Poundian hero. Pound remarks that Napoleon gave to the artist a remarkably high and unique rank in the social hierarchy:

> "Artists high rank, in fact sole social summits
> which the tempest of politics can not reach,"
> which remark appears to have been made by
> Napoleon.
> (Canto XLIV)

Pound pictures Napoleon as carrying on the monetary-economic reforms inaugurated by Pietro Leopoldo and his son, Ferdinando il terzo:

> And 'Semiramis' 1814 departed from Lucca
> but her brother's law code remains.
> monumento di civile sapienza
> dried swamps, grew cotton, brought in merinos
> mortgage system improved
> 'Thank god such men be but few'
> though they build up human courage
> And before him had been Pietro Leopoldo
> that wished state debt brought to an end;
> that put the guilds under common tribunal;
> that left names only as vestige of feudal chain;
> that lightened mortmain that princes and church be under tax
> as were others; that ended the gaolings for debt;
> that said thou shalt not sell public offices;
> that suppressed so many *gabelle;*
> that freed the printers of surveillance
> and wiped out the crime of lèse majesty;
> that abolished death as a penalty and all tortures in prisons
> which he held were for segregation;
> that split common property among tillers;
> roads, trees, and the wool trade,
> the silk trade, and a set price, lower, for salt;
> plus another full page of such actions Habsburg Lorraine

---

[119] Cf. Douglas in *Economic Democracy*, 138: "Since any material received in payment of exported goods would find a distributed effective demand waiting for it, imports would tend to consist of a much larger proportion of ultimate products for immediate consumption than is now the case; thus forcing on the more primitive countries the necessity of exerting native initiative in the provision of distinctive production."

> His son the Third Ferdinando, cut taxes by half,
> improved tillage in Val di Chiana, Livorno porto franco.
> (Canto XLIV)

Semimaris is a reference by Pound to the sister of Napoleon, Elisa, who was given Tuscany to rule. The founder of the great Napoleonic law code, *monumento de civile sapienza* would be certain to agree with the great medieval canonists in their condemnation of usury. Thus, Napoleon Bonaparte would not only be a Poundian hero but a Douglasite one as well. Napoleon, like Douglas, understood that the King must be *boss of the coinage*, not a group of private money manipulators. The fact that Pietro Leopoldo wanted state debt ended is quite in keeping with Douglasite policy. The same is also true of the Leopoldine reforms regarding abolishing many import duties (*gabelle*), ending the jailing for debt, dividing the natural resources (*common property*) among the people, establishing a just price, etc. The same Douglasite approval can be given to Ferdinando III's cutting taxes in half. As we have seen in Chapter II, Douglas had written to Pound and advised him to investigate modern taxation, which he called *highway robbery*.

The last lines of Canto XLIV superpose on the above descriptions of the reforms carried on by the House of Habsburg-Lorraine in Tuscany, in the late 18th century, a brief reference to the Monte dei Paschi of early 17th century Siena:

> 'The foundation, Siena, has been to keep bridle on usury.'
> Nicolò Piccolomini, Provveditore.
> (Canto XLIV)

The inference is that the Monte dei Paschi is in the same socially beneficent tradition as the reforms of Pietro Leopoldo and Ferdinando il terzo.

Canto XLV is the famous usury canto, the best known and certainly most anthologized of Pound's cantos. This canto, along with Canto LI, is the most devastating indictment of usury in all literature. It is important to bear in mind that Pound indicts usury on moral and aesthetic grounds as well as on monetary-economic grounds. In the fully integrated society that Pound envisages, there can be no separation of activity. As pointed out in Chapter II, Pound has a deep-seated antagonism to usury as a sin *contra naturam* which *frustrates the plenitude of nature's abundance* and which acts as *a corrosive force upon nature, art, and man himself.*

Canto XLV sums up in a highly compressed form the many pages of prose, which Pound wrote about usury. Even if one applies the strict distinction between scientific writing and literature to *The Cantos*, one will recognize these lines as poetry of the highest order based upon a monetary-economic objective correlative:

> With *Usura*
> With usura hath no man a house of good stone
> each block cut smooth and well fitting
> that design might cover their face,
> with usura
> hath no man a painted paradise on his church wall
> *harpes et luz*
> or where virgin receiveth message
> and halo projects from incision,
> with usura
> seeth no man Gonzaga his heirs and his concubines
> no picture is made to endure nor to live with
> but it is made to sell and sell quickly
> with usura, sin against nature,
> is thy bread ever more of stale rags
> is thy bread dry as paper,
> with no mountain wheat, no strong flour
> with usura the line grows thick
> with usura is no clear demarcation
> and no man can find site for his dwelling.
> Stonecutter is kept from his stone
> weaver is kept from his loom
>
> (Canto XLV)

Usury causes inadequate and ugly housing that is not made to last for ages, be it the concrete apartments of public housing or the mass trailer parks in North America. These are squalid homes for the working poor. They contrast with the old buildings of the past, which were made artistically beautiful and built to last. It is part of the Douglasite condemnation of economic sabotage to reject such waste of human work and material in the form of *built-in-obsolescence*, so that one always needs to buy again things that used to last for generations. No man has a house of good stone design and good craft. No man is surrounded by religious art that would lead him to *contemplation*, his highest end. Likewise, usury cuts man off from good profane art. It causes paintings to be made for quick sale rather than for permanence and the provision of aesthetic pleasure. Usury is a sin against nature whose corrosive effects cause the sale of inferior, non-nutritious bread, and, at the same time, creates a blurring of aesthetic sensibility, leading to inferior art and non-art. The last lines of the above passage come back to the economic sphere with their indictment of usury for interfering with man's right to find a site for a home, as well as keeping the stonecutter and weaver from their necessary crafts. In other words, usury is the direct cause of sterility in the arts, the crafts, economic life, and religious life.

Canto XLV continues with its indictment of usury:

> WITH USURA
> wool comes not to market
> sheep bringeth no gain with usura
> Usura is a murrain, usura
> blunteth the needle in the maid's hand
> and stoppeth the spinner's cunning. Pietro Lombardo
> came not by usura
> Duccio came not by usura
> nor Pier della Francesca; Zuan Bellin' not by usura
> nor was 'La Calunnia' painted.
> Came not by usura Angelico; came not Ambrogio Praedis,
> Came no church of cut stone signed: *Adamo me fecit.*
> Not by usura St. Trophime
> Not by usura Saint Hilaire,
>
> (Canto XLV)

Usury interferes with the distribution of provisions, it prevents rightful profit, and it has a corrosive and fatal effect on the crafts, especially beautiful public art and buildings. Landini identifies what is mentioned in this passage as follows: "Pietro Lombardo, 1435–1515, architect and sculptor, maker of Dante's tomb at Ravenna; Duccio [Duccio di Buoninsegna], 1278–1319, chief painter of the Sienese school; Pier della Francesca [Piero dei Francheschi], 1420–1492, painter from Rimini; 'La Calunnia,' a painting by Botticelli, 1440–1510, a Florentine; Angelico [Giovanni da Fiesole, Fra Angelico], 1387–1455, Florentine painter; Ambrogio Praedis, [Ambrogio de Predis], 1455–1506, Milanese painter; St. Trophime, a church in Arles, France, constructed between the eleventh and fifteenth centuries; and Saint Hilaire, a church in Poitiers, France, constructed in the eleventh century."[120]

It is significant that all these renowned artists come from a culture that suppressed usury. Pound adverts to this fact, as Landini notes, from Pound's *Guide to Kulchur*: "This total PAIDEUMA, is anti-usura. A tolerance of gombeen men and stealers of harvest by money, by distortion and dirtiness, runs concurrent with a fattening in all art forms."[121]

---

[120] Landini, "A Guide," 111–12.
[121] Pound, *Guide to Kulchur*, 109.

Towards the end of Canto XLV, Pound gives further examples of the corrosive effect of usury on art and craft. Then he repeats his charge that usury is a sin *contra naturam,* which *frustrates the abundance of nature.* In other words, usury is morally evil because it acts *in frustra naturae*; it frustrates nature's plenitude:

> Usura rusteth the chisel
> It rusteth the craft and the craftsman
> It gnaweth the thread in the loom
> None learneth to weave gold in her pattern;
> Azure hath a canker by usura; cramoisi is unbroidered
> Emerald findeth no Memling
> Usura slayeth the child in the womb
> It stayeth the young man's courting
> It hath brought palsey to bed, lyeth
> between the young bride and her bridegroom
> CONTRA NATURAM
> They have brought whores for Eleusis
> Corpses are set to banquet
> at behest of usura.
>
> (Canto XLV)

Usury frustrates the plenitude of nature's abundance in many other ways: by creating monetary-economic conditions that cause the wide prevalence of abortion, late childless marriages, rich old men marrying young girls, the necessity for young newly married couples to refrain from having children, etc. It is obvious that Ezra Pound would be quite impatient with all the anxiety over the *population explosion* and the *threat of world starvation.* It is obvious what his response would be to the much-vaunted contraceptive mentality of today. Pound would see these anxieties and methods as but another example of *the cult of sterility* imposed by usury and the usurocracy; a *Culture of Death* in opposition to the *Culture of Life* which belongs to the Douglas/Pound worldview.[122] As a Douglasite, Pound's solution is to provide *sufficient purchasing power to ensure the distribution and consumption of the world's abundance,* by the world's population, rather than suggesting methods of *levelling population down to existing purchasing power.* In other words, Pound would suggest that *humanity takes precedence over money,* which is only a man-made ticket system, not a product of Divine Revelation inscribed on tablets

[122] Concerning international propaganda and war on families, see: Bonneau, *70 Years of Population Policy*, or the summary from the European Center for Law & Justice (ECLJ), "How WHO and scientific research."

of stone. "'They have brought whores for Eleusis,' meaning that the usurers have profaned a shrine."[123] Money and power are worshiped, not what is life-giving, the eternal *Divinity*.

Canto XLVI was written in 1935, i.e., in the third year of Roosevelt's New Deal. Pound pictures C. H. Douglas in the office of A. R. Orage's *The New Age* engaged in conversation with a "fuzzy bloke":

> An' the fuzzy bloke sez (legs no pants ever wd. fit) 'IF
> that is so, any government worth a damn can
> pay dividends?'
> The major chewed it a bit and sez: 'Y—es, eh . . .
> You mean instead of collectin' taxes?'
> 'Instead of collecting taxes.' That office?
> Didja see the Decennio?[124]
>
> (Canto XLVI)

The *major* is Major C. H. Douglas, and the *dividends* are the Social Credit dividends. The *fuzzy bloke* is normally identified with Ezra Pound himself, a play on his long curly wild hair, but it could likewise be Pound referencing his own lack of knowledge concerning the subject of economics and the proposed Social Credit dividends. The office is *The New Age* office and Pound goes on to describe A. R. Orage at his desk and gives us luminous details in relating his conversation:

> Decennio exposition, reconstructed office of Il Popolo,
> Waal, ours waz like that, minus the Mills bomb an' the teapot,
> heavy lipped chap at the desk,
> One half green eye and one brown one, nineteen
> Years on this case, CRIME
> Ov two CENturies, 5 millions bein' killed off
> to 1919, and before that
> Debts of the South to New York, that is to the
> banks of the city, two hundred million,
> war, I don't think (or have it your own way . . .)
> about slavery?
> Five million being killed off..couple of Max's drawings,
> . . . .

[123] Laughlin, *Pound as Wuz*, 85.

[124] Pound explained the meaning of *Decennio* in one of his radio broadcasts: "And as I stated last time, I am feedin' you the footnotes first in case there is any possible word that might not be easily comprehended. The Decennio, and decennio exposition was the exhibition in Rome at the end of the first ten years of the Fascist regime. Mussolini's fascist regime. They set up the office of the old Popolo d'Italia, very like what had been the New Age Office in London." Pound, "*Ezra Pound Speaking*," 34.

'He ain't got an opinion.'
Sez Orage about G. B. S. sez Orage about Mr. Xtertn.
Sez Orage about Mr. Wells, 'he wont HAVE an opinion.'
(Canto XLVI)

The "heavy lipped chap at the desk" is A. R. Orage, editor of *The New Age* and collaborator with Douglas in the writing of *Credit Power and Democracy*, a Social Credit book. The scene is set in 1919 and Pound points out that by that time Orage had already spent nineteen years studying the great crime of usury. This crime had been going on for two centuries and, by 1919, it had killed off five millions. The reference to the two hundred million dollars in Southern debts to the banks of New York is given as the real cause of the Civil War. Pound believes the slavery question was merely the occasion for the Civil War. A. R. Orage's comments on George Bernard Shaw (G. B. S.), and H. G. Wells are noteworthy. Halloway has given a high rank to A. R. Orage in the field of English literary criticism: "Throughout the nineteenth century, there was a strong tradition (Ruskin, Coventry Patmore, and Leslie Stephen have their places in it, besides [Matthew] Arnold) that the values of life and art were ultimately one. The critical writings of A. R. Orage (editor of *The New Age*, 1908–21) constantly take up problems of moral wholeness ('moral decadence may be discovered in style itself... its sign-manual in style is the diffuse sentence, the partial treatment, the inchoate vocabulary, the mixed principles') and also of cultural decay, commercialization, shortage of serious criticism, and debasement of standards."[125]

Among the great Distributists, Hilaire Belloc and G. K. Chesterton, Alfred Orage was esteemed as one dedicated to the truth, and to the freedom of the press. Belloc dedicated his book, *The Free Press*, to A. R. Orage.[126] Chesterton wrote an obituary for Orage, and granted permission to Philip Mairet to use it in Mairet's biography of Orage.[127] Pound had referred to Chesterton as "like a vile scum on the pond."[128] When asked by Landini about this reference Pound

[125] Halloway, *The Pelican Guide*, 88.
[126] Belloc, *The Free Press*, V.
[127] As mentioned earlier, in the American Jesuit journal *The Commonweal*, A. R. Orage wrote a four part article entitled "An Editor's Progress," in issues from Feburuary-March 1926. Unfortunately, the final fourth part of the article, is not included in reprints of his article. It is in the fourth part entitled "The Quest of God," that Orage gives his current opinion, in 1926, concerning the guild system and Distributism. He also discusses his Catholic and Anglo-Catholic friendships over the years.
[128] Pound, *The Letters of Ezra Pound*, 170–71.

answered: "'Chesterton and I buried the hatchet at St. Margherita,' Italy."[129] Landini then draws our attention to an article from Pound in 1937: "G. K. Chesterton, the great G. K. himself, on his last visit to St. Margherita, admitted to me (in person) that (1) he didn't understand economics; and (2) that his paper was keeping the subject nebulous partly in order not to lose contact with his readers. So far as he had any opinion, he disagreed with NONE of my statements about money, and said that this was the case. He had a theory, probably justifiable, that the British *en masse* were merely put off by clear statement of a case or an idea."[130]

Noel Stock writes similar concerning the reconciliation of Pound and Chesterton, shortly before Chesterton's death in 1936:

> Beginning in November 1934 Chesterton began to publish Pound's articles in G. K.'s Weekly. On 10 May 1935 they had lunch together in Rapallo and Pound discovered that he liked him.
>
> 'G. K. Chesterton here yesterday,' he wrote to Irving Fisher at Yale, 'also finds nothing to contradict in as much social credit as I advocate.' On 30 May Chesterton published Pound's *Child's Guide to Economics* which had previously been turned down by the Morning Post. When towards the end of the year Chesterton had some kind words to say about Pound over the BBC, Pound wrote to thank him, enclosing his sheet of Volitionist questions for Chesterton to answer: 'They have served', he told him, 'to correlate present state of opinion. I don't make out whether there is actually something in Douglas that holds you up, or whether you are working as I am, towards a decent system, but feel the need of something less technical, i.e., some less technical formulation if one is to get it into enough heads for it to take action . . . I should like to see Belloc again, can't make out if his ideas change with state of his liver. At any rate I take it we are all three definitely against Shaw, Wells etc. paucity of perception.' Two years later in a long article on Jefferson and Adams he spoke of Chesterton's whole life as a protest against the 'impoverishment' of the Encyclopaedists and the Enlightenment."[131]

---

[129] Interview at St. Elizabeth's Hospital, Washington, D. C., August 27, 1957: Landini, "A Guide," 43.

[130] Pound, "Why Parliament's Gone to Hell," 7.

[131] Stock, *The Life of Ezra Pound*, 328–29.

Further along in Canto XLVI Pound quotes Paterson, one of the founders of the Bank of England and then goes on to quote from a letter written by the Rothschild Brothers banking firm:

> 17 years on this case, and we not the first lot!
> Said Paterson:
> Hath benefit of interest on all
> the moneys which it, the bank, creates out of nothing.
>
> Semi-private inducement
> Said Mr. RothSchild, hell knows, which Roth-schild
> 1861, '64 or there sometime, "Very few people
> "will understand this. Those who do will be occupied
> "getting profits. The general public will probably not
> "see it's against their interest."
>
> (Canto XLVI)

The quotation from Paterson is from a circular letter soliciting certain monied people to invest in the Bank of England at the time of its founding in 1694. Paterson admits that the bank creates money out of nothing and that it collects interest on this money created out of nothing. Paterson presented this as an incentive to invest in the bank. The letter from Mr. Rothschild is a letter sent on June 25, 1863, from the London banking firm of Rothschild Brothers to the banking firm of Ikleheimer, Morton and Vandergould, Wall Street, New York City. Pound is in fact paraphrasing and summarizing a quotation from the letter in which the writer of the Rothschild Brothers' letter quotes Congressman John Sherman of Ohio, who had introduced the National Banking Act in the United States Congress. Representative Sherman had written the Rothschild Brothers and outlined to them the vast opportunities and profits available in the United States due to the passage of the National Banking Act.[132] Pound presents this evidence and asks if this can be taken to court:

> Seventeen years on the case; here
> Gents, is / are the confession.
> "Can we take this into court?
> "Will any jury convict on this evidence?
> 1694 anno domini, on through the ages of usury
> On, right on, into hair-cloth, right on into rotten building,
> Right on into London houses, ground rents, foetid brick work,
> Will any jury convict 'um? The Foundation of Regius Professors
> Was made to spread lies and teach Whiggery, will any

[132] Overholser, *A Short Review*, 46–47.

JURY convict 'um?
The Macmillan Commission about two hundred forty years
LATE
with great difficulty got back to Paterson's
The bank makes it *ex nihil*
Denied by five thousand professors, will any
Jury convict 'um? This case, and with it
the first part, draws to a conclusion,
of the first phase of this opus, Mr Marx, Karl, did not
foresee this conclusion,
(Canto XLVI)

Pound shows the effects of usury since its enthronement in 1694 by pointing to the shoddy goods and shoddy housing of our modern era, which are the culmination of over 240 years of usury and domination by the Bank of England. The Foundation of Regius Professors, according to Christopher Hollis, was set up in the 18th century to ensure that the teaching of history at Oxford and Cambridge would be properly biased according to the Whig point of view: "Now what was the history which these endowed teachers taught? It was the progressive theory of history—a theory hitherto unknown, a theory soon, as a result of their activities, accepted uncritically, a theory created in the first place quite cynically and clear-headedly in order to cover up the traces of truth."[133] The *Glorious Revolution* of 1688, when William of Orange was invited by the *Immortal Seven* and deposed James II as King, was not mainly about maintaining the dominance of the Protestant religion and the primacy of Parliament over the crown, but more *a conspiracy of financiers.* A contemporary Whig viewpoint admits the same:

> This paper argues the Immortal Seven—those English elite who invited William to invade England—were influenced primarily by economic interests. They could not fail to recognize the shortcomings of their government to protect and advocate for commerce. But the Seven directly reflected the greater commercial concerns of the emerging New London Merchants. The merchants then looked to William of Orange to remedy what was wrong with the English economy and to address specific problems, such as the lack of national debt, national bank, financial products, and the shortage of hard currency, by applying a Dutch model.[134]

---

133 Hollis, *The Two Nations*, 39.
134 Angle, "Glorious Revolution as Financial Revolution," 12.

Hollis explains how, under King Charles II, inflation did not take place, as he kept the paper money supply in proportion to rising productivity. The Bank of England, newly created by English financiers that followed under King William in 1694, would not, within only 6 years of the revolution, be restrained by concerns of price inflation when there was money to be made:

> [B]ecause both Charles and the goldsmiths, divergent as their other interests were, were at least united in their desire that the whole experiment of paper money should not be discredited by a rise in prices. They therefore kept the quantity of it issued strictly proportionate to the increase in productivity. The Bank of England, however, confident that the King [William III of Orange] was impotent against them and that at the same time it was the King who would be blamed by public opinion for a rise in prices, saw now no necessity for restraint. They lent freely—a proceeding which did not cost them a halfpenny—issuing their notes well beyond the country's productive capacity.[135]

As in 1694, as we will read below likewise in 1930, the money that the Bank of England lent was newly created money, by the fountain pen, as has always been the accepted practice of the Bank of England and the other Central Banks it spawned.

The MacMillan Commission on Banking and Finance was set up under the chairmanship of Lord MacMillan by the British Parliament in 1930. C. H. Douglas gave testimony before this commission, as did Reginald McKenna, Chairman of the giant Midland Bank. McKenna wrote the following and would state something similar to the MacMillan Commission: "[E]very new loan or purchase by a bank creates an equivalent deposit, thus increasing the quantity of money, while every repayment to or sale by a bank destroys a deposit and correspondingly diminishes the quantity of money."[136]

As Pound points out, the MacMillan Commission was two hundred and forty years late in getting back to Paterson's admission that the bank creates credit out of nothing, *ex nihilo*. Reginald McKenna's admission of this fact comes two hundred and forty years after Paterson's admission. Pound points out that five thousand professors of *orthodox* economics have denied that the bank creates credit out of nothing. Will any jury convict them? C. H. Douglas had always

---

[135] Hollis, *The Two Nations*, 31.

[136] McKenna, "Midland Bank Limited."

insisted that banks create credit out of nothing. Douglas had always maintained that there was nothing wrong with the creation of credit out of nothing except that this was a prerogative of the supreme public authority and not of private banking interests.[137]

Many dismiss Pound's statements outright, such as "The bank makes it ex nihil / Denied by five thousand professors." Yet it is Pound who is correct. Most people believe there exists a money multiplier, or the so-called fractional reserve system of banking. Contrast the Macmillan Commission, and the clear statement made by McKenna about money creation and destruction above, with a current writer on economics today—Sehgal, who provides this money multiplier, or so-called fractional reserve banking explanation:

> [The Fed] buys $1 million of US Treasury bonds from a bank like Citigroup with new money that it creates out of thin air. The $1 million of bonds are added to the Fed's balance sheet. Citigroup, like all large banks, has an account at the Fed, and its account is credited with the $1 million it received for selling the bonds.
>
> For this new money to circulate more widely through the economy, Citigroup can loan some but not all of it to borrowers. Banks are required to keep a fraction of their deposits, about 10 percent, in the vault or as a deposit with the Fed. Citigroup must keep $100,000 of the $1 million in reserves. It can lend out the remaining $900,000. Let's say someone borrows the $900,000 and deposits it in her account at Wells Fargo. Then $90,000 must be kept on reserve, and $810,000 can be lent. In this way, the "fractional reserve system" enables a multiple expansion of money, as the initial $1 million can be expanded up to ten times: A little money generates a lot of credit. And that's how money is made.[138]

What is wrong with Sehgal's description? Obviously, it denies McKenna's statement, a statement Douglas/Pound likewise affirm, that "[E]very new loan or purchase by a bank creates an equivalent

[137] Editor's note: In actual fact, Douglas was overwhelmingly concerned with the *policy* of the financial system. The financial system should be run for the genuine benefit of the citizens and not be run for the benefit of an oligarchic elite, either private or public. Whether the public authority created the money or private banking interests did was a secondary matter. It would, for example, avail us nothing and would indeed put us in an even worse situation if the public authority created all the money, but then proceeded to impose an anti-social policy on the people.

[138] Sehgal, *Coined: The Rich Life*, 159.

deposit, thus increasing the quantity of money, while every repayment to or sale by a bank destroys a deposit and correspondingly diminishes the quantity of money." All of Sehgal's examples of lending are previously created, not new money created out of thin air. Sehgal is an investment banker who attended the London School of Economics, so does it follow that he *must* be telling the truth? Sehgal's 2015 book was recognized as one of *Business Insider's* top 15 Business books for the year. It was a best seller on the lists of the *New York Times* and *Wall Street Journal.*

The Bank of England Quarterly Bulletin, "Money Creation in the Modern Economy," contradicts Sehgal, as we can demonstrate by providing contrasting statements from the Bulletin:

> 1) "A related misconception is that banks can lend out their reserves. Reserves can only be lent *between banks,* since consumers do not have access to reserves accounts at the Bank of England."[139] Sehgal's example has $900,000 taken from a Federal reserve account and lent to a private individual who deposits it at her Wells Fargo account.
>
> 2) "This description of the relationship between monetary policy and money differs from the description in many introductory textbooks, where central banks determine the quantity of broad money via a 'money multiplier' by actively varying the quantity of reserves. In that view, central banks implement monetary policy by choosing the quantity of reserves. And, because there is assumed to be a stable ratio of broad money to base money, these reserves are then 'multiplied up' to a much greater change in bank deposits as banks increase lending and deposits."[140] Sehgal says banks are required to hold reserves, about 10%, but here the Bulletin contradicts this, stating that there is no required amount of reserve.[141] In the process of making loans (all newly created money *ex nihilo*) the banks actually work in the opposite direction to Sehgal's story; they decide how much they want to place in their own account at the Federal Reserve. The amount is for that individual bank to determine, as implied, after the loan is made.
>
> 3) "Money creation in practice differs from some popular misconceptions—banks do not act simply as intermediaries, lending out deposits that savers place with them, and nor do

---

[139] McLeay, Radia, and Thomas, "Money creation," 16.
[140] McLeay, Radia, and Thomas, "Money creation," 21.
[141] There are probably some minor differences in central bank requirements in different countries, such as the existence of a required amount of reserve.

> they 'multiply up' central bank money to create new loans and deposits."[142] This denies all that Sehgal goes on to say: "Then $90,000 must be kept on reserve, and $810,000 can be lent. In this way, the 'fractional reserve system'" enables a multiple expansion of money, as the initial $1 million can be expanded up to ten times: A little money generates a lot of credit. And that's how money is made."
>
> 4) "Banks making loans and consumers repaying them are the most significant ways in which bank deposits are created and destroyed in the modern economy. But they are far from the only ways. Deposit creation or destruction will also occur any time the banking sector (including the central bank) buys or sells existing assets from or to consumers, or, more often, from companies or the government."[143]

Money creation by banks is as Douglas/Pound contend. All loans are newly created money, all repayments are destruction of that money.

One can argue, until one is *blue in the face*, with economics graduates and others who took a *dismal science* course or read Sehgal's or a similar book. But Sehgal's description of Central Bank workings is not reality, but a farcical fairy tale that is told to the *hoi polloi* and, unfortunately, what is often taught in college economics courses.

On June 28, 2012, Congressman Ron Paul presided over a hearing of the Domestic Monetary Policy Subcommittee to investigate how fractional reserve banking effects the economy. He gave his own statement for the record.[144] The Acton Institute has many articles where it is obvious they believe in the myth of fractional reserve banking.[145] Gary North, who purports to be an expert on Douglas Social Credit, authored a book critical of Douglas called *Salvation through Inflation*. North is identified as a Christian Reconstructionist, i.e., in the Calvinist tradition. North is actively involved in the Austrian School of Economics, and was, at least in the past, associated with the Mises Institute. In North's *Christian Economics*,[146] he speaks against the fractional reserve banking system as unchristian, giving an explanation as to how it works similar to Sehgal's. The American Libertarian Party likewise rales against the fractional reserve system. How is it possible that so many do not understand how modern banking works? As

---

142 McLeay, Radia, and Thomas, "Money creation," 14.
143 McLeay, Radia, and Thomas, "Money creation," 17.
144 U. S. Congress. House, *The Economic Consequences.*
145 See: Carter, "What is the money multiplier?"
146 North, *Christian Economics: Teacher's Edition*, chap. 36.

for those who call Douglas or Pound "Economic Cranks," how is it possible that these two understood the bank creation of money over *a hundred years ago*, whereas many today who disparage their names still don't understand it? Thousands of scholarly papers and millions of dollars are spent discussing or fighting the evil *windmill* of the money multiplier theory—the fractional reserve banking system, all particularly good people like the fictional Don Quixote, but like Quixote's windmills they are fighting a mere illusion. How can one hope to call for change in the banking system, if you do not know how it currently operates?

It is, as Douglas and Pound claim. Every loan is new money, every repayment of that loan destroys that money. If Wells Fargo loans one billion dollars, it is completely new money, not 90% of previously created money, with 10% reserved.[147] When it is paid back, that money is destroyed, just the interest collected is retained. See again the Bank of England article: "[R]epaying bank loans destroys money just as making loans creates it."[148] If the reader learns anything from Pound "the crank" on economics, it is this fact about bank loans, and hopefully the reader will not just accept it, but study further as Pound did. If the reader does so, he will know more than most economics graduates or modern politicians concerning banking practice. If you still do not believe the above, we leave the final word to the Bank of England itself concerning fractional banking (the multiplier effect), probably written with some sarcasm: "While the money multiplier theory can be a useful way of introducing money and banking in economic textbooks, it is not an accurate description of how money is created in reality."[149]

Was there ever fractional banking practiced somewhere? Perhaps. As Douglas explains though, the goldsmiths practiced the same protocol as is followed in modern day banking. Money was created *ex nihilo* as paper receipts. No previously created money, i.e., gold or silver, were loaned, only promises-to-pay:

> There is no doubt that at this point some dishonest goldsmith found that a large number of his clients left their values in his care almost indefinitely. They were safer with him than elsewhere, perhaps even in the castle of the owner, so that

---

[147] Edtior's note: Nor is it the case that 90% of the previously created money serves as backing for the equivalent in bank credit. The system is endogenous. Credit is created by bank loans and purchases and the required reserves for the liquidity of the system are found, borrowed, or created after the fact.

[148] McLeay, Radia, and Thomas, "Money creation," 20.

[149] McLeay, Radia, and Thomas, "Money creation," 15.

> there was always a tremendous amount of wealth in the actual custody of the goldsmiths which apparently was never drawn out. Our dishonest goldsmith had the bright idea of issuing several receipts for one piece of wealth, on the assumption that those receipts would not all be presented at the same time....
>
> ...That process, beginning undoubtedly in fraud, grew so common that it became the convention amongst bankers, who were the descendants of the goldsmiths, to do this thing; and they have always for the past several hundred years been in the habit of issuing more receipts for wealth than the actual wealth which was deposited with them. At the present time it is a well-known convention, not denied by bankers themselves, that for every dollar of legal tender which they have, they issue nine dollars of credit money which they actually create themselves; just as the goldsmith, not by exactly the same process, created those false receipts representing deposited wealth which was not there. Now, no scheme of that kind so obviously fraudulent, in its beginnings at any rate, could have proceeded so long as it did, and for that matter does at the present day, *if it had not served a very useful purpose. In fact the additional receipts were passed as money, facilitated trade, kept goods moving and were in every way an advantage, even to the general population. They were of the greatest advantage, of course, to the banker, but they were also of great advantage to the public, as they provided it with money* [emphasis added].[150]

---

[150] Douglas, "*Money: An Historical Survey*," 25. The question always raised, concerning the Douglasite proposals is, "where will they get the money for dividends, etc.?" Douglas proposed that private banks continue to provide the service they currently do, creating money *ex nihilo (out of nothing)*, as loans to businesses. Private banks are *delegated* this privilege (it is not a right), by the supreme public authority. The nation's treasury, or a new government agency, will likewise create *ex nihilo*, by its prerogative as the supreme public authority, periodic dividends to citizens, to make up for the gap between goods and services available, and money already in circulation. *Ex nihilo*, the consumer price discount will be provided, so that businesses can sell their goods at cost. Finally, *ex nihilo*, the state will create credit to pay for government expenses: employees, needed infrastructure projects, etc. Douglas emphasised that whatever is physically possible and desirable should be financially possible, in the public as well as the private sphere. Money should operate in service to the true good of the community. This is for needed work, not wasteful projects such as new *Towers of Babel*, which would be a waste of human effort and the earth's resources. *Leisure/contemplation* should not be sacrificed to such endeavours. What is the basis of this money creation? As Pound states concerning the Monte dei Paschi: "Credit rests in *ultimate* on the abundance of nature, on the growing grass that can nourish the living sheep" (Pound, *Impact*, 147). And as Douglas

Finally, as to the last quote given from Canto XLVI, Pound alerts us to the fact that the first phase of this opus is concluding. If we follow the Dantescan organization of *The Cantos* into the tripartite *Inferno*, *Purgatorio* and *Paradiso*, we then would be drawing towards the end of the *Inferno*. Pound asks us to look around at the evidence gathered in the case against usury. This first case against usury brings the first part of the opus to its end:

> you have seen a good deal of
> the evidence, not knowing it evidence, is monumentum
> look about you, look, if you can, at St Peter's
> Look at the Manchester slums, look at Brazilian coffee
> or Chilean nitrates. This case is the first case
> Si requieres monumentum?
> . . . .
> Bank creates it ex nihil. Creates it to meet a need,
> Hic est hyper-usura. Mr. Jefferson met it:
> No man hath natural right to exercise profession
> of lender, save him who hath it to lend.
>
> (Canto XLVI)

As evidence in the case against usury, Pound cites the building of St. Peter's Basilica that caused an already heavily indebted Papacy to go even deeper in debt to the usurers. It was to help extricate the Papacy from this debt that the friar Tetzel was sent to preach the ill-fated indulgence in Germany, with its dire consequences for the unity of Christendom.[151] Pound cites the horror of the Manchester slums. He also cites the crime of sabotage as evidenced in the destruction of Brazilian coffee and Chilean nitrates. These goods were destroyed, not because people did not want and need them, but because there wasn't sufficient purchasing power available to buy them.

In the preceding passage, Pound points out that when the bank creates credit from nothing and charges interest for that credit, this is hyper-usury, or super-usury. He quotes Thomas Jefferson who said, "no man has the natural right to exercise the profession of lender, save him who hath it to lend." In other words, Thomas Jefferson attacked

---

states: "[T]he real basis of credit is the producing and consuming capacity of the community" (Douglas, *Monopoly of Credit*, 51).

[151] The unfortunate collection of funds by the Dominican friar Tetzel via the selling of indulgences for the rebuilding of St. Peter's Basilica would, together with Martin Luther's response, never have taken place if it were not for the influence of the Catholic banking family of Jacob Fugger. Fugger directly influenced the Church to soften or at least ignore its traditional stand against usury. Fugger and his banking empire were the *catalyst*. See: Steinmetz, *The Richest Man*.

the bank credit fraud of lending promises-to-pay as if they were real money and charging interest on these promises-to-pay. Jefferson held that lending at a reasonable rate of interest was only justified if the lender did in fact lend out real money, i.e., legal tender. The banks simply lend out bank credit or promises-to-pay. Pound continues with his *first case* against usury:

> Replevin, estopple, what wangle which wangle, Van Buren met it.
> Before that was tea dumped into harbour, before that was a
> great deal still in the school books, placed there
> NOT as evidence. Placed there to distract idle minds,
> Murder, starvation and bloodshed, seventy four red revolutions
> Ten empires fell on this grease spot.
> 'I rule the Earth' said Antoninus 'but LAW rules the sea'
> meaning, we take it, lex Rhodi, the Law Maritime
> of sea lawyers.
> usura and sea insurance
> wherefrom no State was erected greater than Athens.
> Wanting TAXES to build St Peter's, thought Luther beneath
> civil notice,
> 1527. Thereafter art thickened. Thereafter design went to hell,
> Thereafter barocco, thereafter stone-cutting desisted.
> 'Hic nefas' (narrator) 'commune sepulchrum.'
> (Canto XLVI)

Martin Van Buren, like Thomas Jefferson, fought this bank credit fraud. The Boston Tea Party: "[b]efore that was tea dumped into harbour" was simply an effect not the cause of the American Revolution. The true cause of the American Revolution, says Pound, was the suppression of state-issued, debt-free, paper money in Pennsylvania, year 1750: "1750—Sanctions against Pennsylvania, forbidding the colony to issue its own paper money. (A number of different secondary events are mentioned in the obscurantist text-books administered to the victims in the schools and universities of the U. S. A.)."[152]

In this connection, C. H. Douglas himself attacks the control of concentrated economic power through the means of both *education and propaganda*.[153] The *grease spot* of usury has caused the fall of ten empires, murder, starvation, bloodshed, and seventy-four red revolutions. Pound quotes the second century Roman emperor, Antoninus

---

[152] In Pound, *Impact*, this referenced section in the essay "A Visiting Card" is not to be found, but is within the original: Pound, *A Visiting Card*, 10, Money Pamphlets by Pound, no. 4. London: Peter Russell, 1952.

[153] Douglas, *Economic Democracy*, 138.

Pius, on the interconnection between usury and marine insurance. Pound describes usury as having its origin in classical times, from the selling of sea insurance at usurious rates. Pound sees the decline of the Greek city states as linked to usury and the insurance practice for sailing ships. He again repeats his thesis concerning St. Peter's Basilica and once more attributes the decadence of art, design, and craft to usury.

It is interesting that Pound assigns the date 1527 as the turning point in the triumph of usury and the decadence of art. Pound sees the Protestant Reformation as the event which brought on the world-wide triumph of usury. He regards Calvin as the arch-heretic and considers the Protestant Reformation as having its origin not in theological issues but in *monetary-economic* issues, i.e., the desire of a pro-usury conspiracy to topple the Church that had always been an obstacle for the usurer. This usury party, says Pound, gave its support to Luther for this reason. 1527 was also the year that Rome was sacked by troops loyal to Emperor Charles V. That a Catholic monarch would sack the city of Rome would have been unthinkable before. But Luther had undermined the view of the Church as *holy* among Kings and faithful. Many of the unpaid soldiers in the emperor's army would have been followers of Luther. Pound considers the sacking of Rome in 1527 as the death knell to the Renaissance period of cultural splendour. This date is commemorated every year in Rome, where the new Swiss Guards of the Vatican swear to protect the Roman Pontiff, remembering the Swiss Guards who gave their lives in order that Pope Clement VII could flee to nearby Castel Sant'Angelo.

Pound continues with his indictment against usury:

> 19 years on this case/first case. I have set down part of
> The Evidence. Part/coumune sepulchrum
> Aurum est commune sepulchrum. Usura, commune sepulchrum.
> helandros kai heleptolis kai helarxe.
> Hic Geryon est. Hic hyperusura.
>
> (Canto XLVI)

Here Pound states, as part of his evidence, that both gold and usury are a common grave: "Aurum est commune sepulchrum." In other words, both the gold standard and usury bring death. In the Greek phrases quoted, Pound refers to usury as *Geryon* or *Fraud*.

Pound ends Canto XLVI with an indictment of Roosevelt's New Deal in the third year of F. D. R.'s reign, i.e., 1935. The indictment is all the more effective since it takes the form of a description of conditions in the United States in 1935, as described by Roosevelt's uncle, F. Delano:

FIVE million youths without jobs
FOUR million adult illiterates
15 million 'vocational misfits', that is with small chance for jobs
NINE million persons annual, injured in preventable industrial accidents
One hundred thousand violent crimes. The Eunited States ov America
3rd year of the reign of F. Roosevelt, signed F. Delano, his uncle.
CASE for the prosecution. That is one case, minor case
in the series/Eunited States of America, a.d. 1935
England a worse case, France under a foetor of regents.
'Mr Cummings wants Farley's job' headline in current paper.
(Canto XLVI)

Pound would have found this article in an American newspaper, concerning F. Delano: "THE OTHER REPORT—This one confidential—was laid before the president by his uncle, Frederic A. Delano, who is head of the national resources board. This report, titled 'Wastage of Human Resources' lists among other things the following: "5,000,000 youths of working age without jobs. 4,000,000 adult illiterates in the country. 15,000,000 'vocational misfits' workers who have small chance for jobs. 9,000,000 persons injured annually in preventable industrial accidents. Over 100,000 sent to jail each year for violent crimes."[154]

Pound cites Delano's report as one minor case for the prosecution in a series of cases. He cites England as a worse case and describes France as being under a foetor of regents. Richard Sawyer writes of his discovery of the source for this passage concerning France and how that same source's allusions can likewise be found in Cantos 46 and 51.[155] Sawyer found the source for these allusions in a French magazine *VU* in an article published on June 26, 1935: "'Nous n'avons plus de Roi, mais nous avons des Régents. Les vrais maîtres de la France siègent à la Banque de France.' 'We no longer have a King, but we have Regents. The real masters of France sit at the Bank of France.'"[156] Sawyer explains that the author of the article, Francis Delaisi, emphasised twelve of the fifteen Regents, as the true men in power.[157] Pound would likewise emphasise the twelve, as Sawyer quotes from an article Pound wrote: "Five gangs of Swiss Usurers

[154] Pearson and Allen, "Rumored Cummings Wants Farley's," 6.
[155] Sawyer, "The 12 Regents," 1–2.
[156] Sawyer, "The 12 Regents," 3.
[157] Sawyer, "The 12 Regents," 3–4.

came in with [Jacques] Necker. The great banking romance occurred when the Rothschilds did in Napoleon and forced the calvinists [*sic*] to admit them into the holy circle of infamy. These six banking families still direct the Banque de France, along with six industrialists, De Wendel, metallurgy or war material; Voguë, chemicals; Duchemin, chemicals; Poulenc, chemicals; Tinardon, chemicals; Darblay, paper products (P&P 6:333)."[158]

There is a *legion* of misunderstandings concerning Douglas's Social Credit, and Sawyer seems to fall into one of them, implying that Pound, in his backing for Social Credit, should have been happy with the partial nationalization of banks. In 1936, the newly elected Popular Front government of Léon Blum partially nationalized and made many changes in the number of appointed or elected officials at the Bank of France. Pound, following this change, still spoke negatively of the Bank: "[In] 1938, two years after Blum instituted his reforms, we still hear Pound denouncing the Bank of France as 'Europe's worst plague spot,' and he is still holding up Delaisi's outdated exposé as proof (P&P 7:333). Pound was evidently not prepared to let facts foil a good conspiracy plot."[159] In answer to Sawyer, one does not stop the influence of the most powerful bankers and industrialists in France, many of their families in positions of power for over one hundred years, by merely removing them from leadership positions controlling the policy of the Bank of France.[160] Douglas, and Pound in following Douglas, did not desire, as seems suggested by Sawyer, the nationalization of banks:

> Let me say at once that, at any rate, by itself, the nationalisation of banks is no remedy. It is, in fact, very questionable whether the nationalisation of anything is a remedy. Nationalisation is an administrative change, and in most cases is an administrative change for the worse, because, at any rate,

---

[158] Sawyer, "The 12 Regents," 4. P&P refers to the Poetry and Prose collection at ezrapoundsociety.org where this can be viewed. The original article was in *New Age*: Pound, Ezra. "Vu," No. 380, and Subsequent Issues. *New Age*, LVII. 27 (31 Oct. 1935) 218–19. This was a review of the French periodical *VU*, with particular reference to articles by Francis Delaisi.

[159] Sawyer, "The 12 Regents," 9. P&P refers to the Poetry and Prose collection at ezrapoundsociety.org where this can be viewed. The original article was in *Action*: Pound, Ezra. "Infamy of Taxes." *Action*, 120 (4 June 1938) 13.

[160] Perhaps the only book C. H. Douglas translated and then published concerned what took place in France before, during, and after World War I. The book explored the financial betrayal by the banking and armaments sector in France. Chastenet [*sic*], *The Bankers' Republic*. Original French edition: Chastanet, *La République des Banquiers*.

> in the forms in which we know it at present, it involves a highly centralised form of administration, and separates authority very largely from the facts of the situation with which authority ought properly to deal. But whatever views one may have about systems of administration, the essential point to recognise in regard to finance is the question of the beneficial ownership of public credit, whether public credit be administered under a decentralised or private system of administration or by a public authority. To put this matter in a more concrete form, the question at issue, fundamentally, is whether, when a banker creates and issues a loan he should be repaid (which assumes that the loan belongs to him), or whether he should not be repaid (which assumes that credit is a public asset). That is the simple and fundamental issue of this controversy, and upon the answer which is given to it, in my opinion, the present civilisation stands or falls.[161]

Douglas always was clear that what he called the National Credit Office would determine the amount of credit needed but not be a bank as such; private banks would continue to function as they do in loaning to producers. Douglas was no fool. He understood that this power, even by the government, could be abused as a method to control individuals if sane policies were not followed. If it functioned correctly, according to Social Credit principles, the National Credit Office would appoint, as government employees, financial, and other economic experts. These could be, and many probably would be, the same officials who would be hired at a Central Bank, but the difference is these officials could be removed if they fail to meet policy goals. These experts would determine the amount of credit to be issued, as Central Banks do today, but not to fulfill the interests of private banking. Instead, credit is to be created in accordance with the policy goals of *State created credit*, i.e., in the best interests of the nation. This would involve a proper balance between money available and the ability for the public to buy the desired goods and services of the nation. Some credit would be issued as a debt to be repaid (business loans) through private banks. Other credits, as per Social Credit policy, would be issued debt-free to consumers, a *dividend* issued periodically to all, and a *consumer price discount* issued to producers whenever a product is sold. If debt-free credit is not issued when needed to fill the gap between prices and needed goods and services, the monetary system will continue to be unbalanced,

---

[161] Douglas, *Warning Democracy*, 35–36.

whether the banks are nationalized or left in private hands. The goal is to make it possible for all desirable goods and services to be met by the effective demand of money in circulation. Banking is a business and they are entitled to levy fair and just fees for their needed service. But the difference is that under Social Credit they would serve a public policy that recognizes credit as a *public asset.*

In 1945, the Bank of France was fully nationalized. In 1993, it became fully independent or *privatized.* Did anything change in 1936, 1945, and 1993? No, as policy did not change, the system of total debt financing continued as before, with all the booms and busts of the Central Bank system and only the banks benefiting.

You can understand the common man believing today that the Central Banks are part of the government, but even a politician, someone who had worked for stringent regulations on banks following the 2007–2008 financial crisis, still believed in 2014 that the *Federal Reserve* was a government agency: "In a November 2014 hearing of the Senate Banking Committee, Senator Elizabeth Warren of Massachusetts told Bill Dudley, the president of the New York Fed, 'you need to fix it, Mr. Dudley, or we need to get someone who will.' The comment was particularly notable since Congress has no say over appointments at the New York Fed."[162] It should be noted that El-Erian is someone intimately knowledgeable of the international monetary system. Yet he states that he is only *partially exposed* to all that goes on in Basel:

> Of all the economic agencies across the globe, they [central banks] remain the gold standard when it comes to consultation, sharing ideas, and, when needed, applying coordinated action. And what they do is greatly facilitated by one of the best-kept policy secrets in the world of policy coordination — those highly effective and regularly scheduled meetings held in Switzerland.
>
> Having been invited as an external speaker to a few of these meetings, I have come to appreciate their effectiveness, and this despite the fact that I have been only partially exposed to what goes on in that circular building across from the train station in the Swiss city of Basel. Held away from the cameras and fanfare of the press, the BIS [Bureau of International Settlements] gatherings are said to provide for a rather candid exchange of views that in recent years has involved a larger number of systemically important countries. They have also greatly facilitated the critical emergency institutional phone

[162] El-Erian, *The Only Game*, 93.

> calls that are required during periods of crises. Indeed, I have yet to meet a central bank official who has not praised BIS as the best gatherings for frank and effective policy exchanges.[163]

Any government would wish that they had the same privilege, i.e., that their own discussions, meetings, and decisions, could be "[h]eld away from the cameras and fanfare of the press," but fortunately for us, our governments and democratic institutions do not enjoy the same privilege as do the Central Banks and their international organizations.

El-Erian and current central banking officials are intelligent and understand finance extremely well. The problem is private banking has been given control over a nation's credit and the bankers use it to further their own enrichment and policy goals. That control has been wrested from the King, parliament, or State to whom the national monetary policy rightfully belongs. Pound, by his digging into monetary history, wished to show the historical reality of the Douglasite contention: historically, things had once been done very differently, and that financial credit rightfully belonged to the nation's citizens and should be used for their benefit. We should not take for granted that elected officials will reflect the best interests of our nation, and yet, even less so, should we expect private individuals in the banking sector to have the best interests of the nation in their foremost plans and policies. Unfortunately, the end chapter, "In Sum," of El-Erian's book argues that it is not the Central Banks that are to blame for financial instability, as in 2007–08, but rather that the problem is that Central Banks do not yet have enough control over policy: "Central banks have a huge stake in all this. Having been forced into being the only game in town, they now find that their destiny is no longer entirely or even mostly theirs to control. The legacy of their exceptional period of hyper policy experimentation is now in the hands of governments and their political bosses."[164] It would help, after a long book, if El-Erian would state concretely what are the further powers, that he wants Central Banks and their international organizations to be given by the nations of the world. Why these powers? Either El-Erian is afraid to state them, or he is afraid that even with these further powers limiting the democratic rights of nations and individuals, the Central Banks will not have a working system.

---

[163] El-Erian, *The Only Game*, 165.
[164] El-Erian, *The Only* Game, 263.

The main word in El-Erian's book, which is repeated constantly is *growth*. This is the mantra of the Central Bank system. No one asks, "what are the limits of growth?" because according to the current economic model, there can be no limit. No one asks, why is this model, that every decade produces some economic collapse somewhere, accepted as the only model? Why does the Bank of England system, created in 1694, still rule not only Britannia, but every nation? With this system of banking, no growth means a recession or worse.

Douglas always stated that the financial system was purely artificial, and that, as it is practiced today, it does not reflect the real economy, defined as the physical economy of goods and services needed by all. This is what leads to, as Douglas stated, *Poverty in the Midst of Plenty*. This distinction between the artificial and the real economy of goods and services is ancient. In a book by Peter Kreeft, St. Thomas Aquinas is quoted (while quoting the Philosopher, i.e., Aristotle) concerning the distinction between natural and artificial wealth. In a footnote, Kreeft comments:

> The simple and obvious distinction between natural wealth and artificial wealth (and between natural and artificial anything, such as sex, death, and birth control) is largely forgotten, in practice, in a capitalistic and industrial society. In a society like ours, which gives such prominence to artificial wealth, greed is a very great spiritual danger. For the desire for artificial wealth is unlimited, but the desire for natural wealth, however greedy, is always limited . . . *There is never enough money, but there is often enough food* [emphasis added]. The good society would foster neither riches (of excess artificial wealth) nor poverty (of needed natural wealth).[165]

Our financial system is one of hyper mass consumerism, where the media's advertising makes us believe, despite having all we need to live and thrive—food, housing, clothing, entertainment—that there is something we still lack. The banks need us to fill the gap between goods and services and the money available in the economy, by making ever-new credit card purchases, contracting new lines of credit, second mortgages, etc.

There exists only in the Douglasite world of economics a sane proposal that the money system should mirror the natural, real economy. Growth ends when the local community's needs for goods and services are fulfilled by the production of needed goods and the issuing of

---

[165] Kreeft, *A Shorter Summa*, 133.

debt-free credit to fill the gap between prices and money already in the system. Trade with other nations is based on what one's nation truly needs as goods and services from overseas, and/or recognizing there may be unique resources we have that other nations need. All further *growth* is artificial and is a waste of human effort, a waste of natural resources, and the destruction of our planet. This is what happens today under a worldwide Central Bank monetary system that does not reflect reality.

In Canto XLVIII, we have a number of isolated luminous details that show the Douglasite influence:

> And if the money be rented
> Who shd pay rent on that money?
> Some fellow who has it on rent day,
> or some bloke who has not?
>
> . . . .
>
> . . . Bismarck
> blamed american civil war on the jews;
> particularly on the Rothschild
> one of whom remarked to Disraeli
> that nations were fools to pay rent for their credit.
> (Canto XLVIII)

In the first passage, Pound asks, "[w]ho shd pay rent on that money?" Pound is emphasizing that private bankers have been given the power to create money for which they charge interest/*rent* to individuals and governments. This ability to provide the money supply should belong to the state, not to private interests for private gain. In the second passage, the reference to Bismarck's placing of blame for the Civil War must be considered in the light of Pound's contention that the war was not fought over slavery, but was in essence a war between southern debtors and New York City bankers. As to the source of this comment from Bismarck, whatever may be Pound's own direct source, the statement goes back to the recollections of a German American, Conrad von Bauditz Siem, first published in 1915. One may doubt the accuracy of his statement, as it was his personal recollections at the age of twelve. We do know that once the war started, the English Rothschilds and the British in general threw their support behind the Southern Confederacy: "The Civil War in America began not long after Nathaniel entered the firm. He was still very young, but it was said that he was one of the few Englishmen who from the beginning was sure of the victory of the Union. But his views were overruled: and the firm invested largely in Confederate bonds, and lost heavily.

This appears to have disgusted them with American finance, which they left severely alone for many years."[166]

It was to Nathaniel's father, Baron Lionel de Rothschild, that the quote "that nations were fools . . . " is traditionally attributed. As for the continental Rothschilds: "Unquestionably, high finance was largely pro-Union. The Paris and Frankfort branches of the House of Rothschild made no secret of their sympathies. The Paris Rothschild expressly offered his services to the Union, while the Frankfort Rothschild complained bitterly to a lady regarding Baron Erlanger's activity on behalf of the Confederates. A few of the Frankfort banks had branches in New York through which they had already participated in placing the first few war loans."[167]

Bismarck was known to be supportive of the North and the Union. Some attribute this partly to how he saw his own role in creating a united Germany by force. The former U. S. congressman, Richard Bartholdt, related, in his memoirs, an 1895 conversation with Bismarck:

> With regard to the American war loan and Bismarck's opinion of the Civil War, . . . "His reference to the many 'good services' on the part of Germany the advantages of which we had enjoyed, encouraged me to ask him about the Union bonds which the German financiers were said to have bought during the Civil War. 'Yes,' he replied, 'that is true. It was reported to me that Lincoln would be unable to prosecute the war unless Germany helped him. Your commissioners themselves related how they had been turned down in London as well as Paris. Now, we wanted to see the Union preserved. The North, it seemed to me, was right morally, but, aside from that, we were heartily in favor of a strong, prosperous, and united country on the other side of the Atlantic.'"[168]

Pound is returning to the Douglasite contention that wars are financed by the money lenders interested not in the ostensible causes or issues of the war, but in making a profit from the misfortune of war. In financing one side or the other, they were gambling on who would win, or hoping that their *side* at least survived the war and would make full repayment with interest. The Rothschilds of London went on as before despite no repayment from the Confederacy, despite perhaps little monetary interest, if any, received. Only a banking institution can make huge loans and survive the losses, always making

---

[166] Roth, *The Magnificent Rothschilds*, 69.
[167] Stolberg-Wernigerode, *Germany and the* United, 57–58.
[168] Stolberg-Wernigerode, *Germany and the United*, 59.

sure their other loans were in more secure hands — even if that means the opposing side in a military conflict.

The remark attributed to Lionel Rothschild is given as proof of the Douglasite contention that nations are indeed fools to pay rent for their own credit, i.e., having to pay interest and for the loan in full, by borrowing what is rightfully the community's. We are speaking, of course, of the historical and natural right of the community to create money, not the private banks. Pound reinforces this contention by a luminous detail in Canto XLIX on the same point: "State by creating riches shd. thereby get into debt? / This is infamy; this is Geryon." In other words, it is *fraud — Geryon* and an infamy that the state by means of creating wealth should go into debt.[169] Here again is the Douglasite contention that the existing financial system does not reflect the economic facts of life. *The present debt system of financial credit does not truly reflect the real credit on which it should be based.*

Canto L returns to the Italy of Pietro Leopoldo and Ferdinando il terzo of the House of Habsburg-Lorraine. The canto begins with a significant quotation from John Adams:

> 'REVOLUTION' said Mr. Adams 'took place in the
> minds of the people
> in the fifteen years before Lexington',
> That wd have been in Peter Leopold's
> time
> . . . .
> debt when the Medici took the throne was 5 million
> and when they left was fourteen
> and its interest ate up all the best income
> . . . .
> the arts gone to hell by 1750
> and Leopoldo cut down the taxes
> found there was *'Un' abbondanza che affamava'*
> says Zobi
> Leopold cut down the debt interest
> . . . .
> and they brought in Mr. Locke's
> essay on interest
> . . . .
> and Leopoldo meant to cut off two thirds of state debt,
> to abolish it
> (Canto L)

[169] Pound follows his teacher Dante in that Geryon, i.e., *fraud*, and usury should be found together. See: Ravenscroft, "Usury in the Inferno," 110.

The first passage from John Adams is noteworthy because it reiterates Pound's contention that the cause of the American Revolution was not "taxation without representation" or the Stamp Act, but the forbidding of the colonies to issue their own debt-free paper money. Pound bases his contention on the writings of John Adams, Benjamin Franklin, Thomas Jefferson, and others. It is significant that John Adams should claim that revolution took place in the minds of the people in the fifteen years before Lexington, i.e., fifteen years before 1776. In the letter that Pound cites from Adams and his statement "fifteen years before" we read the following concerning the writs of assistance question of 1760 (i.e., "fifteen years before" the 1775 Battle of Lexington) that allowed the British to search homes and vessels without a search warrant or permission and the legal argument from February 1761:

> Mr. Otis displayed So comprehensive a Knowledge of the Subject, Shewed not only the Illegality of the Writt; its insidious and mischievous tendency; but he laid open the Views and designs of Great Britain of in taxing Us; of destroying our Charters and assuming as the Powers of our Government, legislative Executive, and Judicial, external and internal civil and ecclesiastical, temporal and Spiritual; and all this was performed with Such a profusion of Learning, Such convincing Argument, and Such a torrent of Sublime and pathetic Eloquence; that a great Crowd of Spectators and Auditors went away absolutely electrified."[170]

In 1751, the British Parliament had passed an act forbidding "the issue of paper money in the New England colonies except for certain stated objects."[171] This was later followed by the Currency Act of 1764 that forbade the use of this paper money issued by state banks being used as legal tender for private or public debts. C. H. Douglas always insisted that the state should be the lender, not the borrower of money, but British law was enforcing the Bank of England debt system on the American colonies.

The Colony of Pennsylvania issued its own paper currency and loaned it out at a five percent interest. Benjamin Franklin supported this and stated: "There is a certain proportionate quantity of money requisite to carry on trade of a country freely and currently; more than which would be of no advantage in trade, and less if much

---

[170] "From John Adams to Jedidiah."

[171] Channing, *A History*, 501.

less, exceedingly detrimental to it."[172] As with Pound and Douglas, Franklin recognized that there had to be a balance between currency and the goods and services offered, for there to be a healthy thriving economy. This system brought about unprecedented prosperity in Pennsylvania, and Franklin, from at least 1729, would begin his fight to support the issuing of state currency and local control of the same based not on gold and silver, but the natural bounty of the land.[173]

The reference to the heavy interest-bearing debt of fourteen million when the Medici left the throne of Tuscany is noteworthy. The later Medici Dukes of Tuscany lacked the monetary-economic knowledge possessed by Cosimo, the first Duke of Tuscany. When Pietro Leopoldo of the House of Habsburg-Lorraine came to the throne of Tuscany, he was faced with the unhappy situation described by Pound. Leopoldo's solution was to cut down the debt interest and he then planned to cut off two-thirds of the state debt and abolish it. However, these far-sighted Leopoldine reforms were prevented by Leopoldo being sent off to Vienna to be Emperor.

Pound, in Canto L, continues with the monetary-economic situation in Tuscany c. 1800:

> a.d. 1800
>   interest at 24 to the hundred
> and as they say 'commerce languished'
>
> . . . .
>
> And Ferdinando Habsburg (but of the House of Lorraine)
> which is the true name of the clean part of that family
> got back a state free of debt
>   coffers empty
> but the state without debt
> England and Austria were for despots with commerce
> considered
>
> . . . .
>
> and split up Poland in their soul was usura
> and in their hand bloody oppression
>
> . . . .
>
> S . . t on the throne of England, s . . t on the Austrian sofa
> In their soul was usura and in their minds darkness
> and blankness, greased fat were four Georges
>
> . . . .
>
> In their soul was usura and in their hearts cowardice
> In their minds was stink and corruption

---

[172] Channing, *A History*, 503.

[173] Grubb, "Benjamin Franklin," 5–6.

Two sores ran together,
and hell pissed up Metternich

(Canto L)

In the first passage above, Pound points out that in Tuscany, in 1800, the interest rate charged on money was twenty-four percent. Naturally, commerce in the Grand Duchy of Tuscany languished. When Ferdinando III, the son of Pietro Leopoldo, came to the throne of Tuscany, the treasury was empty but there was no state debt. Pound charges England and Austria with conspiring in the promotion of usury. He shows how the hand of oppression fell on Tuscany. C. H. Douglas's affirmation that the veracity of his critique of and solution for the monetary-economic problems of the world could be proved from history is what Pound puts forth in *The Cantos*. Pound's attempt to illustrate the epic struggle against usury from history is difficult to explain except in terms of the Douglasite influence. This affirmation of Douglas is certainly a factor in determining Pound's choice of luminous details:

and that son of a dog, Rospigliosi,
came into Tuscany to make serfs of old Tuscans.

. . . .

'Leave the Duke, Go for gold!'

(Canto L)

Cosimo I de' Medici, had made Tuscany prosperous and ended serfdom. Concerning Rospigliosi, Terrell draws our attention to the writings of Antonio Zobi, for Pound's reference.[174] Rospigliosi would administer Tuscany temporarily for 5 months, but would issue a proclamation that Zobi relates writing in Italian: [N]el quale si legge l'enorme sconcezza, che il *Granducato era patrimonio di stranieri signori*, come se gli stati possano esser un proprio *allodio*, e gli abitanti *servi della gleba*.[175]

For the passage that follows, Terrell draws our attention to Hollis.[176] Christopher Hollis is commenting on the so-called *Great Reform Act* of 1832. Hollis comments that the act, created by the Whigs, "only gave votes to some one in twenty-two of the population. What it did was to register the transfer of political power from the old rich

[174] Terrell, *A Companion*, Vol. I, 195.
[175] Zobi, *Storia Civile*, Vol IV, 24. "[O]ne can read [in the proclamation] the enormous indecency that *the Grand Duchy was the patrimony of foreign lords*, as if nations could be one's own *allotment*, and the inhabitants *serfs*."
[176] Terrell, *A Companion*, Vol. I, 195.

to the new rich . . . it was the Napoleonic Wars and their debt which in reality snatched the power out of the hands of the old landed classes."[177] What follows is where we see Pound's allusion "Leave the Duke, Go for gold!":

> The story of the passage of the Act was perhaps mainly interesting in the light which it threw upon the true virtue of the double-money system in the eyes of its masters. Its virtue was not that it gave the country a stable monetary system but, on the contrary, that it put it within the power of a few determined men to plunge the country into chaos whenever they wanted to. There was after Grey's first resignation a question of the Duke of Wellington forming a Tory Government. The word went out among the reformers, "To stop the Duke, go for gold," and before the threat of a run on the banks the Tory attempt collapsed and the Whigs returned to power.
>
> It would be foolish, in reaction against the drab philistinism of the middle-class Victorian, to indulge in sentimental regrets over the old landed classes who ruled England from 1688 until the Napoleonic Wars. They had a long run for their money, and on the whole they used it without scruple. Yet it was in no sort of way to the advantage of the poor, when power passed out of their hands into that of the masters of the financial system.[178]

Towards the end of the Canto, Pound presents Napoleon Bonaparte as the last hope of the anti-usury forces in the early 19th century, that century which Pound calls *the century of usury*:

> 'From the brigantine Incostante'
> for a hundred days against hell belch
> Hope spat from March into June
> Ney out of his saddle
> . . . .
> Hope
> spat from Cannes, March, into Flanders.
> 'Not'
> said Napoleon 'because of that league of lice
> but for opposing the Zeitgeist! That was my ruin,
> That I ran against my own time, turning backward'
> OBIT, aetatis 57, five hundred years after D. Alighieri.
> (Canto L)

[177] Hollis, *The Two Nations*, 106.
[178] Hollis, *The Two Nations*, 106–7.

Napoleon escaped from the isle of Elba on the vessel *Incostante* in 1815. For one hundred days he fought again, not because he opposed the *League* but because he opposed the *Zeitgeist* of his age, i.e., the enthroning of private banking interests. The French General Ney at an inopportune time was thrown from his saddle at Waterloo, and Napoleon died in 1821 age 57 (Dante Alighieri died in 1321). Napoleon, like Douglas, understood that the King must be *boss of the coinage*, not a group of private money manipulators.

Canto LI, which closes the fifth decade of cantos, is a repetition and emphasis of points made in Canto XLV, the great usury canto. The first part of the canto is almost a direct repetition of Canto XLV. This is quite fitting because Canto LI concludes the *Inferno* of *The Cantos*. It is the conclusion of what Pound calls his *first case* against usury, but it is by no means his last case. Pound is here concluding the first phase of his evidence against usury and its twin Geryon—fraud:

> With usury has no man a good house
> made of stone, no paradise on his church wall
>
> . . . .
>
> Usury is against Nature's increase.
> Whores for Eleusis;
> Under usury no stone is cut smooth
> Peasant has no gain from his sheep herd
>
> . . . .
>
> sang Geryone; I am the help of the aged;
> I pay men to talk peace;
> Mistress of many tongues; merchant of chalcedony
> I am Geryon twin with usura,
>
> (Canto LI)

Most of the lines above have already been set down in Canto XLV. Usury prevents the peasant from profiting from his sheep herd. The lines referring to Geryon (fraud), usury's twin, are of interest. Geryon is the help of the aged because *it weds age with youth*. Geryon is behind the false peace movements, which talk peace without condemning usury, the main cause of war. Geryon masters many tongues in its fraudulent pursuits. The reference to Geryon as the merchant of chalcedony may be because ancient Chalcedon was in Bithynia. In Canto XLVIII, Pound had informed us that twelve percent interest was charged in Bithynia, while only six percent was charged in Rome. This ends the *Inferno* and *first case* against usury.

SUMMARY

Pound has often emphasized that *The Cantos* is an epic. He is convinced that since an epic is a tale of the tribe, it must contain history, and he regards history without economics as meaningless.

In *The Cantos* Pound delves deeply into history and particularly monetary-economic history to support his contention that Douglasism is part of a thought-heritage. Pound's method of historiography is that of the luminous detail and purposeful focus rather than the current method of *multitudinous detail*. The method of luminous detail and purposeful focus can also be described as *ideogrammic* in the manner of the Chinese ideogram, i.e., a composite character symbolizing an idea.

Pound uses the word *periplum* in several places in *The Cantos*. Pound's periplum may be understood as his journey among the islands of personal and intellectual experience. Pound seeks to find the permanent and enduring in the history of civilization, to probe history in search of answers to the problems of his own time, and to determine the *right thinkers* in history whose actions are benevolently directed. Certainly, C. H. Douglas has a remarkably high place in Pound's list of *right thinkers*.

The Cantos reflect the years of *digging down into history* by Pound to corroborate a thesis developed in Douglas's Social Credit theory. The thesis may be broadly stated as follows: "Where in history one finds individual responsibility, beneficent government in control of its own currency, and non-centralization of credit and financial power in the hands of a small group of bankers and financiers, there one finds also economic justice (equitable purchasing power among the whole people), a proper relationship between the ruler and the ruled, and above all flourishing art."[179]

In Cantos V and VII–XI, the *Malatesta Cantos*, Pound gives us a picture of the chaos that results as each of the warring factions in Quattrocento Italy attempts to create a centralization of power, i.e., credit and financial control, in its own state and thus exercise control over the others. Sigismundo Malatesta, Lord of Rimini, sees that the centre of the trouble then, as now, is due to economic chaos and therefore he is made to suffer.

In *The Cantos* as well as in his prose writings, Pound maintains that *usury* and *sodomy* are similar sins in that they are both sins *Contra Naturam*—against the plenitude of nature's abundance. Pound is

---

[179] Landini, "A Guide," 87.

convinced that the Catholic Church got on the wrong track when it softened its stand on usury. The Church's failure to maintain its uncompromising stand on usury, says Pound, has been one of the main causes of the world's woes. Pound, following Douglas, is convinced that the so-called Protestant Reformation was responsible for the acceptance of usury in Christian society. Pound is of the opinion that the Catholic Church softened its strict canonist stand on usury in the post reformation period to accommodate itself to Calvinism, which had come to dominate the commercial world.

In *Cantos* XIV and XV, the *Hell Cantos*, Pound, like Douglas, emphasizes the control of politics and politicians by Finance. He also stresses the financial control of the press and of publicity. Pound is also convinced that Christianity under the influence primarily of Calvinism has focused its attention on condemning sins of impurity rather than sins of usury. Pound condemns to hell all those who interfere with the distribution of nature's abundance and who prevent the dissemination of economic knowledge which could lead to this distribution.

In Canto XVIII, the Geryon or Fraud canto, Pound points out that as far back as the 13th century, Kublai Khan was issuing his own paper money without the aid of bankers. Pound sees this Kublai Khan luminous detail as offering proof of the fundamental Douglasite precept that the state has credit and need not borrow its own credit. Further along in Canto XVIII, Pound reiterates the Douglasite postulate that wars are caused because of the machinations of the Money Power. Pound, like Douglas, sees war as the highest form of sabotage, i.e., the willful destruction of goods to bring about the artificial scarcity of goods and services in line with a chronically and artificially scarce supply of purchasing power.

By means of his prologue to Canto XXXVIII, Pound suggests that Dante's *falseggiando la moneta—falsifying money*, probably refers to usury and usurer's practices, particularly the lending of bankers promises-to-pay as if they were legal tender. In Canto XXXVIII, Pound paraphrases C. H. Douglas's famous A & B theorem. The A+B theorem is Douglas's illustration of the chronic artificial shortage of purchasing power under the present monetary system. Pound intimates that the cause of wars is to be found in this chronic artificial shortage. Pound sees the philosophy and the policy of Social Credit as the only realistic program for true world peace.

In Canto XL, Pound seeks to show that in the United States of Jefferson's day and in the Venice of 1361 there was an awareness that public credit belongs to the people and that currency is *OF* the nation. Pound maintains that if the American nation will assert its sovereignty in monetary matters, as provided for by its constitution, exploiters like J. P. Morgan would be rendered impotent.

In Canto XLV, one of the famous Usury Cantos, Pound indicts usury on moral and aesthetic grounds as well as on monetary-economic grounds. Usury causes inadequate and ugly housing. It cuts man off from both good religious and profane art. It is the direct cause of sterility in the arts, the crafts, in economic life, and religious life. Usury interferes with the distribution of goods, it prevents rightful profit, and it has a corrosive and fatal effect on the crafts. Usury is morally evil because it frustrates nature's plenitude (*frustra naturae*).

In Canto XLVI Pound points out that when the bank creates credit from nothing and charges interest for that credit, this is hyper-usury, or super-usury. He maintains that the true cause of the American Revolution was the suppression of state-issued, debt-free paper money in Pennsylvania in 1750. The "grease spot" of usury, says Pound, has caused the fall of ten empires, murder, starvation, bloodshed and seventy-four red revolutions.

Pound regards the Protestant Reformation as the event that brought on the world-wide triumph of usury. He regards the Reformation as having its origin not in theological issues but in monetary-economic issues, i.e., the desire of a pro-usury conspiracy to topple the Church, which had always been an obstacle to the usurer.

Towards the end of Canto L, Pound presents Napoleon Bonaparte as the last hope of the anti-usury forces in the early 19th century, that century which Pound calls *the century of usury*. Napoleon, like C. H. Douglas, understood that the King (the sovereign public authority) must be *boss of the coinage*, not a group of private money manipulators.

CHAPTER IV
Cantos LII–LXXXIV

I) THE CHINESE CANTOS LII–LXI

Canto LII begins with an allusion to the Monte dei Paschi of Siena and its recognition of the true base of credit in the *abundance of nature and the will of the people*:

> And I have told you of how things were under Duke
>   Leopold in Siena
>   And of the true base of credit, that is
>   the abundance of nature
> with the whole folk behind it.
> 'Goods that are needed' said Schacht (anno seidici)
> commerciabili beni, deliverable things that are wanted.
>   neschek is against this, the serpent
> And Vivante was there in his paradise, the mild air
>   the fields rolling eastward, and the tower half ruin'd
> with a peasant complaining that her son was taken to war
> and he said 'plutocracies were less violent'.
>   (Canto LII)

Pound quotes Hjalmar Schacht, German Minister of Finance, in a luminous detail that stresses the distribution and consumption of goods, i.e., *deliverable things that are wanted.* Pound stresses that *neschek,* the Hebraic Old Testament term for usury, stands between the consumer and production. Pound points out that the poor Jews do not benefit by the system of usury but that they too suffer the ravages of usury just as do the poor Gentiles: "[P]oor yitts paying for — paying for a few big jews' vendetta on goyim."[1] This is important to bear in mind when considering the charges of antisemitism often levelled at Pound. Douglas states that no race is the enemy of any nation, but anyone from any race who would oppose changing the economic system is the enemy: "If he can manage to grasp the fact that the enemies of this and every country are not Frenchmen or

---

[1] Canto LII. Editor's note: When Lorne Reznowski wrote this, circa 1967, *The Cantos* edition did not include all of Canto LII, and showed instead only black lines. It was not until the 1986 edition that the references to *Stinkschuld*, "Pound's pejorative alteration of the Rothschild family name" were included: "Canto LII, Calendar of Composition," 2. Here and in what follows, we have kept it as the text appeared in the 1960s.

Italians or Americans, not dukes, nor employers, or even rich men *per se*, but those people, wherever they may be domiciled and whether Jew or Gentile, who are determined to maintain a system which would destroy all initiative not sanctioned by themselves."[2]

Pound condemns the perverted religion of pecuniolatry, i.e., the worship of money as if it were a thing of value in itself, which he claims has replaced Christianity in the field of economic ethics and morality. He condemns the contemporary Christian Church for having abandoned its concern with economic ethics and morality. He points to the medieval canonists, and to theologians like St. Ambrose as examples for the contemporary Church to follow in this regard. Although Canto LII is the first of the Chinese Cantos, it continues at first to enlarge on the themes mentioned above. Pound also briefly mentions John Adams and quotes his famous statement regarding ignorance of coin, credit, and the circulation of money. John Adams, of course, will be the central figure in the Adams Cantos which follow the Chinese Cantos:

> I think wrote Miss Bell to her mama
> that when not against the interests of Empire
> we shd/ keep our pledges to Arabs.
> Thus we lived on through sanctions, through Stalin
> Litvinof, gold brokers made profit
> rocked the exchange against gold
> Before which entrefaites remarked Johnnie Adams (the elder)
> IGNORANCE, sheer ignorance ov the natr ov money
> sheer ignorance of credit and circulation.
> Remarked Ben: better keep out the jews
> or yr / grand children will curse you
> jews, real jews, chazims, and *neschek*
> also super-neschek or the international racket
>
> governments full of their gun-swine, bankbuzzards, poppinjays.
> Did commit, that he did in the Kingdom of Italy . . .
> of the two usuries, the lesser is now put down.
> that he did in the Kingdom of Britain etc/
>
> (Canto LII)

---

[2] Douglas, *Warning Democracy*, 51. Concerning accusations of anti-semitism against C. H. Douglas, see: Munson, *Aladdin's Lamp*.

The reference to the rigging of the foreign exchange market by the speculators in gold echoes the many statements made by C. H. Douglas on the *gold racket*.[3] Long before C. H. Douglas, John Adams had written that the greatest evil in the young Republic, from which all other evils stemmed, was the sheer ignorance of the people with regard to the nature of credit, coin, and the circulation of money. Pound also quotes Ben Franklin who is supposed to have warned against allowing the Jews into the new republic. Franklin's fears were said to be based on his strong opposition to usury. Chazims (Khazars) are a Turko-Mongol people, and some Khazars may have converted to Judaism as early as the eighth century. They inhabited the area between the Black and Caspian Seas.[4] Super-neschek is another way of saying hyper-usura or super usury. Pound calls this the *international racket* whereby governments have come to be dominated by munition makers—gun-swine, usurers—bankbuzzards, and subservient politicians—poppinjays.

The great heroes of the Chinese Cantos are Kung Fu-Tzu—Confucius and his disciple Mang-Tze—Mencius. Pound has given us the essence of the Confucian ethic in his prose writing. Here we can clearly see the link between Pound's economic beliefs and the Confucian ethic:

> The doctrine of Confucius is:
> That you bring order into your surroundings by bringing it first into yourself; by knowing the motives of your acts.
> That you can bring about a better world government by amelioration of the *internal* government of your nation.
> That private gain is not prosperity, but that the treasure of a nation is its equity.
> That hoarding is not prosperity and that people should employ their resources.
> One should respect intelligence, "the luminous principle of reason," the faculties of others, one should look to a constant renovation.
> "Make it new, make it new as the young grass shoot." . . . .
> "The humane ruler acquires respect by his spending, the inhumane, disrespect, by his taking."[5]

---

[3] Cf. C. H. Douglas in *Brief for the Prosecution*, 49: "the quantity of gold in existence neither varied in any ratio to the possibilities of production nor the necessities of consumption."

[4] Zeidan, "Khazar, people," *Encyclopaedia Brittanica*.

[5] Pound, *Jefferson and/or Mussolini*, 112–13.

Pound's application of the Confucian ethic to the question of world government is quite in keeping with Douglas's basic approach to the problem. Pound, like Douglas, condemned the League of Nations, which claimed to seek *better world government* while the individual nations failed to ameliorate their *internal government* at home.[6] For Ezra Pound, as for Douglas, the amelioration of the internal governments of nations is to be accomplished by their abolishing the debt-money system in favour of the debt-free money system of Social Credit.[7] For Pound and Douglas, this is the only economic foundation upon which world peace can be achieved, and those who seek it in any other way labour in vain. It must also be borne in mind that monetary reform was but one aspect of Douglas's philosophy. Monetary reform for Douglas was the practical application of a policy that was based on a Christian philosophy: the recognition of the dignity and liberty of the individual. In other words, monetary reform for Douglas is the practical means of achieving individual economic freedom and dignity as opposed to the encroachment of a collectivist society on the dignity and liberty of the individual, as in socialism, with its theory of the Supreme State.

In Canto LII, Pound voices his disgust with the way the Catholic Church has abandoned her prerogative to speak clearly on the ethics

---

[6] Cf. Douglas, Approach, 20:

> "The idea of the League of Nations, of course, on the face of it is attractive and is meant to sound attractive. Had we got a reformed financial system, one which did not force exports, one which did not really place everything under the control of finance, one which did not produce frustrations caused by the working of financial institutions: if these things were not so—if, I repeat, we had a reformed financial system—the right kind of internationalism would be fairly sound and proper. But not first, not before the financial system is rectified. The only safeguard against a world governed by international finance is nationalism.
>
> Whatever may be said about the inception of the League of Nations—and some very queer things are being said—there is no doubt whatever that it has been the sport of international financiers from its very beginnings; and while it may be thought the duty of the League of Nations to reform the financial system. I do not think that the League of Nations has either the power or, so far, as it is at present concerned, the desire to do so; but rather so to strengthen itself that it may become a world-government of Finance . . ."

[7] Editor's note: Douglas Social Credit would not eliminate debt-money entirely. Producer credit would be loaned to businesses, etc., as this is a necessary discipline to ensure that only those things that the community wants are actually being produced (if the loan can be paid back under a balanced financial system it would be the key indication that the good or service is actually wanted). What Douglas Social Credit would do would be to ensure that, through the issuance of sufficient supplementary debt-free consumer credits, all production costs and debts can be met as they are presented to the consumer for final liquidation.

and morality of monetary matters and fails to condemn usury as she once did:

> the groggy church is gone toothless
> No longer holds against *neschek*
> the fat has covered their croziers
> The high fans and the mitre mean nothing
> Once only in Burgos, once in Cortona
> was the song firm and well given
> old buffers keeping the stiffness,
> Gregory damned, always was damned, obscurantist.
> (Canto LII)

The reference to the *groggy church* as having gone toothless is interesting in the light of Pound's characterization of Western Civilization as *an old bitch gone bad in the teeth.*[8] The Church no longer speaks out against usury. Monetary-economics is no longer considered a part of moral theology, i.e., as basically involving morality and distributive justice. The powerful image of the fat covering the croziers of the bishops refers to Pound's description of the *Whore of Babylon* as having gone over completely to usury in order to partake of the *sweetmeats at the banquet table.*[9]

The reference to Burgos in Spain, and Cortona in Italy, as places where *once only* the anti-usury stand of the Church was revived, is intriguing. This alludes to the respective bishops of these two sees speaking out loudly and clearly on this issue in modern times, *old buffers keeping the stiffness.* The allusion to Pope Gregory as damned and as an obscurantist may be due to Pound's belief that one of the Gregories compromised with usury. If St. Ambrose and Antoninus Pius are in the Poundian Canon of Saints, Pope Gregory is certainly not.[10] It is obvious that Pound's Douglasite anti-usury criterion

---

8 See Part V, from the long poem "Hugh Selwyn Mauberly." Pound, *Early Poems*, 50.

9 Landini, "A Guide," 20.

10 Besides Pope Gregory I, it is possible this refers to Pope Gregory IX. In Heinrich Denzinger's well-known compendium of official Church pronouncements, there is one referring to usury by Gregory IX, his letter *Naviganti vel*: "Whoever lends a sum of money to someone going to market by sea or by land, and—because he assumes a risk for himself—intends to receive something beyond the capital, should *[not?]* be considered a usurer" (Denzinger, *Compendium*, 275). In a letter, Pound writes: "Only twice in my life have I heard church music achieve true intensity: once in Burgos, Spain, and again, in Cortona, Italy. But it would take too long to explain further what I mean in technical terms. [. . .] Religion is not only depression, sorrow and suffering, it is eternal energy; sometimes even exuberance of energy. This quality is to be found in music, particularly great music, more than in any other art" (Pound, *Ezra Pound and Music*, 361).

plays a preponderant role in the Poundian process of canonization.

It is interesting that while Pound had been critical of the institutional Catholic Church, he also spoke of her contribution to culture: "there is more civilization lying around unused in the crannies, zenanas, interstices of that dusty and baroque fabric than in all other institutions of the Occident."[11]

Towards the end of Canto LII, after Pound has set the canto in the reign of the Emperor Ming T'ang, he returns to his criterion for a good ruler:

> Call things by the names. Good sovereign by distribution
> Evil king is known by his imposts.
> Begin where you are said Lord Palmerston
>   began draining swamps in Sligo
> Fought smoke nuisance in London. Dredged harbour in Sligo.
>   (Canto LII)

Pound once again calls for clarity in language and terminology, *call things by their names*. The good ruler is known by his distribution of goods and services. The evil sovereign is known by his taxes. This echoes the earlier passage in which Pound states: "The humane ruler acquires respect by his spending, the inhumane, disrespect, by his taking."[12] Pound quotes Lord Palmerston to the effect that one must begin where he is. Palmerston began by draining swamps and dredging the harbour in Sligo, Ireland, and fighting the smoke nuisance

---

Taking a possible musical context into account, as above, we may assume that likewise, Pound refers to Pope Gregory I (540–604) due to Gregory's connection to Gregorian Chant, and not a connection to usury. Pound found enough in Gibbon, whom he admired as a writer, to accuse Pope Gregory of being an *obscurantist*, one who had obscured the past glory of Rome by destroying its historical records:

> It is commonly believed that Pope Gregory the First attacked the temples and mutilated the statues of the city; that, by the command of the Barbarian, [i.e., the Christians] the Palatine library was reduced to ashes; and that the history of Livy was the peculiar mark of his absurd and mischievous fanaticism. The writings of Gregory himself reveal his implacable aversion to the monuments of classic genius; and he points his severest censure against the profane learning of a bishop who taught the art of grammar, studied the Latin poets, and pronounced, with the same voice, the praises of Jupiter and those of Christ. Gibbon, *The History*, Vol. VIII, 40.

Whether the above is a reference to music or usury, we need to remember that, for Pound, wherever the corrosive influence of usury did not exist historically, good art (music) flourishes. This may be why he inserts a reference to art—music among many monetary allusions.

[11] Pound, *Guide to Kulchur*, 77.

[12] Pound, *Jefferson and/or Mussolini*, 113.

in London, England. Thus, Canto LII ends with the image of Lord Palmerston as a responsible and ethical statesman who tried to improve the lives of others.

Regarding the influence of C. H. Douglas on the Chinese Cantos and on the Adams Cantos, it would be well to bear in mind the scholastic dictum, *whatever is received is received according to the capacity of the receiver—Quidquid recipitur ad modum recipientis recipitur.* Ezra Pound met C. H. Douglas in 1918 and was introduced to the policy and philosophy of Social Credit. Pound tells us that he became converted to Douglasism at this time. All through the twenties, Pound delved deeply into monetary economics, monetary history, and history, in order to verify the validity of the Douglasite position.

The Chinese Cantos and the Adams Cantos were both written after 1918, i.e., when Pound was already converted to Social Credit. Therefore, in his delving into Chinese History and into American History, Pound was primarily concerned with those events which seemed to him to prove the validity of Douglasism as a thought heritage. It is in this sense that one can speak of the influence of Douglas on the Chinese Cantos and the Adams Cantos.

The Chinese Cantos consist of ten cantos, LII–LXI, "of Chinese history in 'luminous detail,' covering the period from the Age of the Five Rulers (2953–220 BC), through several dynasties and about a century and & half of the Ch'eng to 1735."[13] Pound's source for the Chinese Cantos is the thirteen-volume, *Histoire Générale de la Chine*, translated from Chinese by the 18th century Jesuit, Father De Mailla. Pound took his luminous *details* for the Chinese Cantos exclusively from this monumental work. Pound tells us that: "The dynasties of Han, Tang, Sung, Ming, rose on the Confucian idea; it is inscribed in the lives of great emperors, Tai Tsong, Kao Tseu, Hong Vou, another Tai Tsong, and Kang Hi. When the idea [Confucian] was not held to, decadence supervened."[14]

In Canto LIII Pound moves rapidly through ancient Chinese history using the method of luminous detail. He briefly records the monetary-economic achievements and shortcomings of scores of ancient rulers:

money was in days of Hoang Ti.

. . . .

let his men pay tithes in kind.

. . . .

[13] Landini, *A Guide*, 164.

[14] *Confucius: The Great Digest*, 188.

For years no waters came, no rain fell
for the Emperor Tching Tang
grain scarce, prices rising
so that in 1760 Tching Tang opened the copper mine (ante
Christum)
made discs with square holes in their middles
and gave these to the people
wherewith they might buy grain
where there was grain
The silos were emptied
7 years of sterility
(Canto LIII)

Money was in existence in the days of Emperor Hoang Ti. The Emperor Yu allowed tithes to be paid in kind not in money. This event can be linked with Pound's fundamental distinction of a tithe from a tax as seen in Chapter II. Pound approves of the tithe because it is payable in existing goods, i.e., one-tenth or one-ninth of goods existing. A tax payable only in money most often forces people to pay in that medium which they do not possess or possess in an insufficient amount. This preoccupation of Pound's with the problem of taxation can be traced back to C. H. Douglas who advised Pound "to concentrate on the subject of taxation as a form of modern highway robbery combined with iniquitous interference with the freedom of the individual." This advice has been mentioned in Chapter II in discussing Pound's essay "Destruction by Taxation."

The Emperor Tching Tang in 1766 BC, faced with a shortage of grain and rising prices, issued his own statal copper currency to the people in order to distribute and aid in the consumption of that grain which did exist. In other words, there was a certain amount of grain stored in the silos, but the people could not buy it because of a shortage of currency and the unaffordable prices. Tang issued his statal copper currency to remedy this situation: "Tching Tang: Ch'eng T'ang, who reigned 1766–1753 BC, founded the Shang dynasty (1766–1122). He was a model king who subordinated every passion and feeling to the good of his people. In time of drought he coined money so the people could buy grain, but there was no grain to buy until his sacrifices were accepted by Heaven and rain fell. On his washbasin he inscribed the admonition, 'Make it new'."[15] Tang did not borrow or rent this new issue of currency from the usurers and bankers, but exercised his sovereign prerogative and

[15] Terrell, *A Companion*, Vol. I, 205.

issued this currency debt-free to the starving people of China in 1766 BC. This state-issued, debt-free dividend paid to the consumer differs in no way in principle from the dividend advocated by C. H. Douglas. One begins to understand Pound's preoccupation with Chinese history and the Economic Dialogues of Confucius. As a result of this state-issued debt-free copper currency, the starving people were able to consume what was stored in the silos in this time of famine.

In the modern economy, the recurring need for governments to stimulate or *prime* the economy, by, for example, the US Treasury borrowing money from the Federal Reserve, all point to the already existing reality of a need for a universal dividend. This money is newly created as a debt, when it could likewise have been created, as in the Emperor Tching Tang example, as a credit and debt-free, given as a dividend to citizens as well as used for actual government spending needs. As in Pound's Tching Tang story, copper coinage was created to make it possible to buy the grain available. Likewise, creation of debt-free money has a limit, its limit is the gap between goods and services and money already existing in the economy. More than this would be inflationary. All government borrowing from a Central Bank is bank creation of new money as a debt. The Central Bank *creates this new money* in the very act of making a loan. Repayment of the loan *destroys the money*. Money is also created by private banks; it is not *their* money, but newly created. But the right to create money belongs to the community, through its government, i.e., the Royal prerogative of money creation, which has been forfeited to private interests.

In the imprecise language of economists, they call this new money *printed*, but this money is not *printed* but it is mere fountain pen money, or blips created on a computer, transferring newly created money to the US Treasury, which becomes part of the national debt. Modern day economists defend this separation: "The US Treasury borrows while the Federal Reserve prints money. The separation of these two institutions is designed to prevent the government from using the money printer to pay for government spending and the inflationary consequences that come with it."[16] Pound contends this violates the US Constitution and presents in *The Cantos* the American *paideuma*—this historical tradition that is opposed to the Hamiltonian and Bank of England practice. The Federal Reserve

---

16 Savidge, "Why Does?"

system creates money in the very act of making a loan, it does not *print* money as Savidge states.[17] Savidge must believe US citizens are mere children who cannot exercise their constitutional rights responsibly and therefore must give this right to responsible adults, the unelected and unappointed private money lenders: "The Congress shall have Power . . . To coin Money, regulate the Value thereof, and of foreign Coin, and fix the Standard of Weights and Measures."[18]

In Canto LIII, by the method of luminous detail, Pound gives examples of various Chinese emperors who fulfilled their duty as *distributors of the abundance of nature*:

Saith Tcheou Kong:

. . . .

'A good governor is as wind over grass
A good ruler keeps down taxes.'
Tching-ouang kept lynx eye on bureaucrats
lynx eye on the currency
weight of the tchu was one 24th of an ounce
or one hundred grains of millet
cloth bolt and silk bolt
to be two feet two inches by four tchang (one Tchang equals
four feet)
reigned till 1079
and was peace for the rest of his reign.

. . . .

Honour to Chao-Kong the surveyor.
Let his name last 3000 years
Gave each man land for his labour
not by plough-land alone
But for keeping of silk-worms
Reforested the mulberry groves
Set periodical markets
Exchange brought abundance, the prisons were empty.
'Yao and Chun have returned'
sang the farmers
'Peace and abundance bring virtue.' I am
'pro-Tcheou' said Confucius five centuries later.
With his mind on this age.

. . . .

---

17 Physical money, US coinage and paper money, are *minted* by the US government and *paid* for by the US Federal Reserve. Physical money only enters the economy in place of *ex nihilo (out of nothing)* created money when requested by a financial institution. See: "How much does it cost." *The Federal Reserve.*

18 *The Constitution*, art. 1, sec 8, cl. 5.

Li WANG avid of silver, to whom a memorial
'A Prince who wd/ fulfill obligation, takes caution
à ce que l'argent circule
that cash move amongst the people.
'Glory of HEOU-TSIE is clouded
Deathless his honour that saw his folk using their substance.
The end of your house is upon us.'
b.c. 860 Youi-leang-fou, in memorial.
Said Chao-kong: Talk of the people
is like the hills and the streams
Thence comes our abundance.
To be Lord to the four seas of China
a man must let men make verses
he must let people play comedies
and historians write down the facts
he must let the poor speak evil of taxes.

. . . .

HAN founded the town of Yuei
and taught men to sow the five grains

. . . .

And King Wang thought to vary the currency
μεταθεμένων τε τῶν χρωμένων
against council's opinion,
and to gain by this wangling.

. . . .

Min Kong's line was six centuries lasting
and there were 84 princes
Swine think of extending borders
Decent rulers of internal order

. . . .

Usurpations, jealousies, taxes
Greed, murder, jealousies, taxes and douanes

. . . .

Sou-tsin, armament racket, war propaganda.

. . . .

brain work. POLLON IDEN

. . . .

Yo-Y reduced corvées and taxes.
(Canto LIII)

The reference, in the first passage, to a good ruler being one who keeps down taxes, is completely in harmony with Pound's position. In the "Destruction by Taxation" section of Chapter II, a letter of C. H. Douglas to Pound has been quoted, in which Pound was advised to investigate the modern institution of taxation that Douglas compared to highway robbery. The reference to the Emperor Tching-Ouang keeping a *lynx eye* on the bureaucracy is completely in keeping with Pound's philosophy. Pound had authored an essay against bureaucracy entitled "Bureaucracy, The Flail of Civilization." The point of view expressed in this essay is completely in harmony with C. H. Douglas's hostility to the centralization of power in the hands of an all-powerful bureaucracy.

The reference to the Emperor Tching-Ouang keeping a *lynx eye* on the currency is also completely in harmony with the Douglasite contention that under a monarchy the currency belongs to the king and is part of the royal prerogative. The reference to Chao-Kong the surveyor, who gave each man land for his labour, set periodical markets, and facilitated the exchange of goods, is also in keeping with Douglasite philosophy and policy. The maximum distribution of the benefits of natural resources among the people is both explicit and implicit in Douglas's policy. The facilitating of the distribution and exchange of goods is fundamental in Douglasite policy. The reference to the inscription on Li Wang's memorial to the effect that a prince who would fulfill his obligation is careful to ensure that cash move amongst the people is also in harmony with Douglasism. Douglas's prime concern was the *chronic artificial shortage of purchasing power in the hands of the consumer*. The honour of an emperor is deathless if he saw to it that his folk used, i.e., consumed their substance.

The 860 BC statement of the Emperor Chao-Kong to the effect *that abundance comes from the hills and streams* is simply an early statement of the Douglasite contention that *the real credit of the nation is based on the will to produce and the need to consume.* Here again is the medieval notion of the *plenitude of nature's abundance*, which we see echoed in the writings of Alain de Lille and the School of Chartres. The Poundian–Douglasite hostility to the tyranny of unjust taxation is echoed in the directive that *the emperor must let the poor speak evil of taxes* and in the praising of Yo-Y who reduced corvées and taxes.

It must be emphasized at this point that these passages illustrate Pound's acceptance of certain Chinese ideas that are in *accord* with Douglas's ideas. Pound's endorsement of some practices of Chinese historical figures whose thinking was strikingly similar to Douglas's is noted. Pound's acceptance of Douglas's ideas conditioned his reaction to and evaluation of the incidents from Chinese history. Douglasism had an influence upon Pound's artistic selectivity in choosing these incidents from Chinese history.

In Canto LIV, Pound continues with his luminously detailed survey of the ancient Chinese emperors:

Lieou-pang stored food and munitions
b.c. 202 so that he came to be emperor, KAO,
brought calm and abundance
No taxes for a whole year,
'no taxes till people can pay 'em'
. . . .
Hiao OUEN *b.c.*
179
Prince of Tai to the throne
that was son of KAO TI and a concubine
(no tribute for the first year of his reign)
And the chief of the Southern Barbarians complained
that his silver import was intercepted
circulation of specie impeded
. . . .
And Kia-Y sent in a petition that they store grain against
famine
and HIAO OUEN TI the emperor published:
Earth is the nurse of all men
I now cut off one half the taxes
I wish to follow the sages, to honour Chang Ti by my furrow
Let farm folk have tools for their labour it is
for this I reduce the said taxes
Gold is inedible. Let no war find us unready.
Thus Tchao-tso of his ministry (war)
'Gold will sustain no man's life nor will diamonds
keep the land under culture....
by wise circulation. Bread is the base of subsistence.'
They ended mutilation as punishment
were but 400 men in all jails
Died HIAO OUEN TI, ante Cristum one fifty seven.
After 23 years of reign, that pensioned the elders.
b.c. 146 Great rebels began making lead money
grasshoppers came against harvest
. . . .
and Yang Tchong sent in a placet that food prices had risen
since the start of the Tartar war, taxes had risen
. . . .
and Yang-tchin refused gold of the mandarin
Ouang-mi
. . . .
And HUON gave most of the swag to the people *a.d. 159*
500 million tael
war, taxes, oppression
backsheesh, taoists, bhuddists

wars, taxes, oppressions

. . . .

And TçIN OU exempted the conquered in OU from taxes.

. . . .

And Lieou-Y answered the Emperor:
'Difference, milorr', is that HUON and LING TI
extracted and kept it in public vaults
whereas YR Majesty keeps it in yr/own private

. . . .

TçIN TCHING cared for the people.

. . . .

KAO TSEU preferred distribution

. . . .

Then To-pa-tao went after the shave-heads, the hochang
And the censor finally printed his placet
against extortionate judgements and greed of
the High Judge Yupingtchi *a.d. 448*

. . . .

conscriptions, assassins, taoists
taxes still in the hands of the princes
OU TI had 'em centralized

. . . .

a.d. 'Wheat is by sweat of the people'
503–550

. . . .

and there was a hand-out to the aged

. . . .

Yang-kien of Soui set men to revise his law code
Sou-ouei advised him, grain went into his granaries

. . . .

Ma-tchéou spoke against corvées
that had been under SOUI

. . . .

If a prince piles up treasure
he shares only his surplus

. . . .

And the Emperor TAÏ TSONG left his son 'Notes on
Conduct'

. . . .

the 7th: maintain abundance

. . . .

Honour to HIEUN 'to hell with embroideries, *a.d.*
713–756

. . . .

For five years no taxes in Lou-tchéou
(Canto LIV)

The reference to the Emperor Kao who brought calm and abundance and abolished taxes for a year is in keeping with the Douglasite attitude towards taxation. This is also true of the Emperor Hiao Ouen Ti who declared the earth to be the nurse of men, and cut taxes in half so that the farmers could buy tools for their labour. Hiao Ouen Ti, who flourished c. 179 BC, said that gold is inedible, that neither gold nor diamonds will sustain a man's life. He saw bread, not gold, as the base of subsistence, and encouraged the cultivation of land and the wise circulation of specie. Earlier, we have seen how the chief of the Southern Barbarians had complained that his silver import was intercepted and the circulation of specie impeded. Hiao Ouen Ti died in 157 BC after a reign of twenty-three years in which pensions had been given to the aged. The fifth passage's reference to the newly appointed governor Yang-tchin's refusal of a bribe offered by the mandarin Ouang-mi, c. AD 107, is significant. Pound refers to a similar event mentioned in Chapter II of this book.[19] Pound's point is that the bankers and money lenders in all ages have attempted, in most cases with remarkable success, to bribe political leaders.

However, there have been good emperors like Huon, c. AD 159, who gave *most of the swag* to the people. Tçin Ou, c. AD 274, exempted the conquered in Ou from taxes. Tçin Tchang, c. AD 317, and Kao-Tseu, c. AD 396, *preferred distribution*. Ou Ti took taxes out of the hands of the princes and had them centralized. The luminous detail that "wheat is by the sweat of the people" and that "there was a handout to the aged" are in keeping with the Douglasite concept of the source of real credit and the principle of the dividend.

Canto LV covers the monetary-economic history of China from AD 805 to AD 1172. Here again the method of luminous detail is used so that we can move rapidly and yet not lose the purposeful focus necessary in historical studies. Just as in the preceding canto, there are good emperors who concern themselves with the distribution of abundance, and there are others who engage in heavy taxation:

> And at this time died Ouei-Kao the just taxer
> that set up pensions for widows
> His temple stands to this day
> that his soldiers built for him.
>
> . . . .
>
> And the censors said Liki has hogged ten provinces' treasure
> If these go to the national treasury

[19] Pound, *Impact*, 68.

they will go out of circulation
the people thereby deprived,
so HIEN-TSONG threw this into commerce

. . . .

HIEN reduced the superfluous mandarins
and remitted taxes in Hoai

. . . .

'Men are the basis of empire', said our lord HIEN-TSONG

. . . .

[SIUEN] A man who remembered faces
and had by the taozers
tho' he stood for just price and sound paper

. . . .

a.d. 860

. . . .

HIU cut down taxes and douanes
was hell on extorters

. . . .

TAI TSONG brought out the true BOOKS *a.d. 978*
and there arose in the province of Ssétchuen a revolt
because of the greed of the mandarins.
Not content with their salaries
began to bleed merchants for licences
which new damn tax made money so scarce in that province
that men cdn't buy the necessities. *a.d. 993*
Therefore Ouang Siaopo of the people
demanded just distribution
and they went against Tsing-chin city, and took
Pongchan
by violence and cut open the governor's belly
which they filled up with silver
(bit of what he had extorted)
and TAI TSONG reigned 22 years
caring for field work. Meanwhile Jelly Hugo
the tartar, a Khitan, freed his people of taxes
and started old age relief. Ghengis rising

. . . .

and at this time began Ngan
(or more fully Ouang-Ngan-ché) to demand that they reset
the market tribunals,
posting every day what was on sale and what the right price
of it
as had been under TCHEOU emperors
and that a market tax shd/ go to the emperor from this

thereby relieving the poor of all douanes
giving them easy market for merchandise
and enlivening commerce
by making to circulate the whole realm's abundance.

. . . .

And Ngan saw land lying barren
because peasants had nowt to sow there
whence said: Lend 'em grain in the spring time
that they can pay back in autumn
with a bit of an increase, this wd/ augment the reserve,
This will need a tribunal
and the same tribunal shd/ seek
equity
for all lands and all merchandise
according to harvest and soil
so that the emperor's tithes shd/ be proportionate
to the rarity or the abundance of merchandise
to make commerce more easy, that the folk be not
overburdened
nor yet the imperial revenue be made less.
and Ngan made yet a third point
that was to fix the value of money
and to coin *enough* denars
that shd/ stay always on the same footing.
(Canto LV)

In the passages above, those emperors who lived up to the Poundian ideal have been stressed. For example, Ouei-Ki is a just taxer who set up pensions for widows. Liki, however, has hogged the treasure of ten provinces. Pound points out the concern *that money should not be taken out of circulation* and the people thereby deprived. This concern is identical to the concern shown by C. H. Douglas for the *draining of consumer purchasing power* by the banking system and by iniquitous taxation. C. H. Douglas and the Confucian-oriented Chinese emperors share a belief in the *distributive function of money* that is certainly at variance with the monetary philosophy held by the modern banking system. This concern is based upon that distributive philosophy which C. H. Douglas shares with the wise Chinese emperors. Hien-Tsong put the money back into circulation, reduced the superfluous mandarins/bureaucracy and remitted taxes in Haai. Pound approves of Hien-Tsong's belief that men are the basis of empire. This is in keeping with the Douglasite tenet that *the individual takes precedence over the group* or state. Hien-Tsong would agree with

Douglas that *the individual has a uniqueness and dignity*, which must not be tampered with. Douglasite philosophy stresses the individual rather than the collectivity:

> Systems were made for men, and not men for systems, and the interest of man, which is self-development, is above all systems, whether theological, political or economic.
>
> Accepting this statement as a basis of constructive effort, it seems clear that all forms, whether of government, industry or society, must exist contingently to the furtherance of the principles contained in it. If a State system can be shown to be inimical to them—it must go; if social customs hamper their continuous expansion—they must be modified; if unbridled industrialism checks their growth, then industrialism must be reined in. That is to say, we must build up from the individual, not down from the State.[20]

We also learn from the above passage that the Emperor Siuen stood for *the just price* and sound paper. This is completely in accordance with Douglas's emphasis on *the just price*, and a sound currency based on the real credit of the country.

We learn that Hiu in AD 860 reduced taxes and customs duties. Hiu was also extremely severe with anyone who practiced extortion. In the time of Tai Tsong in c. AD 978 we learn of a revolt because of the greed of the mandarins in Ssetchuen province. The mandarins had imposed a heavy license tax on merchants to supplement their own upper civil service salaries. The burden of this heavy tax fell directly on the consumer. Pound points out how Ouang Siaopo demanded the just distribution of goods and led the people in a revolt. The emphasis on the just distribution of goods and services is completely in harmony with Douglasite theory. Ouang Siaopo, like C. H. Douglas, was a *distributist* in his economic philosophy. Like C. H. Douglas, he emphasized *the distribution and consumption of nature's abundance*. To this extent there is a similarity between the economic philosophy of Ouang Siaopo and that of C. H. Douglas, an economic philosophy which is certainly not held by the *orthodox economist* or those individuals whom Douglas refers to caustically as *economists of repute*. Pound also gives us the example of Jelly Hugo, the tartar, who freed his people from taxation and started old age relief.

We learn that Oung-Ngan-che, in c. AD 1022, demanded that the market tribunals be re-established. He ordered the daily posting of

---

[20] Douglas, *Economic Democracy*, 6–7.

goods for sale and *their prices* and, at the same time, levied a market tax from this. The effect of this market tax was to relieve the poor of paying customs duties and to provide them with a market for merchandise. Pound stresses that the over-all effect of Ngan's policies was to enliven commerce by circulating the whole realm's abundance.

The stress on the *circulation, i.e., the distribution of the realm's abundance*, is completely in harmony with Douglasite policy. Ngan also loaned grain to the peasants in the spring with the understanding that they would pay it back with a bit of an increase to go into the grain reserve. Thus, he promoted a policy of *natural abundance, not artificial scarcity*. Ngan decreed that the emperor's tithes should be in proportion to the rarity or abundance of the merchandise, i.e., that a tithe should consist of a tenth or a ninth of what a man has on hand. Ngan also wanted to fix the value of money and to coin *enough* denars, which should always *maintain* the same purchasing power. This is completely in harmony with Douglas's concept of a balanced economy where goods and services are *balanced* with purchasing power. The very basis of C. H. Douglas's monetary-economic policy is to be found in his insistence upon *closing the gap* between prices and purchasing power by fresh supplies of *debt-free credit, i.e., social credit*. Thus again there is a similarity between the distributist philosophy of certain Chinese emperors, e.g., the Emperor Ngan and that of C. H. Douglas. Douglas would certainly be in sympathy with Ngan's policy of coining *enough* denars and that these denars should maintain the same purchasing power.

Canto LVI covers the period from AD 1206 to AD 1368. This covers the reigns of Ghengis Khan, Kublai Khan, the Twentieth Dynasty Yuen (Mongol), Lady Ouang Chi, Hong Vou (died 1399), and the Twenty-first Dynasty Ming (1368). The canto begins with Pound repeating a reference given in Canto LV to the effect that the Tartars *used paper notes* when coin was too heavy for transport and redeemed these notes at one third:

> Billets, biglietti, as coin was too heavy for transport,
> but redeemed the stuff at one third
>
> . . . .
>
> Sung died of levying taxes
>
> . . . .
>
> and Yeliu Tchutsai said to Ogotai:
> tax, don't exterminate
> You'll make more by taxing the blighters
> thus saved several millyum lives of those chinamen

. . . .

YAO, CHUN, YU controller of waters
Bridge builders, contrivers of roads
gave grain to the people
kept down the taxes
Hochang. eunuchs, taoists and ballets
night-clubs, gimcracks, debauchery
Down, down! Han is down
Sung is down
Hochang, eunuchs, and taozers
empresses' relatives, came then a founder
saying nothing superfluous
cleared out the taozers and grafters, gave grain
opened the mountains

. . . .

Ghenso was for no taxes, grew up as a labourer
A hundred *chi* of rice for ten denars
that is an 1/2 ounce of silver
ZinKwa observed that gold is inedible
Stored grain against famine
observed that jade is inedible

. . . .

and Mengko took off taxes
And in Caï Fong they made a grain dividend
and gave instruction in farming
ploughs, money, ammassi

. . . .

a.d.1278

. . . .

War scares interrupt commerce. Money was now made of brass
and profit on arms went to the government
wine taxed high, settlers licenced.
Lou-chi brought back the grafters (Ahama's)
and boosted the tea tax
Tchin-kin disgusted by the size of the tax receipts
and L Sieuen staved off a war with Japan
staved off a war on Annam
said: Taxes are not abundance
Yeliu resumed the imperial college, gathering scholars
KUBLAI was a buggar for taxes
Sangko stinking with graft
Ouantse made a law code
eliminated 250 tribunals, that mostly did nowt but tax

. . . .

HAN came from the people
How many fathers and husbands are fallen
Make census
Give rice to their families
Give them money for rites
Let rich folk keep their goods by them
Let the poor be provided
I came not against YUEN
but against grafters and rebels
I rebelled not against KUBLAI, not against Ghengizkhan
but against lice that ate their descendants.

. . . .

'Once again war is over. Go talk to the savants.'
He gave fur coats to the troops in Ninghia
Showed no zenophobia. Moguls wd/ not have chinese in office.
In Pekin he paid the soldiers
To peasants he gave allotments
gave tools and yoke oxen
No eunuchs to serve save as domestics
'Don't believe all you are told by officials

(Canto LVI)

The Emperors Yao, Chun and Yu gave grain to the people and kept down the taxes. Thus, these emperors lived up to the Douglasite distributist ideal. Ghenso was against taxes and Zinkwa pointed out that you could not eat gold. Mengko also took off taxes and, in Cai Fong, a grain dividend was distributed. In c. AD 1278 we learn that Tchinkin was disgusted by the size of the tax receipts. This same disgust was to be voiced by C. H. Douglas. D. L. Sieven is quoted as saying that taxes are not abundance. We learn that Kublai Khan was a *bugger for taxes* and that Sangko stank with graft. Ouantse, on the other hand, eliminated 250 tribunals that did almost nothing else except impose taxes. We also learn that Han, c. AD 1312–1320, gave rice and money for their ancestral rites to the families who had lost fathers and husbands in the siege of Peking in AD 1368. It is significant that Han *ordered the rich to keep their goods, and to let the poor be provided for*. This is completely in keeping with Douglasite policy, which maintains that *abundance must be distributed, not that one man's property should be taken and given to another* or to the "state."

C. H. Douglas, repeatedly in his writings, stresses the futility of that policy which would seek to alleviate poverty by redistributing it, i.e., *by making everyone poor*. He stresses, contrary to Marx, that: "The poor are poor not because the rich are rich, but because there is not enough *money*, or, more correctly, purchasing power, to make the poor rich, or even comfortably well off, even if the whole of the money possessed by the rich were taken from them and equally divided amongst the poor."[21]

The proper policy, says Douglas, is to see that all have *security with freedom*. He maintains that this would be possible if only the banking system would not stand between the people and their credit.

Next we learn that the Emperor Hong Vou, died 1399, gave allotments, and yoke oxen to the peasants. This canto ends with a brief account of these sound Douglasite policies of Hong Vou following hard upon the sound policies of the Emperor Han.

Canto LVII deals with the plight of the Emperor Kien Ouen Ti who fled from his uncle. This uncle seems to have been a Chinese version of Richard III. Kien Ouen Ti was the infant son of the Emperor Hong Vou who died at the end of Canto LVI, i.e. in AD 1399. As soon as Hong Vou had died, and Kien Ouen was enthroned, his uncle sought to dethrone him. Kien Ouen Ti, through a secret escape route prepared by his father, fled to the Buddhist temple of Chin Lo-Koan where he and his nine accompanying mandarins became monks, and remained for years. In the meantime, other emperors succeeded to the throne. The Emperor Yng Tsong, in 1452, distributed a grain ration for the famine in Honan and Shantung:

> In '52 was Emperor's grain ration
> for famine in Honan, for famine in Shantung
> a million six hundred thousand measures of grain
> . . . .
> and there were 53 million folk in the Empire
> at tribute average of five measures
> of, say, 100 lbs each
>
> (Canto LVII)

Towards the end of Canto LVII we learn of the massive thefts of gold and silver specie, jewels, pearls, and diamonds by the eunuch Lieou-Kin in the reign of Ou-Tsong, c. AD 1505, and by the eunuch Kiang-ping under the Emperor Chi-Tsong. The Dowager Empress of Tchang Chi had caused this second theft to be discovered.

Canto LVIII deals with Japan, the Tartar Horse Fairs, Tai Tsong, son of Tai Tseu and the twenty-second Manchu dynasty (AD 1625). This canto describes the final triumph of the Manchus over the corrupt Ming dynasty. Canto LIX deals with the translation of the great

---

[21] Douglas, *Warning Democracy*, 126.

Chinese classics into Manchu and with the Russian peace treaty for which the Jesuits Gerbillon and Pereira acted as interpreters in the reign of Emperor Kang Hi. Early in Canto LX Pound then quotes a description of the Ortes, a Mongol tribe:

> Ortes very orderly, have lost none of their mongol habits,
> their princes in concord, no usury.
> . . . .
> And too much rice went to Batavia
> so our lord KANG layed an embargo
> . . . .
> 'no DYNASTY has come in with such justice
> as ours has. I have not wasted the treasures of empire
> considering them as the blood of the people
> 3 million a year on river embankments
> I order that YONG TCHING succeed me
> THOU SHALT NOT
> lend money to sojers.
> (Canto LX)

Pound points out that the orderly Mongol Ortes, whose princes live in concord, do not practice usury. The second passage relates how the Emperor Kang placed an embargo on rice when too much of it was going out of the realm to Batavia, today's Jakarta, Indonesia, the former capital of the Dutch East Indies. Thus Kang shows evidence of the Douglasite preoccupation with the *home market being the best market* and the market that must be looked after first before matters of foreign trade are to be considered. The Emperor Kang, like C. H. Douglas, did not believe in exporting a *false surplus but only a true surplus*, i.e., that which was left when his subjects had truly satisfied their needs and not simply exhausted their pocket-books.

To those who claim gold and silver are *sacred* Pound states that *grain is sacred,*[22] *in* agreement with Kang. In contrast to Emperor Kang in the Orient, Hollis provides the inhumane example in the Occident of trade under Queen Elizabeth I where she traded England's *natural abundance for artificial abundance*:

> The Spaniards, having a surplus of precious metals, developed the habit of purchasing goods with them and of living on foreign imports instead of on the products of their own country. Whether or not this was wisdom in them we need not discuss. But the consequence of it for the English was that they gave the Spaniards consumable goods and received

[22] Pound, *Impact*, 55.

> in exchange for them unconsumable metal. If, as Adam Smith truly says, the one object of production is consumption, it is clear that this exchange was pure loss to the English, and it is not surprising that with such a commerce the reign of Elizabeth should be filled loud with the poor's complaints of their desperate poverty.[23]

As in the Elizabethan economy, so in the modern economy *nations trade true wealth, their goods, even their food, the abundance of nature, for mere artificial wealth*: gold, silver, or as is the norm in the modern economy, *letters of credit, or money transferred via online bank accounts*. The struggle for foreign trade markets in the modern world is due to nations only creating money as a debt, rather than as Douglas/Pound suggest as a credit/dividend to citizens, as the money available in circulation normally is insufficient to meet the flow of goods and services. Douglas/Pound argued that it made sense to export real wealth, i.e., food, oil, gas, timber, etc., for products one's nation does not possess, but to export real wealth in exchange for mere *tickets*, paper money of various kinds, was absurd, especially when a monetary dividend could instead be given to fill any gap between prices and *desired/needed* products and services. It would be the same as saying a rich island nation, that had no foreign market to trade with, could not provide its citizens with food and goods, despite the shelves being full of any product *desired and imaginable*.

The last passage is taken from the Emperor Kang Hi's farewell address to his people. He prides himself on not wasting the treasures of the empire since he considers these treasures to be the *blood* of the people. In other words, to use a famous Douglasite metaphor, the *purchasing power* of the public purse or treasury, *is the life blood of the economic body*.

Canto LXI deals with the Emperor Yong Tching—Chi Tsong Hien Hoang Ti, 1723, and the Emperor Kien Long, 1736. This is the last of the Chinese Cantos. The Emperor Yong Tching was the son of Kang Hi. This emperor is a great Poundian hero because of his wise monetary-economic policies. Pound also admires Yong Tching because of his adherence to Confucian principles:

> Public kitchen in famine
> Public works for the unemployed, 1725,
> a dole,
> . . . .

[23] Hollis, *The Two Nations*, 9.

Officers at Tientsing
who faked rice distribution
and gave bad rice to the needy
can damn well pay up what they have embezzled.
Lieu-yu-y, state examiner said:
Put magazines in the 4 towns of Chan-si
(that there be set up a fondego)
Look whom you choose to administer
that these be not the overworked Governors
To keep out graft . . . if any man have loaned rice in secret . . .
A 100,000 pund capital
wd/ mean Thirty thousand great measures
At moderate price we can sell in the spring
to keep the market price decent
And still bring in a small revenue
which should be used for getting more next crop
AMMASSI or sane collection,
to have bigger provision next year,
that is, augment our famine reserve
and thus to keep the rice fresh in store house.
IN time of common scarcity; to sell at the just price
in extraordinary let it be lent to the people
and in great calamities, give it free
Lieou-yu-y
Approved by the EMPEROR
(un fontego[24*])
. . . .
An' woikinmen thought of. If proper in field work
get 8th degree button and
right to sit at tea with the governor
. . . .
And they druv out Lon Cato fer graftin'
sent him to confino to watch men breakin' ground
He had boosted the salt price.
. . . .
But the population of Yua-nan was growing
and the price of grain kept goin' up.
Lot of land undeveloped
so they opened it
tax exemption for six years on good rice land
and for ten years on dry
and honours in proportion to
how much a bloke wd put under culture

---

[24] ** Canto XXXV

button 8th class for enough, and diplomas
for 15 *arpens*. A peasant got two bouquets for his cap
and a cramoisi scarf and a band to walk home wiff.
And a boost for any mandarin
that wd stake out new settlers
800,000 in doles
a million on canal reparations

. . . .

No house is
durable if perched on yr neighbor's ruin

. . . .

Heaven has scattered riches and poverty
but to profit on other men's loss is no better than banditry
(Canto LXI)

Yong Tching died in 1735 at the age of fifty-eight in the thirteenth year of his reign. In the passages of luminous detail and purposeful focus above, Pound points out how Yong Tching had set up a public kitchen in time of famine, public works for the unemployed, and a dole. He ordered the officers at Tientsing, who had made graft on the rice distribution, to pay up what they had embezzled.

Pound quotes Lieou-yu-y, the state examiner who set up a *fondego* or a chamber for the lending of rice. Pound has already referred to the setting up of a *fondego* or chamber in Canto XXXV in Mantua: "That there be made a *fondego* (a chamber) / to lend money on cloth so that they cease not to labour for lack of money." This *fondego* had been set up in Mantua to aid the cloth industry of that city. Based on 100,000 pounds capital, Lieu-yu-y proposed to sell thirty thousand great measures of rice at a moderate price in the spring. His concern was to keep the market price decent, and still bring in a small revenue to be used for buying more rice from the next crop. Thus, by a state subsidy of 100,000 pounds, Lieu-yu-y sought to have rice sold at the just price, i.e., *at the cost of production*. This is completely in harmony with the Douglasite principle that *the cost of production is consumption*, i.e., that *the just price (the cost of production) should equal the true cost of consumption* and no more.[25]

C. H. Douglas's concept of the *Just Price*, that the cost of production is consumption, was to be applied by means of a *compensated price discount or lowered retail price*. Douglas proposed to increase purchasing power by having retailers sell their products at their *Real*

---

[25] "The true cost of production is consumption." Douglas, *The New and the Old Economics*, 6.

Cost instead of their *Financial Cost*. The difference would be made up to the retailer *by debt-free emissions of credit* placed in the retailer's bank account.

This is *precisely* what Lieu-yu-y did by means of his state subsidy of 100,000 pounds, which ensured that thirty thousand great measures of rice were sold *at the just price*. This state subsidy, like Douglas's compensated price discount, was a subsidy to be paid to the retailer. Douglas always insisted that the Just Price was a *ratio not an absolute measure* and was to be calculated by means of the price factor of Consumption divided by Production, i.e., the C/P ratio. Thus, the Just Price = Present Price × C/P, the Total National Consumption divided by Total National Production. In other words, present prices must be multiplied by the price-factor to reduce them to the desired prices. This calculation is based on the basic Douglasite tenet that the *Real Cost of Production is the Financial Cost of Consumption*.

Lieu-yu-y proposed an *Ammaasi or sane collection* of rice to be kept fresh in the store house. In time of common scarcity, this was to be sold at *the just price*; in more severe times it was to be *loaned*; and in great calamities to be given *free*. Yong Tching's measures to encourage abundance and the distribution of abundance stand out in stark contrast to modern methods. Yong Tching encouraged the farmers to be productive with special awards. Yong Tching did not encourage farmers *not* to produce as is the case today.[26] Lon Cato was imprisoned for raising the price of salt. Thus we can see Yong Tching's zeal in enforcing the just price. Yong Tching's policy of natural abundance as opposed to a policy of artificial scarcity can be seen in his policy of opening undeveloped land. He did not adhere to the cult of sterility that would have sought a remedy in *population control* but he sought his remedy in actualizing the potential of nature's abundance. Yong Tching did not encourage farmers to put their land into a *soil bank*, plough under every third row of cotton, or kill every second suckling pig. Eight hundred thousand denars in doles were given out to the consumers and a million denars were spent on canal repairs. Yong Tching, unlike the modern usurer, believed that *no lasting house could be built on a neighbor's ruin*. He was also completely out of harmony with the sacred tenets of the vested financial interests in declaring that to profit on another man's loss is *no better than banditry*.[27]

---

[26] Example: "Milking Taxpayers," *The Economist*, 26.

[27] The stock market, Canadian RRSPs, US 401(k) profit sharing plans, are mostly mere speculation, taking advantage of another's loss, a change of price for one's

Yong Tching was succeeded by his son Kien Long in 1736. The Chinese had conquered many Muslim towns which possessed extensive treasures. Pound quotes a letter from Tchao-hou, a military governor in Kasgar, Boucaria:

> 'Question of coin in these conquered towns is very important.
> I advise a few of YOUR mintage
> and to leave the old pieces current.
> Those used here,
> *Haskai, yerqui and hotien*
> are of bronze weighing about 1/5th of one of our ounces
> 50 of these mahometan discs make a *teuke*
> about one of our taels.
> There are some useless old cannon here
> which I suggest we melt up for small *cash*
> to keep commerce moving.'
> Tchao-hou
> to his EMPEROR
> from the camp before Hashan
> (or Kasgar, a city in little Boucaria)
>
> (Canto LXI)

Pound stresses the word *YOUR mintage* to emphasize that this is to be regal or statal coinage not a private issue of coinage by private vested interests. The emperor's coins are to circulate to make clear *the emperor's sovereignty in matters of coinage*. This concept of *the regal prerogative* in the matter of coinage is one that is implicit throughout the writings of C. H. Douglas. C. H. Douglas emphasizes that *the state should lend and not borrow*. He constantly reiterates that the creation of credit [or rather the control of the financial system's overall policy—editor] must be a *prerogative of the supreme public authority*,

---

benefit, i.e., *wealth made without making anything of value for the common good*. After the initial purchase by someone of the offered stock, which does go directly to the company, all further purchases or exchanges are between one stock paper owner and the new purchaser. Along with the current banking system model, the stock market model came to England from the Low Countries. In 1997, the Nobel Memorial Prize in Economic Sciences, conferred to those *bringing the greatest benefit to mankind*, was awarded to Myron Scholes and Robert Merton, for their investment model used to determine the value of derivatives. In the following year, 1998, their company Long-Term Capital Management, was responsible for beginning a financial crisis and had to be rescued by the Federal Reserve by a recapitalization of $3.6 billion. Their bailout weakened the financial system, to the detriment of all: Dyer, "The Nobel Bailout." The stock market is artificial and does not reflect nor help the needs of the real economy, *the real world of goods and services*.

i.e. king, parliament, or congress. It was due to Douglas's insistence upon this point that Pound took so great an interest in the works of Alexander Del Mar, who traces the regal prerogative over coinage back to the Byzantine emperor, the Roman emperor and to its origin in the *Pontifex Maximus* or Roman High Priest (to be discussed in this work in reference to Cantos 89 and 104). Tchao-hou does not feel that coinage need *be limited to either silver or gold*, or need be made redeemable in silver or gold.

2) THE ADAMS CANTOS LXII–LXXI

The Adams Cantos run from Canto LXII to Canto LXXI. The central figure in these cantos is, of course, *John Adams* who carries on in America the Confucian principles of right government, which the great Chinese emperors had done before him. This is not to say that John Adams was a Confucian, but he was a man of good will and order, imbued with the spirit of individual responsibility. Pound believes that this is true of the *Adamses, Jefferson, Jackson, Van Buren, Lincoln, John Randolph, and Thomas Hart Benton, among others in American history*. Towards the end of Canto LXI, Pound had prepared us for the Adams Cantos by a one-line luminous detail superimposed on the story of the Emperor Kien Long referring to *the rise of the Adamses —*." In other words, Pound wants to ensure that we realize that the *Adams clan* was rising just in the year that the last emperor with whom he deals came to the throne, i.e., *in the 36th of that century —*", i.e., 1736.

The ten Adams Cantos contain many luminous details taken from the monetary-economic history of the United States. In Canto LXII, Pound touches upon the constitutional problems involved in parliamentary control of the colonies:

> If we be feudatory
> parliament has no control over us
> We are merely
> under the monarch
> allegiance is to the king's natural person
> . . . .
> Local legislation / that is basic /
> we wd. consent in matters of empire trade, It is
> by no means essential to trade with foreign nations at all
> as sez Chas Francis, China and Japan have proved it
> . . . .
> and lastly in superintending the preparation of
> bills of credit, to serve as dollars durin' the struggle

. . . .
spies and persons counterfeiting—or abetting in same—
our continental bills of credit
or knowingly passing the same to be punished
(Canto LXII)

Adams points out that if America is only a feudal domain, then the British parliament has no control over America. The Americans owe their allegiance *directly* to the king's natural person, not to a political body. Adams insists that the Americans must have control over *local legislation* although they would co-operate in matters of empire trade. However, Adams points out that foreign trade is not necessary and gives the examples of China and Japan. The stress on local control of local legislation is in harmony with the Douglasite principle of *decentralization* of political and economic power. Pound stated: "Civilization depends on local control of purchasing power needed for local purposes."[28] Adams's recognition of the fact that foreign trade is not necessary for America is also in harmony with the Douglasite tenet that under a properly functioning monetary system, foreign trade would merely take the form of *exchange of true surpluses between nations*. It would not be necessary for nations to export the *cream of their production* just to acquire sufficient purchasing power to consume the *skim-milk* of their own production. In fact, Douglas stresses that even this objective of foreign trade is not realized since all nations gain by foreign trade is the *raw material* for still further exports, or else they gain *irredeemable export credits*. Thus, Douglas regards foreign trade as another one of the bankers' *hoaxes*. Douglas saw the struggle for foreign markets, caused by an *insufficiency of purchasing power*, as the prime cause of wars; i.e., he saw *commercial warfare as leading inevitably to military warfare*.[29]

The last two luminous details in the passage above refers to the issuing of Continental bills of credit by the Continental Congress during the Revolutionary War. John Adams was active in superintending the preparation of these bills of credit that were to serve as dollars during the war. The reference to spies and persons counterfeiting, abetting in counterfeiting, or knowingly passing counterfeit Continental bills of credit, is of interest. The British under General Howe abetted and patronized those who were engaged in making and pushing

28 Pound, *Impact*, 211.

29 The only known vocal recording of C. H. Douglas is a BBC broadcast where Douglas speaks on the causes of war, a series of speeches during November 1934. See: Douglas "The Causes of War."

spurious issues of Continental bills of credit into circulation. Persons going into colonies held by rebels were supplied with any number of counterfeited Congress notes for the price of the paper per ream. Pound stresses that the thirteen colonies were able to fight and win the Revolutionary War by means of the bills of credit issued by the Continental Congress. Despite the wholesale counterfeiting carried on by the British to sabotage this currency, it never failed the Congress. Even its devaluation, due to British counterfeiting, only acted as an *unevenly distributed tax* on the colonists. This currency was issued *debt-free*, as C. H. Douglas advocates, and therefore the devaluation was really the only tax the colonists had to cope with. Pound's focusing on the debt-free issue of bills of credit by the Continental Congress lends support to his position that *Douglasism is part of a broader thought-heritage.*

Canto LXII continues with luminous details taken from the writings of John Adams:

> 1. Magazines, daily pamphlets in hands of men of no character in fact one bookseller said to me: can get 'em at a guinea a day to write pro or con anything. Hired!
>
> . . . .
>
> 2. a new power arose, that of fund holders
> fond of rotation so that to remove
>   their abuse from me to the President (Washington)
> TO be punctual, to be confined to my seat
>   (over the Senate)
> to see nothing done (by the senate)
> to hear nothing said, to say and DO nothing
> borrow for trading very unmercantile
> by thought, word, never encourage a war . . .
>   horror they are in lest peace shd/ continue
> will accumulate perpetual DEBT
>   leading to yet more revolutions
>
> . . . .
>
> 3. Mr. Jefferson, Mr. Hamilton
> the latter not enjoying the confidence of the people at large
> to oppose Ham to Jeff wd/ be futile
> whereon Ham set to undercut Adams
>
> . . . .
>
> 4. formed own view of Hamilton's game (and his friends')
> which wd/ certainly have tangled with Europe
>
> . . . .
>
> 5. charged course of Ham and his satellites
> to disappointment that they hadn't

got us entangled with Britain
defensive and offensive
Snot, Bott, Cott left over from
Washington's cabinet
and as for Hamilton
we may take it (my authority, ego scriptor cantilenae)
that he was the Prime snot in ALL American history
(11th Jan. 1938, from Rapallo)
(Canto LXII)

In the first passage above, Pound quotes Adams as to the perversion and prostitution of the press and publicity. C. H. Douglas constantly stresses the control of the press and of publicity by the money power. Both Douglas and Pound see the press as a *kept press* in the same way that one speaks of a *kept woman*. The press is supported and maintained by the financial power and therefore prints only what has the approval of the financial power. The press is also able to destroy the reputation of anyone who should raise his voice in protest against the usurocracy. This is what Pound means by the *prostitution of the press* in the first of the Hell Cantos. Adams's reference to a bookseller who claims that the journalists of the day will lie for hire reminds us of Pound's references to the perverters of truth who lie for hire in the Hell Cantos.

The second passage reflects Adams's recognition of the fact that a new power, a *money power*, had arisen. Adams suggests that this new power of *fund holders* already wields great political power in addition to its economic power. He also describes the way the money power has conspired to "kick him upstairs" and thus see that he neither says nor does anything that would encroach on the power of the *fund holders*. He is also made to preside over a senate, which must say or do nothing against the money power. In this same passage, Adams points out that borrowing for trading is very un-mercantile. He adverts to the horror the money power is in lest peace should continue, since *war is the bankers' harvest*. He expresses the opinion that under the private bank credit system, perpetual debt will accumulate, leading to more revolutions. C. H. Douglas also emphasizes that the present bank credit system is designed to accumulate perpetual debt and that it is the prime cause of wars and unrest. This resemblance between the thinking of John Adams and that of C. H. Douglas is significant.

The third, fourth and fifth passages refer to the struggle between Thomas Jefferson and Alexander Hamilton concerning the granting of a charter to the private First Bank of the United States. Jefferson fought for a congressional, or constitutional money system, and Hamilton represented the private banking interests in their successful attempt to seize control of the credit of the United States.

To understand the mind of Hamilton as Secretary of the Treasury, Hollis provides a passage concerning the American loans Congress had taken on to continue the Revolutionary War, interest payments on which Congress had defaulted on and therefore were selling at 20–25% of their par value:

> Alexander Hamilton, the Secretary of the Treasury, gave private information to his financial friends, who therefore bought up the loan at its low market figure. He then announced that the Government would redeem it by paying off the present holders at par plus accrued interest, with the price-level considerably lower than that of the time of the contraction of the debt. To pay them off, he raised a new loan from the New York bankers, thus saddling the new country with a permanent National Debt, which he confessed to thinking necessary in order that finance's mastery of its policies should be unshakable. "He wishes it never to be paid," explained Jefferson at the time, "but always to be a thing wherewith to corrupt and manage the legislature." He thus bound, as Calhoun afterwards put it, "more strongly to the Government that already powerful class by giving them, through its agency, increased profit and a decided control over the currency, exchanges and the business transactions of the country." The interest on the new loan was to be raised by import duties.[30]

Pound's focusing on the struggle over the granting of a charter to the First Bank of the United States, a private bank in all things but its name, lends support to Pound's claim that the struggle between the Money Power and *the man who tries to do a good job* is one of the basic struggles all through history. Thomas Jefferson, like C. H. Douglas, advocated a *Constitutional money system*, i.e., a money system under which Congress issued the nation's money supply debt-free without recourse to the usury of private banking interests. Adams points out that Hamilton does not enjoy the confidence of the people at large. Pound points out that Adams saw through *Hamilton's game* and believed that the Hamilton party sought to entangle America with England. Pound registers his contempt for this *founding father* of America by referring to Hamilton as the "prime snot in all American history." Pound's bitterness towards Hamilton is probably due to a

[30] Hollis, *The Two Nations*, 201.

deep-seated conviction that Hamilton was the agent of the financial conspiracy, and a willing tool of the Bank of England. Pound believes that it is primarily due to the instrumentality of Hamilton that the American Revolution was betrayed at the very beginning. In contrast to Hamilton, Pound describes Adams as the *clearest head in the congress*:

> But for the clearest head in the congress
> 1774 and thereafter
> pater patriae
> the man who at certain points
> made us
> at certain points
> saved us
> by fairness, honesty and straight moving
> ARRIBA ADAMS
> (Canto LXII)

John Adams is a great Poundian hero precisely because his philosophy and policy are similar to those of C. H. Douglas. It should be emphasized that when reference is made to the Douglasite content or emphasis in passages (e.g., those which Pound paraphrases from Adams's writings), it is not being suggested (of course) that John Adams or Thomas Jefferson, etc., were familiar with the writings of C. H. Douglas. It is, however, emphasized, as Pound himself emphasizes, that *Douglasism itself is part of a much older thought-heritage or thought-tradition*. This thought-heritage goes back far beyond John Adams and Thomas Jefferson to medieval Italy and to ancient China itself, to name only two sources.

The first part of Canto LXV deals with the first nomination of Washington. The canto then goes on to discuss John Adams's voyage to France and, as Pound observes in his table of contents for this section, his *not being diddled by Vergennes or plastered by Dr. Franklin*. The canto ends with an introduction to a section dealing with Adams's role in saving the fisheries of the new republic. There are not as many monetary-economic luminous details in this canto as there have been in some others. Here are some of the more prominent:

> We then walked up Broadway
> magnificent building, cost 20,000 pounds
> N.Y. currency
> . . . .
> sez congress shd/ raise money and
> employ men to write in the newspapers (in England)
> (Canto LXV)

The first passage concerns the magnificent building erected on Broadway with New York currency. At this time each of the colonies issued its own paper currency and debt-free New York paper currency had paid for the magnificent building on Broadway. Thus, in New York, as in Pennsylvania, prosperity and progress were being made possible by the issue of debt-free colonial currency without recourse to the usury of the banking system. Adams, like Douglas, recognized the power exerted *by centralized control of the press* as is seen in the second passage. This passage indicates a recognition on the part of John Adams that control of the press is available to whomever has sufficient money to purchase that control.

Canto LXVI opens with Pound's paraphrasing of certain passages taken from John Adams's diary. These recount events in Holland in 1783 and 1784. Pound then brings us to England where Adams observes that:

> A national debt of
> 274 million stg/
> accumulated by jobs contracts salaries pensions in
> the course of a century
> might easily produce all this magnificence
> (Canto LXVI)

John Adams is singularly unimpressed by the magnificence of London when he considers that England has accumulated a national debt of 274 million pounds sterling over a century. John Adams's horror of a national debt is shared by C. H. Douglas, but not by *orthodox economists* and *economists of repute* who maintain that a national debt is so beneficial that we should have to create one if we were not already blessed with one. This is what Alexander Hamilton wrote in a letter to Robert Morris, "A national debt, if it is not excessive, will be to us a national blessing."[31]

Then Pound moves ahead in Adams's diary to July 18, 1784, when Adams was back in America. He arrives back in the United States when everyone's attention is on the coming presidential election:

> 1. Otis full of election: Henry, Jefferson, Burr
> . . . .
> 2. said one thing wd/ make Rhode Island unanimous
> —meaning funding—
> they wanted Hamilton for vice president
> I said nothing.
> . . . .

[31] Gordon, *Hamilton's Blessing*, 20.

3. OB PECUNIAE SCARSITATEM
this act, the Stamp Act, wd/ drain cash out of the country
and is, further, UNconstitutional

. . . .

4. After repeal of American Stamp Act
we have mortification to see one Act of Parliament after
another,
money collecting from us continually without our consent
by an authority
in the constitution of which we have no share
and see the little coin that remained among us
transmitted to distance
with no hope of return

. . . .

5. money extorted from us, appropriated to the augmentation of
burdens upon us
independent of grants of our commons.
(Canto LXVI)

The first and second passages deal with the impending presidential election. We learn that James Otis was excited concerning the election. It is significant that John Adams received with silence James Otis's news that Rhode Island wanted Alexander Hamilton for vice president. He tells us: *I said nothing*. Adams, like Thomas Jefferson, was opposed to Hamilton's plans to grant a charter to the private Bank of the United States. Adams's attitude is completely in accord with the Douglasite position that credit is to be issued by the state debt-free without recourse to the usury of private banking interests.[32]

The third passage starts with the words *OB PECUNIAE SCARSITATEM*, i.e., *due to the scarcity of money*. Adams's objection to the Stamp Act is that it would drain purchasing power out of the country. This emphasis upon the artificial chronic shortage of purchasing power is completely in accordance with Douglasism. Pound chooses these luminous details in John Adams's diary that illustrate the Douglasite position in terms of early American monetary-economic history. Adams emphasizes that the Stamp Act is unconstitutional.

In the fourth passage he points out that after the repeal of the American Stamp Act, one act of parliament after another was passed

[32] Editor's note: The only money to be issued debt-free by the state under Douglas Social Credit would be the compensatory consumer credits, i.e., the dividend and the discount. Credit for production would continue to be issued on a debt basis and most of it by private banks.

to extort money from the colonies without their consent. Pound paraphrases Adams to the effect that the small amount of purchasing power remaining in the colonies was sent to England with no hope of return.

The fifth passage repeats the colonial grievance that the money extorted from the colonies was being used to increase the tax burden on the colonies.

Most of Cantos LXVII and LXVIII deal with Adams's plan for government. However, the first part of Canto LXVII provides more of the monetary-economic background leading to the American Revolution:

> 1. Mr Shirley in 1754 confided to Dr Franklin a secret
> that is a scheme for taxing the colonies by act of Parliament
> WHERETO Ben said: nuts
> in a very accurate manner.
> 'Gevernors' sez he 'whose object is in general to make
> fortunes'
> Shirley a skunk, Pownall a gentleman honest,
> Bernard skilled enough in the law to do mischief
> and thus the total government was to be rendered wholly
> independent of the people
> and the cream to go into their salaries
> (governor's, lieutenant's and judges')
> (signed) *Novanglus*
>
> . . . .
>
> 2. colonization is at common law a *casus omissus*
> no such title is known in that law
> no known punishment at common law even for treasons
> committed out of the realm
> till Hen. VIIIth
>
> . . . .
>
> 3. for 150 years taxed themselves
> and governed their internal concerns
> Parliament governed their trade
> Wales was in some things an analogy
> held of the crown but not parcel
>
> . . . .
>
> AMERICAN governments never were erected by parliament
>
> . . . .
>
> Chester a palatine county and had *jure regalia*
> Great seal did not run into Chester
>
> . . . .
>
> Chester in crown and realm exempt from authority
>
> . . . .

seals, leagues, coin are prerogative absolute
seals, leagues, coin are prerogative absolute
to the king without parliament
not restrained to any assent of the people
homage, fealty are to the person
can not be to body politic
the king might have commanded them to return but he did not
(Canto LXVII)

The first passage refers to Benjamin Franklin's discovery in 1754 that a scheme was afoot to tax the colonies by act of parliament. The government of the colonies was to be made completely independent of the people.

The second passage emphasizes the fact that colonization is not provided for under the common law. The third passage points out that the colonies had taxed themselves and governed their internal concerns for 150 years. Parliament's only concern had been with the foreign trade of the colonies. Adams maintains that Wales provides an analogy to the American situation in that it too was held by the crown, but not as parcel or part of the crown. He stresses the fact that American governments were never erected by parliament. The American governments received their jurisdiction by virtue of the *jure regalia* in the same way that palatine counties, e.g., Chester, received their jurisdiction.

These passages dealing with the controversy over the common law legality of the British parliament imposing internal taxation on the American colonies indicate Pound's continuing preoccupation with the problem of taxation. C. H. Douglas first directed Pound's attention to this problem. Douglas had always maintained that modern taxation, imposed as a form of tribute to the money power and collected by its vassal, the modern state, is absolutely opposed to the freedom and integrity of the individual. He regards taxation as an instrument of policy, a policy pursued by the money power. Modern taxation, as a form of highway robbery, says Douglas, makes war on the individual and is in fact not taxation, but confiscation.

Adams also stresses the fact that seals, leagues, and coin belong to the *absolute prerogative of the king*. These belong to the king without parliament. Adams's stress on coin belonging to the absolute prerogative of the king is similar to C. H. Douglas's stress on *the regal and statal prerogative in the issuing of money*. The king does not require any assent of the people in these matters. Therefore, homage and fealty are owed to the royal person and not to the body politic. Pound is here paraphrasing passages from the letters written by John Adams to the *Boston Gazette* and signed "*Novanglus.*"

The first part of Canto LXVIII deals with Adams's plan of government for the new nation. However, this section is also interspersed with many monetary-economic luminous details:

> 1. in much larger sums than in the ordinary course of
>   business is needed
> Congress having borrowed large sums of this
>   paper money from its possessors
> upon interest
>   and promised payment of that in Europe
>   B. Fr. A. Lee J.A.
>   to Vergennes
> . . . .
> 2.   200 million dollars
> has in general been well rec'd
>   Elbridge Gerry
> demands of the treasury generally answered by warrants
>   @ $40 to 1 in specie.
> Says Vergennes: for strangers?
> 'The depreciation of paper, a tax (T, A, X, tax)
>   the Americans have laid on themselves . . .
> . . . .
> 3. Let me quote you some prices in Boston,
> foreigners have profited by the difference
> between silver and bills of exchange
>   that is paper $25 to 1 of silver
> but no more than   12 paper for One in bill of exchange
> also difference in paper as between Boston and Philadelphia
> If any european merchant can show good cause for
> exception I doubt not we will do justice to him.'
>   1780
> . . . .
> 4. Mr. Bicker:, that I shd/ consider what houses
>   were connected with England
> and also which had 'other connections'
>   equally likely to hinder the loan or defeat it
>   (meaning, I found, the French ministry)
> and which not of credit sufficient
>   (particularly Neufville)
> provision for negotiating the capital 2%
> for undertakers to furnish the capital 2%
> Brokerage 1/2% expenses stamped paper 1/2
> amortization 2 1/4
>   for 3 million guilders

. . . .

5. wd/ be burdensome for us to go on ten years with the war
but for the English equally so

. . . .

6. when England borrows each year a sum equal
to all her exports
shd/ we be laughed at for
wanting to borrow up to 1/12th (one twelfth)
of our exports?

. . . .

7. 'King of Spain so good as to offer his surety
for interest and the capital'
B. Franklin
P.S. I find the sum he wd/ guarantee is
150,000 dollars
payable in 3 years . . . .
No considerable sum here obtainable as Monsieur Necker
is making a loan
(meaning placing one)

. . . .

America is willing to give a just interest

. . . .

'but have never obtained any money
(12 Nov. 1780)
nor the least hope of obtaining'
J.A.
(Canto LXVIII)

The first passage refers to that part of the income of the Continental Treasury, which was derived through loans: "From 1775 to 1783, it is estimated that the income of the Continental Treasury, estimated in specie, amounted to $65,863,825, of which about $37,800,000 was secured through the issue of bills of credit, $19,416,000 through loans, and $5,795,000 through requisitions upon the states."[33] The $19,416,000 was delivered through both foreign and domestic loans. The passage above by Pound refers only to foreign loans from Europe.

The second passage deals with the depreciation of paper money. The ratio of Continental paper money to specie was $40 paper to one of specie. Adams is quick to point out to Vergennes that the depreciation of the Continental paper money is a tax the Americans have put on themselves. This last point will be more fully developed in Canto LXIX.

---

[33] "United States," *The New International Encyclopedia*, 687.

The third passage refers to the monetary situation in Boston in 1780. The ratio of paper money to silver was $25 paper to one of silver. However, the ratio of paper money to bills of exchange was twelve paper for one in bills of exchange. Adams also notes the difference in value of the paper money of Boston as compared with that of Philadelphia. He notes that foreigners have profited on the difference between silver and the bills of exchange.

The fourth passage is interesting in that it shows the degree of sophistication attained by international financial intrigue as early as 1780. Mr. Bicker warns John Adams in Amsterdam against dealing with those financial houses that had English connections. He also indirectly warns him against financial houses that had connections with the French ministry. The interest on the Dutch loan of three million guilders to the United States would have amounted to 7 1/4%.

In the fifth passage, Adams is paraphrased to the effect that ten more years of war would be burdensome for the Americans, but equally so for the English. The English were carrying on the war with borrowed money while most of the money used by the Americans was made up of debt-free bills of credit issued by the Continental Congress. These bills of credit were debt-free in the sense that there was no interest owed on them to private financial interests. This is the type of statal, national, or social credit advocated by C. H. Douglas.

The sixth passage is highly significant in that Adams points out to the Dutch financiers that England borrows each year a sum equal to the total price of all her exports. America is only asking for a sum equal to 1/12 of her exports.

In the seventh passage we learn that it is difficult for America to borrow a large sum in Amsterdam, because Mr. Necker, the French financier, is borrowing a large amount. Monsieur Necker was the father of Madame de Staël and the instrument of the financial power in destroying the state-issued debt-free assignat that the National Assembly in France had issued starting in 1789. These were paper bills, their value based upon the confiscated land of the Catholic Church.[34] As of November 12, 1780, John Adams had not succeeded in borrowing any money in Amsterdam.

In Canto LXIX Pound paraphrases passages of luminous details from the writings of John Adams dealing with diplomatic recognition of the United States, the loan from the Dutch, and the treaty with Holland. Pound, through Adams, takes up again, and in more detail, the question of the depreciation of the Continental bills of credit:

---

[34] Del Mar, *A History of the Monetary Systems*, 470–71.

1. depreciation of money a TAX on the people
paid in advance and
therefore prevents the public from being found in debt, true
it is an unequal tax and causes perplexity
but by no means disables the people from carrying on the war
Merchants, farmers, tradesmen and labourers gain
they are the moneyed men,
The capitalists those who have money at interest
or those on fixed salaries
lose.
England has increased her debt 60 million
ours is not over 6 million
who can hold out the longer?
the depreciation has not tended to make the people
submit to Britain
American exports 1774, 12 million
English debt 200 million
the American debt only six

. . . .

2. Mr. Pitt said that wd/ surprise
people here for that wars never interrupted
the interest of DEBTS

. . . .

3. To T. Jefferson:
'You fear the one, I the few.'
in this matter of redeeming certificates
that were used payin' the sojers
vignette *in margine*
King, Sam Johnson of N. Carolina
Smith (W.) S. Carolina, Wadsworth (Jeremiah
J. Lawrence, Bingham, Carrol of Carrolton
gone piss-rotten for Hamilton
Cabot, Fisher Ames, Thomas Willing
Robt Morris, Sedgwick
natural burella
squad of the pink-haired snot
traitors blacker than Arnold
blacker than Bancroft
per l'argine sinistra dienno volta
behind that mask Mr Schuyler (Filippo)
these the betrayers, these the sifilides
advance guard of hell's oiliness
in their progeny no repentence
quindi Cocito, Cassio membruto

Mr Madison proposed that the original holders
        shd/ get face value,
but not speculators who had bought in the paper for nothing.
ov the 64 members ov the House ov reppyzentativs
        29 were security holders.
                lappin cream that is, and takin it
off of the veterans.
        an' Mr Madison's move wuz DEE-feated.
Maclay and Jim Jackson stood out against dirtiness'
        smelled this stink before Madison
smelt it or before he told Tom about it.
                                        (Canto LXIX)

The first passage re-emphasizes a point made in Canto LXVII concerning the depreciation of the Continental bills of credit. The depreciation of this currency acted as a tax on the people paid in advance and at the same time prevented them from being in debt. This depreciation had not prevented the Americans from carrying on the war. Pound stresses the efficacy of the debt-free bills of credit issued by the Continental Congress in carrying on the War of Independence. This serves as an implicit commentary on the validity of C. H. Douglas's demand for a national credit system independent of the private banking interests.

These Continental bills of credit depreciated due to the wholesale counterfeiting carried on by the British. Nevertheless, this depreciation merely served to act as a tax on the people paid in advance and at the same time prevented them from being in debt. The debt-free Continental bills of credit successfully financed the War of Independence. Adams emphasizes that England had increased her debt by sixty million while the American debt is not over 6 million. The American debt had not increased in proportion to the extent that the British debt had increased because of the issue of the debt-free bills of credit by the Continental Congress. American exports amounted to twice the total American debt.

In the second passage, Mr. William Pitt's comment on wars never interrupting the interest on debts is significant in the light of C. H. Douglas's charge that war is the usurers' harvest. Douglas constantly stresses that the system of usury is the main cause of wars, and that war is the harvest of the usurocracy.[35]

The third passage refers to the notorious scandal of the assumption

[35] Editor's note: C. H. Douglas spoke more in terms of *the Monopoly of Credit* than the usurocracy.

in American monetary history. The veterans of the revolutionary war had been paid off in *veterans' certificates*. These depreciated considerably and were bought up and hoarded by speculating congressmen and others. After they had been purchased by these congressmen, their face value was restored by Congress. The speculating congressmen were also the same men who had fallen under the influence of Alexander Hamilton in his crusade for the banking interests against Thomas Jefferson and the American people. Pound lists these men who have gone "piss-rotten for Hamilton." The list was obtained from a letter of John Adams to Thomas Jefferson. Pound points out that James Madison had proposed that the original bond holders, i.e., the veterans, should get the face value of the certificates but not the speculators who had bought this paper at an extremely low price. However, since twenty-nine of the sixty-four members of the House of Representatives were security holders, Madison's amendment was defeated. This incident from American history illustrates a problem with which C. H. Douglas was very much concerned. Douglas often focused attention in his writings on the use of *bribery* by the banking institutions, with their unlimited financial resources, to corrupt and control members of so-called democratic legislatures.

Canto LXX continues with luminous details from the writings of John Adams that throw light on America's early monetary-economic history:

1. Hamilton's total ignorance (or whatever)
 of practice and usage of nations.

. . . .

2. I leave the state with its coffers full
 Dec 28th 1800

. . . .

3. 2 million issued in bills
old to bind young unconsenting, what right?

. . . .

4. from '61 here in Braintree
was aversion to paper, they preferred to do business by barter
you are right, Rush, our trouble is iggurunce
 of money especially
are still stockjobbers to believe English reports

. . . .

5. (London '85 to Art Lee)
Court as putrid as Amsterdam, divine science of politics.
sale of six million acres to diminish the national debt—

. . . .

6. that there were Americans indifferent to fisheries
    and even some inclined to give them away
    this was my strongest motive
    for twice going to Europe.
fish boxes were rec'd in my absence.
(Canto LXX)

The first passage reiterates Pound and Adams's disdain for Alexander Hamilton. This disdain has its basis in a difference of monetary philosophy existing between Hamilton and Adams. Pound's contempt for Alexander Hamilton is typical of the Social Crediters' contempt for anyone who would betray the public control of credit to private interests.

The second passage indicates Adams's pride on having left the state with its coffers full in 1800.

In the third passage above, Adams protests that policy whereby one generation burdens the generation growing up with a heavy debt load without its consent. He believed it was immoral to burden future generations with debt. In fact, Adams later concluded that the United States should require the amortization of debts in nineteen years' time after their contraction. His thinking on this point is strikingly like that of C. H. Douglas who also condemned the perpetuation of debt. Pound refers to this practice as *eating up one's descendants.*[36]

In the fourth passage, Adams adverts to the distrust of paper currency in his native Massachusetts district of Braintree from 1761 on. The people of Braintree preferred to do business by barter. He maintains, in a letter to Rush, that most of America's trouble is due to ignorance of money. This is a theme Pound will take up in Canto LXXI. John Adams, like C. H. Douglas, believed that ignorance of coin, credit and circulation was the main source of a nation's troubles. C. H. Douglas dedicated his life to removing this pall of monetary ignorance, which he believed was causing mankind to go into slavery.

The fifth passage refers to the corruption of the English court and the sale of six million acres to reduce the national debt. Adams shows monetary literacy in accord with Douglas/Pound in that he notes the difficulty England is in due to her huge national debt with its heavy dead-weight of interest.

In the sixth passage, Adams refers to his role in securing valuable fishing rights off Newfoundland and in the Gulf of St. Lawrence for the United States at the peace commission of 1782. Adams was

---

[36] "[B]ut against lice that ate their descendants." Canto LVI.

acutely aware of the American need to be economically self-sustaining, lest through the want of productive industry, the new nation would become too greatly involved in debt to achieve economic independence.[37] Pound *heartily approves* Adams's aversion to debt, which is completely in keeping with Douglasite philosophy and policy. Adams's desire to protect America's natural resources, in this case her fisheries, is akin to Douglas's insistence on a nation's natural resources being shared among its citizens.

Canto LXXI is the last of the Adams Cantos. This canto sums up and reviews many of the themes dealt with in the earlier Adams Cantos. There are a number of significant monetary-economic luminous details included here:

> 1. depreciated by the swindling banks, a multitude
> of such swindling banks have ruin'd our medium
> Their issues are against gold or on nothing.
>
> . . . .
>
> 2. in '61 came writs of assistance.
> No history of the past 20 years without documents
> especially the circular letters to
> members of congress, without these libels
> no history of these decades '89 to '09
>
> . . . .
>
> 3. Vergennes said to me: Mr. Adams, newspapers govern the world.
>
> . . . .
>
> 4. Funds and Banks I
> never approved I abhorred ever our whole banking system
> but an attempt to abolish all funding in the
> present state of the world wd/ be as romantic
> as any adventure in Oberon or Don Quixote.
> Every bank of discount is downright corruption
> taxing the public for private individuals' gain.
> and if I say this in my will
> the American people wd/ pronounce I died crazy.
>
> . . . .
>
> 5. Taxes laid, war supported. This must be.
> Adams writing in Quincy in 1813
> Histories are annihilated or interpolated or prohibited . . .
> our 'pure uncorrupted uncontaminated unadulterated
> etc'
> Sir Wm. Keith in 1739 proposed such an assembly to the
> ministry

[37] Adams, John, *The Diary*, 306–36.

aiming at stamp tax—he being then, I believe, in Fleet prison
His hint was taken in '54 and in '64

. . . .

6. 'Will his son save 'em (the fishing rights)
for a second time?'

. . . .

7. That is to GET a navy.

JOHN ADAMS FOR PEACE 1800

I believe no printer in Boston wd/ print 'em.
Adams to L. Lloyd, in 1815)
I do not believe they cd/ get printed even today
in any newspaper in Boston. Circular letters, the lot of 'em
are full of as many lies as the Acta Sanctorum.

. . . .

8. Burr folded it with great gravity, saying:
Now I have him all hollow.
(re/ list of Hamilton's delegates)
Walcott persisted for 8%

. . . .

9. money or no money, she can never conquer this country.
'They will print anything that will sell.
'Our correspondence is considered a curiosity by both parties'
Adams to Jefferson 1815
but I do not think that it is tampered with
Your letters seem to get here unopened.

. . . .

10. 'Give more for Jefferson's letters
than for all the rest in his (Morgan's) volume.'

. . . .

11. Credit Otis with a great part of my argument
he showed illegality; toward destroying the charters
Poor soldiers knew not what sent 'em
North called 'em Sam Adams two regiments

. . . .

12. Otis resigned his post (Advocate General)
and was beaten up by coffee house bandits
in good looking clothes.
Otis against the writs, J.A. versus judiciary,
Defended Preston, defended the soldiers;
Fisheries, peace, nomination of Washington, kept peace with

France 1800. Gold, silver are but commodities
Pity, says Tracy, they ever were stamped save by weight
They are commodities as is wheat or is lumber.
. . . .
13. Adams to William Tudor
1818
24 years before Hobhouse.
'Ignorance of coin, credit and circulation!'
(Canto LXXI)

The first passage refers to the depreciation of American currency due to the irresponsible policies of the various state banks, in their issuing of state bank notes during the period 1811–16.

The second passage refers briefly to the writs of assistance of 1761 and then mentions the notorious circular letters that were sent to congressmen in the years between 1789 and 1809. These circular letters were issued by the financial interests and were used to persuade congressmen to vote for the chartering of the private First Bank of the United States in 1791 and for the renewal of its charter in 1811. Adams maintains that these circular letters were full of libels and that there can be no accurate history of this period without knowledge of these libels.

The third short passage has reference to a statement made by the French minister Vergennes to John Adams to the effect that newspapers govern the world. Pound chooses this particular luminous detail because it is completely in accordance with the Douglasite view of the financial control of the press and of other means of publicity.

The fourth passage is strong in its Douglasite content. Adams, like Douglas, abhors the banking system. C. H. Douglas is convinced that the interests of the banking system are incompatible with the interests of the public. The banking system is interested only in the creation and perpetuation of debt, whereas the public is interested in obtaining goods and services. This does not mean that he wishes to do away with all banking any more than Adams does. However, Adams, like Douglas, is convinced that under the present private bank-issued credit system, every bank of discount is downright corruption, taxing the public for private individuals' gain. However, he realizes that due to the frightening monetary illiteracy of the American people, they would pronounce him insane if he were to proclaim this.

In the fifth passage, Adams makes a statement about history, which is completely in harmony with both Douglas's and Pound's views on this subject. Adams maintains that the facts of history are annihilated, interpolated, or prohibited. The Douglasite view is that this is done to keep the people in ignorance of the true monetary-economic facts and forces in history. Anything that might embarrass or weaken the power of the usurocracy is *kept out of the history books*. This is one of the reasons why Douglas refers to the system of general education, in vogue today, as a form of mass hypnotism: "With an overwhelming majority of persons there is (no doubt as the result of the collective hypnotism generally referred to as education), a tendency to uphold a social ideal from which their personal existence is a continuous effort to escape."[38]

In the sixth and seventh passages, Adams refers to his role in saving the fisheries and in providing America with a navy. He then goes on to recall his efforts in keeping the peace and avoiding war with France in 1799. The peace treaty of 1799 with France brought about Adams's defeat in the presidential election of 1800 because his own Federalist party had called for war with the French.

In the seventh passage, Adams refers to the impossibility of getting his publicity published in the Boston press. He again condemns the circular letters.

The eighth passage refers to Aaron Burr's feud with Alexander Hamilton over delegates to a nominating convention. The feud ended with Burr killing Hamilton in a duel.

The ninth passage touches upon the Jefferson-Adams correspondence itself, which was considered a curiosity by members of both the Federalist and Republican parties.

The tenth passage affirms Adams's great regard for Jefferson and his correspondence. This mutual admiration between Adams and Jefferson, even though they belonged to different parties, was largely due to the fact that they shared what Pound calls "monetary literacy," a monetary literacy which Pound sees as the basis of Douglasism.

The eleventh passage has reference to the legal struggle over the writs of assistance referred to earlier in the Adams Cantos.

The twelfth passage describes the beating administered to James Otis who had argued against the petition granting the writs of assistance. Then, in quick review, Pound mentions the great events of Adams's career: the defence of Preston and the soldiers, the fisheries negotiations, the peace with England, the nomination of Washington and the peace with France in 1800. The passage ends with Pound's paraphrasing Adams's remark that gold and silver are only

---

[38] Douglas, *Social Credit*, 221.

commodities like wheat and lumber. This is, of course, a profoundly Douglasite sentiment. C. H. Douglas often ridicules *the fetish of gold and silver* that has been built up and propagated by the banking fraternity. He constantly stresses that financial credit, i.e., the rate at which money can be delivered as, when, and where required, must be based upon real credit, i.e., the rate at which goods and services can be delivered as, when, and where required.

The thirteenth passage is part of one of the most significant monetary-economic luminous details that we have in The Cantos. Adams remarked in a letter to William Tudor in 1818, that ignorance of coin, credit, and circulation is the cause of most of the troubles in America. This is, of course, what C. H. Douglas reiterated constantly between 1918 and his death in 1953, substituting for America the world. It is a theme and a luminous detail which Pound emphasizes often in his prose writing and which, as a luminous detail, he repeats often in *The Cantos*.

The final lines of the Adams Cantos are written in Greek. Pound tells us that these lines are from the "Hymn of Cleanthes," which was part of Adams's *paideuma*.[39] Pound feels that they are perfectly appropriate as a final tribute to Adams: "Glorious, deathless of many names, Zeus aye ruling all things, founder of the unborn qualities of nature, by laws piloting all things."

3) THE PISAN CANTOS LXXIV–LXXXIV

Pound wrote the Pisan Cantos as a prisoner of the American military while held in the Disciplinary Training Centre at Pisa, Italy, in 1945.

By the time the Pisan Cantos were published in 1948, Landini writes, Pound had already proposed his program to reform ethics and economics in seventy-one cantos. Landini states: "In this respect the teacher rested his case. What remained for him as *scriptor cantilenae* was the task of recording the society around him at the D. T. C.: prisoners accused of rape, murder, desertion, plunder, buggary, etc., an ant colony and a wasp hive (Cantos LXXIV, LXXVII, and LXXXIII, for instance)....When the manners and customs of his immediate society grew repetitive and boresome, Pound turned his vision inward, traveling old roads: China, Confucius, Adams, Jefferson, Douglas, Gesell, Eliot, Yeats, Mussolini."[40]

---

[39] See "Table" preceding Canto LII, in which Pound provides his own translation of the Greek text that is quoted. Pound, *The Cantos*, 256.
[40] Landini, *A Guide*, 202–3.

Canto LXXIV contains its share of monetary-economic luminous details. The canto opens with a reference to Churchill's return to the Gold Standard in 1925 and its adverse effect upon the Indian farmers:

> 1. but a snotty barbarian ignorant of T'ang history need not deceive
> one
> nor Charlie Sung's money on loan from anonimo
> that is, we suppose Charlie had some
> and in India the rate down to 18 per hundred
> but the local loan lice provided from imported bankers
> so the total interest sweated out of the Indian farmers
> rose in Churchillian grandeur
> as when, and plus when, he returned to the putrid gold standard
> as was about 1925 Oh my England
> that free speech without free radio speech is as zero
> and but one point needed for Stalin
> you need not, i.e. need not take over the means of production;
> money to signify work done, inside a system
> and measured and wanted
> "I have not done unnecessary manual labour"
> says the R.C. chaplain's field book
> (preparation before confession)
>
> . . . .
>
> 2. and the fleet at Salamis made with money lent by the state to the
> shipwrights
> Tempus tacendi, tempus loquendi.
> Never inside the country to raise the standard of living
> but always abroad to increase the profits of usurers,
> dixit Lenin,[41]
> and gun sales lead to more gun sales
> they do not clutter the market for gunnery
> there is no saturation
>
> . . . .
>
> 3. sd/
> Bunting
> doing six months after that war was over
> as pacifist tempted with chicken but declined to approve
> of war "Redimiculum Metellorum"
> privately printed

---

[41] Cf. Lenin, *Imperialism*, 77: "As long as capitalism remains what it is, surplus capital will never be utilized for the purpose of raising the standard of living of the masses in a given country, for this would mean a decline in profits for the capitalists; it will be used for the purpose of increasing those profits by exporting capital abroad to the backward countries." See a similar allusion in Canto LXXX.

> to the shame of various critics
> nevertheless the state can lend money
> and the fleet that went out to Salamis
> was built by state loan to the builders
> hence the attack on classical studies
> and in this war were Joe Gould, Bunting and cummings
> as against thickness and fatness
> . . . .
> 4. and the Farben works still intact
> to the tune of Lilibullero
> . . . .
> 5. and yet petty larceny
> in a regime based on grand larceny
> might rank as conformity nient' altro
> with justice shall be redeemed
> who putteth not out his money on interest
> "in meteyard in weight or in measure"
> XIX Leviticus or
> First Thessalonians 4, 11
> . . . .
> 6. and all the presidents
> Washington Adams Monroe Polk Tyler
> plus Carrol (of Carrolton) Crawford
> Robbing the public for private individual's gain ΘΕΛΓΕΙΝ
> every bank of discount is downright iniquity
> robbing the public for private individual's gain
> (Canto LXXIV)

The first passage above contains a number of significant monetary-economic luminous details. The "snotty barbarian ignorant of T'ang history" describes the type who contributes to the obfuscation of history and of economics. This can be the *orthodox economist*, the *safe* historian, or the journalist who *lies* for hire. These various types of *snotty barbarians* all contribute to the *stupidity of the populace* and fear nothing more than a *precise definition*, e.g., that handed down by Sigismundo Maletesta.

Pound then refers to the Chinese banker Sung and raises the question as to where Sung had borrowed his money. This luminous detail hints at the high degree of centralized control in international finance. Pound next switches his purposeful focus rapidly to India where the interest on private loans had *dropped* to a mere eighteen percent. However, this *drop* in the interest rate was soon *corrected* by the co-operation of the local moneylenders with foreign bankers. Pound maintains that the total interest rate extorted from the hapless

Indian farmers rose rapidly when Winston Churchill put England back on the gold standard in 1925.

Pound next points out that free speech without free radio speech is pointless. He means that free speech is meaningless so long as the mass communication media and organs of press and publicity are under centralized financial control. Pound stresses the fact that it is not necessary to take over the means of production as the Marxists insist. Douglas had always insisted that it was *not necessary to socialize the means of production*, but that *only the credit of the nation* should be socialized. Richard G. Landini in his otherwise excellent dissertation makes the mistake of claiming that Douglas wanted the socialization of the means of production.[42] Douglas had always maintained that this was unnecessary under Social Credit. Landini has misinterpreted certain passages in Douglas's works and read them out of context.

"I have not done unnecessary manual labour"/ says the R. C. chaplain's field book / (preparation before confession)." Pound is referencing a pocket Catholic prayerbook given to US military personnel, first printed in 1917: *Catholic Prayer Book for the Army and Navy, Pro Deo et Patria*,[43] received from Father Aloysius Vath. It contained a guide to the sacrament of confession on page 32, the question stating: "Have I done unnecessary manual labor?"[44] listed as a sin against the third commandment: "Remember to keep holy the Sabbath day." A certain amount of rest—leisure/contemplation/ recreation ("re-creation," making anew, with the prefix *re* meaning *back* or *again*) is needed by all if we are to live our life to the fullest: *to know, love and serve God*. The traditional monastic dictum *Ora et Labora*, i.e., the "prayer and work" that formed Western Civilization, is not only for monastics, but for all. Traditionally, the monastic day was spent equally in sleep, work, and prayer and contemplation. All should find one's life reflecting a similar healthy rhythm. *Labora* has taken over, and instead of being healthy and holy is mere drudgery due to long hours, repetitiveness, heat, cold, noise, or a dangerous environment. Douglas/Pound did not see any virtue in opposing machinery if it required fewer workers, and would free man from toilsome, repetitive, manual labour. Douglas did oppose the large industrialization of farming, as he understood farming not merely as a science, a technique, but as an art, i.e., a craft that depends on local knowledge and tradition. Douglas supported organic farming in the

---

42 Landini, *A Guide*, 122–23.
43 Baumann, "'In Principio Verbum,'" 255.
44 Baumann, "'In Principio Verbum,'" 241.

early 1940s, when Walter James (Lord Northbourne), authored his well-known book concerning organic farming, based on the writings of Rudolf Steiner.[45] Technology could free the small farmer from dangerous, difficult, and *unnecessary manual labour*, but small family farms were always better for healthy animals, healthy soil, and for the local, rural, cultural life.

Pound confesses to all that whatever sins he has committed, he is not guilty of *unnecessary manual labor*. Pound's statement is purely Douglasite. Pound has not worked more than necessary. He is not a slave but a freeman and indeed an artist who had time for leisure/contemplation. The whole of mankind commits this sin of *unnecessary manual labor*. We are enslaved by a money system that requires us to do additional labour to produce more manufactured products for the home market or for export, just to have *tickets*, i.e., money, to buy and consume our desired but previously unbuyable consumer goods. Trillions of US dollars are created by international banks and their financiers in the search for new investment opportunities. Massive building projects are made: construction of new housing, new factories, questionable infrastructure projects, in the quest for *growth* only to remain either unused or eventually abandoned. Huge projects to aid poorer foreign nations only enslave them to debt and reliance on imports. Physical labour is performed, but is no different, in its value to mankind, than if we were given the job to dig a deep hole and fill it up again. This sin takes us away from all that is holy: family, *re-creation*, the Sabbath rest, and the contemplation of higher things. *Unnecessary manual labour* is built into our system of finance. Our monetary system demands more labour than necessary and the waste of the earth's resources because additional *money created only as a debt owed to the banking system* is the *only means* to obtain manufactured goods that have already been created. The financial system refuses to issue money, created by the stroke of the pen, as debt-free credit—*dividends to all*. To do so would provide the necessary money to buy the goods already sufficient to meet the needs of the local market, the true consumption needs of the community.

The first luminous detail in the second passage refers to the famous sea-battle of Salamis in which the Greeks defeated the Persians and so preserved the cradle of what was to become Western Civilization. Pound points out that the fleet, which won the battle of Salamis, was built by means of money that *the state of Athens had lent* to the

---

[45] James, *Look to the Land*.

shipwrights. Thus, the building of the fleet had been financed by means of statal money. The fact that present-day *orthodox economists* regard state-issued money as *funny money* does not take away from the fact of the sea victory at Salamis. This is another of the great luminous details of *The Cantos*, which is to be repeated very often in subsequent cantos. Pound stresses this particular luminous detail because it provides historical validity for C. H. Douglas's basic postulate that *the state should lend not borrow*. Thus Pound illustrates his contention that Douglasism is itself part of a much older thought-heritage, by tracing back the concept of a statal money system to Ancient Greece.

This same second passage also quotes Lenin to the effect that goods are never distributed inside the country to raise the standard of living, but always abroad to increase the profits of the usurers. Pound ironically points out that gun sales led to more gun sales, and there is never a *saturation* of the munitions market as there apparently is for other markets.

The third passage mentions Bunting. He was a pacifist and had refused to fight in World War I and was imprisoned as a result. He went on a hunger strike and they would daily place a cooked chicken in his cell, to tempt him, and to mock him (since a coward is a *chicken*). Bunting's first poetry collection, the *Redimiculum Metallorum*, translates as *a wreath of chamber pots*. It was printed only by means of private financing.[46] Pound seems to suggest, in homage to his friend Bunting's humble reference to his own verses as *chamber pots*, that it is likewise an apt name — if one expands all possible renderings of the Latin phrase — for the cultural value of weapons of war.

Again, in the third passage, Pound repeats his great *battle of Salamis*, a luminous detail which negates the need and sanity of a privately issued money-system. Pound maintains that classical studies are being de-emphasized in that system of mass hypnotism known as *general education* because the history of Greece and Rome contains too many embarrassing monetary-economic facts for the comfort of the usurocracy. The reference to Gould, Bunting and cummings as being involved in the fight against *thickness and fatness* in literature relates to Pound's belief that the corrosive effect of usury produces an unhealthy *thickness and fatness* in literary works. Pound often refers to the *blurring* effect in the arts and the loss of lines of demarcation.

The fourth passage alludes briefly to the Farben munitions works in Germany that still stand intact. Pound has earlier attacked the munitions makers and has shown their link with the financial interests.

[46] Terrell, *A Companion*, Vol II, 371.

In the fifth passage, Pound points out that one must expect petty larceny under a system based on grand larceny, i.e., usury. He quotes the Old Testament reference to the prohibition of usury and cites, in support, the words of St. Paul: "And that you use your endeavour to be quiet: and that you do your own business and work with your own hands, as we commanded you: and that you walk honestly towards them that are without: and that you want nothing of any man's."[47]

The sixth passage consists of an honour-roll of anti-usury American presidents and statesmen. It concludes with John Adams's powerful indictment of *banks of discount*. This statement of John Adams agrees precisely with Douglas's condemnation of the creation of credit by the banking system. This bank credit system, says Douglas, does in fact rob the public for private individuals' gain.[48]

In Canto LXXIV the monetary-economic luminous details continue:

1. Is downright iniquity said J. Adams
        at 35 instead of 21.65
        doubtless conditioned by what his father heard in
                                        Byzantium
doubtless conditioned by the spawn of the gt. Meyer Anselm
That old H. had heard from the ass-eared militarist in Byzantium:
    "Why stop?" "To begin again when we are stronger."
and young H/ the tip from the augean stables in Paris
    with Sieff in attendance, or not
    as the case may have been,
                                thus conditioning.
Meyer Anselm, a rrromance, yes, yes certainly
but more fool you if you fall for it two centuries later

. . . .

2.   "Thou shalt purchase the field with money."
    signed Jeremiah
from the tower of Hananel unto Goah
unto the horse gate $8.50 in Anatoth
which is in Benjamin, $8.67

. . . .

3.   From the law, by the law, so build yr/ temple
    with justice in meteyard and measure

. . . .

[47] 1 Thess. 4:11 (Douay-Rheims)

[48] Editor's note: Once again it is the fact that the banking system follows the wrong policy by robbing the public for private gain rather than the simple fact of credit creation that Douglas condemns. Indeed, the most serious problem with the policy is the failure of the financial system to automatically provide consumers with sufficient income to offset costs and prices that are simultaneously being generated.

4. and the two largest rackets are the alternation
of the value of money
(of the unit of money METATHEMENON TE TON
KRUMENON
and usury @ 60 or lending
that which is made out of nothing
and the state *can* lend money as was done
by Athens for the building of the Salamis fleet
and if the packet gets lost in transit
ask Churchill's backers
where it has got to the state need not borrow
nor do the veterans need state guarantees
for private usurious lending
in fact that is the cat in the woodshed
the state need not borrow
as was shown by the mayor of Wörgl
who had a milk route
and whose wife sold shirts and short breeches
and on whose book-shelf was the Life of Henry Ford
and also a copy of the Divina Commedia
and of the Gedichte of Heine
a nice little town in the Tyrol in a wide flat-lying valley
near Innsbruck and when a note of the
small town of Wörgl went over
a counter in Innsbruck
and the banker saw it go over
all the slobs in Europe were terrified
"no one" said the Frau Burgomeister
"in this village who cd/ write a newspaper article.
Knew it was money but pretended it was not
in order to be on the safe side of the law."
But in Russia they bungled and did not apparently
grasp the idea of work-certificate
and started the N.E.P. with disaster
and the immolation of men to machinery
and the canal work and gt/ mortality
(which is as may be)
and went in for dumping in order to trouble the waters
in the usurers' hell-a-dice
all of which leads to the death-cells
each in the name of its god

(Canto LXXIV)

The first sentence of the first passage is a repetition of the Adams's reference to the iniquity of banks of discount. The rest of the first passage refers to the revelation of certain monetary machinations on the part of the spawn of Meyer Anselm Rothschild as revealed to a certain *old H.* in Byzantium.[49] The whole tone of this passage is suggestive of a vast international financial conspiracy that starts wars as a matter of policy. This is one of the great themes of C. H. Douglas's writings. Pound points out that the career of Meyer Anselm Rothschild may read like a romance (such as his activities regarding the battle of Waterloo and the London Stock Market) but that we certainly would be fools to fall for such machinations two centuries later.

The second passage is a reference to the Prophet Jeremiah: "And sayest thou to me, O Lord God: Buy a field *for money* [emphasis added], and take witnesses, whereas the city is given into the hands of the Chaldeans?"[50]

The third passage is a paraphrasing of Leviticus XIX. Pound paraphrases this and the second passage mentioned above, both from the Old Testament, to show the standards of economic ethics in the Mosaic Law. The prophet's precept to "so build your temple with justice in meteyard and measure" is indicative of the Old Testament abhorrence for *neschek* or usury. Pound has written elsewhere that the Hebrew word *neschek* has the meaning of a *gnawing into* and thus captures well Pound's idea of usury as a corrosive, non-productive, and destructive force.

The fourth passage begins by naming and condemning the two greatest rackets, i.e., the alteration of the value of the monetary unit and usury. Usury under the present bank credit system takes the form of lending money at sixty percent interest. Pound has already explained, as indicated earlier, that when the bank lends money that it has created out of nothing, at six percent, it is, in fact, receiving sixty percent interest.

Pound next works in a brief uncomplimentary reference to Winston Churchill and then repeats his great luminous detail, i.e., that the state need not borrow. Not only need the state not borrow, but it is also not necessary for private individuals, e.g., the veterans, to

---

[49] Old and Young H are believed to be a reference to Henry Morgenthau, Senior and Junior (Terrell, *A Companion*, Vol II, 379). Senior served as the American Ambassador to the Ottoman Empire during WW I, in Istanbul (Constantinople or Byzantium). Morgenthau, *All in a life-time*, 174. Paris would appear to be a reference to the Paris Peace Conference of 1919. *Augean stables* would not be a kind reference to the Paris Peace Conference because it compares it to the largest mythical barn full of manure that was in need of being cleaned-out.

[50] Jer. 32:25 (Douay-Rheims)

pay usurious rates of interest. C. H. Douglas has always stressed in his writings that the state should lend not borrow. He maintains that the state should lend money to the private banks, not the private banks to the state as is the case today under the debt-money system.

Pound goes on to prove that the state need not borrow, by giving an example from contemporary monetary history. He tells the story of the Tyrolean town of Wörgl and its experiment with scrip money. This Stamp Scrip monetary system was originated by Silvio Gesell, author of *The Natural Economic Order*, which was first published in 1915. Silvio Gesell was for a short time finance minister of Bavaria under a short-lived government. This book has already pointed out that the Gesell plan of Stamp Scrip must be thought of as a supplement to Douglas Social Credit and not as a substitute for Social Credit in Pound's thinking. Pound seems not to have discovered Stamp Scrip until c. 1933, although Gesell's work had antedated Douglas's by several years. Pound's great interest in Gesell scrip was that it was a simple way to teach people about money.

Stamp Scrip is a note or bill produced and issued by the state or governmental issuing agency against the aggregate wealth of the state's production capacity. On each note is an official stamp describing the day, month, and year of issuance. Thirty days after issuance, and each month thereafter, that note depreciates in purchasing power one percent; after five years, it is depreciated by sixty percent. After eight years and four months, that note will have depreciated one hundred percent and is no longer negotiable. Gesell is not adamant concerning depreciation percentage, but suggests about a 5% depreciation, or, as in an example given for American currency, an annual depreciation of 5.2%.[51]

In the Wörgl section of the fourth passage above, Pound takes the time to describe the contents of the Burgomeister's bookshelf. The implication is typically Poundian in that Pound has always maintained that a high level of culture, literary or otherwise, cannot be maintained under the corrosive influence of usury. Herr Unterguggenberger, the Burgomeister, in addition to having clear monetary-economic ideas, also keeps a copy of the *Divinia Commedia* and Heine's *Gedichte*. This is not at all surprising to Pound. One expects this from a man with clear monetary-economic notions. It is the *loan lice* with their perverted system of usury who have blurred and destroyed true culture. In the 1930s the town of Wörgl had issued its own money: "The town had been bankrupt: the citizens had

[51] Gesell, *The Natural*, 270.

not been able to pay their rates, the municipality had not been able to pay the schoolteachers, etc. But in less than two years everything had been put right, and the townspeople had built a new stone bridge for themselves, etc. All went well until an ill-starred Wörgl note was presented at the counter of an Innsbruck bank . . . fulminations, anathema! The burgomaster was deprived of his office, but the ideological war had been won."[52]

Towards the end of the fourth passage above, Pound deals briefly with Communist Russia which had *bungled* and had not grasped the idea of money as a work certificate, i.e., as a certificate of work done. Pound gave the following definition of money: "1) 'Money' as certificate of work done. (2) 'Work done' to be in a sense 'inside a system', that is to say, it must be 'necessary' or at any rate it must be work that someone WANTS done. The product must be what someone lacks."[53]

Due to the Russian Communists not understanding the idea of money as *a certificate of work done*, their New Economic Planning was marred by disaster, and the immolation of men to machinery. Pound accuses Bolshevik Russia of engaging in the usurers's old game of dumping goods on the foreign market. Reference has already been made to Pound's condemnation of Soviet dumping practices in Chapter II of this work. Pound insinuates that this usurers' hell-a-dice game of dumping and fighting for foreign markets represents the commercial warfare which inevitably leads to military warfare, "all of which leads to the death-cells." C. H. Douglas stresses that the struggle for foreign markets, demanded as a *conditio sine quo non* by the bank credit system, is the cause of that commercial warfare which has always preceded military warfare in modern times. Hence, Douglas sees the financial system as constituting the main cause of that continuing warfare which has marred the modern age. The last obvious monetary-economic luminous detail that one finds in Canto LXXIV is a reference to Gesell's role in the short-lived Lindhauer government in Bavaria:

> Gesell entered the Lindhauer government
> which lasted rather less than 5 days
>   but was acquitted as an innocent stranger
> Oh yes, the money is there,
>   il danaro c'è, said Pellegrini
>
> (Canto LXXIV)

---

[52] Pound, *Impact*, 51–52.
[53] Pound, *ABC*, 50.

Canto LXXVI does not contain as many monetary-economic luminous details as the preceding canto. The few that it does contain are mostly repetitions of earlier *luminous details*:

1. So that in the synagogue in Gibraltar
the sense of humour seemed to prevail
during the preliminary parts of the whatever
but they respected at least the scrolls of the law
from it, by it, redemption
@ \$8.50, @ \$8.67 buy the field with good money
no unrighteousness in meteyard or in measure (of prices)
and there is no need for the Xtns to pretend that
they wrote Leviticus
chapter XIX in particular
with justice Zion
not by cheating the eye-teeth out of Don Fulano
or of Caio e Tizio;
Why not rebuild it?

. . . .

2. Washington, Adams, Tyler, Polk
(with Crawford to bring in a few Colonial
families) the unruly
Tout dit que pas ne dure la fortune

. . . .

3. and if theft be the main principle in government
(every bank of discount J. Adams remarked)
there will be larceny on a minor pattern
a few camions, a stray packet of sugar
and the effect of the movies

. . . .

4. Knecht gegen Knecht
to the sound of the bumm drum, to eat remnants
for a usurer's holiday to change the
price of a currency
ΜΕΤΑΘΕΜΕΝΩΝ....
ΝΗΣΟΝ 'ΑΜΥΜΟΝΑ
woe to them that conquer with armies
and whose only right is their power.
(Canto LXXVI)

The first passage begins with a brief allusion to a synagogue service Pound attended at Gibraltar in 1908. He was struck by the general good humour prevailing. He was impressed by the respect shown for the scrolls of the law. Pound also has respect for the scrolls of the law because from these comes redemption. As a Douglasite,

Pound is particularly impressed with the book of Leviticus, Chapter XIX, which expressly forbids and condemns usury. Pound rhetorically asks why this marvellous system outlined by the book of Leviticus is not rebuilt?

The second passage enumerates four presidents and one secretary of the treasury who maintained the proper monetary tradition. The third passage reiterates John Adams's statement regarding the iniquity of banks of discount. Pound again points out that if the main principle of government is based on theft or larceny, i.e., usury, then there will naturally be larceny on a minor scale such as he sees going on in the Disciplinary Training Centre at Pisa. After all, if one accepts the principle of grand larceny, i.e., *usury*, in government, such minor acts of larceny or theft must be considered simply as acts of conformity, not crimes.

The fourth passage claims that usury drives people to consume scraps, if they're fortunate, pitting servant against servant (*Knecht gegen Knecht*), so usurers can continue manipulating currency prices.

The canto ends with a condemnation of the notion that might makes right.

Canto LXXVII also contains its share of monetary-economic luminous details. The following are a select few among many in this canto:

> "And with the return of the gold standard" wrote Sir Montagu
> "every peasant had to pay twice as much grain
> to cover his taxes and interest"
> It is true that the interest is now legally lower
> but the banks lend to the bunya
> who can thus lend more to his victims
> and the snot press and periodical tosh does not notice this
> thus saith Kabir, by hypostasis
> if they can take Hancock's wharf they can take your cow
> or my barn
> and the Kohinoor and the rajah's emerald etc.
> . . . .
> who live by debt and war profiteering
> Das Bankgeschäft
>
> (Canto LXXVII)

The first passage begins by paraphrasing a statement made by Sir Montagu Webb, a monetary reformer who had spent many years in India. Sir Montagu points out that with Winston Churchill's return to the gold standard in 1925, every Indian peasant had to pay twice as much grain to cover his taxes and interest. Pound, following Sir Montagu, points out that while the interest rate did become legally lower on bank loans, the banks simply would lend more to the *bunya* or local money-lender at the lower rate. The bunya thus was enabled to lend more to his victims at a much higher rate. Pound stresses that the *snot press* and *periodical tosh* does not notice the financial exploitation of the Indian peasant.

Towards the end of this passage, he paraphrases a statement concerning *Hancock's wharf* from the writings of John Adams. Pound wishes to point out that if an injustice can be perpetrated against John Hancock it can be perpetrated against the Massachusetts farmer. If an injustice can be perpetrated against the Indian peasant, it can also fall upon the Rajah's emerald. No one's property or rights are safe when a flagrant injustice such as usury is erected into the prevailing form of government.

The second passage records Pound's disapproval of those who live by debt and war profiteering. These two activities fall under the general heading of Das Bankgeschäft, i.e., the banking business.

Canto LXXVIII also continues to keep alive the distributist monetary-economic tradition, which Pound feels must be a part of any true epic:

> Geneva the usurers' dunghill
>   Frogs, brits, with a few dutch pimps
> as top dressing to preface extortions
>   and the usual filthiness
> for detail see Odon's neat little volume
>   , that is, for a few of the more obvious details,
> the root stench being usura and METATHEMENON
> and Churchill's return to Midas broadcast by his liary.
>   "No longer necessary," taxes are no longer necessary
> in the old way if it (money) be based on work done
>   inside a system and measured and gauged to human
>   requirements
> inside the nation or system
> and cancelled in proportion
>   to what is used and worn out
> à la Wörgl   Sd/ one wd/ have to think about that
> but was hang'd dead by the heels before his thought in proposito
>   came into action efficiently
> "For a pig," Jepson said, "for a woman." For the infamies of
>   usura,
> The Stealing of the Mare,.   casûs bellorum,   "mits"

. . . .
and if theft be the main motive in government
            in a large way
there will certainly be minor purloinments
As long as the socialists use their accessories as red herring
to keep man's mind off the creation of money
                                        (Canto LXXVIII)

In the first passage, Pound refers to Geneva, as the *usurers' dunghill*. Geneva is the place that welcomed the Protestant Reformer John Calvin and would be the home of the League of Nations along with International Banking. By the time this canto was published in 1947, it was the United Nations European headquarters.

Pound's views on the League of Nations are identical with those of C. H. Douglas. Like Douglas, Pound does not believe that the League of Nations is an instrument for preserving world peace but rather that it is an instrument of the usurocracy for achieving complete world domination. Pound points out that the French, English, and a few Dutchmen are used as window-dressing in the League of Nations for the usual financial extortion and larceny now practiced by the usurocracy on a world-wide scale. He refers us to *Odon's neat little volume*. Pound translated into English a book by Odon Por that was entitled *Italy's Policy of Social Economics 1939–1940*.[54] Pound implies there is something related to the League of Nations in Odon's writing that supports the charges that the basis of the League is usury and the *metathemenon*. Regarding the *metathemenon*, Pound writes as follows: "METATHEMENON TE TON KRUMENON, as I think Aristotle remarked. The voluntary variation of the value or purchasing power, or the metallic content, or the amount of metal, referred to by a given piece of money has attracted the attention of a great and élite set of people: Demosthenes, Dante, Cleopatra have all found the subject interesting, quite interesting."[55] Pound, like Douglas, can see no hope for mankind in a world organization controlled by the money-power. Pound again briefly alludes to Churchill's return to the gold standard, an event that has appeared before and will appear again in *The Cantos*.

Pound then goes on to quote what he had told Mussolini during an interview which he had with the Italian Prime Minister. On this occasion, Pound had told Mussolini that taxes were no longer necessary in the old way if money were based on work done, measured, and

---

[54] Terrell, *A Companion*, Vol II, 420.
[55] Pound, "*Ezra Pound Speaking*," 263.

gauged to human requirements inside the nation or system. Pound pointed out to Mussolini that the money issued could be cancelled in proportion to what is used and worn out according to the system of Gesell stamp scrip as practiced in Wörgl. In this connection, it is important to reiterate what has already been said in Chapter II. Pound's admiration for Mussolini was based on the hope and belief that the Capo del Governo was moving or intended to move in the direction of Douglasite monetary reform.

It has already been shown by direct quotations from Douglas that Douglas had, from the very beginning, considered Mussolini to be as evil a force as Lenin and Trotsky were. Douglas believed extremes meet and that the extreme left and the extreme right had much in common, including a possible common origin. This possible common origin was to be found in those vested financial interests that had financed both Lenin and Mussolini in their rise to power.[56]

The second passage is partly a paraphrasing of a statement made by John Adams, which has already appeared in *The Cantos*. Pound points out that both grand larceny, i.e., usury, and petty larceny will go on so long as the socialists continue to use various *red herrings* to keep man's mind off *the one big racket, i.e., the private creation of money*. Pound has previously been quoted to the effect that the whole history of the 20th century could be summed up in one sentence, i.e., that "Marx saw nothing wrong with money."

Pound then goes on to include in Canto LXXX by means of his technique of superposition, more monetary-economic luminous details. Some of these are new, others are repeated like the great themes of a marvellous symphony:

1. "Will never be used at home
but abroad to increase the
etc. of the lenders," the eh . . . investors
and is buried in the Red Square in Mosqu[57]
along with Andy Jackson, Napoleon and others
there is according to some authors a partial resurrection
of corpses

---

[56] Cf. C. H. Douglas, *Warning Democracy*, 58: "To a lesser degree, it is also recognised that extremes meet, that the extreme Right Wing reactionary, and the extreme Left Wing revolutionary, are fundamentally similar. There is little but a distance in form and mechanism between the ideas of Mussolini and a Lenin or Trotsky, and they are identical in their contempt for liberty, and passion for the rule of centralised force."

[57] See a similar allusion in Canto LXXIV and the footnote concerning their source in the writings of Vladimir Ilyich Lenin.

on all souls day in Cairo
or perhaps all over Egypt
in identity but not atom for atom
but the Sadducees hardly give credence
to Mr. Eliot's version
Partial resurrection in Cairo.
Beddoes, I think, omits it.
The bone *luz*, I think was his take off
Curious, is it not, that Mr Eliot
has not given more time to Mr Beddoes

. . . .

2. but old William was right in contending
that the crumbling of a fine house
profits no one
(Celtic or otherwise)
nor under Gesell would it happen

. . . .

3. Oh to be in England now that Winston's out
Now that there's room for doubt
And the bank may be the nation's
And the long years of patience
And labour's vacillations
May have let the bacon come home,
To watch how they'll slip and slide
watch how they'll try to hide
the real portent
To watch a while from the tower
where dead flies lie thick over the old charter
forgotten, oh quite forgotten
but confirming John's first one,
and still there if you climb over attic rafters;
to look at the fields; are they tilled?
is the old terrace alive as it might be
with a whole colony
if money be free again?
Chesterton's England of has-been and why-not,
or is it all rust, ruin, death duties and mortgages
and the great carriage yard empty
and more pictures gone to pay taxes
(Canto LXXX)

The luminous detail "Will never be used at home / but abroad to increase the / etc. of the lenders" is a paraphrase of a passage from the writing of Lenin. In this passage, Lenin pointed out that profits will never be used at home to bolster the domestic economy but will always be invested abroad instead. This policy of finance is the direct opposite of the Douglasite contention that the domestic market is the best market and far superior to any foreign market. C. H. Douglas stresses that the struggle for foreign markets, which is a by-product of the system of debt-finance or usury, is the main cause of war. Douglas points out that commercial warfare has always preceded military warfare in modern times. In other words, the money power is never interested in the good of the commonwealth. In fact, C. H. Douglas emphasizes that the welfare of the vested financial and banking interests is completely opposed to that of the public.

Pound then goes on to comment on the fact that Lenin, Andrew Jackson, and Napoleon are all dead. He then suddenly shifts from a discussion of these dead men to a consideration of the resurrection. He mentions various theories regarding the resurrection from the Christian view of Mr. Eliot to the anti-resurrection stand of the Sadducees. Pound mentions the doctrine of resurrection according to identity rather than atom for atom, a view which is also held by many eminent Catholic theologians, e.g., Emmanuel Doronzo O. M. I. Pound probably superposes this discussion of the resurrection after the luminous detail concerning monetary-economic crusaders like Andrew Jackson and Napoleon, in order to bring out the fact that although these men are dead, there may be a resurrection of their ideas. In other words, there may be a resurrection of identity with regard to their ideas, although not with regard to their actual atomic or physical composition.

The second passage refers to a statement made by William Butler Yeats to the effect that the crumbling of a fine house, e.g., a fine manor house, profits no one, "Celtic or otherwise." Pound points out that under the Gesell stamp scrip system this would not happen. C. H. Douglas maintains that the solution to poverty is not to be found in the Marxist policy of redistributing poverty and making every one poor. Douglas is convinced that the poor are poor not because the rich are rich, but because of a defect in the monetary system which causes a break-down in the system of distribution and impedes consumption.[58]

The third passage starts off as a parody of Browning's "Oh to be in England now that Spring is here." In this regard it reminds one of the satiric verse parodies on Social Credit themes "by Alfred Venison"

---

[58] Douglas, *Programme for the Third World War*, 52: "[T]he accepted idea that the poor are poor because the rich are rich has no foundation in fact and therefore class *economic* war has no factual justification."

which Pound wrote in the early thirties. In this passage, Pound longs to be in England given that Winston Churchill was voted out of power in the 1945 election. Since Churchill is out, there is a chance that the Bank of England may in fact be taken back by the nation. Pound, like Douglas, does not want the nationalization of the Bank of England but he does want the state to issue its own credit without borrowing from any private bank. The mere nationalization of the bank building and physical assets, as carried out by the Labour government, for example, would solve nothing as far as Pound and Douglas are concerned. It is the credit that must be nationalized, not the bank buildings.

Douglas never called for the nationalization of the banking industry, as is clear in numerous references. Both those who support Social Credit and those who attack it often confuse the two issues. Douglas clearly states:

> [D]o not be misled by any such phrase as "The nationalization of banking."
>
> The State and the banking system are very nearly one and the same thing at the present time and are wholly one in policy. While the Bank of England is a private bank owned by international financiers, the Treasury plays straight into its hands, and the nationalization of, for instance, the Bank of England, would mean the transfer of the Treasury into the Bank of England rather than the transfer of the Bank of England into the Treasury....
>
> No nationalization of banking will put one penny into the hands of the individuals comprising the countries over whom it rules, so long as this question of the ownership of money is left unaltered. But if it once be admitted that *the community, not its Government,* is the owner of the money, and the individual, as part of the community, is entitled to his share of it, the situation is obviously very different.[59]

Pound, in the same passage, states that it will be interesting to see how the money power will try to hide *the real portent.* He pictures himself watching from the Tower of London where dead flies lie thick over the forgotten Magna Carta. The Magna Carta is forgotten because it has no meaning in a land where the financial power structure rules supreme. He asks if the fields are tilled, and whether the countryside is prosperous—as it might be if money were free again. Chesterton's England of what "has been" and of "why not" should be an actuality in modern trappings if money were only free again. Pound then asks

[59] Douglas, *Dictatorship by Taxation*, 9.

if the true picture of England today is not rather that of "rust, ruin, death duties and mortgages / and the great carriage yard empty / and more pictures gone to pay taxes." This is modern England, due to over two hundred and fifty years of unbridled control by the usurocracy.

Canto LXXXII, like Canto LXXXI, is highly lyrical. There is a passage concerning war of importance:

> there are no righteous wars in "The Spring and Autumn"
> that is, perfectly right on one side or the other
> total right on either side of the battle line
>   and the news is a long time moving
>   a long time in arriving
>   thru the impenetrable
> crystalline, indestructible
>   ignorance of locality
> The news was quicker in Troy's time
> a match on Cnidos, a glow worm on Mitylene,
>
> (Canto LXXXII)

Pound points out in the above passage that there are no righteous wars mentioned in the ancient Chinese chronicle known as *the Spring and Autumn*. There are no wars mentioned as perfectly justified, on the one side or the other. Pound comments on the paradoxical difficulty of communication in the modern world, which makes the possibility of a perfectly righteous war even more remote. This difficulty of communication causes *accurate* news to be a long time in coming. C. H. Douglas emphasizes the blackout of real information that is caused by the centralized control of the press and of publicity. Pound, in support of Douglas, points out that the news was quicker in the time of ancient Troy. The paradox consists in the fact that the pertinent news was more quickly available in ancient times than in the modern world, despite all the new methods of communication. The implication is that the usurocracy has been successful in enforcing a *blackout* of real news and information.

Canto LXXXIV contains this significant monetary-economic luminous detail among others:

> and as to gradations
> who went out of industrials into Government
>   when the slump was in the offing
> as against whom, prepense, got OUT of Imperial Chemicals
> in 1938
> so as not to be nourished by blood-bath?
>
> (Canto LXXXIV)

This passage refers to the investments of high finance being taken out of industrial stocks and bonds and being put into government bonds just prior to the 1929 crash. Pound's statement indicates that high finance knew the crash was coming and acted accordingly. Pound has emphasized repeatedly in his prose writings the Douglasite contention that the 1929 stock market crash and depression were man-made. Both Douglas and Pound have blamed the depression on the banks suddenly calling in their loans. Neither Douglas nor Pound accept the various theories concerning *a loss of confidence*, psychological phenomena, or sunspots, that have been advanced by various *orthodox* economists as possible causes for the depression. The second part of this passage contrasts the machinations of high finance just prior to the 1929 crash with the ethical behaviour of someone who got out of Imperial Chemicals in 1938 so as not to profit from a blood-bath. This person may be Pound himself or someone close to Pound.

One last comment concerning the above. At least one person withdrew their money from stocks due to a warning from Douglas. Charlie Chaplin stated the following in his biography: "During the filming of it [the film *City Lights*], the stock market crashed. Fortunately, I was not involved because I had read Major H. Douglas's *Social Credit*, which analysed and diagrammed our economic system, stating that basically all profit came out of wages. Therefore, unemployment meant loss of profit and a diminishing of capital. I was so impressed with his theory that in 1928, when unemployment in the United States reached 14,000,000, I sold all my stocks and bonds and kept my capital fluid."[60]

SUMMARY

In assessing the influence of C. H. Douglas on the Chinese Cantos and the Adams Cantos, it is useful to recall the scholastic axiom that whatever is received is shaped by the capacity of the receiver. Ezra Pound first met Douglas in 1918, when he was introduced to the programme and theoretical foundations of Social Credit. Pound later indicated that this encounter marked his conversion to Douglas's economic views. Throughout the 1920s, he pursued extensive study in monetary economics, monetary history, and history more generally, seeking to test and confirm the Douglasite position. The Chinese Cantos and the Adams Cantos were both composed after 1918, that is, after Pound had already adopted Social Credit principles.

Accordingly, when Pound investigated Chinese and American history, his attention was directed chiefly toward those episodes that

---

[60] Chaplin, *My Autobiography*, 324.

appeared to substantiate Douglasism as an inherited tradition of thought. His engagement with these historical materials was thus selective, informed by a prior commitment rather than by neutral historical inquiry. It is in this qualified sense that one may speak of Douglas's influence on the Chinese Cantos and the Adams Cantos.

The passages selected from the Chinese Cantos illustrate Pound's acceptance of certain Chinese ideas that are in accord with Douglas's ideas. Pound's endorsement of some practices of Chinese historical figures, whose thinking was strikingly similar to Douglas's, is noted.

The Emperor Tching Tang, in 1766 BC, faced with a shortage of grain and rising prices, issued his own statal copper currency to the people in order to distribute and aid in the consumption of that grain which did exist. This state-issued, debt-free dividend paid to the consumer differs in no way in principle from the dividend advocated by C. H. Douglas. Thus Pound records one of the earliest examples of a state dividend issued debt-free by the statal authority, Emperor Tching Tang.

Pound points out the concern on the part of the distributist Chinese emperors that money should not be taken out of circulation and the people thereby deprived. This concern is identical to that of C. H. Douglas with respect to the draining of consumer purchasing power by the banking system and by iniquitous taxation. It is based upon that distributist philosophy which Douglas shares with the wise Chinese emperors. Douglas and the Confucian-oriented Chinese emperors share a belief in the distributive function of money, which is certainly at variance with the monetary philosophy held by the modern banking system.

In the Adams Cantos, Pound stresses that the thirteen colonies were able to fight and win the Revolutionary War by means of the bills of credit issued by the Continental Congress. Despite the wholesale counterfeiting carried on by the British to sabotage this currency, it never failed Congress. Even its devaluation, due to British counterfeiting, only acted as an unevenly distributed tax on the people paid in advance and, at the same time, it prevented them from being in debt. This currency was issued debt-free as C. H. Douglas advocates, and therefore the devaluation was the only tax the colonists had to cope with. Pound's focus on the debt-free issue of bills of credit by the Continental Congress lends support to his position that Douglasism is part of a thought-heritage applicable to the advance of freedom.

Pound's concern with the struggle over the grant of a charter to the First Bank of the United States, a private bank in all things but its name, lends support to C. H. Douglas's claim that the struggle between the usurer and the man who tries to do a good job is one of the basic struggles all through history. Thomas Jefferson, like C. H. Douglas, advocated a *Constitutional money system*, i.e., a money system under which Congress issued the nation's money supply without recourse to the usury of private banking interests.

John Adams is "the clearest head in Congress" and a great Poundian hero precisely because his philosophy and policy are similar to those of C. H. Douglas. It should be emphasized that when reference is made to the Douglasite influence on passages, e.g., those that Pound paraphrases from Adams's writings, it is because Douglasism influenced Pound to select those passages. Pound wanted to emphasize that Douglas's philosophy and policy is part of a much older thought-heritage. This thought-heritage goes far beyond John Adams and Thomas Jefferson to Medieval Italy and to ancient China itself, to name only two sources.

To repeat a point made earlier, those passages in Canto LXVII dealing with the controversy over the common law legality of the British Parliament's imposition of internal taxation on the American colonies indicate Pound's continuing preoccupation with the problem of taxation. C. H. Douglas first directed Pound's attention to this issue. Douglas has always maintained that modern taxation imposed as a form of tribute to the money power, and collected by its vassal, the modern state, is absolutely opposed to the freedom and integrity of the individual. He regards taxation as an instrument of policy, a policy pursued by the money power. Modern taxation as a form of highway robbery, says Douglas, makes war on the individual and is in fact not taxation, but confiscation.

Canto LXX reiterates Pound and Adams's disdain for Alexander Hamilton. This disdain has its basis in a difference of monetary philosophy that existed between Hamilton and Adams. Pound's contempt for Alexander Hamilton is typical of the Social Crediter's contempt for anyone who would betray the public control of credit to private interests.

John Adams, like C. H. Douglas, believed that ignorance of coin, credit, and circulation was the main source of a nation's troubles. Adams shows monetary literacy, according to Pound, in that he notes the difficulty England is in due to her huge national debt with its heavy dead-weight of interest.

The tone of certain passages in Canto LXXIV is suggestive of a vast financial conspiracy, which starts wars as a matter of policy. This is one of the great themes of C. H. Douglas's writings. Pound points out that while the career of Meyer Anselm Rothschild may read like a romance, such as his activities relating to the Battle of Waterloo and the London Stock Market, we certainly would be fools to fall for such machinations two centuries later.

In Canto LXXVIII, Pound refers to Geneva, the seat of the League of Nations, as the usurer's dunghill. Geneva is the place that welcomed the Protestant Reformer John Calvin and later would be home to the League of Nations. It has long been the headquarters and meeting place for International Finance, even in time of war. Pound's views on the League of Nations are identical with those of C. H. Douglas. Like Douglas, Pound does not believe that the League of Nations is an instrument for preserving world peace but rather that it is an instrument of the usurocracy for achieving *complete world domination*. Pound, like Douglas, can see no hope for mankind in a world organization controlled by the money power.

In Canto LXXXIV, Pound refers to the investments of high finance that were taken out of industrial stocks and bonds and put into government bonds just prior to the 1929 crash. Pound's statement indicates that high finance knew the crash was coming and acted accordingly. Pound has emphasized repeatedly in his prose writing the Douglasite contention that the 1929 Depression was man-made. Both Douglas and Pound blamed the Depression on the banks suddenly calling in their loans. Neither Douglas nor Pound accepts the various theories concerning a *loss of confidence*, psychological phenomena, or sunspots advanced by various *orthodox economists* as possible causes for the depression.

CHAPTER V

Cantos 85–109[1]

I) SECTION: ROCK-DRILL 85–95 DE LOS CANTARES

The Rock-Drill Cantos is steeped in Confucian learning and Chinese classical lore. Pound himself has stated that "Canto 85 is a somewhat detailed confirmation of Kung's [i.e., Confucius's] view that the basic principles of government are found in the Shu, the History Classic."[2] The purposeful focus in the Rock-Drill Cantos is on the United States rather than Europe. Pound derives a good deal of his luminous details from Thomas H. Benton's *Thirty Years' View; or, a History of the Working of the American Government for Thirty Years, from 1820 to 1850.* In Canto 85 there are many Chinese ideograms. Pound has pointed out in his personal note to Canto 85 that the meaning of the ideograms is usually given in the English text. The numerical references in Canto 85 are to Couvreur's *Chou King* and the transliterations are given as in Couvreur and Mathews. In addition to the Chinese ideograms, Canto 85 contains many significant monetary-economic luminous details:

1. Galileo index'd 1616,
Wellington's peace after Vaterloo

. . . .

2. That Queen Bess translated Ovid,
          Cleopatra wrote of the currency,
Versus who scatter old records
          ignoring the hsien form
          and jump to the winning side

. . . .

3. no mere epitome without organization
          The sun under it all:
          Justice, d'urbanité, de prudence

. . . .

4. Hulled rice and silk at easter
          (with the *bachi* held under their aprons
From T'ang's time until now)
That you lean 'gainst the tree of heaven,
          and know Ygdrasail

---

[1] In *The Cantos*, 1970 edition and earlier editions, Roman numerals are used from here forward. The ellipsis format likewise changes.

[2] Pound, *The Cantos*, note for Canto 85.

. . . .

5. Perspicax qui excolit se ipsum,
Their writings wither because they have no curiosity,
This "leader", gouged pumpkin
  that they hoist on pole,
But if you follow this process

. . . .

6. not a lot of signs, but the one sign
    etcetera
  plus always Τέχνη
and from Τέχνη back to *σεαυτόν*
Neither by chinks, nor by sophists,
  nor by hindoo immaturities;
Dante, out of St Victor (Richardus),
  Erigena with greek tags in his verses.

. . . .

7. that they make total war on CONTEMPLATIO.
Not to pamper this squirrel-headedness

. . . .

8. and not to bitch this whole generation in fish-traps

. . . .

9. Not by vain disputations
  nor sitting down on a job that is done

. . . .

10. whereby, in the long run,
reddidit gubernium imperatori

. . . .

11. Alexander paid the debts of his troops.
Not serendipity
  but to spread

. . . .

    tê   thru the people.
The pusillanimous
  wanting all men cut down to worm-size.
Mr. Roosevelt chose Dexter White.
As against culture as quick-sand
  after "'48" (1848)
    philology subdivided,
Nap III had the composition divided,
 to each compositor in the print shop
 a very few lines,
  none seeing the whole Proclamation.
Keep 'em off the market four years
  and leave 'em without understanding,

No classics,
    no American history,
        no centre, no general root,
No *prezzo giusto* as core.
                                        UBI JUS VAGUM.
Alexander paid the debts of his soldiery.
Wishing to bring back T'ang's state of awareness

. . . .

12.   Tch'eng T'ang for guide.

. . . .

13. You will go a long way without slipping,
    without slopping over.

. . . .

14. from Tch'eng T'ang to Ti I
    nullus non splendidas fecit,
    nullus non se sociavit

(Canto 85)

The first passage above refers to the writings of Galileo placed on the Index in 1616. This luminous detail is significant because Pound is concerned with the censorship of significant monetary-economic historical facts by the money power. Pound maintains that the real facts of history are suppressed so as not to weaken the power of the usurocracy. The reference to "Wellington's peace after Vaterloo" is noteworthy in that Pound believes that Napoleon incurred the wrath of the money power by refusing to borrow from high finance and by attempting to assert his sovereignty as emperor over the coinage of the realm. Dr. McNair Wilson deals with this aspect of Napoleon's career.[3]

In the second passage, Pound refers to Queen Elizabeth having translated Ovid, and Cleopatra having written on currency. He contrasts these two queens with those who scatter old records and thus suppress the dissemination of the facts of history. He speaks of those who ignore the *hsien*[4] form and jump to the winning side. He speaks of these as *turbae* or rabble. Pound goes back to Confucian-Mencian lore in the third passage to point out that there is no mere epitome without organization. He stresses justice, urbanity, prudence and the greek *sophia* or wisdom.

The reference to T'ang's time in the fourth passage is significant in that the Emperor T'ang distributed the equivalent of the first state

---

[3] Wilson, *Monarchy*, 33–34.

[4] *Hsien* is "[t]he basic unit of local government in China. The word *hsien* may be roughly translated as 'county,' or 'district.'" "hsien, Chinese government unit," *Encyclopaedia Britannica*.

or national dividend in the year 1766 BC. Thus Pound indicates that Douglasism is part of a much older thought-heritage by showing that the Emperor T'ang distributed the equivalent of the first state or national dividend as early as 1766 BC. This dividend was a debt-free subsidy paid directly to the consumers of China. Reference has already been made to the Emperor T'ang's dividend in Chapter II and in Chapter IV under the section dealing with the Chinese Cantos.

The references in the passage to hulled rice and silk at Easter, etc., are significant in that they emphasize the great stress that the Emperor Tch'eng T'ang put on the distribution of abundance in his realm. Thus the Emperor Tch'eng T'ang, like C. H. Douglas, was a distributist in his economic philosophy. Both Pound and C. H. Douglas have a profound respect for medieval moral theology and canon law because of its emphasis on distributive justice as well as for its emphasis on commutative justice.

In the fifth passage Pound states "[t]heir writings wither because they have no curiosity." According to Pound, this is what is wrong with contemporary literature. Contemporary writers have no curiosity about the things that really matter, e.g., monetary-economics. In this same passage, he describes contemporary *leaders* as being nothing more than *gouged pumpkins* hoisted on a pole. The sixth passage stresses the importance of *Τέχνη* (*techne* or art), and points out that we must go back to Richard of St. Victor from whom Dante derived his philosophy. Pound also praises Scotus Eriugena "with greek tags in his verses." Pound is a great admirer of Scotus Eriugena and of his philosophy. In this passage, Pound is advising would-be leaders to go back to Dante, Richard of St. Victor, and Scotus Eriugena to learn the proper philosophy.

It is because of his great admiration for Richard of St. Victor and Scotus Eriugena that Pound condemns those who make total war on contemplation, as he does in the seventh passage. Richard of St. Victor had divided the stages of the spiritual process into "cogitatio, meditatio, and contemplatio."[5] Dante had read and followed Richard of St. Victor. This tripartite division had a profound appeal for Pound the artist because he saw it as mirroring his own artistic process.

Pound charges that the usurocracy is intent on de-humanizing man by making total war on contemplation, i.e., by creating economic conditions which make it impossible for man to contemplate and thus develop his spiritual nature. Pound's great devotion to Douglasism is largely because he believed that the Douglasite philosophy and policy would set man economically free and allow him to develop

[5] Baier, "Meditation and Contemplation."

his contemplative faculties. As Hugh MacDiarmid, the great Scottish Lallans poet, has said: "The values to be safeguarded in the Douglas Commonwealth are Liberty, Leisure and Culture. The will-to-plenty of the individual is to be given satisfaction, and the whole business and industrial life of society relegated to a subordinate place, somehow as in the economy of the human body many biological processes proceed automatically or semi-automatically, leaving the psychology of the human being free to develop its interests."[6]

Josef Pieper, the eminent German scholastic philosopher, has maintained that leisure is the very basis of culture in his book appropriately entitled *Leisure, the Basis of Culture*. This is in direct opposition to the Puritan doctrine of work for work's sake, and to the Marxist doctrine of the labour theory of value which maintains that all value comes from labour alone. It is no wonder that Douglasism had a powerful appeal for Ezra Pound the artist in a world given over to Marxism and Fabianism. Pound would agree with St. Thomas Aquinas that a certain modicum of well-being is necessary for the spiritual life. In 1922, Pound authored an article titled "Credit and the Fine Arts" in *The New Age*. It clearly shows his attraction to Douglas's scheme because of what it would mean for leisure, contemplation, and the arts:

> The only thing one can give an artist is leisure in which to work. To give an artist leisure is actually to take part in his creation. It is a question of making freemen, in the only sense that that word is worth while. It is NOT a charity. "Bel Esprit" is definitely and defiantly not a charity. It is not based on pity for the human recipient: it has nothing to do with Manchester Liberalism. Civilisation has got to restart. . . .
>
> "Bel Esprit" proposes simply to *release more energy for invention and design;* the practical way (Douglas's scheme does include a man's beginning on his own doorstep, and his own job) is to release those artists or writers who have definitely proved that they have something in them, and are capable of its expression. What we want is not more books, but a better quality of book.[7]

In the same passage, Pound emphasizes the need for clear thinking and clear definitions by asking that *squirrel-headedness* not be pampered. He is concerned lest this whole generation be *bitched* in the *fish traps* of confused and muddled thinking. He cautions against vain disputations

---

[6] MacDiarmid, "The Return," 106–7. See personal letter to Lorne Reznowski from Hugh MacDiarmid, Appendix 1.

[7] Pound, "Credit and the Fine Arts," 284.

and sitting down on a job that is done. He asks in Latin that government, i.e., sovereignty, be returned to the emperor. This sovereignty, of course, involves the emperor's sovereignty over coinage that was given away to private financial interests through the bank credit system. It is this imperial—regal—statal sovereignty over coinage, says Douglasism, which must never be given away to private interests.

In the eleventh passage above, Pound illustrates how this imperial power was exercised in classical times. He points out that Alexander the Great exercised his prerogative over the coinage to pay the debts of his troops. He issued the coinage; he did not borrow it from money lenders. In the words of Alexander as quoted by Arrian of Nicomedia: "[I]f any of you had incurred debts, I paid them off without troubling to find out how they were incurred, though you earn a handsome wage and have had many opportunities to plunder after a siege. Most of you have golden crowns, immortal remembrances of your valor and my esteem. And anyone who has died has met with a glorious end and a splendid funeral; bronze statues of most have been set up at home, and their honored parents are exempt from all public duty and tax."[8] This luminous detail concerning Alexander the Great will be repeated many times in *The Cantos*. Pound emphasizes that this was not a one-off, but was reflective of a general attitude he had toward the people. In other words, the benefits of this imperial issue of money was not mere chance, but was planned to have a distributive outcome, to bring benefit to all:

> Kings therefore needed coins, a responsibility that young Alexander learned from both his father Philip and his tutor Aristotle. The one taught by example, the other by instruction. During Alexander's reign, the treatise titled *Economics* was written down by another of Aristotle's students, perhaps Theophrastus, as a guide to financial management. . . . royal attention was limited to coinage, imports, exports, and expenditures. By modern standards, this is a shallow list of economic responsibilities for the leader of a major state, and we have seen that Alexander may have been lax in his supervision of three of them. What about coinage? The *Economics* advises, "With regard to coinage, the king determines what kinds should be minted and when." This apparently means that monarchs must determine when to strike coins of which denominations, and how much of each.[9]

---

[8] Arrian, *The Landmark*, 287.
[9] Holt, *The Treasures*, 158.

In the same passage, Pound touches upon the cult of mediocrity in modern society. He speaks of the pusillanimous, who want all men to be cut down to worm-size. There is no room for the hero or the heroic in modern society. Pound points out that it was Mr. Roosevelt who chose Harry Dexter White as assistant secretary of the treasury.[10] It was Harry Dexter White who was instrumental in drawing up the Bretton Woods Agreement that Pound, like Douglas, believes to be but another step towards complete world-wide domination by the usurocracy.

In this same passage, Pound stresses the fact that American culture has been subverted since 1848. This was the year that marked the loss of executive control by that group of patriots who had brought Jeffersonian principles into the White House. This line would include Jefferson, Madison, Monroe, Jackson, Van Buren, and Tyler. After this Jeffersonian group lost control of the White House, the usurocracy took over in America.

In this same passage, Pound continues his description of the death of culture. After 1848, philology was subdivided. Pound may be referring here to the dividing of linguistics from philology, which took place by circa 1848. Pound then gives an example of what he calls *obfuscation* by describing Napoleon III's obfuscation of the true facts in a royal proclamation. He bewails the fact that the classics are no longer taught. Pound maintains that the Latin and Greek classics are no longer discussed because they contain too many embarrassing monetary-economic facts of history. For the same reason, no real American history is taught. For instance, the true story of the bank war is not taught. There is no centre, no general root to American culture. There is no *prezzo giusto*, i.e., *Just Price* core. The Just Price was taught and advocated by both the medieval theologians and C. H. Douglas. The concept of the Just Price is, of course, one of the two basic applications of Douglasist policy, the other being the concept of the National Dividend.

In this passage, Pound once again points out that Alexander paid the debts of his soldiery. Here again is the Douglasite emphasis on the royal prerogative in monetary matters. Pound points out that the Emperor Kao Tsoung, 1324–1265 BC, wished to bring back T'ang's state of awareness, i.e., T'ang's state of monetary awareness as seen in his issuing the first consumer dividend in 1766 BC (as

[10] See Whittaker Chambers, *Witness*, where White plays a prominent part in the Alger Hiss spy case. Also see, by Whittaker's son, David Chambers, "The Baffling Harry White."

seen earlier in Chapter II). This act of the Emperor T'ang, as has been pointed out before, is completely in accord with Douglasite policy. By superposing T'ang's state of awareness in 1766 BC, with Alexander's wise benevolence in paying the debts of his soldiery by means of the royal prerogative over coinage, Pound again indicates that Douglasism is part of a much older thought-heritage . . . one that can be traced at least as far back as the Emperor T'ang and through Alexander the Great. In this connection, Pound and the monetary historian Alexander Del Mar would agree that when Christ, taking an imperial coin in his hand, said: "Render therefore to Caesar the things that are Caesar's and to God the things that are God's,"[11] He did indicate *that the coinage was Caesar's* and therefore did not belong to private interests. Del Mar writes: "Julius Cæsar erected the coinage of gold into a sacerdotal prerogative; this prerogative was attached to the sovereign and his successors, not as the emperors, but as the high priests of Rome; it was enjoyed by every Basileus, whether pagan or Christian, of the joint and Eastern empires from the Julian conquest of Alexandria to the papal destruction of Constantinople."[12]

In the passages that follow, Pound speaks of taking this same Emperor Tch'eng T'ang for our guide. With the great monetary wisdom of Tch'eng T'ang we will go a long way without slipping, without slopping over. From Tch'eng T'ang to Ti I (the first), there was nothing made that was not splendid. Thus, monetary wisdom in a culture leads to artistic splendour.

Canto 86, like Canto 85, is heavily laden with Confucian-Mencian allusions. There are not as many direct monetary-economic luminous details here as in subsequent cantos. However, the ones found here are intriguing:

1. Bismarck forgotten, fantasia without balance-wheel,
"No more wars after '70" (Bismarck.)
"Dummheit, nicht Bosheit," said old Margherita
            (or Elenor? dowager)
"Sono tutti eretici, Santo Padre,
            ma non sono cattivi."
Mind (the Kaiser's) like loose dice in a box.
Ballin said: "If I had known,
        wd/ indeed have stuffed all Hamburg with grain."

---

[11] Mark 12:17 (Douay-Rheims)

[12] Del Mar, *A History of the Monetary Systems*, 74. Concerning Silver, copper and bronze, Del Mar asserts that it was a State prerogative which at times was granted to other governing authorities, for example, to the Senate. See p. 35 of this same work.

Bülow believed him. But Talleyrand set up Belgium,
Two dynasties, two buffer states,
    wd/ have set Poland.
So that Belgium saved Frogland; Svizzera neutral.

. . . .

2. It may depend on one man
        . . . as in the case of Edwardus
and von Hoesch on the telephone:
        to good for three years,
            or to evil
Eva's pa heard that on the telephone,
            but forgetful of Bismarck;

. . . .

3. "No wars after '70."
        "Nicht Bosheit, Dummheit!"
"Sono tutti eretici, Santo Padre,
        ma non sono cattivi."
It can't be all in one language"
        "They are all prots YR HOLINESS,
            but not bad.
Yes yr/ Holiness, they are all of them prots."
"Wd/ have filled Hamburg with grain."
"No, Miss Wi'let, on account of bischniz relations."
20 years to crush Bonaparte,
        gold through France into Spain
The purchase and sale of
            Geschäft,
and Buchanan's remark about monarchies
        (1850 to Pierce)
mentioning only those on the Continent
question? England not yet sold for the Suez—
That would have been 20 years later,
        or was it '74?
At any rate, sold down the river,
            passed over Parliament,
    "whatever else he believed in,
it was not representative government"
    Nor visible responsibilities.
All, that has been, is as it should have been,
    but what will they trust in

now?

"Alla non della", in the Verona statement
        οὐ ταῦτα . . . κακοῖσι
    Section Rock Drill.

Alexander paid the debts of his soldiery. They
thought there was a catch in it somewhere, but he set up
the tables
at camp's edge; "Any note will be paid."
OBIT apud Babylonios
(date . . . out of Arrian).
And in the great Hamurabi Inscription:
THEY LIED.
That is the Regius Professorships
(apud Chris. Hollis)
to falsify history
and impose the Whig point of view.
"Such hatred"
wrote Bowers,
and La Spagnuola saying:
"We are perfectly useless, on top,
but they killed the baker and cobbler."
"Don't write me any more things to tell him
(scripsit Woodward, W. E.)
"on these occasions
HE
talks," (End quote)
"What" (Cato speaking) "do you think of
murder?"
But some Habsburg or other
ploughed his Imperial furrow,
And old Theresa's road is still there in Belgium.
Tree-shadowed
and her thalers
were current in Africa,
standard in our time,
"characters by their coinage";
Cleopatra wrote of her coinage.
(Joseph two, verify? ploughed his furrow)
Up out of Tuscany, Leopoldine.
"We don't hate anybody."
Quoted Konody,
"We fight when our Emperor says so."
(Austrians 1914)
"Decent chaps" (Schwartz '43)
"a shame that we have to fight 'em."
"Mais le prussien!
Le prussien
c'est un chic homme."

. . . .

4. "On these occasions
HE
talks,"
end quote, Woodward '36
Eleven literates
and I suppose Dwight L Morrow"
re Senate enrollment
Br . . . C . . . g
question? about '32
"hysteric presiding over it all" '39
House, Foreign Relations.
Bellum cano perenne . . .

(Canto 86)

The first passage paraphrases Bismarck to the effect that there will be no war after 1870. It also paraphrases a remark made to the Pope to the effect that a certain group are all protestants, but not bad. Ballin, the German financier, is quoted as saying that if he had known, he would have stuffed all Hamburg with grain. Pound also points out that Talleyrand set up Belgium and that Belgium saved France. The second passage seems to refer to Edward VIII of England who was known to have quite definite ideas concerning the suffering of his subjects and his desire that something be done.[13] Douglas himself, like Pound, opposed Edward's abdication:

> The issue, whatever the newspapers may be saying, is NOT whether the King should marry Mrs. Simpson or not.
>
> What is being demanded by a curiously unanimous body of newspapers, all of which have financial connections, is, first of all, and as usual, that the interests of the individual must be subordinated to an abstraction, an institution.
>
> Much play has been made of the fact that Mrs. Simpson has two husbands still living from whom she has obtained divorce.
>
> It appears from all the evidence with which we are acquainted that, in this connection, she is singularly free from the unpleasant notoriety which is apt to accompany questions of this kind.
>
> But apart from that it is beyond all discussion that divorce is the law of the land, and to raise such a question is to state in effect that the law of the land is an improper law. This is an aspect of the matter which comes with singularly bad grace from those who are responsible for those laws.

[13] Pound, "Abdication," 82–87.

> Secondly, the storm has burst immediately on top of the King's obvious intention to obtain action to relieve the suffering of the distressed areas.
>
> This is an attack on realism. The row is being made, on formal grounds, by the very people who have been completely unmoved by the continuous suffering of millions of their fellow men.[14]

Douglas saw the immediate cause of the opposition to the King being the King's comment, when visiting the destitute in Wales, that "something must be done," i.e., that he was the only monarch who had shown concern for the poor working man. This was political interference during the Great Depression and was unacceptable to the British government and financial powers.

The third passage again quotes Bismarck and the remark made to the Pope. It also repeats Ballin's remark about Hamburg. There is also a repetition of the luminous detail concerning the twenty years necessary to crush Bonaparte. This has been seen in earlier cantos. There then follow references to the transporting of gold through France into Spain and the purchase and sale of gold. Pound characterizes this as Geschäft or business. He has earlier in *The Cantos* spoken derogatively of *Das Bankgeschäft*, or the banking business. Pound's antagonism to *Das Bankgeschäft* is, of course, fully consonant with Douglasist policy and philosophy.

Pound then moves to a remark made by Buchanan to Pierce in 1850 concerning monarchies, but limits his remarks to those on the continent. Pound then asks if, at this time, the year 1850, England had not yet been sold for the Suez Canal. He then informs us that the selling of England for Suez took place twenty years later or perhaps in 1874. This has reference to Disraeli's purchase of the Suez Canal from the Khedive of Egypt in 1875, a reference to be made again in another passage below.

In this same passage, Pound repeats once again the great Alexandrian theme: "Alexander paid the debts of his soldiery": "He had tables set up in the camp with money on them, and instructed his clerks to pay the debt of any man who presented a promissory note, but not to take down his name."[15]

Pound next maintains the Regius Professorships falsified the great Hamurabi i.e., Hammurabi, inscription. Pound is implying that the Whig point of view could not accept that there was a law more morally

---

[14] Douglas, "The King," 1.

[15] Arrian, *The Landmark*, 280.

exalted in the pagan past than in contemporaneous England. Pound would have found the 48th law of Hammurabi to contrast sharply with the *enlightened* demand for payment by the whiggish banking system: "If a man is liable for interest, and the god Adad [i.e., a thunderstorm] has flooded his field, or the harvest has been destroyed, or the corn has not grown through lack of water; then in that year he shall not pay corn to his creditor. He shall dip his tablet in water, and the interest of that year he shall not pay."[16] As Hollis states:

> Dr. Arnold, the founder of the public-school system, when appointed Regius Professor of History at Oxford, was telling his biographer, Stanley, that he "could not bear to plunge (himself) into the very depths of that noisome cavern", the Middle Ages, "and to have to toil through centuries of dirt and darkness"—centuries in which, as Thorold Rogers was to show, the poor were materially some six times better off than they were in Dr. Arnold's England. In preference to such a painful theme the doctor would prefer to dwell on "the deep calm of the first seventy years of the eighteenth century . . . as containing within itself the seeds of our future destiny."[17]

Pound lends support to C. H. Douglas's view that the system of general education is one of mass hypnotism. Nothing is taught which could lessen the strangle-hold of the usurocracy on society. He refers us to Christopher Hollis for additional information on this point. As noted earlier in this book, in Hollis's *Two Nations*, he shows how the Whig party, in the 18th century, set up Regius Professorships at Oxford and Cambridge for the teaching of Modern History.[18] The avowed purpose of these heavily-endowed professorships was to ensure that the Whig interpretation of history was taught. The Whig interpretation emphasized the fact that every change had been for the better and that all past institutions had been best left buried. Pound then quotes Bowers, the historian, concerning the cruelty in the Spanish Civil War and paraphrases quotations from La Spagnuola.

Then we have a reference to W. E. Woodward, the historian for whom Pound had great respect, and with whom he corresponded. Pound also wrote a number of articles and reviews on books written by Woodward. Pound quotes Woodward as stating "on these occasions HE talks." The *HE* referred to is Franklin Delano Roosevelt. Woodward had written to Pound that there was no use in Pound's

---

16 Edwards, *The Oldest Laws*, 17.
17 Hollis, *The Two Nations*, 87–88.
18 Hollis, *The Two Nations*, 39.

suggesting advice, which Woodward should give F. D. R., because the egotistical President did all the talking. This advice had to do with applying Douglasite policy as a remedy for America's economic ills.[19] This reference will be repeated at the end of the canto with the date 1936 given.

Superposed on this reference to Woodward is an oblique reference to usury. Pound quotes Cato who asks, "what do you think of murder?" This was Cato's reply when asked what he thought of usury. Once again, Pound equates usury with murder as a sin *Contra Naturam*, i.e., a sin that violates the natural order and sanctity of human life. Reference was earlier made to this quotation from Cato in Chapter II of this book.

Thus, we see that the theme of usury underlies this whole section. Pound then moves on to refer to "some Habsburg or other" who had ploughed his imperial furrow. As has been indicated before, when Pound speaks of someone ploughing his imperial furrow, it is used as in the Chinese Cantos, to describe those distributist emperors who exercised their regal prerogative over coinage in the pursuit of a philosophy and policy of abundance.

Pound mentions another Habsburg, Maria Theresa, whose thalers were still current in Africa in our time. In general, Pound does not think highly of the House of Habsburg, and he abominates Franz-Joseph II. However, he has a high respect for the House of Habsburg-Lorraine, which provided him with two of his great heroes in *The Cantos*: Pietro Leopoldo, and Ferdinando il terzo, Grand Dukes of Tuscany. We have seen that this admiration was due to the wise Leopoldine monetary-economic reforms in Tuscany. However, the reference to these two Habsburgs, Joseph II and Maria Theresa, is complimentary. Pound maintains that you are to judge these historical characters by their coinage. Once again, he points out that Cleopatra wrote of her coinage. Joseph II of Habsburg "ploughed his furrow," i.e., did his job properly regarding coinage. Then Pound remarks that it was up out of Tuscany that the Leopoldine reforms took place.

He then quotes Konody and Schwartz to show that the enemy in both World Wars, e.g., the Austrian and the German, was often a "decent chap." The Austrian, of course, contrasts with the Prussian who is a different case altogether. C. H. Douglas had pointed out the deadly combination of Prussianism and State Socialism, which, as

[19] Mullins, *This Difficult Individual*, 258.

early as the time of Bismarck, was already preparing the way for the Servile State. In Germany, this would eventually lead to the rise of Hitler and the Nazi party.[20] Friedrich Hayek in his *Road to Serfdom* (first published in 1944) develops this same theme.[21]

At the end of Canto 86, Pound returns to the quotation from Woodward to the effect that Roosevelt did the talking. Pound also points out that there were about eleven literates in the United States senate circa 1936. Senator Bronson Cutting, the sponsor of a monetary reform bill in the United States Senate in 1936, had made this remark to Pound. Senator Cutting's bill would have put America on a constitutional money system and would have implemented basic Social Credit reforms. He quotes someone to the effect that a hysteric is presiding over the House and Foreign Relations committee in 1939. The last line *Bellum cano perenne*—I sing of perennial war, links up with the anti-usury theme. Pound states that he sings of perpetual war between the usurer and the man who wants to do a good job.

This theme is continually repeated by Pound, as we will see. Again, it is a theme that is based on the writings, speeches, and conversations Pound held with Douglas. The continual divide between prices and real demand available, i.e., money, always makes of the worker a mere cog in the grinding machine of finance that demands work for food and clothing despite the waste of materials and human effort. As Douglas writes: "All these and many other forms of avoidable waste take their rise in the obsession of wealth defined in terms of money; an obsession which even the steady fall in the purchasing power of the unit of currency seems powerless to dispel; an obsession which obscures the whole object and meaning of scientific progress and places the worker and the honest man in a permanently disadvantageous position in comparison with the financier and the rogue."[22]

Canto 87 continues the anti-usury theme of Canto 86. The two opening lines of Canto 87 take us back to the great usury cantos themselves, dealt with in Chapter III of this study:

1. . . . between the usurer and any man who
    wants to do a good job
        (perenne)
without regard to production—
                a charge
for the use of money or credit.

---

[20] Douglas, *Economic Democracy*, 10–12, 23–24, 37–38.
[21] Hayek, *The Road to Serfdom*, 8–9.
[22] Douglas, *Economic Democracy*, 72.

"Why do you want to
" —perché si vuol mettere—
your ideas in order?"
Date '32

. . . .

2. Of Roanoke, EIGHTEEN 31:
"Nation silly to borrow its own."
Polk, Tyler, an honour-roll
paideuma fading,
Buchanan still fairly clean,
Infantilism increasing till our time,
attention to outlet, no attention to source,
That is: the problem of issue.
Who issues it? How?

. . . .

3. The total dirt that was Roosevelt,
and the farce that was Churchill
(vide Grenfell re/ phoney war)
"But", said Antoninus,
"Law rules the sea".
"And that the state shd/ have benefit
from private misfortune,
not in my time, not under me."
Until Salmasius, wanting precision:
Want, χρεία
"Common practice!" sd/ Ari re business;
"Cogitatio, meditatio, contemplatio."
Wrote Richardus, and Dante read him.
Centrum circuli.
Remove the mythologies before they establish clean values.
"Europe" said Picabia
"exhausted by the conquest of Alsace-Lorraine."
Vlaminck: " . . . is local." "Art is."
The pusillanimous wanting all men cut down to a worm size.
Wops, maggots, crumbled from simple dishonesty.
διάΒορον . . . ἐδεστὸν εἐξ αὐτοῦ φθίνει πρὸς κακοίσι
quia impossibile est.
Ver novum
are protected of course,
hic est medium

. . . .

4. Y Yin, Ocellus, Erigena:
"All things are lights."
Greek tags in Erigena's verses.

And when they bumped off Alexander in Babylon
that wrecked, said Gollievski "a good deal".
Greece had no Quattrocento.
Justinian's codes inefficient
"abbiam fatto un mucchio . . .
(a haystack of laws on paper)
Mus. viva voce:
"We ask 'em to settle between 'em.
If they can't, the State intervenes."
They deny, of course, but it percolates,

. . . .

5. "All metal as barter"
Destutt or whomso,
"Pity to stamp save by weight."
Always the undertow,
gold-bugs, against ANY order,
Seeking the common (as Ari says)
practice
for squeeze.
chih4
directio voluntatis.
"An instrument of policy
even more than a measure." Said Douglas (C. H.)
and the squirmers plunder men's mind,
wanting all men cut down to worm-size.

. . . .

6. The tower wherein, at one point, is no shadow,
and Jacques de Molay, is where?
and the "Section", the proportions,
lending, perhaps, not at interest, but resisting.

. . . .

7. But an economic idea will not (Mencken auctor) go into them
in less than a geological epoch.
"Nowt better than share (Mencius)
nor worse than a fixed charge."
That is the great chapter, Mencius III, I, III, 6

. . . .

8. but focus, can they even animadvert on focus?
or true editions?
"or even the use of process?
That fine old word"
sd/ "Stink" Saunders,
"An independence".

. . . .

9. Or as Henry again: "we have, in a manner of speaking,
arrived.
Got to, I think he says "got to, all got to."
The ubicity, ascertaining.
Was De Molay making loans without interest?
Church councils bumbling. Fanatics do not understand
interest.
Justice, directio voluntatis,
or contemplatio as Richardus defined it in Benjamin Major.
(Canto 87)

The first passage is a reiteration of Pound's statement to the effect that he sings of perennial war between the usurer and any man who wants to do a good job. This quote is similar to the words of Pound's epigraph at the start of his collection *Impact*: "Bellum cano perenne, between usury and the man who wants to do a good job."[23] This is an especially important point in illustrating the Douglasite influence on *The Cantos*. Just as Virgil in his great epic poem, *The Aeneid*, stated his theme when he wrote that he sang of *Arma virumque cano*—Of arms and the man I sing,[24] so too Pound, in his great contemporary epic, states his theme when he tells us: "*[b]ellum cano perenne*," i.e., that he sings of perennial war, "*between usura and the man who wants to do a good job*." This statement of theme, echoing that of Virgil's, provides a strong indication of the Douglasite influence and orientation in *The Cantos*.

In the next lines, Pound repeats the definition of usury, which has been quoted towards the end of Chapter II. In his series of essays entitled *Impact*, Pound had defined usury as "a charge for the use of purchasing power, levied without regard to production, sometimes without regard even to the possibilities of production."[25] He inserts the first part of this definition here at the beginning of Canto 87. It is this usurious disregard for economic facts that drives Pound into a fury. Pound, like Douglas, maintains that the existing financial system does not reflect economic reality. The financial system, which is a book-keeping system, does not truly reflect the facts of production and consumption.[26] Pound, like Douglas, maintains that the present financial system is based on a lie.

---

23 Pound, *Impact*, v.
24 *The Aeneid of Virgil*, 1.
25 Pound, Impact, 210.
26 "From one point of view a perfect financial system would simply be a mirrored reflection of every change in physical facts of the economic system. . . ." Douglas, *Warning Democracy*, 35.

The second passage quotes John Randolph of Roanoke, a great figure in American history, who in 1831 said that a nation was silly to borrow its own credit. Thus John Randolph of Roanoke was saying precisely the same thing that C. H. Douglas was to say in 1918, that the state should lend not borrow. The year 1831 was in the time of the great bank war during the presidency of Andrew Jackson. The bank war was the great struggle between the Jackson–Van Buren forces and the financial interests over the re-chartering of the private Second Bank of the United States as the main source of the nation's money supply.

Pound places the names of Presidents Polk and Tyler on his honour-roll of presidents who kept the Jacksonian monetary tradition. He informs us that even Buchanan was "still fairly clean," but that the *paideuma, the teaching or tradition* regarding an honest constitutional money system was fading.

Pound points out that infantilism or monetary-economic idiocy and ignorance kept on increasing until our time. He emphasizes that great attention is paid to the outlet of money or purchasing power, but no attention to the source of purchasing power. The outlets of purchasing power would be the various firms and industries that employ people and pay them salaries and wages. The main source of money and purchasing power, however, is to be found in the banks, which create credit and lend it to industry and business firms.

C. H. Douglas insists that attention must be focused on the banks or the *source* of credit, rather than upon the various firms who act as the *outlet* of credit. The Socialists and Marxists would be the best examples of *reformers* who focus everyone's attention on the outlet of credit rather than the source of credit. Pound indicated in an earlier canto, Canto LXXVIII, that he considers this a red herring to get the people's minds off the problem of issue. Pound sums up the problem of credit issue by asking who issues it and how. This, for Pound and Douglas, is the crux of our monetary, economic, social, and political problems. Until the problem of issue is solved, say Pound and Douglas, there is no use talking of reforms in other spheres.

The third passage above repeats Pound's disdain for both Roosevelt and Churchill. We are referred to a book by Grenfell concerning *phoney war*.[27] Pound then goes on to quote Emperor Antoninus

[27] Grenfell, Russell. *Unconditional Hatred.* Editor's note: Lorne suggested that the Grenfell referred to here and later in Canto 93 was the British banker and politician Edward Charles Grenfell, 1870–1941, but no reasons for his conclusion were provided. It seems certain Pound is alluding to Russell Grenfell as mentioned by Terrell, *A Companion*, Vol. II, 467-68.

Pius, as he has often done before, regarding the distinction to be made between marine insurance and usury. Antoninus maintains that law rules the seas, and that the state should not benefit from private misfortune.

The reference to the Calvinist writer, Claudius Salmasius or Claudio Salmasio,[28] is to *De Modo Usurarum Liber*, a 17th century text justifying usury. This is one of Pound's great sources for the study of usury and one that he always lists in select bibliographies dealing with the subject, as it is from Salmasius that Pound seems to have discovered the history of Emperor Antonius Pius on usury.[29] Pound's *until* as regards Salmasius indicates his respect for Salmasius' clear terminology.

Pound next refers to those who do not translate *χρέια* as Aristotle used it. Terrell explains: "Pound said the word, as used in Aristotle, should be translated as 'demand' and not 'value.' In his opinion, the lack of precision in translating such a key word as this does damage to correct thinking through the ages."[30] Salmasius mentions the Roman jurist Ulpiano's comment concerning the invention of money, and then quotes Aristotle: "διὸ πρὸς τὰς ἀλλαγὰς τοιοῦτόν τι συνέθεντο πρὸς σφᾶς αὐτοὺς διδόναι καὶ λαμβάνειν, ὃ τῶν χρησίμων αὐτὸ ὂν εἶχε τὴν χρείαν εὐμεταχείριστον πρὸς τὸ ζῆν."[31] Jowett's English translation of Aristotle renders it as follows: "[H]ence men agreed to employ in their dealings with each other something which was intrinsically useful and easily applicable to the purposes of life."[32] There does seem to be some understanding, as Pound contends, of the word χρέια being translated as *demand* in Biblical Greek: "[A]lso (by impl.) *occasion, demand, requirement* or *destitution*."[33] One would need to be an ancient Greek scholar of Aristotle's time to be certain. Pound is implying that money

---

[28] Pound can certainly be difficult to understand, even at the best of times. This is especially difficult nowadays, when very few are Latin and Greek language scholars. Pound has respect for Salmasius, as is evident in *Impact*, even implying that reading his work *De Modo Usurarum* provides needed monetary knowledge, and, therefore, that it may have purposely been ignored as no modern reprints are available i.e., post 1639–40 (Pound, *Impact*, 61). Pound likewise implies that due to Salmasius providing clear terminology in his two works, *De Modo Usurarum* and *Dissertatio de Foenore Trapezitico*; various encyclopædias, even if they do mention Salmasius, may not include these two books when listing Salmasius's works (Pound, *Impact*, 185–86). What Pound states in Canto 87 needs further study.

[29] Pound, *Impact*, 240.

[30] Terrell, *A Companion*, Vol. II, 491.

[31] Salmasio, *De Modo*, 97.

[32] *Aristotle's Politics*, 42.

[33] Strong, *The Exhaustive Concordance*, Greek (G) 5532, p. 78.

has no *value* in itself, as Pound understands Salmasius's use of Aristotle's *τὴν χρείαν*. Pound believes it is better translated as *demand*, i.e., money or coinage providing demand for goods and services. Pound is emphasizing the Douglasite understanding that there must be *demand* for a product which includes, besides the desire for the goods or services, the requisite purchasing power. This is referred to by Douglas as *effective demand*. The only thing that gives money usefulness is that there exists desired goods to purchase, as Aristotle explains with the story of Midas.[34] Midas turned all to gold, even food, by his touch. Gold, coinage, or artificial wealth, is worthless without real wealth available, i.e., goods and services to purchase.

Pound next gives an allusion from Ari, i.e., Aristotle; a quote of Pound's also found in *Impact* from Aristotle: "[T]his is a common business practice,"[35] i.e., the story of the philosopher Thales, showing that Thales too could *make money* by what Pound calls "[t]he usual frauds of book-keeping, monopoly, etc. . . . it is precisely for this reason that the usurers are opposed to classical studies."[36] Aristotle himself states of the Thales story: "I was saying, his device for getting money is of universal application, and is nothing but the creation of a monopoly. It is an art often practised by cities when they are in want of money; they make a monopoly of provisions."[37]

Just as Pound believes that the death of classical education is due to the usurocracy fearing the classical monetary-economic *paideuma*, so too he believes that classical mythology makes the usurocracy uneasy. As Pound states in passage three: "Remove the mythologies before they establish clean values." Mythology, too, may establish clean values or clear ideas that have something to teach us today.

Pound emphasizes in the third passage that in this age of mediocrity, with its cult of the sterile and the grotesque, the pusillanimous want to cut down all men to *worm size*. There is no longer any place for the truly exceptional man in the arts, politics, economics, etc. Gone are the Jacksons, the Van Burens, etc. In Pound's view, they have been replaced by "[T]he total dirt that was Roosevelt, / and the farce that was Churchill."

The fourth passage again pays tribute to Scotus Eriugena and quotes Scotus to the effect that "[a]ll things are lights." This Scotistic passage impressed Pound profoundly and he speaks of the Greek

---

34 *Aristotle's Politics*, 43.
35 Pound, *Impact*, 22–23.
36 Pound, *Impact*, 22.
37 *Aristotle's Politics*, 48.

tags in Eriugena's verses. Pound then goes on to quote Gollievski concerning the adverse effect that the assassination of Alexander the Great had on Greek culture. Pound paraphrases Gollievski to the effect that "when they bumped off Alexander in Babylon / that wrecked . . . 'a good deal.'" Terrell explains: "Goleyevsky, a Russian general with an English wife whom the Pounds knew in Paris in the early nineteen twenties. Pound mentions him anonymously: 'To recapitulate, I take it from my ex-Russian ex-General that the fall of Alexander's empire was a disaster.'"[38] This individual is Nikolay Lavrentievich Gollievski. Noted features of his life are his work in the American consulate and his involvement in Freemasonry. He was expelled from France in 1952 on charges of espionage. This former Czarist Russian General returned to Russia, what was the U. S. S. R. under Stalin and lived comfortably in Moscow.[39] Laughlin makes a good point when we may obsess about a reference in *The Cantos* to a person, such as Gollievski, expecting that such knowledge is important in appreciating *The Cantos*: "[H]ow much does it really matter who they were if the lines in which they appear are interesting? Did the readers of Dante know who all those people in the *Commedia* were?"[40] Gollievski only appears in *The Cantos,* as he likewise agreed with Pound concerning Alexander the Great.

Pound goes on to state that Greece had no Quattrocento as did Italy and that the law code of Justinian was inefficient. Pound traces these defects in Greek culture to the assassination of Alexander the Great. Reference has already been made to Pound's great admiration for Alexander's monetary-economic *paideuma* or teaching, in paying the debts of his soldiery. Alexander had shown monetary acumen in utilizing the statal imperial prerogative over coinage. When Alexander was assassinated, Pound believes, as with Gollievski, that Greek culture went into a decline due to the degeneration in the monetary-economic *paideuma*. This link between culture, art, civilization, and a sound monetary-economic *paideuma* is essential to an understanding of Pound. Upon it rests his great interest in Douglas, as the teacher who sought to revive the sound historical monetary *paideuma*, and thus restore art and culture to their former glory.

In this same fourth passage, Pound, as we have said above, maintains that Justinian, the Law-Giver of Byzantium, turned out inefficient law codes. He contrasts the inefficient law codes of Justinian, which are

---

38 Terrell, *A Companion*, Vol. II, 493.
39 Толстой, "Утраченное счастье."
40 Laughlin, *Pound as Wuz*, 109.

likened to a haystack of laws on paper, with what Pound saw as the practical approach of Mussolini. He paraphrases an earlier statement that appeared in Pound's 1933 prose work, *Jefferson and/or Mussolini*:[41] "We ask 'em to settle between 'em. / If they can't, the State intervenes." Pound had explained that the corporate state does not interfere with the matters of individuals and private companies. The corporate state simply asks them to settle matters themselves, and then, if they cannot discipline themselves, the state intervenes. Pound points out that the system works, despite the denials of its critics, i.e., "it percolates."

Pound attributes the fifth passage to "Destutt or whomso." Pound is referencing Antoine Destutt de Tracy, and his Chapter VI entitled *Of Money*. In relation to Pound's statement "All metal as barter," Destutt's description of this chapter states: "Exchange, properly so called, is a simple barter of one money for another." In normal parlance, we usually consider barter as something done not with money, but an exchange of goods and services. Likewise, with respect to Pound's statement "Pity to stamp save by weight,"[42] we read on the same page of the description of Chapter VI in Destutt: "[I]t is to be desired that coins had never borne other names than those of their weight; and that the arbitrary denominations, called monies of account, such as livres, sous, deniers, &c. &c. had never been used."

Pound draws our attention to passages he agrees with in reference to what follows in the canto concerning *metal manipulation*. Pound does not mention Destutt's opinion concerning *paper money*, "A theft of greater magnitude, and still more ruinous, is the making of paper money. It is greater, because in this money there is absolutely no real value;"[43] as Pound would not agree with Destutt. For Pound, as taught by Douglas, neither gold, silver, nor copper are the basis of credit, but as Pound states concerning the Monte dei Paschi: "Credit rests in *ultimate* on the abundance of nature, on the growing grass that can nourish the living sheep";[44] and as Douglas states: "[T]he real basis of credit is the producing and consuming capacity of the community."[45] As referenced before, this is the difference between artificial wealth, i.e., money, and all that acts in its place be it coin or paper, and the true or real natural wealth,[46] i.e., the abundance of nature along with man's ability to work and to produce goods

[41] Pound, *Jefferson and/or Mussolini*, 69.
[42] Destutt, *A Treatise*, xxi.
[43] Destutt, *A Treatise*, xxi.
[44] Pound, *Impact*, 147.
[45] Douglas, *Monopoly of Credit*, 51.
[46] Kreeft, *A Shorter Summa*, 133.

that are needed and useful to society. This arises from living within a nurturing community, a community that is willing to work in solidarity to make possible the natural abundance that comes from the Douglasite *increment of association* and the *cultural heritage*. As noted before, this ancient distinction between artificial and natural wealth is taken from Aristotle.

The Poundian distrust of precious metal manipulation is expressed in the statement that there is "[a]lways the undertow." The gold-bugs, or gold-speculators, are always against any order. Pound paraphrases Ari, i.e., Aristotle, to the effect that the gold-speculators' common practice is to exert a financial *squeeze* through the manipulation of the gold market, partly made possible, as Pound notes from Destutt above, due to coinage not stamped by its weight. As Terrell quotes from Pound: "A [Aristotle] saw 'money as a measure,' which is 'called NOMISMA because it exists not by nature but by custom *and can therefore be altered or rendered useless at will* [Pound's italics]. If we put this 'be rendered comparatively useless' we shall have got the juice out of 'altered and rendered' [which], . . . is now part of the bank wheeze'. 'Wheeze' has an informal meaning of 'trickery.'"[47] C. H. Douglas points out that precious metal manipulation is the primary weapon of International Finance in maintaining its stranglehold on the world's economy. Pound's contemptuous reference to *gold-bugs* characterizes the international usurers and their apologists who insist upon trade among nations being fettered to the artificial fetish of the Gold Standard. C. H. Douglas scoffs at the Gold Standard and maintains that it is one of the main sources of friction among nations.[48]

The sixth passage contains one of Pound's favourite phrases *directio voluntatis*—the direction of the will. This phrase is an important one in Poundian studies since it appears in reference to the *guided intelligence* of Dante and Pound's volitionist economics. Pound stresses the direction of the will in economics because he believes that social and economic reform can be brought about if man truly wills it.

He then goes on to paraphrase C. H. Douglas to the effect that money today is an instrument of policy even more than a measure of value. Douglas emphasizes this point throughout his works and particularly in *Warning Democracy* in the chapter entitled "Government

---

[47] Terrell, *A Companion*, Vol. II, 493.

[48] "Owing to the immense pyramid of purchasing power inverted on a small gold base, exports of gold produce money stringency of a violent character out of all proportion to the amount exported, and bearing no relation either to productive capacity or physical demand." Douglas, *Monopoly of Credit*, 73.

by Money." He stresses that money, i.e., the control of the issue of money, is much more an instrument of financial oligarchical policy than a measure of value. C. S. Lewis notes the following, which can be applied to economics, especially banking: "There is something which unites magic and applied science [economics, banking] while separating both from the 'wisdom' of earlier ages. For the wise men of old the cardinal problem had been how to conform the soul to reality, and the solution had been knowledge, self-discipline, and virtue. For magic and applied science [economics, banking] alike the problem is how to subdue reality to the wishes of men: the solution is a technique; and both, in the practice of this technique, are ready to do things hitherto regarded as disgusting and impious."[49]

For Douglas, it is the banking technique of money creation always as a debt which subdues reality, as it does not reflect the abundance of the *increment of association* and the *cultural heritage* in the current world. The reality of the actual economic world is subordinated to a policy not based on reality or economic facts and geared for the benefit of the individuals who make up the community, but only on the overriding interests of the money lenders.

In this same passage, Pound refers to the *squirmers*, i.e., the pusillanimous, who "plunder men's mind" wanting all men "cut down to worm-size." This is a powerful outcry against our age of the mediocre man. Like Douglas, Pound wants to free and unfetter the uniqueness, the sacredness and dignity of the individual from the morass of grey collectivism in which contemporary man wallows today. The family is the basis of society, but both the family and the community exist to enable the individual to flourish.

The sixth passage references the Masonic hero Jacques de Molay. Pound asks where de Molay stands on this matter of taking interest. Jacques de Molay was the last Grand Master of the Knights Templar. In 1307 he was arrested in France; he confessed to some charges made and was burnt as a lapsed heretic.[50] The Knights Templar and Jacques de Molay evaded the canonical prohibitions against usury: "The method of circumventing this seems to have been that the mortgagees paid to the mortgagors a *nominal* rent which was used towards the reduction of debt. The difference between this and the *real* rent represented the interest."[51] Thus, they did practice an abuse against the spirit of Canon Law which prohibited usury, although they may have appeared

---

[49] Lewis, *The Abolition of Man*, 48.

[50] "Jacques de Molay, Grand Master," *Encyclopædia Britannica.*

[51] "Templars," *Encyclopædia Britannica* Vol. 26, 595.

to be within the letter of the law. This is why Pound highlights the ambiguity of Jacques de Molay's position by asking where he stands on this matter of taking interest. Later in this same Canto, Pound will ask if de Molay made loans without interest. This explains the reference in this sixth passage: "and the 'Section', the proportions, / lending, perhaps, not at interest, but resisting." In other words, the Knights Templar did not lend at interest strictly speaking, but they did resist the spirit of the Canon Law prohibiting usury.

In the seventh passage above, Pound again paraphrases his friend H. L. Mencken, the "old H." of *The Cantos*, to the effect that "an economic idea will not . . . go into them [the people] / in less than a geological epoch." Pound then quotes Mencius, the great disciple of Confucius, to the effect that nothing is better than a share, "nor worse than a fixed charge." This quotation from Mencius is significant since it reflects Pound's own opposition to usury. It is a condemnation of a fixed charge for the use of money or credit without regard to production, or even the possibility of production. It also reflects Pound's distinction between a tithe and a tax on the grounds that a tithe is a share in something existing, i.e., payment in kind, whereas a tax is a charge without reference to whether there is the money available to pay the tax. This, to Pound and Douglas, represents extortion and is a modern form of highway robbery. The example of Confucian/Mencian monetary-economic acumen is important in the light of the fact that from 1957 Pound had been suggesting to interested parties a social-ethical translation and analysis of the writings of Kuan-Tzu.[52] This indicates that, increasingly, Pound finds the monetary-economic history of ancient China a fertile field for his research into the antiquity of Douglasism and it being part of a much older thought-heritage or *paideuma*.

In the eighth passage, Pound asks if the modern reader is even capable of using the process of luminous detail or purposeful focus. Can they even benefit by true editions, untouched by the censorship of the usurocracy? He then recalls that fine old word "an independence" which had formerly been used for someone having an independent means of support quite separate from the wage and salary system. This truly gave one independence, economic freedom, and leisure. Pound is convinced that it is only by possessing *an independence* of some kind that one can benefit by true leisure, not just a weekend off from work. This is a type of leisure that can lead to contemplation

[52] See for e.g., *Economic Dialogues*, Edited by Maverick.

and artistic creativity. This is why Pound the artist is interested in the Douglasite policy of dividends for all, because he sees in this form of economic enlightenment the key to a fuller and more human way of life. He realizes that there is no room for the true artist, in a world devoted to the Marxist philosophy of total work, and to the usurocratic total war on contemplation.

In the ninth passage, Pound once again comes back to Jacques de Molay and asks if he was making loans without interest. He points out that the Church councils have been "bumbling" the question of usury. Fanatics, in general, do not understand loan interest. He emphasizes that the problem of usury relates to that of justice. Pound, like Douglas, sees usury as being opposed to distributive justice. The usury problem is therefore connected with morality and hence Pound, like the medieval theologian, believes *that economics is a part of the whole moral system and does not have a right to be judged on other than a moral basis.* This is pre-eminently true of the monetary-economic question of usury. The problem of usury relates to justice, with the *directio voluntatis* or *contemplatio* as Richard of St. Victor understood it in *The Mystical Ark (Benjamin Major)*. This equating of the *directio voluntatis* with contemplation is important in that Pound constantly emphasizes the need for contemplation, in both the artistic and intellectual sense, as well as the proper use of volition in the solving of the human dilemma. Indeed, Pound himself uses the term *volitionist economics* to distinguish the new economics of Douglas from the *orthodox economics* subsidized by the usurocracy.

Canto 88 derives its luminous detailing largely from Thomas H. Benton's *Thirty Years' View*. Benton was a United States Senator from Missouri for thirty years, from 1821 to 1851. Thus he sat in the Senate during the time when the great bank war was being fought between the Jackson–Van Buren forces and the private Bank of the United States. Canto 88 opens with Pound paraphrasing a section in which Senator Benton recalls how John Randolph of Roanoke came to his room inquiring if he could be Randolph's second in a duel with Henry Clay:

> It was Saturday the 1st day of April, toward noon,
> the Senate not being that day in session . . .
>   came to my room at Brown's asking was I
> Mrs Clay's blood-relation?
> Prompt in agreeing to meet . . . exact in protesting Clay's
>   right to call him. "Col Tatnall, the bearer,
>   is authorized . . .

Was defiance of Adams, not Clay,
in the senate speech, but to Jessup had said
He would waive privilege,
which constitutes a very palpable difference.
Vague report that he had said that Salazar's letter
bore earmarks
("blackleg")
Which led to absolute challenge absolutely accepted,
By which time it had become "forgery"
(Jessup to Tatnall)
"Forged or manufactured"
(Tatnall quoting his principle: Charlotte jury
Wd/ find presumptive strong likeness
"in points of style" to other papers,
Not proof but suspicion, for which he declined to offer
explanation.
Adams and Clay were for entanglement.
Right bank, which is in Virginia*
above bridge of the Little Falls
ten paces
*where there was a law
against duelling.
I alone knew how he meant to avoid that.
I went to Clay's on the Friday, the youngest child
went to sleep on the sofa.
Mrs. Clay, as always since the death of her daughter,
the picture of desolation
But calm and conversable.
Clay and I parted at midnight.
Saturday, Randolph's, Georgetown,
Could not ask him
but mentioned the child asleep on the sofa.
He said:
"I shall do nothing to disturb its sleep
or the repose of its mother",
and went on making codicils for things of slight value;
To Macon, some english shillings to
keep game when he played whist;
Young Bryan sent back to school to
save him shock if . . . and so forth.
(Canto 88)

The background to the Clay-Randolph duel is given by Benton, summarized here by Landini:

> In 1826 the United States sent a mission to the Isthmus of Panama, supposedly at the invitation by letter of "General Salazar, the Mexican Minister at Washington." Henry Clay, who was a member of that mission, felt called upon to challenge Randolph on some comments the latter had made on the floor of the Senate. These comments were understood by Clay as a charge that he had "forged or manufactured a paper connected with the Panama mission" and that Randolph had "applied" to Clay "the epithet of blackleg." Clay emphatically denied Randolph's charges, and Randolph denied the accuracy of Clay's understanding of the comments. An affair of honor developed.
>
> Benton, who could not be Randolph's second because of his blood relationship with Mrs. Clay—obligations of blood, Randolph felt—was present at the duelling site, the right bank of the Potomac which is the Virginia side. Prior to the duel, Benton visited first the Clays and then Randolph.[53]

All this so far has been by way of introduction to an event, which is certainly not without monetary-economic significance, and which illustrates the monetary *paideuma* or tradition of ante-bellum America. Pound now paraphrases a section from Benton regarding Randolph: "He wanted some gold—that coin not being then in circulation, and only to be obtained by favor or purchase—and sent his faithful man, Johnny, to the United States Branch Bank to get a few pieces, American being the kind asked for. Johnny returned without the gold, and delivered the excuse that the bank had none."[54] Pound condenses and paraphrases the passage from Benton describing the incident that followed:

> Wanted gold, coins not then in circulation,
> sent Johnny to Branch bank to get a few pieces,
> who returned, saying they had none.
> "They are liars from the begining. My HORSE!"
> which was brought him, for he never rode Johnny's . . .
> Down Penn. Avenue to what is now Corcoran, Riggs,
> Johnny behind him at 40 paces.
> Asked for the state of his account. The teller
> took up packages of bills and
> asked in what size notes he wd/ have it.
> "I want money."
> said Mr. Randolph,

---

[53] Landini, *A Guide*, 207. Summarized by Landini from: Benton, *Thirty Years' View*, Vol. 1, 73–74.
[54] Benton, *Thirty Years' View*, Vol. 1, 74.

The teller, beginning to understand him, said: Silver?
"My MONEY!" said Mr Randolph.
"Have you a cart, Mr Randolph?"
By that time the cashier
told him there was a mistake in the answer to Johnny
and that he shd/ have what he wanted.
He got it, and closed the account,
Returned and gave me an envelope
to open if he were killed,
And a slip to read before I got to the ground:
to feel in his breeches pocket:
nine pieces, I think It was,
3 for me, Tatnall, Hamilton, each
to make seals of, as mementos.
We were all three then at his lodgings.
He and the seconds took carriage,
I followed on horseback.

(Canto 88)

Pound paraphrases this passage from Benton because it illustrates in a graphic manner the Douglasite charge that banks in fact do not lend currency, but simply lend promises-to-pay. Pound and Douglas maintain that when any real pressure is put on the bank to pay in specie or in legal tender they have always been brought to the point of collapse, e.g., the Bank of England in 1914. No bank is ever able to survive a *run on the bank* because they do not in fact lend money (in the sense of currency), but lend promises-to-pay, which are allowed to circulate as money due to the unfathomable benevolence of governments. Both Pound and Douglas maintain that if the banking system is so sound we should not always be asked to have *confidence* in it.[55]

John Randolph of Roanoake understood very well the banking practice of lending *promises-to-pay* as if they were legal tender. He also understood how little or no legal tender could be redeemed in specie by the *sound* banks. This is why his reaction to Johnny's message that the bank said it had no gold was so violent. His reply to Johnny's message was, "[t]heir name is legion! and they are liars from the beginning."[56] In the Clay-Randolph duel no injuries resulted. Following the duel, Benton relates the following, which is not mentioned in *The Cantos:* "A runner came in from the bank to say that they had overpaid him, by mistake, $130 that day. He answered, 'I believe *it is your rule not*

[55] Cf. Douglas, *The Monopoly of Credit*, 1: "Why should we be asked to have confidence in our money system, if it works properly?"
[56] Benton, *Thirty Years' View*, Vol. 1, 74.

to correct mistakes, except at the time, and at your counter.' And with that answer the runner had to return. When gone, Mr. Randolph said, '*I will pay it on Monday: people must be honest, if banks are not.*'"[57]

This incident, taken from American history, illustrates the very sound monetary-economic *paideuma*, or tradition that existed in *ante-bellum* America. This *paideuma* was lost and betrayed in 1863 with the passage of the National Banking Act, which permanently entrenched private interests in their control of the nation's money and credit.

Following this account of the Clay-Randolph duel in Canto 88, there is a series of monetary-economic luminous details that reiterate points made in earlier Cantos. Pound believes that the truth must be hammered home by reiteration, with the insistence of a rock drill, "drilling it into their heads . . . " much in the way that a composer does in music with the repetition of significant phrases. The German critic Guenther Bloecker, writing in the Berlin *Tagesspiegel*, speaks of the "small units of mathematical-musical composition."[58] The phrase *rock-drill* is derived from a work of sculpture by Pound's good friend Jacob Epstein. One of Epstein's works is called *Rock-Drill* and includes a representation of a rock-drill, i.e., an instrument used by sculptors in their art. The luminous detail quoted below have appeared elsewhere many times in *The Cantos*:

> 1. Bellum perenne:
> 1694: on what it creates out of nothing
> 1750: shut down on colonial paper.
> Lexington;
>   '64 "greatest blessing" said Lincoln.
> 1878: in circulation as currency.
>   *sangue, fatica*, in our time.
> And there is, undoubtedly, blood on their silver,
> Without honour men sink into servitude.
> Responsible, or irresponsible government?
>   Minimum of land without surveillance.
> And as to peerage:
> I. Edward vi, c. 12
> lords of parliament and peers of the realm, having place
>   and voys in parliament may have benefit of their peerage,
>   equiv/ that of clergy, for first offence, though they cannot
>   read, and without being burned in the hand, for all offences
>   then clergyable and also for housebreaking for robbery on the
>   high-ways, horse stealing and robbing of churches.
>   Hal. P.C. 377

[57] Benton, *Thirty Years' View*, Vol. 1, 77.
[58] Quoted from: New Directions publicity on *Section: Rock-Drill*.

The books of a scholar, his countenance (wainagium)
that of a villein.
That these are the Histories
OR
Thus recapitulate:
That T'ang opened the copper mine
(distributive function of money).
Nothing on which he leans, the *chuntze*, under heaven
should have nothing on which he leans,
Or monopoly, Thales, common practice, but dirty,
Antoninus lent money at four percent
that being the summit of Empire
(Roman)
"Trying", he said, "to keep some of the
non-
interest-bearing national debt in circulation as currency.
one, eight, seven, eight,
Mencius on tithing,
PERENNE.
Cano perenne,

. . . .

2. With greek tags in his excellent verses,
Erigena,
In reign of Carolus Calvus.
"Captans annonam
maledictus in plebe sit!"
that was Ambrose:
"Hoggers of harvest!" Delcroix (properly):
"always the same."
Get the meaning across and then quit.

. . . .

3. Antoninus as apex, but on slavery and on bhoogery . . .

. . . .

4. Marse Adams done tol' 'em.
The Major done told 'em
(having a First Folio (Shx) in his lock-box
could afford waiting to see it.
"Every . . . etc. . .
downright corruption". "To the consumer".
Waal, they bust the abundance
and had to pay Europe,
an' Anatole tol' 'em:
"no export? No need to make war."
Ile des Pinguins,
(Canto 88)

The first passage begins with the words *bellum perenne*, perennial war, referring to Pound's great battle-cry in *The Cantos*. This battle-cry has already been paraphrased in English as *I sing of perennial war between the usurer and the man who tries to do a good job*. The luminous detail "1694: on what it creates out of nothing," refers to the founding of the Bank of England in 1694, and to William Paterson's statement that the bank hath the benefit of interest on money which it creates out of nothing. The phrase "1750: shut down our colonial paper," refers to the British Parliament's sanctions against Pennsylvania, forbidding the colony to issue its own paper money. Pound considers this event to be the true cause of the Revolution of 1776. Pound maintains that this event of 1750 led directly to the battle of Lexington.

The phrase "64 'greatest blessing' said Lincoln," has to do with a letter written by Abraham Lincoln to Colonel Richard Taylor and quoted in Emil Ludwig's *Lincoln*.[59] In this letter Lincoln gave Dick Taylor credit for having been the father of the state-issued interest-free greenback. Lincoln recounts how when he came to Dick Taylor for advice in the light of the fact that the Union could not raise money to prosecute the war, Dick Taylor had said: "Why, issue treasury notes bearing no interest, printed on the best banking paper. Issue enough to pay off the army expenses and declare it legal tender." Lincoln goes on to recall that Treasury Secretary "Chase thought it a hazardous thing, but we finally accomplished it, and gave the people of this republic the greatest blessing they ever had—their own paper to pay their own debts." Thus by means of a highly compressed luminous detail Pound reminds us of Lincoln's policy of using state-issued interest-free treasury notes as legal tender. This is precisely the policy which C. H. Douglas maintains should have been followed by the British Cabinet at the time of the run on the banks in 1914. He maintains that a great opportunity to establish a debt-free money system was lost at this time. Instead the British government used an emergency issue of treasury bills to bail the bankers out of their difficulty, by handing these bills over free of charge to the banking institutions.[60] The next phrase "1878: in circulation as currency," has reference to Pound's grandfather, Congressman Thaddeus Coleman Pound. That year, Pound's grandfather, Ezra Pound writes, "expressed or explained his position by saying that he wanted to keep at least part of the non-interest bearing national debt in circulation as currency."[61]

---

[59] Ludwig, *Lincoln*, 448–49.
[60] Douglas, *Monopoly of Credit*, 27.
[61] Terrell, *A Companion*, Vol. II, 503.

In this same first passage Pound goes on to speak of "*sangue, fatica,* in our time." Pound is referring to the tragedy and cruelty of war as "blood, fatigue." Pound also wrote: "Sangue, merda e fatica, was the definition given me by an officer in the last European war. Blood, dung and fatigue."[62] "And there is, undoubtedly, blood on their silver," takes us back to the contention of Douglas that it is by the struggle for markets, that the financial system directly causes wars, and the blood is on all those who operate this system or support it. *Servitude* is related to financial servitude, the *wage slavery* of our economic system that envelops all nations and peoples. He quotes a statute of Edward I, which made members of the peerage accountable at the bar of justice for crimes. This contrasts with modern *justice* which creates a protected class of financiers, who are beyond the law.[63]

Pound also goes on to reiterate the luminous detail concerning the Emperor Tch'eng T'ang who, in 1766 BC, opened his copper mine and coined copper money which was distributed to the people as a state dividend to ease the problem of distribution in the time of a crop failure. Pound points out that T'ang understood the distributive function of money. Thus the Emperor T'ang and C. H. Douglas both emphasize the distributive function of money.

Reference is then made to the practice of monopoly by Thales, and the lending of money by the Roman Emperor Antoninus Pius at four percent (marking the very summit of the Roman Empire). Therefore Antoninus Pius also understood the issuing of money both as an imperial or statal prerogative that leads to prosperity. Pound again quotes his grandfather, Thaddeus Coleman Pound, on his effort to keep some of the non-interest-bearing national debt, i.e., the Civil War greenbacks, in circulation as currency, and makes a brief reference to Mencius on tithing. Mencius's distaste for taxation is completely in keeping with Douglasite philosophy. The first passage ends as it had begun with Pound's epic refrain, *cano perenne*, i.e., a reference to the fuller statement, *I sing of perennial war between the usurer and the man who tries to do a good job.*

The second passage begins with a brief reference to Scotus Eriugena who had flourished in the reign of Carolus Calvus (Charles the Bald), and who had Greek tags in his excellent verses.[64] This passage also

---

[62] Terrell, *A Companion*, Vol. II, 503.

[63] The 2008 financial meltdown only confirms Pound's accusation that the money powers are above and beyond the law. Cf. Cohan, "How Wall Street's Bankers."

[64] Charles II the Bald, king of France, Holy Roman emperor, and the grandson of Charlemagne, placed John Scotus Eriugena at the head of the court school circa 845. "Charles II Holy Roman emperor," *Encyclopaedia Britannica.*

reiterates St. Ambrose's thunderous denunciation of usurers, *Captans annonam maledictus in plebe sit*, (*Hoggers of harvest, cursed amongst the people*). This translation of Proverbs 11:26 into Latin, can be found in Ambrose's Book III of *De Officiis Clericorum: On the Duties of the Clergy*, and in other works by Ambrose, ex. *De Nabuthae*. In *De Officiis*..., Ambrose quotes Proverbs 11:26 three times in short succession in Chp. VI: once in section 37 and twice in section 44, the last of these being "Captans...". All three Ambrose varies in translation. The variation may be due to Ambrose translating himself from the Greek Septuagint and/or providing an already existing Latin translation (pre-Jerome's Vulgate). Ambrose may have been using a Hebrew text of *The Book of Tobit* for "Captans..." as suggested in a comment by a scholar within *De Officiis*.[65] It is apparent that Ambrose considered it important to provide all the possible readings of the text. Pound ends his Latin text from Ambrose with *sit* while Ambrose has *est*. This was probably not a deliberate error, but Pound was known not to check his references, often writing from the memory of a text: "The *Cantos* were written, as far as I could see and I sometimes watched him at work, entirely from memory—more aural than visual memory."[66] St. Ambrose ranks with St. Anselm among Pound's favourite canon of *Saints*.

In the third passage, reference is again made to the Emperor Antoninus Pius as the apex of Roman culture. The brief reference to "bhoogery" i.e., buggery, relates to usury as Pound often equates usury with sodomy; both are sterile, and Dante's Inferno includes them both in the third ring of the seventh circle of Hell.

The fourth passage points out that both John Adams, "Marse Adams," and C. H. Douglas, "The Major," "done told 'em," i.e., had informed people of the real monetary-economic facts. It is significant that Pound mentions that C. H. Douglas had a first folio Shakespeare in his lock-box. This is very much in accordance with Pound's belief that monetary-economic correct thinking goes together with personal culture. As noted in Canto LXXIV, in similar fashion, Pound mentions Herr Unterguggenberger, the Burgomeister who instituted the Gesell scrip, had a copy of Dante's *Divinia Commedia* and Heine's *Gedichte*. The cryptic line "Every... etc... / downright corruption," is a paraphrase of Adams's statement that every bank of discount is downright corruption. The phrase "[t]o the consumer," refers to C. H. Douglas's emphasis on dividends being paid to the consumer, and his emphasis on consumption in economics. Pound then goes on to

---

65 Ambrose, *Opera, Ad Manuscriptos Codices*, 464.
66 Laughlin, *Pound as Wuz*, 8.

state that "they bust the abundance / and had to pay Europe." This statement must be understood in the light of Pound's reference to a passage in Anatole France's *Île des Pingouins* that had shown how commercial warfare leads inevitably to military warfare. Pound paraphrases Anatole France to the effect that if a nation does not export, there is no need for it to make war. These sentiments are completely in accordance with the Douglasite tenet that the domestic market is the best market. We have already discussed this passage from Anatole France in Chapter II.

Canto 89 continues with the monetary-economic luminous detail from Benton:

> 1. This quotation is not from Mr Webster.
> Clay opposed mints in New Orleans and North Carolina.
> The Civil War rooted in tariff.
> Philadelphia did not diffuse,
> France had ten mints, and in Mexico there are 8,
> Every citizen now more or less cheated.
> Mr. B. said he had but two bank-notes
> both of them counterfeit.
> French currency had stood two revolutions, one conquest,
> 20 millions entered that country,
> no interest was paid for its use.
> Land not safe against "issue"
> Crops not safe against "issue"
> Sovereignty is in the right over coinage.
> "All that it (the Bank) creates out of nothing."
> 600 banks to be broken,
> Fictitious woe, and the Senate's organized sorrow.
> "My fellow slave-holder"
> sd/ Mr Randolph
> (masnatosque liberavit)
> "Ef my bull-dog" said Mr Bishop
> to a co-detenuto "had a face like yours, hang'd if
> I wouldn't shave his arse and make him walk backwards."
> And in the time of Mr Randolph, Mr Benton, Mr Van Buren
> he, Andy Jackson
> POPULUM AEDIFICAVIT
> which might end this canto and rhyme with
> Sigismundo.
>
> . . . .
>
> 2. Van Buren already in '37 unsmearing Talleyrand.
> And the elderly Aida, then a girl of 16, in the '90 s,
> visiting some very stiff friends in New England

giggled (and thereby provoked sour expressions)
when some children crossed the front lawn with
a bottle of water strung on a string between them
and chanting:
"Martin
Van Buren, a bottle of urine".
Sagetrieb or the
oral tradition.
(Canto 89)

The first passage quoted refers to a passage above this, in Chinese characters, from *The Works of Mencius*. Pound places in Chinese, the starting lines of Mencius: "Why must [the king] use the word profit?" Mencius goes on to say, "What I am 'likewise' provided with, are *counsels* to benevolence and righteousness."[67] Pound is stating that Daniel Webster, who supported the Bank of the United States and the private banking interests,[68] could never claim, like Mencius, that he was one not interested in providing his nation with unselfish monetary profit and "counsels to benevolence and righteousness." Benton's and Pound's accusations against Webster, against British banking interference in America, and against the banking interests undermining American democracy, are supported by a more current book:

> At first, Peabody merely sent letters to Baltimore friends, scolding them about the need for Maryland to resume interest payments. Then he tired of persuasion and rewarded reporters with small gratuities for favorable articles about the state. At last, in 1845 he conspired with Barings to push Maryland into resuming payment. They set up a political slush fund to spread propaganda for debt resumption and to elect sympathetic legislators; they even drafted the clergy into giving sermons on the sanctity of contracts. By means of a secret account, the two firms transferred £1,000 to Baltimore, 90 percent from Barings and 10 percent from Peabody — a strategy Barings duplicated in Pennsylvania. Most shocking of all, Barings bribed Daniel Webster, the orator and statesman, to make speeches for debt repayment....
>
> Whatever their scruples, the conspiracy thrived: pro-resumption Whigs were elected in both Maryland and Pennsylvania, and London bankers again received payments from both states.[69]

---

[67] Terrell, *A Companion*, Vol. II, 522.
[68] Benton, *Thirty Years' View*, Vol. I, 33.
[69] Chernow, *The House of Morgan*, 6–7.

Henry Clay cooperated with the Bank of the United States in its policy of depleting the South of gold and silver specie by opposing the establishment of mints in New Orleans and North Carolina. Pound claims that the unjust tariff of 1816 was a cause of the American Civil War and paraphrases Benton's following passages:

> Philadelphia could coin, but not diffuse the coin among them. Money was attracted to Philadelphia from the South and West, but not returned back again to those regions. Local mints alone could supply them. France had ten branch mints; Mexico had eight; the United States not one. The establishment of branches was indispensable to the diffusion of a hard-money currency, especially gold; and every friend to that currency should promote the establishment of branches.
>
> Mr. B. said, there were six hundred machines at work coining paper money—he alluded to the six hundred banks in the United States; and only one machine at work coining gold and silver. He believed there ought to be five or six branch mints in the United States; that is, two or three more than provided for in this bill.[70]

Senator Benton is quoted to the effect that the two bank notes in his possession are both counterfeit, because they are promises-to-pay, which are irredeemable in gold or silver specie. Benton then contrasts the soft-money currency of the United States with the hard-money currency of France.[71] "20 millions" and what follows refers to this passage from Benton:

> The effect of the revival of the gold currency was a subject of great congratulation with the President, and its influence was felt in every department of industry. Near twenty millions of dollars had entered the country—a sum far above the average circulation of the Bank of the United States in its best days, and a currency of a kind to diffuse itself over the country, and remain where there was a demand to it, and for which, different from a bank paper currency, no interest was paid for its use, and no danger incurred of its becoming useless.[72]

Benton goes on to stress that neither lands nor crops are safe against the bank's awesome power to issue money. The theme of the role that the money issue played, affecting lands and/or crops can be found in

---

[70] Benton, *Thirty Years' View*, Vol. I, 551.
[71] Benton, *Thirty Years' View*, Vol. I, 552.
[72] Benton, *Thirty Years' View*, Vol. I, 573–74.

several places.[73] The strongest passage is a speech Benton gave in the U. S. Senate, where he begins by first quoting the French writer Voltaire:

> I have a friend, said he [Voltaire], who is a director in the Bank of France, who writes to me when they are going to make money plenty, and make stocks rise, and then I give orders to my broker to sell; and he writes to me when they are going to make money scarce, and make stocks fall, and then I write to my broker to buy; and thus, at a hundred leagues from Paris, and without moving from my chair, I make money. This, said Mr. B., is the operation on stocks to the present day; and it cannot be safe to the holders of stock that there should be a moneyed power great enough in this country to raise and depress the prices of their property at pleasure. The great cities of the Union are not safe, while a company, in any other city, have power over their moneyed system, and are able, by making money scarce or plenty—by exciting panics and alarms—to put up, or put down, the price of the staple articles in which they deal. Every commercial city, for its own safety, should have an independent moneyed system—should be free from the control and regulation of a distant, possibly a rival city, in the means of carrying on its own trade. Thus, the safety of the government, the safety of the people, the interest of all owners of property—of all growing crops—the holders of all stocks—the exporters of all staple articles—require that the regulation of the currency should be kept out of the hands of a great banking company; that it should remain where the constitution placed it—in the hands of the federal government—in the hands of their representatives who are elected by them, responsible to them, may be exchanged by them, who can pass no law for regulating currency which will not bear upon themselves as well as upon their constituents. This is what the safety of the community requires; and, for one, he (Mr. B.) would not, if he could, delegate the power of regulating the currency of this great country to any banking company whatsoever. It was a power too tremendous to be trusted to a company. The States thought it too great a power to be trusted to the State governments; he (Mr. B.) thought so too. The States confided it to the federal government; he, for one, would confine it to the federal government, and would make that government exercise it.[74]

---

[73] Benton, *Thirty Years' View*, Vol. I: 257, 259, 419, 542, 696.
[74] Benton, *Thirty Years' View*, Vol. I, 450.

The above passage summarizes the whole American *paideuma* that fascinated Pound, and which Pound investigated to verify the Douglasite position. The right to issue coinage by the American constitution did not lie with some national or central bank, but with democratically elected officials of the Federal government. They ought not to give it to an unelected body without the power to remove such experts whenever accepted policy is not followed. This is a point that C. H. Douglas makes repeatedly in his writings. He maintains that the banking system's monopoly over credit creation gives it a lien on all property and all production. Nothing is safe from the *neschek,* or corrosive usury inflicted by the banking system on the body-economic. Sovereignty resides pre-eminently in the right over coinage: "[W]e have the situation, that in return for something of which the bank has the monopoly, but yet which cost it nothing, the physical assets of the undertaking have become mortgaged. Further, and taking the industrial situation as a whole, the mortgage can never be paid off, because the mortgagee is in possession of the only medium, i.e. bank credit, by means of which the mortgagor can obtain release."[75]

Pound again superposes part of the quotation from Paterson to the effect that "the bank hath the benefit of interest on money which it creates out of nothing." The phrase "600 banks to be broken," refers to Senator Benton's contention that the State banks throughout the country will either be destroyed or subjugated by the Bank of the United States if its charter is renewed.[76] Next, John Randolph of Roanoke is mentioned as addressing one of the Bank's shareholders as "my fellow slave holder,"[77] when calling someone a *slave holder* was normally used as a reprimand. The implication is that all members of Congress were in some way responsible for slavery, not Randolph alone. Benton relates that Randolph "was one of the large slaveholders of Virginia, but disliked the institution, and, when let alone, opposed its extension."[78]

Related to this is Randolph's response, while in London, to his trading partners who criticized slavery: "[T]he consignees of his tobacco, and the slave factors of his father, urged him to liberate his slaves, he quieted their intrusive philanthropy, on the spot, by saying, 'Yes: you buy and set free to the amount of the money you have received from my father and his estate for these slaves, and I will set free an equal

[75] Douglas, *Warning Democracy*, 184.
[76] Benton, *Thirty Years' View*, Vol. I, 646.
[77] Benton, *Thirty Years' View*, Vol. I, 475.
[78] Benton, *Thirty Years' View*, Vol. I, 474.

number.'"[79] As Randolph notes, not only did the slaveholders profit from the institution, but those in government, merchants, and even merchants overseas. Finance and slavery were tied together. With *masnatosque liberavit* Pound tells us that Randolph freed his slaves. In contrast, the merchants of London experienced no financial loss, and never reimbursed any who they indirectly enslaved. In 1833, when Randolph died, over 350 slaves should have been freed, but his family contested his will in which Randolph had written, "I give and bequeath to all my slaves their freedom, heartily regretting that I have ever been the owner of one."[80] Further along in the passage, Pound again pays tribute to Andrew Jackson who in the time of Randolph, Benton, and Van Buren, had built the nation—*populum aedificavit.*

In the second passage, Pound tells of New England children in the 1890s carrying a bottle of water strung on a string between them and chanting, "Martin Van Buren, a bottle of urine." In his prose writings, Pound has maintained that this *game* did not arise spontaneously but was stimulated by the financial interests: "The war of the 1830s is not to be found in the school books. Jackson is regarded as a tobacco-chewing half-wit, or a tuppeny militarist, the murderer of a few indians, and the victor of New Orleans; Van Buren either vilified or forgotten. Only abnormal Englishmen have ever heard of such presidents."[81] Thus the money-power has been able to pervert and use even the *sagetrieb* or oral tradition for its purposes.

Canto 89 continues with its emphasis upon history as seen from the monetary-economic point of view:

1. Out of von Humboldt: Agassiz, Del Mar and Frobenius

. . . .

2. "We ought not to have turned you out."
        said some old crump to Van Buren
"Great blackguard from Tennessee, by name of Jackson."
"No auction of slaves here in the Capital."

. . . .

3. Slave labour is very expensive.

. . . .

4.   And Disraeli sold the brit fools down the river.

. . . .

5. "And here are Caleb Johnson and two others
as demure" (said T.H.B.) "as three whores at a christening."

---

79 Benton, *Thirty Years' View*, Vol. I, 475.
80 Humphrey, Wallace, "Randolph Slaves."
81 Pound, *Impact*, 151.

That Calhoun called him a quadruped.
Firm taste for good company
evinced by both Benton and Mr Van Buren,
and men even in our time (survivals)
as Domvile and degli Uberti
"His agreeable niece, la Duchesse de Dino."
Betrayed Mihailovitch, assassinated Henriot and Gentile
"China, the longest, and the lowest percent
of burocracy.
(Canto 89)

The reference to Agassiz, Del Mar, and Frobenius having come out of von Humboldt is an important one. Louis Agassiz, the great naturalist, and Alexander Del Mar, the monetary historian, are both Poundian heroes whose works had been reprinted in part by Pound's Square Dollar Series. The quoting of the "old crump's" remorseful statement[82] concerning the defeat of Martin Van Buren is in keeping with Pound's admiration for the former president. The reference to Andrew Jackson as a "[g]reat blackguard from Tennessee" is an example of the usurocracy's perversion and distortion of the *sagetrieb* or oral tradition so that the genuinely great men of American history are either misunderstood or discredited. The phrase "[s]lave labour is very expensive" refers to the usurocracy's preference for wage slavery rather than the older form of chattel slavery.

The luminous detail concerning Benjamin Disraeli selling the British fools down the river has to do with Disraeli's purchase of the Suez Canal. Disraeli did not approach the Bank of England but approached Lionel de Rothschild for the funds to purchase a forty-four percent share from the Khedive of Egypt before the French, who owned the other fifty-six percent, knew of the negotiations. The shares were bought for four million pounds. Lionel received a two and half percent commission, and broke Rothchild tradition by not informing the Paris Rothschilds of the negotiations.[83] This luminous detail arose several times at the beginning of the Rock-Drill Cantos.

The fifth passage begins with Benton's devastating description of Claiborne Jackson (i.e., Caleb Johnson) and his colleagues: "During the campaign on his appeal from the Missouri resolutions in 1849, Claiborne Jackson and two other leading enemies attended one of his meetings and took front seats with a view to interrupting him

---

82 Van Buren, *Autobiography*, Vol. II, 62–63.
83 Bradford, *Disraeli*, 327–28.

with questions, but the interruptions did not occur, after Benton early in his speech said, 'And here are Claib. Jackson [and the others, naming them] as demure as three prostitutes at a christening.'"[84] Benton's animosity against Claiborne Jackson arises from Jackson's pro-Bank position during the great bank war. Benton recorded Henry Clay's U. S. Senate speech where he had claimed that John Calhoun once referred to President Martin Van Buren as a *quadruped.*[85] Calhoun in reply stated that Clay was trying "to cast suspicion on his sincerity or motive,"[86] trying to undermine the credibility of the messenger rather than the message. Calhoun adumbrated the three possibilities that were being debated and his position: "Shall we separate the government from the banks, or shall we revive the league of State banks, or create a national bank? My opinion and course in reference to each are well known. I prefer the separation to either of the others . . . I regard a national bank as more efficient, and a less corrupting fiscal agent than a league of State banks."[87] Pound remarks on the firm taste for good company displayed by both Benton and Van Buren. This is in keeping with Pound's belief that sound monetary-economic principles go together with true personal culture and good taste.

The quotation concerning China having lasted the longest with the lowest percent of bureaucracy reveals Pound's antagonism to bureaucracy. It also reveals his love for the righteous rulers he has noted in Chinese history, especially on account of their regard for economic justice. In our Chapter II, reference was made to an essay entitled *Bureaucracy the Flail of Jehovah* which reveals Pound's views on the subject. This antagonism to bureaucracy is one that Pound shared with C. H. Douglas. In Chapter Two of *Economic Democracy*, Douglas, though he does not call it by name *bureaucracy*, gave pre-World War I Germany as an example of a country where the centralization of power in the government and the control over people's lives had grown to alarming proportions. Pre-World War I Germany had been praised by liberals as the supreme example of *enlightened* social legislation, just as Sweden was praised by liberals for many years and for the same reason following World War II.

As Canto 89 proceeds, Pound introduces other heroes, e.g., President Tyler and Louis Philippe, King of France:

---

[84] Meigs, *The Life*, 456.
[85] Benton, *Thirty Years' View*, Vol. II, 101.
[86] Benton, *Thirty Years' View*, Vol. II, 104.
[87] Benton, *Thirty Years' View*, Vol. II, 105.

1. Mr Tyler

. . . .

2. "even if an independent press cd/ be found to
attempt it"

. . . .

3. The sub-treasury was revived.
Louis Philippe wd/ not let them cut down their notes to 200.
From '34 to '41 our specie rose to 100 million,
"ad valorem" involving a horde of appraisers.
Wright spoke to mind not to passions and
he it was brought in Polk.

. . . .

4. From Charlemagne's grain price Venice, Hansa,
to the forged Donation "of Constantine"
"Perchè in ordine?" (vuol metter la sue idee)
said Mussolini.
Thalers from Maria Teresa,
a road still there in Belgium.
The Emperor's furrow,

. . . .

5. I need add nothing, wrote Van Buren, to the description
by Col. Benton.[88]
"Good-bye Tazewell, good-by Van Buren!"[89]
(that was Randolph)
"on borrowed capital, very unmercantile,"[90]
said John Adams.
Judge Marshall, father of war.

. . . .

6. "Leave the Duke, go for gold."
And they forged those thalers, in our time,
quest'oggi.
Brits did, nacherly Brits did.
"Benton has begun understanding me"
(Randolph)
In Venice the bread price was stable,
ship models still there in Danzig.
Alex said: set up the tables,
any soldier's note will be paid.
Gold was under the Pontifex,
Caesar usurped that.

---

88 Van Buren, *The Autobiography*, 115.
89 Van Buren, *The Autobiography*, 210.
90 Adams, *The Works*, Vol. 1, 466.

Bezants were stable till Dandolo broke into Stamboul,
there had been some arab uneasiness.

. . . .

7. 12 to one, Roma, and about half that in Karachi.
(Canto 89)

President Tyler has already appeared several times in *The Cantos* as a member of an honour-roll including Polk, Monroe, Madison, Jackson, and Van Buren. The second passage refers to a favourite Poundian and Douglasite theme, i.e., the control over our "free press" exercised by the financial interests.[91]

The third passage continues with luminous details from Benton's *Thirty Years' View*. This passage mentions the revival of the sub-treasury during the last year of Martin Van Buren's presidency. Pound points out that Louis Philippe I, King of France during the years when Jackson and Van Buren were in the White House, would not allow the banks to cut their notes down to 200 francs.[92] Pound/Benton stress that from 1834 to 1841, during Andrew Jackson's and then Martin Van Buren's administrations, and after Jackson had destroyed the Bank of the United States, gold and silver specie in the United States rose to one hundred million. Thus Jackson provided America with a hard-money system in a way the Bank never did. Jackson had accused the Bank of failing to provide a sound and uniform currency for the country in his first inaugural address.[93]

In the fourth passage above, Pound mentions Charlemagne's grain price, which was a stable, uniform, and a just price throughout his empire, in contrast to today's fluctuating prices. Pound approves of Charlemagne's grain price because he sees in the medieval managed currency the very mechanism for the just price as recommended by C. H. Douglas.

---

[91] Belloc dedicated his book *The Free Press* to A. R. Orage, a book that is more relevant today than ever: "I PROPOSE to discuss in what follows the evil of the great modern Capitalist Press, its function in vitiating and misinforming opinion and in putting power into ignoble hands; its correction by the formation of small independent organs." Belloc, *The Free Press*, 2. Orage was important in making C. H. Douglas known and understood.

[92] Cf. Benton, *Thirty Years' View*, Vol. II, 391: "The Bank of France lately resolved to reduce the minimum size of its notes to two hundred francs (say forty dollars). The king gave them notice that if they did it, the government would consider it an injury to the currency, and would take steps to correct the movement. The Bank rescinded its resolution; and Louis Philippe, in that single act (to say nothing of others) showed himself to be a patriot king, worthy of every good man's praise, and of every legislator's imitation."

[93] Benton, *Thirty Years' View*, Vol. I, 123–24.

Christopher Hollis in his *Two Nations* explains that prices were kept constant by the following: "In medieval Europe we lived under a managed currency. The way in which it was managed was as follows. From time to time the weight of silver in every coin was reduced. Thus the number of coins that could be coined out of a constant amount of silver was increased, and by this means an increased monetary supply was put out to buy the increased quantity of goods and a fall in prices prevented."[94]

This was a time when theologians concerned themselves with usury and the just price and when economics was considered a part of the system of morality. The references to Venice and the Hanseatic League fill out this medieval economic picture. The lines concerning the thalers from Maria Teresa building a road, which still exists in Belgium, have appeared before. This luminous detail stresses the fact that Maria Teresa built this road in Belgium with state-issued thalers, and not with bank-issued money. The emphasis is on the debt-free thaler as opposed to the bankers' debt-money. This, of course, represents a basic tenet of Douglasism, i.e., public control and issue of the public's credit.

The fifth passage above, mentions Van Buren, Benton, Tazewell, and Randolph. All these men are Poundian heroes and they all fought the money power. Pound quotes John Adams to the effect that it is very unmercantile for the nation to operate on borrowed capital. This is also a basic Douglasist principle. C. H. Douglas stresses that the state should lend not borrow, i.e., that the source of the nation's credit should be the supreme public authority.[95] This is not to involve centralized control of policy, however. Douglas advocates local control of local purchasing power.

The Judge Marshall referred to is John Marshall, Chief Justice of the United States Supreme Court from 1801 to 1835. Pound refers to Marshall as the "father of war" because he feels that Marshall's decisions infringing upon states' rights contributed directly to the American Civil War.

---

[94] Hollis, *Two Nations*, 2.

[95] Cf. C. H. Douglas, *These Present Discontents and the Labour Party and Social Credit*, 14: "[T]here must be somewhere something which stands as Trustee for the unearned increment of association above referred to, the greater part of which is inherited [in the form of the cultural heritage—editor] from a past generation. This Trustee we may call the State, and his agents the banks. Then it must be clear that it is the business of this Trustee to divide amongst the tenants-for-life of the estate, its benefits, i.e., the State should lend, and not borrow, purchasing power, and that for the benefit of individuals, the consumers."

The sixth passage begins with the phrase "Leave the Duke, go for gold," which has already appeared and been commented upon in earlier Cantos. Pound then accuses the British of having forged thalers to undermine the debt-free currency of Maria Teresa. John Randolph of Roanoke is quoted to the effect that Thomas Hart Benton has begun to understand him. Pound then returns to the stability of the medieval price of bread by pointing out the stability of the bread price in medieval Venice. He again refers to the Hanseatic League by mentioning the ship models which are still to be seen in Danzig.

Then Pound reiterates his great monetary-economic luminous detail concerning Alexander the Great having paid the debts of his soldiery. Pound then moves to material taken from Alexander Del Mar that in Rome the issuing of gold coinage belonged to the sacred prerogative of the Pontifex Maximus or Supreme Pontiff, i.e., to the Roman High Priest. This title was adopted by the Christian Bishop of Rome, the Pope of Rome. Pound paraphrases Del Mar to the effect that Julius Caesar usurped the gold coinage prerogative of the Pontifex Maximus.

Del Mar points out that the bezants issued by the Byzantine Emperor in Constantinople were stable until the sacking of Constantinople in 1204.[96] These bezants were large gold coins struck by the Byzantine Emperor that circulated in Europe from the 6th to the 15th or 16th century. The *uneasiness* had to do with Justinian II's coining for the first time coins bearing the image of Christ, rather than just the Emperor's image and the cross. Some assert that the Caliph Abd al-Malik therefore began to coin his own coinage, initially seeming to partially mirror the Roman coins, but ultimately, rejecting any figurative images. The "uneasiness" with the image of Christ, a prophet in Islam, was what some assert, and Pound seems to imply, prompted the Caliph to create his own coinage as a religious and political statement. It should be noted that Del Mar and others assert that it was the Caliph who initiated this religious duel, a coinage war, by minting his own religiously significant coinage, to which Justinian responded.[97]

Canto 89 continues with its heavy monetary-economic detailing:

> 1. Orage remarked on the "recession of power"
> Uncle George said he knew when he came out
> (Lodge, Knox) that there wd/ be one hell of a row in the Se-
> nate.

[96] Del Mar, *A History of the Monetary Systems*, 62–63, 70, 236, 319, 323–24, 334, 341.

[97] Del Mar, *A History of the Monetary Systems*, 134–35.

"offensive, defensive"
and there was one.
"50 mocking birds, 40 robins," wrote Randolph.
and "construe all our liberties from us"
Mazzini: Doveri

. . . .

2. "Shd/have shot Clay and hung John Calhoun."
A.J.'s sole repentance.
And of Antoninus very little record remains.

. . . .

3. Deluged the old hawk at Rip Raps,
Mr Biddle pinching the baby,
"You damn sadist! said mr cummings,
"you try to make people think."
"Yes, Mr Van Buren, the Bank IS
trying to kill me."
Mr Taney's statement was never refuted. Aug. '33
And as to expunging?
that is perhaps prose,
you can find it in Benton.
Securing his (A.J.'s) admiration by the majesty
of his (Dante's) in'elect.

. . . .

4. Make distress, on system, in order to use it.
"The angrier, the cooler he (Benton) became."
We have had one "assumption".
English debt could have been paid by the time of George
Second.
they prefer to send it down to posterity.
And when "EXPUNGED", A.J. sent back the bullet,
which is, I suppose, part of parliamentary history
dull or not, as you choose to regard it.

(Canto 89)

The first passage begins with a reference to A. R. Orage, the editor of *The New Age*, and his remark concerning the recession of power. A. R. Orage, like C. H. Douglas in *Economic Democracy*, had been concerned with the recession of power away from parliaments and cabinet rooms to the boardrooms of the big banking and financial institutions.

The line concerning Senators Lodge and Knox deals with the tumultuous debate in the United States Senate over America's entry into the League of Nations. Pound points out that "Uncle George" was right and there was "one hell of a row" in the Senate. *Uncle George* refers to Congressman George Tinkham, long-time representative from Boston's Back Bay district, who was a friend of Pound's.

Pound then quotes John Randolph of Roanoke to the effect that the United States Congress was made up of "50 mocking birds, and 40 robins," who in effect "construe all our liberties from us." Randolph's statement implies that the Congress by its interpretation of the laws is undermining the liberty of the American people.

The reference to Mazzini is understandable at this point since Mazzini and Cavour are both Italian heroes of Pound. Pound's praise of Mazzini's monetary-economic provisions and the similarity Pound saw between monetary-economic policies of Mazzini and those of Douglas have already been dealt with in Chapter II.

The second passage paraphrases Andrew Jackson to the effect that he should have shot Henry Clay and hung John Calhoun. Both Henry Clay and John Calhoun lined up against Andrew Jackson and Thomas Hart Benton, and on the side of Nicholas Biddle and the Second Bank of the United States, in the great battle over the re-chartering of the Bank.

Pound then shifts from Andrew Jackson to Antoninus Pius, Emperor of Rome. Both Jackson and Antoninus fought against usury and supported the principle of state or imperial coinage. Pound points out that scant record exists of Antoninus's career. The implication is that there is a historical blackout regarding those men who have effectively opposed the forces of usury. Pound is concerned with this historical blackout and its adverse effect on any sound monetary-economic *paideuma*/tradition.

In the third passage above, "Mr. Biddle" is Nicholas Biddle, President of the Bank of the United States during the Bank War. The quotation from H. E. Cummings was addressed to Pound and ironically accuses Pound of sadism, because he tries to make people think. Pound especially tries to make people think in the realm of monetary economics and monetary history. Pound then goes on to quote a statement made by General Andrew Jackson, to the effect that the Bank of the United States was trying to kill him because of his strong anti-bank stand.[98]

This is followed by a reference to the Secretary of the Treasury, Taney, and the fact that his "statement was never refuted."[99] Taney's statement on the floor of Congress was that the Bank of the United States, instead of following its charter that seven directors be present

[98] Van Buren, *The Autobiography*, 625.
[99] Van Buren, *The Autobiography*, 644.

for important money transactions, had an unappointed committee that made decisions, decisions that involved the public interest, but the agents of the government were not even allowed in the decision process.[100] Pound notes the danger Jackson faced, in Jackson's statement to Van Buren, implying that the Banks were behind the effort. Jackson was assaulted once and was the first sitting US president to have an attempt made on his life.

The reference "to expunging" in this same passage alludes to Benton's efforts to have motions of censure against Jackson "expunged" or wiped clean from the records of the Senate.[101] This had been done in the case of Thomas Jefferson and Benton wanted the same to be done in the case of Jackson.

Benton's speech on this occasion was a marvellous tribute to Jackson as the saviour of the people because of his heroic stand against the Bank. Pound goes on to point out that Jackson admired the majesty of Dante's intellect. Again, this is in keeping with Pound's belief that a sound monetary-economic *paideuma* is a prerequisite for true culture. Jackson opposed the corrosive force of usury and therefore he was more likely to appreciate Dante and culture in general.

Pound points out that the usurocracy imposes distress on the present system to its own advantage. In other words, the usurocracy creates chaos in the body-economic and thrives on that chaos. There then follows a description of the coolness of T. H. Benton when in the heat of an argument the angrier he was the cooler he became. Pound points out that America has had one scandal of the "assumption" in her history. This scandal of the assumption has already been discussed in this thesis. This had to do with the hoarding up of depreciated veterans' certificates by speculating Congressmen and others after the War of Independence. The scandal consisted in the face value of these certificates being restored after their purchase by the Congressmen and other speculators. Pound then goes on to point out that the English debt could have been paid by the time of George II, but the English prefer to send that debt down to their posterity. He also recounts how Andrew Jackson sent back the bullet, which had been fired at him in an assassination attempt, to those whom he suspected of arranging the attempt on his life. Jackson did this after Benton had succeeded in having the motions of censure against Jackson expunged from the Senate Record. This is a part of parliamentary history and is dull or not, as one chooses to regard it.

---

[100] Van Buren, *The Autobiography*, 643.
[101] Benton, *Thirty Years' View*, Vol. I, 528.

Canto 90 is preceded by a Latin quotation[102] which provides the major theme for the Cantos as they move into their third and final phase: the "domination of benevolence." The Latin quotation is translated "the human soul is not love, but love flows from it . . . it, cannot ergo delight in itself, but only in the love flowing from it." Pound is a great admirer of scholastic philosophy and of the medieval theologians whom he refers to "as athletes of the spirit."[103] It is quite in keeping with his philosophy that this scholastic dictum should precede this canto. Canto 90 is not as heavy in its monetary-economic detailing as the last few cantos have been. However, even in this canto, Pound does not ignore the enduring monetary-economic *paideuma*:

> 1. That is Sagetrieb,
> that is tradition.
> Builders had kept the proportion,
> did Jacques de Molay
> know these proportions?
> and was Erigena ours?
> . . . .
> 2. Not love but that love flows from it
> ex animo
> & cannot ergo delight in itself
> but only in the love flowing from it.
> UBI AMOR IBI OCULUS EST.
> (Canto 90)

The reference to *Sagetrieb*, or tradition, in the first passage is one that has occurred before in the Cantos. Pound also uses the Greek-based word, borrowed from Leo Frobenius, *paideuma* to describe an inherited culture or tradition. Pound's understanding of the word *culture* is like Eliot's, a broad one. Pound would certainly include the monetary-economic tradition in the overall *Sagetrieb*, *paideuma*, or culture. In the earlier part of Canto 90 he had mentioned certain great works of classical and medieval art and architecture. He now refers to the builders of classical and medieval times who had kept that proportion which is consonant with harmony and beauty. He then asks if Jacques de Molay knew these proportions. Jacques de Molay appeared earlier in the Rock-Drill Cantos. Pound sees a direct connection between the aesthetic perception

---

[102] *Animus humanus amor non est, sed ab ipso amor procedit, et ideo seipso non diligit, sed amore qui seipso procedit.*
[103] Pound, *Impact*, 233.

of proportion and harmony and the degree of one's abhorrence of usury. In Chapter II, Pound's contention that he can tell the degree of tolerance of usury in a particular historical period by closely examining the painting of that period was presented. If art is ugly, out of proportion, then it must have been done in a time of great usury. Pound then asks if Eriugena was ours. He is a great admirer of the philosophy of Scotus Eriugena and of Eriugena's strong stand against usury. Eriugena has appeared many times before in *The Cantos.*

The second passage is Pound's poetic paraphrasing of the scholastic dictum at the start of Canto 90. "UBI AMOR…," and is taken from Richard of St Victor. St. Victor emphasizes that the human soul cannot delight in itself but only in the love flowing from it. As noted above concerning de Molay, "Pound sees a direct connection between the aesthetic perception of proportion and harmony, and the degree of one's abhorrence of usury." Bad art, the ugliness of modern architecture, literature, etc., is due to the corrosiveness of the current banking system, especially how it creates loans as a debt, i.e., money created by a mere fountain pen at a bank. Pound calls this all *usury*, *hyper-usury*. Pound includes its creation, not just the interest itself, as most imply, when speaking of usury. Pound contends that because of usury, much of what we produce is not what we truly desire, which is good art and well-made products for daily use. Others connect St. Victor's passages on love with the ugliness of art today:

> Forming personal relationships cannot be reduced to metrics and algorithms. Instead, forming personal relationships depends on love. And love begins with an appreciation of the beloved's beauty. Nine hundred years ago, Richard of St. Victor wrote *ubi amor, ibi oculus*—"where there is love, there the eye is also."…
>
> I'd like to suggest three ways in which beauty can bring souls into communion with Jesus Christ. The first is the restoration of the beautiful to the world of art, architecture, and culture. We now suffer from a cult of ugliness and utility. And this is manifestly apparent in much of contemporary architecture. The architectural maxim that "form follows function" is a way of saying that design only exists to facilitate production. Architecture is overwhelmed by technocracy. Oscar Wilde recognized the danger of this kind of thinking. "Put usefulness first, and you lose it," he said. "Put beauty first, and what you do will be useful forever."[104]

[104] Conley, "Ubi Amor, Ibi Oculus."

Canto 91 opens with two lines of Gregorian chant written in Italian. This canto also marks the first time that one notices Pound's interest in Egyptology. Pound's son-in-law, Prince Boris de Rachewiltz, was a noted Egyptologist and under his influence Pound was interested in the ancient Egyptian cuneiform script. Pound also translated a series of Egyptian love poems from Italian in collaboration with Noel Stock.[105] Canto 91 contains a number of Egyptian luminous details and references to the Princess Ra-Set. The first section of Canto 91 consists of beautiful and lyrical luminous details taken from ancient Egyptian, Elizabethan, and Anglo-Saxon times. Pound speaks of the Princess Ra-Set entering the protection of crystal, and of her barge on a river of crystal. After these and other similarly beautiful luminous details taken from the days of Francis Drake and of Athelstan before 940 AD, Pound suddenly and violently superposes the following devastating description of contemporary society on the glory of the past:

> Democracies electing their sewage
> till there is no clear thought about holiness
> a dung flow from 1913
> and, in this, their kikery functioned, Marx, Freud
>   and the american beaneries
> Filth under filth,
>   Maritain, Hutchins,
> or as Benda remarked: "La trahison"
>
> (Canto 91)

Pound stresses that under the present form of *democracy* the very worst men or *sewage* are elected. As a result, there is no clear thought about holiness as there was in ancient Egyptian, classical, and medieval times. The "dung flow from 1913" Pound connects with the teachings of Marx and Freud, and with the complete triumph of Marxism and Freudianism in the curricula and teaching of the *American beaneries*, i.e., the American universities and colleges.[106] Pound speaks of this academic decline and corrosion as "filth under filth." Pound mentions the French Catholic philosopher Jacques Maritain and Professor Robert Maynard Hutchins from the University of Chicago and of Great Books[107] fame; both are regarded as 'guilty'

[105] Pound, *Love poems of Ancient Egypt.*

[106] In America, 1913 is significant for two economic events: the year the Federal Reserve system was created and the year Congress proposed the Sixteenth Amendment concerning the imposition of income tax.

[107] Pound had his own multiple recommendations on education, such as Pound's *ABC of Reading,* and had his own *Ezuversity* in Rapallo; he as the instructor. Laughlin, *Pound As Wuz.* Several successful traditional Catholic Colleges in

of an academic treason which turns its back on the great thought of the classical and medieval past, and substitutes for it the ersatz of Marx and Freud. One would think that Pound would find much in common with a neo-Thomist such as Jacques Maritain. Pound may consider Maritain's brand of Neo-Scholasticism as a perversion of the thought of the great Scholastics, e.g., Scotus Eriugena and Richard of St. Victor. Maritain was one of the greatest French Catholic philosophers of the 20th century, uniting medieval Thomistic thought with modern philosophical issues. Maritain was also a friend of Mortimer Adler, who was responsible for developing the Great Books program. This is likely an association of which Pound would not approve. Maritain's involvement in the United Nations and other international organizations may also have been for Pound, who had opposed the League of Nations as an effort to take power away from sovereign nations (away from local control), an additional reason to feel betrayed by Maritain.[108] Pound applies the Jewish French philosopher and writer, Julien Benda's book's title *La Trahison des Clercs: The Betrayal of the Intellectuals* to both Maritain and Hutchins.[109]

Towards the end of Canto 91 Pound comes back to the theme of sodomy which is always in *The Cantos* connected with that of usury:

> 1. And that even in the time of Domitian
>   one young man declined to be buggar'd.
> "Is this a bath-house?"
>
> . . . .
>
> 2.   "Or a Court House?"
> Asked Apollonius
>   who spoke to the lion
>
>   (Canto 91)

Pound's juxtaposition of the themes of usury and sodomy has already been shown in Canto XLI. Appolonius's question concerning whether this is a "bath-house," or a "Court House" suggests the perversion, which is often practised in both places, i.e., in one a perversion of the natural law, and in the other, a perversion of positive/legitimate legal law.

Canto 92 continues with the monetary/historic luminous detail, which has been noted in earlier cantos:

America, and other Colleges, use the canon of *the Great Books*. For a more recent critique, cf. Deneen, "Against Great Books."

108 "About Jacques Maritain."

109 For further inquiry into questions related to Western education or the Great Books, cf. Dawson, *The Crisis of Western Education*.

1. That the Pontifex ceased to be holy
—that was in Caesar's time —
who was buggar'd
and the coin ceased to be holy,
and, of course,
they worshipped the emperor.

. . . .

2. "Two evils:
usury in the bank rot
& theft in les soc/ anonymes".

. . . .

3. And against usury
and the degradation of sacraments,
For 40 years I have seen this,
now flood as the Yang tse

(Canto 92)

In the first passage above, Pound paraphrases again passages from Del Mar to the effect that the office of Pontifex Maximus or Roman High Priest ceased to be holy when it was usurped by Julius Caesar.[110] Del Mar also stresses that, prior to Caesar's innovation, the coinage of gold had been a sacred prerogative of the Roman High Priest, just as it had been a prerogative of the priests among the Greeks.[111] When Caesar usurped the office of Pontifex Maximus he also usurped the sacred prerogative over the coinage of gold. This is what Pound means when he says that the coin ceased to be holy, and emperor-worship began.

The second passage speaks of two evils, i.e., usury as carried on by the banks and theft as carried on by the limited companies, i.e., "les sociétés anonymes." This second passage marks a juxtaposition of time because it obviously refers to the contemporary period.

The third passage is highly significant in that it illustrates Pound's belief that usury is sacrilegious in character and that it is always accompanied by a decline in religious beliefs and values. Pound speaks of his stand against both usury and the degradation of the sacraments. He points out that for forty years he has seen and marked the corrosive force of usury and the degradation of the sacraments. These twin evils Pound compares to the destructive flooding of the Yangtse river in China.

Canto 93 begins with an ancient Egyptian cuneiform inscription and contains several others, once again revealing Pound's growing

---

[110] Del Mar, *A History of the Monetary Systems*, 46–47.

[111] Del Mar, *A History of the Monetary Systems*, 81, 89–90.

interest in Egyptology. This canto also contains passages of great lyric beauty and many luminous details. However, even Canto 93 contains its share of monetary-economic luminous details which continue to show the Douglasite influence:

> 1. Alessandro & Saladin & Galasso di Montefeltro
> and mentions distributive justice, Dante does, in Convivio
> Four, eleven
> "cui adorna esta bontade". Know agenda,
> to the utmost of its virtu,
> of its own.
>
> . . . .
>
> 2. Mr Hoepli sent a small brochure to Svitzerland
> and his banker friend replied "*urgente*":
> "destroy it e farlo sparire."
>
> . . . .
>
> 3. Grenfell's death was (like some others)
> suspiciously sudden.
> The Bard of Avon mentioned the subject,
> Dante mentioned the subject,
> and the lit profs discuss other passages
> in abuleia
> or in total unconsciousness
> Four thousand years after KATI
>
> . . . .
>
> 4. Taffy went putty-colour when I mentioned Zaharoff (1914)
> And general Whoosis, when he read the name, Aquarone,
> 30 years later
> or as Ub said: "ten to charge a nest of machine guns
> for one who will put his name on a chit.
>
> . . . .
>
> 5. Shall two know the same in their knowing?
> You who dare Persephone's threshold,
> Beloved, do not fall apart in my hands.
> E "chi crescerà" they would be individuals.
>
> (Canto 93)

The first passage mentions Alexander the Great, Saladin, and Galasso di Montefeltro in connection with that distributive justice mentioned by Dante in *The Convivio*, 4, 11. Distributive justice in Catholic moral theology is that justice which the community owes to the individual as distinct from commutative justice which exists between persons. Pound is implying that rulers like Alexander the Great and Saladin, who emphasized the distribution of abundance in their realm by a monetary system based on abundance, not on artificial scarcity, were in fact practising that distributive justice mentioned by Dante in *The Convivio.*[112] C. H. Douglas emphasizes distributive justice in his philosophy and maintains that the state fails in distributive justice when it hands over its prerogative of credit creation to private interests.

The second passage mentions Ulrico Hoepli, a Swiss publisher who was known likewise for dealing in antiquarian books. Hoepli died in 1935.[113] Pound tells how Hoepli sent a small brochure that he had published to a banker friend in Switzerland. Whatever the contents of this brochure may have been, they were sufficiently dangerous for the banker to send Hoepli an urgent message to the effect that all copies of the brochure should be destroyed and *made to disappear*. Thus Pound introduces once again the subject of the blackout of history and knowledge caused by the banking interests.

Pound then points out that "Grenfell's death was (like some others) / suspiciously sudden." The Grenfell referred to is Capt. Russell Grenfell of the Royal Navy, 1892–1954, who is alluded to earlier in Canto 87. The inside of Grenfell's 1958 book cover states: "This final book—Captain Grenfell died suddenly of unknown causes in 1954 as he was drafting a sequel to it—is a 21-gun broadside on policy rather than strategy; it touches on so many raw nerves, conflicts with so many prejudices and vested interests, that publication has had to take place in our still largely free and uncensored United States. No English publisher will touch it as of the present—nor has any important American reviewer recognized its existence."[114]

Pound goes on to point out that William Shakespeare, the bard of Avon, had mentioned the subject of usury as had Dante. However, literature professors discuss other passages, thereby displaying their "abuleia" or total unconsciousness. This is even more ironical in the light of the fact that four thousand years have elapsed since Kati, an Egyptian writer, had something negative to say concerning usury.[115]

In the fourth passage, Pound recalls a conversation he, or perhaps someone else, had in 1914 with David Lloyd George. *Taffy* is a diminutive for the Welsh name *Dafydd*, a variant of the name

---

112 Alighieri, *The Convivio*, treatise 4, chp. 11, 280–84.

113 "Ulrico Hoepli."

114 Grenfell, *Unconditional Hatred*, inside book cover.

115 Pound is referring to the letter of King Khety to his son: "The Teaching for King Merikare." No specific passage is explicit in referring to usury, though some imply not taking more than is owed for a loan. Example: "Console him who weeps, and oppress not the widow. / Do not expel a man from the property of his father." *The Literature of Ancient Egypt*, 157.

David.[116] Lloyd George went putty-coloured when the name Sir Basil Zaharoff was mentioned, the banker and munitions king who appears so prominently in earlier Cantos as Sir Zenos Metevsky or Metevsky Melchizedeck. Pound's allusion is possible, as Lloyd George in 1915 would become the first *Minister of Munitions* due to a shortage of artillery shells. Lloyd George would be involved through Zaharoff in the disastrous Greco-Turkish War of 1920–22, again emphasizing the close relationship between the two individuals. Lloyd George was forced to resign as Prime Minister when the massacre by Turkey of the Greek and Armenian Christians in Smyrna became known.[117]

Pound then recalls the same expression on the face of a certain Italian general thirty years later when he read the name of Aquarone, i.e., Duke Pietro Acquarone.[118] Like Sir Basil Zaharoff, Acquarone was a financier in Verona, Italy, a major hub for munitions manufacturing.

While the First World War brought a great loss of life and destruction to Italy, these firms grew rich. The implication seems to be that the usurocracy plays both sides. Their ultimate loyalty is to Mammon, not justice or morality.

He then reiterates a quotation from "Ub" i.e., Ubaldo degli Uberti,[119] to the effect that for every ten men who possess physical courage, who will charge a machine-gun nest, there is only one who possesses financial courage—who will put his name on a chit.

The fifth passage can be paraphrased to the effect that whoever would be someone exceptional must grow as an individual. Here again Pound, like Douglas, stresses the uniqueness and sacredness of the human individual. Greatness depends on the individual not on the collectivity. In this connection, C. H. Douglas devotes an entire chapter of his book *Social Credit* to a discussion of the relation of the group to the individual. In this chapter, Douglas is critical of the contemporary elevation of the group ideal and the minimizing of individuality, i.e., the treatment of individuality as subordinate to group concepts, e.g., nationality.[120]

Canto 94 begins with a number of monetary-economic luminous details taken from American history. Some of these are new and some have been seen before. However, this canto is by no means restricted to the American scene:

---

[116] "Taffy," *A Dictionary of First Names.*

[117] Flynn, *Men of Wealth*, 365.

[118] Terrell, *A Companion*, Vol. II, 565.

[119] Terrell, *A Companion*, Vol. II, 565.

[120] Douglas, *Social Credit*, 30.

1. "Brederode"
(to Rush, Ap 4. 1790)
. . . treaties of commerce only,

. . . .

2. "or whose depreciations are to the favour of the whole people"
Mr Adams saw thru the bank hoax
& Suvitch a century plus 20 years later:
"d- d- d- dina- mite!
sssi si
d-d-
dinamite!
& the Medici failed from accepting too many deposits.
Alex . . . , a respectable
or at least meritorious Biddle,
alive 1890
"& consequently the corruption of history"
J.A. to Rush
18 'leven.

. . . .

3. & then the fun starts
with the "Code"
I. 3, Title:
"feed 'um"

. . . .

4. To Kung, to avoid their encirclement,
To the Odes to escape abstract yatter,
to Mencius, Dante, and Agassiz
for Gestalt seed,
pity, yes, for the infected,
but maintain antisepsis,
let the light pour.

. . . .

5. Said ANTONINUS:
"Law rules the sea"
meaning lex Rhodi

. . . .

6. & do not mow the high stalks
ANTONINUS reigned 138 to 161
SEVERUS and Julia Domna about 198

. . . .

7. That it is of thrones,
and above them: Justice
Acre, again,
with an Eleanor

who sucked the venom out of his wound,
        and came up via Padua,
for a balance of wine & wool,
        distraint and tolls not unbridled

. . . .

8. that the king shd/ be king

. . . .

9. & when Athens exceded the tributes set by Aristides,
Coke, after he got into Parliament,

(Canto 94)

The line, "or whose depreciations are to the favour of the whole people" refers to the depreciation of continental currency during the Revolutionary War working in favour of the whole people since it replaced all other forms of taxation. This point has been discussed in the consideration of earlier Cantos and this same quotation was ascribed to John Adams. Pound goes on to point out that John Adams saw through the bank hoax, as did Suvitch one hundred and twenty years later. "Suvitch" refers to Fulvio Suvitch, an Italian statesman serving Mussolini's government. Pound is referring to a conversation with him, where Suvitch stated, or perhaps agreed, that if people understood the workings of finance it would create an upheaval like an explosion: *dynamite*. Suvitch served as Italy's ambassador to the USA for a short period in the late 1930s, perhaps to get him out of the way, as he opposed the resumption of Fascist Italy's friendly relations with Nazi Germany.[121]

Pound then goes on to reiterate that the Medici banking house failed due to accepting too many deposits. He mentions Alexander Biddle as a meritorious Biddle who was alive in 1890.[122] This Biddle would contrast sharply with Nicholas Biddle, President of the Second Bank of the United States, for whom Pound has no use. The specific line "& consequently the corruption of history" is taken from a letter written by John Adams to Benjamin Rush in 1811.[123]

---

[121] Terrell, *A Companion*, Vol. II, 571–72.

[122] Terrell, *A Companion*, Vol. II, 572.

[123] "Dr. Rush! I request you, or your Son Richard, to write a Treatise or at least an Essay, on the Causes of the Corruption of Tradition and consequently of the Corruption of History. For myself I do believe that both Tradition and History are already corrupted in America as much as they ever were in the four or five first Centuries of Christianity; and as much as they ever were in any Age or Country in the whole History of Mankind. . . . How shall we account for the selfishness, the avarice, the all grasping cupidity of those sublime Genius's. Boerhaave left a Fortune, as great or greater than Franklin or Washington.—And never spent a doit." Quincy 14 August 1811. *Old Family Letters*, Series A, 346–47.

This line obviously refers to that historical blackout and obfuscation of history carried on by the usurocracy, which is one of Pound's favourite themes. Obviously, John Adams agrees with C. H. Douglas concerning the historical blackout and obfuscation of history. This is a very prominent theme in Douglas's writings.

The third passage refers to a section of the Justinian Code that Pound condenses and summarises in the homely expression "feed 'um." Obviously, this section emphasizes the distribution of abundance, which is a favourite theme with Pound and is derived from C. H. Douglas.

The fourth passage recommends Confucius, Mencius, Dante, and Agassiz as writers who will help one escape the encirclement, the "abstract yatter," and infection of the present age. These four writers are praised for their lucidity. Louis Agassiz was the great naturalist who opposed the post-Darwinian school of biology with his emphasis on a creative intelligence behind nature, and on the stability of species.

The fifth passage again reiterates Antoninus Pius's statement to the effect that law rules the sea. Again, Pound points out that the law referred to in reference to Antoninus Pius is the maritime law of the island of Rhodes. The sixth passage gives the dates of Antoninus's reign and one date for his son.

The seventh passage mentions Eleanor of Acquitane who had appeared in the very earliest Cantos. Eleanor is mentioned against the background of the crusades and the battle of Acre. Pound refers to Eleanor in connection with justice, i.e., economic justice as revealed in the balance of wine and wool and the policy of restraining the practice of distraint and tolls. Distraint is that legal action whereby one's goods can be seized and sold for the payment of debt.

The eighth passage emphasizes that the king should be king. This obviously refers to Pound's belief that in a monarchy the king should be *boss* of the coinage. The ninth passage mentions Athens's abuse of the tribute limit set by Aristides and contains a brief allusion to Coke, the great commentator on English common law and another Poundian hero.

Canto 95 is the last of the Rock-Drill Cantos. Its monetary-economic luminous details begins with a reference to Talleyrand:

1. Van Buren unsmearing Talleyrand,
 Adams to Rush before that, in 1811
And there were guilds in Byzantium.
 "Not political", Dante says, a
 "compagnevole animale"
Even if some do coagulate into cities

. . . .

2. Benton: when there was plenty of metal,
Van Buren already desmearing Talleyrand
J.A. "the whole people (devaluation)."
Alexander paid the debts of his soldiery

. . . .

3. And damn it there were men even in my time
Nicoletti, Ramperti, Desmond Fitzgerald
(the one alive in 1919)

. . . .

4. Among all these twerps and Pullizer sponges
no voice for the Constitution,
No objection to the historic blackout.

. . . .

5. The immense cowardice of advertised litterati

. . . .

6. the enormous organized cowardice.
And there is something decent in the universe
if I can feel all this, *dicto millesimo*
At the age of whatever.

(Canto 95)

In the first passage, Pound reiterates a statement concerning Martin Van Buren to the effect that Van Buren *unsmeared* Talleyrand.[124] This luminous detail has appeared several times before and the implication is that Talleyrand has been smeared by the financial interests who control the teaching of history and who are responsible for the historical blackout. This is also, of course, a favourite theme with Pound.

Pound then refers us to John Adams's letter to Benjamin Rush written in 1811, which has been mentioned in Canto 94. In this letter, Adams wrote about the *corruption of history*. In other words, Pound quotes John Adams to prove his contention that the usurocracy corrupts history.

The second passage quoted begins with a reference to Thomas Hart Benton. The phrase "when there was plenty of metal," has reference to Benton's first speech against the Bank of the United States in February 1831. In this speech, which has been discussed earlier in this chapter, Benton mentions that France possessed a hard currency while having no mines of silver and gold, while the United States, where "there was plenty of metal," was forced by the Bank of the United States to use a soft currency.[125] Pound then reiterates the luminous

---

124 Van Buren, *The Autobiography*, 458–59.

125 Benton, *Thirty Years'* View, Vol I, 187.

detail concerning Van Buren already "desmearing Talleyrand." The line "J. A. 'the whole people (devaluation),'" refers to John Adams's statement that the devaluation or depreciation of the bills of credit issued by the Continental Congress was to the favour of the whole people, in that it acted as an evenly distributed tax and was the only tax the people had to pay. This luminous detail has appeared several times before and most recently in Canto 94. Pound then reiterates his great Alexandrine luminous detail to the effect that "Alexander paid the debts of his soldiery."

In the third passage, Pound points out that there have been real men even in his own time, i.e., the time of organized mediocrity. He mentions the Italians Nicoletti and Ramperti and the Irishman Desmond Fitzgerald as contemporary examples, men who rose above the mediocrity of the age.

The fourth passage expresses Pound's contempt for the world of journalism: "these twerps and Pullizer sponges." Pound despises these journalists because none of them has raised a voice for the American constitution. The American constitution states: "The Congress shall have power to coin money, regulate the value thereof and of foreign coin."[126] None of these *kept* journalistic pundits has raised a voice for a constitutional and congressional money system. None of these *Pullizer sponges* has objected to the historic blackout affected by the usurocracy. This historic blackout that caused the American people, since the Civil War, to be completely ignorant of those monetary-economic principles over which the War of Independence was fought. Pound then speaks of the immense cowardice of the advertised litterati who are predestined to glory by having their books reviewed by *Time* magazine and other *learned* journals. The immense cowardice of the advertised litterati consists of their failure to speak out on money matters. Pound has pointed out that for every person with an anxiety neurosis due to a sexual problem there are ten people with an anxiety neurosis due to a lack of purchasing power.[127] Yet contemporary novelists write as if purchasing power magically comes from production, as naturally as the scent from a rose.

In the sixth passage, Pound speaks of this immense cowardice as an "enormous organized cowardice." The inference is that the "enormous organized cowardice" of the litterati has been organized

---

[126] *The Constitution*, art. 1, sec 8, cl. 5.

[127] Pound, *Impact*, 177. Cf. Douglas's statement that: "It is poverty and economic insecurity which submits human nature to the greatest strain. . . . " *Monopoly of Credit*, 89.

by the usurocracy through its control of the academic world, i.e., the publishing houses, and the press. However, in this same passage Pound states that "there is still something decent in the universe / if I can feel all this."

2) THRONES 96–109 DE LOS CANTARES

There is a structural parallel between *The Cantos* and the *Divine Comedy*. This relationship becomes more explicit in *Thrones*, which are named after Dante's *Paradiso*. These new Cantos, like the preceding ones, form a commentary on life and civilization in all its complexity: "And above all there is the dream of the earthly paradise, the '*paradiso terrestre*,' which acceptance of his theories of economic reform might have made possible."[128] Earlier themes are recalled and elaborated, and there are lyric passages as fine as anything Pound has written. However, even in these latest cantos, the distributist and anti-usury theme never loses its intensity.

Canto 96 is one of the most complex and difficult cantos. *Thrones* is complex and scholarly in its cultural, artistic, and monetary-economic luminous details. Pound has answered hostile critics in these words that are inserted as an italicized note in Canto 96:

> *If we never write anything save what is already understood, the field of understanding will never be extended. One demands the right, now and again, to write for a few people with special interests and whose curiosity reaches into greater detail.*
>
> (Canto 96)

Thrones derives much of its luminous details from the works of the great monetary historian, Alexander Del Mar, 1836–1926. He was an American economist, historian, and engineer. He was Director of the Bureau of Statistics of the United States and was a mining engineer for the United States Monetary Commission of 1876. Del Mar amended Theodor Mommsen concerning Roman history and refuted Thorald Rogers: "His thirty volumes may be taken 'as preface to whatever anyone may henceforth write on such subjects.' He was writing on the 'Principles of Taxation' in 1865 and the mystery of his occultation from 1900 until his death in 1926 has yet to be unveiled."[129] Along with Louis Agassiz and Leo Frobenius, he builds

---

[128] Laughlin, *Pound as Wuz*, 115.

[129] This is believed to be a quote from Ezra Pound from a small review of Pound's that was entitled: *Four Pages* (October, 1950). It is partly quoted at the end of a 1975 reprint of Del Mar, *A History of Monetary* Crimes, 98.

upon Alexander von Humboldt's statement of science as "the art of collecting and arranging a mass of isolated facts, and rising thence by a process of induction to general ideas."[130]

Canto 96 takes much of its luminous details from Roman and Greek history. However, many of these luminous details are rich in their monetary-economic significance. This would serve to support Pound's contention that the usurocracy has put an end to classical education because it fears the monetary wisdom that can be obtained from the history and writings of ancient Greece and Rome:

> 1. And the money sellers Ablavius and Marcellus
> thought they would bump off Justinian.
>
> . . . .
>
> 2. an appeal to reason is about a 13%
> appeal to reality,
> job-hunting in our time, and in the 3rd/ year of Justin
> Sophia Augusta
> made the money-sellers cough up something or other,
> pecuniarium venditoribus, and in the 12th
> took over the synagog,
>
> . . . .
>
> 3. and of course there is no local freedom
> without local control of local purchasing power.
> Del Mar spotted "bronze to the cities,"
>
> . . . .
>
> 4. Chosdroes (Second) pro sun
> & melted down the church vessels & coined them
>
> . . . .
>
> 5. The Deacon, col 1026, thinks it "argenteos,"
> nummos aureos et argenteos, HERACLIUS versus Chosdroes
> coined candle-sticks to keep off Chosdroes
>
> . . . .
>
> 6. Anno sexto imperii sui Justinianus (the second)
> pacem, quam ad Habdimelich habuit, ex amentia
> dissolvit, et omnem Cypriorum insulam, et populum
> irrationabiliter voluit transmigrare, et characterem
> qui missus fuerat ab Habdimelich, eum noviter visus
> esset . . . et his auditis Habdimelich satanice stimu-
> latus rogabat ne pax solveretur, sed susciperent mo-
> netam suam, cum Arabes non susciperent Roma-
> norum incisionem in suis nummis. Verum dato
> pondere auri ait: Nullum Romanis damnum effici-
> tur, ex eo quod Arabes nova cuderent . . .

130 Bruhns, *Life of Alexander*, Vol. II, 211.

Quod et factum est, et misit Habdimelich ad aedificandum templum Muchan, et voluit auferre columnas . . .
—col. 1060, The Deacon, Migne's Patrologia.

. . . .

7. the base shall we say, and the slide of Byzantium,
bags, baskets full of, presumably, coinage,
and lured twenty thousand sclavons.

. . . .

8. and the idea of just price is somewhere,
the haggling, somewhere,
(Canto 96)

The first passage speaks of "the money sellers," i.e., the usurers, Ablavius and Marcellus, who thought they would assassinate Emperor Justinian I,[131] the Law-Giver or also called the Great; who ruled the Eastern Roman Empire from 527 to 565. This luminous detail is noteworthy because it reiterates a theme that has often appeared in both *The Cantos* and in Pound's prose writing, i.e., the fact that the usurocracy, whether in ancient or modern times, has often used assassination to attain its ends. Assassination is used after bribery and vilification (in that order) have failed. The expression *money sellers* rather than *money lenders* is important in that it emphasizes that these people, *pecuniarium venditoribus*, i.e., *sell money*, the medium of exchange, as if it were simply another commodity.

The second passage begins with the ironic assertion that an "appeal to reason" is about a "13% / appeal to reality." The reference to "job-hunting in our time" is significant in the light of the Douglasite repudiation of the *jobs for all* philosophy in this age of technology and its replacement by the Douglasite *dividends for all* concept. Pound, following Douglas, regards the policy of *full-employment* and make-work with disdain. It is this frantic Calvinistic philosophy of *total work* which has enabled the usurocracy to stake *total war* on contemplation and thus debase man, religion, and art.

In this same passage, Pound points out that in the third year of Justin II (who ruled 565–578 and was nephew of Justinian I), his wife Sophia Augusta made the money-sellers "cough up something or other." This refers to passages in Migne's Latin patrology where "Sophia Augusta summoned the usurious money-lenders before her and ordered them to treat their debtors better. She restored mortgaged homes to their rightful owners and received great praise from the

[131] Terrell, *A Companion*, Vol. II, 597.

populace."[132] Pound then states that in the twelfth year of Justin's reign the synagogue was taken over.[133]

The third passage contains a direct paraphrasing of a statement made by C. H. Douglas in *Economic Democracy* and elsewhere to the effect that there is *no local freedom without local control of local purchasing power*. This principle of the local control of local purchasing power is fundamental to Douglasism in the light of the fact that Douglas believes that the control over and issue of credit should be decentralized. This passage concludes with Pound's reference to Del Mar who ascribed the prerogative of the bronze coinage to the Senate, whether of Rome or of Antioch.[134] This reference to Del Mar gives historical backing to Pound's insistence upon the local control of local purchasing power.

The fourth and fifth passage recount how the Persian Emperor Chosdroes II who was "pro sun" i.e., a Zoroastrian by religion, directed an insult at the Eastern Roman Emperor Heraclius.[135] The city of Constantinople was in danger of falling to the Persians and Heraclius was planning to flee. The Patriarch of Constantinople Sergius convinced him to stay. Heraclius asked for peace and was made to pay tribute to the Persians. The emperor Heraclius exercised his sovereign prerogative and issued a debt-free currency by melting down the sacred Church treasures such as the "church vessels" and "candle-sticks." From these he made coinage to pay for war. At this point, the tide turned against the Persians. This avowedly distributist philosophy and policy of Heraclius exercising his imperial prerogative by making coinage is looked upon with approval by Pound, as it emphasizes the Douglasite precept that Pound is investigating in history, i.e., that the state has credit and need not borrow its own credit. Heraclius did not have to go begging for loans from the money-lenders, placing him and the empire in debt. Pound's source for this section in *The Cantos*, is Migne's *Patrologia Latina.*

The sixth passage consists of a passage directly from the writings of "The Deacon" as they appear in "Migne's Patrologia." The passage tells how the Arabian Caliph Habdimelich, *"satanice stimulatus"—inspired by the devil*, attempted to violate the sacred prerogative of Emperor

---

[132] Terrell, *A Companion*, Vol. II 598.

[133] This reference is to the building of a church in the Copper Market district of Constantinople, dedicated to St. Mary, *Theotokos*. It was on or near the site of a former synagogue, that may have been torn down to be replaced by this church. Panayotov, "The Synagogue."

[134] Del Mar, *A History of the Monetary Systems*, 35, 48.

[135] Terrell, *A Companion*, Vol. II, 600.

Justinian II over the coining of gold. Habdimelich reasoned that no harm would be done to Rome so long as he put the same amount of gold into his coinage as the Romans.

The seventh passage refers to an edict in the "Eparch's book" concerning the coinage of gold which Pound describes as the base and the slide of Byzantium. In other words, the sacred prerogative of the Basileus, or the Eastern Roman Emperor of Constantinople, over the coinage of gold bezants was the basis of Byzantine power and glory. Throughout the medieval period only the Basileus had the right to coin gold for the whole of Christendom. Del Mar points out that even Charlemagne did not attempt to infringe upon this sacred prerogative of the Basileus as successor to the Pontifex Maximus.[136] This gold coinage prerogative filled Byzantium, says Pound, with bags of what was "presumably, coinage" and lured "twenty thousand sclavons" i.e., Slavs, into attacking Constantinople.

The eighth passage mentions the medieval concept of the just price which was the basis of medieval economic life. St. Antoninus, 15th century theologian and Archbishop of Florence, wrote a great deal on the just price and upon usury. Pound emphasizes the medieval concept of the just price because the just price forms the very basis of C. H. Douglas's monetary-economic policy.[137]

Canto 97 continues the complex monetary-economic luminous details:

1. & there was a good deal of sand-paper ordered,
a staple which seems to move without great publicity.
Mons of Jute should have his name in the record,
   thrones, courage, Mons should have his name in the
                                                            record.
Vasa klipped for the people, Lycurgus, nomisma,
and "limitation is the essence of good nomisma"
but Goertz von Schlitz had not thought of this,
      Sweden, Pultawa, and was in any case,
            executed for something
1745 Copjenhaven, the nine year old bank relieved of conver-
                                                            sion.

---

[136] "Pepin not only refrained from the coinage of gold, he forbade it to the princes subject to his authority. In both these respects he was followed by Charlemagne and all the Western 'emperors' until the reign of Frederick II." Del Mar, *A History of the Monetary Systems*, 63.

[137] Editor's note: For Douglas, the just price has a very definite mathematical definition; it is the price of an article multiplied by the general value of total consumption over the general value of total production.

When kings quit, the bankers began again.
15.08 Denmark and Scandinavs (ratio) in '73
  18, that is 1873
on which Mr Benton would have reflected, as per:
the CONtinuous effort to have it different somewhere or other.
And if these were quarter dhirems in Friesland
  they should be of ratio 6 & one half
to the quarter (talis est) dinars of Spain.
  "The olde double-ducat,
  The olde turkish grouch."
And then Amsterdam (1609) busted the Wisselbank
and said who shd/ deal in exchange,
But Mr Del Mar does not, at this point,
  connect issue with backing,
though he is all for a proper total proportion
  between total issue and buyables,
Ike, '55, had got that far.
  And Baffico had papers, daily papers, giornali.
. . . .
2. "Ad
perpetuam
liberationis divinae memoriam", said the Dutch on white
  pasteboard.
"Rien de ce monde", said Villon, inclusively
  "Godt behoede."
  Pugno pro patria. And
degradations, depradations, degradations whatsodam
of emperors, kings and whatsodam,
Dukes et cetera have since been exceeded,
  Kitson, Fenton & Tolstoi had observed this.
And by curious segregation Brooks Adams ignores him, Del
  Mar,
and he, Adams, so far as I have yet met them,
  despite stylistic resemblance.

(Canto 97)

The passage begins with Pound's satirical comment regarding "a good deal of sand-paper ordered." This sand-paper would be used in the historical blackout to blot out and erase any monetary history which would embarrass the usurocracy. Pound, drawing from Del Mar, mentions Mons of Jute as a man whose name should stand high in the record.[138] Gustavus Vasa of Sweden is then mentioned approvingly as having clipped his coinage "for the people," not for

[138] Del Mar, *A History of the Monetary Systems*, 279.

personal profit, as King Christian had done.[139] Vasa's method was the method used in medieval Europe to maintain a managed currency. Christopher Hollis, in a quote provided earlier, explains how medieval currency was managed. Ever so often the weight of silver in coins was reduced. Therefore, out of the same constant supply of silver, more coins could be made and by this means an increased monetary supply was available to buy the increasing quantity of goods and, at the same time, a fall in prices was avoided.[140]

Pound mentions "Lycurgus" and "nomisma." In a passage from Del Mar, we find where Pound took this from, and a summary of many of the monetary allusions we find in *The Cantos*:

> And let it be remarked that I am not here advocating a policy, but chronicling a historical fact; all the great enfranchisements of society have been accomplished with the aid of fiduciary money. The Spartans won their liberties with the iron discs of Lycurgus; the Athenians, before the Alexandrian period, rehabilitated the republic with "nomisma," a highly overvalued copper issue; . . . the money of the Scandinavian revolution was the "klippings" of Gustavus Vasa, which were issued by the State; . . . the money of the Dutch revolution was the pasteboard "dollars" issued by the city of Leyden; of the American revolution, the paper notes issued by the colonial governments; of the French revolution, the "assignats" and "mandats" issued by the National Assembly; and of the anti-slavery war in the United States, "greenbacks." All these moneys were issued and the emissions were controlled by the State. They were not individual notes, nor private bank-notes, but State notes. Indeed, the issuance of fiduciary moneys by the State has so commonly attended all social enfranchisements, that the occurrence of one of these events is a certain indication of the other.[141]

Pound then states "but Goertz von Schlitz had not thought of this." This is drawn from Del Mar and passages concerning Sweden under Charles XII.[142] Five reasons are asserted by Del Mar for the failure of Schlitz's monetary policy, but it is the second one that Pound is referencing: "Goertz did not place any limitation upon the coinage. This (limitation) is the main principle and essence of money, without which—no matter of what substance the symbols

---

[139] Del Mar, *A History of the Monetary Systems*, 279.

[140] Hollis, *The Two Nations*, 2.

[141] Del Mar, *A History of the Monetary Systems*, 279–80.

[142] Del Mar, *A History of the Monetary Systems*, 295–98.

are made, whether of gold, silver, copper or paper—it must fail to discharge its function equitably."[143] Douglas's credit scheme was often caricatured as "funny money," i.e., that like von Schlitz, the printing presses would have no limit. The volume of compensatory consumer credit to be issued under Douglas Social Credit would be limited by the flow of goods and services available for purchase.

Pound then quotes Lycurgus to the effect that "limitation is the essence of good nomisma," or money. However, Goertz von Schlitz had not thought of Lycurgus's advice. Pound then points out that in 1745, the nine-year-old bank of Copenhagen was relieved of conversion, i.e., of the necessity of redeeming its notes or bank paper in gold or silver specie. This increased the profit of the bank shareholders,[144] but not of the people and nation. The line "When kings quit, the bankers began again," stresses the fact that when kings give up the regal prerogative over coinage, the bankers quickly step in to usurp this prerogative. This relates to what Pound has told us about Denmark. After the king had tried to remedy the depreciation of money, a new private bank was created that again was allowed to operate to the harm of the nation's people.[145]

Pound then gives the silver to gold ratio of 15.08 to one of gold, which prevailed in Denmark and Scandinavia in 1873 and thus deprived silver of monetary value. This was the year that the notorious act demonetizing silver was rushed through the United States Congress and simultaneously imposed the gold standard. This deprived those who held silver coins of the right to use them as legal tender. The demonetization of silver is referred to by monetary reformers as "the crime of '73." Pound then goes on to observe that Thomas Hart Benton would have commented upon the continuous effort to have the silver to gold ratio differ from jurisidiction to jurisdiction in order to allow the gold-speculators to make their profits. The lines "[a]nd then Amsterdam (1609) busted the Wisselbank / and said who shd/ deal in exchange," refer to Del Mar's account of how "the Jews of Amsterdam organized a sort of Wissel bank in 1607; and the bank of Amsterdam, which, under the authority of the city, imitated and then destroyed the Wissel bank and forbade the Jews from dealing in exchange, was established in 1609."[146] Again, Pound chooses this historical fact, as it agrees with the Douglasite position, that the king,

---

143 Del Mar, *A History of the Monetary Systems*, 296.
144 Del Mar, *A History of the Monetary Systems*, 303.
145 Del Mar, *A History of the Monetary Systems*, 303–4.
146 Del Mar, *A History of the Monetary Systems*, 321–22.

state, community, has the right to create money and it is not a right that ought to be given away to private interests.

Pound emphasizes that Del Mar does not at this point connect the issue of money with the backing in goods and services which that money requires. However, he points out that Del Mar is in favour of a proper total proportion between the total issue of money and buyables, i.e., goods and services.

A possible reason for this allusion may be found in Del Mar. He discusses how the "scarcity of money" was a hinderance to trade. Markets and fairs were held "at which merchandise could be permuted without money, and declared trade free of export or import dues."[147] Del Mar states these markets had been an "indispensable institution of European industrial life" and then states: "Nor do we believe with some authors that the permutation practiced at fairs was simply barter. The exchanges were too numerous and important to be made by barter. It therefore seems likely that permutation was a system of clearings. The goods were bought and sold on a credit which was to last during the fair. The prices were couched in £. s. d. or other moneys, and when the fair closed the clearing was made, thus obviating the use of any other money than the final sums needed to effect a balance."[148]

As remarked before, Douglas, in his Social Credit theory, held that there had to be money issued by the state, as a dividend to all, if the dividend was warranted by lack of money available in the economy, in order to bridge the gap between money available and desired goods and services that would otherwise remain unpurchased. Del Mar's example shows that when money was scarce in Europe, markets bridged the gap by using paper ledger entries and minimal cash to settle differences, enabling trade without relying on gold or silver. As Pound remarks, Del Mar wrote of this, but did not "connect issue with backing." That is, money coined must be backed by a commensurate amount of goods and services. This insistence upon the connection between the issuing of money and its backing by goods and services is, of course, pure Douglasism.[149] Douglas maintains *that the total purchasing power in the body economic must equal the total price of goods and services.*

---

[147] Del Mar, *A History of the Monetary Systems*, 194.

[148] Del Mar, *A History of the Monetary Systems*, 195.

[149] Cf. C. H. Douglas, *The Monopoly of Credit*, 56: "On the assumption that the delivery of goods and services is the objective of the industrial system, it is obvious that the rate of flow of purchasing power should be equal to the rate of generation of prices."

Pound comments that even Eisenhower in 1955 had come that far. Pound may be referencing Eisenhower's State of the Union address of 1955: "The recent economic progress in many free nations has been most heartening. The productivity of labor and the production of goods and services are increasing in ever-widening areas. There is a growing will to improve the living standards of all men."[150] It may be farfetched to believe that Eisenhower was referencing the need to make it possible to buy all desired goods and services of the country, but the statement was promising in that it recognized the growing ability of many nations to produce goods and services for their own consumption, rather than relying on foreign imports. Eisenhower's address also included expressions of the desire to end trade barriers in order to bring prosperity to all.[151]

The line "And Baffico had papers, daily papers, giornali" refers to that centralization and control of the press and publicity media that both Pound and Douglas abhor. The lines "'Ad perpetuam / liberationis divinae memoriam' said the Dutch on white / pasteboard," refers to Del Mar's account of how the Dutch issued pasteboard dollars in 1574 during the siege of Leyden. "These 'greenbacks' of the revolution the Hollanders preferred to keep rather than exchange for coins—*ad perpetuam liberationis divinæ memoriam*—in perpetual memory of their divine liberation from tyranny."[152] In a footnote it further explains: "The revolutionary moneys of Leyden were of white pasteboard, round, about 1½ inches in diameter and stamped or embossed to resemble a coin. They took their origin in the first, but were perfected during the second siege—that of 1574. Their denominations were 24 and 40 stivers. The former bore on one side, 'Haec libertatis ergo,' on the other, 'Godt behoede Leyden,' or God protect Leyden. The latter had the city arms on one side and 'Pugno propatria.'"[153]

Pound stresses this luminous detail because it provides an example from 16th century Dutch history of the city of Leyden's exercise of its prerogative over the issuing of currency. The city of Leyden did not

---

150 Eisenhower, 3.

151 C. H. Douglas and Ezra Pound opposed barriers to trade for *needed products* by one's nation, believing that the best market was local and that trade was for goods or services one did not have. It made no sense to trade *real wealth*, actual-physical goods, unless it was for needed goods one's nation did not possess. For Douglas/Pound, why would a nation trade real wealth for the illusion of wealth, i.e., *tickets*, mere paper, and especially for goods one could—should—produce at home?

152 Del Mar, *A History of the Monetary Systems*, 327.

153 Del Mar, *A History of the Monetary* Systems, 327.

borrow this currency from a private bank, but issued it debt-free as an exercise of its monetary prerogative. In this way, Pound provides an example of a basic Douglasite principle being observed in 16th century Holland. Pound also provides us here with an example of paper currency being preferred to metal coins. He maintains elsewhere in his writings that paper currency represents a higher degree of civilisation than the more cumbersome metal coins. "The state has credit. Distribution is effected by little pieces of paper. The best facts of history are not in the school books. The job of this generation is to teach growing children; to make it impossible for any child to arrive at the threshold of manhood, ignorant as my generation arrived there."[154] The lines "'Godt behoede.' / Pugno pro patria" refer directly to the inscriptions on this Dutch pasteboard currency. The lines "degradations, depradations, degradations whatsodam / of emperors, kings and whatsodam / Dukes et cetera have since been exceeded" refer to Del Mar's question:

> Is it yet clearly understood that whatever degradation of money was committed by the emperors, whatever debasement was afterwards committed by the kings, these have since been vastly exceeded by the dishonest use made of "individual" coinage and the control of bank issues? Not at all. The Emperors of Rome controlled the emissions of European money for thirteen centuries, and the kings and dukes for nearly four centuries afterwards; whilst the usurers have held it, to the present time, for about two centuries. It is not too much to say that during these two centuries greater monetary changes have been made and more losses have been occasioned to the industrial classes of the European world than were made by all the degradations and debasements of the Imperial and regal periods put together. Monetary systems have been changed from gold to silver, from silver to gold, and from both silver and gold to paper; tens of thousands of worthless banks have been erected, thousands of millions of worthless notes have been issued, and the entire products of industry have been seized and perverted to the enrichment of a class... The right to issue money needs a radical reform; and the State which reforms it first will secure for its citizens far greater advantages than can be derived from Zollvereins, tariff bills, or any other kind of commercial legislation."[155]

---

[154] Pound, *Impact*, 143.

[155] Del Mar, *A History of the Monetary Systems*, 330–31.

C. H. Douglas would certainly agree with Del Mar, though Douglas did not see himself as a radical, or a Socialist, as some claim: "[T]o the extremely small extent that I can be said to have any party politics, I am a Conservative. In my opinion this is a conservative country, although it has been for many years, and is, governed by Whig policies."[156]

The line "Kitson, Fenton & Tolstoi had observed this" is of note. It is a passage in Del Mar, where Kitson quotes Fenton, who is likewise quoting Tolstoi. Arthur Kitson was the founder of the new economics in England and a forerunner of C. H. Douglas. Del Mar states: "'The control of money' says an eloquent writer on the subject [Arthur Kitson], 'is the ground upon which an international or cosmopolitan combination 'finances' the world and 'farms' humanity'"[157] Del Mar provides Kitson's source as Count Leo Tolstoi, in Tolstoi's *Essay on Money*, in Kitson's *Scientific Solution of the Money Question* (*pref.* and p. 168). Tolstoi stating: "The distribution of wealth and the exploitation of some men by others are dependent upon money."[158]

Pound then goes on to remark that, curiously, Brooks Adams, the author of *The Law of Civilisation and Decay*, ignores Del Mar and Del Mar ignores Adams. Adams's work eloquently shows the role of usury in history from the early Roman times up to the 19th century, which was the century of usury.

Canto 97 continues with its monetary-economic and monetary-historic luminous details among which we find the following:

> 1. 18, CHARLES SECOND c. 5
> In 1816 gave up power over the ratio
> and 1870 gave up the remains of prerogative.
> "Victoria, Victoriaa, w'ere 'ave I 'eard that nyme?"
> Goldsmiths not aiming at
> not ruled by Sophia (σοφία)
> πίστις, σοφία
>
> . . . .
>
> 2. "Duped into double indebtedness",
> "Portcullis" struck by the Crown, but Charles
> let the East Indias do it
> "with the Company's own devices".
> Assyria, Babylon, Macedonia,
> always more somewhere than somewhere,
> but the (*abbreviare*) the great gap declining.
> Steed asked Douglas about the rupee.

[156] Douglas, "Money: An Historical Survey," 23.
[157] Del Mar, *A History of the Monetary Systems*, 331.
[158] Del Mar, *A History of the Monetary Systems*, 331.

1858: End of the Company.
Sylla 9 (ratio 9), Caesar 12
and stayed there till the fall of Byzantium.
"The signal was given by Mr Marble"
(a modest name from some angles)
"Not read except by title". Mr Carlyle:
"This coil of Geryon" (Djerion) said Mr Carlyle,
in Congress,
who later went to the Treasury,
(Canto 97)

The line "18, CHARLES SECOND c. 5" is significant in that it refers to the coinage legislation of 1666–67 brought in under Charles II. Del Mar points out that:

> [T]his iniquitous and mischievous bill.... swept away not only the seigniorage of the Crown, but also its control over the issuance of money, because it left this to the volition and pleasure of those who choosed to bring metal to the mint to be coined, and these were practically the East India Company and the goldsmith class, with which it co-operated and which it influenced. By a rule of the coinage which was afterwards made, refusing any but large deposits of bullion ... the general public was virtually shut out from the mint, which was thus fully subjected to the control of the intriguants.[159]

The line, "[i]n 1816 gave up power over the ratio" refers to what Del Mar calls the "idiotic" mint Act of 1816,[160] whereby the Crown gave up its power over the silver to gold ratio. Pound then goes on to paraphrase Del Mar,[161] to the effect that in 1870 the Crown gave up the remains of its prerogative over coinage. This final stripping of the royal prerogative over silver coinage took place during the reign of Queen Victoria, i.e., in 1870. Therefore Pound asks ironically, of this Queen stripped of her regal prerogative by the usurers: "Victoria, Victoriaa, w'ere 'ave I 'eard that nyme?" Del Mar points out that: "The Mint Law of 1816, section 9, the law which closed the British mints to the private and unlimited coinage of silver, whilst it opened them to the private and unlimited coinage of gold, left it in the power of the Crown at any time (by and with the advice of the Privy Council), to substantially reverse such policy. In other words, down to the year 1870 the Sovereign of Great Britain had the power by proclamation

---

[159] Del Mar, *A History of Monetary Crimes*, 33.
[160] Del Mar, *A History of Monetary Crimes*, 93.
[161] Del Mar, *A History of Monetary Crimes*, 7–8.

to reopen the mints to the private and unlimited coinage of silver."[162] Del Mar states that the mint bill of 1870 destroyed the royal prerogative as to the silver coinage of Great Britain. Del Mar comments this was done by inserting the italicized words into section 12, clause 7, "making the clause read as follows: 'to regulate any matters relative to the coinage and the mint *within the present prerogative of the crown* which are not provided for by this act.'" Del Mar remarks that the addition, inserted in committee without any discussion in the House, worked an entire change of the law.[163]

Thus, the royal prerogative over the silver coinage of Great Britain was destroyed by stealth and in hugger-mugger. Thus Pound, by his method of luminous detail, directs us back to a passage in Del Mar which lends support to C. H. Douglas's charge that the money power controls the decisions of parliaments and their governing policies.[164]

Pound then goes on to point out that the goldsmiths, the first bankers, were not ruled by *Sophia* (Wisdom). He also mentions πίστις or good faith, along with wisdom, which would also be lacking in the goldsmiths. The line "Duped into double indebtedness," is from a statement by Del Mar: "The States which in 1873 were duped into doubling their indebtedness have outlived their resentment, and become reconciled to a loss which has enabled them to dispense for the future with that mischief of Private Coinage, which alone rendered such loss possible."[165]

The lines "Portcullis' struck by the Crown, but Charles / let the East Indias do it / 'with the Company's own devices," directly paraphrases material from Del Mar.[166] Del Mar explains that the East India Company had been given by the crown portcullis coins made in London in 1601. However, by the coinage legislation of 1666–77, King Charles II granted the East India Company the right to strike these portcullis coins with its own devices. Del Mar stresses that the act of 1666 entirely failed to realize any of the expectations that were held out in its title or preamble. It did not increase the coin of the kingdom, but, on the contrary, diminished it. It did not help the State, but on the contrary robbed the State of its prerogative of coinage and the profits it would have made by the Indian exchange.[167] It did not promote the trade and commerce of the kingdom, but only that of

162 Del Mar, *A History of Monetary Crimes*, 78.
163 Del Mar, *A History of Monetary Crimes*, 79.
164 Douglas, *The Monopoly of Credit*, 9.
165 Del Mar, *A History of the Monetary Systems*, 392.
166 Del Mar, *A History of the Monetary Systems*, 395–97.
167 Del Mar, *A History of the Monetary Systems*, 375, 387–88, 395–97, 454.

the East India Company.[168] Thus Pound/Del Mar give another proof from history of C. H. Douglas's charge, that the usurpation of the regal prerogative over coinage by private interests entails disastrous consequences.

The lines "Assyria, Babylon, Macedonia, / always more somewhere than somewhere," refer to the fact that all through history the silver to gold ratio was always higher somewhere, thus encouraging speculation in the precious metals.[169] The line "but the (*abbreviare*) the great gap declining," has to do with Del Mar's observation concerning the silver to gold ratio and its decline:

> Down to the thirteenth century the ratio in the coinages of the northern states of Germany, including Lubeck and Hamburg, varied but slightly from the Roman pontifico-imperial ratio of 12 for 1. During the thirteenth century the influence of the Roman ratio for the first time exhibited signs of decline. Less silver and more gold was now put into the coins of the various Christian states or provinces, and still less into those which, like Pomerania and the Baltic provinces, had been but recently converted to Christianity, and had previously coined at the Gothic pagan ratio of 8 for 1.[170]

The line "Steed asked Douglas about the rupee," refers to C. H. Douglas's being consulted by Henry Wickham Steed, about the intricacies of the Indian rupee. Steed was a British journalist who served as foreign editor of *The London Times* from 1914 to 1918 and as editor of the *The London Times* from 1919 to 1922. Pound stresses that the Indian rupee, because of the mint act of 1870 (which Del Mar refers to as the crime of 1870), also contained an important alteration which destroyed the power of the Crown to make foreign coins, including the Indian rupee, legal tender:

> What has been the result? From the day when the royal voluptuary resigned a prerogative which, more than any other one, pleads for the continuance of kingly rule, to the present time, the commercial community has been subjected to alternate epochs of monetary contraction and expansion, in which much of what it accumulates at one period is insidiously filched from it at a another....
>
> The plain facts are these: two centuries ago the king of England plundered the goldsmiths of London of all their

[168] Del Mar, *A History of the Monetary Systems*, 388–89, 396–97.
[169] Del Mar, *A History of the Monetary Systems*, 393–401.
[170] Del Mar, *A History of the Monetary Systems*, 366–67.

> ready money... his son substantially sold and surrendered to the goldsmiths the State prerogative of coinage. Owing to England's commercial supremacy (due to the energy of her people, not to the plans of goldsmiths) this made the latter the sole arbiters of the Measure of Value, not merely of England, but of the Western world....
>
> ...All that has been perceived clearly, either by them or anybody else, is that since the era of Private Coinage and Private banks of issue the industrial and commercial world has suffered repeated reverses, for which no indemnity has been offered and no practical remedy discovered.[171]

Del Mar concludes with his own treatment, a cure that is both *Poundian and Douglasite*: "That treatment is the resumption by the State of its ancient prerogative of money."[172]

The line "1858: End of the Company," has reference to the end of the East India Company in 1858. The lines "Sylla 9 (ratio 9), Caesar 12 / and stayed there till the fall of Byzantium" refer to the ratio of silver to gold under Sylla (*Sulla*), who died in 78 BC, and that under Julius Caesar, who was assassinated in 44 BC. Pound stresses the conclusion of Del Mar, that the twelve silver to one gold ratio in weight (i.e., for every 1 ounce of gold, you would need 12 ounces of silver to equal its value), which had been adopted by Julius Caesar, was to remain until Constantinople fell to the Latins in 1204.[173] Thus, Pound emphasizes the monetary stability attained by the Emperors of the Roman Empire, for 1246 years, and compares it with the chaos delivered in the modern world by the private bankers.

The line "The signal was given by Mr. Marble," refers to the role played by Mr. Manton Marble, editor, and part owner of the *New York World* in the United States presidential campaign of 1868. The signal given by Mr. Marble was the publishing, by the *New York World* on Thursday, October 15, 1868, of a brief editorial article that advocated for the Conservative candidate for President, Horatio Seymour, to be replaced by a candidate having a better chance of success. The Conservative party opposed the banking interests in this election by advocating that American war bonds be payable in greenbacks, whereas the Radical Party, representing the banking interests, wanted these bonds to be payable in coin. Del Mar stresses that this complete about face by the *New York World* newspaper, which had

---

[171] Del Mar, *A History of the Monetary Systems*, 389–91.

[172] Del Mar, *A History of the Monetary Systems*, 391.

[173] Del Mar, *A History of the Monetary Systems*, 63, 70.

been associated in the public's mind with the Conservative Party, ensured Seymour's defeat. Del Mar maintains that this reversal by Mr. Marble was brought about by the direct intervention of Baron James Rothschild of Paris in the presidential campaign by virtue of a letter of March 13, 1868, to Augustus Belmont, the Wall Street Agent for a European banking syndicate. Mr. Belmont was looked upon in New York as the principal owner of the *New York World*.[174]

The lines: "'Not read except by title'. Mr. Carlyle: / 'This coil of Geryon' (Djerion) said Mr. Carlyle, / in Congress, / who later went to the Treasury," paraphrase the remarks made by Del Mar and by Congressman Carlisle (i.e., "Carlyle") concerning the demonetizing of silver in 1873. So hurried and secret was the passage of this bill through Congress that most members had not read it except by title.[175] In 1878, Carlisle stated in the House of Representatives: "The conspiracy which seems to have been formed here, and in Europe to destroy by legislation and otherwise from three-sevenths to one-half of the metallic money of the world, is the most gigantic crime of this or any other age . . . . It will be observed that in every monetary convention which followed that of 1865 the professed object was the unification of money, whilst the one actually accomplished was the demonetization of silver; that in every case the means employed was indirection and secrecy; and that the vehicle used was always a *New Mint Code*."[176]

Canto 97 continues with its fascinating monetary-economic luminous details. However; the density of the strictly monetary-economic luminous details thins out as Pound begins to include more strictly lyrical passages as well:

> 1. and Raleigh remarked, on Genova's loans non-productive,
> that they had only their usury left,
> and there was that Führer of Macedon, dead aetat 38,
>
> . . . .
>
> 2. faster than it distributes the power to buy,
> but the interval, 15, 16, (vide Benton)
> as from 12 to 6 and one half,
> but by that time they found some other wangle,
> by '78, T.C.P. said "non-interest-bearing"
> as from Adams to Rush, as from Vasa (Gustavus)
> Since when they have had several wars.
>
> . . . .

---

[174] Del Mar, *A History of the Monetary Systems*, 420.
[175] Del Mar, *A History of the Monetary Systems*, 421.
[176] Del Mar, *A History of the Monetary Systems*, 422.

3. "All true," said Griffith
"but I can't move 'em with it."
Ownership? Use? there is a difference.
The temple is not for sale.

. . . .

4. Art is local,
Ike driven to the edge, almost, of a thought.

. . . .

5. and some one has wiped out most of Lucilius
and there is, of course, very little about Antoninus
left in their records,

. . . .

6. And as for the original-sin racket . . . the hex-hoax,

. . . .

7. In a buck-board with a keg of money: Damn you, I
said I would get it (the wages).
The temple is holy because it is not for
sale

. . . .

8. "As THAT!" said Ungaro,
"It is just as hard as that"
(jabbing a steel cube with his pencil butt
and speaking of mind as resistant).

. . . .

9. "Had not *thought* about government", Adams;
"or civilization" said Monsieur Bonaparte,
at least I think it was Bonaparte.

. . . .

10. But that the free-born run wode into slavery
this is not good;
run wode in job hunting,
this is NOT good.

(Canto 97)

The first passage begins by paraphrasing Sir Walter Raleigh to the effect that Genoa's loans are non-productive and leave only their usury. Raleigh's statement is completely in accordance with Pound's own attitude towards Genoa. We will come back to this in Canto 103 and Pound's source for this statement by Raleigh. Pound has stressed in his prose writings that Genoa has not produced the art that cities one-tenth her size have produced. Pound attributes this to the fact that usury prevailed in Genoa to an extreme degree. The Banco Sancto Georgio was the main centre from which this rule by usury emanated. Pound would have found some support for this thesis in Brooks Adams.

Adams claimed that usury had a corrosive effect on the Roman empire and implicitly states something similar with respect to Genoa and art:

> In the commercial cities of the same epoch, on the contrary, the religious idea assumed no definite form of artistic expression, for the Gothic never flourished in Venice, Genoa, Pisa, or Florence, nor did any pure school of architecture thrive in the mercantile atmosphere. Furthermore, commerce from the outset seemed antagonistic to the imagination, for a universal decay of architecture set in throughout Europe after the great commercial expansion of the thirteenth century.[177]

In this same passage Pound mentions "that Führer of Macedon," Alexander the Great who died at age thirty-eight.[178] Alexander, the Poundian hero, exercised his royal prerogative over coinage to pay the debts of his soldiery. Therefore Alexander the Great, like Pound and Douglas, was a distributist. The line "faster than it distributes the power to buy," is purely Douglasite in origin. It refers to the fact that the modern economic system creates prices faster than it distributes the power to buy. This principle is, of course, at the very heart of C. H. Douglas's contention that there is a chronic artificial shortage of purchasing power within the body economic.

Pound then goes on to show how the gap between the gold to silver ratio was slowly bridged. He tells us to see "vide" Benton: "but the interval, 15, 16." Pound is referencing Benton concerning the silver to gold ratio, which was 15 or 16 ounces of silver to buy one ounce of gold. Hamilton proposed fifteen silver to one of gold, while the value in most of the new world, as well as Spain and Portugal, was sixteen to one.[179] Benton states what the problem is with such a ratio: "It is not to be supposed that gold will come from these countries to the United States, if the importer is to lose one dollar in every sixteen that he brings; or that our own gold will remain with us, when an exporter can gain a dollar upon every fifteen that he carries out."[180]

The next passage shifts from Benton to Del Mar. In Terrell's excellent work, he draws our attention to a passage of Del Mar that discusses the twelve to one ratio of silver to gold and the Saracenic Spain ratio of 6½ to one.[181] Del Mar brings up the same matter

---

177 Adams, *The Law of Civilization*, vi.

178 Alexander was nearly age 33 at the time of his death.

179 Benton, *Thirty Years' View*, Vol. I, 441.

180 Benton, *Thirty Years' View*, Vol. I, 443.

181 Terrell, *A* Companion, Vol. II, 617. Del Mar, *A History of the Monetary Systems*, 312.

later on.[182] Pound is emphasizing once again that the ratio is always higher somewhere else, allowing the money changers to make a profit by mere speculation. This is unrelated to money being used for its true purpose: consumption. Pound reveals that this game goes back centuries: "always more somewhere than somewhere", all the way to the 1800s in America with gold and silver. Pound then says: "but by that time they found some other wangle." Again, from Benton: "But, at that time, it unfortunately happened that the paper system, then omnipotent in England, was making its transit to our America; and every thing that would go to establish that system—every thing that would go to sustain the new-born Bank of the United States—that eldest daughter and *spem gregis* of the paper system in America—fell in with the prevailing current, and became incorporated in the federal legislation of the day."[183]

For Pound, these National Banks, the forerunners of the Central Bank system of money creation, is "some other wangle." Benton was voicing his opposition to a National Bank, and the copying of the Bank of England model. This model that has spread worldwide consists of private money interests and their private banks being given the power to create circa 97% of new money by the stroke of the banker's pen by making loans. Of course, the game of gold to silver exchange continues to exist. Along with it is the international currency market and the cryptocurrency bitcoin *kimchi premium*. Trillions of dollars are still bought and sold on currency markets only with the goal of making money. This game does not profit society, but profits only the money changers of today. As Pound states, this is the ancient practice of "always more somewhere than somewhere." Still, for Douglas/Pound, it is the Central Bank enabled money creation practice that is the greater corrosive *wangle*.

The line "by '78 T. C. P. said 'non-interest-bearing,'" refers to the efforts of Pound's grandfather Congressman Thaddeus Coleman Pound and the members of the Greenback Party to keep some of the non-interest bearing greenback currency, that was issued by Abraham Lincoln, in circulation. The line "as from Adams to Rush, as from Vasa (Gustavus)," refers in the first instance to the letter on banking written by John Adams to Rush which has appeared earlier in the Rock-Drill Cantos. Gustavus Vasa also appeared earlier, in Canto 97, in the line "Vasa klipped for the people"; i.e., Vasa clipped his coinage to increase the money supply for the benefit of the people.

182 Del Mar, *A History of the Monetary Systems*, 439.
183 Benton, *Thirty Years' View*, Vol. I, 443.

Christopher Hollis has remarked, as noted earlier, that the method of clipping coinage and thus increasing the money supply, was a common practice in Europe.[184]

As noted before, Pound drew these allusions from Del Mar:

> Gustavus made avail of the monetary device instituted by Christian. The latter had introduced the klippings for the sake of personal profit; Gustavus issued them for the benefit of his country. Christian issued his klippings in the place of the silver coins of the kingdom, which he obtained by taxation, melted down, and sold to foreigners for his own emolument; Gustavus issued his klippings to sustain the cause of liberty....
>
> Such were the klippings of Gustavus Vasa. Greijer says that they were valued in the laws at four times their metallic worth. They were fabricated at Hedemora in 1520, and after having served the objects of the revolution were decried or repudiated in 1524 without any complaint from the people. Indeed, with these klippings, as with the pasteboard dollars of Leyden, the people preserved them in grateful memory of their liberation.[185]

Pound points out, ironically, that since the time of Adams's letter to Rush and since the time of Gustavus Vasa there have been several wars. The third passage begins with the oft-reiterated luminous detail concerning what Arthur Griffiths, the founder of Sinn Fein, had to say about economics. The lines: "'All true,' said Griffith / 'but I can't move 'em with it,'" indicates that Griffiths admitted the validity of Pound's Douglasite arguments, but contended that he couldn't move the Irish with a *cold thing* like economics. In the circle of Irish nationalists familiar with Social Credit, there may have been a source for this allusion. W. B. Yeats seems most likely. Yeats's *muse* Maud Gonne, founder of *Inghinidhe na hÉireann — the Daughters of Ireland*, and the writer Eimar O'Duffy, who was intimately involved in the 1916 Easter Rising, both became ardent supporters of Douglas's Social Credit. O'Duffy was an early writer of science fiction that was inspired by Social Credit:

> Social credit provided the central theme of Eimar O'Duffy's mythical science-fiction fantasy trilogy. Published in three volumes, it is a comic indictment of politics and economics in the contemporary world. *King Goshawk and the Birds*

184 Hollis, *The Two Nations*, 2.

185 Del Mar, *A History of the Monetary Systems*, 279–81.

> (1926) portrays the philosophy of the capitalist financial system followed through to its logical conclusions: a monopoly has been established over song-birds and wild flowers. The second book, *The Spacious Adventures of the Man in the Street* (1929) portrays a world where a sane credit system, offering sufficiency and leisure for all, is viewed through the unsympathetic eyes of a speculative opportunist. Finally, in *Asses in Clover* (1933) the god-hero travels through the kingdom of Assinaria. There professors of the dismal science discuss how far the standard of living must be lowered in order to raise it, and the impossibility of providing an income for all in a land of plenty when there is no demand for labour.[186]

Pound then remarks that there is a difference between ownership and use. This distinction between ownership and use appears in the writings of C. H. Douglas. C. H. Douglas maintains that *public ownership* is a hoax because ownership without control is meaningless.[187]

The third passage ends with Pound's reiteration of the Confucian luminous detail to the effect that the 'temple,' the holy place, is not for sale. This Confucian luminous detail must be understood against the background of Pound's contention that usury, working through Calvinism and the Protestant Reformation, has destroyed the mysteries within the bosom of the Church. Pound, like Tawney, and Brooks Adams, is of the opinion that the Protestant Reformation was primarily inspired by economic motives rather than theological. He sees usury as a powerful force behind the Protestant Reformation. In Del Mar,

---

[186] "The Goshawk Trilogy," *The Social Credit Secretariat.*

[187] C. H. Douglas, Warning Democracy, 7–8: "Speaking to Labour and Socialist audiences I have been struck with the hypnotism exercised by such phrases as 'Public Ownership'. It never seems to penetrate the minds of the large numbers of people who clamour for Public Ownership of this, that, or the other, that they already have public ownership of such things as the Army, Navy, Post Office and many other services. I should like to see one of the public owners step upon a battleship of the Royal Navy with a view to removing his bit of property or making some use of it. The real fact is that the word 'ownership' is quite meaningless when it is applied to the relations between any undertaking and a large number of what the law calls 'tenants-in-common'. It is quite impossible for a hundred people to own a piece of land, although there is a legal fiction to the effect that they can. Either they have to let it, and divide the rents, or each one of them can walk about on it, in which case there is no rent and nothing to divide. Even a Public Park is subject to regulations which the individuals using it are generally powerless to alter as individuals. It is a fact inherent in the nature of the case that ownership must vest in an individual, and any attempt to get away from this law of nature results as a practical consequence in the appointment of an administrator whose power increases as the number of appointers increases."

Pound would have found the sacred character given to the coining of gold, which was often chronicled in the ancient world, duly emphasized. Monetary instruments were a right exercised by sovereigns and by the state. But it was especially Rome (*Roma Amor*) that Pound investigates. The imperial treasury was a sacred institution coining gold. Silver coinage was a secular prerogative of the government.[188] In all cases, monetary instruments were a right, a sacred privilege, of those who governed, not to be given to private interests.

The fourth passage states: "Art is Local." This is a simple statement from Pound, but contains a deep meaning. Man's skill and imagination reflect his own locality, tribe, family. Pound's first love, like Dante's, was for the Troubadour poetry of the Provençal region of France. It had its own distinct culture, language, traditions; every poet reflected his individuality. The modern state makes war on individuality by destroying locality and the family. Culture, traditions, knowledge of farming, and weather, are either shared or lost locally. For Douglas, there is no local freedom without local control of local purchasing power. It cannot be taken away from King or parliament and given to Central Banks, i.e., international financial institutions, without a loss of personal rights and freedom. This globalism means destruction of all that is unique. Without a return of credit to control by the State and its use in line with reality and natural law for the benefit of the common citizen, the continual destruction of the small and beautiful farms and villages, the forced migration to cities, etc., will all continue unabated. Pound and Douglas would agree with G. K. Chesterton:

> We are in the strict sense conservatives; because we hold that the old creed and culture of Christendom realise for men, relatively to all that is reasonable and possible, the great art of life which we call Liberty. The truth has made us free; the tradition has given to men the sort of liberty they really like; local customs, individual craftsmanship, variety of self-expression, the presence of personality in production, the dignity of the human will. These are expressed in a thousand things, from hospitality to adventure, from parents instructing their own children to children inventing their own games, from the village commune to the *vin du pays*, from practical jokes to pilgrimages and from patron saints to public-house signs. The mark of all these things is variety and spontaneity, the direct action of the individual soul on the material environment of mankind. The result is a rich complexity of common things,

[188] Del Mar, *A History of the Monetary Systems*, 79.

> a wealth of work and worship, a treasure which we refuse to abandon and are resolute to defend.[189]

Terrell states the following in connection with an earlier passage in the Cantos, where Pound also states "Art is local": "Vlaminck: Maurice de V., 1876–1958, was one of the fauvist painters influenced by Van Gogh, a group that included Derain and Matisse. Pound knew them in his Paris years. Perhaps the 'Art is local' is a response to W. C. Williams's [William Carlos Williams's] attribution of the idea to John Dewey. In the 'Author's Note' to Paterson, WCW said that Dewey had said: 'The local is the only universal, upon that all art builds.'"[190]

Likewise, in the fourth passage, the line concerning "Ike," must be understood in the light of the earlier reference to President Eisenhower in this same Canto. In this earlier reference, Pound had begun by stating that Del Mar at a particular point in his *A History of the Monetary Systems*... does not connect the issue of money with the backing of money by desired goods and services available for purchase in a nation. However, Pound points out that Del Mar is all for "a proper total proportion / between total issue and buyables." Then Pound remarks that "Ike, '55 had got that far," i.e., that even President Eisenhower by 1955 had got to the point where he realised that there must be a proper total proportion between the total issue of money and the goods and services available. This is what Pound means when he says, "Ike driven to the edge, almost, of a thought." This thought is a profoundly Douglasite thought.

The fifth passage mentions the writings of Lucilius and the Emperor Antoninus Pius and says that little remains of "their records." This passage is in keeping with Pound's belief that there has been a historical blackout particularly with reference to the monetary history of the classical period. Gaius Lucilius wrote cutting satire and only fragments remain, some concerning money and wealth, while Antoninus Pius has been referenced before concerning usury.

The sixth passage's reference to "the original sin racket," "the hex-hoax" must be understood in the light of Douglas's impatience with those who would insist upon the impossibility of a properly working monetary system due to the ravages of original sin. Some Christians seem happy to see their fellow man burdened due to a misunderstanding of the passage "with labour and toil shalt thou eat thereof all the days of thy life."[191] They avoid helping their fellow man to perform

---

[189] Chesterton, "Straws in the Wind," 213.

[190] Terrell, *A* Companion, Vol. II, 492.

[191] Gen. 3:17 (Douay-Rheims). C. H. Douglas is accused of rejecting Christian

physical labour and believe it is all *God's will* that someone perform backbreaking labour—as long as it is not themselves. Such Christians honestly think that modern *wage slavery* was what God had planned all along in Genesis. Pound draws this from Douglas's numerous references to fellow Christians who opposed Social Credit based on a misunderstanding of human nature, scripture, and theology.[192]

The seventh passage begins with the line "In a buck-board with a keg of money," which might have reference to wagon loads of hard currency transported out of colonial Massachusetts by the British. This passage concludes with the oft-repeated Confucian luminous detail that the "temple is holy" and "not for sale."

The eighth passage consists of Pound's paraphrase and description of a statement made by Filippo Ungaro, an Italian journalist,[193] concerning the resistance of the mind and the difficulty of penetrating it. It is reasonable to assume from the whole context of *The Cantos*, that Ungaro was referring to the difficulty of making people understand the truth concerning monetary matters.

The ninth passage cryptically paraphrases and compresses statements made by John Adams and Napoleon concerning someone not having given any thought to government or civilization. Again, in the context of this section and of *The Cantos* in general, it is reasonable to assume that it is the usurocracy that does not concern itself with honest government nor civilization.

The tenth passage emphasizes that it is wrong that "the free-born" should run "into slavery." The slavery Pound is speaking of is wage-slavery, which the usurocracy has found to be more profitable than the older form of chattel slavery. Pound also stresses that it is wrong that

---

teaching concerning the effects of Original Sin, when what Douglas rejected is the Calvinist interpretation of Original Sin, i.e., the total depravity of mankind. Pound's hex-hoax reflects Douglas's influence. Investors do not question their own right to periodic dividends, but they are unwilling to extend this right to all; to receive periodic dividends; as such will only lead "the dregs of society" into sin and depravity. Unsurprisingly, this thinking can be found among "righteous" Socialists and Capitalists; they both have their own warped elitist views concerning work-labour.

192 Cf. C. H. Douglas, *The Monopoly of Credit*, 5: "Unable effectively to isolate the cause of the trouble, a large section of the general public, while recognising the increasing gravity of social maladjustment, has fallen back on the assumption that human nature is at fault—a comfortable theory which, while excusing the necessity for further mental effort, goes some distance towards assuring popularity in circles well able to reward it . . . all the more immediate difficulties which threaten us are in the nature of technical defects, requiring for their adjustment rather a change of head than a change of heart. . . ."

193 Terrell, *A Companion*, Vol. II, 625.

"the free-born" should run into "job-hunting." This equation of wage-slavery[194] and "job-hunting" with chattel slavery is fundamental to an understanding of the Poundian and Douglasite position. Pound believes with Douglas that the philosophy of *total work* and *full-employment*, advocated as a desirable end by the usurocracy today, is calculated to make total war on contemplation and to dehumanize man. Pound sees the philosophy and policy of Douglas as making possible a world in which man would have leisure for contemplation, just as he had in the medieval period. The Douglasite concepts of the *Consumer Dividend* and the *Just Price* would free man and combine the best features of medievalism with the best features of ultra-modernism.[195]

Canto 98 contains some significant monetary-economic luminous details:

1. But the lot of 'em, Yeats, Possum and Wyndham
        had no ground beneath 'em.
        Orage had.

. . . .

2. "Eleven literates" wrote Senator Cutting,
        "and I suppose, Dwight L. Morrow".

. . . .

3. The King's job, vast as the swan-flight:
thought built on Sagetrieb:

. . . .

4. They destroy the 5 human relations,
mules saddled with trappings,
        deeper in debt every day
and next they are selling their farmsteads.

. . . .

5. Antoninus and Leo got down the percentage
and, as Stock says, "the historians missed it".

. . . .

6. And as Ford said: get a dictionary
        and learn the meaning of words.

. . . .

7. And Byzance lasted longer than Manchu
        because of an (%) interest-rate.
Thought is built out of Sagetrieb,

. . . .

---

194 The Catholic Distributist writer Hilaire Belloc may have been one of the first to speak of *wage-slavery* in his book *The Servile State.* He viewed wage-slavery and servility as arising from the growing threat to the rights of all to possess private property.

195 Cf. C. H. Douglas in *Economic Democracy*, 100–101.

8. Sixteen bitched by an (%) interest rate
Byzantium rather more durable.

. . . .

9. And XVth. Not a fixed charge.
This is from Mang Tzu
(Canto 98)

The first passage is of immense significance in the light of the Douglasite influence on Pound's writings. Pound points out that William Butler Yeats, Possum, i.e., T. S. Eliot, and Wyndham Lewis, had no ground beneath them, but that Alfred Richard Orage did have ground beneath him. Alfred Richard Orage was the editor of *The New Age* and an exponent of Social Credit. *The New Age* was an expression of Orage's personality. In 1918, Orage met C. H. Douglas and became convinced that Social Credit was a sound economic scheme. He was a strong advocate of the theory. In 1932 he "founded the *New English Weekly*, which became the organ of social credit and also a forum for many good writers."[196]

Chesterton called Orage "the most vigorous and lucid exponent of economic philosophy in our time."[197] However, it is not because of Orage's literary ability and editorial talent that Pound places him ahead of such literary giants as Yeats, Eliot, and Lewis. When Pound accuses these three great luminaries of not having any ground beneath them, and when he praises Orage for having ground beneath him, he is not thinking of literary ability. The ground that Orage had and which Yeats, Eliot and Lewis lacked, was the *solid ground*—Douglasite philosophy and policy. Pound stresses that Douglasism, as a philosophy and policy, gave a solidity and stability to Alfred Richard Orage, which Pound's three great literary friends and luminaries lacked. This luminous detail is one of the most eloquent expressions of Pound's faith in Douglasism in *The Cantos*.

In the second passage, Pound paraphrases Senator Bronson Cutting, a Republican from New Mexico, to the effect that there were only eleven literates in the entire United States Senate. Terrell explains that Cutting mentioned in a letter to Pound[198] that there were nine such Senators, "and I suppose Dwight L, Morrow". As Terrell states, if you add Morrow to the nine plus Cutting himself that equals eleven.[199] Senator Cutting introduced a bill calling for monetary

---

196 *The Dictionary of National Biography*, 659.
197 Mairet, A. R. Orage. v.
198 Pound, *Guide to Kulchur*, 260.
199 Terrell, *A Companion*, Vol II, 629.

reform along Social Credit lines within the United States Senate in 1935. When this Social Credit bill failed to pass the Senate, Senator Cutting described the mental acumen of the Senate in terms of the luminous detail cited by Pound.

The third passage begins with a Confucian reference to the fact that the job of the king is "vast as the swan-flight." One of the most important aspects of a king's job for Pound and for Douglas is that of being "boss of the coinage." Pound goes on to point out that formal thinking or thought is built on *sagetrieb* or the oral tradition. One of the most important aspects of this s*agetrieb* or oral tradition is that monetary wisdom which opposes itself to usury.

The fourth passage refers to the Taoist priests of ancient China who are regarded with contempt by Pound as they were by Confucius. These Taoist priests are accused of having destroyed the five human relations mentioned earlier in *The Cantos*. They lack that monetary wisdom which would protect them against usury and they therefore go "deeper in debt every day."

The fifth passage points out that both Emperor Antoninus Pius, 138 AD–161 AD, and the Byzantine Emperor Leo VI, 886 AD–912 AD, commonly called *Sapiens* or the Wise, managed to get the interest-rate down. Pound then quotes the critic Noel Stock to the effect that historians had missed this point.

The sixth passage paraphrases Ford Madox Ford's advice to "get a dictionary / and learn the meaning of words." This emphasis upon precise and clear definitions is an important one for Pound, as he has often accused orthodox economists of failing to define their terms and of using the same word in ten different ways in a single textbook. In his *ABC of Economics* Pound lacerates the orthodox economists for their fussy and sloppy use of words, e.g., credit, money, etc. He has often said that it would be a wonderful thing if the orthodox economists would define what they mean by money.

The seventh passage points out that Byzantium lasted longer than the Manchu dynasty in China because of a lower interest rate. Again, Pound reiterates that thought is built out of *sagetrieb* or the oral tradition.

The eighth passage points out that sixteen civilizations were *bitched*; i.e., they collapsed because of an exorbitant interest rate. Pound sees usury as having the potential to bring about the collapse of any civilization. Usury is a corrosive force which undermines society. He points out that Byzantium lasted longer than the other civilizations because it had a lower interest rate.

The ninth passage paraphrases Mencius, the great disciple of Confucius, to the effect that a tithe differs from a tax in that it is not "a fixed charge." In other words, a tithe is a ninth or tenth of something that exists, such as a tithe of one's rice harvest, not a fixed charge on something that may or may not exist and is therefore unpayable. A requirement to pay in money-coinage is a tax on something which no farmer grows. In other words, in this paraphrasing of Mencius's Rule XV, Pound is emphasizing the iniquity of taxation as a fixed charge on money that is often not even available. This attack on taxation was mounted by Pound from the very time C. H. Douglas had directed him to investigate modern taxation as a method of highway robbery. Pound has faithfully carried on the attack ever since. The directive in question was quoted in Chapter II.

Canto 99 in general contains many more lyrical luminous details than monetary-economic luminous details. However, here again, there are some significant monetary-economic luminous details in Canto 99:

1. Crusaders' bows gnawed by gold-lice,
   Normandy pawned,
"some of the non-interest-bearing"
   (T.C.P. '78)

. . . .

2. Taxes, for public utility,
   a share of a product,
People have bodies
   ergo they sow and reap,

. . . .

3. the k'ao ch'eng is according to harvest,
the tax as a share of something produced.

. . . .

4. the land has been ploughed
   t'ien^2 ti4
& there have been taxes in kind, and by (liang^2) measure
This is important
   as to the scope of such taxes
all Courts have levied them
   the right pattern of levy is yang4 cheng^1
   id est: for use
not a fountain of folderols
for top poppinjays.
   Wranglings won't get you out of it
High & low, top & under
   INCORPORATE
& one body.

. . . .

5. The State is corporate
as with pulse in its body
& with Chou rite at the root of it
The root is thru all of it,
a tone in all public teaching:

. . . .

6. CHÊN, *yo el Rey*, wish you to think of this EDICT.
4.
Having heard that provisions are the root of the people
(logistica)

. . . .

7. From of old the sovereign likes plowing
& the Empress tends trees with reverence;

. . . .

8. (interest)
not for a quick buck at high interest
the legal rate does not exhaust things
(Byzance did better)
Don't burn to abandon production and go into trading,
Dig up root to chase branches
vide Michelet & Ambrose "De Tobia"
The rate in Byzance was lower,
as can continuous far
(*que ça doure*)
Established that everybody got some education
AND you had literate Confucians
in the burocracy,
(Canto 99)

In the first passage, Pound, drawing from Brooks Adams, tells us about the "Crusaders' bows gnawed by gold-lice." This refers to Pound's and Adams's contention that the effectiveness of the later crusades was destroyed by the corrosive effects of usury.[200] Pound is pointing out that the "gold lice" (i.e., the money lenders) ate away at the archers' efficiency by saddling both Christendom and the Church with a heavy debt. This debt had been assumed to finance the crusades. This passage goes on to mention the historical region of Normandy, which was larger than its modern-day counterpart. It was pawned to the "gold-lice" in order to fight the crusades: "The first symptom of disorder seems to have been a rise in the purchasing power of both the precious metals, but particularly of gold, which rose in its ratio to silver from

[200] Adams, *Law of Civilization*, 169–71.

about one to nine and a half, to one to twelve. At the same time, the value of commodities, even when measured in silver, appears to have fallen sharply. . . . Everywhere there was a deficit, almost everywhere ruin. Amiens, Soissons, Roye, Saint Quentin, and Rouen were all in difficulty with their loans, but Noyon was perhaps the worst of all."[201]

The passage ends with a reference to the fact that Pound's grandfather, Thaddeus Coleman Pound (TCP), tried to keep "some of the non-interest bearing" greenback money in circulation in 1878. This superposition of Thaddeus Coleman Pound's monetary wisdom on the depressing story of usury's destruction of the crusades is impressive from the Douglasite point of view.

The second passage presupposes Pound's distinction between a tithe and a tax. A tithe is a ninth or a tenth of something that exists, i.e., "a share of a product," while a tax is a fixed charge on something that may, or may not, exist. Pound paraphrases a passage of Confucian-Mencian lore to the effect that taxes should be for public utility and therefore "a share of a product."

The third passage reiterates this piece of ancient Chinese wisdom, by pointing out that "the k'ao ch'eng," i.e., the tithe, is calculated according to the harvest, and that the tax is a share "of something produced."

The fourth passage mentions the right pattern for levying taxes: *for use*, i.e., for constructive purposes not to maintain an arrogant bureaucracy. This passage also stresses that there have been taxes "in kind," and by "measure." The passage ends with a plea for the corporate state.

The fifth passage points out that the state is corporate, i.e., it is a body politic and economic, with a "pulse in its body."

The sixth passage reiterates the strong distributist position of the Emperor Chen to the effect that provisions are regarded as the root of the people. This once again emphasizes the distributist doctrine of utilizing the plenitude of nature's abundance, which is fundamental to Douglasism.

The seventh passage continues this theme of the plenitude of nature's abundance by pointing out that "[f]rom of old the sovereign likes plowing / & the Empress tends" the mulberry "trees with reverence."

The eighth passage returns directly to the theme of usury. Pound points out that the interest rate must not be set up with a view to making a "quick buck." It must not be a high rate of interest as the

---

201 Adams, *Law of Civilization*, 169–70.

legal rate must "not exhaust things." Pound cautions against abandoning "production" for the false lure of foreign trade. He compares this neglecting of the home market for the nebulous benefits of foreign trade, to the digging up of a root just to chase the branches.

C. H. Douglas constantly attacks this *myth of foreign trade* and insists that the home market is the best market. Douglas stresses that the only valid foreign trade is to be found in the exchange of *true surpluses* between nations. A nation would only have a true surplus of a particular product when its own domestic market had been saturated with that product. Douglas insists that nations mostly trade in *false surpluses* which their domestic consumers want, but cannot buy, because of the built-in shortage of purchasing power in the body economic. He distinguishes very clearly between demand as *desire* to buy and demand as *ability* to buy. Demand in this latter sense can best be described as *effective demand*. Douglas claims, as does Pound, that the orthodox economist never makes a distinction between these two entirely different kinds of demand.

Pound refers us to Michelet and St. Ambrose's *De Tobia* for further information on the evils of usury. We have already seen Ambrose on usury. In Jules Michelet's writings, in *History of the Roman Republic*, we can find some statements concerning the effects of usury on Rome. In *The People*, writing of France in the 1840s and prior, we see Michelet's views concerning the effect of usury and industrialization on the French villages and towns at the start of the modern industrial age. Michelet provides a vibrant image of village life on the seacoast; families working together to benefit from the abundance of nature:

> I HAVE long studied the ancient associations of France. The most charming of all, in my opinion, is that of the fishing-nets, on the coasts of Harfleur and Barfleur. Each of these vast nets (of a hundred and twenty *brasses*, or six hundred and twenty feet long) is divided into several portions, which descend by inheritance to the girls as well as to the boys. The girls, inheriting this right, but not going to fish, nevertheless assist in it by weaving their share of the nets, which they confide to the fishermen. . . .
>
> Here my heart fails me, and my pen stands still. I must confess that the country and the family profit but little by it now. Those net-associations will soon exist only in history; they are already succeeded, in many parts of the coast, by that which takes the place of every thing—the bank and usury.[202]

[202] Michelet, *The People*, 131–32.

Pound concludes this section by reiterating that the interest rates in Byzantium were lower and it was for this reason that Byzantium lasted longer than other civilizations.

Canto 100 is much heavier in its monetary-economic luminous detail than Canto 99, and once again returns to American history for many of its details:

> 1. "Has packed the Supreme Court
> so they will declare anything he does constitutional."
> Senator Wheeler, 1939.
> —and some Habsburg ploughed his imperial furrow
> Eu ZoOn—
> Not that never should, but if exceeding and
> no one protest,
> will lose all of your liberties.
> "Would have thought of something"
> said Joffre of
> Napoleon.
> . . . .
> 2. And small bank accounts are now guaranteed.
> By increase of debt? strengthen??
> . . . .
> 3. "not a trial but a measure" committed Danton.
> And which Henry committed Jo Skelton?
> Wiseman to Isaacs, Aug 18, 1918
> "try to shift power to the Executive"
> i.e. out of Congress.
> No french public debt before Francis
> (at 8½ to the hundred)
> — S...W...[203] fished out of a duck-pond —
> After Mazarin over 400 million,
> I think four hundred and thirty
> (Canto 100)

The first passage begins with a luminous detail in which Pound paraphrases a statement made by Senator Burton K. Wheeler in 1939. This statement has to do with Franklin Delano Roosevelt's packing the Supreme Court with his own political appointees and hangers-on. Senator Wheeler maintained that the Supreme Court would declare anything Roosevelt did constitutional since it was a creature of Roosevelt's.

The line: "—and some Habsburg ploughed his imperial furrow" has been encountered already regarding the royal thalers issued by

[203] Sumner Welles. Terrell, *A Companion*, Vol. II, 645.

Maria Theresa. Pound uses the Confucian expression "to plough his imperial furrow,"[204] in the sense of the monarch exercising his royal prerogative over coinage. This, of course, is a key point with Pound, as it is with Douglas. The lines: "Not that never should, but if exceeding and / no one protest, / will lose all of your liberties," must be understood in the light of Pound's insistence upon the fact that the usurocracy, through its imposition of a crushing debt structure on society, eats away not only at economic freedom, but also at political freedom. C. H. Douglas insisted that "[p]olitical democracy *without* economic democracy is dynamite."[205]

The lines: "'would have thought of something' / said Joffre of Napoleon," refers to Marshall Joseph-Jacques-Césaire Joffre, the French commander in chief during World War I. From its place among other economic allusions, it could be referencing a comment by Joffre that Napoleon would have thought of something to beat the usurers, if he had only been given time. As a general facing a German onslaught in WW I, Joffre's statement could be honouring France's greatest general, i.e., Napoleon, and his ability to always snatch victory from the jaws of defeat. It has already been pointed out that Napoleon is a Poundian hero primarily because of his stand against the usurocracy.

The second passage: "And small bank accounts are now guaranteed," must be understood in the light of Pound's antipathy to the financial power structure which urges people to save and then cuts the buying power of their savings by means of that built-in inflation which is part of the banker credit system. In his prose writings and particularly in the Alfred Venison poems mentioned in Chapter II, Pound charged that England's First World War veterans had been subjected to this cruel hoax by the usurocracy. They had been told to work hard and save and then the buying power of their savings had been decreased.

Again, the second passage: "By increase of debt? strengthen??" is an ironic line, in that Pound is asking whether one can strengthen either the nation or the individual by increasing either national or personal debt.

---

[204] "The frontispiece of a book by Mirabeau, *Philosophie Ruräl [Rurale]* (1764), showed a Chinese emperor plowing an imperial furrow to hearten his subjects and to carry on an age-old ritual. Hence the young Dauphin was required to hold a toy plow in his delicate hands to show princely sympathy with the French peasants. In 1769 Joseph [II] went the whole way: he took a real plow and plowed some real land to show he meant business." Terrell, *A Companion*, Vol. II, 486–87. Note, that the only complete I–III volumes of *Philosophie Rurale* by Mirabeau, at archive.org, are from the library of President John Adams, located at the Boston Public Library.

[205] Douglas, *The Monopoly of Credit*, 42.

The third passage: "'not a trial but a measure' committed Danton," is a luminous detail taken from the history of the French Revolution. R. McNair Wilson points out that Robespierre claimed that Danton was in the pay of foreign bankers. Danton led the attack on the Republicans by insisting that Louis XVI be brought to trial:

> The Government, therefore, tried to prevent the King's trial. Instantly they were accused of treachery. The names which, under Necker's guiding hand, they had flung at King, priests, and nobles were flung at them. It was asserted by Robespierre at a later period, that Danton, who led the attack on the Republicans, was in the pay of foreign banking houses. It is certain that he served their ends. The King's trial effected a further fall in the purchasing power of the Assignat; his execution continued the process. The Government passed from anxiety to despair. Their money was ceasing to command confidence and they had a great European war on their hands. So evil did their plight seem that revolt against their authority was everywhere stimulated. Both Lyon and Marseilles declared for the King's son, *Louis XVII.*[206]

This trial was "'not a trial but a measure'" by Danton, states Pound, i.e., a calculated plan. It contrasts with a beneficial "measure," earlier under the French monarch, that led directly to conflict between the French King and the financiers. Wilson tells us of a "measure" by the French King through the French finance minister Turgot, to aid the French people:

> Turgot immediately decided to remove the restrictions on the free sale of wheat throughout France, so that in times of famine, such as he had experienced at Limoges, wheat might be brought easily from districts where it was plentiful to districts where it was scarce. The effect of this measure was to cause an immediate fall in the price of bread at a moment when, thanks to a bad harvest, the price was very high. Necker and the other bankers who financed the grain trade were filled with alarm. Necker at once composed a pamphlet against Turgot's policy and caused it to be widely circulated.[207]

McNair Wilson,[208] who is one of Pound's sources and whose name appears in *The Cantos*, stresses the fact that the banking system is of

---

[206] Wilson, *Monarchy or Money Power*, 25.

[207] Wilson, *Monarchy or Money Power*, 14.

[208] Robert McNair Wilson was born in Glasgow 1882, and educated at Glasgow University. He edited for nine years the Oxford Medical Publications. Wilson

its very nature antipathetic to monarchy. They are antipathetic to any righteous sovereign, ruler, or government that would actually *feed the people*, i.e., that would make it possible for the nation's abundance to supply the needs of the community. This is the Douglas contention that Pound explores historically in *The Cantos*.

The lines: "Wiseman to Isaacs, Aug. 18, 1918 / 'try to shift power to the Executive' / i.e. out of Congress," have reference to Pound's belief that the usurocracy is opposed to the tripartite division of powers: legislative, judicial, and executive, that was created by the Founding Fathers of the United States. The usurocracy wishes to filch power away from the legislative arm and place it entirely in the executive or presidency. It desires this because it is easier to control the executive branch. The usurocracy favours centralization of power and it is precisely this centralization of power that both Pound and Douglas oppose.

In August 1918, Sir William Wiseman, a British intelligence agent, and banker at Herndon's of London, spent a week-long vacation with the American President Hoover Wilson. Though Pound's source of the August 18 letter, or more likely a telegram to Rufus Isaacs, cannot be found, the time frame is probable. Concerning Wilson we read:

> He went to Magnolia on August 15 for a few days' vacation with House. Wiseman, not accidentally, was also at Magnolia. On August 17 he received a cable from Balfour for House which again raised the question of economic policy. Balfour intended the cable as a courtesy and an indication of the British willingness to confide in Wilson. But the subject of the cable, a contemplated interference in Mexico to "secure honesty and order in the public administration" (i.e., to protect British oil investments), could hardly have been better calculated to anger Wilson. Here shortly after Wilson's announced determination to avoid interference in the domestic affairs of Siberia and only days after his criticism of Lloyd George's talk of commercial ambition, the British revealed they might support a revolution in Mexico in order to improve their commercial position there.[209]

The line "No french public debt before Francis," refers to the fact that there was no French national debt before King Francis I.[210] Pound

---

published several books on Napoleon Bonaparte, Bonaparte's family, and monetary history and reform. He published under several pseudonyms, such as *Anthony Wynne*. "Wilson, Robert McNair," *Who's Who 1956*, 3229–30.

209 Fowler, *British-American Relations*, 211.

210 Francis I lived from 1494 to 1547 and reigned from 1515 to 1547. He was a patron of the arts and of the letters. "Francis I, king of France," *Encyclopaedia Britannica*.

then mentions that the interest rate at this time was 8 percent, i.e., "8 to the hundred." The lines: "After Mazarin over 400 million, I think four hundred and thirty" refers to the regime of the first minister of France, Cardinal Jules Mazarin, 1643–61. Mazarin caused the French public debt to increase to four hundred and thirty millions, according to Pound. Canto 100 continues with its luminous details taken from 19th century European history and with Pound's comments:

> Oh GAWD!!! that tenth section . . .
> "any portion of . . . "
> DAMN IT.
>
> (Canto 100)

These lines record Pound's deep-seated antagonism to any legislation that would curb the monetary sovereignty of the state. The tenth section referred to here is Article I, Section II of the Constitution of the United States, which prohibits the States from exercising certain powers. The first paragraph of Section 10 reads: "NO State shall enter into any treaty, alliance, or confederation, grant letters of marque and reprisal, coin money, omit bills of credit, make anything but gold and silver coin a tender in payment of debts, pass any law of attainder, ex post facto law, or law impairing the obligation of contracts, or grant any title of nobility." This prohibition of control of their money systems by the various states is clearly opposed to the fundamental Douglasite principle of local control of local purchasing power, and therefore Pound damns it.

Canto 100 continues with its monetary-economic luminous details. However, as in the passage above, there are many purely lyrical passages:

> and J. Austin, an Englander,
> attempted to separate law from moral philosophy.
> Of which the value . . .
> said Frank Harris, they deal in things,
> always, the value of which is unknown.
> No greek sells a slave out of Hellas
> Silk news came up, by monks, out of India,
> Shingled flakes on a moth's wing. monetary (218 a.D.)
> commission, Belisarius
> forbade cavalry to damage any man's standing grain.
> "NO, not THAT boat"
> shouted his captain at Ratto, when the latter had
> nicely aimed his torpedo
> at a Lloyd Triestino
> in which wops held certain shares.
> Wanted her (%) interest, De Stael did.

"More" said Santayana "for Rome than three Napoleons".
I suppose he meant than Nap had done for Paris.
(Canto 100)

The lines "and J. Austin, an Englander, / attempted to separate law from moral philosophy," refers to that dichotomy between the natural and positive law which is such a sore point with Pound, and which he charges is found in the writings of Jane Austen. The lines "Of which the value . . . / said Frank Harris, they deal in things, / always, the value of which is unknown," refers to the usurocracy's dealing in such commodities as gold and silver, the value of which varies from place to place. The lines "Belesarius / forbade cavalry to damage any man's standing grain," are in harmony with Pound's distributist sentiments. The lines: "'NO, not THAT boat' / shouted his captain at Ratto, when the latter had / nicely aimed his torpedo / at a Lloyd Triestino / in which wops held certain shares," illustrate Pound's deep-seated conviction that wars are dictated by economic reasons. The line "Wanted her (%) interest, De Stael did," has appeared before and refers to Madame de Stael, the daughter of the financier Necker. Madame de Stael wanted her interest even when her investment was with an enemy country:

> Money reacted against Bonaparte with all its strength. Necker remained in Switzerland, but his daughter, Madame de Staël, was in Paris. . . . A second line of attack consisted in showing Bonaparte as an ignorant provincial. Madame de Staël and her friend, the beautiful Juliette Recamier, wife of the banker of that name, proclaimed themselves citizens of Europe, and cried that Bonaparte's methods were shutting France in an "iron cage." Men, they urged, must be free to follow their own ideas. (This meant that rich men must be free to move their money about.) Men must be free, too, to produce, to buy and to sell where and when they chose. (This meant that bankers must be free to stimulate the export trade by foreign lending).[211]

The lines: "'More' said Santayana, 'for Rome than three Napoleons'. / I suppose he meant than Nap had done for Paris," refers to George Santayana's praise of Mussolini, who had done more for Rome than the three Napoleons: I, II, and III, had done for Paris.

Canto 100 continues with more lyrical luminous details and with Confucian-Mencian material as well. However, although the monetary-economic luminous detail thins out as the Canto progresses, nevertheless there are some highly significant lines:

---

[211] Wilson, *Monarchy or Money Power*, 33.

1. "They miss Tyler"
(Stock wrote)
as well as Polk and VanBuren."

. . . .

2. "A DICtionary
and learn the meaning of words!"

. . . .

3. Durch das Bankhaus Pacelli kompromettiert
and B. Swan thought civil war was the only means of getting
(from Spaniards)
five bucks ($) for one buck's worth of petrol.

. . . .

4. Stead asked Douglas about the rupee . . .

. . . .

5. Erigena,
Anselm,
Cherbury,
Rémusat,
Thiers was against income-tax
"the portal to inquisition"

(Canto 100)

The first passage refers to a statement made by the critic Noel Stock to how historians miss or overlook the great roles played by Presidents Tyler, Polk, and Van Buren. Stock was referring to these men in their roles as champions of monetary integrity. Pound has emphasized in his prose writings that Tyler and Polk continued the Jackson/Van Buren tradition of monetary integrity during their own administrations. Both men opposed the encroachment of the usurocracy.

The second passage paraphrases a statement made by Ford Madox Ford to the effect that it is necessary to have a dictionary and learn the meaning of words. This luminous detail must be seen against the whole background of Pound's insistence upon clear definitions and the avoidance of sloppy language. Pound particularly applies this insistence upon clear language to the writings of the orthodox economists who constantly use words, e.g., credit and money, with several different meanings and in several different ways.

The third passage begins with a luminous detail in German that may be translated as "through the Banking House, Pacelli compromised." This would seem to refer to a compromise made by Eugenio Pacelli, who became the future Roman pontiff Pius XII, 1939–58, with the banking interests. This may have more to do with distrust by

Fascist Italy of the new Pontiff, than Pound's own beliefs. Nevertheless, Noel Stock writes concerning the following response by Pound:

> When he received a request from the editors of a book containing biographies of Catholic authors, asking whether he was a Catholic, he replied on 5 February: 'It is up to you. The late Pope was pleased that I remembered to send him my *Make it New,* but he played safe and "marvelled" at my "versatility."' He had immense respect for what he believed to be the true work of the Church, but could not support an institution that was too cowardly to preach its own doctrine and acted as mere lackey to international usury. Until Pacelli (Pius XII) damned the men who had caused the war and branded it largely as a crusade for money-lending and metal monopoly, he would have to remain, he said, among the 'doubtful adherents'.[212]

On the other hand, the previous Roman pontiff, Pope Pius XI had openly attacked the monopoly of credit in the encyclical *Quadragesimo Anno*. What Pope Pius XI wrote is in full conformity with Douglas's and Pound's thinking, including the attack on the monopoly of credit, the mention of the use of economic warfare for power and wealth, the bemoaning of loss of the supremacy of the State-Monarchy and its right to coinage, and the enslavement of individuals and nations to international finance. A long quote is necessary to understand the thrust of the encyclical, released in 1931, during the Great Depression:

> 103. But, with the diffusion of modern industry throughout the whole world, the "capitalist" economic regime has spread everywhere to such a degree, particularly since the publication of Leo XIII's Encyclical, that it has invaded and pervaded the economic and social life of even those outside its orbit and is unquestionably impressing on its advantages, disadvantages and vices, and, in a sense, is giving it its own shape and form.
>
> 104. Accordingly, when directing Our special attention to the changes which the capitalist economic system has undergone since Leo's time, We have in mind the good not only of those who dwell in regions given over to "capital" and industry, but of all mankind.
>
> 105. In the first place, it is obvious that not only is wealth concentrated in our times but an immense power and despotic economic dictatorship is consolidated in the hands of

212 Stock, *The Life of Ezra Pound*, 377.

a few, who often are not owners but only the trustees and managing directors of invested funds which they administer according to their own arbitrary will and pleasure.

106. This dictatorship is being most forcibly exercised by those who, since they hold the money and completely control it, control credit also and rule the lending of money. Hence they regulate the flow, so to speak, of the life-blood whereby the entire economic system lives, and have so firmly in their grasp the soul, as it were, of economic life that no one can breathe against their will.

107. This concentration of power and might, the characteristic mark, as it were, of contemporary economic life, is the fruit that the unlimited freedom of struggle among competitors has of its own nature produced, and which lets only the strongest survive; and this is often the same as saying, those who fight the most violently, those who give least heed to their conscience.

108. This accumulation of might and of power generates in turn three kinds of conflict. First, there is the struggle for economic supremacy itself; then there is the bitter fight to gain supremacy over the State in order to use in economic struggles its resources and authority; finally there is conflict between States themselves, not only because countries employ their power and shape their policies to promote every economic advantage of their citizens, but also because they seek to decide political controversies that arise among nations through the use of their economic supremacy and strength.

109. The ultimate consequences of the individualist spirit in economic life are those which you yourselves, Venerable Brethren and Beloved Children, see and deplore: Free competition has destroyed itself; economic dictatorship has supplanted the free market; unbridled ambition for power has likewise succeeded greed for gain; all economic life has become tragically hard, inexorable, and cruel. To these are to be added the grave evils that have resulted from an intermingling and shameful confusion of the functions and duties of public authority with those of the economic sphere—such as, one of the worst, the virtual degradation of the majesty of the State, which although it ought to sit on high like a queen and supreme arbitress, free from all partiality and intent upon the one common good and justice, is become a slave, surrendered and delivered to the passions and greed of men. And as to international relations, two different streams

> have issued from the one fountain-head: On the one hand, economic nationalism or even economic imperialism; on the other, a no less deadly and accursed internationalism of finance or international imperialism whose country is where profit is.[213]

Interestingly, paragraph 105 was included at the end of the Social Credit Party of Alberta leader's booklet, the then Premier of Alberta, William Aberhart.[214] This was remarkable in 1940 Alberta, when it was predominately a Protestant province, and Premier *Bible Bill* Aberhart was a Baptist minister.

This passage concludes with a reference to B. Swan,[215] whose opinion regarding the reason for the Spanish Civil War seems to relate to the profit motive. This would be in keeping with Pound's and Douglas's constant emphasis on the link between profiteering and war.

The fourth passage is directly concerned with the Douglasite influence upon Pound. Pound states that Stead asked Douglas about the rupee. Pound writes "Stead" but he is probably referring to Henry Wickham *Steed*, an eminent British journalist who was born in 1871. He was educated at the Universities of Jena, Berlin, and Paris. He served as foreign editor of *The London Times* from 1914–19 and as editor of *The London Times* from 1919–22.[216]

The passage is significant in that it clearly shows the extent to which Douglas was consulted on monetary matters by the most eminent men in England. That Steed asked Douglas about the rupee, is significant by virtue of the royal prerogative. The British Monarch, up to 1870, could have decreed that the Indian rupee be accepted as legal tender in England, and thus augment England's money supply.

The fifth passage begins by seeming to provide a historical line from the past into Pound's lifetime of heroes, i.e., those he seems to admire for their clear philosophical writing and vision and whom he deems worthy to sit on *Thrones*: Eriugena, Anselm, Cherbury and Rémusat. Scotus Eriugena in the ninth century, and St. Anselm who flourished in England in the eleventh century, both were unalterably opposed to usury: "Medieval christianity is held in high esteem by Pound because it has 'taught us that usury was an evil.' His opinion of the modern church, however, is very low, for 'in our day Rockefeller and the church eat from the same manger . . . . ' To Pound, usury

---

213 Pius XI, *Quadragesimo Anno*, para. 103–9.
214 Aberhart, *National Monetary Reform*, 48.
215 Terrell, *A Companion*, Vol. II, 650.
216 "Steed, Henry Wickham," *Who's Who 1956*, 2826.

is not an isolated economic disease. Once usura starts to grow, the corruption of a society and the withering of a civilization can be predicted."[217] Charles de Rémusat wrote a book concerning Lord Herbert de Cherbury[218] and a book on the life of Saint Anselm of Canterbury;[219] Thiers and Rémusat were friends and political allies.

Pound then ends this line with Marie Adolphe Thiers, the 19th century French historian and one time President of France, who opposed income-tax and called it *the portal to inquisition*. Terrell states that in Thiers's *Defense of Property*, Thiers opposed "taxation of income or wealth."[220] Thiers wrote and spoke on his opposition to income-tax and most famously against the efforts of the socialist-anarchist Pierre-Joseph Proudhon to impose such a tax in France in 1848, the year of European revolutions. For this, to this day, Thiers is smeared as the protector of landowners and the rich. There are comments that were made by Thiers that are similar to the one Pound quotes. In a publication written on the centenary of income-tax in France, a short summary of its history from 1914–2014 is provided. There's a quote from Thiers, who stated that income-tax was "immorality written in law."[221] Most French people today would probably agree, be they rich or poor.

As has been referenced before, C. H. Douglas also condemns income-tax as an infamy and as being opposed to the economic freedom of the individual. Douglas was the one to draw Pound's attention to the history of taxation. Pound, through his allusions concerning the devaluation of silver, then events leading to the formation of national banks, the forerunners of the central bank system, and now with the spread of income-tax on a global scale, provokes the following question: Why and how were all of these economic events and/or acceptance of these economic tools spread, and why/how were they accepted by nations, nations that if not at war with one another, at least were diametrically at odds with one another?

It was not mere happenstance, but shows how closely the various banking houses of Europe, the Americas, and those of the British Empire, despite their competitive nature, worked in unison from the 19th century, into the 20th. New methods had to be found to keep their model of banking functioning, finding new methods for governments:

---

217 Tay, "Between Kung and Eleusis," 38.
218 Terrell, *A Companion*, Vol. II, 652.
219 Terrell, *A Companion*, Vol. II, 650–51.
220 Terrell, *A Companion*, Vol. II, 651.
221 André and Guillot, "1914–2014: One Hundred Years," 2.

national, state-provincial, county-municipality, and city-town, to finance government projects and debt. The so-called *Tax Freedom Day* is the first day in each year that a nation, by the cumulative income of its citizens, has managed to pay all the taxes expected for that year. It may be an imprecise tool for an individual, but does give the larger picture of a nation's *wage-slavery*. On average, most Americans are working until early April, as of 2025, to pay all government taxes, while in most other countries of the world, that date is much later, even coming as late as July, as is the case, for example, in Austria and Belgium.[222] This does not include the personal debt of individuals: mortgages, car payments, credit cards, etc. Debt has truly become a form of modern slavery, both government debt and personal debt.

Personal debt and national debt are inescapable. Concerning income-tax, we can take the United States today: "Interest on the federal debt is now so immense that it's consuming 40% of all personal income taxes. The largest source of revenue for the federal government is increasingly being devoted to just servicing the debt, not even paying it down."[223] The National debt in the US is over 36 trillion dollars,[224] and just the interest payments on the debt are now over one trillion dollars a year, averaging over two billion dollars a day towards interest.[225]

Under our current banking system, no one ever talks about paying the debt completely off, and while many support *balanced budgets* it is rare for them to be implemented, and even if they are, it does not stop the growing national debt. How is this possible for society and its citizens to continually carry and pay this debt, and survive financially? Debt has become another form of slavery that denies many people the opportunity to enjoy private ownership. Even most homes are mortgaged; i.e., the banks really own them until the mortgage is paid off. In contrast, we have the financial sector, the banking industry. Their profits are *legally* hidden, along with criminal elements, in the many island tax havens, especially British ones: Jersey, Guernsey, the British Virgin Islands, etc. It is estimated that the wealth hidden in these havens is from six to thirty-six trillion US dollars.[226] Among these banks are ones most of us ourselves use. As can be seen by the estimates given, this is a secret world that only the privileged are allowed to enter. The upper number, thirty-six trillion, would

---

222 "New study compares tax," *Brussels Report*.
223 Antoni, "American Taxpayers Are Now Slaves."
224 "What is the National Debt?" *Peter G. Peterson Foundation*.
225 Conte, "U. S. Debt Interest Payments."
226 Shaxson, "The City of London."

more than pay off the current US National Debt. Despite the 2008 financial crisis that brought unwanted attention to these tax havens and calls for reform, the havens seem to be reaching out again to the banking sector, as "Havens Of Calm In Volatile Times."[227]

C. H. Douglas did not advocate for the redistribution of the wealth of others, but rather the *distribution* of wealth from source. This would make it possible for all to own private property, by instituting, through a National Credit Office, periodic credit payments to all to bridge any gap between prices for goods and services and wages, salaries, and dividends. Douglas noted that banks also try to bridge this gap by encouraging the capture of foreign markets, by issuing loans to businesses to produce items that, at least hitherto, have little demand, or by issuing loans to individuals: mortgages, credit cards, etc. Governments inject billions into economies by funding military equipment production, which is later destroyed in training or war, sold abroad, or replaced and upgraded. What could be a dividend to all and debt-free is wasted in this massive creation of national and personal debt.

101 is a short canto and was written after 1958. Pound provided a date for the ending of Canto 100, i.e., "1 Jan '58." Canto 101 continues with the monetary-economic luminous detail seen in the earlier cantos:

> 1. Kublai,
> Te Te of Ch'eng, called Timur, 1247, came hither
>
> . . . .
>
> 2. Talleyrand, Thiers, tried to get sense into princes.
> 6 to the public; 3%, and then one to the state
> (Simon admits it)
> 4 letters patent, 5 seals
> after the 4th year of Yung-lo
> 12th May, 1406, and a gold belt
> inlaid with flowers, pay for the troops holding
> passes; rations, chair-coolies, horses.
>
> . . . .
>
> 3. and, going toward slavery, have mislaid family names.
> 40 years trailer life, non-productive,
> non-agricultural
>
> . . . .
>
> 4. tho' avoiding the squalor of taxes
> by cretins imposed;
>
> . . . .

---

[227] Burroughes, "Havens of Calm."

5. "la bêtise humaine."
That one dollar's worth of oil sell at 5 dollars.
Talleyrand, Austerlitz, Mme Rémusat:
"90 francs fee for obtaining gold for
a one thousand franc note" (1805) . . .

. . . .

6. Gaudin did not pay interest on government credit. Nor did
Kang Hi.

. . . .

7. "Sort of ignorance," said the old priest to Yeats in a railway train,
"is spreading every day from the schools!"

. . . .

8. and they pay the land tax in buckwheat.

. . . .

9. "No money, no swiss" quoted Wilson (McN.)
(Canto 101)

The first passage begins by mentioning Kublai Khan, who had issued the first paper currency, as has been pointed out in Chapter II.

The second passage begins with a reference to Talleyrand and Thiers who tried to get some sense into the minds of princes. The sense Pound is speaking of has to do with monetary sense, particularly regarding the issuing of currency. The line "6 to the public; 3%, and then one to the state / (Simon admits it)," refers to a passage written by Jules Simon, concerning the government under Thiers: "Nous avions emprunté 1,330 millions à la Banque, au taux réductible de 3% Nous voulions porter, et nous portâmes en effet, notre emprunt avec elle à 1,500 millions. La Banque, qui prête au public à 6%, prêtait à l'État à 3% en 1871, et lui prêta à 1% les années suivantes, parce que l'État l'avait autorisée à porter successivement le chiffre de ses émissions."[228]

The lines: "4 letters patent, 5 seals / after the 4th year of Yung-lo / 12th May, 1406, and a gold belt / inlaid with flowers, pay for the troops holding / passes; rations, chair-coolies, horses," refers to the exercise of the regal prerogative over coinage by the Emperor Yung-lo in 1406.[229] Yung-lo exercised this regal prerogative over coinage to pay for his troops and military supplies. Just as Alexander the Great had paid the debts of his soldiery by exercising the regal prerogative over coinage, so too had Yung-lo in 1406. Thus, monetary sanity has existed in both the East and the West.

In the third passage, Pound points out that as we move toward slavery, a slavery imposed by the usurocracy, we tend to mislay our

[228] Simon, *Le Gouvernement de M. Thiers*, 197–98.
[229] Yung-lo was the younger brother of the founder of the Ming dynasty.

family names. This loss of family names is symptomatic for Pound of that loss of a sense of tradition and history, which both he and T. S. Eliot lament. The lines: "40 years trailer life, non-productive, / non-agricultural," comments upon this nomadic aspect of American life, which nevertheless can avoid the squalor of taxes imposed by cretins, i.e., morons, mentioned in the cited fourth passage. The lines: "'la bêtise humaine.' / That one dollar's worth of oil sell at 5 dollars," refers to Pound's impatience with the lack of ethics in the economic sphere. Pound refers to this lack of ethics in the economic sphere as "human stupidity"—"la bêtise humaine."

The lines: "Talleyrand, Austerlitz, Mme Rémusat: / '90 francs fee for obtaining gold for / a one thousand franc note' (1805)...," refers to a passage, from the French writer Mme Rémusat, concerning speculation in gold: "'Money had become still more scarce; in fact, it attained such a price that... I had to pay ninety francs merely for obtaining gold for a thousand-franc bank-note.'"[230]

Concerning passage five and six, Talleyrand is a Poundian hero in contrast to Metternich, who is despised by Pound. Pound points out that Napoleon's Secretary of the Treasury, Gaudin, did not pay interest on government credit, nor did the Chinese Emperor Kang Hi. This monetary-economic luminous detail is of great significance from the point of view of the Douglasite influence on Pound since it emphasises the Douglasite principle of debt-free and interest-free government credit.

The lines: "'Sort of ignorance,' said the old priest to Yeats in a railway train, / 'is spreading every day from the schools!'" This reflects Pound's contempt for the system of general education which only succeeds in disseminating ignorance, particularly about monetary-economic and monetary-historic matters. C. H. Douglas had referred to the system of general education as one of mass hypnotism, as has been mentioned earlier.

The eighth passage consists of one line: "[A]nd they pay the land tax in buckwheat." This is a reference to the system of paying taxes in ancient China. Pound stresses here and elsewhere that taxes in ancient China were paid in kind, instead of in money. Pound sees this as a much more humane method because it represents paying a tithe, i.e., one-ninth or one-tenth of something which exists rather than paying a fixed charge in something which may or may not exist in the pocket of the tax-paying victim.

---

[230] Terrell, *A Companion*, Vol. II, 655.

This luminous detail must be seen against the background of Pound's constant attack upon taxation. This campaign against the modern form of taxation as being equivalent to highway robbery dates from the time of C. H. Douglas's letter to Pound advising him to investigate the modern form of taxation. This letter of Douglas to Pound has been quoted and dealt with in Chapter II. The one-line luminous detail "'No money, no swiss' quoted Wilson (McN.)," refers to a passage in the writings of the monetary historian McNair Wilson, whose name has appeared several times before in earlier cantos. This allusion is probably from the following passage from Wilson, illustrating how domestic and foreign banking interests work together. Those at home can deny loans if they do not like government policy, and then, by their international reach, see to it that foreign banking houses, such as the Swiss banking houses, also deny the government financing:

> The Whigs drew a great part of their support from the merchant bankers of the City of London, whose financial operations extended over the whole world; the French nobility and higher clergy, as a consequence of their extravagance, fell into the hands of the Swiss and Dutch bankers. Thus, in these two countries, the internationalism of Money challenged the power of the Throne and began to exert influence on national policy.
>
> So far as Money was concerned there was neither England nor France. Close relations existed already between the banking houses in all European centers. Thus the firm of Thelusson and Necker financed the grain trade in France and England and was connected both in France and England with the trade with the East Indies. This Swiss firm of Geneva had offices both in Paris and London. It made numerous loans to Louis XV and was interested at the same time in loans made to the British Government.[231]

Pound corresponded with Robert McNair Wilson for many years. T. S. Eliot invited Wilson in 1934 to write a review of C. H. Douglas's books and pamphlets, those from Stanley Nott publications. Wilson, who had his own suggestions concerning monetary policy, would agree at times in his *Criterion* article with Douglas: "Thanks to his [Douglas's] brilliant and searching analyses of the existing financial system, millions of men and women in all parts of the world have been brought face to face with the supreme political and economic

---

[231] Wilson, *Monarchy or Money Power*, 9.

issue of this time and have learned that, in the absence of national control of money, national control in almost any form is impossible."[232]

Canto 102 is also a short canto which contains a number of significant monetary-economic luminous details, one of which is particularly Douglasite:

1. But the lot of 'em, Yeats, Possum, Old Wyndham
had no ground to stand on

. . . .

2. Barley is the marrow of men,
40 centess' in my time
an orzo.
At Procope, one franc fifteen for a luncheon
and ten centimes tip for the waiter. Noi altri borghesi
could not go down into the piazza. We thought we could
control . . .

. . . .

3. seed barley with the sacrifice (Lacedaemon)
But with Leucothoe's mind in that incense

. . . .

4. Antoninus;
Julian
would not be worshipped

. . . .

5. Assyrios fines ingressus,
Built granaries, sueta annona,
naturally labled "apostate".
Quem mihi febricula eripuit
Domitian, infaustus
tried to buy peace with money.
(Canto 102)

The first passage reiterates a powerful Douglasite luminous detail. Pound once again points out that William Butler Yeats, T. S. Eliot, and Wyndham Lewis, had no ground to stand on. When this luminous detail first appeared in an earlier Canto, Pound had pointed out that A. R. Orage did have ground to stand on. The ground which Orage had, and which the three great literary giants lacked, was the solid ground of Douglasite policy and philosophy. As Pound stated: "Orage's *rectitudo* demanded justice, justice in the division of the 'eredità culturale,' the cultural heritage; of the increment of association."[233]

---

232 Wilson, "Review of C. H. Douglas'," 342.
233 Pound, *Impact*, 161.

The second passage continues the theme of abundance, which is in accordance with Pound's distributist philosophy. It points out that barley is the marrow of men, which is an allusion to a passage taken from Homer's *The Odyssey*, the words of the goddess Athena to Telemacus.[234] This passage ends with a mention of the fact that certain forces thought they could control Mussolini before he came to power. The line: "We thought we could control," has appeared in Canto 98 and has been linked with the control which the chemical combines thought they could exert on Mussolini before his coming to power.

The distributist theme of the plenitude of nature's abundance reappears in the third passage, with the Poundian emphasis upon the sacredness of grain. The lines: "seed barley with the sacrifice (Lacedaemon) / But with Leucothoe's mind in that incense." Food provides nourishment and life for man, a gift from the Divine one, a sacred gift.

The fourth passage mentions the Emperor Antoninus Pius and Julian the Apostate. Both Antoninus Pius, emperor from 138–61 AD, and Julian the Apostate, are Poundian heroes because of their wise monetary policies. Pound goes on in the fifth passage to mention that Julian built granaries, and made the grain crop his concern. This is an allusion to Gibbon:

> When the luxurious citizens of Antioch complained of the high price of poultry and fish, Julian publicly declared that a frugal city ought to be satisfied with a regular supply of wine, oil, and bread; but he acknowledged that it was the duty of a sovereign to provide for the subsistence of his people. With this salutary view, the emperor ventured on a very dangerous and doubtful step, of fixing, by legal authority, the value of corn. He enacted that, in a time of scarcity, it should be sold at a price which had seldom been known in the most plentiful years; and, that his own example might strengthen his laws, he sent into the market four hundred and twenty-two thousand *modii*, or measures, which were drawn by his order from the granaries of Hierapolis, of Chalcis, and even of Egypt.[235]

Pound goes on to comment ironically, that naturally Julian has been labelled "apostate." Pound ends Canto 102 with a reference to the unwise Emperor Domitian "infaustus," i.e., unsuccessfully, "tried to buy peace with money." This allusion is to the payment yearly of eight million sesterces to king Decebalus of Dacia to maintain peace.

---

[234] Terrell, *A Companion*, Vol. II, 659.

[235] Gibbon, *The History of the Decline*, Vol. 4, 112.

Canto 103 continues with the great anti-usury theme and interesting monetary-economic luminous details:

> 1.   Homestead versus kolschoz
>   Rome versus Babylon
> no sense of quidity in the sovreignty
>   i.e. the power to issue
> The slaves were red herring,
>   land not secure against issuers
> Emerson, Agassiz, Alcot
>   at Hawthorne's funeral
> . . . .
> 2. land to all veterans: Mommsen
>   160 acres, 33rd congress
> "I see its relation to one thing,
>   Yu sees its relation to ten."
> Monetary literacy, sans which a loss of freedom is consequent
>   (Canto 103)

The lines: "Homestead versus kolschoz / Rome versus Babylon," refers to the age-old struggle between the individual and the group. Whereas the American frontier tradition had emphasized the uniqueness and sacredness of the individual by the grant of homesteads, the new collectivity would organize mankind into the kolschoz, kibbutz, or commune. The kolschoz is, of course, a collective farm in the Soviet Union.

C. H. Douglas devotes Part I, chapter III in his book *Social Credit*, to a discussion of the tensions between the group and the individual. Pound expresses this Douglasite dichotomy in terms of Rome versus Babylon, as representing the traditions of the individual versus the group respectively. Rome has upheld the uniqueness and sacredness of the individual, whereas Babylon has emphasized the collectivity. Pound, like Douglas, is aware that Western civilization has been built upon the individual and not the group.

We cannot speak of the individual today without understanding its Christian meaning; it must be in the context of the family. Douglas is criticised for his emphasis on the individual, especially in the context of the global spread of American individualism. It can be an unfair criticism, in that the whole justification for the issuing of *Social Credit* debt-free dividends to individuals on a regular basis has to do with the fact that it is a shared heritage that grows and expands from living within a community. A dividend that belongs to all within a nation, whatever their race, colour, or creed. This does not mean that a credit payment to a family rather than an individual does not have merit and would perhaps be more just and equitable. A family of ten, does not need over three times more a dividend than a family of three, though it does need more. And a family of three with a child with a severe physical disability, does need more than a family of three all in good health.

This is where Catholic Social Teaching, concerning its four major pillars, provides needed guidance: the dignity of the human person, subsidiarity, the common good, and solidarity. In reference to solidarity, there are nations such as small Pacific island nations, that would rely on solidarity from nations with abundance. They are rich culturally, but poor in natural resources. The nation of Nauru is an example, where their one main item of trade, phosphate, has already been heavily exploited. The trade wars of the Central Bank Economic model, based on endless growth, must be substituted by solidarity. As for understanding in a correct way Douglas and his emphasis on the individual within a community, one must look to the *individuation* philosophy of a medieval Franciscan Friar:

> Throughout history the human being is a predominantly tribal creature. Most of the great cultures of this world are familial and tribal. In the rising tide of the Far East today, the greatest honor in work is to sacrifice one's more personal desires for the sake of the family business. The Hispanic culture is a family first tradition.
>
> Furthermore, most ancient civilizations were built around the centrality of the temple. Religion is what held them together. Only modern western civilization has adapted a more secular and pagan model. . . .
>
> . . . In the west the individual stands in ideological preeminence over the community. We have embraced individualism. We have become the culture of "me," and self, over really sacrificing for the sake of "us." This kills the possibility for any stable social relationship. IT has vast ramifications throughout a culture. To quote John Paul II, we have become a "culture of death."
>
> The Franciscan, John Duns Scotus (1266–1308 AD), taught the venerable notion of "individuation." Individuation rightly recognizes the unique, and unrepeatable gift, of each individual human person. It creates a positive attitude of reverence for human life, and its entire process from beginning to end, and a further appropriate love and respect for all life.
>
> But "individualism" is individuation "gone bad." Individualism places the rights of the individual over anything else.

> This creates a society of self. This manifests in hedonism, consumerism, economic inequality, and violence. Death is the result, whether through gangs and domestic violence in the streets and homes of our cities, the lost youth in our schools, or with the unborn and elderly in the wards of hospitals and nursing homes. Individualism is the root of it all.[236]

The first passage: "no sense of quidity in the sovreignty / i.e., the power to issue," refers to the Douglasite/Poundian insistence upon the essence of sovereignty consisting in the power to issue money. This is a major theme in the works by Alexander Del Mar, which Pound uses readily in *The Cantos*.

The lines: "The slaves were red herring, / land not secure against issuers," refers to Pound's belief that the American Civil War was not fought over the slavery question but was fought because the southern land-owners were hopelessly in debt to the large New York banking houses. It was because of this southern indebtedness that the land was not secure against the issuers of money. Christopher Hollis is the probable source for much of Pound's argument:

> [T]he true source of those loans was not New York, which it could perhaps conquer, but London, which it could not reach. If the piper would not dance to his master's tune, the master would not pay at all. Thus the money-power of New York was able to dictate the development both of the West and of the South. We have spoken in another chapter of the system under which development is dependent upon loans of bank-created money which have to be repaid long before the goods for whose manufacture they were issued come on the market....
>
> This southern debt to New York is the explanation of much. The debts were bank-debts. They were short-term debts. They had to be repaid, and yet they never really could be repaid. They could only be nominally repaid by further borrowings. And the price of the borrowings was the acceptance of the lender's terms. It is common enough for the books to describe to us how the area of cotton-cultivation spread in the years before the war. But cotton no more spreads of itself than gold flows into a country unasked. The area of cotton spread because the banks lent money to those who would grow cotton and forced into bankruptcy those who refused.[237]

---

236 Talbot, "Community of Disciples."
237 Hollis, *The Two Nations*, 206, 208–9.

Hollis is explicit that the cause of slavery should not be looked for only in the south, but the cause and blame lay likewise in the large banking institutions of Yankee New York City. C. H. Douglas maintained that property rights, as with the southern farmers, are never secure against the unlimited power of those who have a monopoly over the issue of money, as seen above.

The lines: "Emerson, Agassiz, Alcot / at Hawthorne's funeral," superpose a literary luminous detail on the dense monetary-economic luminous details which have preceded it. Pound saw these individuals as worthy of honour. Pound would have agreed with Hawthorne's worries about "the healthy state of the writer or artist in the aggressive marketplace" and Hawthorne's description of Andrew Jackson, as "one of the greatest men we ever had."[238]

The lines in passage two: "land to all veterans: Mommsen / 160 acres, 33rd Congress," recall the grants of quarter-section homesteads to war veterans by the thirty-third congress. Mommsen is the monetary historian whose work was debunked by Alexander Del Mar. Here though, Pound is agreeing with Mommsen, who had noted that the Roman Empire had likewise strengthened society by settling veterans in newly conquered territory.[239] The individual and their family are the strength of the community, the reason a nation exists.

The lines: "I see its relation to one thing, / Yu sees its relation to ten," are Sinological luminous details and stress the Confucian insistence upon seeing the relation of one thing to another: "Pound is asking the reader to act like Hui [Yu] and see how many random things relate in a dramatic way; how states and governments rise and fall, not by the well considered merits of their causes, but by what ought to be minor matters."[240]

Finally, the line "Monetary literacy, sans which a loss of freedom is consequent," is of tremendous importance from the point of view of the Douglasite influence on Pound. Pound, like Douglas, maintains that without monetary literacy there cannot be lasting freedom in which the individual can flourish. Like John Adams, Pound would insist that ignorance of coin, credit, and circulation is the greatest evil of the age. Monetary illiteracy brings about the enslavement of the individual to the usurocracy.

In Canto 103, the density of the monetary-economic luminous details continues:

---

238 Hussey, "Hawthorne's 'Dangerous Soul,'" 25.

239 Terrell, *A Companion*, 664–65.

240 Terrell, *A Companion*, 665.

1. Bismarck thought centralization bitched France

. . . .

2. Absolutely drop idea of putting Chase
into the Treasury

. . . .

3. A.J. to Buchanan: unable to perceive that U.S. interests
will be safer in other hands than her own.

. . . .

4. Napoleon's taxes less than ½ now at Bergheim."
Buchanan got a treaty out of the hRooshuns
"worst the art of man" (speaking of bank system)
could devise,
English income tax odious, has risen to seven pence in the
pound

. . . .

5. Raleigh noted that Genova's loans were not productive
"all they have left is their usury"

. . . .

6. Das Leihkapital.
And there is, of course, the Mensdorf letter
that has had (1958)
no publicity.
(Canto 103)

The first passage refers to the fact that Bismarck thought centralization had *bitched* France. This luminous detail is completely in harmony with the Poundian/Douglasite antipathy to the centralization of power. C. H. Douglas in his very first book *Economic Democracy* speaks of the growing menace of centralization of power in politics, finance, industry, and the press. Pound would find confirmation for Douglas's conclusions in reading Brooks Adams, who dedicates chapter XI, to his own inquiry into "Modern Centralization."[241] Douglas, in contrast to this reference to Bismarck, saw the prime example of centralization of power as being Germany itself, before World War I and after, especially through the influence of Prussianism that exalted the power of the State and made the Teutonic race servile to authority.[242] C. H. Douglas sees this phenomenon as a manifestation of the will-to-power and in its place advocates a policy of the decentralization of power.

The second passage concerns the absolute necessity of not putting Salmon Portland Chase into the treasury. Chase was secretary of the

---

241 Adams, *The Law of Civilization and Decay*, chp. XI.
242 Douglas, *Economic Democracy*, 10–12.

treasury under Lincoln and was responsible for the National Bank Act, which Pound despises. Pound then paraphrases and condenses a communication of Andrew Jackson to Buchanan concerning the Panama Treaty: "I cannot see, for my part, how it follows that the primary interests of the United States will be safer in the hands of others than her own; or, in other words, that it can ever become necessary to form treaties, alliances, or any connections with the governments of South America, which may infringe upon the principles of equality among nations which is the basis of their independence, as well as all their international rights."[243]

This communication to Buchanan stresses the fact that American interests must not be left in the hands of a foreign oligarchy, and at the mercy of this oligarchy, and likewise freedom from foreign control should be the respected right of every nation. This is in accordance with C. H. Douglas's insistence that the independence and peaceful harmony of all nations is foremost based on each nation's control and issue of local purchasing power.

In the fourth passage, Terrell, in his Vol. II, indicates that Pound draws this allusion from a passage in George Ticknor Curtis's *Life of James Buchanan*. In a passage, Buchanan relates what he hears while among the Germans of the Cologne region in the Summer of 1833: "They all refer to the days of Napoleon; and compare their situation then with what it is at present. The old maitre d'hotel at Bergheim, who has kept a public house for fifty years, and who seems to be a sensible and honest-hearted old man, told me that the taxes were not half so heavy under Napoleon as they were at present. That he was the greatest man there had ever been in the world, and they loved the French much better than the Prussians."[244] As has been noted, Napoleon is a great monetary hero of Pound's, and the only serious challenge to the usurocracy in the 19th century. Pound finds in the living oral tradition Buchanan encountered confirmation of Pound's own delving into history. Even a German innkeeper, the presumed enemy of the French, remembers Napoleon with fondness for his low taxation.

Pound then paraphrases a statement made by Buchanan that he had completed a commercial treaty with the Russians in 1832.[245] Then he alludes to a speech by Buchanan in 1838 in the US Senate: "It is true that at the special session I did endeavor to prove that the

---

[243] Terrell, *A Companion*, Vol. II, 672.
[244] Curtis, *Life of James Buchanan*, 219.
[245] Curtis, *Life of James Buchanan*, 171.

present banking system, under its existing regulations, was one of the very worst which the art of man could devise. Under it, ruinous expansions and revulsions must continue to succeed each other at stated periods, and many of the best and most enterprising men of the country must become its victim."[246]

Pound further paraphrases Buchanan:

> The income tax of England has never been resorted to except in cases of extreme necessity. That tax at present in existence imposes seven pence per pound.... Under the British government, they have adopted the means necessary to secure a just return of all incomes; under ours, this, in many cases, would prove almost impossible, without resorting to an inquisition unknown to our form of government. Indeed, as far as I know, our present taxes on income are eluded to a most shameful extent. The income tax has always been odious in England; and it would prove to be so, if carried to anything like the same extent, in this country.[247]

It is to be noted that both Pound's allusion to the French politician Thiers and Buchanan's own statement refer to income tax as an *inquisition*. The modern world lambasts the Spanish Inquisition, but individuals universally submit yearly to their own governmental *inquisition*. With fear and trembling, they fill out their income tax forms lest they may have paid one penny more, or paid one penny less. These luminous details are completely in accord with Douglasite philosophy and policy. Again, Pound has been guided in his artistic selectivity of luminous detail by Douglasism. Thus we see Douglasism as providing a focal point for *The Cantos*.

Pound goes on to reiterate a luminous detail having Sir Walter Raleigh as its central figure. It is a repetition of the same paraphrase from Canto 97. It is taken from a letter written by Sir Walter Raleigh to King James I of England: "There was an Intercourse of Traffick to *Genoa*, and there was the Flower of Commerce, as appeareth by their ancient Records, and their sumptuous Buildings, for all Nations Traded with Merchandize to them, and there was the Store-house of all *Italy* and other places; but after they had set a great Custom of 16 *per Cent.* all Nations left Trading with them, which made them give themselves wholly to Usury."[248] The implication is that Genoa's custom duty destroyed any trade and manufacturing within their

---

246 Curtis, *Life of James Buchanan*, 438.
247 Curtis, *Life of James Buchanan*, 527.
248 Raleigh, "Select observations," 3.

city, leaving only money-lenders and their usury. As Pound rightfully paraphrases, "all they have left is their usury."

The sixth passage contains a reference to "Das Leihkapital," i.e., "Pawn Capital" or the capital of the pawnshop. This luminous detail represents the supreme attitude of disdain expressed by Pound for the present monetary-financial system. In other words, Pound maintains that the financial system is without dignity and equates it with the system of a pawnshop. Both the usurocracy and the pawn-keeper prey on the misfortunes of others and thrive upon debt.

The very last luminous detail of Canto 103 refers to the famous Mensdorff letter. This letter to the Carnegie Endowment for International Peace was drafted jointly by Pound and Count Mensdorff in 1928. The letter suggested studying the causes of war rather than investigating the effects of war. It stated that some of the causes of war were: "1. Intense production and sale of munitions; the whole of the trade in munitions and armaments might be subjugated to contemporary, not retrospective investigation via trade channels. 2. Overproduction and dumping, leading to trade rivalries and irritation. 3. The intrigues of interested cliques. All these are general and constantly active forces towards war."[249]

Canto 104 continues with the fascinating monetary-economic luminous details we have learned to expect from Pound. This Canto is also rich in political luminous details taken from the world of contemporary politics:

1. But when the young lout was selling the old lout
the idea of betraying Mihaelovitch[250]
The air of the room became heavy so that young S.
Resigned from the F.O. and "went into the City" —
Banners they took after Lepanto
but now obtain "control of the outlets"
to keep down printed quality

. . . .

2. And a $ to look like a franc,
the franc worth a centesimo

. . . .

3. "Good chaps" said Schmidt
"damn shame we have to fight 'em."
Hate is not born in the trenches
nor among 2nd. lieutenants.

. . . .

---

249 Stock, *The Life of Ezra Pound*, 276.

250 Later editions of *The Cantos* spell his name *Mihailovitch*.

4. But in Venice more affirmations
                    of individual men
From Selvo to Franchetti, than any elsewhere.
. . . .
5.   Lar-
ranaga
saw fashion an element:
          No science without clear definitions.
. . . .
6. Moral scruple unknown to financiers
                                        at THAT time
a common custom in business.
. . . .
7. Pulchra documenta
          Bülow from agencies
                    "don't waste time getting into papers"
Get the agencies.
          and to summarize:
Gold was in control of the Pontifex,
          standard at Byzance
                    and El Melek
until 1204.
     kalos kagathos
Del Mar cites 12 cases of tickets
          as from Iron in Spartan coinage
. . . .
8. Mond killed the English Review
          and Ford went to Paris (an interval)
Village festival on the Quatorze
Brits paid out of french pocket
          one whole installment;
Alex, the debts of his soldiers
And as for what happened after the king lost exclusivity
          even Del Mar gasps with astonishment
McNair Wilson, Larranaga, or Tremaine at 2 in the morning
                                        (Canto 104)

The first passage quoted above refers to the selling out of General Dragoljub "Draža" Mihailović, the leader of the Yugoslav Chetniks who was loyal to the exiled King Peter. This luminous detail takes us right into the machinations of the British Foreign Office where a "young lout" was selling an "old lout" on the idea of abandoning Mihailović. Pound tells us that old and young have the same last name, "lout," or someone uncouth. The "old lout" is Winston Churchill, and the "young lout" is his own son, Randolph Churchill, who, like his father, many found to be brutish and a heavy drinker. As in any good spy novel, Pound does not reveal the man on the inside who is sharing these secrets. He says only that the young man, known by the code name "S.," found the atmosphere so oppressive that he resigned from the Foreign Office and "went into the City." It is Pound's reference to the *City* that reveals the identity of "S.": "Frank Kermode in his essay, 'Mr. Waugh's Cities,' points out Waugh's very real tendency in his writings generally to identify the 'Catholic City' (of Faith) with a secular order of reason, clarity, and beauty—in fact, Kermode might have added, even with the West, or Western Europe alone. The critic then observes that in Waugh's writings the Great House becomes a 'type', a symbolic representation, of the Catholic City, and, like Hetton, must be defended against barbarism."[251]

Pound, in good spy fashion, does not even with "young S." betray this individual's identity. It may be Waugh's code name in the Foreign Office, or a peculiar nickname devised by Pount himself, like many of the others he has bestowed, especially to those in the literary community. Waugh was known for his writing on various saints, but more importantly, his full name is *Evelyn Arthur Saint John Waugh.*[252] He was christened and given the name *Saint John*, not just named after a saint, as *John*. So "S." refers to Pound's own code name for Pound's man on the inside, the *young Saint.*[253]

In being an allusion to Waugh, it is also an allusion to Leslie Charteris or Leslie Charles Bowyer-Yin, the British-Chinese author who created the fictional character, Simon Templar, initials S. T., also known as *the Saint*. It is understood that Canto 104 was completed in 1959. If not with the books themselves, Pound may have been more familiar with the movie films, some created pre-World War II, and certainly he would have heard the dramatized radio programs with Vincent Price while at St. Elizabeth's Hospital in Washington, D. C.[254]

The English writer, Evelyn Waugh, was personally involved in the British mission to Yugoslavia. We learn from him, many of the details surrounding the events in Yugoslavia. Waugh, on March 30, 1945, submitted a report titled "Church and State in Liberated Croatia." In

---

251 Brown, *The Major Works*, 33.

252 "Waugh, Evelyn Arthur St. John," *Who's Who* 1956, 3126.

253 Based on private correspondence from Pound, it is suggested by others that the identity of "S." is not Waugh, but Captain Robin Sanderson, who left the Foreign Office and became a stockbroker in the city of London. Henderson, "Exploring Permanent Values," 232–233.

254 "Charteris, Leslie," *The Encyclopedia of Science Fiction*. Pound listened to radio dramas, such as *Dragnet*, on the hospital ward's radio at St. Elizabeth. See: Swift, *The Bughouse*, 24.

the report, Waugh provided evidence of Tito's direct persecution of religion in the territories that partisans controlled. But "Waugh was discharged from the mission before submitting his Report to the Foreign Office."[255] In this same year, Waugh's book, *Brideshead Revisited*, would be published with his most famous reference to a *City*: "Oxford, in those days, was still a city of aquatint. In her spacious and quiet streets men walked and spoke as they had done in Newman's day."[256]

The City Waugh "went into," as the quote above from Brown suggests, could have several meanings for Pound in reference to Waugh. Perhaps it is the simplest and the one with the deepest meaning, the one that Pound would have most respected. Waugh, like Odysseus in the Odyssey, returned from his *periplum* in service to his country among the islands and lands of the eastern Mediterranean, to his own home, his *Great House* of Piers Court, a beautiful country house near Stinchcombe in Gloucestershire. He returned to his wife and children. Pound's use of Waugh's other given name, *Saint*, is not merely an effort to cloak Waugh's identity, but perhaps an indication of Pound's respect for Evelyn Waugh in this historical event. Waugh is included in Pound's list of *Saints* or righteous individuals.

The report by Waugh seems to only address the Croatians, who were a concern of Waugh's as fellow Catholics. But in his own diary he writes the following, showing his support for the Serb Mihailović and his concern with government tyranny in controlling the media, "I read a report in the *New Statesman* of an interview with returned Serbian guerillas—anti-Mihailović propaganda. It read like an official interview and my first thought was, 'How has this been allowed to appear?' That, on second thoughts, showed how used one has become to governmental tyranny."[257]

In 1946, Waugh writes concerning Randolph Churchill's earlier effort, the date not stated, to convince his father Winston *at the crucial time*:

> Monday 10 June 1946
>
> Bill Deakin and his wife came for the night. Maclean had that morning published an apologia in *The Times*, dishonest in two ways: (a) in claiming to have originated the mission and discovered Tito when in fact Bill had done all the early and dangerous work; (b) in saying no pretence was ever made that the movement was not Communist, when in fact *at*

---

[255] Borden, "Evelyn Waugh's Yugoslav Mission," 4.
[256] Waugh, *Brideshead Revisited*, 21.
[257] Waugh, *The Diaries of Evelyn Waugh*, 539.

> *the crucial time* [emphasis added] Randolph was empowered by him to act as public relations officer and sent to Rome and London, seeing the Pope and Winston, to assure them that the 'whole trend' was towards liberal democracy. Meanwhile the trial of Mihailović is being staged as a fraudulent 'exposure' of British intrigue. The General has plainly been offered his life if he will pretend he was put up to fight the Partisans by English Fascists.[258]

Finally, we have the following in a biography written on Randolph Churchill. In it, we are told that in early January 1944 Randolph was in Marrakesh, then part of the French Protectorate in today's Morrocco. He had travelled there to see his father Winston:

> Churchill [Winston] dictated a memorandum to Anthony Eden in England based on the discussions he had had with Randolph about the situation in Yugoslavia. In it he advised that positive action be taken against Mihailović by both the British Government and the exiled King Peter. He included the arguments that Randolph had put to him concerning the harm that would be done to the young King's reputation if Mihailović were not repudiated. He agreed with them wholeheartedly. 'Let me know . . . ' his letter to Eden concluded, 'the form in which you will repudiate Mihailović, and invite the King to do so. It is, in my opinion, Peter's only chance.' Randolph's propaganda activities had, it seems, already started.[259]

The mystery: How did Ezra Pound know all this in 1959? Waugh spoke in Baltimore, near Washington D. C., in late November 1948. On February 10, 1949, Waugh was in Washington itself to speak at Georgetown University. Is it possible that Waugh visited Ezra Pound at St. Elizabeth Hospital?[260]

Again, we see treason as a theme in *The Cantos.* Pound regards those who allow the private creation of money through the modern central banking system to be guilty of treason, in keeping with Sir Edward Coke's legal opinion. Pound himself had been accused of treason,

---

258 Waugh, *The Diaries of Evelyn Waugh*, 651–52.

259 Roberts, *Randolph: A Study*, 254.

260 A more likely avenue. Pound was a correspondent with Robert McNair Wilson, from 1934 to 1959. Cf. Pound and Preda, *Ezra Pound's Economic Correspondence*, 285. Wilson was a friend of Christopher Hollis. He dedicated his work *The Two Nations*, on page vii, to R. McNair Wilson. Christopher and his brother Roger Hollis, the Director General of MI5 from 1956 to 1965, were friends with Waugh. See: Waugh, *The Diaries of Evelyn Waugh*, 164, 189. Is it possible that Wilson may have known and shared information concerning Waugh, with Pound?

but here Pound mentions a greater treason committed not just by an individual but by a nation, the betrayal of the Royalist, mostly Serb forces fighting with the Allies. Treason begets treason. In a year after the war ended, Tito's government wanted Mihailović to save his life by blaming *English Fascists* for encouraging him to fight Tito's Partisans. Mihailović was loyal to the end and paid with his life rather than falsify historical facts. Britain chose its own path of betrayal. The Yugoslav government did not collaborate with the Axis powers, but became, with much of eastern Europe, victims of Allied treachery. This was the cause of their future subjugation to Stalin and/or communist tyranny. Eastern Europe to this day is still a source of continual turmoil that is directly due to the imposition by the Allied powers of new governments and often new borders. The invasion of Poland by both Germany and the Soviet Union in 1939 was the cause of the war, but, if the war was to free Poland, it was lost, not won, in 1945. The West is rightfully horrified by the ethnic cleansing that took place in the Balkans when Yugoslavia began to collapse in the early 1990s, but it stood by while Stalin did the same to various nations and people in Eastern Europe and beyond. Actions have consequences, and, if one does not bring them to light and condemn them, they will rise again. Pound will not hide this crime of betrayal by the Western powers.

Not noted by Pound directly in his reference to Mihailović, but implied and stated clearly elsewhere in *The Cantos*, is control of the media to bring about a determined policy. The BBC is held to be a bastion of truth and democratic values. Their mast head proclaimed: *Nation shall speak peace unto Nation*. But during the war, the BBC would falsify reports, attributing actions within Yugoslavia to Tito's partisans when they knew they were performed by Mihailović's Chetniks. The final statement about this betrayal by the media, of Mihailović and the legitimate Yugoslav government, is best voiced by George Orwell. In what was to be his English language preface to *Animal Farm* for the 1945 edition:

> The Russians, who had their own Jugoslav protege in Marshal Tito, accused Mihailovich of collaborating with the Germans. This accusation was promptly taken up by the British press: Mihailovich's supporters were given no chance of answering it, and facts contradicting it were simply kept out of print. In July of 1943 the Germans offered a reward of 100,000 gold crowns for the capture of Tito, and a similar reward for the capture of Mihailovich. The British press 'splashed' the reward for Tito, but only one paper mentioned

> (in small print) the reward for Mihailovich: and the charges of collaborating with the Germans continued.[261]

Orwell's statement above was not published until 1972. The *Free Press*, the grand institution of British democracy, falsified reality during the war and suppressed the truth. Orwell,[262] in the original unpublished 1945 preface, explained further how censorship works in Great Britain:

> The British press is extremely centralised, and most of it is owned by wealthy men who have every motive to be dishonest on certain important topics. But the same kind of veiled censorship also operates in books and periodicals, as well as in plays, films and radio. At any given moment there is an orthodoxy, a body of ideas which it is assumed that all right-thinking people will accept without question. It is not exactly forbidden to say this, that or the other, but it is 'not done' to say it, just as in mid-Victorian times it was 'not done' to mention trousers in the presence of a lady. Anyone who challenges the prevailing orthodoxy finds himself silenced with surprising effectiveness. A genuinely unfashionable opinion is almost never given a fair hearing, either in the popular press or in the highbrow periodicals.[263]

As mentioned before, Douglas drew Pound's attention to the manipulation of the press by finance and its control in favour of their own policy objectives. In 1937, the duly elected Social Credit government of Alberta had passed the "Act to Ensure Publication of Accurate News and Information." This act required newspapers to provide sources for statements made and allowed the government to print a

---

261 "The Freedom of the Press," *Orwell News, the Orwell Foundation.*

262 Orwell identified as a Socialist. Nevertheless, he is respected across the political spectrum, as a prophetic voice, warning of *Big Brother's* efforts to manipulate society, suppress the truth, and suppress fundamental human rights. Did Orwell ever express his opinion concerning Douglas Social Credit? The most explicit statement is in a private letter, dated June, 1933: "Do you ever see the *New English Weekly*? It is the leading Social Credit paper. As a monetary scheme Social Credit is probably sound, but its promoters seem to think that they are going to take the main weapon out of the hands of the governing classes without a fight, which is an illusion . . . the entire population reduced to docile wage-slaves, our lives utterly in the hands of the bankers . . . in the name of progress." Orwell, *The Collected Essays*, 120–21. Orwell's warning would soon play out in the province of Alberta, Canada, where any Douglas Social Credit monetary policy was rejected by the power of the legal system. Nothing similar in the number of policies disallowed has ever happened in Canada. The modern legal system is simply the handmaiden of finance.

263 "The Freedom of the Press," *Orwell News, the Orwell Foundation.*

correction for any false statements. The Supreme Court of Canada declared the act to be unconstitutional. Often in Canada this act is brought up as an example of the government trying to control the press, but it was not so. Hooke, who was a Social Credit MLA at the time, explained: "It was widely misrepresented by the press as a 'muzzling Act'. Actually, it was the reverse. It did not prohibit the press from publishing anything it wanted. It merely provided that the public be told all the facts, not what a particular newspaper thought fit."[264]

William Aberhart had led the Social Credit Movement in Alberta to power using the new medium of radio. His Baptist radio program brought mass attention to Douglas Social Credit in Alberta and beyond. In response to the Social Credit 1935 election victory, the Government of Canada, in 1936, would create a federal government media empire, replicating the BBC: the Canadian Broadcasting Corporation (CBC). "[T]he CBC was given the responsibility of establishing and expanding Canada's national radio network while also serving as the regulatory body for privately owned stations."[265] Aberhart had shown the power of radio in politics, and the Federal Government needed to gain control of this medium of communication. The federal government wanted control of media sources and output. "The regulations prohibited political addresses during religious programs."[266] One would have been a fool not to recognize that the regulation was directed personally at Aberhart. The radio transmission Aberhart used was powerful, allowing Aberhart to reach into large swaths of Western Canada, beyond Alberta, and even into the US. The government broadcast regulations were an opportunity to restrict Aberhart's impact.

In January 1939, with war approaching in Europe, "H. Milton Martin, who served on the Western Regional Advisory Council, wrote Murray to say that he was frequently asked 'why it is that Mr. Aberhart is allowed to say things which nobody else is allowed to do on the air.'"[267] Not only was the federal government creating a huge monopoly for itself in radio communication, but it also wanted to control what others said. As a 1962 thesis concerning broadcasting regulation in Canada writes: "William Mallone argued that the CBC had learned from the CRBC and that 'up to 1939 there was no particular problem' with political programming. As previously

---

264 Hooke, *30 + 5*, 139.
265 Graham, "As Canadian as Possible," iii.
266 Graham, "As Canadian as Possible," 127.
267 Graham, "As Canadian as Possible," 220–21.

discussed, the corporation wanted to earn the support of as wide a base as possible—placing such a priority on this that it was not firm in its enforcement of the regulations. In order to fulfill its goal of connecting Canadians, however, the corporation felt it needed to air commentaries on current events by, what it determined to be, qualified speakers, frequently university faculty."[268]

The qualified speakers were obviously those who would transmit what was in accord with the government's objectives. Graham goes on to mention, that "some took the CBC's actions as evidence of government censorship and left-wing propaganda."[269] But even those on the Left, confirm Pound's and Douglas's contentions about the media and the Alberta Social Credit experience in the Canadian context. This is not a Right versus Left debate, but has to do with a universal concern regarding political control of the media. Siegel comes to the same conclusion concerning the control of the media in Canada:

> The media . . . are not an independent source of power, in the words of Denis McQuail, "the political and economic influence which flows through the media has origins in the power centres of society."
>
> McQuail's statement raises questions about the nature of the connection between the public and the Establishment provided by the media. Does it favour the status quo, so that the media are agents of conservatism rather than of social change? Is it designed to mobilize the population in support of policies affecting the interlocking political, business, and media elites? Noam Chomsky provided affirmative answers to these questions. In his CBC Massey Lectures, Chomsky referred to the process of mobilization of support as the "engineering of consent". This propaganda model of communications provides a problematic perspective on the exercise of freedom and views the media as instruments of thought control.[270]

As stated before, Social Credit policies cannot be judged based on what happened in Alberta, where any Douglas Social Credit policies were declared null and void. What happened in Alberta leads to confusion concerning Douglasite/Poundian contentions and policies, especially the belief by some that Gesell scrip is a policy from Douglas. Even so, the Alberta party did accomplish much in following Social

---

[268] Graham, "As Canadian as Possible," 221.
[269] Graham, "As Canadian as Possible," 222.
[270] Siegel, *Politics and the Media*, 23.

Credit philosophy. Until recently, it had been the longest serving political government in Canada, lasting over 35 years. It was only superseded as the longest by the Progressive Conservative Association of Alberta and their later name formulations. Even the Progressive Conservative Party in Alberta, it can be contended, was and is the continuation of Social Credit philosophy, partly a result of former premier Ernest Manning's book: *Political Realignment: A Challenge to Thoughtful Canadians*. It argued for the uniting of Canadian conservatives in one party, which undermined the Social Credit movement.[271] What remains from a party that fell out of power in 1971? It is portrayed today as a Canadian anomaly, a *flash* in the pan, though a *35 year* flash.

Monetary reformers often complement the Bank of North Dakota as a State-owned bank that can leverage its own funds as the depository of State funds. At the same time, they ignore the Alberta Treasury Branch (ATB) established by the Alberta Social Credit government in 1938, which likewise leverages its own provincial funds to create financial benefits for Albertans and is "seven times larger in terms of assets (loans) than its peer, the Bank of North Dakota."[272] As emphasized earlier, Douglas did not believe in the establishment of one National Bank, or the nationalization of the banking system, but wanted private banks operating as they do today, loaning to producers, but making a profit by serving the common good under a National Monetary Policy. That policy would be overseen by the treasury, a government credit office, or other designated office. Consumer incomes would be supplemented with debt-free money creation, i.e., new credit issued directly to businesses and consumers whenever there exists a gap between goods and services available and consumer purchasing power. Finally, there would also be money creation by the state for actual government expenses (to be recovered by taxation). Within the unfortunate context of the reigning private banking practice, the creation of a Provincial Bank, where the government can use its own deposits to leverage money creation, is still an act in conformity with the Social Credit distributist philosophy.

Since 1937, due in large part to Social Credit party governance, Alberta has not had a provincial sales tax. The province was originally the first province to introduce a sales tax in 1936, as it had defaulted on debt payment, but after the initial year, the province did not collect a sales tax. Many contend that Alberta's rich oil profits made it possible to not have a sales tax, and likewise that oil led to Social

---

271 Bell, Edward. "The Rise of the Lougheed Conservatives," 474.

272 Ascah and Anielski, *Alberta's Public Bank*, 1.

Credit's long continual election success, but the oil boom did not start until 1947. For the other provinces in Canada it would be unthinkable to end the sales tax as Alberta had done. Social Credit created the mentality/philosophy among its residents that would not allow a sales tax to return to Alberta. As in Poundian parlance, a just historical precedent had taken root; a *paideuma* had been established. The currently resource rich neighbour east of Alberta, i.e., Saskatchewan, should be able to do the same. But even with long-term economic success, Saskatchewan maintains the provincial sales tax.

Beyond Alberta itself, there is a direct line to the Alaska Permanent Fund, a fund that provides yearly a dividend to every resident, child or adult, from the State's oil revenue. This was in keeping with Douglas's proposal that every individual is entitled to a dividend, but Douglas based his dividend on any gap between money in existence, in the economy, and the prices for goods and services available. Such Social Credit policies of money creation were not capable of being implemented in Canada on the provincial level. But under a Social Credit government in Alberta, it was decided to issue, on an irregular basis, a dividend from the oil revenue, but only to adults. In a paper written in 2002, comparing the current Alberta practice of placing money in the so-called *Heritage Fund* in contrast to Alaska, reference is made to the Social Credit dividends issued in Alberta: "It is ironic that in the mid-1950s, just prior to an election, the Alberta Government of the day issued a $25 'oil dividend' to every (adult) person in the province. Today, the State of Alaska pays a dividend to individuals but Alberta persists with the policy that government knows best. Oddities abound: Alberta was the first province in Canada to impose a sales tax; it was removed in the midst of the 1950s oil boom. Currently Alberta is the only province without a sales tax."[273] This passage is misleading, implying that a sales tax was collected up to the 1950s. The tax was collected only in the year 1936, though the income tax law remained legally in effect until it was repealed in the 1950s.

The *Alberta Heritage Savings Trust Fund* of 1976, referred to above, was created by the Conservative Party of Alberta. It has been argued that this is certainly in name and practice a reflection of the *Cultural Heritage* philosophy of Douglas and was due to the Conservative party's almost wholesale appropriation of the Social Credit party machine in the 1970s. The Social Credit party did not create the *Heritage Fund* directly, but it certainly influenced its creation *via* Douglas's philosophy that emphasized the rights of the individual

[273] Warrack and Keddie, *Natural Resource Trust Funds*, 14.

and defended the right of all members of society to share in the abundance created by the Cultural Heritage. The current fund is meant to provide Albertans a guarantee that wealth will be available in the future, despite the expected future fall in oil and gas revenue. This Heritage Fund, as referenced above by Warrack, is criticized for not being as successful as the Alaska option. Indeed, even from the point of view of Social Credit philosophy, the Alaska practice is a better distributist option, giving the people their wealth as a dividend. This has even been suggested by an *Edmonton Journal* article.[274] In summary, while what happened in Alberta and Alaska was not Douglas Social Credit policy (which the courts had disallowed in Alberta), it did reflect the Social Credit distributist philosophy.

If one wishes to experience the effect that a periodic issue of money as a credit, rather than as a debt, creates, as advocated by Douglas/Pound, one needs to visit Alaska in Autumn. This is the season during which the Alaska Dividend is released each year for each child and adult.[275] It is not something that Alaskans will allow to be taken from them; they understand that this is their rightful dividend, as citizens of the State of Alaska. Again, a thought heritage has been created, a Poundian *paideuma*. It is an autumn feast of *Thanksgiving*—true financial abundance in Alaska, while most of the developed world experiences autumn as a season of increased credit card debt, leading into the Christmas season.

Pound's passage continues with a reference to banners that were taken after the sea battle of Lepanto. Pound perhaps had seen these banners: "One of Ali Pasha's banners is in the Church of Santo Stefano in Pisa. Another is in the Palazzo Ducale of Venice. Pasha's flagship banner decorated with Quranic verses from the 48th surah Al-Fath (The Victory) hung near the tomb of St. Pius V in Santa

---

274 "If Alberta had followed Alaska's model since inception in 1976/77—including 25 percent annual resource revenue contributions, inflation-proofing and annual dividends—the Heritage Fund would be worth approximately $234.2 billion today compared to $16.2 billion. In total, it could have paid out $101.5 billion in dividends to Albertans, which would average $1,018 (inflation-adjusted) per Albertan annually." Hill, "Dividends to Albertans."

275 Cf. Waldholz, "Alaska's annual dividend.": "[T]he dividend is overwhelmingly popular. That may seem obvious, but it's interesting, given a second point: the dividend matters a lot more if you're poor than if you're rich. For the 20 percent of Alaska households averaging $35,000 a year or less, the PFD is a major source of income. That's one reason Alaska has one of the most equal—or least unequal—distributions of wealth in the U. S., Knapp said, 'there's many other things that enter into income equality, but certainly we know that the dividend is a contributing factor.'"

Maria Maggiore."[276] This is the Poundian device of juxtaposing the past with the present to the detriment of the present. He juxtaposes this affirmation of the sovereignty of the individual nations of Europe that had willingly united in the Holy League, the *Allies* of that time, to sacrifice their lives against a common enemy. The result was they freed the many Christian galley slaves held by the Ottomans and they ended centuries of Ottoman Muslim encroachment on Christian lands. Pound contrasts this with the contemporary situation of the World War II *Allies*. Within the Greek waters of the Gulf of Patras, the site of the sea battle of Lepanto is found. Unfortunately, the current rulers of Europe, so-called *Western Civilization* or the heirs of Rome, had surrendered their fellow Christians along with their Muslim neighbours in the Balkans, the land just north of Greece, to an atheistic empire with more in common with Tolkien's fictional Mordor than any past historical empire. Likewise, that same Western Civilization had surrendered the issuing of money "control of the outlets" to private banking interests. For Pound, the moral corruption, and the spiritual weakness of these once Christian nations, their betrayal of half of Europe, are caused by their monetary surrender to the usurocracy who have the financial power to determine state policy. The "printed quality" is kept down, as it is not state coinage nor even paper money, but mere bank cheques and bookkeeping numbers, reflecting no historical pedigree nor beauty.

The second passage begins by giving examples of just how this is done, e.g., by making a dollar look like a franc and making the franc worth a centesimo: "[the] results of a managed and calculated depreciation of the currency."[277] The implication is that the banks, to their advantage, can use the currency exchange rate to make a profit by planning a rise or fall in the exchange rate.

The third passage begins with a series of luminous details which reflect Pound's hatred of war. Pound paraphrases a statement made by second lieutenant Schmidt to the effect that the enemy are "'[g]ood chaps'" and that it's a shame "we have to fight 'em." Pound's *Scriptor Cantilenae* emphasizes that "[h]ate is not born in the trenches / nor among 2nd. lieutenants." Pound's hatred of war is intensified by his conviction that war is the usurer's harvest and by his strong belief that the usurocracy is directly involved in the munitions industry.

The fourth passage pays tribute to Venice. Venice had been the largest contributor of ships to the Holy League at Lepanto. Pound

[276] Rutler, "The Banners of Lepanto."
[277] Terrell, *A Companion*, Vol II, 676.

states that Venice produced more great individual men in its history from Selvo to Franchetti than any other state. This affirmation of the individual is important to Pound as it is to Douglas, since both believe in the uniqueness and sacredness of the human individual. A nation will only flourish if it makes possible for individuals to have the ability to flourish through leisure/contemplation.

The fifth passage makes mention of Larrañaga, i.e., Pedro Juan Manuel Larrañaga, the Peruvian economist and monetary reformer whose definitive work in the field of monetary reform is entitled *Gold, Glut and Government: a New Economic Dawn*. Larrañaga was familiar with C. H. Douglas's writings and quotes him as an authority in his book. Pound's reference to "fashion" in Larrañaga, seems to be drawn from this passage: "[The] maintenance of a bare subsistence does not suffice to keep our industrial producing plant fully occupied. New appetites must be discovered. Fashions are not enough. The state must intervene with its appetites, no longer warlike and conquering in the military sphere, but conquering in the sphere of constructive social service. Public works, schools, communications, health, irrigation . . . . The question is to share equitably in the unearned increments and increase of value created by the State and by the community itself without withholding due reward from those who excel in their labour and exertions."[278]

"[U]nearned increments," from other evidence in Larrañaga, is certainly a reference to C. H. Douglas's famous use of the term. Despite Larrañaga's references to Douglas, and praise by Pound in *The Cantos*, one must be careful not to interpret the whole of Larrañaga's economic vision as in full harmony with Douglas or with Pound. Larrañaga, as an admirer of Douglas, also expresses even more admiration for J. M. Keynes, an admiration not shared by either Pound or Douglas, as has been seen previously. Earlier in the book, Larrañaga, refers to the need for modern economists to think, among other suggestions, like a "French dress designer." Larrañaga goes on to state: "The dress designer would remember the economic worthlessness of last year's models, the incalculable effect of demand upon all new 'creations' of human ingenuity, art, and propaganda; the precariousness of assets based on a frozen inventory, the importance of goodwill and fickleness of markets."[279]

As shown earlier, Douglas stressed the waste of human effort induced by the need to create demand *via* new products: the constant change

---

[278] Larrañaga, *Gold, Glut and Government*, 97–98.
[279] Larrañaga, *Gold, Glut and Government*, 22–23.

of designs to create new demand, rendering past technology obsolete by inventing something new, and the need of advertising to generate demand for new goods and services. Douglas also stressed how finance will invest capital into new machinery production, even though the old machinery is still capable of production and in good order.

All of this, according to Douglas, plays into the need in Orthodox economics to keep society on the work treadmill, as only future borrowing for production and consumption can normally pay for present debts to the banks. So often new *fashions* are not what we need, nor are they worthy of consumption, but the new money and treadmill of wasteful production must be maintained to avoid economic collapse.

The fifth passage goes on to reiterate the fundamental Poundian position: that there can be no science without clear definitions and there can be no progress in understanding and practice without common definitions of words in order to make discussion of science fruitful. As always, Pound applies this principle pre-eminently to the science of economics.

Likewise, as with Pound and Douglas, Larrañaga also criticizes the economists who make it impossible to comprehend what they are saying, especially for the average person. Larrañaga quotes in his book the wise words of Mr. Piero Straffa from an issue of the *Economic Journal*, and Straffa's criticism of Dr. Hayek's lecture on Prices and Production: "For, however peculiar and probably unprecedented their conclusions may be, there is one respect in which the lectures collected in this volume fully uphold the tradition which modern writers on money are rapidly establishing, that of *unintelligibility*."[280]

The sixth passage emphasizes the lack of moral scruples among financiers at that time, i.e., in the 19th century, and speaks of this lack of moral scruples as being common business practice.

The seventh passage contains advice from Bülow, i.e., Friedrich Wilhelm Freiherr von Bülow, the Prussian general who aided the defeat of Napoleon, about not wasting time in getting into newspapers, but rather to get control of the news agencies. C. H. Douglas constantly stresses the centralization and control of the press by the financial interests, particularly through their control of the news agencies. Pound then gives us a summary of much of the monetary-historical lore which has preceded. As mentioned earlier in reference to Canto 89, Pound emphasizes that gold was under the control of the Pontifex or Roman High Priest until the time of Julius Caesar who had usurped this priestly prerogative. Pound then mentions the twelve silver to

---

[280] Larrañaga, *Gold, Glut and Government*, 8.

one gold exchange rate in weight of Byzantium, where the emperor had inherited the prerogative of the Roman High Priest with respect to the coinage of gold. He then mentions the Caliph Abd-el-Melik who set up the Muslim ratio of six silver to one gold in opposition to Rome. These standards held firm until the sacking of Constantinople by the Venetians in 1204. Pound then goes on to point out that Del Mar cites twelve cases of tickets or non-precious metals being used for coinage.[281] The first of these was the use of iron in Sparta.[282]

The eighth passage mentions "that Mond killed the English Review," whose editor was Ford Madox Ford. Sir Alfred Mond was the board chairman of the Imperial Chemicals combine who offered financial backing to Ford Madox Ford's *English Review*. Once he had control of the publication, Mond dismissed Ford as editor and then discontinued the publication of the periodical. Because of this, Ford would take a dozen years, an "interval," before he would go to Paris and edit a publication again.[283] Further along in this passage Pound reiterates that great monetary luminous detail concerning the fact that Alexander the Great paid "the debts of his soldiers." He then goes on to point out, with respect to what happened after the king lost the exclusive right over the power of issue, that even Alexander Del Mar "gasps with astonishment."

Pound then mentions three monetary reform writers, i.e., McNair Wilson, Larrañaga and Tremaine, who also are astonished that the *Royal Prerogative* is no longer the right of the King or the Nation to be used for the benefit of the citizens. Instead, private individuals, through the banks they control, are allowed to practice money creation for their own benefit, personal wealth, and private ends. Pound's reference to "2 in the morning," indicates that Pound believes McNair Wilson, Larrañaga, and Tremaine have in some way contributed to bringing us past the darkest hour of midnight, closer to a new economic dawn.

---

281 "Numerary Currency": Del Mar, *A History of the Precious*, 352–55.

282 Lycurgus, of Sparta, whose laws in the ninth century "interdicted the working of the mines, and even forbade the importation of gold and silver into Greece. This was after coins of these metals had circulated in that country for many centuries; and when this currency was superseded by the iron numeraries (not coins, as is commonly supposed) of the great lawgiver." Del Mar, *A History of the Precious*, 344. Del Mar ends chapter XXXIX, pages 353–55, by noting that silver and gold mining was often historically forbidden due to their evil influence and subsequent environmental degradation. Del Mar argues that, just as America abolished the cruelty of slavery and ended the suffering caused by the British Poor Laws, the negative moral impact of gold and silver mining can only be addressed by ceasing these activities entirely.

283 Terrell, *A Companion*, Vol. II, 681.

The Douglasite policy of returning control of monetary policy to the state for the benefit of the common citizen, as expressed in Douglas's policy of filling the gap between goods and services and that of money in circulation by issuing periodic dividends to all citizens, is often dismissed as mere utopian policy. Pound delved deeply into history to show that it was not utopian at all, but was the *norm*, whenever and wherever there was a just government that served the common good of the community. It was the norm in Medieval times. Most men in the medieval period worked with their wife and children on the land, or in a shop below or by their home, as was the custom worldwide. The Scottish Highland clearances are symbolic of what was to follow, especially with the Industrial Revolution, and were a direct result of the establishment of the new Bank of England. Dispossessed people were forced to move from their home villages to larger towns for work and/or to migrate overseas. This mass migration, due to economics and war, continues unabated. Societies, cultures, and languages suffer, but it is individuals and families who are the victims. Modern societies, as part of government planned policies, continue the attack on families by making the houses empty during *work* hours. The old are placed in senior housing and children are taken to schools, which have become mere places to keep children out of trouble, so that their parents can work. Infants go to day care. Mothers are expected to find work and this *employment* is often to be had in these newly created jobs that never existed: public schools, day cares, old age homes, etc.

The effects of the Douglas Social Credit policies are hard to predict. At a minimum, as with Odysseus, Social Credit would allow all to return home, if they so desired. Paid work would still need to be done, but for the mass of the community it would either be performed by individuals working fewer hours, and/or by some choosing to remain at home and live off their dividends. Such a plan could be subsidised by working a small plot of land or developing a craft. This artistic element was one of the attractions for Pound to Social Credit. One would likewise be able to choose to care for elderly parents or instruct their children at home, instead of opting for state or private schools. In an age when millions are expected to be replaced by technological advances, such as artificial intelligence, Douglas offered and still offers the only solution to the Central Bank's unending mantra for its all-devouring golden calf: ceaseless *economic growth* and *job creation* to obstruct the financial reality of what could be, i.e., a *culture of leisure*.

Canto 107 is primarily a tribute to Sir Edward Coke, the great 16th and 17th century commentator on English common law:

1. they had not Magna Charta
in ver l'estate, Queen of Akragas
resistent,
Templum aedificavit
Segesta
hospitality . . . of the ancient ornaments and
commandations of England
II. Inst. xxi

. . . .

2. so that after one set of damned scoundrels (tonsured)
another set of damned scoundrels
(untonsured)
the foulest of all these Jimmy Stuart.
Coke: the clearest mind ever in England

. . . .

3. That is our PIVOT
Statute de Merton:

. . . .

4. corruption of Symbol
then the invasion of Bede's time
and the hog-wash with King James
his "version"
till in 1850 to unfashion the lingua latina;
to drive truth out of curricula.
Coke's quotes might have told something.
Alex, Antoninus in blot-out
and Randolph,
not to distreine corne in sheafes
Edward "Mirror of Princes"
Statute of Merton, Cap. Five.
5 groats to an ounce of silver
not subject to forrein lawes.
One thousand two sixty seven
King Henry's 52

(Canto 107)

The first passage employs a typical Poundian device of juxtaposing the past with the present to the detriment of the present. The French did not have the Magna Carta, so they did not have the possibility of making a stand against financial tyranny based on common law: "Coke says the statute applies to all nobility but 'extendeth not to any person ecclisiasticall,' and, 'all this . . . was (. . . for the advancement and maintenance of that great peacemaker, and love-holder, hospitality) one of the auncient ornaments, and commendations of the kingdome of

England' [Chap. XXI]."[284] The English Common Law system as commented on by Coke in his *Institutes*, says Pound, provides a bulwark against financial and monetary oppression. Pound's emphasis upon the literacy and clarity of thought possessed by Coke is interesting in the light of C. H. Douglas's condemnation of the modern legal system as being simply the handmaiden of finance.

C. H. Douglas devotes Chapter I of Part II of *Social Credit* to the close link between Law and Finance. He emphasizes that a vast amount of the contemporary legal system has developed to aid the financier in his harvest of debt. He points out that a great deal of modern *justice* exists to guarantee the safety and security of what is an unjust financial system. Pound shares with Douglas this attitude towards the modern legal system and, like Douglas, he has a profound respect for medieval common law based, as it was, on the clear thinking of the canon lawyers. The soundness of Coke's thinking stands in contrast with the perversion of truth, which in Pound's view, passes for modern law. The greatest proof, says Pound, of the decay of the modern legal and educational system is that Coke has been driven out of the curricula. For Douglas, both modern law and modern education exist to make the world safe for the financiers and not to disseminate justice and truth.

The second passage also contains a reference to King James I, as the "foulest of all" the new breed of untonsured scoundrels who descended upon England like a brood of vipers. This new set of untonsured scoundrels is probably in reference to the seizing of estates of Bishops and monasteries by James, especially early on as King of Scotland. As under Henry the VIII, the seizing of Church property and turning it over to the favoured nobility continued unabated. *Tonsured*, a sign of consecration, that something is set aside as holy, refers to the rightful owners, the deprived monastics and clergy, or those who should be holy if performing a holy function.

Sir Edward Coke was removed in 1616 from the Court of King's Bench for his opposition to the transferring of ecclesiastical property to Richard Neile, a "tonsured scoundrel," who was given a bishopric and its revenue though he did not reside there, by "Jimmy Stuart" i.e., James I, the foulest of the untonsured scoundrels. "Coke: the clearest mind ever in England," is called thus by Pound because his judgements are based on upholding the laws of England against the King's unlawful commands: "These lines express the attitude of Coke during his struggles against the ecclesiastical courts, when they were taking jurisdiction in cases Coke believed should be tried under the

---

[284] Terrell, *A Companion*, Vol. II, 696.

common law. In King James's time both church people (tonsured) and nonchurch lawyers (untonsured) tried to play safe by pleasing the king, who promoted the ecclesiastical courts."[285]

The third passage refers to the Statute of Merton as "our PIVOT," i.e., the foundation upon which any system of financial and monetary justice must be based. Pound refers to the Statute of Merton as "our PIVOT" just as certain writings of Confucius were referred to by Pound as our "unwobbling pivot."

The fourth passage speaks of the corruption of symbol, the invasion in the time of the Venerable Bede, and the hogwash of the King James's English version of the Bible; all contributing to what Pound earlier called the "brain-wash." The connection with the Latin tongue, and thereby with the historical past of Western civilization, were being replaced in the name of progress.

The 1850 reference to the *lingua latina* is an allusion to a 1917 article in *The Atlantic Monthly*. For Pound, who loved Roman civilization, and loved the Greek and Latin languages, such an article titled "The Case Against Compulsory Latin," would have drawn his ire: "No one can reasonably maintain that the American educated generation today is less well equipped for its life work than the generation which graduated from the American colleges in 1850. On the contrary, all the old professions maintain a much higher standard for admission and in practice than they maintained in 1850, and a large group of new professions has been added to the old."[286]

For Pound, without Latin and Greek, we cannot understand the writings and heritage of Rome, and he saw this as something planned, as if the knowledge from the past is something dangerous to those in power. We cannot understand Coke whose "quotes might have told something." The history of Alexander the Great is cut off from us. The deeds and history of Antoninus Pius, and John Randolph of Roanoke were also blotted out of the curricula. In *Impact* quoted in section II of this book, Pound stated "Latin is sacred, grain is sacred. Who destroyed the mystery of fecundity, bringing in the cult of sterility?"[287] Pound then goes on, in the same page, to list the things that had led to Bolshevik *atheism* in the modern world wiping out "the consciousness of the greatest mystery" (Greek: *mysterion*, Latin: *sacramentum*, a visible sign): the Catholic Church. The history of the past, the ability to receive life-giving truth, ideas, culture from our ancestors comes

---

285 Terrell, *A Companion*, Vol. II, 697.
286 Eliot, "The Case Against," 360–61.
287 Pound, *Impact*, 55.

from language. Sterility for Pound is due to a monetary system that, since the creation of the Bank of England, has created wars, taxes, economic booms, and busts, as the only sure thing in life. Many contend that the loss of knowledge of Latin in the Eastern Empire, and loss of knowledge of Greek in the Western Empire, were major causes of the great schism between Constantinople, i.e., the Orthodox Church, and Rome, i.e., the Catholic Church. The sacredness of Latin for Pound (Pound not being a Catholic) is not only because it is the traditional liturgical language of the West, but is one of two vessels that transmits the wisdom of our classic Roman heritage. Pound is returning to the vindication of a basic Douglasite postulate concerning the system of general education, and media, as a system of mass hypnotism,[288] that no longer transmits the wisdom of past cultures and civilizations. Such knowledge of the past may cause us to question policies, laws, ideas, and opinions of our current modern culture.

Pound goes on in this passage to refer to a prohibition in the Statute of Merton against the distraining of corn in sheafs. Terrell explains that this was to protect a widow from paying rent in sheafs of corn. Instead, she was to have the protection of the law, so that she pays only when the corn is gathered and therefore properly weighed. Edward is "Mirror of Princes," i.e., what a prince should be, because of his prohibition of usury: "but Coke notes in 'Statute of Merton,' Chap. V, that, nevertheless, England had great profit because of usury at a time when 'the ounce of silver was five groats.'"[289]

Nevertheless, the edict of King Henry emphasizes the regal prerogative over coinage and the necessity of this regal prerogative not being subject to foreign laws but only to local control. This emphasis upon the regal prerogative over coinage and the necessity of independence from foreign financial control is a theme in C. H. Douglas's writings. He emphasizes that, in England, the state has given away the sovereign right over coinage: "since the Bank Act of 1928, the State has resigned its sovereign rights over Finance in favour of the international private organisation known as the Bank of England."[290] For Pound and Douglas, the king must be *boss* of the coinage and not a gang of international usurers using the deceptively named Bank *of England* as their instrument of subjugation.

---

[288] Cf. Douglas, *Social Credit*, 202–03: "With a majority of persons there is (no doubt as the result of the collective hypnotism generally referred to as education) a tendency to uphold a social ideal from which their personal existence is a continuous effort to escape."

[289] Terrell, *A Companion*, Vol. II, 699.

[290] Douglas, *The Monopoly of Credit*, 49.

Canto 107 continues with its fascinating monetary-economic luminous details:

> Was new coin 1560,
>   '65, dutch weavers in Norwich
> at terms, whores in St Paul's,
>   Trinity, Michaelmas,
>   Hillary is from Jan 23rd.
> Each wench to a pillar
>   "as do the Serjeants at lawe".
> To use grain for food only;
>   build no more houses in London
> de heretico comburendo
>   Bacon for, Coke opposing.
> In a white sheet in the Savoy
>   500 marks, be imprisoned
>   Sir Henry (1628) Martin gave sentence.
> Invasion of the rights of his subjects
>   3 months to *habeas*
>   B. 18.
>
> (Canto 107)

The passage above makes mention of the new coin issued by Elizabeth in 1560, which replaced the degraded coinage.[291] Most of the passage is referenced by Terrell. Coke remembers as a youth how Dutch weavers fleeing religious persecution had settled in Norwich and revived the town. Next, Pound is referencing Coke, who refers to "whores," i.e., women who were in economic distress that would hang around the court houses. Those in "high" repute would debase women in financial distress. Finally Pound stresses that grain is to be used for food only, referencing a law that prohibited grain following a bad harvest to be used "for starching clothing or for any purpose except that of food."[292] Pound then mentions the difference of opinion that existed between Francis Bacon and Coke "de heretico comburendo", which concerned the burning of a heretic. Under Henry IV in 1401, an English statute was passed for the burning of heretics. This was a secular law, not ecclesiastical, targeting the Lollards of the time. But the law was used by the established Church of England: "'of burning heretics.' The name of a writ issued by a bishops court in 1612 sentencing Bartholomew Legate and Edward Wrightman to be burned as heretics. They were. Coke opposed the 'monstrous writ,' saying the bishops court did not have jurisdiction. Francis Bacon and others said

291 Terrell, *A Companion*, Vol. II, 699.
292 Terrell, *A Companion*, Vol. II, 700.

conviction in bishops court would suffice."[293] Pound is underlying the perversion of the legal system. One man, Coke, upheld the legal rights of the accused, while all others, sworn to uphold the same, accepted the unjust decision. This allowed an ecclesiastical court's ruling to be upheld, when such a court had no jurisdiction to pass a capital sentence. Pound is emphasizing the righteousness of Edward Coke, the great English legal authority, who declared concerning money: "It is misprision of High Treason, for forging of money, which neither is the money of this Realm of England nor currant within the same."[294] Many central banks are government owned and therefore we can't accuse them of forgery when they create the currency.

The passage ends with the story of Frances, the daughter of Coke, being forced to wear "a white sheet" and walk to the Savoy, as punishment for being found guilty of adultery. The sentence of public penance was imposed by the judge Sir Henry Martin in 1628.[295] These same legal officials may have debased women in financial distress, as Pound earlier alludes to by "wench to a pillar." And yet they sit in judgement for similar crimes they or their fellow legal officials likewise frequently commit. C. H. Douglas constantly attacked the legal system as the handmaiden of Finance. Both Pound and Douglas are convinced that the real criminal is the usurer, but as with Sir Henry, or his fellow *respectable* members of society, no one will prosecute them, for whatever criminal immorality they commit.

In Canto 108, contrary to the wishful thinking of certain critics, the monetary-economic and Douglasite themes continue to be emphasized:

1. COMMINUIT
            there is frost on the rock's face
nurse of industry (25 Edward III)
            BRUM
"alla" at Verona
            of courage
having none hath no care to defend it

. . . .

2. From the Charter to the Petition 1628
            in June and toward twilight
                                    DROIT FAIT
Statutum Tallagio
                        Lambarde on Valla
                                        "all monopolies"

---

[293] Terrell, *A Companion*, Vol. II, 700.
[294] Pound, *Impact*, vii.
[295] Terrell, *A Companion*, Vol. II, 700.

"nor against his will into Ireland"
autarchia
not cloth from out of the Realm
Owse, Wherfe, Nid, Derwent,
Swale, Yore & Tine
Post Festum Sancti Hilarii
mults de mals et disherisons
18 E. 1 a.d.
1290
ne curge de S. Edward
prochainement
and his father H. 3 before him
ne quis injuriam —
salvum conductum
18 die Jul. 11, 18
E.1
die decimoctavo
was 15 000 three score.
Divers had banished
but the usuries, no King before him.
Holl fol 285
Wals hypod
Florilegius Dunstable
Angliae exeuntibus,

(Canto 108)

The first passage refers to a judicious decree of King Edward I Longshanks, referred to by some as Edward III, a degree Pound characterizes as the nurse of industry. This statute was issued in 1297: "Loans against the will of the subjects are against reason and the franchises of the land." "Coke quoted it in a House of Commons session during which Dudley Digges said: 'meum and tuum ... [is] the nurse of industry, the mother of courage; for if a man hath no property, he has no care to defend it.'"[296] The English law confirmed the right to private property, even against any possible future law, that might take away the rights of individuals and family to property.

The second passage begins with a reference to the time from the Magna Carta to a petition Coke made in 1628. The lines: "all monopolies" stress Pound's contempt for monopolies of which the most nefarious is the money monopoly. In the words of Edward Coke: "Generally all monopolies are against the great Charter, because they are against the liberty and freedom of the subject and against the law

[296] Terrell, *A Companion*, Vol. II, 704.

of the land."[297] The passage goes on to paraphrase certain decrees of King Edward I forbidding the importing of cloth from outside England: "In the past, kings had imposed a custom on wool, to which Parliament had assented. The wool was converted into cloth and often exported. When attempts were made to extend this tariff to wool already made into cloth, they protested."[298] Individuals were punished for creating products of greater value to trade, manufacturing cloth at home rather than exporting their raw resource, i.e., wool. Pound's constant emphasis upon the domestic market rather than foreign trade is purely Douglasite.

Pound in this Canto stresses the necessity of medieval England to be self-sufficient in economic matters. Why export an unfinished raw material when you can manufacture the raw material into finished products of greater value for use at home? Overseas trade is only for what you do not possess and need for the local market, exchanged for finished goods when your home market is sufficiently saturated. C. H. Douglas constantly emphasizes that, in modern times, foreign trade is pursued as a means whereby nations sell the cream of their production to get enough purchasing power into the country so that their citizens can buy up the skim-milk of their own production. Douglas maintains that the system of foreign trade does not alleviate the shortage of purchasing power within the body economic. Nations, says Douglas, simply are paid for their exports by more raw materials with which to manufacture more exports, or are paid in irredeemable export credits. This is why Douglas refers to *foreign trade* under the present system of debt-finance as a myth or a hoax. All through his writings Douglas constantly reiterates that the home market is the best market and that competition for foreign markets, necessitated by the domestic lack of purchasing power in every country, is the direct and foremost cause of war. Douglas maintains that commercial warfare is always preliminary to military warfare.[299]

This passage ends recalling that King Edward I banished the usurers from his realm by a decree in the year 1290. The decree speaks of, mults de mals et disherisons — many evils and disinheritings, caused by usury. Pound mentions that "15,000 three score;" Jews, "left the

[297] Terrell, *A Companion*, Vol. II, 705.

[298] Terrell, *A Companion*, Vol. II, 705.

[299] Cf. Douglas, *Monopoly of Credit*, 94: "[T]he financial *system*, . . . is, beyond question, the chief cause of international friction. Since . . . no nation can buy its own production, a struggle for markets in which to dispose of the surplus is inevitable. The translation of this commercial struggle into a military context is merely a question of time and opportunity."

country under the anti-usury law."[300] and gives Hollinshed's chronicle, folio 285, as the source. Terrell quotes the legal scholar J. M. Rigg: "This statute [Edward I] forbids usury but also forbids the persecution of the Jews. As Coke points out, many had decisively banished the Jews and discriminated against them racially but Edward I saw the injustice of this and merely made a law against usury.' He also made a law assuring those Jews who wanted to leave England that 'they might have the king's writ to the sherifes for their safe conduct."[301]

The basic and fundamental Douglasite theme of the statal or regal nature of coinage, i.e., currency and credit, re-appears further along in Canto 108:

> Nor set any stone in gold
> except it be natural
> 28 Edward I, a.D. 1300
> auxy soit signe teste de leopard
> and false stone not set in true gold
> Pertaine to the King onely
> to put a value to coin
> And to make price of the quantity
> Cap xx
> . . . .
> ELIZABETH
> Angliae amor,
> ad valorem reducta.
> To take wood to melt ore
> non extat memoria
> . . . ardendam, fundendam
> (Canto 108)

"Cap. xx" refers us to King Edward the I's, Law entitled "Vessels of Gold shall be essayed, touched, and marked. The King's Prerogative shall be saved." The law is provided in English and French and the cited words can be found in the text or in the side comments.[302] Pound's lines: "Pertaine to the King onely / to put a value to coin / And to make price of the quantity," are derived from the writings of Sir Edward Coke.[303] Coke confirms the regal prerogative over coinage. These lines stress the fact that only the king can put a value on coin and stipulate what the buying power of that total coinage shall be.

---

300 Terrell, *A Companion*, 706.
301 Terrell, *A Companion*, 706.
302 Ruffhead, *The Statutes at Large*, 146–47.
303 Terrell, *A Companion*, Vol II, 708.

These lines of Coke interpret and confirm the conclusion of the law stated in Cap. XX, which was not quoted by Pound: "(13) And if any Goldsmith be attainted hereafter, because that he hath done otherwise than before is ordained, he shall be punished by Imprisonment, and by Ransom at the King's Pleasure. (14) And notwithstanding all these Things before-mentioned, or any Point of them, both the King and his Council, and all they that were present at the making of this Ordinance, will and intend that the Right and Prerogative of his Crown shall be saved to him in all Things."[304]

Thus the *scriptor cantilenae*, in the persona of Ezra Pound, is once again proving the veracity of the Douglasite position concerning the regal prerogative over coinage by appealing to English history and the legal patrimony of England. Pound continues the theme of the royal prerogative with a reference to Elizabeth I in the lines: "ELIZABETH / Angliae amor, / ad valorem reducta," i.e., "Elizabeth / the love of England, / to the reduced value." This refers to Elizabeth's exercising the royal prerogative by restoring the English debased coinage during her reign. This is partly a phrase derived from an inscription on Queen Elizabeth's tomb: "Moneta ad suum valorem reducta, 'she brought money back to its true value.'"[305]

Canto 108 continues with its monetary-economic luminous details:

> 1. & souls of the dead defrauded
>   35 Edward
> send or cause to be sent out of the
>   Kingdom
> and that the seal be in custody of four men dignioribus
>   & the prior
> alien abbots may visit;
> . . . .
> 2. damnable customs introduc of new in Roma.
> . . . .
> 3. HORSEFAIRE from 10 of the clock before noon
>   until sunset
> the queenes dominions
>   Phil, Mar
> Colour, with one speciall mark at the least
>   of every such horse, mare, colt, gelding
>   on paine of default 40 shillings
>   ridden openly for one hour
>   and after 10 in the morning

304 Ruffhead, *The Statutes at Large*, 147.
305 Terrell, *A Companion*, Vol. II, 709.

as might be for Cadilacs, Fords & such other
ridden, led, walked or kept standing
& in free markets to the book-keeper one penny
no toll

Coke, Iong Ching
responsabili
par cretance del ewe which is
french for floodwater.
Who for bridges
reparando;
For every new cottage 4 acres
Stat. de 31 Eliz.
Angliae amor.
(Canto 108)

Pound by "35" is noting he is referring to a law in the last year of King Edward I, his 35th year of reign, 1307. From Cap. I: "Alms being not given to the Poor, the Sick, and Feeble, the Healths of the Living and the Souls of the Dead be miserably defrauded, Hospitality, Almsgiving, and other godly Deeds do cease."[306] From Cap. II: "[S]ecretly or openly, by any Device or Means, carry or send, or by any Means cause to be sent, any Tax imposed by the Abbots, Priors, Masters or Wardens of Religious Houses their Superiors, or assessed amongst themselves, out of his Kingdom and his Dominion."[307] From Cap. IV: [S]hall hereafter have a Common Seal, and that shall remain in the Custody of the Prior of the Monastery or House, and four of the most worthy and discreet Men of the Covent of the same House.[308] As the law is also provided in Latin, Pound states *dignioribus* as his preference instead of the English language, *worthy*. From Cap. IV: "But it is not the Meaning of our Lord the King to exclude the Abbots, Priors, and other Religious Aliens, by the Ordinances and Statutes aforesaid, from executing their Office of Visitation in his Kingdom and Dominion; but they may visit at their Pleasures."[309] Money was endowed to a monastery for a specific purpose, for the good of the spiritual and physical needs of the local community, including prayers to be offered for the souls of the dead and for the physical benefit of the poor and all of the local community, *via* the monastery. English laws were created to prevent abuse, especially to prevent donations not being used for the reasons they were given.

---

[306] Ruffhead, *The Statutes at Large*, 160.
[307] Ruffhead, *The Statutes at Large*, 161.
[308] Ruffhead, *The Statutes at Large*, 162.
[309] Ruffhead, *The Statutes at Large*, 162.

The second passage, referring to Rome, takes us to 1350 and a law under King Edward III:

> [T]he Bishop of *Rome*, accroching to him the Seigniories of such Possessions and Benefices doth give and grant the same Benefices to Aliens, which did never dwell in *England*, and to Cardinals, which might not dwell here . . . if they should be suffered, there should scarcely be any Benefice within a short Time in the said Realm, but that it should be in the Hands of Aliens and Denizens by virtue of such Provisions, against the good Will and Disposition of the Founders of the same Benefices . . . and Goods without Number should be carried out of the Realm, in Adnullation of the Estate of the holy Church of *England*."[310]

Edward III was enforcing a previous law made by Edward I. The above-noted abuse deprived the country of England of local control of its patrimony, and especially the law notes the harm the abuses especially inflict on those in need: "[A]nd the Alms, Hospitalities, and other Works of Charity, which should be done in the said Places, should be withdrawn."[311]

This all underscores the Douglasite contention that no nation can be truly independent and prosperous without local control of its purchasing power, its moveable and immovable property. Neither can a properly governed family flourish without purchasing power, nor the *family* of a monastery, nor the larger *family* of the nation, without the independence that property and the King's right to coinage bring, especially the right to increase or decrease the nation's purchasing power.

Passage 3 tells of various laws, the first dating from Queen Mary I. This is the law from "2 & 3 Phil & Mac [*sic*, Mar] Cap 7,"[312] the Sale of Horses Act of 1555. At Horse fairs the law was to protect buyers from unjust practices of sellers:

> We see here how much the whole idea of complete protection and fairness has developed from the earlier charters into the later statutes such as this one. Equity has awareness even here in the humblest rural paths. This bears out the Chinese idea that the constructive idea of the rulers will affect the lives of all. As Pound points out, why can't this be seen in its present application anywhere and anytime, in Iong Ching's China or Cadillac's America?

---

310 Ruffhead, *The Statutes at Large*, 268–69.
311 Ruffhead, *The Statutes at Large*, 268–69.
312 Gordon, "The Azalea Is Grown," 294.

> And the canto ends with the responsibility of repairing a broken bridge. In the statute on that subject " . . . concerning the repairing of decayed Bridges in Highwaies, and by whom," those inhabitants of the county or shire where the bridge is used are responsible because it is for the common good "and ease of the whole country." This comes near the corporate responsibility in the *Sacred Edict*, and the common good of the common law, for the ease of the whole people.[313]

The passage, "& in free markets to the book-keeper one penny / no toll," in reference to the horse fair, emphasises the Douglasite contention that the financial system is simply a book-keeping system and that the financiers' profit should be a just return for a service provided, but not excessive, hindering trade. The lines: "Coke, Iong Ching / responsabili," pays tribute to Iong Ching, but, in this context, also to the great 16th–17th century commentator on the Common Law, Sir Edward Coke, whom Pound lists with the "responsabili." Again, Pound's admiration for Sir Edward Coke is due to Coke's clearcut commentaries, the four-volume *Institutes of the Lawes of England*, and his equally well-known *Reports*. Thus, the later interest of Pound's can also be ascribed to the influence of Douglas.

Pound emphasises that the American constitution was based on Sir Edward Coke's writings and less on the Magna Carta. He is furious with the educational system because he only learned about Coke and his importance during his last years in Washington. Pound considers Coke's works to be the legal foundation of Anglo-Saxon civilization.[314] Pound was not the only one who believed this. In 1769, a future Supreme Court Associate Justice of the United States, John Rutledge, wrote his brother Edward, a future signer of the Declaration of Independence and participant in the American Revolution: "[W]ith regard to particular law books—Coke's Institutes seem to be almost the foundation of our law. These you must read over and over, with the greatest attention, and not quit him till you understand him thoroughly, and have made your own everything in him, which is worth taking out."[315]

The lines: "For every new cottage 4 acres / Stat. de 31 Eliz. / Angliae amor," refers to a statute of Elizabeth I which stipulated that every family was to have at least four acres of land. Pound chooses this luminous detail because it is completely in harmony with C. H.

---

[313] Gordon, "The Azalea Is Grown," 295.

[314] Mullins, *This Difficult Individual*, 318.

[315] O'Neall, *Biographical Sketches*, 124.

Douglas's philosophy which advocated as wide as possible a distribution of the ownership of land and a sharing in natural resources among the citizens of a commonwealth. Douglas ridiculed the Marxist concept of public ownership which he said was impossible because this type of *ownership* was completely divorced from control. Ownership without control, says Douglas, is a myth. Douglas advocated the maximum decentralization of ownership of land and natural resources, not the maximum centralization provided by that monopoly which goes under the name of Socialism: "International Socialism is simply world monopoly. It is propagated by International Financiers everywhere, and an elaborate organisation of teaching bodies, such as the London School of Economics, is subsidised by them to turn out quantities of 'intellectuals' with no practical knowledge of any economics other than the rules of the Gold Standard."[316]

Canto 109 is the last Canto of *Thrones* and the last Canto published by Pound as of the year 1967. Yet even in this last canto the influence of Douglas can be clearly seen and the monetary theme prevails:

1. Pro Veritate . . .
            curtilagia teneant,
                  enough land about each of them
16 foot and a halfe to the pole
                  exception if sailor, etc
town, seaside or brickworks
                  Idlenesse, mother of pickings
                                    EPARXON
Do sell the same in the realme and buy english
            not carry coin, plate or masse out of the country,
      Donaison, denizen
            8H. 6 for cash in exchange
            5H. 4. three months credit
                  and books not brought in bound.

. . . .

2. afraid he will balk and not sign mobilization,
                  got, said Monro, to get rid of him
                                                (Eddie)
He has been around in the hospitals

. . . .

3. Erigena, Anselm,
                  the fight thru Herbert and Rémusat
                                    (Canto 109)

---

[316] Douglas, *The Big*, 52.

The first passage refers to the amount of land to surround each family dwelling in medieval England: "curtilagia teneant: . . . '[those] living in cottages.' The statute prescribes the ideal and goes on to allow exceptions to some who cannot afford '4 acres' or would otherwise be harmed."[317] The harmony of this regulation with Douglasite philosophy has been pointed out in reference to Canto 108 above.

The passage then continues with a reference to the Byzantine Book of the Eparch,[318] which has appeared in the earlier Cantos. English medieval commercial regulations are quoted which are like those in the Book of the Eparch, e.g., the prohibition against carrying coin or plate out of the country.

The references to "cash in exchange," "three months credit," and "books not brought in bound" are purely Douglasite, a thought heritage found in Coke's writings. These refer to three past policies of foreign trade in English law that were quite rational. Douglas always criticized the practice of nations exporting their real physical wealth in exchange for mere tickets or money tokens used only to bridge the disparity between domestic prices and available money in the local economy. As Coke writes: "By the said Act of 8 H.6, no Englishman should sell within this Realm to any merchant alien any manner of merchandises but only for ready payment in hand or else in merchandises for merchandises, to be paid and contented in hand."[319] Real money is to be accepted as payment-in-hand, not foreign loan borrowers's promises-to-pay.

The reference to "merchandises for merchandises" aligns with the subsequent mention of "three months credit." Statute 5 H.4, from the parliament of King Henry IV, concerned foreign merchants who, having sold their imports in England, were given three months to buy English goods of nearly equal value, retaining only the amount needed for their return expenses.[320] Today, under the banner of free trade, nation-states struggle economically for foreign markets, lamenting when another nation sells more goods to them than they buy in return. Nations also use tariffs to reduce the ability of foreign nations to sell

---

317 Terrell, *A Companion*, Vol. II, 710.

318 Cf. *The Oxford Dictionary*, "Book of the Eparch." "Tenth-century regulations governing certain guilds in Constantinople. Administered by the city prefect (eparch), they protected guild members from competition, regulated the quality and quantity of production, supervised prices and salaries, and controlled the activities of foreign traders."

319 Coke, *The Second Part of the Institutes*, 742. Concerning Pound's reference to three months credit and unbound books, it is drawn from the same, 742–44.

320 Giuseppi, "Alien Merchants in England," 84.

products cheaply, increasing costs for all, especially the end consumer. Trade should not be accepted for goods already sufficiently produced locally. These ideas are distinctly Douglasite.

The final reference to "books" pertains to a law supporting local English production. Bookbinding could be done domestically by English binders using English materials. Allowing foreign books to be imported already bound increases costs for English consumers, who must pay for the added expense of transporting bound books. These were rational laws that respected reciprocal practices by other nations. What exists today largely stems from an artificial need for growth, leading to a few powerful nations emerging as winners in the global struggle for markets. Under either free trade or tariffs, local production for local consumption suffers, in contrast to the old legal statutes referenced.

The second passage reiterates the luminous detail concerning Edward VIII's opposition to the Second World War. Both Pound and C. H. Douglas opposed King Edward VIIIs abdication. Pound maintains that the usurocracy had the stage set for war in 1938, but that Edward VIII refused to sign for the commencement of the war. Edward VIII had visited the hospitals during the First World War and, from what he saw, had no desire to send men to war. Pound maintains that the young Windsor gave us three more years of peace, 1936–1939.[321] Pound cites the Georgian poet Harold Monro as his source for this information. Monro had contacts with people highly placed in the British government.

The third passage traces what Pound refers to as the life-giving tradition and clear thinking through Scotus Eriugena and St. Anselm, through Herbert and Rémusat, as referenced in Canto 100. The whole purpose of *The Cantos* has been to chronicle this life-giving tradition through the ages and record its struggle against the death-dealing blight which has its source in usury. Scotus Eriugena and St. Anselm represent the life-giving tradition as it existed in medieval times. Rémusat, the chronicler of Napoleon's struggle against the usurocracy, represents the anti-usury *paideuma* as it existed in the 19th century. Pound's interest in Napoleon and his presentation of Napoleon as a hero in *The Cantos* can be traced back to the influence of Douglas. Napoleon as Emperor had insisted upon exercising his imperial prerogative over coinage in the best Douglasite tradition. The fact that Napoleon insisted on being *boss of the coinage* was enough to endear Napoleon to a Douglasite, such as Pound.

---

[321] Mullins, *This Difficult Individual*, 195–96."

Canto 109 is the last of the *Throne* Cantos and the last Canto to be published so far by Pound as of the year 1967. It thus marks the last Canto of the *Paradiso* which the literary world has thus far received from the pen of the maestro and *scriptor cantilenarum*. Pound, of course, has gone beyond Canto 109 in his continuing *work in progress*. Some years ago he celebrated his birthday by finishing Canto 111. He had said that the Cantos will now probably go to 120. In any case, it is almost certain that the influence of C. H. Douglas will be seen in these latest Cantos, as has been the case thus far throughout Pound's great epic.

SUMMARY

The link between culture, art, civilization, and a sound monetary-economic *paideuma* is essential to an understanding of Pound. Upon it rests his great interest in Douglas as the teacher who sought to revive the sound monetary *paideuma* and thus restore art and culture to their former glory.

C. H. Douglas points out that precious metal manipulation is the primary weapon of International Finance in maintaining its stranglehold on the world's economy. Pound's contemptuous reference to "gold-bugs" in Canto 87 characterizes the international usurers and their apologists, who insist upon trade among nations being fettered to the artificial fetish of the gold standard. C. H. Douglas scoffs at the gold standard and maintains that it is one of the main sources of friction among nations.

In Canto 87 Pound paraphrases C. H. Douglas to the effect that money and the money-system today are an instrument of policy even more than a measure of value. Douglas emphasizes this point throughout his works and particularly in *Warning Democracy*, in the chapter entitled "Government by Money." He stresses that money, i.e., the control of the issue and distribution of money, is much more an instrument of financial oligarchical policy than a measure of value.

Like Douglas, Pound wants to free and unfetter the uniqueness, the sacredness, and dignity of the individual from what Pound and Douglas consider the morass of grey collectivism in which contemporary man wallows today.

Pound is convinced that it is only by means of one having an independence of some kind that one can benefit by that true leisure, not just a weekend off from work, which can lead to contemplation and artistic creativity. This is why Pound the artist is interested in the Douglasite policy of dividends for all, as he sees in this form of economic enlightenment the key to a fuller and more human way of life. He realizes that there is no room for the true artist in a world devoted to the Marxist philosophy of total work and to the usurocratic total war on culture and contemplation.

Pound emphasizes that the problem of usury relates to that of justice. Like Douglas, he sees usury as being opposed to distributive justice. The usury problem is therefore connected with morality, and hence Pound, like the medieval theologians, believes that economics is a part of the moral system, and does not have a right to be judged on any basis other than a moral basis. This is pre-eminently true of the monetary/economic question of usury.

In Canto 88, Pound illustrates in a graphic manner the Douglasite charge that banks in fact do not lend money, but simply lend promises-to-pay. Pound and Douglas maintain that when any real pressure is put on the banks to pay in specie or in legal tender they have always been brought to the point of collapse, e.g., the Bank of England in 1914. No bank is ever able to survive a *run on the bank* because they do not in fact lend currency but lend promises-to-pay. These promises are allowed to circulate as money due to the unfathomable benevolence of governments. Both Pound and Douglas maintain that if the banking system is so sound, we should not always be asked to have *confidence* in it.

In Canto 89, Pound/Benton stress that neither lands nor crops are safe against the Bank of the United States's awesome power to issue money. This is a point which C. H. Douglas makes repeatedly in his writings. He maintains that the banking system's monopoly over credit creation gives it a lien on all property and all production. Nothing is safe from the *neschek* or corrosive usury inflicted by the banking system on the body economic. Sovereignty resides pre-eminently in the right over coinage.

Pound maintains that the usurocracy prefers the system of usury and wage slavery to the older form of chattel slavery. The system of usury and wage slavery is preferred, because under it one does not have to feed the slaves.

In Canto 91 Pound stresses that under the present form of *democracy* the very worst men or "sewage" are elected. As a result there is no clear thought about holiness, as there was in ancient Egyptian, classical, and medieval times. The "dung flow from 1913", the year that marked the creation of the modern Federal Reserve Bank, relates, according to Pound, to the teachings of Marx and Freud, and to the complete triumph of Marxism and Freudianism in the curricula and teaching of the *American beaneries*, i.e., the American universities and colleges. Pound speaks of this academic decline and corrosion as "filth under filth."

In Canto 96 Pound directly paraphrases a statement made by C. H. Douglas in *Economic Democracy* and elsewhere to the effect that there is no local freedom without local control of local purchasing power. This principle of the local control of local purchasing power is fundamental to Douglasism in the light of the fact that Douglas believes that the control over and issue of credit should be decentralized.

In Canto 97, Pound points out that Del Mar is in favour of a proper total proportion between the total issue of money and "buyables", i.e., goods and services. He also comments that even Eisenhower in 1955 had come that far. This insistence upon the connection between the issuing of money and its backing by goods and services is, of course, pure Douglasism. Douglas maintains that the total purchasing power in the body economic must equal the total price of goods and services.

In Canto 97, the line "faster than it distributes the power to buy" is completely Douglasite in its origin. It refers to the fact that the modern economic system creates prices faster than it distributes the power to buy. This principle is, of course, at the very heart of C. H. Douglas's claim that there is a chronic artificial shortage of purchasing power within the body economic.

In Canto 97, Pound emphasizes that it is wrong that the free-born should run into slavery. The slavery Pound is speaking of is, of course, that wage slavery which the usurocracy has found to be more profitable than the older form of chattel slavery. Pound also stresses that it is wrong that the free-born should run into job-hunting. This equation of wage slavery and job-hunting with chattel slavery is fundamental to an understanding of the Poundian and Douglasite position. Pound believes with Douglas that the philosophy of total work and *full employment*, advocated as a desirable end by the usurocracy today, is calculated to make total war on contemplation and to dehumanize man. He sees the philosophy and policy of Douglas as making possible a world in which man would have leisure for contemplation as he had in the medieval period. The Douglasite concepts of the *consumer dividend* and of the *just price* would free man and combine the best features of medievalism with the best features of ultra-modernism.

The lines: "Homestead versus Kolschoz / Rome versus Babylon" in Canto 103 refer to the age-old struggle between the individual and the group. Pound, like Douglas, comprehends that Western civilization has been built upon the individual, and not the group.

CONCLUSION

THE PHILOSOPHY AND THE POLICY OF C.H. Douglas had a profound influence on the writings of Ezra Pound. It is important to emphasize that this philosophy and policy were by no means limited merely to the question of monetary reform and economic considerations. C.H. Douglas has always insisted that monetary reform is but one aspect of Social Credit. He has constantly referred to Social Credit as the policy of a philosophy. He sees this philosophy as having its roots in a firm belief in the uniqueness and sacredness of the human individual:

> Although the fact is a little obscured at the moment, the human individual is the highest manifestation of divine attributes with which we are in day-to-day contact. What differentiates him from the lower orders, when he is different, is his initiative—the fact that he manoeuvres under his own steam. I am confident that there is an organised attempt to drive him down the scale of existence, so that he becomes primarily a number on a card index, by taking away as far as possible any recognisable initiative, his potentially divine attribute.[1]

Douglas has always insisted upon the Christian concept of the individual as opposed to mass collectivism, which is advocated by various forms of materialistic messianism, e.g., Marxian Socialism.

C. H. Douglas regards the continuing warfare against the dignity, liberty, and sanctity of the individual and the move towards the centralization of power in industry, finance, and government to be the great crisis of our time. He sees the centralization of financial power as a key factor in this war upon the individual. This centralization of financial power is possible because of the complete domination of the existing monetary system by usury.[2] The existing monetary and financial system is based upon a system of usury that in no way takes into consideration real economic facts.

Ezra Pound first met C. H. Douglas in *The New Age* editorial offices of A. R. Orage in 1918. He therefore met Douglas at the time when Douglas's first articles on Social Credit were beginning to

---

[1] Douglas, *The Big Idea*, 6

[2] Editor's note: Once again, Douglas's analysis of what is wrong with the financial system goes far deeper than the question of usury, even in the broadest of senses that might be implied here.

appear in *The New Age*. Because of his meeting and continuing contact with Douglas, Pound plunged into a lifetime of research, one of the objects of which was to verify the truth of the Douglasite philosophy.

This research carried him very deeply into the realm of world history and particularly monetary-economic history. It took him on an intellectual *periplum* or voyage of discovery into the work and careers of: Confucius, Malatesta, Cosimo de' Medici, Ferdinando il terzo and Pietro Leopoldo of the House of Habsburg-Lorraine, Napoleon, John Adams, Thomas Jefferson, Randolph of Roanoke, Abraham Lincoln, Benjamin Franklin, Scotus Eriugena, St. Anselm, St. Ambrose, Alexander Del Mar, Thomas Hart Benton, Sir Edward Coke, Agassiz, etc. The purpose of *The Cantos* has been to record and chronicle this life-giving tradition based upon the dignity of the human individual and upon the philosophy of abundance. This philosophy of abundance is the distributist philosophy, which prevailed whenever and wherever economic justice prevailed in history. This distributist philosophy was always connected with that monetary literacy and wisdom which opposed usury. As a philosophy of abundance, it is the very philosophy upon which the monetary-economic aspects of Douglasism are based. Hence Pound sees Douglasism as part of a much older thought-tradition or paideuma.

Opposed to this life-giving tradition is the death-dealing blight which manifests itself in collectivism, but whose very heart and soul is the system of usury. Pound sees usury as the great sin from which all other sins flow and upon which they feed. Pound's interest in *Usura* and in the anti-usury paideuma throughout history can be ascribed to the influence of C. H. Douglas, especially since it did not exist before Pound met Douglas. Pound's interest and respect for medieval thought was encouraged by the fact that it equated usury with sodomy, as both were opposed to the abundance of nature.

Even Pound's great interest in the preservation of peace and in world peace was influenced by C. H. Douglas. Pound's contempt for the munitions makers and his conviction that they were intricately connected with the usurocracy goes back to C. H. Douglas's contention that war is the usurer's harvest. The Douglasite warcry articulated by A. R. Orage: "In the gap between purchasing power and prices is enough gun-powder to blow up the world," had a profound effect on Pound, who had seen war destroy men of promise like T. E. Hulme and Gaudier-Brzeska. The Douglasite claim that commercial warfare is the cause of military warfare could not fail to impress Pound, with his Quaker background and heritage. Before Pound met Douglas in 1918,

Pound had already "been researching the causes of war since shortly after Gaudier's death."[3] Pound's friend, Henri Gaudier-Brzeska, died fighting the Germans in the French army, 5 June 1915.

The influence of C. H. Douglas upon the prose of Ezra Pound can be readily seen in his collection of essays: *Impact: Essays on Ignorance and the Decline of American Civilization*. These essays are heavily Douglasite in their philosophy and reflect Douglas's preoccupation with the chronic artificial lack of purchasing power within the body economic. Pound constantly stresses the Douglasite theme of poverty amidst plenty due to a faulty man-made *ticket system*, i.e., money system. Pound deals directly with the Douglasite concepts of the *cultural heritage* and the *increment of association* in these essays. In addition to these essays, Pound's *ABC of Economics* is based upon Douglasite philosophy and policy. His prose work *Jefferson and/or Mussolini* also reveals his preoccupation with Douglasite themes. The Rome radio broadcasts, for which he was imprisoned for thirteen years without being brought to trial, are greatly inspired by Douglasism and are arguably part of Pound's prose output. These broadcasts usually only depart from Douglasite themes when dealing with strictly literary or artistic topics. In addition to these works, Donald Gallup's *A Bibliography of Ezra Pound* reveals an enormous prose output on Douglasite themes contained in personal letters, articles, letters to the editor, essays, etc. This prose output starts soon after 1918 and continues well up to Pound's last years.

The great epic masterpiece, *The Cantos*, shows the same powerful influence of C. H. Douglas. Pound incorporates Douglas's A+B theorem which illustrates the chronic gap between prices and purchasing power into Canto XXXVIII. It is no exaggeration to say that Douglasism is the focal point of *The Cantos*. The Douglas philosophy and policy of Social Credit acts as the thematic centre of *The Cantos* and gives a unity to this vast epic. Pound does not merely reflect the Douglasite opposition to usury in his work but also reflects a *positive alternative* to the debt-money system. This positive alternative is found in the system of *debt-free money* advocated by Douglas.[4] This system presupposes *a return* to the royal prerogative over coinage in the case of a monarchy, and to a congressional or parliamentary

[3] Laughlin, *Pound as Wuz*, 94.

[4] Editor's note: The Douglas Social Credit system is debt-free in that sense that sufficient debt-free compensatory consumer credits are to be issued in the form of the dividend and the discount to balance the price system and to eliminate the need for compensatory government, business, and consumer debt. Producer credit would still be issued as a loan, i.e., as a debt.

money system in the case of a democracy. Pound constantly asserts the Douglasite theme that the essence of sovereignty consists in the power to issue money. He insists, following Douglas, that this power to issue money must never be surrendered by the king or parliament to private interests. He insists that the public credit must never be monopolized by private interests.[5]

In his desire to prove the validity of Douglas's position, Pound incorporates the ideas of Confucius, Jefferson, Adams, Del Mar, Coke, etc., into *The Cantos*. He shows that the American Revolution was fought over the principle of debt-free money against the powerful forces unleashed by the Bank of England with its debt-money system. He borrows heavily from the Jefferson-Adams correspondence, the work of Thomas Hart Benton, and the writings of Alexander Del Mar, to show the constant epic struggle between the usurer and the man who wants to do a good job. In the works of Del Mar he traces the Douglasite concept of the royal prerogative over coinage as far back as the Pontifex Maximus or Roman High Priest.

Pound also shows the influence of Douglas in his disdain for the system of general education which fosters a blackout of learning. This blackout of learning shows itself particularly in the areas of history, economics, and monetary history. Even the classics and the work of Sir Edward Coke have been dropped from the curricula because they contain ideas which would embarrass the usurocracy. Pound also reflects C. H. Douglas's disdain for *Orthodox Economics* and such founts of financial orthodoxy as the London School of Economics.

Pound's insistence upon clarity of language and of definitions has its counterpart in Douglas's impatience with the jargon of *Orthodox Economics*. Douglas maintained that the London School of Economics taught nothing about practical economics but only taught how the gold standard works.

Finally, Pound's emphasis in *The Cantos* on the necessity of monetary literacy and sanity for the creation of an atmosphere conducive to great art reflects his conviction that Douglas is the only reformer in whose policies and philosophy the artist is considered.

Pound's constant emphasis upon the benefits of leisure, contemplation, in both his prose and in *The Cantos* reflect the influence of Douglas whose philosophy and policy would make possible an age

---

[5] Editor's note: The key question for Douglas is what is the policy of the financial system, not who creates the money supply. The financial system should serve the common interest, not monopoly or oligopoly private interests (whether private or public).

of leisure in the midst of abundance. Pound's disdain for the Marxist concept of full employment and the labour theory of value also have their source in Douglas.

Douglas's preoccupation with the individual as opposed to the collectivity can be seen in *The Cantos*, e.g., in Pound's presenting the choice of homestead vs. kolschoz, i.e., a collective farm and in Pound's praise of Venice as the civilization which fostered and produced the greatest individuals.

Ezra Pound shows the influence of C. H. Douglas in his emphasis upon the fact that the State should lend, not borrow. Pound, like Douglas, maintains that the creation and control of credit belongs, by necessity, to the supreme public authority, whether this be king or congress. He stresses that the public credit must never be allowed to fall into private hands.

Pound, following Douglas, maintains that the main cause of the world's woes is the fact that the nations of the world have surrendered the control of their own credit to the vested banking interests, i.e., to what Pound calls the usurocracy. This bank-credit or debt system of finance is responsible for the built-in real inflation and discrepancy between total prices and total purchasing power from which the world suffers.

Ezra Pound also shows the influence of C. H. Douglas in charging that the usurocracy, i.e., the big usurers in conspiracy, have *appropriated to themselves* both the cultural heritage and the unearned increment of association. Pound has defined the Douglasite increment of association as the advantage men get from working together instead of each on his own. He has defined the Douglasite cultural heritage as the increment of association in the form of all past inventiveness. Pound maintains, following Douglas, that both the unearned increment of association and the cultural heritage belong, of necessity, to humanity not to vested financial interests.

Pound, following Douglas, advocates the application of both a *national dividend* paid directly to the consumer, and a *compensated price discount* paid to the seller of goods. These are to be paid with *debt-free credit created* by the supreme public authority through a monetary commission or credit board. Both the national dividend and the compensated price discount are how the *gap between total prices and total buying power* will be bridged.

Douglas/Pound maintain that *consumption* is the minimum price we must pay for production. Pound, following Douglas, claims that the *just price* of any product is the *real cost* of production and that the real cost of production is thus the financial cost of consumption. Douglas/Pound maintain that goods should be sold to consumers at their real cost, instead of as now at their financial cost, and that the sellers should be reimbursed by the treasury or other duly appointed national authority for the amount they were consequently out of pocket.

Pound, following Douglas, stipulates that these fresh debt-free issues of credit must not come out of production, i.e., out of wages paid to workers. These fresh debt-free issues of credit must always be based upon a technical estimate of the total prices of goods and services available. Therefore financial credit, the rate at which purchasing power can be delivered as, when, and where required, must be based upon real credit, i.e., the rate at which goods and services can be delivered, as, when, and where required. Real credit must be the only basis of financial credit, not the fetish of gold.

Pound, following Douglas, is completely opposed to the system of foreign trade whereby nations attempt to sell the cream of their production to import enough purchasing power into the body economic so that their consumers can buy up the skim-milk of their production. Pound, like Douglas, maintains that the home market is the best market. He sees the struggle for foreign markets as creating that commercial warfare which has always been the prelude to military warfare in modern times. Therefore Pound, like Douglas, sees the system of usury as being the main cause of warfare. Like Douglas, Pound sees no hope for world peace until individual nations free themselves from the debt-money system.

Pound, following Douglas, sees the only valid foreign trade to consist in the exchange of true surpluses between nations, e.g., Canadian wheat for Indian cotton. He stresses that these surpluses must be true surpluses not false surpluses, i.e., that the home market has bought up all it really wants and needs, not all that it can *afford* to buy, as is the case under the present banker credit system. Here Pound follows the basic Douglasite distinction between *demand* and *effective demand.* Effective demand for Douglas would be the demand for a particular product *plus* the purchasing power with which to buy that product.

Pound, following Douglas, sees *unemployment* as a blessing and mark of progress, not a curse. He, like Douglas, opposes the Marxist philosophy of total work, make work, and *jobs for all.* He, like Douglas, sees the philosophy of *work for work's sake* as resulting in the brutalizing of humanity and the destruction of contemplation.

Pound, like Douglas, views leisure as being necessary for human, cultural, and artistic development. Leisure, says Douglas/Pound, does not consist in a weekend *off* from work, so that the wage slave may attack his task with renewed vigour again. Pound has defined leisure as *Time plus Money*, i.e., time free from money worries and cares. It is obvious that this leisure is sorely lacking today in our "affluent" society. Pound maintains that the best thing you can give an artist is leisure. When you give an artist leisure, says Pound, you have a share in his creation. Pound is convinced that C. H. Douglas is the only reformer who truly has a place for the artist in his vision of society. In this connection, Pound has written: "As for proposed remedies, C. H. Douglas is the first economist to include creative art and writing in an economic scheme, and the first to give the painter or sculptor or poet a definite reason for being interested in economics; namely, that a better economic system would release more energy for invention and design."[6] Like Hugh MacDiarmid, Pound sees the Douglas Commonwealth as being based upon Liberty, Leisure, and Culture with *the will-to-plenty* supplanting the collectivist *will-to-power*.

Pound, following C. H. Douglas, maintains that the usurocracy is in complete control of the press, publicity, and the entire communications media. Like Douglas, Pound believes that there has been an historical blackout particularly regarding the monetary-economic facts of history. The usurocracy has arranged this to make the world safe for bankers. Pound would agree with Douglas that the system of general education is one of mass hypnotism. Douglas/Pound see financial control over academic teaching as consisting in the fact that universities and colleges are dependent upon subsidies from government, or from vested financial interests. The governments, in turn, are extremely responsive to the wishes of the usurocracy, since the usurocracy holds first and second mortgage on government debts.

Douglas/Pound believe that there is no hope for world peace unless the monetary system is reformed. Douglas/Pound saw the League of Nations as an organ of that centralized financial control which is vital to the existence of the usurocracy. Douglas/Pound oppose the centralization of power and maintain that decentralization of finance, politics, and industry is essential to individual freedom and development. Douglas/Pound regard all peace movements which do not consider the necessity for monetary and financial reform as *ersatz*. Pound advocates Confucius's formula for world peace, i.e.,

---

[6] Pound, *Impact*, 90.

"to promote the peace of the world by the good internal government of one's country."

The policy and philosophy of C. H. Douglas provides a dominant theme for much of Pound's prose writing and provides the focal point or unifying theme for his great epic masterpiece, *The Cantos.*

Leave the words to me.
Leave me to explain myself.
I made the song of eternal war
between the light and grime.

(Canto LXXII)

APPENDIX I

Letter of the Scottish Poet Christopher Grieve

Hugh MacDiarmid

The famous Scottish poet, Christopher Murray Grieve, known by his pen name Hugh MacDiarmid, wrote to Lorne A. Reznowski the following letter, concerning the influence of the writings of C. H. Douglas and Social Credit upon literary figures.

Gratitude is expressed to his widow, Mrs. Deirdre Grieve and family, for permission to include her late husband's letter in this work.

Brownsbank
Biggar
Lanarkshire
Scotland
17/10/68

Professor Lorne A. Reznowski
St Paul's College
Winnipeg 19,
Canada

Dear Professor Reznowski

Many thanks for your letter of 3rd inst and your kind remarks about my essay on Ezra Pound.

I am indeed interested to know of your projected thesis on C. H. Douglas, of whom a biographical study is certainly long overdue and so far as I know not yet contemplated by anyone. I knew him well and have written a good deal about him in various quarters. In my book, "The Company I've Kept" (Hutchinson, London, 1966) there is a chapter entitled "Major Douglas and Social Credit" and throughout the book various other references. This chapter also contains references which go to bear out my claim that, as you say, Douglas represents the very culmination of Scottish genius in its contribution to the Anglo Saxon world and thought. That is, of course, in the sphere of economics in which Douglas came at the end of a long line of Scottish thinkers on the subject and carried their ideas to their logical conclusion. There are numerous references to Douglas also in an earlier book of mine, "Lucky Poet",

(Methuen, London 1943), and I had an obituary article on him in "the Scottish Journal", a now defunct periodical a copy of which I'll try to get and send you.

I expect you know the two recent books *Orage and the New Age Circle*, by Paul Selver (Geo. Allen and Unwin, London, 1959), and "The New Age under Orage" by Wallace Martin (1967) — this last published in America by Barnes and Noble inc., 105 Fifth Avenue, New York, N.Y. 10003. There are also two earlier books, Philip Mairet's biography of Orage, and the Selected Essay of A. R. Orage, edited by Denis Saurat and (afterwards Sir) Herbert Read, both of whom are now dead. I would have to write you a long separate letter about the line of Scottish economic thinking and banking practice which found its culmination and crown in Douglas.

So far as Douglas's influence on the British literary world is concerned, that is mainly found in connection with T. S. Eliot, Ezra Pound, Arnold Bennett, Liam O'Flaherty, Ruth Pitter, AE (G.W. Russell), and a few others — and, of course, you know of the association with the "New Age" in its heyday of G. Bernard Shaw, G. K. Chesterton, and Hilaire Belloc.

If you have not these books and cannot get them in Canadian libraries, I would be glad to lend them to you, if you let me know.

. . . The Herbert Read and Edwin Muir pamphlets on Social Credit (and all the Social Credit pamphlets published by Stanley Nott Ltd) were reprinted by the poet Pete Russell. I should have copies somewhere here but cannot lay my hands on them yet. Russell now lives in Florence and I can write to him for copies. There is material about the New Age, Douglas etc in Professor Pete Butter's "Edwin Muir, Man and Poet" (Oliver & Boyd, Edinburgh 1966) and in Edwin's widow, Willa Muir's autobiography, "Belonging" (Chatto and Windus).

Muir's pamphlet was "Social Credit and the Labour Party", published by Stanley Nott, London, 1935.

On Envelope:

To: Professor L. A. Reznowski,
St Paul's College,
University of Manitoba, Winnipeg
Canada

Hugh MacDiarmid (Christopher Grieve), Brownsbank, Biggar, Lanarkshire, Scotland

APPENDIX II

What is Douglas Social Credit?

M. Oliver Heydorn

[*Douglas Social Credit is, of course, the original Social Credit and is the very opposite in intent to the faux CCP totalitarian reward and punishment system which goes by the name 'social credit.'* —*Ed.*]

1. THE TERM 'SOCIAL CREDIT' REFERS, IN THE first place, to the power of human beings, working in association, to achieve intended results. It is a power that is operative in all human societies. When capitalized, 'Social Credit' may refer either to the study of this social power (i.e., an investigation of its general nature, including how it may be maximized, what weakens it, and what its limits are, etc.) or else to any individual action or organized movement which aims to safeguard and increase the social credit of a given society as a fixed policy.

2. Since it is centred, above all, on how the general society functions in view of the fundamental purposes of human association, Social Credit is chiefly concerned with the nature and functionality of association for the sake of economic ends and with the nature and functionality of association for the sake of political ends. Such a study presupposes specific philosophical views regarding the general characteristics of reality, of knowledge, of scientific methodology, and of human nature, as well as a particular type of social philosophy. It also gives rise to a distinctive manner of understanding history and of interpreting historical events.

3. Although the basic philosophy and policy of Social Credit were not predetermined to satisfy the tenets of Christian belief, that philosophy and policy turned out, retrospectively, to be an organic expression of the Christian worldview. Christianity, correctly understood and practised, is the primary metaphysical inspiration supporting Social Credit.

4. As far as its underlying social philosophy is concerned, Social Credit holds that associations, of whatever kind, exist for the purpose of making it as easy as possible for human beings to achieve the fundamental purposes of the respective associations in an effective and equitable manner. That is, the group exists for the sake of the well-being of each and every individual and not as an end in itself,

nor as a means of advancing the anti-social interests of any oligarchic elite who may have gained control of the group and its activities. Each common member of a particular association is best served when the intended results of the association in question can be properly actualized with the least amount of trouble to everyone.

5. With regard to economic association, the economic system which governs a society should allow for the fulfillment of the true purpose of economic association, i.e., the delivery of goods and service as, when, and where required with the least amount of trouble to anyone, to be achieved to the extent that this is physically or realistically possible.

6. Social Credit notes that it is chiefly on account of the nature of the present financial system that economic associations fail to deliver the intended results. It is also chiefly on account of the financial system that economic associations typically yield a number of undesired outcomes, some of which go beyond the realm of economics proper. In sober truth, there is, in the modern, industrialized world, no good reason for poverty, or for a policy of full employment (with its consequent lack of leisure), or for inflation, or for alternating cycles of boom and bust, or for economic waste and sabotage, or for inhuman financial pressures, or for personal indebtedness, or for chronic public debts, or for high levels and/or unjustifiable forms of taxation, or for social turmoil, or for cultural decay, or for the forced (economically induced) migration of persons from their native lands, or for environmental degradation, or for international economic and political conflict culminating in that form of collective insanity otherwise known as war, etc.

7. The faulty nature of the financial system has two fundamental and complementary aspects. On the one hand, the financial system, as it presently operates, generates an ever-increasing gap between the rate at which the prices of ultimate goods and services are produced and the consumer incomes that are simultaneously liberated in the course of their production. This is primarily, though not exclusively, due to the way in which real capital (machines and equipment) are financed and their costs accounted for under existing financial and industrial cost accountancy conventions and the concomitant displacement of human labour. On the other hand, a particular monopoly, i.e., the monopoly of credit creation currently exercised by banking institutions, makes use of this artificial scarcity of consumer credit to enforce a self-serving policy on the members of economic associations. They relieve the lack of consumer credit (chiefly by issuing loans), but only on asymmetrical terms that transfer purchasing power, property, and control over the economic policy of governments, businesses, and individuals to themselves.

8. The solution to these problems is to create and issue a sufficient volume of debt-free money in the form of the compensated price and the National Dividend to equate the rate of flow of final prices with the rate of flow of consumer purchasing power. This would restore balance or financial equilibrium to the circular flow while simultaneously ensuring that all prices are fully liquidated as they come on to the consumer market. A sufficiency in the rate at which consumer credit is injected into the economy would also provide adequate support for the issuance of additional producer credit up to the physical capacity of the economy or the psychological satiety of the consumer. The rate of flow of producer credit would be released so as to finally correspond isomorphically to the real demand of consumers. Whatever production is physically possible and desired by the population could be made financially possible.

9. In its purely economic dimension, Social Credit may therefore be described as a radical type of monetary reform that is specifically designed to subordinate the activities of the group to the well-being of each individual member of economic association (thus liberating the individual from the domination of the group—and from the domination of the elite who control the group—that currently characterizes economic life). The delivery of goods and services as, when, and where required to the extent that this is physically possible, and this with the least amount of trouble to everyone, may be expected as the natural consequence of such a reform.

10. With regard to political association, the political system that governs a society should allow for the fulfillment of the true purpose of political association, i.e., the maximization of each individual's effective sovereignty over his own affairs with the least amount of trouble to everyone, to be achieved to the extent that this is physically or realistically possible.

11. The conventional financial system and the resulting economic order have profound political implications. On the one hand, the existing system generates a great deal of economic conflict which often translates into political and even military conflict between nations and within nations. To take just one example, it is impossible for all nations to have 'favourable balances of trade' and yet each of them strives very hard to achieve such a result in order to compensate for their internal lack of consumer purchasing power (or at least seek to minimize their unfavourable trade balances). The transformation of this clash of objectives into economic and even military warfare is only a matter of time and opportunity. On the other hand, the same system concentrates a

great deal of financial wealth, privilege, and power at the apex of the socio-economic pyramid. This centralization of financial and economic clout puts the chief beneficiaries of the disordered financial system in such an advantageous position that they are capable, by various means, of obliging or at least heavily pressuring (under various guises) political associations to adopt those policies that are most congenial to this elite: i.e., the policies that will transform their credit monopoly into a total social monopoly: economic, political, and cultural. Social Credit notes that the failure of political associations to achieve their intended results in modern 'democratic' countries is chiefly due to a poorly designed political system which is harnessed, by the power of money, to serve an end which is alien to the true purpose of political association.

12. In the first place, conventional 'democracy' does not allow individual citizens to establish a political association which would permit and support the maximum decentralization of effective sovereignty to each individual over his own affairs simply because it does not even aim at this objective and, in consequence, is not designed to achieve it. According to liberal democratic theory, the true objective of government is to adjudicate or strike a balance between competing group interests in the state who have incompatible ends: 'politics is the art of compromise'. On the basis of this conception it is inconceivable that there should be a unanimous general or common will in favour of an overriding general objective such as the maximization of effective, individual sovereignty over one's own affairs to the extent that this is objectively possible and with the least amount of trouble to everyone. The possibility of there being a truly common policy is discounted from the very beginning. As a result, such 'democracies' do not even aim at fulfilling the true purpose of political association even though many ordinary citizens take for granted that in a democracy the policies of the government should reflect the general will of the common people. In the second place, and as a consequence of this first point, the mechanisms of conventional democracy (its voting systems and its multi-party systems) do not deliver to individuals real, i.e., effective, control over their governments.

13. To further complicate matters, the monopolistic financial system, especially at the levels of 'High Finance' and 'International Finance' in conjunction with 'Big Business' make use of the flaws in the conventional democratic system to impose their own self-serving policy on individuals: the increasing centralization of political power in their own hands. Control of the creation and issuance of money is the power to reward and punish; it is the power to control or at least

exert pressure on state institutions, governments, political parties, and individual politicians. It is also the power to control or at least heavily influence public opinion by funding news media, education, and entertainment industries. High finance is thus in a position to push society from above and pull it from below to embrace those intermediate policies which will further centralize political control in the hands of those who are interested in monopolizing power. The logical endpoint of a policy of political centralization, the greatest degree of centralization possible, would be the establishment by International Finance of a one-world totalitarian dictatorship: 'The New World Order.'

14. The solution to these failures of conventional democracy is to rehabilitate democracy by introducing a political system which is explicitly aimed at the true purpose of political association and is then judged and regulated by the individual citizens themselves in terms of its capacity to decentralize effective sovereignty of the individual over his own affairs.

15. Such a system would need to have a tripartite structure. Effective democracy does not mean the right of the people to dispose over other people's affairs or over the objective functional necessities of political association (which are grounded in natural law and can only be disregarded at a very high price); it means the right and the real power of individuals to ensure that all activities of a public nature will deliver the maximum benefit to the individuals who comprise the public. In order to achieve this end, there must be an effective constitutional framework, in the care of a Guardian Chamber or Upper House, which limits the power of the state and governments in order to protect as sacrosanct those legitimate individual rights that are God-given and are thus prior to the state. There must also be a series of civil service administrative hierarchies that are fully and personally responsible to the citizens for carrying out (not determining) policy-decisions. Finally, there must be a set of mechanisms put in place by means of which individual citizens can either directly or *via* their parliamentary representatives initiate policies and sanction the administrative hierarchies in terms of results. Such mechanisms may include voting for independent as opposed to partisan candidates (the end of the political party system), the right to recall Members of Parliament, citizen's initiatives and referenda, the responsible vote (the end of the secret ballot), and, most importantly, the widest possible latitude to contract out or opt out of government services/programmes.

16. The Social Credit philosophy and policy regarding the nature and proper orientation of economic, political, and cultural associations

constitutes an Archimedean point against which the history of civilization can be analyzed and evaluated and by means of which the future of civilization can be re-oriented towards the common good and the general satisfaction.

17. In the first place, it must be recognized that much of what has occurred in the history of civilization was caused or at least conditioned by the specific policies that were adopted by various human associations. History is correctly described, therefore, as crystallized politics rather than as a series of disconnected episodes.

18. In the second place, it must be recognized that the history of policy is a history of conflict between two diametrically opposed social policies: the policy of domination which animates despotic associations (and which most often is, in practice, an oligarchic policy) and the policy of freedom which lies at the foundation of the authentically democratic association. In the case of the despotic associations, the history of civilization is also the chronicle of an internecine war between ideologically similar if not identical individuals and groups who are competing with each other for the power to administer the policy of domination and to enjoy its ill-gotten fruits.

19. It would seem that the first conflict of history, the struggle between oligarchy and the mass of common individuals, is reaching its culmination point in the contemporary world. The almost exclusive vehicle by means of which the policy of domination and hence of despotic association is presently being imposed on the world is that of finance; and finance, improperly regulated, is the most powerful instrument the mind of man has ever conceived for imposing policy on his fellows.

20. Accordingly, it is important for people to be aware that the way in which history is conceived by the general population has powerful political implications and that those who would wish to usurp the unearned increment of an association have a compelling incentive to ensure that the telling of history in the public forum is conducive to the maintenance and augmentation of their societal hegemony. The representation of history can, like the practice of empirical science, be easily politicized, i.e., employed to promote beliefs which, although they are at odds with objective reality, are nevertheless useful in the attainment of certain political ends. As George Orwell noted in his novel 1984: "Who controls the past . . . controls the future: who controls the present controls the past."[1]

[1] George Orwell, *1984*, 30. This principle was actually one of the slogans of the totalitarian Party which was in almost total control of the fictional superstate of Oceania.

BIBLIOGRAPHY

Aberhart, William. *National Monetary Reform, Canada's Urgent Need*: Commentary by L.D. Byrne. Edmonton: Today & Tomorrow, 1940.

Adams, Brooks. *The Law of Civilization and Decay: An Essay on History*. 2nd ed. New York: Macmillan, 1897.

Adams, John. *The Works of John Adams, Second President of the United States*. Vol. 1. Boston: Little, Brown, 1856.

Adams, John Quincy. *The Diary of John Quincy Adams, 1794–1845: American Diplomacy, and Political, Social, and Intellectual Life, from Washington to Polk*. Edited by Allan Nevins. New York: Charles Scribner's Sons, 1951.

Alighieri, Dante. *The Convivio of Dante Alighieri*. Edited and translated by Philip H. Wicksteed. London: J.M. Dent, 1903.

———. *The Inferno*. Translated by John Ciardi. New York: New American Library, 1954.

Ambrose, Saint, Bishop of Milan. *Opera, Ad Manuscriptos Codices, Vaticanos, Gallicanos, Bellgicos, &c.* Vol. 3. Venice: Typis F. Petteri, 1781.

Anderson, David. *Pound's Cavalcanti: An Edition of the Translations, Notes, and Essays*. Princeton: Princeton University Press, 1983.

André, Mathias, and Malka Guillot. "1914–2014: One Hundred Years of Income Tax in France." *Institut des Politiques Publiques, IPP Policy Briefs*, no. 12 (July 2014): 1–8.

Angle, John David. "Glorious Revolution as Financial Revolution." *History Faculty Publications*, no. 6 (Spring 2013): 1–15.

Antoni, E.J. "American Taxpayers Are Now Slaves to Interest Payments." *The Heritage Foundation*, November 28, 2023.

Aristotle. *Oeconomica*. Translated by E.S. Forster. Oxford: Clarendon Press, 1920.

———. *Politics*. Translated by Benjamin Jowett. Oxford: Oxford University Press, 1916.

Arrian. *The Landmark Arrian: The Campaigns of Alexander (Anabasis Alexandrou)*. Edited by Pamela Mensch and James S. Romm. New York: Anchor Books, 2012.

Ascah, Bob, and Mark Anielski. *Alberta's Public Bank: How ATB Can Help Shape the New Economy*. Edmonton: Parkland Institute, University of Alberta, August 2018.

Baier, Karl. "Meditation and Contemplation in High to Late Medieval Europe." In *Yogic Perception, Meditation and Altered States of Consciousness*, edited by Eli Franco, 325–49. Vienna: Verlag der Österreichischen Akademie der Wissenschaften, 2009.

Baumann, Walter. "'In Principio Verbum': Seminar on Canto 74, Lines 76–145." *Lingue e Letterature*, 234–56.

Bell, Edward. "The Rise of the Lougheed Conservatives and the Demise of Social Credit in Alberta: A Reconsideration." *Canadian Journal of*

Political Science / Revue Canadienne de Science Politique 26, no. 3 (1993): 455–75.

Belloc, Hilaire. *The Free Press*. London: George Allen & Unwin, 1918.

———. *The Servile State*. London: T.N. Foulis, 1912.

Benton, Thomas Hart. *Thirty Years' View; or, A History of the Working of the American Government for Thirty Years, from 1820 to 1850*. 2 vols. New York: Appleton, 1854–56.

Bonneau, Louis-Marie, and Grégor Puppinck. *70 Years of Population Policy: History of the Human Reproduction Program of the World Health Organisation, 1950–2020*. Cambridge: Ethics International Press, 2024.

Borden, Milena. "Evelyn Waugh's Yugoslav Mission: Politics and Religion." *Evelyn Waugh Studies* 49, no. 1 (Spring 2018): 1–25.

Bradford, Sarah. *Disraeli*. New York: Stein and Day, 1983.

Brown, Richard. *The Major Works of Evelyn Waugh: Brideshead Revisited, Decline and Fall, A Handful of Dust, The Loved One, a Critical Commentary*. New York: Monarch Press, 1971.

Bryan, Charles S., and Shane R. Mull. "Pellagra Pre-Goldberger: Rupert Blue, Fleming Sandwith, and The 'Vitamine Hypothesis.'" *Transactions of the American Clinical and Climatological Association* 126 (2015): 20–45.

Burckhardt, Jacob. *The Civilization of the Renaissance in Italy*. New York: Modern Library, 1954.

Burroughes, Tom. "Havens of Calm in Volatile Times: The Channel Islands." *Wealth Briefing: News Insight Intelligence*, September 6, 2022.

"Canto LII, Calendar of Composition." *The Cantos Project*. Accessed December 14, 2024. http://ezrapoundcantos.org/canto-lii.

Carter, Joe. "What Is the Money Multiplier?" *Religion and Liberty Online*, April 9, 2019.

Carter, Zachary. *The Price of Peace: Money, Democracy, and the Life of John Maynard Keynes*. New York: Random House, 2020.

Casillo, Robert. "The Italian Renaissance: Pound's Problematic Debt to Burckhardt." *Mosaic: A Journal for the Interdisciplinary Study of Literature* 22, no. 4 (1989): 13–29.

The Catholic Encyclopedia. New York: Robert Appleton Company, 1907–1912.

Chambers, David. "The Baffling Harry White." *Whittaker Chambers Official Website*, May 22, 2012.

Channing, Edward. *A History of the United States: A Century of Colonial History, 1660–1760*. Vol. 2. New York: Macmillan, 1937.

Chaplin, Charlie. *My Autobiography*. Brooklyn: Melville House Publishing, 2012. "Charteris, Leslie." *The Encyclopedia of Science Fiction*. Accessed March 17, 2025. https://sf-encyclopedia.com/entry/charteris_leslie.

Chastanet, J.L. *La République des Banquiers*. Paris: Les Éditions Georges-Anquetil, 1925.

———. *The Bankers' Republic*. Translated by C.H. Douglas. London: Cecil Palmer, 1926.

Chernow, Ron. *The House of Morgan: An American Banking Dynasty and the Rise of Modern Finance*. New York: Atlantic Monthly Press, 1990.

Chesterton, G.K. "Straws in the Wind: The Aggression of Plutocracy." *G.K.'s Weekly*, June 12, 1926, 212–13.

Chinese Classics: Containing the Works of Mencius. Vol. 2. Translated by James Legge. London: Trübner, 1861.

Cohan, William D. "How Wall Street's Bankers Stayed Out of Jail: The Probes into Bank Fraud Leading Up to the Financial Industry's Crash Have Been Quietly Closed. Is This Justice?" *The Atlantic*, September 2015.

Coke, Edward. *The Institutes of the Laws of England, Containing the Exposition of Many Ancient and Other Statutes*. 4 vols. London: Printed by W. Rawlins, for Thomas Basset, 1681.

———. *The Reports of Sir Edward Coke Kt., in English, Compleat in Thirteen Parts: Her Majesty's Attorney General*. London: Printed by E. and R. Nutt, and R. Gosling, 1738.

———. *The Second Part of the Institutes of the Laws of England [...]*. 6th ed. London: W. Rawlins, 1781.

Confucius. *The Great Digest, the Unwobbling Pivot, the Analects*. Translated and commentary by Ezra Pound. 8th ed. New York: New Directions Publishing, 1969.

Conley, James D. "Ubi Amor, Ibi Oculus." *First Things*, July 21, 2015.

Constitution of the United States with Index and the Declaration of Independence. 26th ed. Washington, DC: Government Publishing Office, 2017.

"Consultation on Fighting Predatory Lending by Lowering the Criminal Rate of Interest." *Department of Finance Canada*, 2022.

Conte, Niccolo. "U.S. Debt Interest Payments Reach $1 Trillion." *Visual Capitalist*, edited by Dorothy Neufeld, April 16, 2024.

Corey, Lewis. *The House of Morgan: A Social Biography of the Masters of Money*. New York: Grosset & Dunlap, 1930.

Couvreur, Séraphin. *Cheu King: Texte Chinois avec une Double Traduction en Français et en Latin, une Introduction et un Vocabulaire*. Ho Kien Fou: Imprimerie de la Mission Catholique, 1896.

Curtis, George Ticknor. *Life of James Buchanan, Fifteenth President of the United States*. New York: Harper & Brothers, 1883.

Dawson, Christopher. *The Crisis of Western Education*. With specific programs for the study of Christian culture by John J. Mulloy. New York: Sheed and Ward, 1961.

Del Mar, Alexander. *A History of Monetary Crimes: A Faithful Copy of the Edition of 1899 Entitled Barbara Villiers or a History of Monetary Crimes*. Washington, DC: Cleaners' Press, 1975.

———. *A History of the Monetary Systems of France, and Other European States*. New York: Cambridge Encyclopedia, 1903.

———. *A History of the Precious Metals, from Earliest Times to the Present*. London: George Bell and Sons, 1880.

Delaisi, Francis. "Nous n'avons plus de ROI mais nous avons des RÉGENTS: Les vrais maîtres de la France siègent à la Banque de France." *VU* 380 (June 26, 1935): 837–39, 863.

Deneen, Patrick J. "Against Great Books: Questioning Our Approach to the Western Canon." *First Things*, January 2013.

Denzinger, Heinrich. *Compendium of Creeds, Definitions, and Declarations on Matters of Faith and Morals*. Edited by Peter Hünermann. 43rd ed. San Francisco: Ignatius Press, 2012.

Destutt de Tracy, Antoine. *A Treatise on Political Economy*. Georgetown, DC: Joseph Milligan, 1817.

Dictionary of National Biography, 1931–1940. Edited by L.G. Wickham Legg. London: Oxford University Press, 1950.

Douay Rheims Catholic Bible. Baltimore: John Murphy Company, 1899.

Douglas, C.H. *The Approach to Reality*. London: K.R.P. Publications, 1936.

———. *The Big Idea*. Liverpool: K.R.P. Publications, 1965.

———. "The Causes of War." Part 1. YouTube. https://www.youtube.com/watch?v=sw28HmmvNNs.

———. *The Control and Distribution of Production*. London: Cecil Palmer, 1922.

———. *Credit, Power and Democracy*. London: Cecil Palmer, 1921.

———. *Dictatorship by Taxation*. London: K.R.P. Publications, 1936.

———. *Economic Democracy*. New York: Harcourt, Brace and Howe, 1920.

———. "Evidence Submitted to the MacMillan Committee of Finance and Industry by C.H. Douglas." May 1, 1930. https://thepeoplescredit.com.au/wp-content/uploads/pc-pdf/longform/MacMillian-Committee-Of-Finance-and-Industry.pdf.

———. *The "Land for the (Chosen) People" Racket*. London: K.R.P. Publications, 1943.

———. *Major Douglas Analyzes 'Social Credit' in Alberta: What Went Wrong?* London: K.R.P. Publications, 1948.

———. "Money: An Historical Survey." *The Fig Tree*, no. 2, September 1936, 139–47. Reprint issue, 23–27. Accessed December 12, 2024. https://thepeoplescredit.com.au/wp-content/uploads/pc-pdf/the-fig-tree/The-Fig-Tree-No-02-Sep-1936.pdf.

———. *Money and the Price System: A Speech Delivered at Oslo on February 14, 1935, to H.M. The King of Norway, H.E. The British Minister, the President, and Members of the Oslo Merchants' Club*. Liverpool: A.W. Duncan & Co. Ltd., n.d.

———. *The Monopoly of Credit*. 3rd rev. ed. London: K.R.P. Publications, 1958.

———. *The New and the Old Economics*. London: K.R.P. Publications, 1933.

———. *Programme for the Third World War*. London: K.R.P. Publications, 1943.

———. *The Pyramid of Power*. London: K.R.P. Publications, 1936.

———. *Social Credit*. London: Cecil Palmer, 1924.

———. "Lord Keynes." *The Social Crediter*, March 4, 1950, 1.

———. *These Present Discontents, and the Labour Party and Social Credit*. London: Cecil Palmer, 1922.

———. *The Douglas Theory: A Reply to Mr. J.A. Hobson*. London: Cecil Palmer, 1922.

———. *Tyranny: Taxation System a Device for Exercising Despotic Pressure.* London: K.R.P. Publications, 1936.

———. *Warning Democracy*. 3rd ed. London: Stanley Nott, 1935.

"Dr. Richard Pollard Receives University of Paris Degree." *The South Coloradan* 23, no. 14 (January 31, 1961): 1.

Dyer, Nat. "The Nobel Bailout." *Earth Rise Blog*, August 19, 2019.

Economic Dialogues in Ancient China: Selections from the Kuan-Tzu. Edited by Lewis A. Maverick. Translated by T'an Po-fu and Wen Kung-wen. Carbondale, IL: Lewis A. Maverick, 1954.

Edwards, Chilperic. *The Oldest Laws in the World: Being an Account of the Hammurabi Code and the Sinaitic Legislation with a Complete Translation of the Great Babylonian Inscription Discovered at Susa*. London: Watts, 1906.

Eisenhower, Dwight D. *Annual Message to the Congress on the State of the Union*. January 6, 1955.

El-Erian, Mohamed A. *The Only Game in Town: Central Banks, Instability, and Avoiding the Next Collapse*. New York: Random House, 2016.

Eliot, Charles W. "The Case Against Compulsory Latin." *The Atlantic Monthly*, March 1917, 352–61.

Eliot, T.S. *After Strange Gods: A Primer of Modern Heresy*. The Page-Barbour Lectures at the University of Virginia, 1933. London: Faber and Faber, 1934.

———. *The Rock: A Pageant Play, Written for Performance at Sadler's Wells Theatre, 28 May–9 June 1934*. New York: Harcourt, Brace, 1934.

Encyclopaedia Britannica. Chicago: Encyclopaedia Britannica, Inc., 2025. Accessed April 25, 2025. https://www.britannica.com.

European Center for Law & Justice (ECLJ). "How WHO and Scientific Research in Human Reproduction Are Instrumentalized in the Service of Depopulation." *European Center for Law & Justice*, February 2024.

Flynn, John T. *Men of Wealth: The Story of Twelve Significant Fortunes from the Renaissance to the Present Day*. New York: Simon and Schuster, 1951.

Fondazione Antiusura San Nicola e Santi Medici. "L'Usura." *Fondazione Antiusura San Nicola e Santi Medici*. Accessed July 21, 2024. https://www.fondazioneantiusurabari.com/index.php/l-usura.

Fowler, Wilton B. *British-American Relations, 1917–1918: The Role of Sir William Wiseman*. Princeton: Princeton University Press, 1969.

"The Freedom of the Press: On George Orwell's Unused Preface to 'Animal Farm.'" *Orwell News: The Orwell Foundation*, August 17, 2022.

"From John Adams to Jedidiah Morse, 29 November 1815." *Founders Online*, National Archives. Accessed April 17, 2025. https://founders.archives.gov/documents/Adams/99-02-02-6547.

Galbraith, John Kenneth. *Money: Whence It Came, Where It Went*. Boston: Houghton Mifflin, 1975.

Gallup, Donald. *Ezra Pound: A Bibliography*. St. Paul's Bibliographies, vol. 7. Charlottesville: University Press of Virginia, 1983.

Gesell, Silvio. *The Natural Economic Order*. Translated by Philip Pye. London: Peter Owen, 1958.

Gibbon, Edward. *The History of the Decline and Fall of the Roman Empire*. Edited by J.B. Bury. Introduction by W.E.H. Lecky. New York: Fred de Fau, 1906.

Giuseppi, Montague S. "Alien Merchants in England in the Fifteenth Century." *Transactions of the Royal Historical Society* 9 (1895): 75–98.

Gordon, David M. "The Azalea Is Grown." *Paideuma* 4, no. 2/3 (1975): 223–99.

Gordon, John Steele. *Hamilton's Blessing: The Extraordinary Life and Times of Our National Debt*. New York: Walker, 1997.

Graham, Sean. "As Canadian as Possible: The Canadian Broadcasting Corporation, 1936–1939." PhD diss., University of Ottawa, 2014.

Grenfell, Russell. *Unconditional Hatred: German War Guilt and the Future of Europe*. 4th printing. New York: Devin-Adair, 1958.

Grubb, Farley. "Benjamin Franklin and the Birth of the Paper Money Economy." *Federal Reserve Bank of Philadelphia and the Library Company of Philadelphia*, 2006.

Halloway, John. *The Pelican Guide to English Literature: The Modern Age*. Vol. 7. Edited by Boris Ford. Harmondsworth, UK: Penguin Books, 1961.

Hamilton, John. *The Catechism of John Hamilton, Archbishop of St. Andrew's, 1552*. Edited by T.G. Law. Oxford: Clarendon Press, 1884.

Hanks, Patrick, Kate Hardcastle, and Flavia Hodges. *A Dictionary of First Names*. 2nd ed. Oxford: Oxford University Press, 2019.

Harris, T.M. *Assassination of Lincoln: A History of the Great Conspiracy: Trial of the Conspirators by a Military Commission, and a Review of the Trial of John H. Surratt*. Boston: American Citizen Company, 1892.

Hayek, Friedrich A. *The Road to Serfdom*. Foreword by John Chamberlain. 2nd impression. Chicago: University of Chicago Press, 1944.

Henderson, Archie. "Exploring Permanent Values: Canto 104," *Astern in the Dinghy: Commentaries on Ezra's Pound's Thrones de los Cantares 96-109*. Glossator Vol. 10. Edited by Alexander Howard. CreateSpace Independent Publishing Platform, 2018.

Hill, Tegan. "Dividends to Albertans Would Ensure Better Maintenance of Heritage Fund." *Fraser Institute*, August 19, 2021.

Histoire Générale de la Chine: ou, Annales de cet Empire; Traduites du Tong-Kien-Kang-Mou. Translated by Joseph-Anne-Marie de Moyriac de Mailla. 13 vols. Paris: Ph.-D. Pierres, 1777–1785.

Hollis, Christopher. *The Two Nations: A Financial Study of English History*. London: George Routledge and Sons, 1937.

Holt, Frank Lee. *The Treasures of Alexander the Great: How One Man's Wealth Shaped the World*. New York: Oxford University Press, 2016.

Hooke, Alfred John. *30 + 5, I Know, I Was There*. Edmonton: Co-op Press, 1971.

Humphrey, Jim, and Rich Wallace. "Randolph Slaves." *Traveling Through Time: Archived Articles of Shelby County People, Places and Events*. Shelby County Historical Society, February 1997.

Hussey, James. "Hawthorne's 'Dangerous Soul' and Jacksonian Individualism: Artist Isolation in Fanshawe and 'The Artist of the Beautiful.'" *IJAS Online*, no. 7 (2018): 23–33.

Irving, John A. *The Social Credit Movement in Alberta*. Toronto: University of Toronto Press, 1959.

James, Walter (Lord Northbourne). *Look to the Land*. London: J.M. Dent & Sons, 1940.

Jefferson, Thomas. *The Writings of Thomas Jefferson*. Vol. 15. Washington, DC: Thomas Jefferson Memorial Association of the United States, 1903–04.

Kearns, George. *Guide to Ezra Pound's Selected Cantos*. New Brunswick, NJ: Rutgers University Press, 1980.

Keynes, John Maynard. *The General Theory of Employment, Interest and Money*. London: Macmillan, 1936.

Kimpel, Ben D., and T.C. Duncan Eaves. "Some Curious 'Facts' in Ezra Pound's Cantos." ELH 50, no. 3 (1983): 627–35.

Kreeft, Peter. *A Shorter Summa: The Essential Philosophical Passages of St. Thomas Aquinas' Summa Theologica*. San Francisco: Ignatius Press, 1993.

Landini, Richard G. "A Guide to the Economic Thought in Ezra Pound's Cantos." PhD diss., University of Florida, 1959.

Larrañaga, Pedro Juan Manuel. *Gold, Glut and Government: A New Economic Dawn*. London: G. Allen & Unwin, 1932.

Laughlin, James. *Pound as Wuz: Essays and Lectures on Ezra Pound*. Saint Paul: Graywolf Press, 1987.

Lenin, Vladimir Ilyich. *Imperialism, the Highest Stage of Capitalism: A Popular Outline*. London: Lawrence & Wishart, 1948.

Leo XIII. *Rerum Novarum: Encyclical Letter of His Holiness Pope Leo XIII on the Condition of the Working Classes*. Boston: St. Paul's Editions, 1942.

Lewinsohn, Richard. *Basil Zaharoff, Munitions King*. Philadelphia: J.B. Lippincott, 1934.

Lewis, C.S. *The Abolition of Man: Or Reflections on Education with Special Reference to the Teaching of English in the Upper Forms of Schools*. New York: Macmillan, 1947.

Literature of Ancient Egypt. Edited and introduction by William Kelly Simpson. Translated by Robert K. Ritner, William Kelly Simpson, Vincent A. Tobin, and Edward F. Wente Jr. New Haven: Yale University Press, 2003.

Love Poems of Ancient Egypt. Translated by Ezra Pound. Edited by Noel Stock. New York: New Directions Publishing, 1962.

Löwenberg, J., Robert Avé-Lallemant, and Alfred Dove. *Life of Alexander von Humboldt: Compiled in Commemoration of the Centenary of His Birth*. Edited by Karl Bruhns. Translated by Jane and Caroline Lassell. Vol. 2. London: Longmans, Green, 1873.

Ludwig, Emil. *Lincoln*. Translated by Eden and Cedar Paul. Boston: Little, Brown, 1930.

MacDiarmid, Hugh. "The Return of the Long Poem." In *Ezra Pound—Perspectives: Essays in Honor of His Eightieth Birthday*, edited by Noel Stock, 90–108. Chicago: Henry Regnery, 1965.

Maino, Thomas. "What Benedict XVI, Francis and Other Popes and Councils Say About Usury." *National Catholic Register*, October 31, 2022.

Mairet, Philip. *A.R. Orage: A Memoir*. Introduction by G.K. Chesterton. London: J.M. Dent, 1936.

Manning, Ernest. *Political Realignment: A Challenge to Thoughtful Canadians*. Toronto: McClelland and Stewart, 1967.

Mathews, R.H. *Mathews' Chinese-English Dictionary*. Cambridge, MA: Harvard University Press, 1943.

Mazzini, Joseph. *The Duties of Man*. London: Chapman & Hall, 1862.

McKenna, Reginald. "Midland Bank Limited: Ordinary General Meeting: Friday, January 28th, 1927: Speech of the Right Hon Reginald McKenna, Chairman." *Churchill Archive*. Accessed February 11, 2025. churchillarchive.com/catalogue-item?docid=CHAR18_40_62.

McLeay, Michael, Amar Radia, and Ryland Thomas. "Money Creation in the Modern Economy." *Bank of England Quarterly Bulletin* 2014, no. Q1: 14–27. Accessed April 25, 2025. bankofengland.co.uk/-/media/boe/files/quarterly-bulletin/2014/money-creation-in-the-modern-economy.

Meigs, William M. *The Life of Thomas Hart Benton*. Philadelphia: J.B. Lippincott, 1904.

Merriam-Webster Dictionary. Springfield, MA: Merriam-Webster, 2025. Accessed April 25, 2025. https://www.merriam-webster.com/dictionary.

Michelet, Jules. *History of the Roman Republic*. Translated by William Hazlitt. London: David Bogue, 1847.

———. *The People*. Translated by Charles Cocks. 3rd ed. London: Longman, Brown, Green and Longmans, 1846.

"Milking Taxpayers; Farm Subsidies." *The Economist*, February 14, 2015, 26.

Minton, Edward. "Keynes and Douglas." Accessed May 5, 2024. thepeoplescredit.com.au/wp-content/uploads/pc-pdf/shortform/Keynes-and-Douglas.pdf.

Mirabeau, Victor de Riquetti, Marquis de, and François Quesnay. *Philosophie Rurale; ou, Économie Générale et Politique de l'Agriculture: Réduite à l'Ordre Immuable des Loix Physiques & Morales, qui Assurent la Prospérité des Empires*. 3 vols. Amsterdam: Les Libraires Associés, 1764.

Mullins, Eustace. *This Difficult Individual, Ezra Pound*. New York: Fleet Publishing, 1961.

Munson, Gorham. *Aladdin's Lamp: The Wealth of the American People*. New York: Creative Age Press, 1945.

Neault, D. James. "Richard of St. Victor and 'Rock-Drill.'" *Paideuma* 3, no. 2 (1974): 219–27.

Neumann, Robert. *Zaharoff the Armaments King*. Translated by R.T. Clark. London: Reader's Union, 1938.

"New Study Compares Tax Freedom Days in Europe and Around the World." *Brussels Report*, July 22, 2021.

North, Gary. "Christian Economics: Teacher's Edition." Chapter 36: Banking. garynorth.com/public/16782.cfm.

———. *Salvation Through Inflation*. Tyler, TX: Institute for Christian Economics, 1993.

O'Duffy, Eimar. *Asses in Clover*. 2nd ed. Oxfordshire: Jon Carpenter Publishing, 2003.

———. *King Goshawk and the Birds*. London: Macmillan, 1926.

———. *The Spacious Adventures of the Man in the Street*. London: Macmillan, 1928.

Old Family Letters: Copied from the Originals for Alexander Biddle. Series A. Philadelphia: J.B. Lippincott, 1892.

O'Neall, John Belton. *Biographical Sketches of the Bench and Bar of South Carolina*. Vol. 2. Charleston: S.G. Courtenay, 1859.

Orage, A.R. "An Editor's Progress." *The Commonweal Weekly Review of Literature, The Arts, and Public Affairs* 3, nos. 14–17 (February 10–March 3, 1926): 376–79, 402–4, 434–35, 456–57. Accessed April 25, 2025. archive.org/details/sim_commonweal_1926-02-10_3_14.

———. "Letter from Hobson to Orage." University of Leeds Alfred R. Orage Archive.

Orwell, George. *The Collected Essays, Journalism, and Letters of George Orwell: An Age Like This, 1920–1940*. Vol. 1. Edited by Sonia Orwell and Ian Angus. New York: Harcourt Brace Jovanovich, 1968.

Overholser, Willis A. *A Short Review and Analysis of the History of Money in the United States with an Introduction to the Current Money Problem*. Libertyville, IL: Progress Publishing Concern, 1936.

Oxford Dictionary. Oxford: Oxford University Press, 2025. Accessed April 25, 2025. https://www.oxfordreference.com.

Panayotov, Alexander. "The Synagogue in the Copper Market of Constantinople: A Note on the Christian Attitudes Toward Jews in the Fifth Century." *Orientalia Christiana Periodica* 68 (2002): 319–34.

Patrologia Latina. Edited by Jacques Paul Migne. 221 vols. Paris: Garnier, 1865.

Pearson, Drew, and Robert S. Allen. "Rumored Cummings Wants Farley's Job." *Waterbury Evening Democrat*, November 27, 1935, 6.

Penguin Random House. "The Inferno by Dante Alighieri." Publisher's description for The Inferno. Accessed December 13, 2024. https://www.penguinrandomhouse.ca/books/304807/the-inferno-by-dante-alighieri/.

Phillips, Walter Alison. "Templars." In *The Encyclopædia Britannica*, 11th ed., 26:1–10. Cambridge: University Press, 1911.

Pieper, Josef. *Leisure: The Basis of Culture*. Translated by Alexander Dru. New York: New American Library, 1963.

Pius XI. *Quadragesimo Anno: The Reconstruction of the Social Order*. May 15, 1931.

Pollard, Hazel M. Batzer. "From Heroics to Sentimentalism: A Study of Thomas Otway's Tragedies." In *Poetic Drama & Poetic Theory*, edited by James Hogg, vol. 10. Salzburg: Institut für Englische Sprache und Literatur, Universität Salzburg, 1974.

Pollard, Richard. "The Electra Theme: A Comparative Study of Three Treatments in Drama." PhD diss., University of South Dakota, 1949.

Pollard, Richard, and Hazel Batzer Pollard. *From Human Sentience to Drama: Principles of Critical Analysis, Tragic and Comedic*. Athens: Ohio University Press, 1974.

Polo, Marco. *The Travels of Marco Polo, the Venetian*. Introduction by John Masefield. London: J.M. Dent & Sons, 1954.

Por, Odon. *Italy's Policy of Social Economics, 1939–1940*. Translated by Ezra Pound. Rome: Istituto Italiano d'Arti Grafiche, 1941.

Pound, Ezra. *ABC of Economics*. London: Faber and Faber, 1933.

———. *ABC of Reading*. New York: New Directions Books, 1960.

———. "Abdication." *Globe* [Milwaukee, WI] 1, no. 1 (March 1937): 82–87.

———. *A Visiting Card*. Money Pamphlets by Pound, no. 4. London: Peter Russell, 1952.

———. "Credit and the Fine Arts . . . A Practical Application." *New Age* 30, no. 22 (March 30, 1922): 284–85.

———. *Early Poems*. Dover Thrift Editions. Edited by Thomas Crofts. New York: Dover Publications Inc., 1996.

———. *Ezra and Dorothy Pound: Letters in Captivity, 1945–1946*. Edited by Omar Pound and Robert Spoo. New York: Oxford University Press, 1999.

———. *"Ezra Pound Speaking": Radio Speeches of World War II*. Edited by Leonard W. Doob. Westport, CT: Greenwood Press, 1978.

———. *Guide to Kulchur*. 4th ed. London: Peter Owen, 1966.

———. "I Gather the Limbs of Osiris, I." *The New Age* 10, no. 6 (1911): 130–31.

———. *Impact: Essays on Ignorance and the Decline of American Civilization*. Edited and introduction by Noel Stock. Chicago: Henry Regnery, 1960.

———. "Infamy of Taxes." *Action* 120 (June 4, 1938): 13.

———. *Jefferson and/or Mussolini: L'idea Statale Fascism as I Have Seen It*. New York: Liveright, 1970.

———. *Letter to Lorne Reznowski*. Rapallo, Italy. April 20, 1965.

———. "John Buchan's Cromwell." *New English Weekly* 7 (June 6, 1935): 149.

———. *The Letters of Ezra Pound*. Edited by D.D. Paige. London: Faber and Faber, 1951.

———. "Questions." *New Democracy* 1 (October 10, 1933): 4.

———. *The Cantos of Ezra Pound*. New York: New Directions Publishing, 1970.

———. "The Central Problem." *Townsman* 4, no. 13 (March 1941): 13–17.

———. *Ezra Pound's Economic Correspondence, 1933–1940*. Edited by Roxana Preda. Gainesville: University Press of Florida, 2007.

———. *Ezra Pound and Music: The Complete Criticism*. Edited by R. Murray Schafer. New York: New Directions Publishing, 1977.

———. "Vu, No. 380, and Subsequent Issues." *New Age* 57, no. 27 (October 31, 1935): 218–19.

———. "Why Parliament's Gone to Hell." *Action* 98 (December 30, 1937): 7.

Prince, Paul. *Think and Conquer! Collection of CKRC and/or CKRX Radio Broadcasts, Feb. 19 to Oct. 07, 1944*. Vol. 1. Winnipeg: Manitoba Social Credit Organization, 1944.

Raleigh, Walter. "Select Observations of the Incomparable Sir Walter Raleigh Relating to Trade, Commerce, and Coin, as It Was Presented to King James." In *Early English Books Online*. London: Printed by T.N. for G. Calvert, 1653. name.umdl.umich.edu/A57605.0001.001.

Ravenscroft, Simon. "Usury in the Inferno: Auditing Dante's Debt to the Scholastics." *Comitatus: A Journal of Medieval & Renaissance Studies* 42 (2011): 89–114.

Reznowski, Lorne. "Letter to Ezra Pound." Beinecke Rare Book and Manuscript Library, Yale University, New Haven, CT, YCAL MSS 53, box 15, folder 380.

Roberts, Brian. *Randolph: A Study of Churchill's Son*. London: Hamish Hamilton, 1984.

Roth, Cecil. *The Magnificent Rothschilds*. London: Robert Hale, 1939.

Ruffhead, Owen. *The Statutes at Large: From Magna Charta, to the End of the Last Parliament, 1761*. Vol. 1. London: Mark Basket, 1763.

Rutler, George W. "The Banners of Lepanto." *Crisis Magazine*, October 7, 2016.

Salmasio, Claudio. *De Modo Usurarum Liber*. Leiden: Ex Officina Elseviriorum, 1639.

———. *Dissertatio de Foenore Trapezitico, In Tres Libros Divisa*. Leiden: Ex Officina Joannis Maire, 1640.

Sancti Victoris, Richardi. *Benjamin Minor*. In *Patrologiae Latina Cursus Completus, Series Secunda*, edited by Jacques-Paul Migne, vol. 196. Paris: Migne, 1855.

Savidge, Thomas. "Why Does the Federal Government Borrow?" *American Institute for Economic Research (AIER)*, May 30, 2024.

Sawyer, Richard. "The 12 Regents in Canto 51." April 2020. Accessed May 27, 2024. https://drive.google.com/file/d/1xkE1N82JoGKz-e9I66X2FP-dk5uIsqmpn/view.

Sehgal, Kabir. *Coined: The Rich Life of Money and How Its History Has Shaped Us*. New York: Grand Central Publishing, 2015.

Shaxson, Nicholas. "The City of London Is Hiding the World's Stolen Money." *The New York Times*, October 11, 2021.

Siegel, Arthur. *Politics and the Media in Canada*. 2nd ed. Toronto: McGraw-Hill Ryerson, 1996.

Siem, Conrad von Bauditz. *The C.S.L.T: Containing Views on Abraham Lincoln as Expressed by Bismarck in 1878, from the Recollections of Conrad von Bauditz Siem*. N.p.: n.p., 1915.

Simon, Jules. *Le Gouvernement de M. Thiers: 8 Février 1871 – 24 Mai 1873*. Vol. 2. Paris: Calmann Lévy, 1880.
Smith, Adam. *The Wealth of Nations*. Vol. 1. Introduction by Edwin Seligman. London: J.M. Dent & Sons, 1964.
Snyder, Timothy. *The Red Prince: The Secret Lives of a Habsburg Archduke*. New York: Basic Books, 2008.
"Social Credit and the Catholic Doctrine." *La Semaine Religieuse de Montréal*, November 13, 1939. Accessed April 25, 2025. michaeljournal.org/articles/social-credit/item/social-credit-and-the-catholic-doctrine.
Steinmetz, Greg. *The Richest Man Who Ever Lived: The Life and Times of Jacob Fugger*. New York: Simon & Schuster, 2015.
Stolberg-Wernigerode, Otto zu. *Germany and the United States of America During the Era of Bismarck*. Reading, PA: Henry Janssen Foundation, 1937.
Strong, James. *The Exhaustive Concordance of the Bible*. New York: Abingdon-Cokesbury Press, 1890.
Stock, Noel. *The Life of Ezra Pound*. San Francisco: Northpoint Press, 1982.
Swift, Daniel. *The Bughouse: The Poetry, Politics and Madness of Ezra Pound*. London: Harvill Secker, 2017.
Talbot, John Michael. "Community of Disciples." *John Michael Talbot*. Accessed May 24, 2024. https://www.johnmichaeltalbot.com/community-of-disciples.
Tawney, R.H. *Religion and the Rise of Capitalism: A Historical Study*. 12th ed. New York: New American Library, 1963.
Tay, William. "Between Kung and Eleusis: 'Li Chi,' The Eleusinian Rites, Erigena and Ezra Pound." *Paideuma* 4, no. 1 (1975): 37–54.
Terrell, Carroll F. *A Companion to the Cantos of Ezra Pound*. 2 vols. Berkeley: University of California Press, 1980–84.
Thiers, M.A. *De La Propriété*. Paris: Paulin, Lheureux, 1848.
Tolstoy, Ivan. "Utrachennoe Schast'e" [Lost Happiness]. *Radio Svoboda/Radio Liberty*, Russian language edition, December 5, 2017. Accessed March 4, 2025. https://www.svoboda.org/a/28901507.html.
Townshend, Jules. *J.A. Hobson*. The Lives of the Left Series. Edited by David Howell. Manchester: Manchester University Press, 1990.
"Ulrico Hoepli (1847–1935), Bookdealer." *Institute of English Studies, School of Advanced Study, University of London*. Accessed March 7, 2025. https://ies.sas.ac.uk/research-projects/cultivate-mss-project/cast-characters/ulrico-hoepli-1847-1935-bookdealer.
United States Congress. "Nye, Gerald Prentice." Accessed April 22, 2025. https://bioguide.congress.gov/search/bio/N000176.
U.S. Congress, House. "The Subcommittee on Domestic Monetary Policy and Technology of the Committee on Financial Services Fractional Reserve Banking and the Federal Reserve." *Fractional Reserve Banking and the Federal Reserve: The Economic Consequences of High-Powered Money*. 112th Cong., 2nd Sess., June 28, 2012. congress.gov/event/112th-congress/house-event/LC3666/text.

United States. The New International Encyclopedia. Vol. 19. Edited by Daniel Coit Gilman, Harry Thurston Peck, and Frank Moore Colby. New York: Dodd, Mead, 1905.

Van Buren, Martin. *The Autobiography of Martin Van Buren*. Vol. 2. Edited by John C. Fitzpatrick. Washington, DC: Government Printing Office, 1918.

The Aeneid of Virgil: Books 1–6. Edited with introduction and notes by R.D. Williams. London: Macmillan, 1972.

Waldholz, Rachel. "Alaska's Annual Dividend Adds Up for Residents." *Marketplace*, March 16, 2016.

Warrack, Allan A., and Russell R. Keddie. "Natural Resource Trust Funds: A Comparison of the Alberta and Alaska Resource Funds." *Education and Research Archive, University of Alberta*, no. 72, September 2002.

Waugh, Evelyn. *Brideshead Revisited: The Sacred and Profane Memories of Captain Charles Ryder*. Boston: Little, Brown, 1945.

———. *The Diaries of Evelyn Waugh*. Edited by Michael Davie. New York: Penguin Books, 1979.

"What Is the National Debt Today?" *Peter G. Peterson Foundation*, April 22, 2024.

Who's Who 1938: An annual Biographical Dictionary With Which is Incorporated "Men and Women of the Time." London: Adam & Charles Black, 1937.

Who's Who 1956: An annual Biographical Dictionary With Which is Incorporated "Men and Women of the Time." London: Adam & Charles Black, 1955.

Wilhelm, James J. *The American roots of Ezra Pound*. New York: Garland Publishing, 1985.

Wilson, R. McNair. *Monarchy or Money Power*. 2nd ed. Reprint. London: Eyre and Spottiswoode, 1934.

———. "Review of C.H. Douglas's Stanley Nott publications". *The Criterion* 15, no. 60 (April 1936): 342–345. Edited by T.S. Eliot. London: Faber & Faber, 1967.

Zobi, Antonio. *Storia Civile della Toscana dal MDCCXXXVII al MDCCXLVIII*. Vol. IV. Firenze: Presso Luigi Molini, 1852.

FURTHER READING

Adams, John. *The Works of John Adams with a Life of the Author, Notes and Illustrations. Second President of the United States: with a life of the author*. Edited by Charles Francis Adams. Boston: Little, Brown and Co., 1854–1856.

Ambrose, Saint, Bishop of Milan, and Lois Miles Zucker. *S. Ambrosii De Tobia: a Commentary, With an Introduction and Translation*. Washington, DC: The Catholic University of America, 1933.

Anderson, Thornton. *Brooks Adams, Constructive Conservative*. Ithaca: Cornell University Press, 1951.

Bolles, Albert S. *The Financial History of the United States, from 1774 to 1789: Embracing the Period of the American Revolution.* 3rd Ed. New York: D. Appleton and company, 1892.

Cunningham, W. "The Perversion of Economic History." *The Economic Journal.* Vol. 2, no. 7 (Sep. 1892), 491–506.

Deutsche Bundesbank. "The Role of Banks, Non-Banks and the Central Bank in the Money Creation Process." *Deutsche Bundesbank Monthly Report.* April 2017, 13–33.

Finlay, John L. *Social Credit: The English Origins.* Montreal: McGill – Queen's University Press, 1972.

Gordon, Armistead C. *Congressional Currency.* New York: G.P. Putman's Sons, 1895.

Hamilton, James A. *Martin Van Buren's Calumnies Repudiated: Hamilton's Conduct as Secretary of the Treasury Vindicated.* New York: Charles Scribner & Co., 1870.

Heydorn, M. Oliver. *Social Credit Economics.* Ancaster, Canada: Create Space Independent Publishing Platform, 2014.

———. *The Economics of Social Credit and Catholic Social Teaching.* Ancaster, Canada: M. Oliver Heydorn, Create Space Independent Publishing Platform, 2014.

Kimpel, Ben, and T.C. Duncan Eaves. "The Sources of Cantos XLII and XLIII." *Paideuma* 6, no. 3 (1977): 333–58.

———. "The Sources of the Leopoldine Cantos." *Paideuma* 7, no. 1/2 (1978): 249–77.

Klinck, Dennis R. "Pound, Social Credit, and the Critics". *Paideuma.* 5 (1976): 227–40.

Kunitz, Stanley J., ed. *20th Century Authors.* New York: H.W. Wilson Company, 1959.

Mengozzi, Narciso. *Il Monte dei Paschi di Siena (1625–1921).* Firenze: R. Bemporad & Figlio, 1922.

Norman. Charles. *Ezra Pound.* New York: The Macmillan Co., 1960.

Pound, Ezra. *The Posthumous Cantos.* Ed. Massimo Bacigalupo. Manchester: Carcanet Press Ltd., 2015.

Reznowski, Lorne A. "The 'Chesterbelloc' And Ezra Pound." *Paideuma* 13, no. 2 (1984): 291–95.

Sawyer, Rollin Alger. *Social Credit: A Reading List.* New York: The New York Public Library, 1936. babel.hathitrust.org/cgi/pt?id=uiug.30112117983723&seq=1.

Sheard, Paul. "Repeat After Me: Banks Cannot and do Not "Lend Out" Reserves." *RatingsDirect, Standard & Poor's Ratings Services.* August 13 2013.

Woodward, Guy. "'Conducting his own Campaigns': Evelyn Waugh and Propaganda." *The Review of English Studies,* Volume 73, Issue 308, February 2022, 144–164.

WEBSITES

Aberhart Foundation: aberhartfoundation.ca/Pages/Premier.htm#Social-CreditPublications.

Alexander Del Mar Letters: library.syracuse.edu/digital/guides/d/delmar_a.htm.

Alfred R. Orage Archive: explore.library.leeds.ac.uk/special-collections-explore/7315.

The Archives of the Morgan Library & Museum: themorgan.org/collection/archives.

Bank of England resources related to money creation: bankofengland.co.uk/quarterly-bulletin/2014/q1/money-creation-in-the-modern-economy.

The Bilderberg Meetings: bilderbergmeetings.org.

The Cantos Project: ezrapoundcantos.org.

Center for Financial Stability, Bretton Woods Documents: centerforfinancialstability.org/brettonwoods_docs.php.

The Clifford Hugh Douglas Institute for the Study and Promotion of Social Credit: socred.org.

Defense News: defensenews.com.

The Ezra Pound Society: ezrapoundsociety.org.

The Fugger Archive: https://fugger.de/en/archive.

Gorham Munson Papers on the American Social Credit Movement: archives.wesleyan.edu/repositories/ua/resources/gorham_b_munson_papers_social_credit.

The John Adams Library at the Boston Public Library. Books available at archive.org: archive.org/details/johnadamsBPL.

The Peoples Credit: thepeoplescredit.com.au.

Rothschild Archives: rothschildarchive.org.

The Social Credit Secretariat: socialcredit.schooljotter2.com.

The University of Pennsylvania online list of Del Mar's publications: https://onlinebooks.library.upenn.edu/webbin/book/search?author=Alexander+Del+Mar.

The World Economic Forum: weforum.org.

ACKNOWLEDGMENTS

Grateful acknowledgment is given to New Directions Publishing Corporation and Faber & Faber Ltd. for permission to quote from the following copyrighted works of Ezra Pound:

ABC of Economics. London: Faber and Faber, 1933.
ABC of Reading. New York: New Directions Books, 1960.
"Abdication." *Globe* [Milwaukee, WI] *1*, no. 1 (March 1937): 82–87.
A Visiting Card. Money Pamphlets by Pound, no. 4. London: Peter Russell, 1952.
"Credit and the Fine Arts… A Practical Application." *New Age 30*, no. 22 (March 30, 1922): 284–85.
"Ezra Pound Speaking": Radio Speeches of World War II._ Edited by Leonard W. Doob. Westport, CT: Greenwood Press, 1978.
Guide to Kulchur. 4th ed. London: Peter Owen, 1966.
"I Gather the Limbs of Osiris, I." *The New Age 10*, no. 6 (1911): 130–31.
Impact: Essays on Ignorance and the Decline of American Civilization. Edited and introduction by Noel Stock. Chicago: Henry Regnery, 1960.
"Infamy of Taxes." *Action 120* (June 4, 1938): 13.
Jefferson and/or Mussolini: L'idea Statale Fascism as I Have Seen It. New York: Liveright, 1970.
"John Buchan's Cromwell." *New English Weekly 7* (June 6, 1935): 149.
Letter to Lorne Reznowski. Rapallo, Italy. April 20, 1965.
The Letters of Ezra Pound. Edited by D. D. Paige. London: Faber and Faber, 1951.
"Questions." *New Democracy 1* (October 10, 1933): 4.
The Cantos of Ezra Pound. New York: New Directions Publishing, 1970.
"The Central Problem." *Townsman 4*, no. 13 (March 1941): 13–17.
Ezra Pound's Economic Correspondence, 1933–1940. Edited by Roxana Preda. Gainesville: University Press of Florida, 2007.
Ezra Pound and Music: The Complete Criticism. Edited by R. Murray Schafer. New York: New Directions Publishing, 1977.
"Vu, No. 380, and Subsequent Issues." *New Age 57*, no. 27 (October 31, 1935): 218–19.
"Why Parliament's Gone to Hell." *Action 98* (December 30, 1937): 7.

Scripture quotations are taken from the Douay Rheims Bible (Baltimore: John Murphy Company, 1899).

INDEX

F

U

Y

Z

ABOUT THE AUTHORS

REVEREND DEACON, DR. LORNE A. REZNOWSKI received a Bachelor of Arts degree from Loyola College, Montreal, 1950. Licentiate in Sacred Theology from Catholic University of America, Washington, D. C., 1957. Master of Arts English Literature, thesis: *The Death of Hope in H. G. Wells*, University of Ottawa, 1961. Doctor of Philosophy in English Literature, dissertation: *An Examination of the Motifs of Contempt of the World and of the Exaltation of Chastity over Marriage in the Old Slavonic Paterikon, and the Middle English Katherine Group*, University of Ottawa, 1980. Lorne taught for several years at the University of Ottawa, then from 1966 to 1992 at St. Paul's College, University of Manitoba in Winnipeg.

THEODORE D. REZNOWSKI received a Bachelor of Arts degree from St. Basil College, Stamford, Connecticut, 1987, Bachelor's in Sacred Theology from St. Thomas Aquinas University, Rome, Italy, 1990, Bachelor of Science in Nursing, Colorado State University, 2008.

* * * * *

M. OLIVER HEYDORN, Ph.D., is the founder and director of the Clifford Hugh Douglas Institute for the Study and Promotion of Social Credit (www.socred.org). He has published several books and articles on Social Credit theory, including *Social Credit Economics*, and *The Economics of Social Credit and Catholic Social Teaching*. He obtained a Bachelor of Science in Life Sciences from McMaster University in 1997, a Master's in Philosophy from the Franciscan University of Steubenville in 2002, and a Ph.D. in Philosophy, *summa cum laude*, from the International Academy of Philosophy at the Pontifical University of Chile in 2005.

www.ingramcontent.com/pod-product-compliance
Lightning Source LLC
Chambersburg PA
CBHW031319230926
51848CB00001B/10